T&T Clark Social Identity Commentaries on the New Testament

Series Editors

Kathy Ehrensperger
University of Basel, Switzerland

Philip Esler
University of Gloucestershire, UK

Aaron Kuecker
Trinity Christian College, USA

Petri Luomanen
University of Helsinki, Finland

J. Brian Tucker
Moody Theological Seminary, USA

Recent volumes in the series

2 Corinthians: A Social Identity Commentary
Luke: A Social Identity Commentary

Forthcoming volumes in the series

Mark: A Social Identity Commentary
Hebrews: A Social Identity Commentary
The Pastoral Epistles: A Social Identity Commentary
1 and 2 Thessalonians: A Social Identity Commentary
John: A Social Identity Commentary
1 Peter: A Social Identity Commentary
Galatians: A Social Identity Commentary
Ephesians: A Social Identity Commentary

Romans

A Social Identity Commentary

William S. Campbell

LONDON • NEW YORK • OXFORD • NEW DELHI • SYDNEY

T&T CLARK
Bloomsbury Publishing Plc
50 Bedford Square, London, WC1B 3DP, UK
1385 Broadway, New York, NY 10018, USA
29 Earlsfort Terrace, Dublin 2, Ireland

BLOOMSBURY, T&T CLARK and the T&T Clark logo are trademarks of
Bloomsbury Publishing Plc

First published in Great Britain 2023
This edition printed in 2024

Copyright © William S. Campbell, 2023

William S. Campbell has asserted his right under the Copyright, Designs and Patents Act, 1988, to be identified as Author of this work.

For legal purposes, the Acknowledgments on pp. xiii–xiv constitute an extension of this copyright page.

Cover image © Shutterstock

All rights reserved. No part of this publication may be reproduced or transmitted in any form or by any means, electronic or mechanical, including photocopying, recording, or any information storage or retrieval system, without prior permission in writing from the publishers.

Bloomsbury Publishing Plc does not have any control over, or responsibility for, any third-party websites referred to or in this book. All internet addresses given in this book were correct at the time of going to press. The author and publisher regret any inconvenience caused if addresses have changed or sites have ceased to exist, but can accept no responsibility for any such changes.

A catalogue record for this book is available from the British Library.

A catalog record for this book is available from the Library of Congress.

ISBN: HB: 978-0-5676-6942-1
PB: 978-0-5677-0996-7
ePDF: 978-0-5676-6943-8
ePUB: 978-0-5677-0995-0

Series: T&T Clark Social Identity Commentaries on the New Testament

Typeset by Newgen KnowledgeWorks Pvt. Ltd., Chennai, India

To find out more about our authors and books visit www.bloomsbury.com and sign up for our newsletters.

To the memory of
Anthony Tyrell Hanson
Teacher, Mentor, and Friend

Contents

Series Preface	xi
Preface and Acknowledgments	xiii
Introduction	1
Setting the Scene	1
Reception History	10
Approach to the Letter	16
Translation and Terminology	32
Excursus I Paul's Use of Diatribal Style in Romans	33
Diatribe and the Interpretation of Romans	33
Paul's Use of Rhetorical Questions in Romans	44
Conclusion	48
Romans 1	49
Romans 1:1-7: Paul the Apostle, to the Beloved "Gentiles" in Rome	49
Romans 1:8-12: The Thanksgiving—Paul's Relationship with the Romans	57
Romans 1:13-18: The Beginning of the Body of the Letter	59
Romans 1:19-32: God's Wrath against the Gentile World Revealed in the Gospel	69
Excursus II The Wrath of God against All Idolatry—A Trajectory from Zephaniah to Romans	77
Romans 2	83
Romans 2:1: The Transition from Romans 1:19-32 to Romans 2	83
Romans 2:1-5: The First Apostrophe—"To the One Who Judges"	88
Romans 2:6-16: Commonality under Divine Judgment and Impartiality	93
Romans 2:17-29: The Second Apostrophe—"If You Call Yourself a Jew"	97
Romans 2:1-24: Paul's Interlocutor and the Dynamics of Group Identity at Rome	103
Romans 2:25-29: Paul and the Circumcision of Non-Jews	108

Romans 3	113
Romans 3:1-2: The Advantage of the Jew and the Value of His Circumcision	113
Romans 3:3-8: The Advantage of the Jew and God's Covenant Faithfulness—Gentile Reactions to Paul's Gospel	115
Romans 3:9-20: Scriptural Reasoning—The Whole World Living under the Power of Sin	119
Romans 3:21-26: The Revelation of God's Rectifying Power in Christ	125
Romans 3:27-31: Drawing Accurate Inferences from the Revelation of God's Rectifying Power in Christ	132
Romans 4	139
Romans 4:1-8: Abraham, the Forefather "According to the Flesh" of Those Ἐν ἀκροβυστία?	139
Romans 4:9-12: "Not Only but Also, οὐ μόνον ἄλλα καὶ" Paul's Inclusive Argument	143
Romans 4:13-18: Abraham, the Promise, and the Inheritance	149
Romans 4:17-25: Abraham, the Forefather of Israel, and Father of Many Nations	160
Romans 5	165
Romans 5:1-11: "Now That We Have Been Reconciled, Let Us Enjoy Peace"	165
Romans 5:12-21: The Rule of Grace through Christ Overcomes the Rule of Sin and Death	173
Romans 6	181
Romans 6:1-14: "Should We Continue in Sin in Order That Grace Might Proliferate?"	181
Romans 6:15-23: You Are Slaves to Whom You Obey—Putting Your Bodies at God's Disposal	190
Excursus III Slavery to God	199
Romans 7	205
Romans 7:1-6: "You 'Gentiles' Have Died to the Law So That You May Belong to Another"	205
Romans 7:7-25: Paul's Use of Speech-in-Character to Represent the Confused "Gentile"	211
Subsection A	212
Romans 7:7-12: The "Gentile" on His Own with the Law and without the Spirit	212

Subsection B	216
Romans 7:13-25: The Conflicted Self—The Good, then, Brought Death to Me, Did It Not?	216
Romans 8	221
Romans 8:1-11: The Law of the Spirit of Life in Christ Jesus	221
Romans 8:12-17: A New Identity—Adopted into the "Family of God" as Those from the Nations	226
Romans 8:18-30: The Creation Waits for the Revealing of the Children of God	233
Romans 8:31-39: "If God Is for Us, Who Is Against Us?"	238
Romans 9	245
Romans 9:1-5: Sorrow for Israel and Israel's Heritage	245
Romans 9:6-13: But It Is Not as Though the Word of God (to Israel) Has Failed	248
Romans 9:14-29: The Sovereign Creator, the God of Israel—"I Will Have Mercy on Whom I Will"	258
Romans 10	267
Romans 9:30–10:3: Israel Stumbling but Still in the Race	267
Romans 10:4: For the Goal of the Law Is Christ	271
Romans 10:5-10: How Christ Is the Goal of the Law	275
Romans 10:11-13: For with God There Is No Discrimination	280
Romans 10:14-21: "His Hands Are Stretched Out Still"	282
Romans 11	289
Romans 11:1-10: "God Didn't Cast Off His People, Did He?"	289
Romans 11:11-16: Israel's Stumbling: The Kindness and Severity of God	293
Romans 11:17-24: "You Were Grafted In"—an Apostrophe Reprimanding the Wild Olive Shoot	301
Romans 11:25-36: Israel Will Be Restored but only after the Fullness of the Nations	305
Excursus IV Supersessionism at Rome	317
Do the Ethnē in Christ Have a Connection to Any of the Synagogues at Rome?	317
Supersessionism at Rome? The Influence of Roman Imperial Ethos among the Ethnē in Rome	318

Romans 12 — 323

    Romans 12:1-2: Offer Your Bodies as a Living Sacrifice—a Distinctive Ethos — 323

    Romans 12:3-8: The Alternative Pattern of Life for a Community in Process of Transformation — 334

    Romans 12:9-21: The Response of Trust—Overcome Evil by the Good — 337

Romans 13 — 343

    Romans 13:1-7: "Pay All, What Is Due to Them" — 343

    Romans 13:8-14: The Link between the Law and Ἀγάπη—Love Fulfills the Law — 351

Romans 14:1–15:6 — 357

    Romans 14:1-4: Welcome "The Weak"—Paul's Measure of Strength — 357

    Romans 14:5-12: "The Weak"—Not a Temporary Phenomenon — 359

    Romans 14:13-16: Guarding the Holiness of the Ethnē in Christ Community — 368

    Romans 14:17-23: The Way of the Kingdom—Walking in Love — 370

    Romans 15:1-6: He Did Not Please Himself—Christ the Exemplar — 375

Romans 15:7-13 — 383

    "Rejoice, Ethnē Together with His People"—the Dual Outcome of Christ's Servanthood — 383

    Romans 15:7-13: The Conclusion to the Argument of the Entire Letter — 393

Romans 15:14-33 — 399

    Romans 15:14-21: Reiterating and Expanding on His Plans — 399

    Romans 15:20-24: Not Where Christ Has Already Been Named—Paul's Prioritizing of Pioneer Areas — 403

    Romans 15:25-29: "I Am Going to Jerusalem in Service of the Saints" — 405

    Romans 15:30-33: "Join Me in Earnest Prayer to God" — 408

Romans 16 — 411

    Romans 16:1-2: "Now I Recommend to You Phoebe, Our Sister" — 411

    Romans 16:3-16: Paul Requests the Roman Ethnē to Transmit Greetings to Numerous People in Rome — 414

    Romans 16:17-20: Warning and Assurance — 418

    Romans 16:21-23: Paul Conveys Greetings from Colleagues with Him — 421

    Romans 16:25-27: The Final Doxology — 422

References — 423

Index of Ancient Sources — 447

Index of Biblical Texts — 449

Index of Modern Authors — 460

Series Preface

The **T & T Clark Social Identity Commentaries on the New Testament (SICNT)** is a series that presents readings of the New Testament focussed on identity. In the last three decades biblical studies have seen a marked upsurge of interest in questions of identity in the ancient world, both of groups and individuals. The Hebrew Bible and the New Testament are replete with phenomena that are embedded in and impact on issues of identity. A primary narrative of the New Testament concerns the processes in the first century CE by which eventually a new socio-religious Christ-movement formed within the populous and long-established Judean/Jewish groups. It developed, interacting with Greek, Roman, and other traditions, on trajectories of its own until, at some stage, to be both Judean/Jewish and a Christ-follower became difficult, resulting in rapidly increasing social and intergroup complexity. Central to that process was the way participation in various Christ-following assemblies cultivated in the minds and hearts of their members aspects of identities that eventually became distinct from Judean/Jewish identities. These aspects expressed distinctive beliefs, attitudes, and behavior, which Christ-followers traced back to the ministry, teaching, death, and resurrection of Jesus Christ. Since the 1990s that branch of social psychology known as social identity theory, originally developed by Henri Tajfel and John Turner at the University of Bristol in the 1970s and 1980s—now deployed by hundreds if not thousands of psychologists across the world—has proven a remarkably rich theoretical resource for probing these inter- and intra-group dimensions of aspects of the social identities of Christ-followers as exposed in the books of the New Testament. A torrent of books, articles, and essays has appeared and continues to appear applying social identity theory to the biblical texts, not least the *T & T Clark Handbook to Social Identity in the New Testament* (Bloomsbury, 2014). This series of commentaries testifies to the extent to which the application of social identity theory has become established as one of the liveliest sub-fields of New Testament research and to the resulting need to make available to scholars, students, and the general public detailed treatments of each text from this perspective. The authors of each volume, all well-recognized scholars in the area, while engaging with existing scholarship as they move through the text *seriatim* in commentary style, will apply distinctive social identity ideas and other perspectives on group behavior, generating fresh but well-founded interpretations of the New Testament's twenty-seven constituent books. The series aims to demonstrate how much New Testament interpretation can benefit from the application of the expert investigation into the social realities of groups and group and individual identities undertaken by social identity psychologists and other social-scientific specialists.

Series Editors

Kathy Ehrensperger
University of Potsdam, Abraham Geiger College

Philip Esler
University of Gloucestershire

Aaron Kuecker
Trinity Christian College

Petri Luomanen
University of Helsinki

J. Brian Tucker
Moody Theological Seminary

Preface and Acknowledgments

My interest in Paul preceded my study of Romans. I have written particularly on his relation to the varied communities he founded, and felt most at home in this milieu. However, Romans has always fascinated me, especially its status as a letter rather than a theological treatise. I began with a BD dissertation on "Election and Predestination in the Theology of John Calvin and Karl Barth" (Trinity College, Dublin). This was followed by research begun for an MTh at the University of London with Professor C. F. Evans, who kindly suggested that I upgrade to a PhD. Then followed three years of research supervised by Professors Hugh Anderson and Robin Barbour at the University of Edinburgh half of which were spent at the University of Tübingen, Germany. There I continued my research under Professors Otto Michel and Ernst Käsemann on the topic "The Purpose of Paul in the Letter to the Romans with Special Reference to Chapters 9–11" (completed 1972). Thus, the study of Romans laid the foundation for my understanding of Paul. Unlike many others, I did not start with Galatians and then come to Romans. This letter always took top priority for me and enabled me to be a regular participant in its academic discussion—first in the decade-long Pauline Theology Consultations of the Society of Biblical Literature and second in the Romans through History and Cultures project (AAR and SBL) both resulting in the publication of a series of volumes from 1993 to 2013.

Since the completion of a previous book, *The Nations in the Divine Economy* (2018), I have spent the past four years drawing together the most recent research related to Romans. Two of these years, confined through Covid-19, both assisted and hindered research. On the one hand, the lack of travel to conferences and so on hindered conversations with colleagues but enabled focus on this task. This has been not only an exciting but also a most demanding project. I have come to a greatly increased admiration and respect for all who have completed a commentary on this marvelous literary achievement of Paul, and most of all for Paul himself. What a privilege to spend so much time learning of one of the greatest of scholars and missionary entrepreneurs. The literature on Romans is enormous in extent, apologies to those whose commentaries and other writings I have not space to include. But what I do include indicates the great debt I owe to many, especially innovators such as Robert Jewett, Daniel Patte, Ekkehard W. Stegemann, and Neil Elliott. I have been in conversation with too many other colleagues over the years to name them all, but I would like to mention Brian Tucker, Robert Brawley, Mark Nanos, and Paula Fredriksen whose opinions I greatly value. Many colleagues and friends have read and commented on the preliminary versions of chapters. Special thanks are due to Patrick McMurray, David Neville, Hans Förster, Marius Felderhof, John Dunlop, and John Grove. I very much appreciate the careful review of the entire manuscript by Philip Esler and Brian Tucker, and their invaluable expertise, particularly in the area of SIT. But most of all I owe so much to

Kathy both in terms of her own intensive scholarship and also the mechanics of getting scholarship into print." To whom much is given of them shall much be required. Special thanks also to Juni Hoppe, whose technical expertise in finalizing the manuscript was invaluable. At Bloomsbury T&T Clark, Dominic Mattos, editorial director and publisher, and Sarah Blake, commissioning editor who have been most helpful and supportive throughout the entire project. Saranya Manohar expertly and efficiently oversaw the copyediting, typesetting, proofing, and indexing of the manuscript. My commentary presented here is the fruit of all those who have inspired me, including Charles Cranfield, Ernst Käsemann, Markus Barth and especially Anthony Hanson who invited me to give my first seminar paper as a guest at the SNTS Meeting, Durham 1979, and who also initiated the proposal for my SNTS membership when he was already severely ill with cancer. Finally, I must acknowledge that it was the scholarly and friendly community of learning at New College, University of Edinburgh that launched me on my academic career.

William S Campbell
Basel,
October 27, 2022

Introduction

For the interpretation of any letter, as much knowledge of the context and circumstances as possible is essential. In recent years, the awareness of the relevance of the context of Paul's letters has expanded to include not only his personal circumstances but also the wider cultural and sociopolitical context within which both the addressees and Paul and his colleagues lived and operated. For a letter of antiquity, the reconstruction of context and circumstances is necessarily built on fragmentary evidence, but this should not hinder the inclusion of all relevant information available or its critical assessment.

Setting the Scene

The Beginnings of the Messianic Movement at Rome

Whatever approach is taken to the interpretation of Romans, the historical setting as far as we can ascertain it remains primary. The beginnings of the Christ-movement in Rome are unclear, and many possibilities lend themselves to investigation. Lampe shows that the likely arrival of the Christ-movement in Rome was in the 40s of the first century at the latest. It came probably through large Roman households with connections to the East who brought with them their families and slaves, some of whom were Jews. The latter commenced their own synagogues with the permission of their heads of houses, these probably constituting the earliest known synagogue groups in Rome. Other Jews, some of whom were Christ-followers arrived later and joined the growing number of synagogues. At this point, there is no evidence that Christ-following Jews worshipped separately from other Jews, and it appears that when non-Jews joined the Christ-movement, they also associated with Jews as God-fearers tended to do. Although the Jews as the entire Christ-movement were very poor, there were some Jews and Christ-following ethnē who were slightly more affluent, these being linked in some capacity with the leading family houses. Lampe gives one example of a Christ-follower, Valerius Biton, who was part of the delegation bringing *1 Clement* to Corinth in the 90s of the first century. He was described as an elderly man, which indicates that he was growing up in Rome at the time the Christ-movement had its beginnings in the 30s or 40s of the first century. It is thus possible that despite its growing diversity, the Christ-movement at Rome had early and ongoing links with

Jerusalem (Brown 1983: 103–4, Longenecker 2011: 146). Lampe concludes that despite patchy source material, at least it can generally be surmised that Jewish Christianity in the 30s and 40s of the first century found one of its paths from the Syrian-Palestinian East into the city of Rome through some of the aforementioned Roman households, through their Jewish slaves, freed persons, and their descendants (Lampe 2003: 143–8).

A conflict emerged among one of the Roman synagogue groups prior to the year 49 CE. At this time, Paul's ἐκκλησίαι were just beginning to be founded in the East. Jewish Christ-followers, probably arriving from the East, caused disputes focusing around someone called Chrestus (Suetonius, *Claudius* 25:4, Acts 18:2). This figure most likely refers to Christ, since the spelling Chrestus is permissible (compare Chrestianos Acts 11:26, 28; 1 Pet. 4:16 Codex Sinaiticus). The phrase used by Suetonius, *impulsore Chresto* need not mean that Chrestus was thought to have been present in Rome but can be translated as "because of the instigator Christ" (for a different view, see Slingerland 1997: 159–63). The key persons, among them Aquila and Prisca, tentmakers from linen like Paul, were expelled by Claudius. This incident meant that later Jews and Jewish Christ-followers in Rome had to be careful as regards their behavior before the authorities. The conflict over Chrestus marked the public awareness of the arrival of the Christ-movement at Rome prior to the year 49 BCE. Much speculation continues over whether the expulsion of leading Jews, Christ-followers, and others allowed the ethnē in Christ, who were a subgroup among the synagogues at Rome, to gain more influence over their fellows in the forced absence from Rome of the Jewish leaders (Wiefel 1991: 100, Longenecker 2011: 136, 146).

Also what would be the effect of exiles rejoining the synagogue communities after their return at the beginning of Nero's rule in 54 CE, following a five-year absence? This outcome of earlier inter-Jewish conflict may have left a legacy of animosity in Rome which would influence Jewish–non-Jewish relations, particularly when gentile Christ-followers later became more numerous.

The manner of its arrival from the East in important households to some extent determined the designation of the meetings of Christ-followers as house ἐκκλησία, in that the members were able to meet under the auspices of their head of house. The fact that Paul only gives this designation to one of the many groups he names in Rome may indicate that his use of ἐκκλησία indicated a group meeting under a patron, rather than a more unspecified entity. When other non-Jewish Christ-followers arrived from the East, and when the Christ-movement increased in numbers, it is quite possible that workers lived and socialized in tabernae close to the tenements where most of them lived. Jewett envisages that these people would share their food and eat together in a kind of love-communalism (in contrast to the love-patriarchalism of the home governed by the head of the house) (2007: 66–9).

It may be that some of the various groups Paul names in Romans 16 may live as groups of "brothers" where none of them is designated as the head or leader. In some cases, the named persons in Romans 16 do fit the pattern which centered on the patronage of the head of the house, for example, "those of the domestic staff of Aristobulus" or Narcissus (16:10-11) (Lampe 2003: 127). There are some people mentioned at the end of Romans 16 who probably do not all belong together but of whose social groupings Paul does not tell us much, except that they can apparently be listed together and that other unnamed "saints" associated with them (16:15). It is noteworthy that a common factor uniting all the people named here is some previous relation—family, work, friendship, and so on with Paul himself and his mission. Paul may be indicating how many friends and associates he has already in Rome or demonstrating what human resources he will be able to draw upon for future work. Notable is the number of women and the important roles and descriptions Paul gives them, including Prisca, Phoebe, Junia, and the mother of Rufus. Less prominence is generally attributed here to named men than women. This is a significant list, especially in Rome at this time when female leadership and influence were not unknown.

How Paul presents his named list of people suggests that Roman gentile Christ-followers were fractionalized like their Jewish counterparts, acting as independent units and only loosely connected to each other. This was in contrast to the Jewry in Alexandria where the various synagogues constituted one political body, a *politeuma*, under an ethnarch (Schwartz 2016: 127). This points to at least seven groups of named Christ-followers in Rome when Paul wrote his letter. This variegated diversity, including only one group actually labeled ἐκκλησία, denotes varieties of work, residence, and possibly social stratification and outlook. It seems that Paul's letter would be read to each group who, in turn, would deliver it to the next group, so that all the ethnē in Rome would hear it. Whether some Jewish individuals might also listen in is an unknown, but in any case, they were not addressed. This applies also to those named people in ch. 16 to whom Paul asks for greetings to be sent. God-fearers and proselytes could participate in certain aspects of synagogue activity and may have been included in the audience Paul addressed. To outsiders, these also may have appeared as Jewish.

Synagogues and Craft Guild Associations in Rome

Varying numbers of assembly places have been cited for the city of Rome at the time of Paul's letter. But the numbers of those specified are determined obviously by the definition given for this assembly or meeting place. When the term "synagogue" is used, some of the same issues arise as happens when "church" is used to signify the ἐκκλησίαι of the first century. Ralph Korner has decided to avoid "the problematic translation 'church' for ἐκκλησία, not least since ἐκκλησία never refers to the building or structure in which the ἐκκλησία gathers" (2015: 3–78, 54, n6). An overload of modern meaning is added to the term that Paul or his associates could never have envisaged or intended. Some scholars have argued similarly in relation to the term "synagogue," which in the first century differed greatly from its meaning in our contemporary era. "Calling ancient groups 'synagogues' necessarily transports a variety of modern connotations and sets these groups apart from similar social phenomena."[1] Korner continues to use the term "synagogue" but intends by that "not simply a specific reference to the Greek term συναγωγή, but rather a global reference to all terms used by Jews when describing their meetings, their communities, or places of meeting, for example, σύλλογος,

---

[1] Here Eckhardt acknowledges agreement with Richard Last (who has written extensively on this issue) "The Other Synagogues" (2016: 330–63), Eckhardt (2017: 248).

συναγωγή, ἐκκλησία, and προσευχή" (Korner 2015: 60). "The ancient designation may be closer to what would now be termed a "community center." "Religion" is today explicitly identified as separate from many activities that were closely interconnected in the first-century world (cf. Korner 2015: 1, n2; 75). For Jews, particularly since they were spread widely throughout the Diaspora, the synagogue served as a link between isolated Jewish communities. Josephus emphasizes the synagogue as a place to assemble, to live according to or maintain ancestral traditions, to collect money for the Temple, and possibly to store money safely.[2] Elaborating on the contribution of the synagogue, Ehrensperger makes the expansive claim that

> the powerful networks that connected local Jewish groups across vast swathes of territory and different sociopolitical realities thus provided various forms of mutual support, enabling the exchange of goods, traditions, and information, providing hubs on the road, and making it possible to maintain contact despite distance and local diversity. (2022b: 297)

Ehrensperger bases this claim on Josephus (*Ant.* 14:258-60, 16:43) and Cicero (*Flacc.* 66–69). She also interacts with the recent research by Collar (2013). Paul would doubtless have taken advantage of the wide range of facilities which the synagogue complexes offered to travelers such as him.

The ancient synagogue thus served a number of purposes for Jewish groups. Its primary function was as a meeting place for Jewish people. It is not the building or place of meeting that is the significant focus, but the assembly of Jewish members who constitute a synagogue. However, the term προσευχή is also used and this appears to denote some sort of physical structure or place in which Jews assemble for prayer (Philo, *Legat.* 132) and/or public decision-making. Josephus mentions προσευχή both in Alexandria (*Ap.* 2:10) and in Galilee (*Vita* 276–81, 294–5). In Tiberias, the προσευχή was large enough to contain the entire βουλή, which numbered around six hundred persons. It seems, therefore, that Josephus's προσευχή are purpose-built communal buildings and likely to have been used for public communal gatherings (Korner 2015: 60, n29). For various reasons, we will continue to use the term synagogue, but keeping in mind the range of options that may have been included in the first century. The place of meeting was not strictly limited to Jews, but others interested in Jewish tradition and practice could participate in accordance with their status. Though proselytism to Judaism was not generally encouraged or promoted, and though the core membership would remain Jewish, non-Jews could meet as "God-fearers" honoring the Jewish God and, if desired, after instruction could convert to become proselytes leading to eventual full membership of the assembly. We will not discuss this option now, but only later in relation to Romans 2 at the appropriate point.

As noted, there was no overarching structure encompassing all Jewish synagogues in Rome as there was in Alexandria (Schwartz 2016: 153–66). They seem to have been

---

[2] Thus, money stored in a building serving as a synagogue would be protected in Roman law: Philo, *Legat.* 156–158; Josephus, *Ant.* 16.163-171; Cicero, *Flacc.* 66–69. See also Ben-Zion Rosenfeld and Joseph Menira (1999) and Levine (2005: 81–134).

widespread all over the city, as the dispersed location of Jewish catacombs of later centuries clearly indicates. Thus Paul may have been in contact with some synagogue groups but not others (as seems to be the pattern in relation to assemblies of Christ-followers according to Romans 16). In Paul's case as a frequent traveler of long journeys, synagogue communities would be an invaluable asset not only to facilitate his travel but also in his apostolate to the nations. Indeed, it seems that most of Paul's potential converts already had had some contact with Judaism. It is likely that these became part of the network that he gradually established from Jerusalem to Corinth and elsewhere. This means that when we consider the likely venue for the meeting place for the ethnē in Christ at Rome, it is hard to discern whether a synagogue meeting place is or can be assumed or not. The fact that at times, in moments of crisis, *collegia* gatherings were banned in Rome, and that some Jewish (leaders?) had recently been exiled (Acts 18) makes certainty in relation to venues for meeting very difficult to ascertain. The Jewish origin of the messianic movement in Rome can be asserted with relative confidence, but whether the subsequent vicissitudes resulted in separate gentile Christ-following groups cannot confidently be assumed.

The current debate on the terminology for Jewish assemblies focuses not so much on whether or not there were ancient communities that may be called synagogues. But the designation "synagogue" has itself been challenged, not on the basis of its existence but on the scope of the designation. Richard Last proposes that every private group known to have at least one Judean member (and hence to be connected with *Ioudaismos*) "should be categorized with the same name that we give to ethnic associations devoted to the Judean deity," that is, "synagogues."' Last's skepticism regarding the term synagogue has been recognized as valid on both terminological and categorical grounds, but not without some qualification. Naturally, as Eckhardt notes, "this way of thinking would result not so much in the extension of the 'synagogue' category to encompass associations of craftsmen, but in the abandonment of the category and its replacement by a broader label, for which Last offers the suggestion 'private Judean-deity associations'" (2017: 247–8). There is evidence to support the designation of *Ioudaioi* as associations/collegia according to Roman law as a normal form of categorization. But this limited approval of a certain skepticism regarding its meaning does not warrant widening the scope of the term "synagogue" to such an extent as to render it meaningless.[3]

According to Philo, Augustus had written to the governors of Asia "so that they should allow solely the *Ioudaioi* to assemble in the synagogues" (*Leg.* 311). The first time that the association category is encountered in the sources points to a similar conclusion not in contradiction but in support of ethnically homogenous groups concerned with upholding their own customs. Thus, it can be asserted that "the Romans saw the Judeans as legitimate associations only in so far as they could plausibly regard them as ethnically homogenous groups" (Eckhardt 2017: 250). The aspect of worship was an important part of that definition since Josephus reports that *Ioudaioi*

---

[3] Last's research is based on recently offered taxonomies of ancient private groups that view all private voluntary cult groups as falling under the rubric of Greco-Roman associations (2016: 334).

are freed from Roman military service "who are Roman citizens and have Judean rites in Ephesus and are used to practicing them" (*A.J.* 14.228-29, 240).

Not only is the right for Jews to have an association, σύνοδον ἔχειν, Latin *collegium habere*, attested in legal texts of the Imperial period, but also Eckhardt cites a letter of 50/49 BCE in which Lucius Antonius confirmed the Jews' right to have these things. Another more direct reference is offered by Octavian in his letter to Parion/Poros where he notes that Jews should be allowed to come together according to their native tradition and collect money. What is significant is that he (Octavian) reports that though both he himself and Julius Caesar had put a ban on all associations (θίασοι) in Rome "these (associations) alone" (τούτοις μόνοις) are exempt from that ban due to the status of the *Ioudaioi* as friends and allies (Eckhardt 2017: 249).

Where disagreement in relation to the designation "synagogue" or "association" arises is particularly in relation to ethnic identity markers. Eckhardt, as noted, acknowledges that the transmission of Judean ancestral traditions need not be limited to the traditional role of synagogal Judaism, but that these could be honored in several ways and gives the example of the occasion when a markedly Judean commemoration was carried out not by the local group called συναγωγή, but by the local purple dyers and carpet weavers. Yet this did not constitute them Judean-deity associations, and he asserts that "Last goes too far in his attempt to eradicate any difference between groups using an ethnic marker of identity and those using a professional one" (Eckhardt 2017: 259). On the other hand, Richard Ascough may be correct to challenge any heuristic category that creates a sharp distinction between "associations" and "synagogues" (2015: 27–52).[4]

From the discussion of one aspect of recent debate about the use of synagogue terminology especially with reference to Rome, we conclude that it is still useful to continue to use the traditional term "synagogue." This can only be done with care, especially to avoid anachronism with respect to its difference from modern usage, and (some) assumptions of close parallels that may not be warranted. Last holds that if the exclusion of guilds from the synagogue category is allowed to persist, the insights gained from critical theory for understanding the fluidity and heterogeneity of Judean identity, ethnicity, and cult practice will be counteracted (2016: 330). We need to keep an open mind on this matter, but for our immediate purpose, we are swayed in our judgment by the fact that ethnicity and particularity receive specific attention from Paul in Romans, and that we see him in this letter as combining "impartiality and no discrimination" in relation to both Jews and the nations. He is moving toward the proper recognition of ethnicity among gentile Christ-groups rather than moving toward assimilation of these within broader non-ethnic associations. Though our approach does not require any specific connection of the ethnē in Christ at Rome with a Jewish *synagogue*, we are especially concerned both with how Paul navigated the intricate issues concerning difference between Jews and non-Jews in his mission and, in relation to current scholarship, how to adjust the pattern of a Paulinism that has tended to depict Paul "outside the synagogue." Our approach views the image of Paul

---

[4] Cf. also Korner's published McMaster's 2017 dissertation.

as "apostle to the nations" as constituting him an unlikely candidate for the blurring of ethnic realities in a universalizing direction to make him more amenable to our contemporary visions of unity.

We are in broad agreement with Eckhardt's claims that "*Ioudaios* is first and foremost an ethnic designator and, of course, encompasses forms of worship, but is never completely separated from *Ioudaia*" (Eckhardt 2017: 258). He does advise taking into account the indisputable fact that people could become *Ioudaioi* under certain circumstances and acknowledges that a broader use of the term after 70 is conceivable, yet claims "but it never lost its ethnic connotations" (2017: 258–9). The city of Rome, like the Greco-Roman world generally, was inhabited by a plethora of groups and knew numerous forms of social aggregation offering many options. Eckhardt concludes, "We should not condense this immense and interesting variety in an overarching supercategory for the sole purpose of denying any special traits to *Ioudaioi*" (Eckhardt 2017: 260).[5]

Assemblies in Rome?

One of the most tantalizing facts about Romans is the single reference to an assembly, ἐκκλησία—the one in the home of Aquila and Prisca (Rom. 16:3-5). This must indicate a self-conscious choice on the part of Paul. He would not have chosen the designation *synagogue* because his converts were not Jews, and his policy is always to distinguish Jew and non-Jew. The argument from silence suggests that Paul does not call the entire community of Christ-followers at Rome an ἐκκλησία, but only the subgroup in this home.

It may even be concluded from this fact that the other groups in Rome preferred other designations and resisted the appellation of ἐκκλησία. One implication of this could be that the term ἐκκλησία was inseparably related to Paul's gentile mission and the social patterns associated with it. There is evidence in the New Testament to support this. Not all Christ-followers across the Diaspora are explicitly identified as ἐκκλησία. James and Hebrews use the term but not necessarily as a permanent group identity. The absence of ἐκκλησία from 1 Peter is striking as Korner notes: "given the fact that 1 Peter addresses Christ-followers across Asia Minor, which is where Paul established ἐκκλησίαι (Galatia, Roman Asia) and where, only a few decades later, the author of Revelation writes to seven ἐκκλησίαι (Roman Asia)" (2015: 70).

Korner argues that if the description by the author of Acts concerning pre-Pauline communities in Judaea is regarded as a provincial or anachronistic usage, "then Paul's communities are the only subgroup within the pre-70 Jesus movement which

---

[5] Similar to Eckhardt, Clemens Leonard investigated whether Rabbinic Havurot were Greco-Roman Associations but concludes that the

> search for structures of Greco-Roman voluntary associations did not yield reliable results. … The rabbis do not pass on bylaws of an association or describe its social function in a way that requires the reconstruction of cultural borrowings in this respect … Havurah was just not a technical term for "Greco-Roman association" and haverim were not associates in this sense. The rabbis did not regard themselves as such. They were not regarded as such by Romans and they cannot be classed as such in modern scholarship. (2019: 205)

self-designated collectively as ἐκκλησίαι … [T]his group designation predominates within writings attributed to or associated with Paul" (Korner 2017: 70). Esler, however, is not convinced and argues that the term is rooted in some passages of the LXX, 1 Sam. 19:20 in particular. He concludes that ἐκκλησία was used "by Christ-groups of Judea which Paul and other Judeans after him persecuted" (2021c: 124). Esler interestingly argues that despite its Septuagintal origin, the term ἐκκλησίαι as used by Paul "acquired connotations from the role of ἐκκλησίαι in the cities of the Greek East. This allowed the Christ-movement to continue developing an identity distinct from ethnic Judeans and recognisably similar to Greco-Roman voluntary associations" (2021c: 130).

It could be that some of the Christ-followers at Rome were the fruit of the ministry of other apostles, especially those sent to "the circumcision" such as Peter (Campbell 2010: 178–9). Thus some may have heard the Christ-message in Jerusalem (cf. Fitzmyer 1993: 29) or elsewhere and, in the Diaspora, possibly through Paul and his associates, prior to their arrival in Rome or their return there (Esler 2003: 101); similarly, Richard Longenecker cites evidence from Eusebius and Ambrosiaster, favoring the latter's claim that the gospel was introduced in Rome by native Jews (2011: 71–3). In any case, there is reasonably strong evidence of a Jewish origin of the Christ-following groups at Rome which helps to explain ongoing issues surrounding proselytes and God-fearers.

We need to question why it was that Paul does not refer to all the Christ-following groups at Rome as ἐκκλησίαι, but only those in the home of Prisca and Aquila. The Christ-followers at Rome were a long-established group prior to Paul, and thus had developed their own patterns of *didache* and association with non-Jews. This would have followed the normal pattern of Christ-following Jews who continued to assemble with other Jews, and who would allow proselytes, God-fearers, and ethnē in Christ to join them. How could Paul be viewed as in opposition to this? He does acknowledge preexisting *didache* in 6:17 in a typical Pauline pattern of the "now" in Christ contrast with the "once" when you were slaves of sin. Where Paul seems to differ is that in contrast to existing patterns, he ruled that ethnē in Christ must cease to honor the Roman gods, thereby cutting them off from their pagan *habitus* while simultaneously preventing them from becoming proselytes to Judaism. Thus Paul, in this respect, would be viewed as a troublesome innovator because he interrupted the perception of ethnē in Christ viewing themselves, and being viewed as, either equivalent to God-fearers or in the process of becoming Jewish as proselytes.

Paul's perspective was determined by his conviction that a new era—Messianic Time—had dawned in the life and death of Jesus of Nazareth and its interpretation as the Christ-event. Paul was particularly concerned with the meaning of this for the ethnē. He may earlier have preached circumcision as a route to become a proselyte but turned away from this because he now realized it was both invalid and ineffective. Since the coming of Christ had actualized the promises of Abraham to the nations, those from the nations should no longer seek to become proselytes. Through trust in God's righteousness revealed in Christ, ethnē no longer had to come to God via Judaism; they could be accepted via Christ as non-Jews through trust—this was what the promises intended. What was distinctive about Paul's message for ethnē was that he taught that there was no point in their attempting to keep Israel's Law. Though not becoming Jews, they would become an associate gentile people of God alongside the Jews. This message was to be understood not in a supersessionist displacement manner but aggregatively—they would be blessed alongside the Jews (Tucker 2018, McMurray 2021). Nor did this message indicate the termination of Jewish law and practice. Paul did teach that God-fearers and proselyte circumcision were no longer necessary for non-Jews but not that the Jewish people had no future as Jews or should cease to live as Jews. The Law did have some significance for the ethnē, but not as a way of gaining access to the promise. It remains a Law given to and for the people of Israel. However the ethnē used it, it would never be possible for them to achieve its goal without trust in Christ. The Law had been given to Jews, but non-Jews were outside of God's gracious covenant, brought up amongst sinful people living as slaves to sin, without the aid of God's grace. In this state, no amount of effort would enable them to fulfill the Law as it would be perverted by sin in the process. To seek to use it to achieve access as ethnē to the people of Israel is mistaken effort—the call of God to Israel was by grace and likewise the call of God to ethnē is by grace, a call to trust in Christ as the way to God for non-Jews.

Paul's gospel effectively closed off access for the ethnē to the God of Israel via Judaism.[6] The path for ethnē should now be only through God's revealed pattern—through trust in Christ. He seems to be pessimistic concerning gentile sinfulness, but this is overshadowed by his optimism through Christ. So, if the term, ἐκκλησία is inseparably related to Paul's ministry, and many of the Christ-followers at Rome were not, this would partly explain Paul's limiting the term ἐκκλησία. It would give some substance to the phrase "Paul's gospel" of which he is far from ashamed. Paul's supporters possibly differentiate themselves from those who do not oppose the making of proselytes or the acknowledgement of God-fearers, both parts of the process of ethnē becoming Jews. Paul's "people" are categorized as either Jews or gentiles whether Christ-followers or not. Paul's deliberate emphasis on difference between Jew and non-Jew derives from the God of Israel's covenant with the Jewish people. The Christ-event did not annul this difference, though it did confirm the access of "gentiles" as "gentiles." In addition, what we find in Romans is evidence for differing forms of Christ-following groups with specific patterns for their members to follow. Paul can only acknowledge this diversity of identity and corresponding practice. He could not and dare not attempt to make it uniform across all the differing groups, whether meeting in tabernae or households. Rather, Paul locates himself and his co-workers in association with those many already known to him in Rome with particular reference to their prior and ongoing links with him (cf. 16:1-16). Diversity in patterns of following Christ are acceptable, so long as there is mutual recognition. He notes differing groups centered round particular individuals probably meeting in dispersed groups across Rome. Whether this indicates groups living in their leader's, possibly their master's house, a synagogal community or an association in a workshop setting is almost impossible to determine, but suggests a reasonable number of gentile adherents to Christ-trust even if there were only a few situated at each focus of meeting.

Paul's stance against gentile participation in what he viewed as potential idolatry constituted another problem, in that if the ethnē in Christ did consent to the Pauline pattern of nonparticipation, they would thus arouse resentment among their fellow ethnē who would view their disrespect for the gods as a threat to the safety of the city.

---

[6] I will discuss this further in a forthcoming article.

Reception History

Notable Emphases in the Reception of Romans Since 1970

In theory, Romans 1–11 or Romans 1–14 could be a self-standing argument to which chs. 12–16 or 15–16, respectively, were added to fit the exigency, that is, the perceived need calling forth this letter to Rome (Minear 1971: 84; Song 2004: 46). Indeed, it could even be claimed that it is only chs. 14–15 that give evidence of real interaction between Paul and the context of the Roman Christ-followers (Minear 1971: 84). In earlier debates, these chapters became the focal point in the issue concerning the epistolary nature of the letter. The sustained pattern of argumentation maintained through chs. 1–8 was commonly used as evidence for the dogmatic stance that tended to view Romans as an outline of Christian doctrine on the presumption that, for varied given explanatory reasons, Paul here offered a "theological self-introduction." This perspective, typical of the majority approach to Romans prior to the 1970s, was suggestive of writing theology free of constraint and did not adequately reflect the historical Paul but rather academic theology from the "ivory tower" divorced from historical context. Indeed, it is perhaps not too extreme to claim that "a text without a context (historical, social, literary, and rhetorical) is just a pretext for whatever the individual reader wants it to mean" (Witherington 2004: 16).

But, beginning in the 1970s, in response to the historical neglect of Romans as a letter to Rome, and of chapters Romans 9–11 in particular, a new impetus emerged, exemplified in the volume of essays, *The Romans Debate* (Donfried 1977, 1991). The volume represents the lasting contribution of Karl Donfried (deceased February 2022) to the interpretation of Romans. This research had the effect of leading to a fresh attempt to view the letter historically and contextually as presenting a coherent argumentation addressing the Roman context (Donfried 1991: 103). Harry Gamble's thorough research of the manuscript evidence led him to affirm the unity of all sixteen chapters of Romans as an address to Rome (Gamble 1977). The newer approach, typified particularly by the work of Jewett *Paul's Anthropological Terms* (1971), and others, including my own research and that of Donfried In *The Romans Debate* (1991), sought to view Paul's statements in his letters as particular, contextually related statements, rather than as *only* theological proclamation (to artificially exclude the theological is to fail to fully understand Paul's thought) (cf. Longenecker 2011: 305).[7] Failure to view Paul in his Jewish context and also to view him in light of what was later to be designated as the "Paul within Judaism" (Zetterholm 2015) approach meant that prior to the arrival of this, the concentration on the Jewish people in Romans 9–11 was often portrayed as a digression from the ascribed emphasis on Paul and his gentile gospel in the previous chapters. Reginald H. Fuller, one of my predecessors at the University of Wales, Lampeter, later of Virginia alerted me to the deficiencies in the existentialist approach to Romans 9–11 (1963: 72). It was this perceived neglect that led me into my research on "The Purpose of Paul in the Letter to the Romans: A

---

[7] Longenecker's is one of the most useful and comprehensive introductions to research on Romans (2011: 341–4).

Survey of Romans 1–11 with Special Reference to Chapters 9–11" in my unpublished doctoral dissertation (University of Edinburgh, 1972, cf. also Campbell 1982: 121–31, 2013: 1–17.)

Current and Backwater: The Relation of Romans 1–8 and 9–11

In the history of reception, there has been an ongoing tendency to deny full significance to chs. 9–11 within the argument of the letter, which led Bent Noack to coin the image Current and Backwater (Noack 1965). In my own research on Romans, I came to the conclusion that Romans is best represented as a letter to Rome and that not only were chs. 9–11 an intrinsic part of the letter, but more than that, they were the climax of its accumulated argumentation (Campbell 1981 and 1991). Later, the publication of Krister Stendahl's *Paul among Jews and Gentiles* (1976) gave impetus to this reading and, indeed, of the whole of Romans as a letter to Rome. Despite criticisms of its radically new approach in viewing Romans 14–15 in particular as addressing actual congregations in Rome, Paul Minear's innovative and imaginative monograph, *The Obedience of Faith* (1971), signaled a transition from reading Romans as more or less contextless, systematized theology to reading it in a similar vein to Corinthians or Galatians. Robert Karris opposed Minear's conclusions, arguing that Rom. 14:1–15:13 has no specific referent within the Roman community, and disputing the nature of the paraenesis in 14–15 in particular (1991: 84). Although not concentrating specifically upon Romans, E. P. Sanders's *Paul and Palestinian Judaism* (1977) combined with other currents of research, to point the way to a fresh approach to the content of Romans. When some continuity with Judaism, rather than mainly contrast was emphasized, both chs. 9–11 and chs. 14–15 demanded the fresh attention and significance which has to some extent been subsequently realized. It was F. C. Baur (1831) who pioneered the way to a historical interpretation of Romans and, as Käsemann has noted, whose important recognition of 9–11 as the climax of the letter was annulled by his mistaken view of the audience as predominantly Jewish Christian (1980: 253–4). Although disagreeing with Baur's posited opposition between so-called Christian universalism and Jewish particularism, his emphasis on the Sitz im Leben pointed me toward an historical approach to the letter (Campbell 1991a: 2). But it was Johannes Munck who gave his full "historically oriented" attention to Romans 9–11 viewing these chapters as Paul's reconstruction of events in "Heilsgeschichte" in light of the Jewish failure to recognize Jesus as Messiah and in light of Paul's own successful gentile mission (1967: 22–3).

As the exegesis will demonstrate, I have not changed my view of the significance of Romans 9–11, but I would wish to insist that the climactic nature of its contents emerges fully only with 12:1–15:13 in the praising God together of the Jewish people and the nations, thereby fulfilling the requirement of "ongoing ethnic plurality" (McMurray 2021: 2). Chapters 9–11 can be linked to chs. 1–8 in various ways, depending on scholars' approach. Witherington, followed to some extent by Elliott, offers an interesting suggestion that "Romans provides a *refutatio* of gentile misunderstandings about Jews and Jewish Christians" (2004: 17). Elliott agrees but claims that these "gentile misunderstandings constitute not just one aspect of the situation addressed by Romans, but the primary exigence of the letter" and "that Paul never addresses himself to actual Judeans, but to the contrary, explicitly directs the climactic warning in 11.13-24 to non-Judeans" (2008: 20). With this I am in full agreement. The effect of this perspective noted above is, as I have continued to stress, to regard chs. 1–8, not as the core of the letter, but as constituting an extensive *insinuatio*, the subtle or indirect approach recommended by ancient rhetoricians in situations in which the speaker's voice was expected to be controversial or unpopular. I can agree that it is not until Romans 9, that "Paul has finally arrived at what has concerned him the most about the theological misunderstanding in Rome" (Witherington 2004: 17).

However, to stress 9–11 does not demand the diminishment of 1–8. Because these latter chapters also relate to the exigency at Rome, however, indirectly; they have their own inherent significance not least of these being that they lay the groundwork on which 9–11 may be adequately understood. What must not be allowed is a preeminence attributed to 1–8 so as to neglect 9–11. Structurally, the use of μὴ γένοιτο as a characteristic response, ties Romans 9–11 inseparably to 1–8, and its contents cannot rightly be separated or diminished in relation to these— they must be attributed a significance at least equal to that of chs. 1–8 (Campbell 2013: 10–11). Through my exegesis, I have come to regard the refutation of the misunderstandings prior to ch. 9 as presenting Paul's own understanding in ways that prepare for 9–11: "Paul's strategy appears to be to highlight his own stance by a categorical rejection of extreme positions adopted by, or available to, at least some of the Roman Christ-followers" (2013: 43). These corrections to misunderstandings tell us not only what Paul did not believe but also indirectly what his own convictions were concerning these issues, thus contributing with chs. 12–15 to a cumulative argument focused around 9–11. The rhetorical questions enable Paul to voice stances he himself would have been unable to express so forthrightly to an audience that originated outside his own initiative.

The Nature of the Paraenesis in Romans: General or Particular?

We aim to give full recognition here to the epistolary diatribal style in which Romans is written, so we will keep before us our findings in the Excursus on Diatribal style, particularly on the relation of style to content, as we proceed. This is partly because we view this relation as indicative of Paul's mediation of his apostolic authority, in fact as signifying a leadership issue. Although Paul in 2 Corinthians does not respond to the same exigency as in Romans, we recognize that Esler's valuable portrayal of Paul's leadership (and issues attached to this) strengthens our emphasis on Paul's apostleship and resonates at this point with our research on Paul's leadership in Romans (Esler 2021a: 49–53, 161–6, 269–305).

The fact that Paul has not yet visited Rome has had various outcomes in the letter's content, the most obvious being that he cannot refer back to encounters on previous visits and that he has to rely on reports for the information concerning the situation at Rome. This limits Paul's use of his authority and demands a careful approach appropriate for one who has not worked in Rome, even though he claims authority in relation to the Roman ethnē in Christ as apostle to the nations. Commentators have sought to overcome this deficiency in Paul's relation to the Romans by viewing the letter's content as arising out of Paul's previous mission experiences in particular places, such as Corinth (best exemplified by Tobin 2004) or in the gentile mission generally (Manson 1991: 3–15). Alternatively, Paul's proposed visit to Jerusalem has been viewed as having triggered some of the topics discussed in the letter (Suggs 1967: 289–312; Jervell 1991: 53–64). As noted above, Paul Minear's study opened up new approaches to Romans in its depiction of a situation where differing groups disputed contemporary live issues in Rome. Its impact was not as great as it might have been due to its relative neglect of chs. 9–11 and its underestimating the diatribe features of the letter in seeking too precisely to identify the "you" to whom Paul is speaking at any given moment (Patte 2018: 86, n50).[8]

The question was raised earlier whether the content of chs. 14–15 was, as Bornkamm claimed, a revamping of 1 Corinthians, elevated from the sphere of the particular to the universal? Thus, Karris maintained that "Rom. 14.1-15.13 is a generalized adaptation of a position Paul had earlier worked out respecting actual known situations, especially in Corinth" (1991: 71). But, partly as a result of the ongoing "Romans Debate" in which I have been a regular participant, I am convinced that particularity is the chosen form of address in Paul's letters and that Romans is not different in this respect. Particularity in address does not mean that everything in a letter is entirely new or that part of the content has not been used before. Essentially, it means that the content is directed or specifically targeted to apply, in this form, to the exigence that caused the construction of the letter. Paul must be allowed to reuse his own expressed thoughts, but his unique pattern was to so relate to the exigencies targeted as to transform earlier conceptions in response to a new context.

This particularity can be demonstrated in several examples of items both included and omitted. The first possible instance is a certain gentile group calling themselves Jew(s) (2:17). This self-designation would have little credibility if this entity were merely something Paul imagined, and there is no sign of the phenomenon in Corinthians. Also, there is no warning against ethnē accepting circumcision in Romans as there is in Galatians—why did Paul omit this in Romans, and include "the value of circumcision" in Rom. 3:1-8? Why does Paul specify his addressees so specifically as "gentile" in Romans 1, 11, and 15? Also why did Paul carry through this gentile differentiation so precisely at varying points so that he avoids including himself in a "mixed" group of Jews and non-Jews in his use of pronouns to distinguish ethnic origin? In addition, we need to ask where Paul learned about the claim of the wild olive shoot to displace others, that is, the Jews. Moreover, where and how did the people listed by name in differing ways in ch. 16 originate? The best explanation of Paul's specific inclusion of topics or failure to include them, as well as in the presentation of these, is that he was informed by colleagues and friends in Rome with information that enabled or caused him so to do. As we proceed in the exegesis of the letter, we will draw attention to

---

[8] This work is an outcome of Patte's decade-long initiative and involvement in the Romans Through History and Cultures SBL Seminar and the series emerging from it with the same title, which he edited together with Christina Grenholm, beginning in 2000.

unique or unusual features that distinguish Romans from all Paul's other letters, as, for example, 6:3, 7:14a, and 8:29.

These distinguishing features of Romans indicate not generalities of paraenesis but interaction by an apostle who, though he had not visited Rome, yet in whose sphere of apostleship the city has already been included, for perhaps up to a decade. These factors just noted do not explain all the peculiarities of Romans but they do demonstrate its lack of similarity with Paul's other letters sufficiently to resist it being subsumed under vague generalizations.

Having stressed its distinction in relation to Corinthians or other Paulines, account must be taken of the nature and distinction of Romans itself. We will devote some attention to its diatribal style of presentation at many points throughout the letter, particularly in relation of style to content and interpretation (see Excursus I). We will discuss throughout our exegesis to what extent the fact of Paul's never having visited Rome is a sufficient reason to explain its divergence from other Paulines. Also, we will consider whether the diatribal style is primarily polemical or pedagogical and how our decision on this influences our reading of the letter. One feature will emerge in our discussions, that is, Paul's authority as an apostolic leader of the ethnē in Christ and how this leadership is expressed through the varied rhetoric in Romans. Thus, there is some similarity between Romans and Corinthians regarding some of the issues that affected Paul's leadership of the gentile mission (Esler 2021a).

Romans Addresses Ethnē in Christ in Their Roman Context

As we have just insisted above, the actual context to which Romans is addressed must influence to some extent the form and content of Paul's teaching in the letter. Also, as I have argued consistently throughout my academic career, this contextual factor has not been sufficiently addressed in the vast amount of literature on the letter, mainly because of the attribution of its paraenesis to general contexts rather than specifically to Rome.

I have concentrated in my research on the text and content of Romans itself, particularly on how ethnic and theological (i.e., covenantal) issues relating to Israel and the nations have determined its content. In the past two decades, especially, wider contextualization of the letter has opened up new vistas, though strong evidence in the text of Romans has, as yet, not always been easily deduced in their favor. The application of theories to the actual text of Romans must have priority however much contextualization is required, and no commentary is adequate that does not give a viable interpretation of the essential contribution and characteristics of all sections of the letter.

My own approach to Romans has been enhanced, I believe, through the activity and outcomes of the "Paul and Politics" Seminar at the Society of Biblical Literature (SBL).[9] Richard Horsley, Robert Jewett, Neil Elliott, Ian Rock, and others have demonstrated the need to place Paul contextually within the real political world of his day and to

---

[9] See, for example, Horsley (1987, 2000). For a comprehensive listing of the published papers of this seminar up to 2008, see Elliott (2008: 173, n22).

read his letters against this background (rather than in a political, social, or ideological vacuum). For my part, I have concentrated on how the politics of the first century impinged on Jewish and, specifically, ethnic issues and how this has influenced the understanding of Paul both then and today. Though not all scholars have responded equally or similarly to this challenge, I have come to view the wider context of first-century social (and political) life as one of the formative influences that shaped the presentation of Paul's gospel. There has been an ongoing widening and development in the meaning of the phrase Sitz im Leben "the historical context" from F. C. Baur until today, and New Testament Studies in particular is the richer and the more historical because of this.

As James Harrison has noted, in addition to the literary texts, Jewish and Roman, a whole new arsenal of equipment to study the Roman context is now available in the archaeological, epigraphic, numismatic, and iconographic evidence. Also, new methodologies such as visual exegesis and a consideration of the subliminal messages embodied in the urban landscape need to be brought into play (2020: xii). Thus, the challenge facing the interpreter of Romans is greater than ever and involves bringing these insights into a close correlation with the text.

This is a problem that is not really new, but the challenge that has been intensified by these new vistas is how to incorporate their insights emanating from a great diversity of sources such as Social Identity Theory (SIT), meaningfully and coherently into the understanding and interpretation of the text.

Robert Jewett's massive Hermeneia commentary (2007) represents a valiant attempt to do just this, and to a great extent he has succeeded, though new publications quickly date even the most up to date research. Neil Elliott also represents an approach to Romans that takes the Roman context very much into account particularly how it would have been read in the 50s from the context and categories of Roman state/imperial ideology (2008, but cf. also 1994 and 1990/2007). As Elliott claims, "The argument of Romans as a whole collides inescapably with the claims of empire even if that collision is never expressed in explicit terms." (2008: 14). These were already proving somewhat seductive to the emergent gentile Christ-groups. Ian Rock, my former doctoral student stands in this political/ideological line of interpretation and has brilliantly demonstrated its application to Roman imperialism (2012). What is significant in Jewett's and Elliott's readings, as also with Rock, is the application of their findings to contemporary politics.

Elliott's approach is challenging in its integration of (contemporary) Roman texts and imperial ideology with the interpretation of the letter. An additional merit is that it, simultaneously with this, presents a Jewish Paul. It was partly the neglect of a positive reading and understanding of Judaism that first drew me to research Romans 9–11. Already in 1996, Mark Nanos had drawn attention to the Jewish context and content of Romans, emphasizing Paul's roots in Jewish tradition and the close relation of the Christ groups to synagogue communities. Elliott argues that this Jewish teaching and alternative ideological outlook is clearly visible in light of the all-pervasive domination of the Roman Empire. This emerges particularly in his perspective upon how Roman imperial ideology impinged with corrosive effect upon the members of the gentile assemblies whom Paul addresses (2008: 9). As he claims, "I suggest that the letter confronts both the 'boast' of supremacy over Israel and, by necessity, the attitudes in the wider environment that nourished that boast" (Elliott 2008: 20).

Already the recent emphasis upon "Paul within Judaism" has developed links with current interpretation of Romans. I have found it fruitful in this research to develop the line of thought espoused by Rajak (2009: 154) and Ehrensperger (2013: 146–8) that Paul's use of the language of the LXX indicates both "playing and not playing the game of acculturation." Thus Paul uses Greek linguistic terms with added meaning in a particular context derived from filling these Greek terms with Jewish meanings to convey a certain resistance to imperial ideology in light of commitment to the God of Israel. This approach to Paul's vocabulary and awareness of difference between Jewish and Greek cultural emphases has supported earlier research that focused upon Paul's ethnic differentiation in relation to the covenant and people of Israel. Because recent interpretation of Romans has read Romans as a letter to non-Jews, this has strengthened insights into Paul's ethnic thought (e.g., McMurray 2021), as well as contributed to avoiding supersessionist readings (Tucker 2018).

Approach to the Letter

Important in my approach is to read Romans as noted in its sociohistorical context. This implies development in interpretation across the centuries. My approach emphasizes continuity over against discontinuity. This is because any interpretation includes presuppositions that are informed and formed within and by the sociohistorical and cultural context of the author, and authors live and write in diverse cultural contexts. Creative thought normally occurs most easily and fruitfully in conversation with others, far and wide, across the centuries as well with contemporary colleagues. Reading scripture is always a communal endeavor in process, continually in need of critical evaluation in a responsive concert of diverse voices.[10] So among the many voices relevant for my approach are, for example, Nicholas of Lyra, the Franciscan scholar and biblical exegete (*c.* 1270–1349), who wrote a famous and highly influential first full commentary on Romans (1329). He claimed that the Jewish people surpassed other peoples in knowledge of divine law. As a dedicated student of the Hebrew Bible and Rabbinic interpretation of it, Nicholas assumed that Jewish scholars, both biblical and contemporary, held unique insights into divine truth. He emphasized continuity rather than opposition between what he called Old and New Law (Klepper 2007). This was in spite of the fact that he was as supersessionist as any of his contemporaries and wrote at a time of Jewish expulsion as, for example, from England in 1290. A similar noteworthy example is Heinrich Bullinger, 1504–75, the Swiss Theologian, successor of Huldrych Zwingli in Zurich (Opitz 2008). In his 1533 commentary on Romans,[11] he succeeded in holding together Law and Gospel in a way that few have managed so successfully since the Reformation, setting a pattern that

---

[10] Patte and Grenholm labeled this process "scriptural criticism" (2007, Preface to Vol. 1 *Reading Israel in Romans*, 2000: 5).
[11] Latin title, *In sanctissimam Pauli ad Romanos epistolam … commentarius* (Zurich: C. Froschauer).

is still evident in traditions that followed this trajectory of interpretation (Campbell 2007, 2008). In the more recent past, I acknowledge the innovative work of Anthony Tyrell Hanson, who was instrumental (with others) in the founding of the annual conference titled "The Use of the Old Testament in the New," the predecessor of the British New Testament Society.

But it was primarily through the decade-long project, Romans through History and Cultures, jointly led by Christina Grenholm and Daniel Patte, that I was able to develop and deepen my understanding of Romans in ongoing conversation with a diversity of international expert scholars. Primarily, I came to see more clearly that interpretation is communal, that a diversity of plausible readings is normal in scholarly interpretation, and that those who differ in stance should not be regarded as enemies but as colleagues in seeking understanding. Because of this another element in reading Paul in particular emerges, that reading scripture is not only a collegial but also an ethical process. As scholars we are responsible for the impact of our interpretations in social interactions of the societies in which we live (Patte 1995). The ethics involved in the reading and teaching of Paul could not be more demanding than at present— "an age of Fake News and Alternative Facts" (Patte 2018: xiv). Jews and others who differ in what are perceived to be significant ways from "the rest of us" are often treated in prejudicial ways, and Paul in Romans offers us something better in his "welcome one another therefore just as Christ has welcomed you" (Rom. 15:7). It is incumbent upon biblical scholars as Paul's students never to inflame passions prejudicial to those perceived as "weak," particularly in those societies that still claim to have some form of Christian civilization. Certainly, the kingdom of God is primarily justice and peace and joy in the Holy Spirit (Rom. 14:17-18).

In as much as contemporary interpretation is a communal process, for Paul too his activities and teaching were communal, as is evident in his normal form of address to "you" plural, rather than to the singular individual. Paul's teaching is surely relevant for the individual but only insofar as the individual is part of a community, in the sense of the French philosopher Jean-Luc Nancy, one can only be individual in the plural (Nancy 2000).

The Significance, Effect, and Outcome of Paul's Addressing Only "Gentiles" in Romans

Those addressed in the plural by Paul in Romans are "gentiles," that is, non-Jews.[12] We will consider in detail through our exegesis how Paul addresses this selected and designated gentile audience. But even a quick glance at the significant texts demonstrates without ambiguity that Paul explicitly addresses the ethnē in Christ at Rome. Paul has received grace and apostleship to bring about ὑπακοὴν πίστεως the "hearing in trust," among all the nations ἐν πᾶσιν τοῖς ἔθνεσιν, including yourselves (Rom. 1:6). The expanded address "to all God's beloved in Rome" (v. 7) is not an address to another group as yet unaddressed but an elaboration of the previous verse (for detailed discussion of the issues involved in this verse see the exegesis of Rom

---

[12] For a good overview of predecessors of this stance see Zetterholm 2009: 127–63.

1:5-7, pp. 54–6). In Rom. 1:13 Paul explains his desire to "reap some harvest among you as among the rest of the ethnē (ἐν τοῖς λοιποῖς ἔθνεσιν)." Also, here Paul's own particular calling, not to the whole world of peoples but only to the ethnē, is specifically noted—he is a Jewish apostle to the nations.

Again, somewhat unexpectedly, in 11:13, Paul pauses to remind his addressees that "I am speaking to you ethnē," and elaborates on this in his appropriate designation of the ethnē as a "wild olive shoot" (11:17). At the conclusion of the letter, Paul is once again explicit about the limitation of his ministry to the ethnē, λειτουργὸν Χριστοῦ Ἰησοῦ εἰς τὰ ἔθνη, "a minister of Jesus Christ to the ethnē," and follows this with a reference to ἡ προσφορὰ τῶν ἐθνῶν the offering of the ethnē (15:16). A further comparison between poor Jews (ἅγιοι) in Jerusalem and the Christ-followers of Macedonia and Achaia (who appropriately share their resources with their Jewish Christ-followers) leaves no doubt that Paul explicitly here compares Jewish and gentile responses to the gospel, with the Christ-followers at Rome being unequivocally classed as ethnē. Where this focus differs from most earlier interpretive stances (Stowers 1994 and Rodriguez 2014 being notable exceptions) is that we stress and seek to consistently adhere to the view that Jews are not addressed but only ethnē in Christ. Even Patte who is very alert to the significance of our approach, and regards the letter as "primarily addressed to Gentile Christ-followers," still adds "with the expectation that Jewish Christ-followers overhear this conversation and are secondary addressees" (2018: 192).

The fact that Paul addresses only ethnē in Christ does not mean that Jewish Christ-followers are not presupposed and present or that they did not meet together or interact with ethnē in Christ. Historically, it is evident that there was and had been significant numbers of Jews living in Rome; this cannot be disputed. But that does not mean that Paul must write to them. His concerns are only with ethnē in Christ. The argumentation of the letter as we will see is designed to make a case for ethnē in Christ linking themselves in some association with the Jewish people. Whether or not there were mixed communities in Rome, Paul chooses to write only to the ethnē in Christ.

Having established that Paul addresses only the ethnē at Rome, we need to consider what the social, political, and theological significance of this is. We do not think that Paul, at this point, is seeking to establish the equal rights of Jews and non-Jews in Christ. That has already been established, but the question is whether the groups, in addition to acquiring their own distinctive identity in Christ, should be required to have any association with each other. If they each have their own identity, do they need one another in the future? One issue in Rome must be a *consistent understanding of gentile identity in Christ*.

We consider that Paul's writing a letter to such a group among the Christ-followers at Rome would have major side effects, one of which would have been to contribute to the conception of themselves in their own eyes or in the eyes of others as a particular, already formed group, a cohesive unit, distinct from other similar entities. In the writing of such a letter, Paul cannot avoid addressing these as a distinct group and thus directly contributes to their "entitativity" (Hogg 2006: 118), which in the long term may have signaled the beginning of gentile alienation from the people of Israel.

Thus, Paul contributes to their entitativity by addressing only the ethnē, hence the increased possibility of these being conceived or of conceiving themselves as distinct from other Christ-following groups including, or perhaps even especially, Jews. This is a serious step to take, not one Paul would have taken lightly. He needed to address the ethnē in Christ because of their mistaken conception that they had taken the place of the Jews as God's servants in the world. We conclude, therefore, that Paul must have felt obligated to do this as the lesser of two possible evils. The situation must have been such that Paul felt he could not do otherwise than intervene. We do not consider Paul would knowingly have encouraged a sense of self-awareness among Christ-followers as non-Jewish, even though he strongly differentiated between Jews and ethnē. As far as we can see, the ethnē in Christ at Rome were already quite self-aware as ethnē without Paul's accentuating this (though the fact that some considered calling themselves Jews indicates deficiency in ethnic understanding). We conclude, therefore, that Paul took the crucial step of addressing ethnē in Christ separately from Jews not willingly but out of dire necessity. This leads us to the conclusion that there was a critical exigency at Rome in which Paul as the apostle to the nations was involved because he was perceived as encouraging the view that Israel had been surpassed and displaced. The reporting of Israel's reaction to the message about the Christ-event must underlie some of the opinions expressed in Rome. The proclaimed opening of the kingdom to the nations caused diverse reactions in the gentile world. Some gentile Christ-followers went in one direction in viewing themselves as "true Jews" possibly, as we have noted, because they saw themselves as replacing Israel.

Others probably held on to Roman God-fearer patterns of life in which the honoring of the gods was normal in everyday life, thus enabling them to socialize better with their gentile neighbors. This would avoid associating with some who were still concerned about participating in anything associated with idolatry. Surprisingly, the Roman ethnē in Christ probably did not perceive themselves as anti-Jewish—they were not proposing the complete demise of Israel, only that their group had now become a mainly gentile entity through Christ in light of Israel's perceived failure. This meant that implicitly, even explicitly, the Roman ethnē must have regarded themselves as heirs through Christ to all the inheritance of Israel. In future, the blessing of God and his purpose for the nations would proceed through the ethnē, not Israel. So, it was not that the ethnē sought complete separation from the Jewish people and Jewish tradition. It was partly that they were misinformed about the identity of Israel, and hence about their own identity as a satellite group of people associated with Israel. The fact that Paul draws an analogy in ch. 8 between the attributes of Israel and those of the ethnē in Christ is warrant for designating the ethnē an associate people with Israel. But the association with Israel is more than analogical; it is intrinsic to the identity of the ethnē in Christ as we will demonstrate throughout the commentary.

The significance of Abraham was crucial here—he could easily be depicted as the first non-Jew who was called by God. To claim to be heirs of Abraham through Christ might suggest that the acceptance of the promises by the ethnē could facilitate bypassing the people of Israel. If Abraham were truly our fleshly forefather, does this not legitimate a claim that ethnē can call themselves Jews, even without circumcision? The Christ-movement at Rome was in danger of confusion because of its deficient understanding of Jewish traditions in this area, and thus of attracting unwanted attention from Nero and the Roman authorities. To call oneself a Jew while being born a "gentile" could lead to Jews being persecuted. Again, to call oneself a Jew, as some obviously did, did not require a wholly negative view of Israel, though some interpreted the outcome of Israel's refusal to be persuaded by the Christ-event as resulting in her rejection and bypassing by God from his purposes.

To take Israel's place, in one respect, not only indicated appreciation of this particular people but also simultaneously implied only a previous honorable history that was now *passé*. And if it is permissible for some to take on the title of Jew though of gentile birth, then in light of this newly acquired Jewish identity, issues could arise concerning such rituals as circumcision? Can this any longer function as a badge of identity, or should it now be spiritually/internally interpreted? This suggests there must have been powerful reasons for Paul's writing—his mission and reputation were already involved in debates at Rome, causing him to intervene. Paul has no authority over Jewish people in Rome—his apostleship, as he underlines this, is to the ethnē. It is primarily the content of what needs to be said to the ethnē to correct their self-understanding as ethnē in Christ that makes them the only addressees of Paul's letter. The content of Paul's letter to Rome does not indicate that Jews were addressed at any point—rather the opposite. It would have been unlikely that Jews would boast over other Jews (11:17-24). Also, Jews could not be criticized for calling themselves Jews (2:17). Paul could not have addressed himself so explicitly and so strongly if the congregation addressed were mixed—Jews and non-Jews.

It is Paul's gentile mission and his entire perspective upon the ethnē that is required to explain the content of Romans (rather than any failings imagined or real on the part of Jews resident at Rome). Gentile Christ-followers and their noted deficiencies by themselves offer an adequate subject matter. This implies that Paul's visit to Jerusalem and his safety on arrival there might be affected by Paul's writing or not writing to the Romans. His already projected image is in serious need of correction. Whether Paul's intervention caused further gentile "separateness" at Rome or overcame the divisive ideology noted above is not clear. What must be clear is that Paul's addressing of ethnē in Christ as a separate entity would help to crystallize/confirm a gentile identity as such, and thus he may also have (unwillingly) contributed to the conception of what may be termed a "supersessionist people of God self-understanding" favored by the Roman ethnē (Tucker 2018). As a minimum, we must envisage the ethnē in Christ at Rome as having a sufficiently specific identity as non-Jews to be identifiable as a subgroup within synagogues (if they were attached to such) and to continue to be recognized as such. These would most likely have produced leaders of the group who could represent their opinion to other assemblies.[13] Thus, it may be feasible to agree that Romans is directed to non-Jews, but precisely those non-Jews who had been or still were operative within a Jewish community in Rome (Thorsteinsson 2003: 121).

One scenario that can be envisaged is that in order to assert their own identity as ethnē in Christ, and because of growing gentile arrogance, the ethnē in Christ at Rome to whom Paul writes may be in process of separating from a Jewish synagogal group(s). It may also be likely that Paul and his gentile mission were becoming a

---

[13] I reach this perception by assuming that some of "the strong" are putting pressure on "the weak" to conform to patterns of conduct that they resist (1995: 56–8).

focal point of contention, leading to Paul's being slandered in the process (3:8). This misunderstanding of Paul and his mission is perfectly understandable in light of conflictual issues that had already arisen elsewhere. If, as Nanos has argued, the ethnē in Christ remained within the synagogue context, then it is possible that they were beginning to consider separation, or found they could no longer live in harmony with their fellow Jews and ethnē in Christ. It seems that some leaders were expelled in 49 CE, leaving a leadership vacuum for ethnē associated with the synagogue (1999: 283–304; 2012: 12–16). This expulsion would have involved only separation from common meeting places, but could have been interpreted both as self-sufficiency from the synagogue and as superiority because of the supposition that Jewish people had lost their way. The ethnē, in contrast, had responded positively to the message about the Christ. If Paul and his mission were being used as a lever in Rome, particularly by those Christ-followers who, for various reasons, thought themselves superior to Jews, Paul's gospel in relation to both Jews and non-Jews would necessarily be a subject of discussion, possibly something of which to be ashamed of (1:16).

Some such scenario would contribute to a solution of certain issues requiring explanation sought by many Roman commentators. The perceived double character of Romans as very explicitly addressed to ethnē only, but containing many features that, despite this, have led many to refuse to give up the concept of a mixed body of Jews and non-Jews as the actual addressees.

Paul carefully limits his apostolic authority only to the nations. Even if the addressed ethnē in Christ were operating as a subgroup of a synagogal association and, as such, would not be subject to normal discipline for Jews, the latter would still be held responsible for any disturbances that would bring attention from the authorities. My view is that since Paul's guidance is that they should not separate from Jews, he would seek to be really careful not to give or to be any cause of separation from, or criticism of, Jews or Jewish tradition. In fact, it is legitimate to claim that it would be Paul's normal policy not to needlessly antagonize his fellow Jews. Paul always tempers his critique of Jewish tradition or of Jewish identity so that he is never guilty of unwittingly encouraging anti-Judaism or of allowing his concentration on the gentile mission to be interpreted as opposition to Jewish tradition or its Law (Campbell 2006: 110–11).

Thus, Paul elaborates on his call as apostle to the nations in such a way in Romans as to demonstrate his Jewish roots (9:1-4) and to explain that this concentration does not allow the inference that Israel has been bypassed. Such an explanation would have been an essential element in any guidance to encourage ethnē in Christ to maintain links with Jews and Jewish tradition but could have been counterproductive if misunderstood.

The question that is very difficult to answer, but that requires some response, is what difference would it make for ethnē in Christ to separate from an existing association with a Jewish synagogue group, in terms of visible social relations. They would still be perceived by outsiders as a Jewish group except that they now adopted patterns of life that were explicitly non-Jewish, for example, by participating in worship at local shrines. It is likely, except they were very cautious, that they might soon be categorized by outsiders as non-Jewish, in which case they would have no protection because of their supposed adherence to ancestral Jewish law and custom. Paul, I think, was very aware of the growing discontent in Judaea, at this time, and fearful that the Roman ethnē would attract attention from the civic authorities as a new "superstition," especially as they were disputing among themselves. Also, their departure from synagogal association might not encourage local Jewish neighbors to dispel any rumors that they were not really "Jewish." In any case, Paul is quite clear that in terms of a secure identity as ethnē in Christ, as well as for their political security, they ought to maintain links with Jews and together though distinct to praise the God of Israel.

Social Identity Theory

Reading Romans through the lens of SIT requires some clarification of my particular grasp of those aspects of the diverse field of SIT that I consider most relevant and illuminating for this task. Since its emergence in the 1970s, SIT has developed in various ways, so that there is now not just one strand but significant diversification in critical interaction with the paradigms set by Tajfel and Turner. To focus on the importance of groups for understanding social interaction was a great achievement, but its findings need to be broadened and critically discussed in diverse cultural, social, and political settings (Reicher 2004). Generalizations over time and space are also questionable in this field. In view of the application of SIT to texts of antiquity, this is particularly important in order to avoid potential anachronisms. Nevertheless, since Paul's letters evidently address and deal with group-related issues, using SIT alongside other methods promises valuable insights into the group dynamics that may not be otherwise noted (Clarke and Tucker 2014: 23).

Human beings only thrive in relation to others. A space of belonging is vital for the survival of biologically prematurely born humans. Thus, at the heart of life is the relation to the other—the inimical bonding of the newborn to primary carers—from which its differentiation in the course of the first few years of life a sense of self can only emerge. The relationship emerges as a relationship precisely through the difference—in the space between humans who are different. Relationality, belonging, and commonality are based on difference; they are nurtured and grow in this space (Buber 1937, Levinas 1969, Arendt 1979). Although one of the first words a child may say is "no," she or he can only say so due to the safety of belonging, a committed relationality. Thus differentiation or individuation can only emerge based on the symbiosis of the earliest months of life, but even separation, although a process of differentiation, is inherently relational and based on the trust in which parent and child are commonly held together. Difference and differentiation may lead to conflicts and distancing, but all of these processes happen grounded in the commonality of trust and the sense of belonging. When a child in the process of growing up moves further away from the family group, this again is based on the safety of this unquestioned place of belonging, to which she or he can return. This basis of trust enables the child to experiment through trial and error on how to relate to others, individuals and groups—and thus negotiate nearness and distance, commonality, and difference in circles beyond the immediate in-group of the family.

The need to belong is related to the interrelatedness of life—no life and no group can exist in isolation. This is recognized by most behavioral scientists. Human beings are group beings. The physical endowments of humans—weakness, hairlessness, and extended infancy—what has been labeled by Adolf Portmann (1971, 1973) as socially premature-born beings, clearly indicate that we cannot survive as lone individuals, or even as small family groups. Key characteristics that have contributed to the adaptation of humans to a wide range of physical environments are based on interdependence, collective knowledge, and cooperative sharing of information (Kameda and Nakanishi 2003). Thus, interrelatedness not only applies to individuals but also to groups that differ in analogy to individuals who differ, but whose difference is the basis of them being able to relate to others as others. They do not do so in a binary fashion but in a network of multiple relations, in analogy to a rhizome (interconnected root system). There seems to be an analogy with individuals to the interrelatedness of groups, which exist in their difference/diversity but as such are necessarily related. This is of significance for the commentary, in that we do not see groups and aspects of identity as necessarily mutually exclusive. We note Paul's tendency to formulate arguments in a "not only but also" inclusive pattern.

Social Identity Based on Group Conflict

We do not attempt here to give a justification or defense of the use of the social identity approach in biblical interpretation. This has been very thoroughly exemplified by many scholars as, for example, in the comprehensive volume in the *T&T Clark Handbook to Social Identity in the New Testament* edited by Coleman A. Baker and J. Brian Tucker (2014), but most recently by Robert Philip F. Esler in the previous volume in this series, 2 Corinthians (2021a). Most of the significant issues in relation to the social identity approach to the New Testament have been already addressed by Brawley (2020), Tucker (2011), Esler (2003, 2021a), and others to whom we will refer at relevant points in our interpretation of Romans.

In SIT, there has been a strand/tendency to view in-group identification as basically implying bias or antagonism against out-groups or other groups. The theory emerged through research that tried to understand group behavior—that is, the behavior of individuals when identifying as a group member, which in certain contexts and cases differed from when these individuals acted outside the group in question. Its research focus was on understanding conflict between groups—how they emerged and how such conflicts could be resolved (Tajfel and Turner 1979: 7). Based on the horrors of the Shoah, minimal laboratory experiments tried to understand intergroup interaction between groups, even where no specifically context-related characteristics were attributed to the groups whose members were to interact either in the in-group or with members of the out-group (cf. Esler 2021a. 22–4). In-group favoritism was observed and mostly competition or antagonism against the out-group. This leads some SIT researchers to the conclusion that group identification or group formation is inherently competitive and antagonistic or, in a milder version, requires a negative discernment of other groups in order to be able to support the self-esteem of the in-group members. Positive in-group bias is seen as inherently linked to negative or even derogatory out-group perception (Tajfel 1978, Tajfel and Turner 1979, Turner 1975). The formation of groups as such was seen as a negative differentiation from others, with the primary function of enhancing or stabilizing the self-esteem of the individual (Abrams and Hogg, 1988, Turner and Reynolds 2001).

In this strand of SIT, this is actually considered to be the motivation for groups to be formed. However, it has been demonstrated convincingly that this model only captures one aspect of group formation, namely, in specific contexts and under specific conditions (Brewer 2010). The minimal laboratory experiments were set up with the specific aim to analyze the reasons for intergroup conflicts. This is certainly valuable but can hardly explain all aspects of group formation. Critical questions have subsequently been raised about the setup of minimal laboratory experiments per se, in that they create a researcher-controlled environment and do not take into account cultural, power-related, gender-related, and sociopolitical factors that impact on human behavior (Maddux and Brewer 2005, Magnusson and Marecek 2017). The conclusions drawn based on experiments under laboratory conditions (see Hodson and Earle 2017: 3) in Western societies of the late twentieth century need to be seen as precisely that. The predominantly male participants in these experiments are socialized in the particular way of Western societies, that is, societies that are permeated with an ethos of competition, and not only at the economic level. This context is the practical and hermeneutical presupposition of the theory and needs to be consciously reflected upon when drawing conclusions that claim significance beyond this particular context. It is questionable to draw general conclusions from experiments in such a particular setting and then generalize across different periods to other times and places.

The universalization of some aspects of the theory that the rationale for group formation is self-enhancement—and thus antagonism toward other groups (Hogg 2016: 16)—needs then to be questioned from within SIT, as well as in light of gender-critical and certain philosophical insights. Thus, it has been argued that in modern societies "singular ingroup–outgroup differentiations (dramatic and powerful as they maybe) may be more the exception than the rule" (Brewer 2010: 11).

It has been argued in other strands of SIT that the central motivation for group formation is not the enhancement of self-esteem of its members or differentiation from another group but rather cooperation between members of a group for mutual support and/or to achieve common goals. Human beings are inherently interdependent on each other, and their cognition, motivation, and emotion are evolving in relation to social interaction and social requirements in groups. The main primary purpose of group formation is thus internally oriented rather than outward to other groups. Cooperation between members is necessary and beneficial irrespective of the existence of an out-group. Intergroup conflict is thus not the presupposition of in-group formation (Brewer 2007: 731). Positive identification with the in-group is, of course, assumed, but this is a consequence rather than the motive for belonging to a group. A group or community provides some security through cooperation and trust. There is no inherent connection between positive in-group perception and negative out-group perception. These aspects can be, but do not need to be, interconnected. As noted, the identification with the group to which one belongs does not require a negative or derogatory attitude to an out-group. The prioritizing of the in-group and discrimination against an out-group are different phenomena, which need to be analyzed as such, rather than seeing them intrinsically linked where group formation is observed. The mere fact that a group forms, thus, does not mean that it understands itself in opposition or antagonism against another group, even if it differentiates itself from such (Brewer 2007). Clearcut boundaries have the potential to promote positive intergroup relations (Jonas and Mummendey 2008: 213).

This does not mean that such antagonism cannot occur at all. But it needs to be carefully investigated under which circumstances, internal and external, intergroup relations turn into conflict, rather than assuming that groups are in conflict per se. Given that groups provide security in the self-perception of its members, that is, affirm their social identity, any threat to such, externally or internally, can lead to antagonism. This can happen at the collective level (Jetten, Spears, and Postmes 2004) as well as at the individual level (Pickett and Brewer 2005). Such threats can be real or perceived at the level of real life or at symbolic level (Stephan et al. 2002). Despite her emphasis on the nonconflictual model of the emergence of groups, Brewer does not downplay the risk of intergroup hostility. But she differentiates the latter from the formation of groups and draws attention to the various different circumstances under which differentiation can turn into hostility, and in turn how such hostility can be reduced or overcome.

Two aspects discussed in SIT are particularly relevant for reading a text from antiquity through the lens of SIT: the concept of complex social identity and the concept of superordinate identity.

Complex Social Identity

It is evident that in-group membership of one person is not restricted to merely one group. Research into bilingualism/multilingualism demonstrates that it is perfectly possible for one person to be at home, even if to different degrees, in more than one language community, which implies also in more than one cultural context. And even within the same linguistic context, people identify in different ways, as, for example, the example of the dual identity of German Jews up to the Shoah demonstrates (Mendes-Flohr 1999). Belonging to and identifying with more than one group does not mean that these are then being fused or converge within this person, but they are different and differentiated aspects of the identity of this one person. Sociolinguistic research demonstrates that bilinguals/multilinguals are well aware of the differences associated not only with the different languages in which they are proficient but also the respective cultural aspects (Pavlenko 2005, 2006). There is no fusion or convergence of the different languages in which a bi- or multilingual person is at home. Being familiar and aware of different expressions and perceptions of life, as well as different ways of life enables bilinguals/multilinguals to negotiate between these diverse "worlds" as part of their own identity. The diversity they embody indicates that belonging to different groups not only does not threaten their identity but rather is an inherent and positive part of bilingual identity. As such it contributes to openness toward difference (Ehrensperger 2013: 39–62).

Such insights from sociolinguistics resonate with the notion of complex social identity in SIT. The fact that people belong not merely to one group leads to the question how they perceive these different aspects of their social identity. It could be demonstrated where the awareness of a complex social identity leads to the recognition that in-groups are also diverse, in that not all aspects of one in-group overlap with other aspects. To be part of multiple groups means that in- and out-groups cannot be clearly delineated. What is an in-group in one sense is an out-group in another. Applied to bilingualism, this means that for someone who is French, German, and Italian speaking, these are all in-groups; however, for someone who is French and German speaking, Italian is an out-group, and for a German-speaking monolinguist, the others are out-groups.[14] Hence, for the person who embodies the three languages and cultures, members of an out-group could be in-group for him or her. They can be A and B at the same time without this constituting a contradiction (Brewer and Pierce 2005).

Diversity is thus integrated within the person and part of his or her social identity. A high awareness of this nonconvergence of diverse group membership leads to a higher level of openness and acceptance toward out-groups, more generally, as these are not seen as inherently and necessarily in opposition to the multiple membership one embodies or integrates in one's own social identity (Bodenhausen 2010). Thus, complex social identity leads to a higher openness to others who are and remain different. It appears that people who integrate diversity in their social identity have a high awareness of their complex social identity and that diversity within a group may mutually contribute to reduce potential intergroup tensions (Bodenhausen 2010: 16).

Superordinate Identity

Another concept of overcoming intergroup hostility is referred to as a common in-group identity model. Different groups are recategorized to see themselves as part of a larger superordinate group that would allow them to stress their commonality rather than their difference. The in-group boundaries seem to be redefined in that the boundaries of the distinct group are seen as relativized or indifferent in light of the superordinate group (Gaertner and Dovidio 2000). By redefining the group boundaries, the former bias against out-group members would be dissolved in that they would now be seen as in-group members, as one of us rather than one of them. It can be demonstrated that such recategorizations can actually reduce intergroup tensions or problems in a number of culturally diverse settings (Dovidio et al. 2009). However, the limitations of the promotion of a common in-group or superordinate identity have clearly emerged. There are a number of aspects that need to be noted here, since it has been proposed especially in the reading of New Testament texts and research into processes that lead eventually to the emergence of Judaism and Christianity, that possibly the model of superordinate identity may provide helpful clues (e.g., Tucker 2018). It has been noted that "blurred intergroup boundaries or superordinate categorizations are not necessary preconditions … for positive intergroup relations, and that maintaining salient group differences in the intergroup context can in appropriate circumstances provide a basis for such positive relations" (Jonas and Mummendey 2008: 213).

---

[14] For this discussion of recent linguistic research, I am deeply indebted to Ehrensperger (2013: 39–62), especially in its relevance for an SIT approach.

A superordinate identity can lead to the perceived erasure of the distinctiveness of one or more of the groups subsumed under the superordinate category, which leads to a sense of threat to the subgroup's identity that can enhance intergroup tension or conflict rather than reducing it (Dovidio et al. 2009). Moreover, it can also lead to groups competing against each other in their attempt at embodying the superordinate category in more perfect ways than co-subgroups within the overarching or common category. Thus, threats to subgroup identities, competition between subgroup identities triggered by the promotion of a superordinate identity, can have the opposite of the intended effect and actually contribute to an emphasis on the distinct identity often associated with the resurgence of negative intergroup relations (Neufeld and Schmitt 2019).

In scenarios where superordinate identities appear to provide a way out of intergroup tensions, the issue of power asymmetry is easily overlooked. Hardly ever are groups encouraged to form units under a superordinate identity without any power dimension being involved. Thus, claims to more accurate embodiment of aspects of superordinate identity can easily turn into denigration of other groups under the overarching umbrella who, in the perception of the more dominant group, embody these ideals in a less appropriate or less prototypical form. This can lead to assimilation pressure (Wenzel, Mummenday and Waldzus 2007) of one group against others, or by subsuming all subgroups under the superordinate identity aspect, there is a risk of creating an abstract identity with no grounding in concrete embodied identities (Neufeld and Schmitt 2019: 599–616). An abstract disembodied superordinate identity would be the result, a rather empty shell that only encompasses generalities with no basis in any reality. Taking such problems into account, variations to the initial recategorization models have been proposed that have promising potential for Pauline research in particular. These more recent approaches have similarities with findings of sociolinguistic research into bilingualism, as noted above, and they are also related to the concept of complex social identity.

A key aspect in relation to this is that superordinate identity or common in-group identity cannot replace or override subgroup identities in its realm. The concept of dual identity (which as noted is not new at all, but actually discussed by Mendes-Flohr in 1999) is introduced into SIT and expressed in SIT terms. But it has a history in other disciplines and interdisciplinary conversation and, in this respect, is highly constructive. It is thus now recognized in SIT also that although a superordinate or common identity contributes to the reduction or overcoming of intergroup tensions, this cannot happen at the expense or relativizing of the respective subgroup identities. The primary identifications need to be recognized and valued as part of the superordinate aspect. This implies that no one group or aspect of one group can be seen as representing the superordinate identity as such. The superordinate aspect is not representing prototypicality. The superordinate aspect can only be represented or embodied in the diversity of the subgroup identity. Thus, diversity and difference, recognized and valued, are at the center of superordinate or common identity. There can be no commonality except in diversity (Neufeld and Schmitt 2019). Interestingly, this SIT model proposed in diverse ways in the publications of Dovidio et al. resonates with aspects of the political philosophy of Hannah Arendt—who maintains that the presupposition of political cooperation is diversity; or of the philosophical approach by Emmanuel Levinas who refers to ethics as the first philosophy, in that the other in his or her difference calls me to re-spond, be respons-able. Thus, relationality begins with the other, in his or her difference (Ehrensperger 2009: 166–78).

Relating Social Identity Theory to Romans

Philip Esler has pioneered the application of SIT to Romans already in 2003. He particularly used the concept of superordinate identity to explain Paul's relationship to and reorientation of differing groups among the Roman Christ-followers. Although I am indebted to Esler for exemplifying an SIT approach to Romans at a much earlier stage, because I take a different view of the groups Paul addresses in the letter, I will also necessarily make a differing application of SIT. The major difference is that I read Romans as addressed only to the ethnē in Christ at Rome, so I do not read Romans 14–15 as necessarily presenting issues of interethnic conflict. Ethnicity is a major factor in Romans, and that is not a point of disagreement with Esler. But the fact that the addressees are entirely non-Jewish means that I cannot view ethnic conflict in the way I would if I had posited an ethnic dispute between Christ-following groups in Rome. Such a scenario has led in the past to many useful insights in the interpretation of the letter, and I do not overlook or disregard other scholars from F. C. Baur until the present who have focused on the relation of Jew and "gentile" in the letter. We will later note how Munck, Minear, Brown and Meier, Stendahl, Stowers, Esler, and others have interpreted Paul's dealings with differing and disputing groups in Rome. The fact that Paul does not address Jewish groups, whether Christ-following or not, in Romans stands in some contrast to the actual situation on the streets of Rome.

Ancient tradition has it that Christianity in Rome emerged out of the synagogue context, and recent scholarship has posited the view that Christ-followers continued to participate in synagogue activity possibly as subgroups (Nanos 1996, Thorsteinsson 2003). There was a large population of Jews in Rome at this time. These were known to the authorities who intervened in the dispute about Chrestus by banning the leaders, as they had done earlier in sending Jewish men to fight in Sardinia. Jews suffered victimization as did other minorities who persisted in being different. Nevertheless, some non-Jews chose to follow Jewish life patterns, even to call themselves Jews. Some became proselytes, others remained on the margins of synagogal life, but were influenced by it. So, although Paul chose not to address Jews in Rome, this does not mean that they are not an important element in the Roman context. He sends greetings to numerous people, many of whom he identifies, or can be identified, as Jewish. The Christ is identified with the house of David, and as the Jewish Messiah (1:4-5, 9:5, 15:3, 15:7). Paul himself underlines his Jewish ancestry, even as he plans to visit Jerusalem with the collection (15:25). So, although the nations are the addressees in Romans, they are presented with a Jewish Christ, and a Jewish apostle who delivers a gospel concerning the God of Israel.

The Jewish people, "my kinsmen according to the flesh," feature explicitly in Romans 9–11, where their place in the divine narrative of the Creator God's relation to Israel and the nations is a burning topic. So, although the ethnē are addressed in Romans, they are not addressed as a separate, free-standing group but as "gentiles" who are viewed through the lens of God's narrative with Israel. Thus, the God of Israel is very much present in Romans, and not merely indirectly through the reported Christ-event, and the referenced narrative concerning Israel. Israel, as Israel, is also presupposed in Romans, in the sense of being present in order to be displaced according to some of the ethnē in Christ, "Branches were broken so that I might be grafted in" (11:19). So, Israel is at least negatively present at this point. Even if the ethnē only are addressed in Romans, this happens in the context of Israel, and of Israel's God. Above all, Israel is supremely present in Paul's own symbolic universe into which he is trying to introduce the Roman ethnē. As apostle to the nations, the Romans as ethnē also occupy Paul's mind, but only in positive association with Israel. As noted above, in any co-operative relation, primary identities remain crucial.

Several differing groups seem to be competing in Rome for the honor of being recognized as the people of God. The ancient traditions of Abraham and the Jews, and the newly created gentile Christ-following communities define the two poles of the discussion, with various combinations of claimed identity and practice occupying the spaces between.

A common in-group identity in its inclusiveness may be fruitful in reducing the conflict between differing groups, but it can also operate so that it becomes a denigration of another group under its overarching umbrella. It seems that being Jews acquired ambivalent evaluations in this debate, with the ethnē in Christ claiming to most perfectly incarnate the common in-group identity. In such a setting, animosity and increasing distancing is the result. Paul seeks to restore the equilibrium at Rome among those ethnē in Christ by respecting primary identities, including stressing his own belonging in the people Israel, and Israel's continuing relation to her God. Surprisingly, Paul does not explicitly name Jewish Christ-followers as a group, though such may have existed within the varied synagogal assemblies. We interpret this to indicate that all the Jews, Christ-following or not, continued their adherence to the synagogue, and that, historically at least, interaction with non-Jews also continued in connection with synagogues. Paul does not draw a boundary between Christ-following ethnē and Christ-following Jews (this is probably implicitly assumed); instead, his boundary marker is drawn between Jews as a corporate entity and ethnē in Christ.

The great new event, according to the gospel, passed on to Paul was the acceptance of non-Jews through the Christ-event. Thus, those outside were now also able to relate to the God of Israel, and those far way were brought near (Eph. 2:12-14). Paul's proclamation proceeded from his own particular call to be "apostle to the nations," and his teaching included making these equal with the Jewish people in every respect, relating them to the covenant with Israel. But Paul retains differentiation between ethnē in Christ and Jews in the covenant with Israel, opposing circumcision and assimilation for ethnē in Christ to Israel and thereby supporting primary identities. To this we will return later in the exegesis of chs. 9–11. Proceeding from the receipt of the covenant with Israel, Paul insisted on the retention of Jewish and non-Jewish ethnicity and the recognition of differing roles in the divine purpose.

The incoming of the nations meant another corporate entity to be considered in relation to God's purpose. Probably in the earliest days, the ethnē were regarded as proselytes though without the necessity of circumcision. It was Paul who became their theologian, particularly in Romans, to present the ethnē in Christ as an associate people alongside Israel, but not as Israel and certainly not in place of Israel. Thus, however appropriate it might sound to speak of the Judeo-Christian reality in relation to modern Europe, this is not an adequate description of two historically distinct, self-differentiating world religions. The affinity and the difference between Jews and ethnē in Christ began to cause problems already at this early date, particularly, the non-Jew calling himself a Jew and those ethnē who boasted in being Israel's replacement. Paul seeks to relate Jews and non-Jews positively but also to differentiate them within the divine purpose. The arrival of ethnē in Christ in a Jewish context, especially in Rome, demanded explanation and clarification, and ongoing identity differentiation offers promise in this respect. The entire exercise upon which Paul embarks in Romans is addressed to the ethnē, and it is all for their education and illumination (not for Jews who might happen to be listening in).

So, the ethnē in Rome are lacking in self-understanding, reflected particularly in their mistaken view of Israel. These two entities, ethnē in Christ and Israel trusting in her God but responding negatively to the Christ-event, comprise the scenario that Paul addresses in Romans. Israel as a whole has not been persuaded by the Christ-event, and the ethnē have jumped to the conclusion that just as victorious Roman armies regarded subjugated nations as nonentities whose Gods had been defeated, so too with Israel.

From a SIT perspective, it seems that the ethnē in Christ perceive the people Israel negatively in relation to themselves. They think they possess what Israel lost. They have an inflated self-estimate based mainly on the supposed demise of Israel, a sign of in-group favoritism in relation to themselves, most likely resulting from their trusting in Christ, and social discrimination against Jews also related to Christ, but negatively. If the ethnē are correct, the resulting image of Israel's God requires correction, and his character needs careful distinguishing from the Roman deities particularly in relation to such things as shared cultural conceptions of 'glory'. Paul seeks to do this particularly in regard to the divine faithfulness to his covenant as the required correction concerning Israel's present status. Thus, Paul presents the Creator God as Israel's God, the God of all peoples, who revealed himself to Abraham and the prophets but most distinctly to Israel. The God whom Paul claims has revealed himself in the Christ-event and called the nations is thus a glorious God already known to Israel. He already exists in a covenant with the people Israel as he does similarly with those ethnē who have trusted in Christ. Contrary to Roman boasts, Israel's God has not rejected her, nor annulled his covenant, but is faithful to his promises that will lead to Israel's secure future. In this, Paul acts in conformity with the insight that the most effective way to improve relations between groups is to "promote awareness of a common superordinate identity, while at the same time preserving the integrity of valued subgroup identities" (Hornsey and Hogg 2000: 243).

What Paul does is to focus on the character and activity of the God of Israel in association with the people Israel. These oppose idolatry and seek to worship their God alone. So, Paul stresses this as a commonality between Israel and the ethnē in Christ. (In this instance, it is not a Christological distinction in that the majority of Israel are not convinced of the full significance of the Christ-event.) But exclusive worship of the one God of Israel can be an identity norm despite differentiation concerning the meaning of the Christ-event (Sterling 2019: 262). By stressing common belonging to God, he (Paul) is able to include the gentile Christ-followers alongside the Jewish people under the superordinate belonging to the one God. They are not included as individuals but corporately as representatives of the nations, a people through Christ closely associated with the people Israel, neither replacing nor becoming part of this people. This representation should indicate to the ethnē in Christ that trusting in this Christ is not in opposition to belonging together with Israel in the common allegiance to the one God. By distinguishing the ethnē from Jews and yet at the same time including them in the worship of the one God, Paul affirms the identity of both the ethnē in Christ and also that of Israel (as a related rather than as an oppositional activity). This will be exemplified in our exegesis of the relevant texts throughout the letter.

Doxological Social Identity

Tucker has recently proposed a title for the (future) social identity of the ethnē in Christ, viewed in their proposed Pauline relation to Israel, describing this as a doxological social identity (2018: 223–4). This innovative identification is supported by the fact that Paul in our view opposes a realized eschatology perspective that seems to presume that because Israel was not persuaded first (i.e., before the ethnē) by the Christ-event, she has been bypassed.[15] It is to be noted that Paul does not regard the promises given to the ethnē as having received final fulfillment but rather as being confirmed as an expansion that includes the ethnē (Tucker 2018: 236). So, if the promises await final realization in God's consummation of history, then a doxological social identity makes sense and especially as a continuation of Israel's covenantal identity signaled by Paul's citation of the Song of Moses (Tucker 2018: 231–6). For Paul, God is still at work among the people of Israel, and Israel's identity is still a salient identity, part of a doxological superordinate identity along with the ethnē in Christ (Tucker 2018: 242–3).

This designation is particularly appropriate to our reading of 15:7-13 as Paul's conclusion to Romans, drawing the ethnē into a joint praise together within a superordinate social identity alongside Israel rather than seeking to praise God by themselves. Importantly, in Paul's scenario of this superordinate identity, the integrity of both Israel and of the nations is likewise preserved as those recent SIT theorists whom we have included in this discussion here have strongly insisted (e.g., Neufeld and Schmitt 2019: 611–13). Such a participation in a joint scenario will enable the ethnē in Christ to discover both who they were and who they now are in God's continuing purposes. This is, in fact, the proper thankful response of ethnē in Christ to God's mercy on both Jews and themselves (Witherington 2004: 344, Tucker 2014: 52). These are no longer "the defeated nations" but "for Paul they are part of the restoration of Israel, the consummation of his (God's) purposes for the world" (Tucker 2018: 252). This views the actual bringing in of the ethnē in Paul's time not as the end of a process

---

[15] See my essay on 2 Cor. 3 (Campbell 2016: esp. 143–50).

but as the continuation of God's purposes yet to be finally consummated. It stresses that these purposes are Israel-centric rather than ethnē-centric as was the view of some of the Romans (cf. 11:17-19). These were overimpressed by the competitive search for glory at the expense of others typical of Romans at this time (Tucker 2018: 223–4). Thus, these ethnē were also prone to the concomitant cultural boasting as we will argue in more detail in relation to a section of our exegesis of Romans 14 ("The Inversion of Roman Imperial Influence"). Paul does not dismiss this quest but redirects it, pointing them instead to seeking not Roman glory but the glory of the God of Israel (15:9-12), that is, when God's purposes will have come to fruition/consummation.

As we proceed with the exegesis of the chapters throughout the letter, we will consider these with a SIT lens as appropriate. As noted above, since Baur's stress on the Sitz im Leben, the historical must still have preeminence in the reading of an ancient text such as Romans, and as underlined again in the Romans Debate (1977 and 1991), the historical is a necessary starting point in all investigations (Donfried 1991: 103). Additionally, "the claim is that contemporary social theories are especially useful tools when they provide an appropriate framework and language for interpreting the historical evidence" (Clarke and Tucker 2014: 42–7). SIT as any other approach cannot apply equally fruitfully to every pericope in Romans (Esler 2021a: 35 cf. also 28), and in light of this, we will use, eclectically, alongside our selected approach, other illuminating lenses wherever necessary in light of the nature and content of the text. A literary perspective will require to be salient throughout in view of the rhetorical skills and devices that Paul uses to such great advantage to present his argumentation in the letter.

Translation and Terminology

I will provide my own translation of the text of Romans unless stated otherwise. Since many of the terms Paul uses have overtones of later Christian perception, I will leave some of these untranslated. I will use the transliteration ethnē for ἔθνη throughout, occasionally translate it as "nations" and will use "gentiles" only with a small letter and normally only as an adjective. The term ἐκκλησία will either be left in Greek or translated as assembly.

Normally I will use the term Jew and Jewish rather than Judean, in that I consider the former links the present and the Second Temple period rather than indicating a break in tradition. This does not mean that traditions do not change (cf. Levine 2006: 164–5, Reinhartz 2014). Where I discuss other authors, I will retain their specific terminology.

I will retain the androcentric language of antiquity for sociohistorical reasons, that is, where Paul uses the term ἀδελφοί, I translate this as "brothers."

Where νόμος clearly refers to the Torah we use Law (capital), otherwise we use law.

We will translate ὑπακοὴ πίστεως as "hearing in trust" to avoid the negative overtones of obedience language to emphasize the call and response aspect of Paul's understanding of divine–human relations.

EXCURSUS I

Paul's Use of Diatribal Style in Romans

Diatribe and the Interpretation of Romans

An important area of research on Romans concerns its distinctness from and commonality with other Pauline letters. Identifying where it differs will help us to discover its particular character. One aspect is particularly distinctive, that is, the number of questions that proliferate its contents. These consist not merely of routine questions of meaning or substance but are often vivid, reactionary, and even negative. They represent an ongoing response to Paul's statements as a speaker might interact with his audience. Questions such as these find their closest parallel in speech and writing, particularly in rhetorical patterns known as the diatribe. Although not equally distributed through Romans, these (diatribal) questions often are closely interwoven with the pattern and progress of argumentation so that a full understanding of the letter's content requires an understanding of the role these play in the structure and argument of the letter. Our aim is first to discover the nature of the diatribe, second to check its presence and function within Romans, whether as a formal style or pattern of argument, and third to consider how the use of diatribal style affects or determines the interpretation of the letter.

The Diatribe and Romans in the History of Interpretation

The present discussion of the diatribe and its influence on Paul in Romans goes back mainly to Rudolf Bultmann's doctoral research, *Der Stil der paulinischen Predigt und die kynisch-stoische Diatribe* (1910).[1] Bultmann, relying heavily on earlier research such as that of E. Weber, regarded Paul's diatribe as reflecting a popular preaching style similar to Stoic street preachers, whereas more recent research such as that of Abraham Malherbe has argued that "the formal and functional agreements between Paul and Epictetus are more far-reaching than Bultmann demonstrated" (1989: 32–3). The issue was reactivated by Karl Donfried's response to Bultmannn's work on the diatribal aspects of Romans. Donfried insists that "Bultmann never defines precisely

---

[1] Malherbe claimed that only in Epictetus's *Discourses* is there a real parallel to Paul's use of μὴ γένοιτο (1989: 32–3). Further on Bultmann, see Donfried (1991: 112–21). Cf. also Stowers (1981: 21), also Song (2004: 1 and 11).

or critically what the form of the diatribe is and what justification there is for talking about it as a *Gattung*" (1991: 113). In the introduction to *The Romans Debate*, Donfried opposed the perception of Romans as a diatribe, maintaining that the "so-called diatribe is not a literary genre but rather a series of rhetorical devices" (lxx). Donfried's concern, continued in the 1991 revised and extended *The Romans Debate* (102–25), was that the historic specificity of Romans should be recognized, rather than it being perceived as a summary of Paul's earlier theology, "elevated above the moment of definite situations and conflicts into the sphere of the eternally and universally valid" (Bornkamm 1991: 28). Failure to recognize the significance of diatribe in Romans assists inevitably in its designation as a "theological report." As Käsemann claims, "If this epistle is constitutively distinguished from all the other Pauline epistles by its reflective character, mirroring earlier experiences and being interspersed by what are for the most part only invented objections, this is to be understood under the category of a 'theological report'" (1980: 404). Donfried's article and responses to Karris in *The Romans Debate* originated from Karris's strong reaction (1973) to Paul Minear's "situational" approach to Romans (1971). This discussion became more nuanced in the revised edition of *The Romans Debate* (Karris 1991b) in which I was one of the contributors (Campbell 1991). Thus, the diatribal style of Romans in this discussion originated as part of the discussion about its epistolary character and the historical context to which it may have been addressed. The present discussion of diatribal elements in Romans continues to have close links with these same issues.

Taking account of this discussion, I prefer to use the description, "diatribal style" since Romans remains a letter addressed to a specific audience in Rome, while exemplifying many of the characteristics and techniques of diatribe. Diatribal features are now generally recognized in scholarship on the letter but, as Stanley Porter points out, scholars have been slow not only to recognize the status of Romans as of diatribe genre but also in determining the significance of the diatribal features in the letter, irrespective of the category to which it is assigned (1991: 655).

Although not always in agreement, it is significant to my mind that a significant number of recent commentators on Romans agree on taking this aspect into account (e.g., Donfried 1991, Porter 1991, Stowers 1994, Elliott 2004, Song 2004, Tobin 2004, Keck 2005, Jewett 2007, Wengst 2008, Matera 2010, Rodriguez 2014, Hultgren 2011). There is also some agreement that the diatribal style of Romans is not reflective of Paul's preaching, but rather of Paul's teaching. This emerges from the growing awareness that in Romans Paul presents himself more as a teacher or a philosopher rather than as an evangelist. This correlates with his emphasis on his own leadership of the mission to the nations as "apostle to the nations" which includes the Romans and all the other gentile assemblies.

Diatribe—a Distinct Genre or a Rhetorical Style?

A major tendency after the Second World War was to identify diatribe not as a distinct genre but as a literary style or set of techniques often found in rhetorical philosophical prose. Porter wishes to challenge this consensus, arguing strongly that Romans is part of a recognizable diatribal genre, despite the rejection of diatribe as a genre by many, but not all, classical scholars (Judge 1972: 33).

Here, we take into account Donfried's response to Bultmann's study of the diatribe which was skeptical with regard to the claim regarding the posited existence of a genre that can accurately be designated as such (i.e., a genre), and the scholarly research of Malherbe (1980), Stowers (1981), Thorsteinsson (2003), and Aune (1991) in more recent years. We recognize that Donfried was resisting the posited genre of diatribe in relation to Romans because this perspective had been used to oppose the reading of Romans as a particular rather than a general letter. This stance was influenced by Martin Dibelius's long-standing view that Paul's paraenesis is aimed at the general rather than the particular situation. This is similar to Bornkamm's stance noted above that the "objections arise out of the subject matter, or rather out of a misunderstanding of it, and not an actual historical situation" (1971: 12). But the possibility of a more contextually grounded view of Paul's paraenesis emerged with Victor P. Furnish's volume, *Theology and Ethics*, particularly in his emphasis on the connections of Rom. 12:1-2 with what precedes, and especially with Romans 6 (1968: 68–92). Thus, we hold that the recognition of diatribal style in Romans is not subject to the same sort of critique as Dibelius's view of paraenesis, that is, that the use of diatribal style indicates only general paraenesis with no close relation to the situation at Rome. Hence our agreement with Aune is in relation to diatribal style as being particularly suited for use in *logoi protreptikoi* (1991: 283),[2] and also especially Donfried (1991) and Stowers (1981, 1994) whom we will discuss later.

Diatribe—a Controlling Feature or a Rhetorical Teaching Style in Romans?

However, we still need to take account of and evaluate the significance of Paul's deliberate and sustained use of the particular rhetorical style of the diatribe, but within the context of a real letter to the Romans. First, I wish to clarify my own presuppositions and starting point. I do not agree with Changwon Song's view that, as a diatribe, Romans cannot be relied upon to give any real insight into the situation of the Roman Christ-followers (2004: 46). From this perspective, the diatribe style coupled with the fact that Paul has not previously visited Rome in his mission work could be seen to give some credibility to the older view of Romans as a theological treatise rather than a letter (which was dominant prior to Donfried's first publication of *The Romans Debate* in 1977). My concerns remain similar to the historical and epistolary interests of Donfried, and though disagreeing with Song (2004), must acknowledge the profitable insights that his thorough study has provided.

George Kustas has defined diatribe as "a specific mode of rhetoric, characterized by the simulation of dialogue, which functions to manipulate the 'real' constraints of a rhetorical situation by inviting the audience into a set of 'hypothetical' constraints and premises of the speaker's design" (1976: 12). Thus, the subtitle of Runar

---

[2] On diatribe style, rather than the diatribe as a genre, see Donfried's suggestion that it is perhaps better to speak of "Diatribenartiges," that is, as a diatribe style that is represented in a variety of genres (1991: 118).

M. Thorsteinsson's monograph on *Paul's Interlocutor in Romans 2*, significantly reads, *Function and Identity in the Context of Ancient Epistolography*. Thorsteinsson argues,

> While uses of such interlocutors show basic formal and functional similarities with the "diatribe style," the specific identity of an epistolary interlocutor may normally be determined according to the following procedure. As a rule, the interlocutor is meant to speak for or represent the letter's recipient(s), and thus to function as an object of identification for the latter. (2003: 150)

It is from this perspective that we consider diatribal style in Romans. Stanley Stowers has demonstrated the origins of this dialogical style of debate in the context of the philosophical school, and his work has been a reliable source in a very disparate area of research, despite some (few) of his conclusions being modified (for their recent use in a commentary on Romans, see e.g. Rodriguez 2014). Indeed, Stowers's views have been broadly accepted except on the point that the interlocutor may vary in ethnicity.[3] Rodriguez with Thorsteinsson claims as I do that the interlocutor is always the same throughout, that is, of gentile origin (Rodriguez 2014: 48–50, Thorsteinsson 2003: 150). But taking into account the accumulated research since Bultmann, it now seems justified to posit a view of Romans in which Paul uses diatribal style in a letter to Rome. Here the diatribe patterns are still subordinated to Paul's epistolary address to the Roman gentile Christ followers, but in a style that enables him to say indirectly things that he would be unable to say explicitly in normal address. To this extent, it is clear that Paul in Romans is dependent on the dialogical element of the diatribe. But peculiar to Romans is the fact that "only in this letter is the dialogical style employed throughout the major portion of the letter's body, rather than in a few isolated texts … the dialogical element is closely tied to the development of the argumentation in Romans" (Stowers 1981: 179). *This is a significant factor that must not only be listed but also taken fully into account in every aspect of the letter's interpretation.*

A main feature of the recent discussion of the diatribe on which some agreement has been achieved is on its pedagogical function where a student is encouraged by his teacher and pedagogically instructed via a developing dialogue rather than in mainly polemical exchange; the schoolroom rather than the law court becomes the venue, with encouragement and guidance, including censure, rather than accusation typifying the mode. Dialogical style is fundamental to the diatribe[4] even though it may not always be oppositional. It may not be too speculative to suggest that Paul used dialogical exchanges as a teaching style in his communities. In Romans, Paul presents himself as a teacher. The dialogical element is neither "Paul's preaching style unconsciously slipping through" nor a "marginal stylistic phenomenon … but 'is central to this self-presentation'" (Stowers 1981: 179). Diatribal significance is

---

[3] Others like Changwon Song disagree with Stowers on detail, that is, that ἄνθρωπε is not one of the more neutral expressions among the diatribe vocatives, but rather a harsh censuring expression as is clear in 2:1–3 and 9:20 (2004: 39, 46, cf. also 80).

[4] The interlocutor can speak hypothetically as an opponent, but can also do so as a helper or even *for* the author. Porter's article demonstrates the significance of diatribal features as, for example, in confirming the subjunctive reading ἔχωμεν in 5:1 (Porter 1991: 661). Cf. also Aune (1987: 200–2).

underlined in Jewett's description of what he terms "The Third Pericope" beginning with "Diatribe and Enthymemes Concerning the Death of the Sinful Self and the New Life in Christ" (2007: 390).

This factor is important for the interpretation of Romans since the sharp rejection in the μὴ γένοιτο (far from it!) passages in diatribe style may give the (false) impression that the letter is a polemical confrontation between Paul and the Romans, an opinion gaining or retaining significance when joined with the thesis that the audience addressed is considered primarily of Jewish origin. A similar impression may likewise be registered by the effect of the typical vivid, abrupt, and incisive retorts designed to enforce progress to the next stage of an argument by means of a false inference. Abraham Malherbe has demonstrated that the μὴ γένοιτο response is not a single exclamation of rejection but part of a larger form, which includes "an introduction to an objection with a characteristic particle, a false conclusion, the rejection μὴ γένοιτο, and a shift to another theme using a particle such as ἄλλα, γάρ, and δέ" (1989: 232). Speeches-in-character, in which the writer or speaker takes on the character of someone else, were also fairly common in diatribes. Stowers himself has, in later articles, shown more awareness of the rhetoric of speech-in-character which was often associated with the use of diatribe and is likewise valuable in its interpretation (1995: 180–202).

Should Romans Be Designated as a Diatribe?

We need, therefore, to respond to a recurring question in this discussion. Is Romans in total a diatribal writing or only sections of chs. 2–14? Thomas Tobin notes obvious similarities between the conventions of the diatribe and the body of Paul's letter to the Romans. He is open to the view that in Romans we have a diatribal body situated within an epistolary frame, and that Paul's hearers would have recognized the diatribe style even though Paul has turned the conventions of the diatribe to his own purposes (2004: 97). Tobin notes Paul's use of many of the same rhetorical devices found in the diatribe (2004: 95–8) and also concurs with my earlier research findings that Rom. 1:16–11:36 alternates between argumentative and more expository passages as in several of Epictetus's diatribes (Campbell 1981: 22–40).[5] In this earlier research, I had drawn attention to two differing styles in Romans which I described as "diatribe style" sections in contrast to other "kerygmatic, declaratory" sections, questioning which of these was the more significant for interpreting the letter historically (1981: 29–31).[6] Paul's use of expository/declarative sections and those more argumentative has been confirmed, and found to be similar to Epictetus's pattern in which the more expository serve as the bases and support for the more argumentative. The relative proportion of

---

[5] Tobin helpfully discusses both the similarities and differences between the conventions of the diatribe and the body of Romans (2004: 95–8). As noted, I prefer to speak of diatribal style within the constraints of a Pauline letter (cf. Stowers 1981: 178–84).

[6] Though its main thesis remains salient, particularly in regard to the two differing styles of Romans (as declarative/expository and argumentative question and response), and the significance of Rom. 3:1-8 as the structural center of the letter, this essay is now somewhat dated in that its publication coincided with Stowers's ground-breaking volume (1981), so I was unable to have access to his contribution.

expository/declarative sections both in Epictetus and Paul is similar, roughly about a quarter of the text as in Romans. In addition, Romans, though longer than most diatribes, still falls within the range of what would be thought a normal length for a diatribe (Tobin 2004: 95, Song 2004).

An important issue is not just whether scholars today regard Romans as a diatribe but, equally important, would Paul's audience in Rome have recognized Romans as a diatribe. We should bear in mind that though we think of Romans in terms of a written text, it would have been delivered orally, and its rhetorical presentation would have been crucial to its interpretation. Familiarity with Greco-Roman diatribal techniques need not imply a highly educated or sophisticated audience since oratory and the practice of oral/aural interpretation were pervasive in that period in popular culture in Rome (Achtemeier 1990: 20). I think there is a strong possibility that at least a substantial portion of Paul's designated audience would have been capable of hearing his message, and that Paul's style of argument would have been influential in this communication (Tobin 2004: 95).

Changwon Song regards Romans as an Epictetus-like diatribe implying a schoolroom context that explains the parallels between Epictetus and the apostle (2004: 122). This teaching context coheres better with Paul's letters than his image as a street-preaching evangelist similar to Stoic/Cynic popular "Volkspredigt" (Donfried 1991: 112). Some scholars see 1:16-17 as the theme or thesis of the diatribe, and 1:18-32 as an indictment (e.g., Stowers 1981: 79, Song 2004: 82). Chapters 3–4, 6–7, and 9–11 have many features which are recognizably identifiable as clearly in diatribe style. But other sections, not so obviously in diatribe style have been identified as broadly diatribal. Stanley Porter argues that Romans 5 and Romans 13–14 are both diatribal. Despite Stowers's claim that "there is no typical structure to a diatribe," Porter, in his detailed exegesis of Romans 5, provides a cumulative argument that demonstrates that many recognizable elements of its typical and normative pattern can be discovered there. He points out that Romans 5 has three rhetorical questions, uses the exhortative subjunctive in 5:1-3, uses ἀλλὰ καί and πολλῷ μᾶλλον (four times in vv. 9-17), and several sets of parallel statements, as well as an *exemplum* in vv. 12-21, all of which when taken together are strongly indicative of the diatribe (1991: 655–77). As Porter claims, "All of these elements, noted individually by others, combine to point to Romans 5 as reflecting the rhetorical conventions of diatribe" (1991: 677, 1990: 113–37). A genre has been defined as "a fairly stable clustering of different conventions such that they formed a commonly recognized pattern. These patterns then informed the ways in which authors composed, and hearers understood, these compositions" (Tobin 2004: 90). My position is that whilst acknowledging diatribal patterns and conventions as noted above, I view these as indicating not that Romans is a diatribe, but that it is replete with diatribal style used in the service of an epistle addressing a historical exigency as perceived by Paul as existing at Rome.

We can, therefore, conclude that through the diatribal argument beginning in 1:16 (Song 2004: 65),[7] and continued in 2:1-6 where Paul initiates a dialogue, directly

---

[7] Song argues that the diatribe starts not with verse 18 as Stowers argues, but with verse 16, at the very beginning of the 'body' of Romans (2004: 65).

addressing someone in the second-person singular (ὦ ἄνθρωπε, cf. also 9:20), Paul constructs substantial elements of his argument in this particular diatribal style. Some diatribal features may also be discernible throughout Romans including chs. 13–15 (Schmeller 1987: 70–1), though these are most strongly obviously accentuated in the body of the letter in that there they are structurally and inherently related to the progress of its argument (Stowers 1981, Campbell 1981). In the discussion of 3:1-8, we note that the μὴ γένοιτο diatribal-style question and retort occur a total of ten times in Romans 3–11. Paul is not easily fitted into any one pattern rhetorical or theological. His distinctive characteristic was his exceptional ability to use material from differing sources for his own purposes but to simultaneously stamp his own unique mark upon it. Paul's epistolary use of diatribal rhetoric is distinctly his own, but still clearly recognizable as such. One good example of this by Paul is in his use of scriptural citations. Like Epictetus, he uses citations from authoritative figures, not Homer or Euripides, but the narratives and *exempla* of Israel which make Rom. 1:16–11:36 look very different from Epictetus's discourses. But both make use of authoritative texts, even though these play a more significant role in Paul because of his reverence for the scriptures of Israel (Tobin 2004: 97). More work needs to be done to demonstrate the rhetoric of Romans and especially its relation to the theological content of the letter. We now need to offer a sufficient reason why Paul should use this particular style in writing to Rome, since others were also available.

We need first to be more precise about what constitutes diatribe or diatribal style. In a neat description of diatribe, George Kustas notes that there are notable characteristics, the most important being that "it functions to manipulate the "real" constraints of a rhetorical situation by inviting the audience into a set of hypothetical constraints and premises of the speaker's design" (1976: 12). This could mean that it does not reflect any real situation or context, but may be entirely hypothetical. But it is no more hypothetical or contrived than a conversation with the personified righteousness that comes by trust (10:6). The other main feature of diatribe that we wish to stress is its dialogical style, since the simulation of a dialogue is a significant element of diatribal style also in Paul. Yet the use of this element in Paul does not reflect simply a circumscribed mode of oratory. In Paul's case, the hypothetical presentation has a relation to the actual purposes he has in mind. It is designed to reflect back upon the situation of the addressees after the rhetorical effect of the dramatic hypothetical "context" has worked its influence. Thus, Paul uses diatribe, but is not strictly bound by its "normal function," if we can really speak about such. We prefer to regard him using diatribal style rather than diatribe itself. We will demonstrate in at least one example how Paul combines actual and hypothetical addressees (i.e., 11:13-24). Song has claimed that "the diatribe is too well structured to remain as a mode or a style" (2004: 58–62). He points out that it contains four distinct markers characteristic of Epictetus's diatribe, that is, vivid dialogues with fictitious interlocutors, the exemplary singular "you," the use of μὴ γένοιτο with its characteristic rejection formula, and a diatribe vocative "o man (ὦ ἄνθρωπε) (2004: 46). However, our decision not to follow this view that Romans itself is a diatribe is based on Paul's activities and goals as apostle to the ethnē as well as on his characteristic tendency to transform everything he uses to become uniquely his own creation. Thus, we have presupposed that Paul would not take over all the constraints of a particular form of rhetoric, but rather subordinate and adapt these to suit his own epistolary purposes. The content must be geared to the epistolary and apostolic purposes.

The Function of Diatribal Style in Romans

An important reason for Paul's use of this style of approach, rather than genre, is that Paul can use indirect speech, speaking in the voice of an imaginary interlocutor, rather than criticizing or disputing directly with the Roman ethnē in Christ, whom at this point he had not yet visited. Kustas holds that "we would be helped toward an appreciation of diatribe if we thought of it less as literary type and rather as literary mode" (1976: 14). But Malherbe's view is more persuasive in that he argues in light of the original oral setting of "diatribal" discourse that we should prefer to speak of "rhetorical" rather than "literary mode." This concern with style or genre, particularly the emphasis on an imagined interlocutor, may give an impression that we are presenting Paul more as a rhetorician rather than a busy apostle. If it is kept in mind that Paul's goal was primarily persuasive communication, then the relevance of rhetoric may be more obvious. Rather than as a speaker to unknown people in the public space,[8] Paul emerges primarily as a teacher using rhetoric in relation to the communities he founded or addressed. David Aune notes the terminology Luke uses to describe Paul's activity, particularly lecturing (διαλεγόμενος) and pleading (πείθειν) which he notes belongs to the same semantic subdomain as προτρέπειν to urge a particular course of action (1991: 289–90). The presence of diatribal style, rather than being indicative of bitter polemics, may indeed suggest something about Paul's teaching pattern, his classroom style (cf. 6:17). The content of Romans and the style in which it is presented indicate patterns that most likely preceded the writing of and extended far beyond the specific content of the letters, but it was probably these teaching patterns that enabled the creation of such contextually focused letters. Thus, the view of Paul proposed here is that Paul uses diatribe functionally rather than slavishly following a known cultural pattern. Speech-in-character and the rhetoric of diatribe would have been familiar to Paul's addressees at Rome. Thus, we can assume that Paul shared with the Romans his commitment to the Christ-movement and its central tenets, knowledge, and experience of daily life in the multicultural environment of the Roman Empire, but also pervasive aspects of Greco-Roman culture such as oratory and popular diatribal techniques. "Familiarity with Jewish and Greco-Roman diatribal techniques need not imply a high level of literacy ... since oratory and the practice of oral/aural interpretation were pervasive in ancient Greco-Roman society" (Casson 2019: 53). Casson also notes that her personal experience of contemporary cultures with a high degree of orality suggests a much greater capacity for retention and memorizations of information communicated orally than in high literate cultures.

---

[8] While designating Romans as a *logos protreptikos*, Aune is open to the view that it contains shorter literary units of various types including diatribes. The strength of Aune's perspective is that it shows awareness of, and fits well with, the fact that the *logos protreptikos* continued to be used by later writers such as Clement of Alexandria (1991: 284–5).

Thus, Paul employs these communication techniques as part of his letter and, within the letter context, the apostle addresses whether directly or indirectly, a specific exigency at Rome. This disposes us to agreement with Aune's perspective that the terms genre or *Gattung* in relation to diatribe are not appropriate and that the diatribe *style* was eminently suited for use in *logoi protreptikoi* (1991: 283). The use Paul makes of diatribal style is not inconsistent with or distanced from the situation of the Romans, for example, Stowers states that the advice given to the interlocutor is really meant for the hearers of the letter (1981: 100). Thus, when Paul addresses the interlocutor, "he is not directly addressing the letter's audience but a fictitious individual whose participation in the discourse is meant to say something to the audience" (Thorsteinsson 2003: 116). Again, as Elliott claims, "The interlocutor reflects the speaker's construal of a particular audience" (2007: 125).

As noted above, Stowers's insights have been generally affirmed with the exception of his identification of more than one interlocutor in Romans which goes awry in his construal of the interlocutor (Rodriguez 2016: 106). This modification allows for a more consistent reading and for greater emphasis upon its epistolary character. Thus, we have come to the conclusion that in all of these addresses to an imagined interlocutor, Paul addresses a figure who represents his gentile readers and their response to or perspective on his (Paul's) argument. Unlike Song, we do not posit a rift between the rhetorical style and the contextual information it transmits.

But what evidence or sources did Paul use to reach his construal of the exigency at Rome? Even if somewhat exaggerated, Paul's recognition in Rom. 1:8 of the widespread reputation of the Christ-followers in Rome must have some basis, in fact, and be capable of verification from the extensive group of friends whom Paul greets in ch. 16. Paul can use the reported knowledge he has about the Romans and their circumstances to dialogue pedagogically in diatribal style to persuade them to develop and adjust in the direction of his teaching and mission. And this persuasion need not always be negative (cf. Rom. 1:8-12) since Paul also emphasizes what he holds in common with them, as indicated by the use of οἴδαμεν (and related terms), for example, in 2:2, 3:19, 7:14, 8:22, 28 (cf. Tobin 2004: 120). Probably, the use of the term "objections" (rather than inferences or questions and responses) encourages too much concentration on polemics, especially where the rhetorical distance between the interlocutor and the audience addressed is not kept in mind. There need be no suggestion of contradiction in goals here since Paul is clearly seeking to influence the gentile Christ followers in Rome and chooses the diatribal style of pedagogical argumentation as the best form of argument to achieve this. Paul has a very specific focus on whatever style he uses to reach this goal, and from what we have learned of him from his letters, his use of diatribal style is more than ornamental. "He rarely uses comparisons as ornamental flourishes, rather his use of comparison (*synkrisis*) *is normally subservient to the purpose of his argument*" (Forbes 2016: 225). As Wilhelm Wuellner insists, "Argumentation never develops in a vacuum, but in a situation that is socially and psychologically determined" (1991: 143).

In view of the factors noted above, it is our conclusion that Rom. 1:15 to 15:13 is not best described as a diatribe in spite of demonstrating many of the features of that form of rhetoric. My main rationale for this opinion is based on Paul's interaction with the context and exigencies of his audience at different points in Romans which seem to confirm the priority of the letter genre. As Tobin notes,

> For the most part, diatribes, including those of Epictetus, are not addressed to a particular audience or to a particular situation. Their advocacy of virtues and rebuke of vices are usually at a more general level and appropriate to a school context. Romans on the other hand, seems much more specific in the way Paul addresses the issues of a particular community, ... (2004: 97)

Only in one respect does Paul use diatribal style for deliberate anonymity, that is, in relation to certain opinions that were circulating (according to Rom. 3:8) among his Roman gentile addressees concerning his mission and its significance for the Jewish people.

While we are aware that Murphy O'Connor has argued that the diatribe style betrays Paul's lack of familiarity with the actual situation of the Roman communities (1996: 334), we would wish to stress that though this is a legitimate inference, it is not the only or the best explanation. It is equally possible to maintain as we have done that it is Paul's delicate relation to the Romans as apostle to the ethnē (yet never having visited them) that is primary, and that this relation does not require precise information on every issue. This diatribal style enables Paul to achieve entry into a rhetorically imagined scenario in order to discreetly air opinions without precisely naming the source personally,[9] that is, whether these represent the opinion of the Romans or his own opinion. It enables Paul at delicate points, or in relation to disputed opinions strongly held, to air the particular viewpoint without disclosing or offending its perpetrator, or incriminating himself. Although we do not disagree with Keck's correct observation that following the argument does not require knowing exactly who says what, it is an enormous help in many places to have (the many) rhetorical clues concerning the speaker that assist in clarifying Paul's many complicated arguments, especially in Romans (2005: 90). Matera offers a very helpful chart where he traces the questions and responses in the rhetorical flow (2010: 79). On the same issue, we are assisted by Stowers's proposal that, like Epictetus, Paul so designed the exchanges that the interlocutor admits Paul's basic points and so moves the argument forward (1981: 89–90).

Diatribal Style Functioning in a Letter: Romans 11:11-32 as an Example

This pattern can be demonstrated in that there are several sections of Romans where Paul, though clearly using diatribal style, nevertheless, sets this in a letter framework that applies the outcome of the argument directly to the situation of the Romans. We will note these in passing at the appropriate points in our exegesis, but will consider first the most significant example in 11:13-32. In 11:13, Paul directly addresses the Romans as ethnē, and relates this status, as a wild olive shoot, to his own gentile

---

[9] Jewett has carefully explored this and most other aspects of Paul's use of the diatribe at the relevant points in his commentary, see particularly Jewett (2007: 25–7, 33, and ad loc.).

mission. Then in 11:17, he addresses an apostrophe (i.e., as if he were talking) to the wild olive shoot. Here it could be argued that the address in 11:17-24 does not apply directly to the Romans and might support a claim such as that of Song that Romans as diatribe tells us nothing about the Romans (2004: 122). At a minimum, the presence of diatribal elements does lead scholars to some uncertainty about passages such as 11:17-24. Barclay is cautious about asserting anything directly from Rom. 11:17 due to the singular form of address in diatribe style. He thinks it is "unclear" whether "believers in Rome boasted over taking the place of Jews." Yet he does see that the "impression of supersessionism" could easily arise from the better reception of the good news among "gentiles" rather than Jews, and Paul's own insistent self-presentation as "apostle to the Gentiles" (2015: 459, cf. also 552).

I think we can be more confident. What must be stressed is that the *indirect* address to the wild olive shoot, is situated in a *direct* address within the context of 11:13-24 beginning "it is to you ethnē that I am speaking." Then in 11:25 a resumption of direct address to ἀδελφοί confirms that the same manner of address has continued from 11:13 and that the address to the personified wild olive shoot is to be bracketed within the wider context in which it stands. *This illustrates what we are claiming, that is, that the diatribal element is subsidiary to, and serves the aim of, the direct epistolary address in which it is enclosed.* If Paul had not contextualized 11:17-24 within the direct address section 11:13-32, then it could be claimed that the diatribal element is determinative, but since the discussion at this point is set within a context of very explicit direct address to the Romans, the diatribal style clearly serves the principal function which is that of *directly* persuading Paul's audience.

A similar example is to be found in Romans 14 where the diatribal style is visible at several points throughout the chapter in the use of the singular when addressing more than one addressee as in 14:4, 10, and possibly 22. Yet this style is intermingled with normal direct address in second-person plural indicating that the total paraenesis relates to Rome and is applicable to the Roman context with careful enunciation even in this indirect style.

Examples such as this, in my opinion, confirm Romans as a letter to Rome, rather than a diatribe, and answers the objection that Romans is no less a diatribe because it is set in an epistolary framework (contra. Tobin 2004: 96). Rodriguez is able to recognize the clear differentiation between diatribal and epistolary function "that Paul continues to speak in the manner of a letter-writer even after he finishes speaking in the manner of a rhetorical instructor" (2014: 37, n40). It is also to be recognized with Tobin that Stowers, who has made the strongest case for diatribal elements in Romans, is nevertheless reluctant about claiming that 1.16–11:36 as a whole should be seen as a diatribe (1981: 178–84).

But what did the Romans know about Paul whether reliable or exaggerated? Paul himself had never taught most of the Christ followers in Rome. He knows some individuals but has never taught his message there. His gospel is known only by hearsay, by reports from Corinth, Jerusalem, or elsewhere, and has not always been accurately reported (*c.* 3:8). As Sandnes notes, Paul "had already faced objections elsewhere (Galatians), and he is concerned that his Roman audience is susceptible to charges against him and his theology" (2018: 97). He goes on to insist that the diatribe style is *not* pure imagination because "behind any imagined interlocutor lurk opinions, misperceptions, or rumors concerning Paul and his relationship with his addressees." Paul was known to some of the Romans at least and had shared experiences in previous encounters with some of them as is illustrated by his added notes on named individuals in Romans 16 such as Andronicus and Junia. It appears that he may have lost some prestige in Rome in that he seems to have to apologize for not having come earlier as he had led them to anticipate (15:22). As noted, Paul also has to explain that it is not his policy to enter the mission area of another apostle, but that he intends to go via Rome for further mission work in Spain.

Thus, it is a delicate situation where Paul needs the Romans and wishes to work with them. As apostle to the nations, they come within the area of his apostolic remit. But since they were for Paul, a relatively unknown group of Christ followers whose support he must solicit, Paul is obliged, if possible, also to simultaneously correct the mistaken reports of his message and activity. If one deals with issues directly or in a straightforward manner, it will be evident what one supports or promotes but not perhaps so *clear what one rejects*. The advantage of Paul's dialogical approach in Romans is that alongside the letter he actually wrote, we can to some extent envisage the letter *he chose not to write*.[10] This situation accounts for Paul's use of the diatribal style by means of which the exaggerated reports of his gospel and activity can be voiced and sharply repudiated without directly accusing or offending needlessly (individuals in) his Roman gentile audience. In the interpretation of Romans, it has always to be remembered that the voice of the person speaking is not necessarily that of Paul but of the imagined interlocutor whom Paul creates to voice an issue or to object to such. This is clearest in Rom. 7:7-25, where the "I" who speaks cannot, without strong contradiction, represent the voice of Paul himself. Although it is not always unanimously agreed at which points Paul speaks in his own voice, it is significant how much agreement (despite great divergence) emerges in recent studies concerning the major passages in question.

Paul's Use of Rhetorical Questions in Romans

To the best of my knowledge, few scholars have noted the peculiarity of Romans in the abundance of questions it contains. Apart from 1 Corinthians, Galatians, and James, all of which are influenced by diatribe techniques, questions are relatively rare in New Testament letters, and some reveal no questions at all. But in Romans, Paul engages in lively dialogues with questions and answers, created by himself (Song 2004: 22). These are clear evidence, as we have noted, of diatribal style. However, there is another aspect of dialogue questioning also often neglected, that of rhetorical questions.

Collins Dictionary defines a rhetorical question as follows: "a question asked solely to produce an effect or to make an assertion and not to elicit a reply" (2019).

---

[10] In a section of an earlier essay, I refer to "The Diatribe Style as an Indirect Witness to What Paul Is Not Saying" (Campbell 2013: 42–3). Cf. also Elliott's insightful comment on the diatribal apostrophe 'that serves to contain and control the range of possible interpretations' (2007: 164).

First, it is to be noted that a rhetorical question is not the same as a normal question. If it is treated as no different from other questions, then its rhetorical effect is denied. The definition given above has two essential elements: (1) a reply is not necessary and (2) the intention is to make an assertion. If treated merely as a question, the rhetorical effect of the implied assertion is entirely overlooked. In the context of persuasion, a rhetorical question may be a delicate way of introducing a controversial assertion without being seen to make such explicitly.[11] The rhetorical presentation deliberately leaves the answer open. But why then make it? In Paul's case, these are made to lead the thinking of the audience in a direction the speaker wishes them to travel without risking a definite statement revealing explicitly his own stance. At this stage in the discussion, the speaker may not be ready, or consider his audience is not ready, to face a dialogue on this issue because it is so controversial. What he can do in a rhetorical question is to put in question form an assertion that leads his audience to take into account the issues raised by the tentative assertion, which otherwise they might not consider. Israel is just such a controversial issue in the Roman context, and we will investigate the place this theme occupies in the distribution of rhetorical questions. What we are tentatively considering is whether Paul, who has never been to Rome and whose reputation may be and probably is in dispute there, is obligated to discuss Israel's negative response to the Christ message yet must tread very carefully as he does so. He needs to be cautious in how he presents his own stance regarding Israel, otherwise he may cause division rather than heal it. Thus, Paul puts two rhetorical questions about Israel in Rom. 10:18-19 that illustrate the rhetorical process in that he really does not give proper explicit responses[12] at this stage, but simply points to relevant scriptural passages, citing Ps. 18:4 (LXX), Moses (Deut. 32:21), and Isa. 65:1-2 to form the basis of a reply, rather than his own words (Keck 2005: 260–1). Though it is clearly understandable that translators do not want to leave such serious questions unanswered, the very negative answers usually given are not demanded by these rhetorical questions in Rom. 10:18-19.

Rhetorical questions are unusually frequent in Romans, especially in Romans 9–11, but also throughout the letter. For example, there are some twenty examples of rhetorical questions in Rom. 8:31–11:36 (Tobin 2004: 300).[13] If rhetorical questions are such a frequent feature of this letter, then it becomes exceedingly important how they are translated and understood. A primary issue is that these must be treated as such—rhetorical questions—and not translated and read as conceptual statements. This becomes most notable in questions such as 3:3 or 11:1. A number of commentators (e.g., Elliott 2007: 263, Tobin 2004: 300, Keck 2005: 98, Matera 2010: 79, Rodriguez 2014: 61) from differing perspectives agree on translating these texts as proper rhetorical questions: for example, 3:3 "Their failure to trust will not nullify God's trustworthiness, will it?" The same we will argue, applies to 9:6b "For all

---

[11] Though the rhetorical question by the inclusion of μή can indicate that a negative reply is expected.
[12] Μενοῦνγε (10:18, cf. 9:20) cannot be regarded as the substance of a proper/full response.
[13] Tobin lists 8:30, 31, 32, 33, 34, 35; 9:14, 19, 20, 21, 22, 30; 10:8, 14, 15, 19; 11:1, 2, 7, 11 (2004: 300). To these we add also 9:6b.

those from Israel are Israel, are they not?" and to 11:1 "God did not cast off his people, did he?"[14] Porter (1991), Jewett (2007), Caragounis (1985) and Rodriguez agree on reading 5:15a as a rhetorical question, 'But isn't the gift just like the transgression?' (Rodriguez 2014: 106). As with 9:6b, this effectively results in the opposite of the traditional reading, and it is therefore very significant how such rhetorical questions are translated and interpreted.[15]

It is extremely important likewise to pay close attention to the grammar of each sentence which will indicate whether Paul (whether as interlocutor or in his own voice) addresses someone directly in second-person singular or plural, or speaks about someone as a third person(s) whom he is not actually addressing. For example, in several places in Romans, Paul may be speaking *about* Jews in the third person, but not dialoguing directly with them as, for example, in most of chs. 9–11. Yet despite the Jewish content of the topic at this point, the addressees here, as throughout the letter, are actually non-Jews, "I am speaking to you, ethnē" (11:13). While the theme or agenda may frequently be Jewish the addressees are gentile throughout.

The significance of reading a text as a rhetorical question rather than as a conceptual statement will be fully demonstrated when we consider Rom. 9:6b, which can and, I think, should be translated "For all those from Israel are Israel, are they not?"[16] This has traditionally been translated as "For not all Israelites truly belong to Israel" (New Revised Standard Version [NRSV]). The contrast between these differing renderings of the same text, without any textual variant as a rationale, is exceedingly strong and points to differing presuppositions as controlling the process, determined by what one brings to Romans 9–11 rather than by its inherent content or argument. One aspect of the presuppositions involved relates, of course, to the literary question as to which questions may clearly be classified as rhetorical. This can be discussed freely since its resolution ought not to depend on theological stances as it is primarily a literary question. The significance of reading a text as a rhetorical question rather than, for example, as a conceptual statement, will be fully demonstrated when we consider the text of Rom. 9:6b, which can arguably be translated as "For all those from Israel are Israel, are they not?" We will return to Rom. 9:6b at the appropriate point but have noted it here as an illustration of how the understanding of rhetorical questions, as indeed other related diatribal rhetorical issues, can alter the reading at important junctures. What has emerged from the consideration of Paul's use of rhetorical questions is that we have found that these occur, significantly, where Israel is discussed as, for example, at 3:3, 9:6b or 11:1. Note below our list of rhetorical questions with a focus on Israel. These questions are selected because of their proximity to μὴ γένοιτο constructions in the text which occur at regular intervals through chs. 3–11, that is, at 3:4, 6, 31; 6:2, 15; 7:7, 13; 9:14; and 11:1, 11.

We noted another related pattern in Paul's letter construction, that is, his use of the phrase τὶ οὖν ἐροῦμεν—"what then shall we say?" This characteristic formula

---

[14] Compare Keck (2005: 98), Wagner on Rom. 11:1 (2003: 219), Elliott (2007: 263), Matera (2010: 79), and Rodriguez (2014: 61–2).
[15] Note the helpful chart of questions and responses in the rhetorical flow of 3:8 (Matera 2010: 79).
[16] Wengst translation reads Rom. 9:6b as "Sind denn nicht alle aus Israel eben Israel?" (2008: 293).

occurs six times in Romans, in every case except 8:31 standing alone as a complete sentence. It occurs at major breaks between/within chapters, at 4:1, 6:1, 7:7, 8:31, 9:14, and 9:30. A variation is found in 11:1 and 11:11 where λέγω οὖν is its equivalent. What must be emphasized here is that the question following "what, then, shall we say?" is a rhetorical question. The follow-up question normally presents a false inference to which Paul explicitly objects. This is the rationale for our interest in rhetorical questions throughout the letter.

This may lead us to an initial assumption that Paul deliberately asks a rhetorical question at these points in order to keep the conversation about difficult issues open, especially about Israel and the character of her God implied by his relation to this people. Paul wants to continue to educate the ethnē by encouraging further investigation of the issue under discussion. To assist our focus on the content of the more important of Paul's rhetorical questions, we will list selected translations of these questions by recent differing authors.

Various Readings of Paul's Rhetorical Questions in Romans 3–11

Rom. 3:3: "Their unfaithfulness does not nullify God's integrity, does it?" (Elliott 2007: 139)
 3:5: "God is not unjust when he inflicts wrath, is he?" (Matera 2010: 82)
 9:6b: "All Israel are Israel, are they not?" (Wengst 2008: 293)
 9:14: "There is no unrighteousness with God, is there?" (Rodriguez 2014: 178)
 10:18: "They haven't really heard, have they?" (Keck 2005: 260)
 10:19: "Israel did not understand, did it?" (Keck 2005: 261).
 11:1: "God has not rejected his inheritance, has he?" (Wagner 2003: 219–20)
 11:11: "They haven't stumbled so as to fall, have they?" (Wagner 2003: 266)

This list of rhetorical questions which indicates that there is a concentration of topic in these confirms our intuition that many of these focus around the theme of Israel, particularly where Paul responds with the negative retort μὴ γένοιτο.

It is clear that the occurrence of numerous rhetorical questions in conjunction with the μὴ γένοιτο retort denotes a planned framework by Paul in order to enable him to get a hearing in Rome for those views of his that may have been, and most likely will be, misreported and misunderstood. There is widespread recognition of these rhetorical questions by leading scholars of diverse viewpoints; this is evidence that my reading of Rom. 9:6b as a rhetorical question is fully warranted.

We have listed scholars from differing perspectives and approaches in order to check whether Paul in the wording of these as rhetorical questions deliberately presents them in the form of open-ended questions (irrespective of what "answers" he is interpreted as having given to each), and whether it indicates that he wishes to keep the issue of Israel and her future open during his arguments throughout Romans 3–11. We have selected these questions because of their closeness in the text to μὴ γένοιτο retorts, which we recognize as serving a significant function in Paul's construction of the letter. Rom. 9:6b is not immediately adjacent to the latter rhetorical phrase which next occurs in 9:14, but is nevertheless closely related. On the issue of rhetorical questions generally, we have reached the conclusion that Paul deliberately uses these open-ended questions to facilitate his ongoing conversation concerning Israel and related delicate issues without getting personally polemically involved, and to encourage the Romans to reflect on the significance of this (open) stance in order to further investigate this serious issue (Campbell 2021: 165–86).

Conclusion

The diatribal style is a subtle approach by Paul in dialogue with a group of Christ-followers over whom he is lacking the authority of one who had first brought to them the message of Christ, and hence is unable and unwilling to reprimand them directly for such failings of theirs as he is currently aware. Instead, he directly confronts and criticizes an imagined interlocutor, who bears the force of Paul's piercing critiques, encouraging the audience to align themselves, both intellectually and emotionally with what, through the interlocutor, Paul commends or repudiates (Tobin 2004: 102–3). Paul cannot be too presumptuous or too prescriptive but has to lead the Romans gently through a progressive argumentation, in a cumulative argument. This may be partly because the Romans' experience of following Christ is proclaimed "throughout the world," such that Paul, however much he may hope to teach them, must acknowledge that he hopes that he and they "may be mutually encouraged by each other's trust, both yours and mine" (1:12). Rather than denying or ignoring the presence of diatribal elements throughout Romans, we conclude that these support the view that Romans is created as a circumstantial letter written in response to the actual situation of the Roman ethnē in Christ, rather than only a rhetorical or theological argument where Paul reflects his stance on important issues not intrinsically connected with the situation at Rome (cf. Aune 1991: 278–96).[17]

---

[17] These contrasting views of Romans and differing rhetorical approaches are well noted by Aune who views Romans as Paul's general theological views not as reflecting a specific epistolary situation but as including a range of possible objections (1991: 278–96).

Romans 1

As Ernst Käsemann has noted, "Romans reveals a close-knit argumentation which is hidden only to those who do not exert enough effort over it" (Käsemann 1980: 324).

Paul writes letters according to the conventions of his time, which, as here in Romans, usually contained first a prescript (Latin *praescriptio*) (1:1-7) in which to identify the writer (named in the *superscriptio*), named the addressee (identified in the *adscriptio*) and conveyed a greeting (the *salutatio*). After the prescript, a thanksgiving section (1:8-15) can be identified, giving thanks for the trust/πίστις of those addressed and Paul's plans concerning them (and himself). The thanksgiving corresponds loosely to the *exordium* as used in orations to secure the goodwill of the audience. The third segment of a letter opening usually identified is the thesis *propositio*, a focused statement of what the author intends as the theme of the body of the letter. Our working hypothesis at this point is to propose that the body of the letter proper begins at 1:13 where Paul takes up again a theme first announced in 1:5, the apostleship to the nations. But though we recognize Paul as a letter writer in accord with the main conventions of his day, what he writes should be evaluated more in terms of oral and rhetorical conventions rather than only in terms of epistolary features (Longenecker 2011: 224–5).

It is worthy of note that the opening greeting in Romans is more elaborate than in any other of Paul's letters. It contains much more than the typical identification of the senders, recipients, and grace wish. But surprisingly, there is no reference to an ἐκκλησία—a term that does not appear until ch. 16.

We will deal with Romans 1 in four main sections, 1:1-7, 1:8-12, 1:13-18, and 1:19-32.[1]

Romans 1:1-7: Paul the Apostle, to the Beloved "Gentiles" in Rome

¹Paul, servant of Jesus Christ, called to be an apostle, set apart for the gospel of God,
²which he proclaimed beforehand through his prophets in the holy scriptures,

---

[1] I have availed myself of Rodriguez's heading at this point (2014: 1) in that it highlights the gentile addressees of the letter at the same time as it uses the translation of the term ἀγαπητοῖς θεοῦ, which carries resonances of God's choice of Israel, even as it refers specifically to non-Jews.

> ³*the gospel concerning his Son, who was from the seed of David according to the flesh* ⁴*and was declared Son of God with power according to the spirit of holiness by the resurrection of the dead, Jesus Christ our Lord,* ⁵*through whom we have received grace and apostleship to bring about the hearing in trust among all the ethnē for the sake of his name,* ⁶*among whom you are, you called to belong to Jesus Christ,* ⁷*To all who are in Rome, beloved of God who are called to be holy. Grace to you and peace from God our Father and the Lord Jesus Christ.*

Romans 1:1

In the first verse of this long letter, Paul introduces himself factually and confidently, yet not in an authoritative fashion. He presents himself not as an unknown outsider, but as one whose name and status will resonate with at least some of the Roman Christ-followers. In contrast to five of the seven undisputed letters in which Paul's opening greeting includes the names of co-senders, Romans alone mentions no co-senders at the outset. This is probably because here Paul wishes to stress his own unique calling as apostle to the nations, surpassed only by the elevated description of Jesus Christ on whom attention is quickly focused in 1:3-6.

The two key terms Paul first uses to introduce himself are slave δοῦλος and apostle ἀπόστολος, both linked to Χριστοῦ Ἰησοῦ and κλητός, "called," respectively. The term δοῦλος is significant both here and later in ch. 6, and its first introduction must be understood in its immediate context where Jesus is acclaimed as Messiah. This suggests that its use resonates with the meaning supplied by the background of Hebrew *ebed*, "servant" as well as by that of "slave" in contemporary Roman culture. Whether translated as "slave" or "servant," in either case the term δοῦλος indicates a subordinate relationship in which the one person with his entire existence is bound to the other. The people of Israel are designated as servants or slaves (δοῦλοι) in the Hebrew Bible/LXX and other Jewish writings (LXX Deut. 32:36; Josh. 14:7; Isa. 48:20; 2 Macc. 7:33; 8:29). In Jewish tradition, *ebed* is the term for the prophets (Am. 3:7; Zech. 1:7; Isa. 45:9; Jer. 7:256; 25:4; Ezek. 38:17), also for kings (2 Sam. 7:5; Ezek. 34:23; 37:24), and for Israel as a whole (Jer. 26.27; Ezek. 28:25; 37:25), and this tradition strongly resonates in the second term of Paul's self-description, κλητὸς ἀπόστολος, "called to be an apostle" (Ehrensperger 2022b: 1–2).

Esler considers the role of apostles is best regarded as a subgroup identity. They were a select few within the wider group of Christ-followers (2021a: 35). Paul in Corinth claimed to be an apostle of Christ Jesus (2 Cor. 1:1), but so did his opponents whom he labeled as false apostles. By linking with call terminology, Paul consciously situates himself within the covenantal traditions of those who stand in the service of God, such as the people of Israel, but especially of prophets such as Jeremiah. The prophet is told, "I have set you over the nations and over the kingdoms, to pluck up and to break down, and to destroy and to overthrow; to build and to plant" (Jer. 1:10). "Being an apostle was the foundation of Paul's claim to exercise authoritative leadership; to this extent there is an element of his being a leader which does not depend on group processes but on external warrant from a supernatural source" (Esler 2021a: 35). Esler adds that there is really nothing like this in the social identity approach, except to the extent that the claim only functioned if the Christ-followers considered it was true. He notes, however, that this is one instance of the fact, very common in social-scientific interpretation, that sometimes there is not a perfect fit between social theory and empirical data (2021a: 35). This is something that we will need to keep in mind as we continue the exegesis of the letter.

Jewett argues that Paul's self-designation as δοῦλος here may include elite imperial slaves who operated as "king's officials," diplomatic ambassadors (1982: 13). If, as we shall note later, Paul regards the Christ as of the royal lineage of King David, this would cohere with the covenantal and liturgical emphases visible in Romans. Paul claims that he was set apart (ἀφωρισμένος) for the gospel of God (1:1), for proclaiming it specifically to the nations. Paul does not limit the use of δοῦλος, servant/slave, to himself, but uses the term for others (1 Cor. 7:22; Phil. 1:1) who also serve (δουλεύειν) Christ (Rom. 12:11; 14:18; 16:18), God (1 Thess. 1:9), or the Lord (Rom. 12:11). By calling himself a "servant of Christ," Paul identifies himself at the outset as a "fellow-servant" with all other Christ-followers, including those at Rome. The fact that Paul himself had never been a slave in the socioeconomic sense may indicate that he derives the term primarily from the Jewish self-designation of the people of God, but the term nevertheless would resonate with the Christ-followers at Rome with experiences of slavery (Hultgren 2011: 41).

In Greek and Roman contexts, the term δοῦλος, "slave" indicates the status of one who is not perceived as fully human and designates absolute dependence. It is a status that can never be entirely overcome, even upon manumission. The status a former slave could achieve upon manumission was not that of a *vir* but that of a "*libertus*/freedman" (Ehrensperger 2019: 77–8). Δοῦλος refers to Paul's self-perception as being bound and responsible to someone else, and the term ἀπόστολος refers to the role that is commissioned to him by the one to whom he is bound (2019: 77–8).

How Paul's message would be understood in the context of first-century Rome will obviously be interpreted not only in relation to its predominantly Jewish source but more immediately in relation to its target audience, the ethnē in Christ at Rome. Ἀπόστολος, as noted, can designate a mediator or go-between, an ambassador in diplomatic service as Jewett has demonstrated (1982: 10–11).[2] The word εὐαγγέλιον is a highly political term, used to designate a proclamation by the Roman authorities, in particular of a victory by leading personalities, often the emperor himself. The fact that Paul stresses the *ebed*/δοῦλος aspect of his call indicates that he considers himself commissioned to a specific task that he did not choose himself, but that is given to him by someone else—he is a broker, not the instigator of the message he conveys, a mediating go-between between the commissioner, God, and those to whom he transmits the message, the nations (Ehrensperger 2022b: 3–6). The mediating go-between role of Paul is one that surfaces in many aspects of his life and writings.

Paul's message is not his own, it is "God's gospel" that he is commissioned to carry and to which he has been set apart a very significant role indeed. Influential slaves in Roman imperial society, especially those of the *Familia Caesaris*, the slaves and freedmen

---

[2] Jewett maintains that the notion of "emissary" or "ambassador" is integral to the definition of "apostle."

of the emperor's household, were the elite status group in the slave–freedman sections of Roman imperial society. Thus, Paul as δοῦλος of Christ, may be read as a conscious parallel to the proudly borne slave description, "slave of Caesar." He thereby emphasizes that he is the slave only of this Lord not of any other. Jewett makes the significant claim that this juxtaposition of slaves of differing masters "sets an agenda pursued throughout the letter concerning whose power is ultimate, whose gospel is efficacious, and whose program for global pacification and unification is finally viable" (2007: 100–1). Even within his immediate contemporary context that included other apostles and evangelists of the Christ message, Paul understands himself as having been given a very specific task to explain how the action of God in his Messiah Jesus relates to the non-Jewish world (Cranfield 1975: 53). Only in Romans, does Paul elaborate in full on the specifics of this commissioning. Over half a century ago, Johannes Munck drew attention to Paul's special status in stressing his heightened self-understanding as "apostle to the ethnē." This special role in relation to the ἔθνη, in this instance in Rome, gains increased significance in that here, following Munck (1959: 50, n41, 200–7),[3] we regard this letter as addressed to "gentiles" only rather than to a mixed body of Jews and non-Jews.

The Christ as Seed of David and Son of God

Romans 1:2-4

Paul first presents Christ Jesus as descended from David by human lineage, a glorious pedigree in Jewish perspective. Not only this, Paul also claims that Christ "was designated Son of God in power according to the Spirit of holiness by the resurrection of the dead, Jesus Christ our Lord" (1:4). A crucial issue that arises here concerns the point in time at which Paul intends to claim Jesus Christ's identity as "Son of God in power" is made manifest; is it at or by, Jesus Christ's own resurrection, as in the Revised Standard Version (RSV) text, "by his resurrection from the dead," or rather, at the general end-time resurrection of the dead? Fredriksen has argued strongly for the latter reading based partly on the fact that Christ's manifestation in *power* normally in Paul is tied to the general resurrection, to the coming of the Kingdom at the End. He is, of course, already designated Son of God, but the general manifestation of this is yet to come. This reading fits better the parallelism in the pre-Pauline text of Rom. 1:3-4, which Paul may cite here to indicate common ground with his addressees (Jewett 2007: 103–8, but cf. Fredriksen 2017: 142). These verses may be rendered as follows:

> The good news concerning his son,
> > the one born according to flesh by the seed of David,
> > the one appointed SON Of GOD IN POWER according to spirit by the resurrection of the dead.

Fredriksen maintains that this rendering shows that

---

[3] Munck's innovative work (1959) has stood well the test of time. His other important publication on Romans *Christ and Israel* (1967) still holds interest for its fresh insights on Romans 9–11.

flesh expresses Davidic genealogical descent, and *spirit* expresses appointment as the eschatological messiah by the End-time resurrection of the dead—a very public event, and one that Paul and others still awaited. Special insiders (such as those listed in 1 Cor. 15:5-8) knew that the Kingdom, thus the general resurrection, was close, because they themselves had seen the risen Christ. (2017: 142–5)

The use of the genitive plural, *of the dead*, following ἀνάστασις, his term for resurrection, shows that Paul chose not to use ἐκ because he wanted to say "of the dead" rather than "from the dead." Fredriksen notes that this reading was proposed already in Augustine's unfinished commentary on Romans, *Epistulae ad Romanos inchoate expositio* (394/95 CE, 2017: 142–3). This supports the reading proposed by Fredriksen.

The good news Paul is called to proclaim concerns God's Son (1:3) and with this elevated title Paul begins to elaborate on the significance he wishes to have attributed to Jesus as the Messiah. Paul and those he worked alongside were convinced that Jesus was the promised Messiah. Χριστός was not simply a proper name with no messianic content, a view that Matthew Novenson has shown to be inadequate, demonstrating that "Christ" in Paul serves as an honorific (like Antiochus Epiphanes or Caesar Augustus), with clear messianic meaning (2012: 95–7). As Fredriksen notes, "That Jesus was *ho christos*, the messiah … was an identification that Paul took to heart: in his seven undisputed letters, he repeats the term 269 times" (2017: 133–4). Romans contains the two occasions when Paul designates Jesus explicitly as the *Davidic* messiah, the royal messiah (the most widely attested of the varied messianic-related expectations). These form a "kind of messianic *inclusio*, at the beginning and towards the end of the letter, 1.3 and 15.12, both being immediately tied to Paul's own mission to the nations. Thus, Paul's commission to the nations originates in his recognition of Jesus as the scion of David's house" (Fredriksen 2017: 137) but presented as such in a specific Roman context. This form of presentation that combines a royal connection with the epic and heroic King David would affirm the Jewishness of the message as well as Paul's Jewish identity but would not necessarily suggest any conformity with Roman ideology, rather the opposite since it claims royalty not approved by Rome.

There can be little doubt that with the attribution to Jesus of this title, Paul, from his scripturally based prophetic background (e.g., Ps. 2:7), is deliberately resonating with the use of Son of "God" in Roman political life in all its utter ubiquity and diversity of expression. Michael Peppard finds warrant for this resonance "in the context of Roman imperial ideology, a powerful, almost all-pervasive web of motifs, images, narratives, and words that established and delimited the theatre of discourse in the Roman Empire." Following in the steps of Adolf Deissmann (1910), Peppard finds imperial theology manifested in innumerable ways: coins, temples, milestones, processions, statues, standards, priesthoods, sacrifices, compital altars, household shrines, battlefield rituals, legal proceedings, mealtime libations, feast days, birthdays, auspices, augury, omens, games, ecologues, hymns, and so on (2019: 135–57, 149). Thus, it is legitimate to conclude that though Paul's view of Χριστός emerged out of his Jewish tradition, its expression in his letters, is cognizant of the all-pervading context of Roman imperialism.

What conclusions may be drawn from Paul's apparent explicit awareness of the profound contrast between Roman ideological claims and his presentation of the gospel? Whether the apostle may have intended to subvert these Roman claims needs to be kept in mind and further explored at relevant points throughout this commentary.

To the Beloved "Gentiles" in Rome: Romans, a Letter Addressed *Only* to Those from the Nations

Romans 1:5-7

Paul, along with others included in the "we," has received χάρις, "grace," and ἀποστολή, "apostleship," through his Messiah, Jesus. Thus, in a statement of authority that excludes the audience addressed, Paul with reference to himself is here deliberately inclusive, he emphasizes his sharing of grace and calling with others even as he notes his own distinctive commission to those from the nations. More attention has recently been focused on his network of co-workers, and their working together as a mutually supporting team to communicate the gospel (Hanson 1974: 45, Collar 2013). We will return at differing points to consider the tension that arises from the use of "obedience-related language" in relation to δικαίωσις (Ehrensperger 2008: 166–71). This is to bring about the "listening" or "hearkening"—"the obedient hearing/positive response that arises from trust among all the nations for the sake of his name, including yourselves who are called to belong to Jesus Christ" (1:5-6). This Greek phrase ἐν οἷς ἐστε καὶ ὑμεῖς κλητοὶ Ἰησοῦ Χριστοῦ can be interpreted broadly as indicating only that the Romans addressed lived in the gentile world, rather than in the more specific sense that they were non-Jews. But Godet has identified a syllogism here based on Paul's apostleship. The major premise is "Christ has made me the Apostle of the Gentiles"; the minor: "ye are of the number of the Gentiles" and conclusion: "therefore, in virtue of the authority of that Christ who has called you as he has called me, ye are the sheep of my fold."[4] This syllogism, based on Paul's apostleship as directed only to the "gentiles" is limited to "gentiles" and therefore indicates clearly as do other references later in this letter that the Romans addressed here are explicitly designated as non-Jews. It is the fact that the Romans come within the sphere of Paul's apostleship, *not their geographical context*, which confirms them as being of gentile origin, read in concert with other similar references in the letter. What Harry Gamble asserted with respect to the Roman addressees, we reiterate only with reference to the Roman ethnē: "It is clear that no interpretation of Romans will be adequate if it fails to make sense of the fact that in Romans, we have a letter addressed to a specific community, and, as it appears, only to that community" (Gamble 1977: 137).

On the other hand, the address "to all God's beloved in Rome, who are called to be saints" raises the issue of whether Paul may not also include within his addressees those other Christ-followers of Jewish origin who most certainly were part of the wider

---

[4] Godet's correct recognition of a syllogism here strengthens the emphasis upon Paul's gentile apostleship (1883/1977: 83). Godet is here followed by most modern commentators (cf. Jewett 2007: 112, n165). Similarly, see Thorsteinsson (2003: 84).

Christ-communities at Rome. Did he possibly write to the ethnē in Rome and add greetings to those of Jewish extraction in ch. 16 (Minear 1971: 77–8)? Theoretically, this would have been perfectly acceptable, even though the latter group were not the primary addressees. I have seriously considered this as a perfectly reasonable option, especially in light of 11:28 where the Jews are ἀγαπητοὶ διὰ τοὺς πατέρας. But after careful reflection, I have concluded that an address to "gentiles" only carries the most weight in light of the fact that ἀγαπητοί is also used in Rom. 12:19. The decisive passage is 9:25, "those who were not my people I will call 'my people,' the one not beloved I will call beloved." I have previously demonstrated that Paul uses the Hosea citation primarily with reference to Israel, clarifying that Israel will be restored. So here we have an expression of hope for all Israel. And alongside Israel, another non-people, that is, the ethnē (in Christ) will by analogy also become a "beloved" people (Campbell 2000: 199–200). The point of the non-people citation is that the ethnē through Christ are now also "beloved." Thus, the term "beloved" in 1:7 and 12:19 indicates in light of 9:25 that the ethnē in Christ though differing from Israel are nevertheless still entitled to this designation. I do not consider it a serious problem for a gentile-only address for Romans that Paul should send greetings to others whom he will not address, whether in ch. 1 or ch. 16, so long as it is clear whom he is actually addressing. Paul makes it clear throughout that he addresses the ethnē. There are good reasons why Romans should not be read as a letter to all those who are in Christ, both Jews and those from the nations. The first and obvious reason is that Paul actually states that it is those from the nations whom he specifically addresses, though it may be that others, that is, Jews, may be listening in (Campbell 2013: 195). While he refers to Jews, to Jewish heritage and genealogy, even to someone "calling yourself a Jew," we must respect Paul's clear demarcation between a *dialogue about Jews and Jewish tradition* and *a dialogue with Jews*. The former is clearest in chs. 9–11 where the theme involves Israel, including Israelite genealogy, heritage, and hope, but the addressees are gentile (11:17-24).

The second main reason why Paul must be addressing non-Jews in Romans is that he is clear that his apostolate is not to the whole world but only to the gentile part of it. He respects the Jerusalem summit agreement that

> when they saw that I had been entrusted with the gospel for the foreskin, just as Peter had been entrusted with the gospel for the circumcision … and when James and Cephas and John recognized the grace that had been given to me, they gave to Barnabas and me the right hand of fellowship, agreeing that we should go to the ethnē and they to the circumcision. (Gal. 2:7-10)

It is significant that here we have a distinction between two missions that are mutually exclusive in their designated addressees, one described as the ἡ περιτομή, the circumcision, and the other as τὰ ἔθνη, the nations. Paul recognizes that he has no apostolic authority over Jewish Christ-followers, and he is careful to distinguish ἐκκλησίαι where he is the founder, as in Corinth, from Rome that he did not found and has not yet visited. It is notable how careful Paul is here to stress his limited purpose and plans in relation to his planned visit to Rome. Thus, he may know a number of Jewish Christ-followers in Rome as indicated in ch. 16, but though he asks for greetings to be sent to them *via those ethnē whom he specifically addresses*, they are not necessarily present when his letter is read. In any case, they are not addressed by Paul; otherwise there would be no cause for singling them out from the gentile addressees for special mention.

So it may readily be acknowledged that the reference to "all God's beloved in Rome" is, when read in isolation, broad enough to include Jewish Christ-followers, particularly as the phrase "God's beloved" might seem appropriate for Jews (Campbell 2010: 67–82; also Rock 2012: 20–96). But, for the explicit reasons given above, Romans must be regarded as written exclusively to those from the nations who live in Rome. This is further supported by the use of ὑμῖν in vv. 6 and 7. It clearly refers to ethnē in v. 6. They are called in Christ (κλητοὶ Ἰησοῦ Χριστοῦ) and directly addressed as "you" in second-person plural, that is, those among whom Paul is called to exercise his ministry (i.e. the ethnē). But Paul in v. 7 conveys "grace and peace" greetings to "all God's beloved who are in Rome," "called to be saints," which might well include Jewish Christ-followers. But they are not the addressees, though nevertheless their presence may be acknowledged by Paul through these greetings as well as those in ch. 16. We read the letter's context as that of all the Christ-followers at Rome, with Rome itself as the determining context. Although some early manuscripts lack the precise address "to you also who are in Rome," this omission should be regarded as a later attempt to widen the letter's address to claim for its wider relevance (Gamble 1977). A letter with no particular addressees in the text is hard to imagine as Pauline. Paul in Rom. 15:16 presents himself in the role of the officiating priest who presents the "offering of the ethnē." Our approach is that of a coherent Roman-focused reading, context-specific and context-shaped (cf. Casson 2019: 267, 272). Since Paul had not yet visited Rome at the time of writing, his argument cannot be as interactive as, for example, in 1 and 2 Corinthians. So, he makes it interactive and dialogical in another way, by writing in parts in diatribal style. Thus, Romans presents Paul as actually producing a dialogical argument within the format and constraints of a letter. In this respect, he consciously produces argumentation, which by its nature ought to produce a coherent example of reasoning in relation to context, not just a series of unrelated proofs or responses. Since I have always argued consistently that Romans is a context related document, not a theological or other form of abstract treatise, I continue to view Romans as offering *a coherent argumentation*, sometimes including diatribal elements, that Paul sent to Rome. This does not conflict with its designation as a real letter addressing a historical exigency.

Paul's Use of Diatribal Style in Romans 1 and Ethnic Specificity

The recurring diatribal style[5] frequent throughout Romans reinforces rather than undermines the claim to ethnic specificity of address that will be noted at many points in the commentary. Diatribal style is, in fact, used by Paul in Romans, among other things, to assist in maintaining an ethnic distinction between himself, a Jewish author,

---

[5] Cf. Excursus I.

and his gentile readers. Paul is very clear about this in his use of pronouns and forms of address. Rodriguez recognizes a pattern in which Paul's "second person plural rhetoric distinguishes himself from his gentile readers, and his first-person plural rhetoric circumscribes himself and his readers within the same rhetorical space" (2016: 110). In this Paul shows a consciousness of differentiating between his own Jewish ethnic status as distinct from that of gentile Christ-followers (Rodriguez and Thiessen 2016: 101–31). This aspect has been well demonstrated in the introductory essay, which includes Thorsteinsson (2016: 1–37), as well as in several of the other essays, for example by Novenson and Garroway. This volume offers strong evidence that a careful, rhetorical-conscious consideration of Romans confirms that it is, beyond doubt, Paul's most ethnic-conscious letter because of its specific designation to "gentiles" only, and its consistent differentiation of Jew and Greek. We hope to demonstrate from the exegesis of its content that the gentile address of Romans permeates far beyond even the several significant mentions of ethnē that it instances.

There seems to be a secondary ascription to "all God's beloved in Rome," which we have noted above. This designation resonates with the call of the prophets, with Paul's own call, and even with the declaration of Christ Jesus as Son of God in power in the previous verses (1:1-4). The Romans as called to be holy—κλητοῖς ἁγιοῖς—have a prehistory that binds them to the faithful who preceded them, and with whom they share God's call to holiness. This title resonates with the concept of God's people as a holy people, as Ehrensperger has clearly demonstrated (2010: 104–5). James Hester views the opening greeting as a dramatizing message that reminds the Romans of the history of the promises of God, and the prehistory of the gospel of God that he promised beforehand through his prophets, including a narration of the ancestry and destiny of the Son of God (2004: 83–105). It contains a series of insider cues that include code words such "apostle," "gospel," "prophets," "Holy Scriptures," "son of David," "resurrection," and "lord." These words refer to concepts that were all part of the content of Christ *paideia* for the nations and send a powerful signal to the Romans that Paul has something in common with them. But what is common is not, at this early period of the messianic movement, so much the commonality of a body of doctrine as the commonality of a pattern of activity, norms for behavior patterns rather than doctrinal patterns.

Like Paul they are separated to a life of trust and obedient hearing to the one God. The end of the opening salutation is signaled by Paul's characteristic "grace" wish in v. 7b, "Grace and peace from God our Father and the Lord Jesus Christ."

Romans 1:8-12: The Thanksgiving—Paul's Relationship with the Romans

⁸First of all, I thank my God through Jesus Christ for all of you, because your trust is proclaimed throughout the whole world. ⁹For God, whom I serve with my spirit by announcing the gospel of his Son, is my witness that without ceasing I remember you always pleading in my prayers, ¹⁰that by God's will I may somehow at last be granted success in coming to visit you. ¹¹For I long to see you so that I may share with you some spiritual charisma to strengthen you—¹²or rather so that we may be mutually encouraged by each other's trust, both yours and mine.

Romans 1:8-9

Unlike in his other letters, Paul is not able to refer to a previous period when he first came to meet the Romans and enjoy their friendship. Instead, Paul refers to a distance relationship that already exists between him and them. He is well acquainted with the fact of their trust in Christ, acknowledging that it is "proclaimed throughout the whole world" (v. 8). Before God he vows that he unceasingly remembers them in his prayers. The strength of his assertion might indicate that because he had promised to come previously, but not done so, this could have led to the Romans becoming somewhat skeptical concerning his interest in them. But the fact that Paul remembered them always in his prayers denotes his awareness of their existence and prehistory. This clearly implies that Paul was kept informed about the Romans—he must have had strong connections among the Christ-followers in Rome to be well enough informed to pray continuously for them and that he might, at last, be able to visit them. His prayer suggests that his eventual arrival in Rome may be far from straightforward—"asking that somehow he may be granted success in coming to visit you," due to factors beyond his control. Paul presents himself as one under authority, someone who offers worship λατρεύω to God,⁶ not someone free to plan his own life, hinting that the demands of the gospel and of his God may have to take priority to his own planning. Paul will later (15:22-24) go on to explain both why he has not yet come to Rome and also why he should want to come *in the first place* (Elliott 2004: 81). It is Paul's faithful execution of his divine calling to preach the gospel that has hitherto hindered his coming to Rome, and it is his call to continue to "have some fruit" among them as among other ethnē that maintains the saliency of his goal.

Romans 1:10-12

"At last" (1.10) denotes his consciousness that his delay in his planned visit may seem unreasonable from the Romans' perspective. Paul, for whatever reason then proceeds to stress his longing to see them, "so that I may share with you some spiritual charisma to strengthen you" (1:11). But having stated this, he feels it may sound somewhat pompous in view of the purported universal reputation of their *trust* (1:8), or that his statement might suggest that Paul considers inadequate the pattern of Christ-trust already planted in Rome. So he adjusts his statement to become "so that we may be mutually encouraged by each other's trust, both yours and mine" (1:12). In this cautious retraction, we see Paul's careful approach to the Romans, particularly as regards his

---

⁶ The LXX offers insights into λατρεύω and related terminology. Of the nine uses of λατρεία (worship), eight refer to the cultic service associated with either the tabernacle or the Jerusalem temple. Paul describes himself as a λειτούργος, a servant or one of the personnel of the temple (Rom. 15:16, cf. 12:2). Of the thirteen uses of this term in the LXX, Rodriguez notes that six certainly refer to temple personnel, two probably do, and the remaining five refer to a prophet's or king's servant (or a political official) (Rodriguez 2014: 20–1).

status and anticipated activity with them. We note also here that there is no mention of evangelization of those outside of Christ, only of strengthening and encouraging those already committed (1:11). His goal is simply to strengthen them (εἰς τὸ στηριχθῆναι); we note the resonance with the weak in trust "τὸν δὲ ἀσθενοῦντα τῇ πίστει"(14:1, 15:1) and οἱ δυνατοὶ "the strong" in 15:1.

We see here how Paul has used the thanksgiving to emphasize his unquestioning appreciation of the Romans' trust in God, despite the omission of the term ἐκκλησία, the reason for which we can only speculate.

Romans 1:13-18: The Beginning of the Body of the Letter

¹³I want you to be aware, brothers, that I have often planned to come to you [but thus far have been prevented], in order that I may reap some harvest among you as I have among the rest of the ethnē. ¹⁴To both Greeks and to barbarians, to both wise and uneducated I am indebted ¹⁵—hence the eagerness on my part to proclaim the gospel to you also who are in Rome.
¹⁶For it is not as if I am ashamed of the gospel, am I? For it is God's power for rescue of everyone who trusts, to the Jew first and also to the Greek. ¹⁷For in it God's righteousness is being revealed through trust for trust; as it is written, "The righteous lives by trust."¹⁸For the wrath of God is being revealed from heaven against all impiety and wrongdoing of humans who by their unrighteousness suppress the truth.

The important issue to be decided at this point is precisely where we ought to locate the beginning of the body of the letter. Our starting point is Elliott's argument that 1:13-17 has to be seen as a unit, but we will include 1:18 along with 1:13-17. Elliott identifies here a "disclosure formula, alerting the readers to what will follow, or as a transition to the letter body (2007: 80–4). We agree with his claim that units usually separated (1:13-15, 16-17 and 18-32) are integrally related, and therefore it is arbitrary to isolate 1:16-17 from their functional roles within the *exordium* of the letter (2007: 83) because "the period marked by subordinating conjunctions (γάρ) in 1:13-18 bears a rhetorical significance that is neglected when vv. 1:16-17 are extracted from their context as the 'theme' of an exposition in the following chapters" (2007: 80). Elliott's insights have been developed and strengthened in several ways by Sarah Casson's recent study, which likewise concentrates specifically on the use of γάρ, "for" (but throughout the letter), yet suggesting fresh significance for 1.19a. She also warns against imposing artificial breaks on the text, for example, at 1:16 and 1:18 (2019: 268).

This attention to the context and progression of 1:13-18 effectively requires a reevaluation of 1:13-18/19 accepting that there is little grammatical or rhetorical justification to isolate 1:16-17 as the *propositio* thesis for the entire letter. Elliott had previously argued that it is arbitrary to isolate 1:16-17 from their functional roles within the letter *exordium*, for this is to break apart the rhetorical exigence of the letter and the divine κλῆσις that claims apostle and Christ-followers alike. He insists "that the proper interpretation of Romans is impossible apart from the insight that in the lengthy disclosure period (1:13-17), the 'deep exigence', God's redemptive purpose as this has claimed Paul *and* the Romans, is fused together with the immediate epistolary exigence that now brings them together." From this Elliott reaches the very significant conclusion that we support that "the letter is directed to perform the very function that Paul would have performed in person had he not been hindered" (2007: 83–4).

The Letter as Paul's Gift to the Romans in Lieu of His Personal Presence

If we view the letter as Paul's gift to the Romans in lieu of the strengthening activity he had intended to pursue when he had first planned to visit them, then we have a certain correlation between the letter contents and Paul's plans for mutual strengthening. This can be used to illustrate how Paul operated when resident in a particular city in that it may indicate something about his teaching methods. Without discussing these directly, his use of the dialogical element in this letter must offer certain clues as to how he perceived the needs of his audience, and whether, for example, he uses the style of indictment and protreptic in this teaching, since it was within the Christ-movement (and not in the public arena) that he used such patterns (Stowers 1981: 181–3, Longenecker 2011: 224, 336).

Romans 1:13

With the direct address to ἀδέλφοι brothers (v. 13), Paul begins to explain his purpose in writing, indicated here by the disclosure formula "I want you to know" (Mullins 1964: 44–50). The use of ἀδέλφοι brothers at this point implies a family relationship (in Christ) and connects Paul closely with his gentile audience. This introduces what appears to be an apology for being unable to fulfill, as yet, his long-intended plan to visit them (Lütgert 1913: 36–8). Thus, v. 13 changes from describing Paul's present attitude and activities in relation to the Romans, to his past concerns, "many times I have longed to come to you." This is indicated by the shift from present tense in 1.8-12 ("I make mention of you in my prayers, I long to see you" to past tense "many times I have longed to come to you"). Paul has thus far been prevented from fulfilling his desire to have some fruit among the Romans as among the rest of the nations. In 1:13, Paul explains both why he has not yet visited the Romans and why he still wishes to come. The accent here falls not on his being hindered (καὶ ἐκωλύθην) but on his hitherto postponed desire to visit them. The hindrance, elaborated in terms of "Greeks and barbarians, wise and uneducated" (1:14) and "identified at the end of the letter as preoccupation with other mission areas (15:22), springs from the same motive that continues to drive him towards Rome" (Elliott 2007: 81–2). Paul's commission causes him to be indebted, not to all people, but more specifically, "to Greeks and barbarians" (Harrison 2020: 167–8). This makes him eager to teach the meaning of the gospel, εὐαγγελίσασθαι, to you also who are in Rome (1:15) (Stegemann 2010:19, Nanos 1996: 233). This moreover, includes "strengthening" and "encouragement" (1:11-12), rather than only *protrepsis*, speech of exhortation to adopt a new way of life (Elliott 2007: 85, contra. Klein 1991: 32). Paul may even be preparing here for the introduction of his plans to travel later via Rome to Spain since the Spaniards, along with Africans and Gauls, were identified as typifying the barbarians, the 'uncivilized' who could not speak Greek or Latin, and concerning whom the Romans regarded themselves as divinely appointed to subjugate (Jewett 2007: 130–1).

The Beginning of the Body of the Letter in 1:13

As noted above, there is an ongoing debate about how 1:13-15 relates to 1:16-17 and the body of the letter generally. If as we have done, we take Paul's statement "I want you to know, brothers, that I have often planned to come to you" as a disclosure formula, it could be maintained that this disclosure is closely related to Paul's purpose in writing, and hence can be viewed as the beginning of the body of the letter. Later in the letter at Rom. 9:3, Paul will refer to his Jewish ἀδέλφοι and his συγγενεῖς according to the flesh, but here he is implying an argument about gentile Christ-followers' relation to Jewish kinship (Rainey 2018: 230).[7] Through the Spirit, they are Paul's adoptive brothers though non-Jews, and as such Paul is indebted to them. Hester explains, "Paul has learned from his experience (1:14) and is eager to build on it (1:15). The presence of the inferential particle γάρ 'for' in 1:16 indicates the conclusion of a case-result argument begun in 1:14" (2004: 93–95). Hester insists that there is no reason, based either on epistolographic or rhetorical features, to locate the opening of the letter at v. 16. In his view, the body of the letter opens at 1:13. This is the point at which the principal occasion for the letter is usually indicated and lays the foundation from which the superstructure may grow (Elliott 2007: 81, n1). The gospel of God was first mentioned in 1:2-6, and again in 1:13-15, so it is already a significant theme that Paul returns to consider further in 1:16-17. We can then translate v. 16 as "For it is not as if I am ashamed of the gospel, am I?" which enables Paul to focus attention by using a rhetorical question to stress his claim (Song, 2004: 92). Further evidence for v. 13 as the beginning of the body of the letter will be considered below.

If Paul is involved in a mutual exchange with the Romans, συμπαρακληθῆναι, to be mutually encouraged (1:12), then he must invest something as his part of the transaction. If he had not been hindered, this would already have been given. But since this is the way things are, then Paul is indebted to them, and it looks like he intends the expression of the gospel as a kind of *paideia* to be his gift to the Romans. He will "evangelize" them through this gift even though not being able to be personally present. Thus, the "gospel" which is a central feature of Romans is not something for the non-committed only, but includes both the first turning to God through Christ and the subsequent returnings. In short, the gospel according to Paul includes the whole of the life in Christ, but obviously the commencement of a new way of life has special significance. He sees his task as sharing with the addresses in the process of transformation through the message of the gospel. This will bring mutual encouragement to both and strengthen them in the confidence that their common trust in Christ creates. The content of the gospel is identity shaping in that it provides the narrative and ethos for them as a corporate

---

[7] The Deuteronomistic tradition repeatedly uses the term "brothers" *ahim* to denote ethnic kinship (cf. Rainey 2018: 230). Paul's consciousness of *ethnic* issues is thus hard to deny.

entity as ethnē in Christ. The importance of shared beliefs in group formation and in the nature of social reality that groups construct has been shown to be of primary significance. But it is particularly the awareness of sharing beliefs that turns sharing into a powerful psychological mechanism that can have crucial effects on a group or society (Bar-Tal 2000: 3). This understanding of the gospel as applying to the entire life span of its adherents explains Paul's role as a teacher who can use innovative rhetoric to present his teaching. As Stowers has noted, "in the letter, Paul presents himself to the Romans as a teacher. The dialogical style of the diatribe is central to his self-presentation" (1981: 179). If we have now identified Paul's teaching in Romans as the content of the "evangelizing" he would have done if he had been able to come in person (Dahl 1977: 77), then it is not surprising that Paul moves directly from speaking about his eagerness to come to Rome (1:15) to the content of the gospel as the power of God working towards rescue (1:16-17).

Achtemeier's Reading

Romans 1:14-16

Can we be more precise about where Paul's teaching properly commences in Romans or, in other words, where does the body of the letter actually begin? We have noted above that the term "gospel" has already been introduced prior to 1:16, which continues this strand of thought rather than being an entirely new theme. Here we consider Achtemeier's thesis. He has noted that Paul, after having completed his introduction in 1:13, returns in 1:14 to his *previous* statement in v. 5 that he has been set apart to preach the gospel to the ethnē; so Paul's "indebtedness to all" elaborated here, proceeds from 1:5 and is the beginning of an interconnected argumentation proceeding to the end of the chapter and further (1985: 35). Achtemeier offers an expanded paraphrase of 1:14-22 in which the translation of the repeated γάρ is rendered as "because":

> v. 14 Both to Greeks and barbarians, both to wise and foolish, I am under obligation (to preach the gospel, so vv. 5 and 15). For that reason, my purpose also to preach the gospel even to you who are in Rome (Why even in Rome?). 16 *Because* I am not ashamed of the gospel. (Why am I not ashamed of it?) *Because* it is God's power for salvation for everyone who trusts Jew first and also Greek.

Although many commentators, for example, Jewett argue that 1:16-17 constitute the *propositio* of the letter, we are convinced by Achtemeier's argument that the grammatical subordination of v. 16 to v. 15, and the subsequent dependence of v. 17 on v. 16, and v. 18 on v. 17 indicated by the repetition of γάρ (I prefer 'for' rather than 'because') precludes the possibility that vv. 16-17 function as the theme of the letter (1985: 35–6).

Achtemeier's view gets strong support in various ways from Rachel Casson's research, particularly in the stress on the interconnectedness of vv. 15-18 via the repeated use of γάρ ("for"). Casson seeks to provide "a coherent and integrated understanding of the entirety of verses 15-18" in keeping with the guidance signposts given by the chain of γάρ clauses to be read as tightly knit and coherent complexes of thought (2019: 239).

What is being emphasized here is that a long sequence of subordinate clauses all connected by γάρ ("for") begins with the words "hence my eagerness to preach the gospel to you": *it is in support of this statement that all the rest has been written.* After v. 15, there is no break in the sequence of argument at v. 16 as often claimed.[8] Paul's method of argument is to make a statement followed by γάρ "because" (Achtemeier), which gives his reason for making the claim so that a whole sequence of subordinate clauses is thus interdependent. Rom. 1:16-17 is a part of this sequence, not a separate statement. "Paul's grammar alone all but precludes such a division" (Achtemeier 1985: 36). As asserted above, after 1:15, there is no break in the argument. Verse 15 begins with οὕτως, "hence," indicating its dependence on v. 14. It is because Paul is a debtor to Greeks and barbarians that he is eager to teach the gospel also in Rome.

If in 1:15, Paul emphasizes strongly his desire to teach the gospel in Rome, the first occasion to do so occurs immediately in v. 16, the following verse, which could possibly for this reason be regarded as the beginning of this gospel teaching. The content of the teaching is further expressed in 1:17, for ἐν αυτῶ (in it) the righteousness of God is revealed, and this verse is directly connected to 1:18, which further develops the revelation of God that is revealed. However, there is no grammatical indication to justify making a break after 1:15 (which is what effectively happens when we isolate vv. 16-17 as a theme or *propositio* for the entire letter).

We have greatly valued Achtemeier's reasoning for locating the beginning of the body earlier than v. 16. He concludes that the body of the letter begins with 1:14, but we prefer to identify this as beginning at 1:13, which effectively sets in motion the sequence of thought that explains Paul's gospel and his eagerness to come with it to Rome. We have not identified a *propositio* in 1:16-17, but it is not normal to identify a theme or *propositio* for each of Paul's other letters. Second Corinthians is also a long letter but has no regularly identified thematic verses. The outdated tendency to regard Romans as a theological treatise would favor the view that it must have an identified theme in 1:16-17. Jewett tries to avoid the normal pattern of separating 1:16-17 since he notes, as we have done, that this section began already in 1:13 with no identifiable breaks apart from the disclosure formula commencing in v. 13. Despite being aware of the difficulty of artificially separating 1:16-17 as the theme, Jewett makes these verses the theme of the rest of the letter (2007: 135). But, to my mind, this loses the specificity of these verses within the body of the letter, so that they cannot really function as thus intended. We will now return to consider the content of these verses in the context described above.

Verse 1:16 begins, as noted, with a connection (οὐ γάρ) to the previous statements in 1:14 15. Here Paul acknowledges he is a debtor both to Greeks and to barbarians, to the wise and the uneducated including "virtually every imaginable gentile person" (Hultgren 2011: 66). He is indebted to differing groups of people, and therefore he is eager to proclaim the gospel also to you who are in Rome. It seems that Paul feels

---

[8] "Grammatically, verse 17 is formed as a subordinate clause to verse 16, as verse 16 in its turn is grammatically subordinate to verse 15. That construction does not end with verse 17, however. Verse 18 is shaped in such a way as to be subordinate to 1.17, 1.19b is subordinate to 1.19a, and 1.20 in its turn is subordinate to 1.19b" (Achtemeier 1985: 35).

indebted not only to God for his grace and commission but also to those to whom he has been sent (which includes the Romans). The Greeks, as the parallelism indicates, represent the 'cultured' peoples in contrast to the barbarians, those people who spoke neither Greek nor Latin, both clearly being non-Jews.

There are overtones here of hierarchies, that is, the wise and the uneducated, and Paul acknowledges indebtedness to both, implying that he does not simply adopt the Roman pattern that categorized Romans as first, Greeks a poor second, and all the rest as subjugated nations.

Paul's approach is inclusive, his gospel has an outreach to everyone, hence "everyone who trusts" παντὶ τω πιστεύοντι (v. 16). This means not simply an undifferentiated *homo sapiens*, but specifically both Greeks and barbarians, a phrase typifying peoples in Greek speech, but here putting emphasis on the conquered peoples, the nations, including their varied languages. Having resisted one form of hierarchy, it seems Paul then proceeds to another in claiming his gospel is "for the Jew first and also the Greek."[9] The πρῶτον here may refer to a precedence for the Jews arising from the fact that they are in covenant with the God of Israel—whose Son Paul has announced in the first few verses of his letter as being both descended from David and declared to be Son of God (Ehrensperger 2013: 217–22).

In making a connection between vv. 13-15 and what follows, Paul strongly affirms his pride in the message he has been given to proclaim, "For it is not as if I am ashamed of the gospel" (cf. Song 2004: 65). It implies that Paul asserts here that he speaks openly and candidly about this declaration of good news (εὐαγγέλιον). As Wolter notes, this ought to be interpreted as a rhetorical emphasis formula: a "rhetorische Bekräftigungsformel" (2019: 114–15).

Paul's Gospel "to the Jew First and Also the Greek"

Romans 1:16-17

It might seem somewhat surprising in a letter that we have argued is addressed only to the ethnē in Christ at Rome to find a claim early in the first chapter that Paul's gospel is first to the Jew and only then for the "Greek." An explanation is required because of this disparity between addressees and the priority of the gospel, and this is all the more pressing because of Paul's specific emphasis upon his own apostolate to the nations. When items that seem so incongruous are closely related in one letter, this can only mean that attention is being drawn to this unusual coincidence. We cannot solve this issue at this point, but we suggest that there must be some lack of understanding at Rome about the relation of the gospel to the Jewish people, otherwise it seems unwarranted to stress this aspect (of Jewish priority) to a gentile audience. In fact, it could be perceived as extremely provocative.

---

[9] Cf. Rainey's comment, "In an ancient context, the word means 'fairness' with respect to 'hierarchy.' Someone getting their *due* is contingent on what is *due* to that person as a member of a particular group. It is 'fair' and 'just' treatment, but it is by no means equal treatment" (2018: 236).

Having argued for the unity of 1:13-17, it is noteworthy that 1:18 also links with 1:13-17 through the repetition of γάρ:

> The statements in verses 15-18 are bound together by the procedural guidance given by γάρ. Consequently, they should not be separated from one another in interpretation by the imposition of major section breaks in the text. The fourfold strengthening of γάρ clauses leads back to verse 15, supporting the claim (eagerness to proclaim the gospel to you in Rome) in that verse and underlining its argumentative salience." (Casson 2019: 243)

Casson claims that within Romans γάρ functions consistently as a procedural textual signpost that leads addressees to draw inferences that reinforce prior contentions Paul has just made. This is similar to Achtemeier's explanation of how Paul through the subordinate γάρ clauses gives reasons for claims he has just made. Thus 1:16-17 is included in the section beginning at 1:13 and probably concluding with the διότι that commences v. 19. Based on the analysis of 1:15-18 as a connected interlinked text, a fresh line of thought is perceived as being introduced only in 19-32, a basis that is itself strengthened by γάρ clauses in vv. 19b and 20. This leaves vv. 16-18 to find their full expression at this point, *joined as they are with Paul's long-held desire to visit Rome*. As Casson claims, "Verses 16-17 need to be interpreted as strengthening material within the context of Paul's desire to preach the gospel to those in Rome, rather than regarded as an isolated thesis statement that summarizes a gospel of justification by trust and thereby announces the epistle's theme." Investigation shows that "all occurrences of γάρ clauses in Romans can be accounted for in terms of core procedural instructions toward background strengthening. It follows from a uniform reading of these signals that reinforcement is primary (Casson 2019: 21). It is his eagerness to visit that Paul wants the Romans to be fully aware of, and it is this that constitutes the explanation of all that follows, including the gospel as the power of God leading to rescue. Although not viewing vv. 16-17 as the *propositio* for the entire letter, this does not reduce their value or their significance. This value comes from their inherent content and actual context. Verse 18 is connected also with Paul's goal to visit Rome: "Verse 18 should be interpreted as part of the complex of assumptions in verses 16-18 marshalled to bolster Paul's claim in verse 15 and not as a heading for a new section describing God's wrath against mankind." Thus, 1:16b-18 represent a powerful theological rationale backing up the claim in v. 16 concerning the gospel (Casson 2019: 243).

For it is not as if I Am Ashamed of the Gospel

Paul has no reason to fear being put to shame because it is God's δικαιοσύνη—integrity—that is revealed in the proclamation of the gospel from "trust to trust" that is, the trustworthiness of God creating trust so that "out of trustworthiness the righteous lives." It is the character of the God of Israel whom he proclaims that gives Paul confidence. In his claim "For it is not as if I am ashamed of the gospel" (1:16), which comes at the end of a listing of reasons why he is eager to come to Rome, Paul is claiming both his right and his determination to speak out the gospel message to the Greeks and barbarians. In his contemporary context, the term "shame," the Latin *pudor*, was regarded as one of the inhibiting emotions. "*Pudor* was the shyness that caused one to draw back before another, the fear or respect that caused one to make way for another even when one was within one's rights, one's *libertas* or *ius* ... *Pudor* was the emotion that constrained speech, that bridled the tongue" (Barton 2001: 202–5). Whatever responses might be encountered by it in Rome, Paul is committed to the value system of the gospel as expressed in his message about Christ the Messiah of Israel. Paul is committed to its proclamation because it is the power of God that leads to rescue for everyone who trusts "the Jew first and also the Greek." He strongly affirms that he will not hold back from proclaiming the message of the one whom the Romans crucified, but God vindicated in the resurrection.[10] The very reference to being ashamed alerts Paul's audience to undercurrents in Rome that might find his value system out of harmony with their cultural *habitus*, indicating that at least some of the ethnē in Christ may have been not as distant in perspective from imperialist Roman values as Paul himself appears to be (Elliott 2008: 202). Rome's boast of supremacy over Israel and other subdued nations must not be allowed to influence the relation of the ethnē in Christ in their attitude towards Israel, especially if there were undercurrents of anti-Judaism among the Roman gentile population that were already encouraging the despising of Jews (Wiefel 1991: 79). In full contrast to this, Paul unequivocally claims that the gospel of divine blessing is oriented to the Jew first even in face of Roman supremacy.

Paul refers to the message proclaimed by the term "gospel," εὐαγγέλιον, literally good news. It is probable that its background lies in the "emperor ideology" in which the "good tidings" of the dawn of a new era are proclaimed with the accession of an emperor to the throne. Similarly, it is a term in which a victory in a battle is proclaimed.[11] Thus, Paul in Romans proclaims the good news that "the God of Israel reigns" (Isa. 52:7 cf. Rom. 10:15), a new era has dawned. This good news is not merely new information but the power of God operative through Paul, his co-workers, and others in the proclamation of the message about Jesus as the Christ. The word order in 1:16b puts the emphasis upon the gospel as liberating power (δύναμις), a performative utterance that carries emancipation from the powers of sin and death under which the ethnē have been living in bondage (Elliott 2007: 111). It leads to rescue (εἰς σωτηρίαν) for everyone, because this message is effective in releasing God's power to everyone who trusts, including even the ethnē. God's salvation is divine action denoting ongoing activity, not a thing that we possess but a relation of trusting in God (Käsemann 1971: 82). Positively, as Paul will later elaborate, σωτηρία is family oriented—it consists in membership in the family of God through Christ, reconciliation to God, being

---

[10] Setzer (2001: 65–102). Setzer presents a fresh ideological approach to the doctrine of resurrection as a tool that was ultimately concerned with vindication of the righteous and the dispensation of God's justice and was utilized by communities on the peripheries of existence to help them cope with the lived realities of this world (87–9).

[11] Cf. Friedrich, εὐαγγέλιον, *TDNT* 2:724-725. This form of the term does not derive from the LXX, but the verbal form εὐαγγελίζομαι—to proclaim good news—is used more than twenty times in the LXX.

conformed to the image of God's Son, the firstborn of many brothers, and eventual bodily resurrection (8:23-29).

The Gospel as an Alternative to Roman Imperial Ideology

Neither the good news εὐαγγέλιον nor rescue/restoration σωτηρία is explained by Paul—it is assumed that the Romans will be able to understand what he means, indicating a supposition that these terms circulated widely in Pauline circles and elsewhere. By the end of Augustus's reign, generally perceived deterioration in social life, resonated with hopes of a return of a golden age (Stowers 1994: 124). There are indeed good reasons for suggesting that Paul's terminology would have resonated with the Romans. As Harrison claims, Roman auditors would have noticed a terminological overlap between Paul's proclamation

> of the gospel and the inscriptional propaganda of Augustus and Nero. The early Christians were heralding the advent of a new Benefactor, whom they credited with the same honorifics as the Caesars and whose benefits (they claimed) surpassed the imperial household. (Harrison 2011: 185)

Paul does not explicitly mention the emperor Nero whose first five years were, by some, regarded as most promising.[12] It was a time when new benefactions were expected according to the poet Virgil in the *Aeneid*, the hope of a golden age of human flourishing and fertility made possible by the Augustan peace. It is indeed possible that one of Virgil's sources was the Jewish *Sibylline Oracles*, through which he derived eschatological and paradisal images from Isaiah (cf. Stowers 1994: 123, also Bremmer 2013: 157–64). The emphasis upon *pietas* (piety) included a range of connotations, including loyalty and devotion to the gods, emperor, nation, and family. *Pietas* was esteemed as one of the quintessential qualities that distinguished the Romans from other nations and so legitimated their imperial rule over such inferior barbaric peoples (Hoklotubbe 2017: 53).

Although it is clear that Paul's terminology resonates with imperial terminology, and though we are not asserting that Paul explicitly opposes the rule of Rome, it is likely that he was intending to make his readers aware of the challenge that the claims about Christ posed to this rule. Thus, Elliott reads Romans "as a Judean critique of an incipient non-Judean Christianity in which the pressures of imperial ideology were a decisive factor" (2008: 15). The Jewish pattern of critical distancing from idolatry and its claims might not be familiar to all the ethnē in Rome, and a variety of stances to cultic participation and performance would have been common (cf. Rajak 2009: 154–5; also Taubes 2004: 13–16). Paul's radical claim "to the Jew first" (1:16) would have revealed one point where Paul diverged from Roman norms, and where

---

[12] Golden-age ideology and hopes may have reached their highest peak since Augustus around the time that Paul wrote Romans, when Nero's tutor Seneca presents Nero as the one who has the potential to save the empire from sin and usher in the golden age (cf. Stowers 1994: 124, Rock 2012: 59–65).

there was divergence of opinion among Christ-followers. Because it comes so early in the letter, is specifically emphasized, and is so radically innovative in content, this emphatic stress upon the role of the Jew must be taken as evidence that this is a crucial element in Paul's understanding of his gospel.[13] His gospel includes ethnic issues and new perspectives on the future of Jews and the nations in the divine economy as now revealed through Jesus as the Christ. The formula "to the Jew first and also to the Greek" seems almost like a counter-assertion to the emerging fact of non-Jews responding to the "good news" and many Jews remaining unpersuaded (which may be evidenced later in 11:17-24). It is difficult to presume the attitude of the Roman ethnē in Christ to this divergent interpretation of apparent responses, but Paul's emphasis, taken along with 11:13-24, suggests that these Christ-followers may have been influenced by everyday attitudes in Rome to Jews as one of the groups somehow perceived as inferior.

In contrast to Roman subjugation of the Jews and other nations, Paul makes an explicit reference to the special relation that Israel enjoyed with her God and, in contrast to Roman control over the nations, Paul claims that Israel is not inferior to Rome and the other nations. Instead, in contrast to Rome's boasts of favor by the gods, Paul regards Israel as chosen for special purposes by her God who gives her a certain priority in these plans (as already indicated by his presentation of Christ as the seed of David). He depicts this as "to the Jew first and also to the nations (the Greek)." Only in Romans does Paul make this radical claim and three times within the first two chapters (1:16, 2:9-10). This indicates that the priority and place of Israel in the purpose of God has specific significance in this letter. Also, this claim to priority emerges in the context of a radical critique of gentile idolatry. What is noteworthy is that this context suggests that in Paul's mind, as he addresses the Roman ethnē in Christ, there is a link between God's purpose with Israel and his opposition to gentile idolatry. Roman idolatry stands on one side and on the other, in opposition and contrast to this, is Israel (and other subjugated ethnē in Christ).

Core to this εὐαγγέλιον about which Paul talks freely (is not ashamed) is the proclamation of the resurrection (1:4) of the one crucified by the Roman authorities. As Claudia Setzer has stressed, the belief in resurrection is mainly a symbol for Jewish groups, being inseparable from the knowledge of scripture, particularly the interpretation of the Torah, and trust in God's power and his involvement in human affairs (Setzer 2001: 87–9). Resurrection implies the crucifixion of Jesus by Roman law as a rebel for treason, and an overturning of this verdict by God through his justice and power. Thus, resurrection contrasts with the understanding of the Roman emperor as the one who controlled life and death for the nations as Nero had claimed in his accession speech (Rock 2012: 115–18). It is hard to avoid the conclusion that this presentation of Jesus as Son of God is not meant to declare a deliberate contrast and challenge to the ubiquitous description of the Roman emperor, though it is not so much an "emperor alone" challenge, but the emperor as the ruler of a system of beneficence sanctioned by Roman deities, considered a system of idolatry in Jewish eyes, which

---

[13] For this focus on Israel, see last section Excursus I.

gave Rome its specific ethos.[14] Jews living in Rome, as elsewhere in the Diaspora, had to learn how to play and not to play the game of acculturation to enable some kind of participation without compromise in everyday life. Through the translation of the LXX into a special kind of Greek "which respects the peculiarity of the source language, a bridge between cultures was built which connected and separated at the same time" (Ehrensperger 2019: 152, Rajak 2009, Cohen 1995).

Romans 1:18

For Paul, the God of Israel is not distant from the world that he created as in some philosophical perceptions. The God of Israel is not remote and removed from human activity in the created world. On the contrary, the wrath of God is revealed in the gospel against all ἀσέβεια, impiety, and ἀδικία, injustice (1:18). Although the opposition of God to all impiety and injustice is clear in Romans, the formulation of the critique here, as the terms indicate, is specifically directed against *gentile* idolatry, as primarily but not exclusively represented by the emperor and the hegemonic system of which he was the head. This gentile focus is because it is the nations that Paul directly addresses in Romans, as he has clearly indicated earlier in this chapter, and also because he will differentiate explicitly his statements concerning the nations and those concerning the Jews throughout this letter.

Romans 1:19-32: God's Wrath against the Gentile World Revealed in the Gospel

[19]For what can be known about God is evident among them, because God made it evident to them. [20]For ever since the creation of the world his invisible qualities are perceived through created things; they are clearly discerned—namely his eternal power and divine nature. So they are without excuse; [21]for though they knew God, they did not glorify him as God or give thanks to him, but they were made futile in their thinking, and their senseless minds were darkened. [22]While claiming to be wise, they were made witless; [23]and they exchanged the glory of the imperishable God into a likeness of an image of a perishable human and birds and four-legged animals and reptiles. [24]God therefore handed them over to the desires of their hearts for impurity of their bodies, being dishonored among themselves, [25]those who exchanged the truth about God for a lie and venerated and worshiped the creature rather than the Creator, who is blessed unto the ages! Amen. [26]For this reason God handed them over to degrading passions. For their females exchanged natural use for the unnatural, [27]and likewise also the males, after they abandoned natural use with females, were inflamed with their lust for one another, males committing shameless acts with males and received the recompense that was required for their mutual deception.

---

[14] Cf. Peppard (2019: 135–757). Ehrensperger points out that the element of subversion in Paul's language and discourse to which scholars like Georgi, Horsley, and Elliott have drawn attention is decisively indebted to the Jewish Greek resistance discourse (2013: 219).

²⁸And since they did not see fit to acknowledge God, God handed them over to a debased mind and to things that are improper, ²⁹having been filled with all manner of wrongdoing, evil, greed, malice. Persons full of envy, murder, strife, treachery, malevolence, they are gossipers, ³⁰slanderers, God-haters, bullies, arrogant, braggarts, contrivers of evil deeds, disobedient to their parents, ³¹senseless, faithless, heartless, ruthless, ³²those knowing God's decree that those who practice such things deserve to die— yet not only practice them but even applaud others who are doing them.

Rom. 1:19-32 is critically situated in Paul's address to the ethnē in Rome. Paul has claimed in vv. 1:16-17 that he is proud to proclaim the gospel for in it the saving power of God for everyone who has trust is being revealed (present tense). The same connection (γάρ) with the gospel is now made with the wrath of God in v. 18. This continues the argument in 16-17 beginning with the same γάρ, resumed also in vv. 19-20. Paul's point is that just as the gospel is God's power for *all* who trust, so God's wrath is against *all* human ἀσέβεια and ἀδικία. Ἀσέβεια denotes irreverence towards the Creator particularly in the worship of idols (v. 25), impiety towards the sacred.[15] According to Paul's argument here, to know what God is revealing is to know seemingly contrasting aspects of his character. The God of Israel, the Creator God revealed in the traditions of Israel, is now being more fully revealed in the gospel. Thus, the nature and character of the God of Israel whom previously the gentile world knew only indirectly and partially, Paul claims is now being revealed through his gospel. We should anticipate that Paul's teaching in this letter will have much to say about the understanding of the God of Israel and how this God is revealing himself through the gospel. We *could* note first that we are considering here not the god of philosophical enquiry but the God of Israel, the Creator of the world. Yet that emphasis would only be partly true. It appears that the character of the God of Israel met with some incomprehension in Rome due to the cultural presuppositions of the ethnē, as would emerge later in Marcionite and other controversies. But Paul is more adaptable than simply to directly repudiate these, though he will do so indirectly. Instead of viewing his critiques of the gentile world as the reaction of a devout Israelite to various forms of idolatry, these critiques reveal that "philosophical arguments about cosmology, first principles and causality were being productively expropriated and applied to the God of Jewish ethnic tradition" (Wasserman 2018: 164–72). Also, since Paul's comments in Romans 1 reveal parallels with the polemics of Philo and Pseudo-Solomon, these polemics are suggestive insofar as "they furnish evidence of other Jewish intellectuals appropriating from philosophical cosmology in ways that expand their polemical arsenals." Thus, Paul takes seriously the questions emerging from the pagan cultural context when considering the challenge of relating the traditional Roman gods to the good news of the Christ, but in this he was participating in an ongoing Jewish critical tradition (Wasserman 2018: 171; also Öhler 2016).

---

[15] Ehrenkrook notes that "both *before* and *after* 70 AD, the dominant tendency was to restrict the scope of the second commandment to images that had some kind of cultic association … whether formally consecrated or otherwise deemed an object of worship. Iconolatry rather than iconography was the issue" (2011: 97).

So, we assume that in v. 19, the people under discussion are "gentile sinners" (Gal. 2:15) in that these are referred to in the third person, that is, "they are without excuse" (1:20). This does not mean that there may not be echoes of Sodom traditions here, especially given the reference to same-sex relations (Esler 2003: 149; contra Rodriguez 2014: 26). Paul does not directly accuse the Roman Christ-followers of these things,[16] but for such critiques to be relevant, there must be persons in Rome who could be viewed as being involved in such or similar activities, or at least in danger of becoming so. So, the accusations are not just complaints against non-Jews generally but against the sin of idolatry, misdirected λατρεία particularly representative of the nations, and one that has, in Paul's view, probably some resonance in popular discussions in Rome. It is interesting that Abraham in Romans 4 is presented as trusting in a God who "gives life to the dead and calls into being things that do not exist." In scriptural reception, Abraham was depicted, especially since the period from the Maccabean revolt, as trusting in the living God having turned from idols. This explains the strange statement in 4:5, "who justifies the impious" (ἀσεβής, cf. 1:18) in relation to Abraham. Thus, Abraham is presented here as an anti-type to the gentile idolators in 1:19-32, in his being able to reason from the created world back to the Creator (Esler 2003: 193, following Adams).

Thus, 1:19-32 can be viewed as a somewhat accentuated, that is, diatribal, indictment against the sinfulness and corruption of the gentile world as it was typically viewed from a Jewish perspective. There are parallels with Wisdom of Solomon 13–16 (Wasserman 2018: 168), but Keck notes that although Paul agrees that idolatry is the beginning of corruption, he differs in that he traces the error to disobedience (Keck 2005: 60–3). Here in Romans, the indictment is much accentuated in its concentration upon idolatry. Misdirected *latreia*, therefore, is the fundamental problem (Fredriksen 2017: 118, McMurray 2021: 49–52), so that 1:19-32 represents a rather negative introduction to the body of Paul's letter. This may be explained by noting that it bears some of the characteristics of diatribal style with its intensity and accumulation of critique, especially of inconsistency, and other features such as lists of virtues and vices leading up to the direct addressing of the man, ἄνθρωπε, in 2:1-5 (Stowers 1981: 19–25, 71, 111). Although there is little consensus about the rhetoric of 1:18-32, several scholars have noted diatribal characteristics at various points. Song, as noted (2004: 82), suggests that a diatribe commences at 1:16, rather than at 1:18, as Stowers holds. Douglas A. Campbell views much of 1:18–3:20 as speech-in-character in which Paul is mimicking the hypothetical perspective of an opponent (2009: 519–600). I differ in that I do not support the hypothesis concerning opponents of Paul in Romans. "If we accept that the diatribe techniques permeate in Romans, then there is no real opponent in Romans; the epistle is only pedagogical, not polemic; and the seemingly harsh tones and apostrophes are only rhetorical" (Song 2004: 8; cf. also Rodriguez 2014: 37). In broad agreement concerning diatribal style, Thiessen regards 1:16–2:16 as diatribe

---

[16] "Even though there are numerous examples in the Hebrew Bible of Israelites engaging in forbidden religious practices, Israel's current situation (in contrast to the nations) is, in Paul's perspective, not connected with idolatry. He appears to agree with the Book of Judith that Jews in the present day, do not worship idols (Jud. 8.18)" (Rainey 2018: 230).

(2016: 46). Thus, despite little precise agreement on reading 1:16–2:16 as diatribal and, in the absence of any other convincing consensus, there are sufficient grounds in the content and form of 1:19-32 to merit a consideration of the diatribal aspects of Paul's arguments.

Romans 1:19-32 Diatribal Indictment Concerning the Worship of God

We note the course of Paul's thought here. In 1:16, it is Paul himself who is speaking in the first-person singular, and the theme of 1:16 continues directly through 1:17. But after 1:18, there is a transition from first- and second-person addresses as in 1:15-17, to third-person plural continuing throughout 1:19-32, thereby giving this a certain unity. If, despite unclarity as to its extent, 1:16 is taken as the commencement of a diatribe, then this must extend through to 1:32 or further (Elliott 2007: 147, Song 2004: 65). This does not necessarily conflict radically with the common reading of this passage as referring to the idolatry of the gentile world. The third-person plural continues throughout indicating a continuous subject and common critiques.

The indictment Paul denoted by the ongoing use of third-party language that emerges with 1:19 is specifically against gentile *idolatry*, not all aspects of gentile society, and thus not surprisingly, it shows little specific attention to Roman virtues except by their absence or perversion. In diatribal style, it focuses sharply upon certain characteristic inconsistencies, its concentration on these giving the impression of intensification or exaggeration. This could perhaps be explained as a feature of the diatribe, if there is sufficient agreement on the evidence to support this. The indictment focusses on the behavior of those who do certain things, and although the reference to humans, ἀνθρώπων in 1:18, could suggest all humanity is in view, the third-person reference to "among them," and "because God made it evident to them" (1:19, cf. 1:20-22) indicates that it is specifically *gentile* idolatry that Paul critiques. At this point, he does not speak of "us" or of "you," as is common in the diatribe but from v. 19, of "them." For example, he stresses the triad of ὑβριστής, ὑπερήφανος, and ἀλαζών in 1:30 and thus connects the fall of the ethnē to the current state of their society (Stowers 1994. 122–3). Some gentile Greco-Roman intellectuals no less than Jews ridiculed idol worship as vulgar superstition (Goodwin 2001: 82, n23); yet nonetheless everyday life in Rome was dominated by reverence for the gods and those who claimed to represent them. Denial of the reality of the gods, apparently, did not cause any cessation of their ongoing worship in everyday life, which was virtually universal as Ehrensperger has noted (2019: 159–80).

One aspect of idol worship that none could escape was the offering of sacrifices designed to ensure the ongoing favor of the gods to the Romans; and because, like Philo and the author of the Wisdom of Solomon, Paul traces all immorality to failure to give God his due honor, idolatry is a fundamental cause of corruption. Rock claims that "what has not received sufficient attention is how both literary creations (Romans and the Wisdom of Solomon), sought to address similar concerns (i.e., a critique of gentile idolatry)" (2012: 252). In some respects, Paul's critique of idolatry in Romans can be viewed as the way of life of faithful Israelites honoring the God of Israel in fundamental contrast to idolators.

God's dealing with the gentile world surfaces clearly in Rom. 1:19-32 in the claim that by their wickedness, the nations "suppress the truth." It is to be noted that Paul offers not only a critique of gentile idolatry but also an explanation to show that they are responsible for their practice of it. If we had decided that Paul is simply outlining the well-known errors of the gentile world from the perspective of his Jewish symbolic universe, then it might seem warranted to read the second half of Romans 1 simply as an anti-idolatry diatribal statement. But the content of Paul's claims, even as read through a diatribal lens, does not fully explain why Paul deals so specifically with the attributed gentile sins. As noted above, why does Paul not simply give examples of idolatrous practice but proceeds to explain that it need not have been like this. He seems to be attributing gentile responsibility and also foolishness simultaneously. The point is that knowledge of God need not have been absent or confused (Rom. 1:20-21). Wasserman sees a contrast between Paul's references to so-called gods and lords—στοιχεῖα, εἴδολα, and δαιμονία in Gal. 4:1 and 1 Cor. 8–11:1—where these are used largely as foils for exploring the exceptional status of Israel's deity.

> In some contrast, Rom. 1:18-25 reviles gentiles for misapprehending the created order, failing to perceive the true divine power that stands supreme over that order, and perversely worshipping the creation in place of its Creator. In this remarkable turn, Paul thus neatly avoids other gods by explaining the origins of idolatry as a form of intellectual error or confusion about the nature of reality. (Wasserman 2018: 164)

What emerges from this analysis is that Paul not only is content to describe the errors of the ethnē but also consistently avoids attributing any real function to the Roman pagan gods in his explanation of human sin, even where it involves their worship. Paul's analysis not only announces a wrathful punishment against impiety (ἀσέβεια) and wickedness (ἀδικία) but also explains that these alleged evils all derive ultimately from a single cause: the failure to worship the supreme divine Creator. In reaction to such confusion, Paul's response is to maintain that they should have known better because knowledge of God was clearly displayed to them (v. 21). God displayed it to them since his invisible attributes—his eternal power and godliness—are discoverable. Knowledge of God has been disclosed to human beings ever since the creation of the cosmos. His invisible attributes of power and godliness could be intellectually discerned in the created order in that the divine power and nature, though invisible, are discernible through the created things. Jewett is one of very few Pauline scholars who have considered how the doctrine of God concerning nature and its corruption relates to the understanding of God and environmental issues (2004: 25–46). As Wasserman maintains, "In this line of argument, gentiles should have observed the world around them and come to intuit an unseen creator outside of it" (2018: 41–64). So, they could have come to the right conclusion about God and honored him respectively. However, they opted instead to worship the created, misdirecting their honor and thus living in a wrong relation to the created world and its God. "The primary problem is that of misguided gentile cult with Paul's emphasizing the behaviors of 1.26-32 as being a secondary consequence of this" (McMurray 2021: 6).

Paul's Strategy in Critiquing the Gentile World: What Paul Is Doing through What He Is Saying

Building on this analysis of Paul's argumentation in Romans 1, we have realized that Paul here offers the gentile audience an indirect description of the God of Israel. By analysis of the ascribed failure of gentile comprehension, Paul offers a vista of what should have been evident—the image of the Creator God whose being is the explanation of the cosmos. *The Creator God is thus indirectly presented via Paul's response as what the idolators had failed to comprehend.* Via the narrative of what the gentile world did not grasp, Paul seizes an opportunity to present the God of Israel in his relation to the creation. Paul's verdict is that they, the nations, are without excuse, ἀναπολογήτους (v. 20). Although they knew God, they did not honor him as God, or give thanks to him, and their whole understanding was affected, so that whilst claiming to be wise, they became fools and they exchanged the glory of the immortal God for images resembling human beings, or animals and reptiles (Carter 2008: 57). The reference to images, including birds (viewed as omens), four-footed animals (whose entrails were studied), and reptiles (frequently depicted as household gods), brings to light the presence and pattern of the gentile way of life, dominated by gods of all kinds, including household deities and sacrifices to these at important sites in the community area.[17] The summary of gentile failure is epitomized in idolatry, worshipping the created rather than the Creator, but in this diagnosis, Paul also points to its solution, the revelation of the Creator God of Israel. His primary interest is not on the failings of the gentile world but on their explication.

One of the qualities of the diatribal style we note in our Excursus on this topic is that it offers an opportunity to raise controversial issues without precise attribution of their sources. By formulating his description of gentile culture as characterized by wrong λάτρεια, that is, idolatry, as he has done here, Paul enables his understanding of the God of Israel to be presented indirectly at an early point in the letter under the guise of what the idolators failed to comprehend. What he is apparently saying is that the idolators as a penalty for their mistaken worship have confused the nature of reality. What Paul is doing, through what he is saying, that is, his rhetorical strategy, is using this explanation to explain the Creator's relation to the created world, particularly its gentile inhabitants, so that indirectly he is providing here a vehicle for explaining the gospel to the nations. Hence, the logical connection (in our construction) of 1:19-32 to 1:16-18 is the reflex of the gospel proclamation. It is significant, however, that as noted, Paul does not accuse his Roman gentile audience of idolatry. It seems that he is warning them indirectly to be aware of the imperial ethos in which they live and whose influence they cannot escape. Most likely, he is offering them here his view of the world as an alternative explanation of reality in contrast to the dominating narrative of Rome's claimed "gods-given" role. This leads into the issue of how to act to escape the just wrath of the God of Israel against all unrighteousness and impiety. Apart from Paul's gospel, the only way for the ethnē to escape the judgment of the God of Israel against the gentile world would be to take on the yoke of the Law and thus to

---

[17] Cf. Rock on birds and animals in Roman idolatry (2012: 256-8).

join the Jewish people. This will be considered in the next chapter, especially in relation to 2:17-29.

Conclusion to 1:19-32

As a Jewish person, Paul sees the improper worship of God as the marker of gentile deviance, and the dividing line between Jews and non-Jews. This boundary line, determined by idolatry, puts the Jews and Christ-following ethnē on one side and gentile idolators on the other. It is not a new dividing line but part of an alternative discourse that we have outlined as advocated by Paul, which subverts the hegemonic claims of the empire (Greek first, followed by Rome). What is new in the subversive use of the language of power by Paul is that he communicates to non-Jews the significance of this discourse. The ethnē need to know that this alternative discourse has its roots in exclusive loyalty to the one God of Israel through the inauguration of the Christ-event that includes them as well (Ehrensperger 2008: 138–58). The gentile Christ-followers in Rome must determine where their loyalty lies, with Israel and her God through Christ or with Caesar and the ethos of associated idolatry.

Ehrensperger stresses how this discourse of power that was formerly exclusive to Jews has been brought by Paul to those from the nations giving them a fresh alignment with the God of Israel. "The exclusive loyalty claim at the heart of the Christ-movement to the One God of Israel, and the understanding of the crucifixion of Christ in the context of the resistance discourse of the Jewish scriptures was distancing the Christ-movement decisively from the dominating power system. Any totalizing power-claims were subverted by the exclusive loyalty claim of the One God" (2008: 157–8). Through Christ, the ethnē are now linked with Israel and her God in distinction and implicit resistance to Roman domination. Later, in ch. 2, Paul will show more appreciation of some aspects of gentile patterns of morality, but this does not mean any lessening of his opposition to idolatry. The fact that he takes up this theme so early in the letter must be taken into account as we seek to relate his rhetoric to daily life among the ethnē in Christ at Rome. Paul's apparent critique of mistaken worship as stemming from idolatry, when carefully considered, reveals that this is his way of telling the Romans about the supreme God of the cosmos who in Paul's mind is the Creator God of Israel (Wasserman 2018: 169). *The Romans need to learn not only of Jewish opposition to idolatry but indirectly via the critique of idolatry the true nature of Israel's God and how he operates in the world.*

EXCURSUS II

The Wrath of God against All Idolatry—A Trajectory from Zephaniah to Romans

Is Paul's critique of gentile idolatry in Rom. 1:19-32 typical of the apostle's line of thought?

In some respects, it seems somewhat extreme and lacking in appreciation of the non-Jewish world. It is for this reason that we need to look for precedents for his perspective.

Paul asserts that the wrath of God, ὀργή, is revealed against all ἀσέβεια, impiety, and ἀδικία, injustice, of those who by their wickedness suppress the truth (1:18). In the scriptures, the demonstration and execution of this wrath often involve the interaction of one nation against another, whether in victory or subjugation, functioning as a critique of national leadership and of political alignment with the will of God as expressed within the covenant. Quite often, the wrath of God has a specific reference to the powerful enemies of Israel, proud despotic rulers who do not recognize Israel's God. The wrath of God does not denote an irrational or irresponsible outburst of rage, a capricious or arbitrary anger against human beings; nor is it to be associated with the Greek idea of angry deities who have to be placated. It is linked to monotheism and to the covenantal relationship of God in which Israel is bound up with her God so that this wrath represents the anger of a righteous and impartial God. Thus, Wisdom 13:1-9 condemns πάντες ἄνθρωποι "all people," but nonetheless refers only to the gentile world, and though he does not explicitly say so, it appears that in Rom. 1:19-32 Paul also can only have non-Jews in mind in the twenty-seven references to "they," "their," or "them" (Campbell 2009: 357). It is significant that Paul's earliest readers universally read these in the same fashion, that is, as referring to non-Jews (Gaca 1999).

Stowers has noted Paul's use of texts and association of ideas from Zephaniah in Romans 1. This is despite the fact that none of the echoes of Zephaniah in Romans is a convincing quotation in itself, since individual elements of the language of judgment appear widely in Jewish literature. We have found these parallels convincing, especially the fact that Romans 1 is the locus classicus for much of this language. Moreover, the accumulation and combination of features found within it make Zephaniah a work with which Romans connects, particularly in its emphasis upon God's judgment and redemption of Israel and the gentile nations (Stowers 1994: 118). The "wrath of God" in Rom. 1:18 and "day of wrath" in Rom. 2:5 echo the language of LXX Zeph. 1:18, cf. 2:2 (ἐν ἡμέρᾳ ὀργῆς κυρίου). The crucial point for reading Romans is that

Zephaniah, even while using the language of "all humanity," does not reduce Israel and the various non-Jewish peoples to abstract individuals-in-relation-to-God. Both works view individuals as members of human communities and treat individual relations to God under the larger category. Like Romans, Zephaniah begins with oracles of judgment and admonition by proclaiming that God's wrath will soon be poured out on all humankind, but like Paul in Romans this is a differentiated humanity. Zephaniah and Romans distinguish the particular sins of the nations as well as those of Israel, and each of these as differentiated peoples.[1] Stowers views Zephaniah as a text from the Greek Bible upon which Paul likely drew for narrative patterns, metaphors, and motifs, using the sacred Jewish writings to think about the gentile problem (1994: 118). This indicates that Paul saw parallels between the critiques of Zephaniah concerning Israel's enemies and that which he himself is making concerning Roman arrogance. In Zephaniah the gentile nations are accused of having "taunted my people and made boasts against my borders" (Zeph. 2:8). Thus, Paul drew upon a Jewish tradition that offered him an alternative perspective on the relation of powerful nations to the people of Israel and their God. Paul must have thought this behavior somehow resonated with the situation of the ethnē in Rome. Because of their ὕβρις, arrogance, Zephaniah even pronounces an oracle of doom against the gentile nations because they taunted and boasted against the people of the Lord of hosts (LXX 2:10, cf. Rom. 11:18, 25). The arrogant ones have said, "I am and there is no longer anyone else" (2:15). The pride of the arrogant nations against the God of Israel and his people led Paul to see in Zephaniah evidence of the coming wrath of God against imperial rulers like Rome. In Rome's arrogant self-understanding, Rome is the ultimate power, the final authority, "they taunted my people." In Paul's reading of scripture, Zephaniah's reference here to the people of Israel reflects the opposition between the God of Israel and imperial rulers' self-understanding.

Paul's use of Zephaniah then gives us some insight into Paul's own negative understanding of Roman/political imperialism and the diametrical opposition it represented to the claims of Israel's God through Christ. If Paul reads these verses in relation to imperial rulers like Rome, he must be thinking broadly of the people of God on one side and the Roman Empire on the other. The Roman ethnē are called to worship the Creator God of Israel, the God and Father of our Lord Jesus Christ who opposes such idolatry rather than giving their loyalty to Rome and its gods. Already in 1:16, Paul has made the radical claim that the gospel is the power of God unto σωτηρία "to the Jew first and also to the 'Greek,'" so the Roman ethnē cannot turn their back on their Jewish foundation, as Rome's influence might encourage them to do. In this letter to Rome, Paul seems to be trying to address an early loosening from Jewish roots, not only in the sense of Jewish traditions but including also the Jewish people (cf. Rom. 11:1). If the Roman ethnē were to echo the insolent views of the nations in Zephaniah, "I am and there is no one else," this would be pure idolatry. Instead of this, Paul offers an alternative view of the cosmos, in "which philosophical arguments circulating at this period about cosmology, first principles, and causality were being expropriated

---

[1] That Israel will not be excluded from the judgment of God is presumed, but in my view, Paul's use of Zephaniah connects more closely with God's wrath against the hybris of the gentile nations.

and applied to the God of Jewish ethnic tradition." Emma Wasserman sees Paul's language, though often brief and allusive, as indicative of links with the polemics of Philo and Pseudo-Solomon, thus providing a helpful context for considering Paul's intellectual practices, appropriate interests, and habits. "These are suggestive insofar as they furnish evidence of other Jewish intellectuals appropriating from philosophical cosmology in ways that expand their polemical arsenals" (2018: 171). Thus Paul, even though not identical in approach with Philo and other intellectuals, shares with these a world of thought in which the God of Israel is set in opposition to all idolatry.

This type of political thinking implicitly reclassifies other gods so that they are imagined as subordinates to the Jewish God. Paul does not represent those from the nations as handed over to other gods, spirits or ἄγγελοι as do texts such as Deuteronomy 32 and *Jubilees* 15. Instead, he repeats three times that the supreme deity intervened directly to give them over to the desires of their hearts (Wasserman 2018: 169–70). Significantly, even when describing the failings of idolators, Paul ascribes all the initiative and power to the God of Israel, leaving no political space for the idols made with hands. In this he shows a similar response to Philo who goes so far as to justify the death sentence for idol worshippers. "For it is right that he who honors lifeless things should have no part in life, especially if he has become a disciple of Moses" (*Spec.* 2:255-256) (Wasserman 2018: 166). In this, we find evidence of Paul's gospel's embeddedness in the Jewish tradition of resistance to the dominating imperial discourse, which we have illustrated above. This was particularly relevant for Jewish Diaspora communities who had to relate as positively as possible to their non-Jewish neighbors. In this respect, Paul's resistance to the imperial discourse of violent domination is explicable in association with his Jewish roots rather than in opposition to them. Nor can Israel's failure to be persuaded by the Christ-event be used as a rationale for anti-Judaism. In Paul's perception, those from the nations cannot bypass Israel; their call is inherently linked to Israel through Christ.

That Rom. 1:19-32 should not be considered as an isolated text can be easily demonstrated. These verses share some basic ideas with Jer. 10, Isa. 44:6-18, and Ps. 115. As well as the parallels observed between Zephaniah's opposition to idolatry and that of Paul in Romans, scholars have noted similarities between Paul and the Wisdom of Solomon 12–14 (15), especially in relation to gentile idolatry as depicted in Wis. 13:1-19 and 14:22-31.[2] Rainey sees similarity between Rom. 1:18-32 and Wisdom of Solomon 13–14 in their shared characteristic as a recast icon polemic because "in the Hellenistic period, the anti-*icon* polemic morphs into an anti-*idolatry* polemic" (2018: 231). Also, Rock maintains that what has not been given sufficient attention is how the two texts Wisdom of Solomon and Paul's letter to the Romans both face similar concerns, that is, a critique of gentile idolatry (2012: 252). Rock places Wisdom of Solomon in the context of the reign of the emperor Caligula (37–41 CE) when the Jewish community at Alexandria were under severe threat with regard to their political rights and their synagogue worship. I am not convinced we can be so precise about the

---

[2] Ben Witherington III drew up a table indicating the parallels between Romans 1:19-32 and the Wisdom of Solomon (2004: 63). Rock extended these parallels incorporating Witherington's insights (2012: 327).

historical context, but see such texts as evidence of an ongoing anti-imperial discourse in which Paul was a discreet participant. We can agree that

> Wisdom of Solomon may best be regarded as a case of the conventional application of Jewish Wisdom as a bulwark against Roman cultural imperialism, and it was that, along with the restatement of the cause of Israel, which attracted Paul as an integral part of the tradition that gave rise to his citing this work. (Rock 2012: 254)

The ethos of Roman cultural imperialism was almost all-pervasive and therefore could not be omitted from Paul's critique. But this continued a long line of prophetic and Jewish Wisdom traditions as an alternative discourse visible in the background of Paul's condemnation of idolatry resulting from imperial claims to absolute power. It is significant that Paul turns to the Wisdom of Solomon in apparent agreement concerning the indictment of the nations, rather than reading Paul as overturning one of the key beliefs of its author (Thorsteinsson 2003: 190–4, contra Dunn). Paul is similarly in agreement with Jer. 10:6-8 that the nations who do not fear God, are insolent, denying him the honor that is due. Paul recognizes that God deals differently with his people Israel with whom he is in covenant than with the pagan nations who oppress his people. It is therefore not surprising that in this aspect of Jewish covenant theology Paul finds himself in agreement with other Jews including the author of Wisdom of Solomon. Romans 1 is evidence of Paul's active participation in this strand of Jewish thought rather than of his opposition to it (Thorsteinsson 2003: 190–4). Interestingly, J. M. Reese also finds parallels with Paul's use of diatribe in Wis. 1:1-6, 11; 6:16-20, and so on (1970: 117–21, cited by Aune 1991: 284).

It is notable here that Paul in addressing the ethnē in Rome refers to God as the Creator whose knowledge is available ever since the creation of the world, and who ought to be worshipped rather than the things he has created. This God is closely related to and involved in his creation from whom knowledge of his ways can be discerned. Thus, judgment arising from the worship of idols and other animal images had the result, according to Paul, in that "he (God) gave them up," repeated no less than three times in vv. 22-26. Although they did not acknowledge God as God, they could not escape his response to their ἀσέβεια and ἀδικία so that they were given up—παρέδωκεν—to the degrading of their bodies among themselves, to degrading and unnatural passions, to the catalogue of sins listed in vv. 27-29, including murder, strife, slander, rebellion against parents, and lack of compassion.[3]

What is significant is that Paul traces gentile immorality entirely to idolatry as a result of disobedience. Thus, the nations are responsible, and culpable because they did not acknowledge what God disclosed to them. They knew that the created world is *not* God but did not worship him as its Creator. Thus, the refusal to honor God as

---

[3] Thus. παρέδωκεν, "giving them up," indicates that God is not passive, allowing the world to go its own way, but actively involved in the outcome of human sin (cf. Stowers 1994: 93). Rainey sees here a parallel with the former inhabitants of Canaan who suffered permanent, hereditary defilement as a result of committing abominations in the land of Israel. Paul thus views all gentiles as handed over to impurity ἀκαθαρσία, a defilement that connotes both deep moral transgressions and also overlaps with the realm of ritual practice (2018: 232, also McMurray 2021: 47–52).

God, and its corollary, the creature's contingency, did not result in agnosticism or in a "secular" life, but in a debased religiosity that "exchanged the glory of the immortal God" for images of mortal humans, birds, quadrupeds, and reptiles (Keck 2005: 64). The reference to reptiles shows that Paul has specific examples of idolatry in mind (1:23). Wrong worship is obviously fundamental to Paul's view of gentile confusion, the solution to which he will set out in 12:1, as a presenting of their bodies to God as a living sacrifice. Here Paul links in to Jewish versions of world decline, which claim this is evidenced in a loss of reason and corresponding unnatural behavior (Stowers 1994: 122). Paul's main emphasis here is the Roman ethos of gentile idolatry. His foundational critique is the error of worshipping the creation rather that its Creator, which he obviously knows to be prevalent in Rome (1:21-23, 28).[4]

---

[4] Rock finds possible references to Nero in these verses, particularly in relation to homosexuality and the introduction of Greek-styled games. He regards the vice lists in 1:27-29 as directed against Neronic immorality, particularly as critiqued by Suetonius (Rock 2012: 258–65).

Romans 2

Romans 2:1: The Transition from Romans 1:19-32 to Romans 2

¹Therefore you are inexcusable, whoever you are, all of you who judge; for by that in which you pass judgment on another you are condemning yourself, because you, the one who passes judgment, practice the same things.

It is gentile behavior that is being condemned in Rom. 2:1 as indicated by the particle διό, "therefore." This particle serves the normal function of relating directly to and drawing a conclusion from what has preceded it, as well as linking to what succeeds. There is no change of topic or audience. Neil Elliott critically notes in some depth how a scholar such as Anders Nygren used Jewish tradition in the Wisdom of Solomon to seek to justify a presupposed change of address to Jews from the ethnē in 1:19-32. The fact that from 2:17 onward Paul engages with someone who "calls himself a Jew" does not give any real reason for the view that 1:19-32 is universal in application to Jews and non-Jews, or that Paul already in 2:1 addresses Jews. Charles Cranfield, despite being a most careful exegete, simply presumes Paul is apostrophizing the typical Jew in 2:1 since he finds no indication to the contrary (1975: 137–9). Thus, his exposition proceeds as if Paul had the Jew, and the Jew exclusively, in mind (Thorsteinsson 2003: 180–220).

To the contrary, it can easily be shown that 2:1-16 does not require a Jewish addressee. Jewish or scriptural affinity, especially in Paul's letters, need not mean that Jews are the addressees. It is noteworthy that it is an unspecified man, ὦ ἄνθρωπε whom Paul addresses in 2:1. This indictment functions "to bring home, to concretize and to sharpen the indictment in 2.1 for Paul's audience. It takes the indictment of 'them' in 1:19-32 and makes it into a personal indictment of any of the audience to whom it might apply." Here the interlocutor's identity remains indeterminate by intention (Elliott 2007: 126–7). We take this to refer to gentile people generally "you, man whoever you may be." It is a nonspecific person possibly of a philosophical discussion, a rhetorical figure in the typical pattern of the diatribe.[1]

---

[1] Romans "shares many of the distinguishing conventions of Epictetus' diatribe; i) vivid dialogues with fictitious interlocutor(s); ii) the generalizing second-person singular; iii) the μὴ γένοιτο rejection; the characteristic vocatives," cf. Song (2004: 46).

Because Paul in 2:17-29 addresses someone "who calls himself a Jew," this does not mean we can presume the apostle has already changed his envisaged audience from addressing ethnē in 1:19-32 to addressing Jews from 2:1 onward. As Stowers notes, "It is anachronistic and completely unwarranted to think that Paul has only the Jew in mind in 2:1-5 or that he characterizes the typical Jew" (1981: 112).

It is actually the pretentious judging person that Paul has in mind in 2:1-5. But, as Stowers has noted, "No one in the first century would have identified the *ho alazon* i.e., the pretentious person, with Judaism" (1994: 13, 101). Such an identification was unseen until Augustine, and that only in his later writings (Thorsteinsson 2016: 184). It is therefore both wrong and anachronistic to hold or to continue to hold that Paul changes from gentile addressees in 1:19-32 to Jewish addressees in 2:1. Scholars are deeply indebted to Thorsteinsson for his thorough investigation and frequent demolition of the ingenious arguments that have been raised, and sometimes still are raised, in support of reading 2:1 as having a Jewish addressee; he concludes as follows:

> In sum there are many weighty reasons to refute the common view that Paul has a Jewish interlocutor in mind in 2.1. A linear and progressive approach to the text, in which full account is taken of the inferential function of διό, suggests instead that the interlocutor is ... a gentile. (2003: 188, cf. also Dabourne 1999: 108)

It has sometimes been overlooked that Romans is a publicly spoken address. Since this is so, the addressees could not possibly have known in 2:1 that Paul would address a so-called Jew in 2:17, so the gentile address must continue from ch. 1. A linear and progressive approach rules out this modern regressive reading of introducing a Jew without any evidence for such in the text.

Jews have been frequently stereotyped in biblical interpretation and elsewhere as those who judge others, but it is only the viewing of the stereotypical judging as *specifically* Jewish that would make a link to Jews in any way comprehensible at 2:1-5. As Esler notes, "It is hard to see why there should be a fierce debate about whom Paul is addressing here. A large number of scholars consider that the ἄνθρωπος is a typical Judean. Others see a non Judean interlocutor. The latter position is correct, and the widespread support for the former is a cause for wonder" (2003: 151). It is only because of a history of biased interpretation based on Jewish stereotypes that this view carries conviction, built on the assumption that it *must* refer to a Jew who judges others. Simon Gathercole, following the pattern of Dunn, thinks that in 2:12-13 Paul is operating in categories that *could only be Jewish* (2002: 198–9). But assumed content should not predetermine audience, nor should a stereotypical image of the Jew. It was Hans Lietzmann in his commentary on Romans who argued that the person addressed in Rom. 2:1 is not the wrong-doer of 1:32, but is instead "der selbstgerechte Jude," the self-righteous Jew (Lietzmann 1971: 37–9). Lietzmann gives no weight to the διό in 2:1—it is only "eine farblose Übergangspartikel," a colorless transitional particle, hence our attention to γάρ and διό despite both being tiny particles. We emphasize here, and will continue to do so throughout this commentary, that one ought not to separate what Paul's argument and the normal grammatical signposts indicate to be a continuous and ongoing argument, as Casson has demonstrated.[2]

Many commentaries in these and in differing ways still reveal the continuation of a common anti-Jewish prejudice, severely condemned by Sanders in his devastating critique of Ferdinand Weber's presentation of Judaism as a legalistic religion, the antithesis of Christianity. Sanders notes that this negative view of Judaism has continued to be voiced despite being shown by outstanding scholars such as George Foot Moore to be massively mistaken (1977: 33–59). Any suggestion of anti-Jewish sentiment is particularly serious if it is introduced at this point early in the reading of Romans, which misleadingly suggests to the reader that there might be reason to anticipate anti-Jewish argument later throughout its contents. Thorsteinsson criticizes Dunn (along with other well-known interpreters) in relation to this passage as one of the more extreme negative examples (2003: 186–8). According to Dunn, Paul in 2:1-16 presents "a spiral that consists of the increasing specificity of the Jewish identity of the viewpoint rebutted" (1988: 1.76–77). There is, however, as little evidence for the "spiral" as there is justification for the view itself!

Here in 2:1-5, we have the amazing spectacle of an image of the stereotypical Jewish person supposedly introduced in a Pauline passage *concerning typical gentile sins, including idolatry*. It is difficult to comprehend how such obviously gentile-targeted material could be so transformed by the lack of attention to the διό, which connects the two chapters in normal grammatical fashion, into a record of continuing Jewish stereotyping. Similarly, many other commentaries follow this route (Schreiner 1993: 14–41). Despite this, there can be no doubt that the most accurate reading is that the construction with διό indicates that 2:1 continues the argument begun in 1:19—it continues the address to non-Jews. Since there is no explicit indication before 2:17 that it is a so-called Jew Paul has in mind, there is no real justification for introducing Jews in 2:1 by a regressive reading back from 2:17, except for the continuation of older patterns of interpretation in which their presence was *assumed* as essential in an argument for the universality of sin.

In any case, as we shall see, the person in 2:17-25 is not a Jew but only one who "calls himself a Jew," as is to be anticipated in a letter that explicitly targets the ethnē. However, it is important to state that whatever reading one gives to 2:17, its content cannot be read into 2:1-16, so it is still inaccurate to introduce a "Jew" at this point, that is, at 2:1. It could be argued that it may be the same figure who will be addressed in 2:17-24, and that therefore it is not wrong to use here the extra information that will be later acquired. But the audience cannot know in advance where the conversation leads. It is the speaker who has the initiative in guiding the audience, not the one who seemingly interrupts the flow of argument with interjections (Dabourne 1999: 106). So, it is Paul who has decided to introduce a differing gentile conversation partner at 2:17, and we must not predetermine the outcome by assuming to be wiser than Paul.

---

[2] Casson's study (2019) is most useful in dealing with the use of γάρ throughout Romans particularly where scholars have tended to ignore its force in the ongoing argumentation of the letter.

Romans 2 Interrogating the Text: From Literary Figures to Social Reality?

Paul created an amazingly rich text when he dictated the letter to the Romans, not least ch. 2, which has puzzled even the best Pauline interpreters, and led to confusion as much as clarification in the exposition of its content.[3] As Sanders rightly noted, this chapter focusses on obedience to the Jewish law, not as the theoretical standard, but as something that must be practiced, put into action if it is to lead to salvation (1983: 130–2). To try to make more sense of Romans 2 in coherence with Paul's thought elsewhere, we must locate and take into account all the cues, literary, rhetorical, grammatical, and so on to provide some factual basis to guide us through the maze of Paul's narrative.

Some clues are provided in the fact that Paul's writing differs substantially at many points from his usual pattern. His long-accentuated concentration on gentile failure to worship the Creator God rather than the creation is unique to Romans and could give the impression that Paul was anti-gentile, and at best one-sided rather than balanced. But its very distinctness offers us a clue that Paul is writing here in a particular, sometimes exaggerated, vein. Literary style such as that of diatribe is not given a stylistic introduction such as "and now we turn to diatribal style," but emerges directly through the text, and thus is dependent on the awareness of the reader to uncover its message. We have therefore listed the characteristics of diatribal style in our Excursus I, which has confirmed that there is some rationale for reading Rom. 1:16–2:29 as at least in parts presenting its arguments in diatribal style.[4]

But how then do we move from a literary personification or textual reality to the actual social reality, which we assume Paul was seeking to influence? Perhaps we are anticipating too much from our investigation, and maybe Paul does not provide us here with sufficient information so that we must forcibly remain at the theoretical level. Our assumption is that Paul as letter-writer, traveler, and networking apostle views these differing roles as combining to produce social change among his addressees, that is, transform their identities through his personal and communal intervention (cf. Ehrensperger 2022b: 269–305).

When we look at Romans 2 and take into account the actual clues that Paul provides in the text, we find that he does not leave us without guidance as to how to read. There are, in fact, numerous signs as to how to differentiate and interpret his writing. In the apostrophe of 2:1-5, the addressee is a rather undefined individual who in judging others thereby renders himself without excuse and so condemns himself. But Paul uses here a participle construction, that is, ὁ κρίνων, the one judging, which is less specific than addressing a particular individual, and *identifies only on the basis of the judging activity* rather than on any other quality. This allows us in our reading to consider the addressees here possibly as consisting of a group of people engaged in judging rather than an individual. Esler has clarified the difference between prototypes and groups. Following Hogg and Smith, he notes that

---

[3] Sanders found Romans 2 so different from the rest of the content of Paul's letters that he dealt with it in a separate appendix (1983: 123–35).
[4] We recommend that Excursus I on diatribal style be read at this point.

people cognitively represent a social group (e.g., a religion, an organization, a team) as a category prototype—a fuzzy set of attributes that are meaningfully inter-related, and simultaneously capture similarities within the group and differences between the group and other groups, or people who are not in the group. (2021: 33–4)

A prototype differs from a norm because "it is the member's cognitive representation of the normative properties of the group," and because "it is an assemblage of group attributes that will nearly always encompass more than one norm or even several norms, including features such as beliefs, attitudes and feelings characteristic of the group" (Hogg 2012: 262). Since Paul addresses groups of ethnē in Rome, this leads us to propose that among them may be some people, not just an individual, who fit the category of those judging others, and who therefore consider themselves superior to these.

Another example of how to interrogate Paul's text comes from categorizing oneself in relation to how one would prefer to be identified. "But if you (singular σύ) call yourself a Jew" (2:17) leading into an idealized portrait of the so-called Jew, then the "you" singular suggests that we are again encountering a specific (diatribal) style in which the singular "you" does not necessarily refer only to one individual interlocutor, but could refer to "some people," that is, a group. (Modern English, unfortunately, no longer distinguishes the singular and plural forms of "you"). We must remember that Paul most commonly addresses the group so that the plural form of "you" is the normal, and the singular use is saying something to be specifically noted.

Thus, a major issue emerges in ascertaining whether the one judging means the judging individual or rather whether it points to anyone who fits the description, that is, "anyone judging" (paying attention to the participle). I think it unlikely Paul would attack an individual in Rome even if he had reports to confirm such. Again, an individual on his own rather than the representative of a group is unconvincing. The diatribal singular pronouns in 2:25-29, where normal second person address would be anticipated, cannot be ignored and likewise the repetition of participles indicating a general categorizing rather than a specific addressee. The grammatical and rhetorical significations are too explicit to be explained away. They are saying something, that is, this is not normal address to an individual who is a Jew, just as in 2:1-5 the one judging can indicate a group. The continuity in form of address is further indicated by the repetition of the participial formation πᾶς ὁ κρίνων (2:1) and ὁ οὖν διδάσκων (2:21), neither specifying an address to a particular individual, but precisely something other than this, that is, indirect address in diatribal style. It may legitimately be read as indicating a social group of ethnē who choose to be identified as "Jews" even though they had been born "gentiles."

Again, we might question that when Paul refers to people who judge or who view themselves as teachers of those less knowledgeable, he is not merely differentiating or categorizing people into different social groups in a theoretical fashion that does not have any basis in social reality? The groupings represent more than mere literary categorization but suggest that Paul was well enough informed by his friends in Rome to link his literary creations to an actual context. We will, therefore, not refer to "the implied reader" but to the ethnē in Christ as the normal anticipated readership, and any other interlocutor or rhetorical *persona* will be identified in context as these arise.

Romans 2:1-5: The First Apostrophe—"To the One Who Judges"

¹Therefore you are inexcusable, whoever you are, all of you who judge, for by that in which you pass judgment on another you are condemning yourself, because you, the one who passes judgment, practice the same things. ²But we all know that God's judgment is according to truth on those who practice such things. ³Do you imagine, whoever you are, that when you pass judgment on those who commit such things and yet practice them yourself, you will escape the judgment of God? ⁴Or do you scornfully presume upon the riches of his kindness and his forbearance and patience, failing to comprehend that the kindness of God is meant to lead you to repentance? ⁵But by your hard and impenitent heart you are storing up wrath for yourself on the day of wrath and revelation of the righteous judgment of God.

The second chapter opens with an apostrophe, an address to an imaginary interlocutor or conversation partner.[5] This will be followed by a second apostrophe at 2:17ff addressed to a different interlocutor. Because Paul's letter to Rome is addressed to a group of gentile Christ-followers whom Paul has not yet visited in Rome, Paul makes full use of a range of rhetorical possibilities such as diatribal style and the use of speech-in-character to facilitate the communication of his message. Since Paul cannot refer to how the Christ-movement in Rome began or to any activity on his part to found it, he interacts with the addressees partly through imagined scenarios and the speech-in-character of an envisaged *persona*. But, as we have asserted above, this indirect address is not purely imaginary but based on information from Paul's close friends, co-workers, and other contacts in Rome, indicated by the large number of people greeted in ch. 16. It should also be borne in mind that indirect diatribal-style speech can be valuable in sharpening the address to the audience, especially where diatribal mini-dialogues or addresses were used as a teaching device on difficult issues (Dabourne 1999: 105).

As Thorsteinsson has noted, "Paul's Discourse in Romans 2 is characterized by a dialogical style replete with uses of the second person singular … which both distinguishes and unites Romans 2" (2003: 152–3). The use of the vocative of 2:1 continues in 2:3 with the specific address to the interlocutor σύ "you" (singular), which, with the participle ὁ κρίνων "the one judging," is indicative principally of the diatribe style (Stowers 1981: 100). But some scholars such as Rodriguez go further and consider this particular vocative to be an indirect address via an interlocutor (also) to an individual teacher (2014: 47–72). Although this interpretation can offer a potential reading of Romans, and has some support, I am not fully convinced that

---

[5] "Apostrophe is a 'turning away' from the actual audience to address absent persons as if present, or things as if listening," cf. Quintilian, *Inst.* 4.1.63-70 cited by Tobin (2004: 110, n14).

we can claim with confidence that this is the best reading of Paul's diatribal vocative singular address. Song has argued, convincingly in my opinion, that such vocatives are not factual but fictitious (2004: 38). This form of address here is weak evidence for an address to an individual, and it is not good exegesis to read into Paul's criticisms of this *persona* a sense of jealousy or competition over against Paul's designation as "apostle to the ethnē."

Romans 2:1-5

Normally, diatribal vocatives are used in the singular and seldom occur in the plural. Paul is consistent with this as is evident in Rom. 2:1-3 and 9:20. Song notes that although Epictetus often used second-person plural expressions as well as the singular, in his (Epictetus's) *Discourses*, the vocatives are almost always used in the singular forms (2004: 42–6). Thus, the vocative singular address to the ἄνθρωπος in Rom. 2:1 need not, as noted above, designate an address to a single individual, but could signify a group in that the diatribal, vocative style of address would not necessarily distinguish between the two in this instance. In Paul, the best example of this phenomenon is Rom. 11:17 where Paul argues that "if some of the branches were broken, and you (vocative singular σύ) a wild olive shoot were grafted in among them to share the riches of the olive tree …." Here Paul clearly uses the singular vocative address to speak to *some* of the gentile Christ-followers in Rome, in the *persona* of a wild olive shoot (a group rather than an individual), and this pattern gives supports for our positing a similar group address in Rom. 2:1-6. This perception of the vocative σύ representing a group rather than an individual need not rule out the possibility that there did exist such a contemporary person with views in opposition to those of Paul. But to posit a leader without a group cannot carry conviction. It is from groups that leaders emerge. We must consider this "leader" from a social identity perspective as encapsulating and thus representing prototypically the stance of his group (rather than as an individual promoting his own views as distinct from those of the group). "Leaders gain power not by possessing resources in a manner separate from group dynamics but by representing and working for group values and identity" (cf. Esler 2021a: 30–45). One pattern Paul uses to indicate diverse groups is by denoting their opposites, that is, circumcision and uncircumcision, or hearers versus doers of the law and those who fulfil the law rather than breaking it (cf., e.g., 2:27). There have been earlier attempts to identify groups in Rome, five groups in all according to Paul Minear (1971: 1–2, 46). Similarly, later Raymond Brown tried to delineate diverse groups and types of Christ-followers in Rome (1983: 74–9).

Paul interrupts this address briefly in 2:2 to indicate that from the perspective of his dialogue partner's stated position ("you say"), "we, (now inclusive of Paul), know that God's judgment on those who commit such things," that is, on the evil doers reported in 1:19-32, is "in accordance with truth." This indicates that here, in 2:1-6 in contrast to the idolators in ch. 1, there is some agreement. Paul and the *persona* he addresses in the apostrophe in 2:1-6 have something (possibly reverence for the Law), in common. In 2:7-10, in order to extend the second-person singular critique to everyone who fails to worship God, Paul returns to the third-person plural "they," which continues until the introduction of a second apostrophe concentrating on "you" at 2:17-29.

The first apostrophe begins in 2:1-6 and focuses on the accusation of hypocrisy/inconsistency, a typical diatribal theme. It is this judgment that explains Paul's critical accusation in 2:1, "Therefore you are inexcusable, whoever you are, all of you who judge; for by that in which you pass judgment on another you are condemning yourself, because you, the one who passes judgment, practice the same things." In light of the idolatrous behavior condemned in 1:19-32, this is a very harsh verdict and requires explanation. What seems surprising is that though Paul's conversation partner, his interlocutor, agrees with Paul's stance in judgment, he is nevertheless judged in the process for doing "the very same things" as those judged in Rom. 1:19-32. In light of this accusation, Paul asks how can the judging person suppose he will escape the judgment of God revealed according to 1:18 in the gospel since "He (God) will repay according to each one's deeds," when the wrath of God against all ungodliness and wickedness is revealed (2:6). Significantly, here judgment is universal, it is according to works, the Law must be practiced (Sanders 1983: 130–2) and demands repentance.

We are still seeking clarification of how Paul can accuse those who condemn the gentile world, and in that respect consider themselves different, by indicting them with doing the very same things? According to Paul's concluding summary given in 1:22-28, the reason for the gentile world's immorality is that God handed them over to a new custodian to cosmic slavery resulting in impurity, degrading their bodies, and debased thinking—παρέδωκεν (1:24, 26, 28) (McMurray 2021: 47–9). Paul's perspective is clear. The moral failings of the ethnē, their "degrading passions," are the symptoms of incorrect worship and sin as a power itself is not the root problem, but the outcome of incorrect worship. The chapter ends with the charge that although the nations know God's decree that those who commit such things deserve to die—yet they not only do them, but even applaud others who practice them. Here, strikingly, even more condemnation is heaped upon those who by their approval encourage the transgression of others. This emphatic denunciation could apply to the leaders of gentile groups (not, as traditionally, to Jewish stereotypes) and must be kept in view even if the ethnē operated as subgroups attached to synagogal communities.

What is more significant is that, though aware of God's judgment, these people have not responded with the appropriate outcome, repentance, but with a hard and impenitent heart are storing up judgment for themselves (2:4-5). Despite the emphasis on their different perspective in contrast to the idolators previously condemned, and despite the knowledge of God possibly acquired as God-fearers,[6] these ethnē have not repented in face of the gospel. This suggests that Paul not only has in mind groups of ethnē in Christ, linked loosely to synagogal communities, but also other ethnē interested in Jewish tradition who have not accepted Paul's message about the Christ-event.

This indicates, in our analysis, that they are God-fearers, sympathizers who acknowledge Israel's God in their perception of the world but do not do so to the

---

[6] Our assumption here is that God-fearers did exist in sufficient numbers and over a long period of time making the attribution of a specific designation meaningful, cf. the title of Paula Fredriksen's interesting essay "If It Looks Like a Duck, and It Quacks like a Duck ... on Not Giving up on the Godfearers" (2015: 17–24).

exclusion of other deities. This means that, as unrepentant ethnē, in Paul's perspective they are still under the judgment of God, even though God-fearers with some marginal affiliation with Jews. Though they judge those who worship idols, but do not repent in face of the gospel, they too remain sinners despite other differences between their behavior and the foolish idolaters in 1:19-32. Though we categorize here a group of people, we do not imply that they are a coherent entity having much in common. They may be an indiscriminate entity who are categorized under a common feature. The primacy of rituals as generators both of experience and meaning in a religious world that lacked official theological systematization and teaching must be acknowledged. For example, a study of the nature of the *lares* (together with their frequent companions, a *genius*, and a pair of snakes) raises many questions about the most frequently practiced rituals that shaped the everyday life of ordinary Romans at home and in the local neighborhood (Flower 2017: 2–4). Were the *lares* guardian gods identified with places (and therefore with the roads between these)? Or were they the (potentially restless) spirits of deceased family members, which would make them underworld spirits?

Whether they should be associated with place, or with the head of the household, or with the dead is unclear. Again, did the Romans trust and celebrate their *lares* or fear and appease them? (Flower 2017: 2–4). Some ethnē may be philosophers who recognize gods of wood and stone as just that. But the key factor is that they have not ceased to participate in honoring such deities and still join in the communal practice of their worship. Although they differ in that they do not share the common beliefs about the gods, in other respects in the practice of everyday life they are no different. Like the other worshippers of the gods, though they are aware of the Creator's existence, they do not worship the God of Israel exclusively, in Paul's perspective they are unrepentant.

The divine judgment is also in accordance with knowledge and will therefore, both in good deeds and evil, apply "to the Jew first and also the Greek" (2:9, 2:10). God will reward "good" and condemn evil irrespective of the doers, "for God shows no partiality" (2:11). We must point out that here the inclusion of the Jew with reference to liability to judgment is demanded not because Paul addresses Jews in Romans, he does not, but for the sake of the argument about divine impartiality Jews are necessarily included within its scope. This does not constitute an address to Jews—it only denotes that God's judgment is all-inclusive. One can distinguish Paul's addressees as ethnē but simultaneously recognize that the Jewish world is Paul's thought-world. I can agree that "the horizon of Paul's theology surpasses that of his intended addressees, and that the overall aim of his gentile mission as the ultimate redemption of his fellow Jews must be accounted for" (Sandnes 2018: 27). But this in no way prevents the view that only ethnē are addressed in Rome. The stress on the doing of the Law rather than its possession, that is, hearing but not doing, strongly indicates God-fearers. So, we have reached the conclusion that this "hearing but not doing" group depicted particularly in 2:1-6 is most likely to be identified as God-fearers in some relation to a synagogue community, though not as proselytes or as Christ-followers. Whether it may include educated people such as philosophers who rightly denounce the idolatrous beliefs of the common people may be disputed. These educated people might also be included in this group labeled as God-fearers, and of which the main critique by Paul is that they have not repented (2:4). In any case, it is clear that "despite their common judgment against idol-worship and its immoral consequences, the elitism of gentile moral philosophy runs counter to the God of Paul's gospel" (Rodriguez 2014: 40).

Romans 2:6-16 Indications of Group Affiliation

One of the useful clues to group identity in Romans 2 may be that Paul has the interlocutor report someone as claiming that they recognize that God's judgment on idolators such as in 1:19-32 is "in accord with truth" (2:2). Here Paul describes a criticism of one person or group upon another who differs, thus indicating two discernible stances or categories of value judgment. This must indicate someone who acknowledges the truth of the verdict of Torah upon sinful behavior, in addition to those he criticizes. Who are these critics? One hypothesis is that these acknowledge that the Law opposes such sin but think that it no longer applies to them, possibly because they believe that they are former idolators, who now no longer fall under its verdict. These categorize themselves wrongly and fail to realize they still belong to the idolatrous nations reported in 1:19-32. Being a God-fearer is, in Paul's view, no substitute for responding in trust to Christ. As Thorsteinsson claims, "The interlocutor invented by Paul is a person of gentile origin who fails to recognize that his ethnic roots put him in ranks with the people described in 1.19-32 whose existence is still affected by the divine punishment once imposed upon them." This means that both God-fearers and would-be proselytes get to know that circumcised ethnē do not have grounds for judging uncircumcised yet Law-abiding ethnē, as if the former were in a more advantageous position (2003: 232–3).

The accusation against a group of ethnē styled as an individual in 2:1-6 is that though they differ from those ethnē mentioned in 1:19-32 and have some knowledge of God, they still continue, according to Paul's perspective, to be idolators (2:3b). These are not identical with the first group of people negatively described in 1:19-32, the group in 2:1-16 are hearers of the Law (2:13); but since they have not totally turned away from idols, nor repented (2:4), they are storing up wrath for themselves.[7] The text points particularly to God-fearers, with possibly some diversity in their opinions. As God-fearers, they were not required by Jews to separate themselves from any involvement in idol worship as were Jews. But Paul did not consider his communities of gentile Christ-followers to be identical with God-fearers and had strong convictions as regards any association with idolatry.

Thus, from our reading of the vocative singular as addressing a group distinguished by the fact that they differ in certain respects though not all, from the sinful "gentiles" in 1:19-32 but mainly in their judging of these for their sinfulness, we can already posit two groups of ethnē. The first group consists of those sinning, described throughout simply in the third-person plural as "they," contrasted and judged in relation to another group who are better informed concerning the divine judgment

---

[7] Barrett titled the section 2:1-11 as "Judgment and the Critic" and describes the critic Paul has in mind as considering himself "superior to the idolator"; the second "you" is emphatic (2:3) and stresses that in the very act of judging, the judge is involved in the sin of idolatry in putting "himself in the place of God," even though *ex hypothesi* he knows the law (1962: 42–3).

and acknowledge its reality (2:3). As noted, the latter may well be God-fearers who regard themselves as superior in that they no longer do precisely the same things as the group described in 1:19-32, though they have not embraced the gospel concerning Christ (cf. Witherington 2004: 79, Thorsteinsson 2003: 233). This suggests contact and interaction between at least two groups of ethnē both also under some Jewish influence but differing in their response to the significance of Christ for ethnē (especially in relation to participation in everyday honoring of the local deities what Paul perceives as idolatry. Contra Stowers 1994: 103, see Witherington 2004: 79).

The Relation of 2:1-5 to 2:6-16

To summarize our findings on 2:1-16 concerning those addressed, we note that Paul, in 2:1-6 and in 2:17-29, uses the second-person singular form. Only in 2:7-16 does he use plural forms. The overall structure of Rom. 2:1-29 is thus indicated by two apostrophes, one beginning in 2:1-6 directed to those judging, and the other more precisely marked, the apostrophe to the so-called Jew. The elevated style and the exaggerated, idealistic portrait of the so-called Jew in 17-29 indicates a change of addressee and topic after 2:16. By distinguishing it from the sections on either side of it, this division somewhat isolates 2:6-16. The best understanding of 2:6-16 is that this is a continuation of 2:1-5 that brings out more of the reasons why those who are judging are misled. This is because the distinctions they draw between themselves and those others whom they are judging are not really significant in light of God's impartial judgment. Paul is highlighting internal disputes and group categorization in Rome among non-Jews, but claiming that they are not the same distinctions as divine impartiality demands (Bornkamm 1969: 46–70). The question remains how the arguments used here will relate to or differ from those outlined in 2:17-29.

Romans 2:6-16: Commonality under Divine Judgment and Impartiality

⁶For he will recompense to each according to their deeds: ⁷to those who persistently pursue glory, and honor, and incorruptibility by steady perseverance in good work, he will recompense eternal life; ⁸on the other hand to those who disobey the truth and instead obey unrighteousness, wrath and fury, ⁹affliction and distress for everyone who works evil, the Jew first and also the Greek, ¹⁰but glory and honor and peace for everyone who practices the good, the Jew first and also the Greek. ¹¹For there is no partiality before God.
¹²All who have sinned outside the law will also perish outside the law, and all who have sinned in the law will be judged by the law. ¹³For it is not the hearers of the law who are righteous in God's sight, but the doers of the law who will be set right. ¹⁴When ethnē, who do not possess the law by nature, do what the law requires, these, though not having the law, are a law unto themselves. ¹⁵Such people demonstrate that the work of the law is written on their hearts, to which their conscience testifies on their behalf; and their conflicting thoughts will accuse or perhaps excuse them

¹⁶on the day when, according to my gospel, God will judge the secrets of people through Jesus Christ.

Romans 2:6-16

Paul's response to this paradoxical situation in Rome in which his gospel is implicated, and of which he has possibly been informed by his friends there, is to stress the universality of the Torah's application—absolutely no one, Jew or ethnē, is beyond its rule. Surprisingly, in a context where Paul differentiates between Jews and the nations, he has to begin by repeating the traditional emphasis upon the universality of divine judgment. This is, as already noted, because he believes there are some people in Rome who, for ethnic or theological reasons, believed the judgment of God against sin and revealed in the Torah, did not, or now did no longer, really apply to them. There is diversity in Rome in the realm of Jewish communities and in the ethnē loosely relating to them; there are even some who are not Jews but call themselves such (2:17), and Paul is very aware of all this. But for him there is an unavoidable common element in that the Law's judgment will apply to all, whoever they are, or in what relation to the Law they exist or may have chosen to situate themselves, even though some think they will escape its verdict (2:3). Rather than accentuate distinctions among themselves as the Romans are doing, Paul finds a source of commonality in their status under God in relation to the performance, the actual doing of the Law.

Divine judgment, though universal, is not undifferentiated according to Paul—he recognizes that some sin "apart from the Law" while others sin ἐν νόμῳ "in the law" (2:12). Even non-Jews who do not possess the Law are not entirely lawless, but their conscience can operate so that they are "law unto themselves" (2:14). The Law will apply in a differentiated form to people according to their status in relation to it, but it will still apply to all. The common basis of judgment is whether the Law has been practiced—whether "what the Law requires" is written on their hearts (2:15), "He will repay according to each one's deeds" (2:6). In order to underline the universality of the application of the judgments of God, Paul twice repeats very deliberately, first in relation to doing good and then in relation to those who disobey the truth, that the verdict will bring its due outcome "to the Jew first and also to the Greek" (2:6-11). Possession of the Law is recognized but as bringing increased responsibility because of the greater knowledge it provides. In any case, "God shows no partiality" (2:11).

Romans 2:12-16

Neil Elliott has demonstrated that the argumentative flow of 2:11-16 is not from other premises toward "impartiality," but *from God's* impartiality as an axiom *toward* the main thesis, which is that there is no excuse before God's judgment. "The offence at the center of Paul's apostrophic indictment is nothing other than considering oneself 'excused' from God's righteous demand" (2007: 123). Elliott paraphrases the criterion for divine judgment as "the doing of what the Law requires." In Rom. 2:12-16, Paul argues, that those who sin are judged, whether they sin "outside the Law" or "in the Law." Not those who have heard the Law, but those who have *done* what the Law requires are justified before God (2:13). Elliott perceptively notes that Paul is not so concerned here as he was in 2:9-11 to sustain a careful balance between Jew and non-Jew but seems to be more concerned in 2:12-16 to argue that the ethnē who, although they do not "have the Law," are no less accountable before God's righteousness for not "having the Law" (2:15-16) (2007: 122–3). "Whatever else is true of God's mercy, it does not provide exemption from absolute accountability to God's judgment according to works" (2007: 122–3).

Paul is concerned to demonstrate that God shows no partiality whether to Jew or Greek/Roman. In the context of their self-understanding as having been granted a covenant with the Creator God, the people of Israel looked to their God to protect them against their enemies, and thus to ensure for them great blessing. But in the Roman context, the imperial ideology of Roman election cannot be ignored. In this ideology of Rome's election by the gods, its emperor symbolizes the will and rule of the gods, and thus demands submission. This rule was a pervasive ideology that functioned to explain Roman military success, to guarantee the social blessings of security, justice, peace, and fertility for Rome's submissive subjects and defeat for Rome's enemies (Carter 2006: 83). There may also be a deliberate impreciseness in Paul's claim that there is no favoritism with the God of Israel. Whether to Jew or Roman, the God of Israel will not show partiality. The same applies to God's covenant with Israel—that covenant also includes commitment to the righteous rule of God over all the peoples of the world.

There may also be some ambiguity about whether Paul means to address God-fearers or gentile Christ-followers in 2:1-16. Paul may deliberately at this stage be imprecise because he wants to stress the universality of divine judgment irrespective of the group commitment involved. The decisive division between people is whether they worship the Creator or worship what he has made. In this distinction, Jews, God-fearers, proselytes, and gentile Christ-followers, though differing in group loyalty would share a recognition of the Creator of all things without being precisely differentiated. Thus, some categorizations among the ethnē in Rome draw lines of distinction that Paul views as invalid in view of the ultimate divine categorization of all being judged on the basis of doing or not doing the Law.

But it may also be possible that Paul wanted to draw a clear demarcating line between those who worshipped the Creator and those who continued to worship idols. There were likely God-fearers who were impressed by the ethical and cultic practices of the Jews. Also, there were former God-fearers who, contrary to Paul's pattern, were perceived as participating in the worship of the gods even after they had turned to Christ, and Paul may wish to indicate the inconsistency in this pattern. If this supposition is correct, though it cannot be proved, it would mean that even though those God fearers do not do the immoral things reported in 1.19-32, they are still perceived as remaining part of the disobedient idol worship that Paul views as the root cause of all immorality.

Impartiality and Ethnicity

In a context typified by diverse groups, including Jews, God-fearers, proselytes, and Christ-following ethnē, Paul stresses commonality—that is, that commonality ensured by the impartiality of God, who is no respecter of people's ethnicity or Law possession when he makes his judgments—these are truly universal. There are no exemptions; all, whether Jews or the nations, come under divine judgment. On the other hand, it is wrong to use the universality of God's judgment as an argument against the recognition of ethnicity as such, because God's judgments are differentiated (even though there is no discrimination against anyone in relation to the gospel, cf. Rom. 3:22, 10:12). People of differing ethnicity are not discriminated against, not because God is unobservant of ethnicity, but because his nature is such that he is impartial—he sees and recognizes the difference but he is just and never discriminates on the basis of it. Hence Paul can reiterate "to the Jew first and also the Greek." Paul further exemplifies how God's impartial judgment operates in 2:12-16.

In fact, the exercise of impartiality implies, even demands, a context where difference is exemplified. As J. Christiaan Beker has noted, "Just as Karl Barth and Ernst Käsemann are wrong in characterizing the Jew in Romans as the *homo religiosus* in general, so it is wrong to suppose that the emphasis on πᾶς or ἄνθρωπος blots out the ethnic specificity of two different peoples, Jews and Gentiles" (1986: 330). Beker rightly affirms that Paul's (and other Jewish forms of) universalism is not in contrast to but inclusive of ethnic specificity. For him Christology also, properly understood, requires not uniformity but unity in diversity. Thus, it cannot be too strongly stressed that in relation to ethnicity, God's impartiality is anti-discriminatory rather than anti-ethnic. Indeed, a charitable reading of claims that Paul is anti-ethnic would suggest that some of those who claim Paul is anti-ethnic would be more accurately categorized as stressing that he is anti-discriminatory.

To read Romans, therefore, from the contextuality of Paul's form of universalism is not to avoid reference to ethnicity or ethnic-specific texts, or to ignore these in favor of an undifferentiated humanity—it is Paul, not his readers, who presents human beings as either Jew or Greek with their attenuated cultural characteristics and patterns. Not to recognize Paul's diverse presentation is to decontextually and inaccurately use his letter in the service of producing an artificial "cultural melting pot" form of society unwarranted by and in contrast to Paul's gospel. This occurs when Paul's οὐ γάρ ἐστιν διαστολή is read as "there should be no distinction" (Rom. 10:12) rather than "there should be no discrimination," and when his gospel is characterized as universal, non-ethnic, and concerned only with equality rather than including also ethnic differentiation (Campbell 2018: 129–35). What Paul claims is that grace may be distributed according to Rom. 10:12-13 "without discrimination" to Jew and non-Jew (Barclay 2015: 543, 566–7).

The emphasis is not upon "hearers of the Law, but the doers," so that those "without the Law by nature," that is, non-Jews, and those "in the Law,"[8] will be judged accordingly. Those ἐν νόμῳ (Jews) will judged, whereas those who sin ἀνόμως, that is, those who sin outside the Law, will perish. The nations, those not ἐν νόμῳ, will be "law unto themselves," showing what the Law requires is written on their hearts and their

---

[8] We distinguish those ἐν νόμῳ from "those under the Law," we take the latter to mean non-Jews who have chosen to take on the Law. Cf. 1 Corinthians 9 where Paul differentiates between those under the Law (ὑπὸ νόμον) and those without the Law (ἀνόμος).

conscience operating in relation to this (2:14-16). But significantly, although ethnicity is taken note of, the universal judgment of God does not operate simply on the basis of whether one is or is not a Jew. It might seem as if the reference to Jew and non-Jew in 1:16 has been ignored. Yet in the reading of Romans, ethnicity can never be ignored, and it recurs again as an ongoing element in 2:9-10. Also, since 1:16-17, Paul has not explicitly mentioned his gospel, it might seem as if the conversation about the Law and its judgments against idolatry has become a separate topic of discussion. However, in 2:16 Paul does return to the theme of the gospel, "my gospel," according to which "God, through Jesus Christ, will judge the secret thoughts of all" (2:16).

Paul stresses the impartiality of the God of Israel as this is expounded in the Law, rather than impartiality understood as a self-standing universal principle. Viewed thus, it can sometimes be combined, for example, with "no distinction" as slogans to be used ideologically in discussions about Paul (Campbell 2018: 129–52) and as a slogan against minorities, Jews, or others, who are marginalized because of their "odd" particularity in relation to the majority (cf. Elliott's discussion of Bassler, Elliott 2007: 122–3).

Romans 2:17-29: The Second Apostrophe—"If You Call Yourself a Jew"

^{17}But if you were to call yourself a Jew and you were to find your comfort in [the] law and you boast in God ^{18}and you know the (divine) will and you approve the good, having been instructed in the law, ^{19}and if you have persuaded yourself that you are a guide to the blind, a light to those in darkness, ^{20}a tutor of the foolish, a teacher of children, possessing in the law the embodiment of knowledge and truth, ^{21}as one, therefore, who teaches the other, will you not teach yourself? The one who preaches not to steal, do you steal? ^{22}The one who says not to commit adultery, do you commit adultery? The one who abhors idols, do you commit sacrilege? ^{23}You who boast in [the] law, do you through transgression of the law dishonor God? ^{24}For, as it is written, "Because of you the name of God is slandered among the ethnē."

Romans 2:17

A significant factor here is a shift to a new conversation partner. This is indicated at 2:17 by the words εἰ δὲ σὺ "but you, for your part" (cf. 2:1) (Elliott 2007: 127). The second apostrophe differs markedly from the first both in terms of conversation partner, this one *calls himself* a Jew, as well as the tone in which he is addressed. But we must be careful not to leap from the ascription in the rhetorical presentation of someone in the speech-in-character of an imagined person, *prosōpopoia*, to the assumption that now we address real Jews and not, as is the case here, *non-Jews rhetorically representing themselves as Jews*. As Keck notes, "With this technique, the speaker depicts an entity or an imagined person, a 'type' outfitted with traits selected to advance the argument" (2005: 83). We must clarify at this point that, in the second apostrophe, though we encounter a new conversation partner, we do not mean that the interlocutor has switched from being "gentile" to here becoming a Jew. Unlike in the other places in Romans where Paul specifically refers to Jews (3:1-3, chs. 9–11), the form of address differs here. Paul does not refer to "them" or "they" but here addresses "the one" in diatribal style in second-person singular σύ "you" the same pattern in which he addresses ethnē frequently throughout the letter (Rodriguez 2016: 161–2). We still maintain our avowed stance that the interlocutor remains of the same non-Jewish ethnic origin throughout the letter. If the entire letter is addressed to the ethnē, then the imagined interlocutor must reflect the designated audience, otherwise there would be no consistency, whether in content or imagined addressee. The interlocutor may take up differing stances at various points to progress the argument, but always as a gentile and never as a Jew.

Here, in the second apostrophe, we meet a "person" who prides himself in taking on the name of a Jew (2:17). But the depiction of this so-called Jew indicates by the form of rhetoric that this is not a born-Jew but *one who prides himself on the adoption of Jewish life and practice*. This is indicated by the idealized exaggerated portrait of the Jew as one who "knows God's will and approves the good, being instructed from the Law" (Novenson 2016: 139). We meet here the use of the singular σύ (2:17), τέ (2:19), σου (2:25), and σέ (2:27) accompanied by the frequent use of participles such as ὁ λέγων, denoting the continuance of diatribal style, and clear proof that the singular addressee here cannot be claimed to be a φύσει Ἰουδαῖος. The clauses that follow here characterize the so-called Jew in explicit contrast to the nations (Elliott 2007: 127–8). The nations "suppress the truth" (1:18); their thinking has become futile, and their minds darkened (1:21), and so on; in short, they break God's Law, whereas the so-called Jew "and if you have persuaded yourself that you are a guide to the blind, a light to those in darkness, a tutor of the foolish, a teacher of children, possessing in the law the embodiment of knowledge and truth" (2:19-20).

We might well ask "who calls oneself a Jew anyway?" Certainly not someone who *is recognized* as Jewish by birth (Gal. 2:15, Rom. 11:1, 2 Cor. 11:22 Israelite being equivalent), but rather a non-Jew who has taken to practice certain elements of Jewish observance and thus has chosen to claim that self-definition as a personal achievement (Frankfurter 2001: 4030–425). There simply was no way, whereby a non-Jew could convert to Judaism through "social conversion," that is, the integration of the convert into the Jewish community (Cohen 1999: 169).[9] Indeed, the distinction between Jews and proselytes tended to be retained, thus an epitaph in Rome refers to *Iudeus proselitus* (Thorsteinsson 2003: 203). Righteous "gentiles" might find favor with God, but this did not mean they would be viewed by Jews as Jews, though they may have been thus viewed by the Roman authorities (Cohen 1999: 14, 168, 219). Paul alerts us to how he views this self-designation as a Jew by reporting it in an idealized, exaggerated form, *implying a distancing critique even in its presentation*. Paul hints that the man's self-image does not square with reality (Novenson 2016: 140). But it is the (gentile) "one called a Jew" from whom Paul is distancing—not Jews or Jewish tradition as such. As previously noted, it has clearly been established both that this chapter is not targeted at

---

[9] This is a disputed issue, to which we will return to later.

Jews and that the one who is only called a Jew is clearly a gentile interlocutor. Building on the work of Stowers, Thorsteinsson's lead (followed by Thiessen and Rodriguez, Novenson, and others) in the identification of the interlocutor has greatly assisted the interpretation of Romans 2, and thus of the whole of Romans. I myself was convinced by Thorsteinsson's arguments, that is, being called a Jew, and found his exegesis illuminating in several essays (2013: 1–37, 220, 260), but am surprised that it has not found wide recognition until now.[10]

Recently arguments confirming (Novenson 2016) and challenging the identity of the one calling himself a Jew have been elaborated (Öhler 2021, following Dochhorn 2018[11]). In response, we will briefly summarize some of the issues raised. The first issue is the translation of εἰ δὲ σὺ Ἰουδαῖος ἐπονομάζῃ, which Novenson renders "If you call yourself a Jew" (2016: 139), but which Öhler translates "If you are called a Judean" (2021: 224). Öhler cites Epictetus who normally adds a reflexive σεαυτόν to indicate that a particular identity, for example, Stoic, is reflexive. But though Paul does not have a reflexive here, he has the emphatic diatribal σύ (and an instance of σεαυτόν appears in v. 19). The best rendering of 2:17 is therefore "If you call yourself a Jew" (Jewett 2007: 219–37). There is no major problem for our reading if the person here is only "called a Jew," but is this the best reading? One would not say to a person born in Glasgow "if you are called a Scot," since that would be tautologous. But if someone said "if you call yourself a Scot," this could introduce any hypothetical inference that followed, and imply a preference or choice, indicating that this "one" might not be called, recognized as a Scot (or a Jew).

This, I think, is the emphasis here. But the significance of being called a Jew is treated by Öhler and others as possibly indicating that not only is the *persona* called a Jew, but that in fact he is or may be a Jew. As several scholars have pointed out, this was noted as early as Origen, "First of all it must be observed that he has not said of him 'But if you are a Jew,' but rather 'if you call yourself a Jew.' This is because to be a Jew and to be called a Jew are not the same thing" (*Commentary on Romans* 2.11.4). Both Origen and others, for example, Keck, go on to claim that the interlocutor should be understood as an ethnic Jew but one who because of his moral failings Paul denies the right to claim the name "Jew" (Keck 2005: 83). Some ninety years ago, Dodd spoke of "Paul's fiercely satirical attack" on this Jew (1932: 38). If we have here, even in an address to non-Jews, a polemic against Jews, and this were the accepted reading, it would open the door to Paul being perceived as making radical critiques of a Jew "by nature," similar to what we have shown above to be without foundation. So, the issue is not merely the translation of 2:17, which Novenson had already clarified (2016: 139) but of whether the chosen reading fits with the rest of Romans both in tone and in content. I find readings such as those by Thorsteinsson and Novenson to be very consistent with my view of Romans, but there may still be other unanswered issues.

---

[10] Recently Thorsteinsson joined with Matthew Thiessen and Rafael Rodriguez to write a substantial introductory chapter to a book of essays on Romans (2016: 1–37).

[11] Dochhorn (2018) views this incident of temple robbery as helpful for positing a Roman source of this use of ἱεροσύλειν.

The charge of "sacrilege," as Novenson renders, is that Rom. 2:21-22 is particularly attractive as an explanation of Paul's accusation (2016: 145–7).

A merit of Öhler's study is that a good overview of relevant texts is supplied, particularly a story told by Josephus. This is a reference to an incident from the year 19 CE of a deceitful Judean who had fled to Rome, falsely claiming to be a teacher of the Law. He and his three henchmen persuaded a Roman proselyte named Fulvia to donate purple and gold for the Jerusalem Temple, but dishonestly kept these riches for themselves. When Fulvia's husband Saturninus found out, he reported this to the emperor Tiberius who reportedly banished the whole community of Jews from Rome, and 4,000 Judeans were conscripted as soldiers to Sardinia. The reputation of Jews in Rome was damaged for years following this scandal in the eyes of mocking ethnē (Josephus *Ant.* 18:81-84). The withholding of the donated property in this story is nothing other than theft from the Temple, so this element may explain Paul's allusion to "You that abhor idols, do you rob temples?" The strange term ἱεροσύλειν (2:22b) that Paul uses (but not Josephus) may resonate with some such setting. Öhler views this story as historically plausible allowing for some dramatization by Josephus (2021: 231). The rare accusation, plausible or not, might denote ongoing inter-ethnic slandering of competing groups in Rome.[12]

However, although the analogy reported in this story is useful, it is not without problems when viewed as a possible reference to an incident used by Paul as part of his argument in Romans 2. I remain unconvinced that "Paul can safely assume that Roman readers of the letter recognized that the brief description in Rom. 2.21-24 contains an allusion to a teacher who strove to teach non-Jews but was a deceiver. Against such a *Ioudaios* the polemic is directed" (Öhler 2021: 231). In my view, the only real effect this allusion could ensure is a blow against the moral integrity of Judeans/Jews (note Öhler's use of "polemic"), something that would not be helpful in Paul's argument. Paul is not using polemic in Romans against Jews or Judaizers, and the diatribal style does not warrant this long-standing presupposition here. The reported incident could even be heard as a warning against itinerant Jewish teachers among whom Paul himself could be included, thus proving to be counterproductive.

It may be questioned as Öhler notes, whether we have here a self-designating identity claim to be categorized as Jewish or whether the passive indicates that Ἰουδαῖος was used also to label proselytes. Notably, Paul does not use the term proselyte, and Acts might indicate that "Jews and proselytes" denoted differentiation by "outsiders." We also point out that to become a full proselyte was a long process. There was no question of instant conversion by ethnē, and so there would continue to be ethnē en route to becoming full proselytes who have not yet realized their goal. They would continue to be differentiated as proselytes by Jews, if not by others. Whether Ἰουδαῖος was a claimed title given by outsiders to include proselytes, the main point, which Paul makes clear, is a challenge of ethnē breaking the Law of circumcision. By whatever route, the "one calling himself a Jew" came to be so recognized, Paul's conclusion is that for non-Jews to seek to achieve recognition as Jewish is a mistaken goal now that Christ

---

[12] On interethnic slandering, see also Marcus (1989: 67–81) and Wendt (2016).

has come. In any case, seeking Jewish recognition as a non-Jew would be an extended process and would have to be in accordance with normal Jewish practice, not simply a matter of being called a Jew by non-Jewish neighbors or the civil authorities. The addressees of Romans are non-Jews, and in this context there is no polemic against Jews as such. The pedagogical, diatribal teaching is directed only to ethnē wanting to call themselves Ἰουδαῖος.

Paul in ch. 2 is respectful of the Jewish Law, which he insists must be done rather than merely owned (Sanders 1983: 130–2). He has just ended a sharp critique of gentile life without the Law. If there is no basis for an anti-Jewish Paul at this stage in Romans, it would be unlikely that Paul himself would repeat the story of a false Jewish teacher, a Law-breaker who robs temples, to a group of ethnē in Christ who need convincing about his own reliability. The implied reference to a narrated incident involving a Judean in Rome does not have the credibility or relevance to make Paul use it critically of his own tradition at the commencement of a crucial argumentation. No wise rhetor would risk such a negative reference unless he were not genuine in his own self-presentation as deeply concerned about the future of his own people (9:1-3).

In the first apostrophe on the one judging in 2:1-5, the tone was sharply critical, and the attitude somewhat suspicious (cf. Cranfield 1975: 164), as if Paul were not fully convinced of the integrity of those judging their fellow "gentiles" possibly still fully participant in the worship of the gods.[13] But in 2:17-29, it is only open questions that are put, not necessarily impugning sincerity or integrity. Only on one point may there be a hint of implied criticism—there may possibly be a critique of boasting in the Law and in one's relation to God. The idealized, somewhat exaggerated image of "you that teach others" (2:17) is due mainly to the diatribal style, the rhetoric of which conveys here, in view of the high ideal presented, a suggestion of improbability as, for example, "do you commit sacrilege?" The questions are mostly simply interrogative. What is most significant is that Paul's first rhetorical question in 2:21 expects an affirmative answer. To the question "therefore, you who teach another, do you not teach yourself?" the normal anticipated response, would be, "of course I do." If Paul had expected a negative answer as elsewhere, he would have chosen to introduce the question with the term μὴ rather than οὐ, BDF §427 (Rodriguez 2014: 54, n29). The same does not apply to the other questions where μὴ is actually included, "you who preach 'Do not steal, do you steal?': You who say, 'Do not commit adultery, are you adulterous?' and 'You who abhor idols, do you commit sacrilege?' " Here the expected answer would be "of course not."

We hold that it must be an imagined gentile proselyte that is addressed here in that "he" is referred to in 2:27 as "you who through the letter and circumcision" are a transgressor of the law, and as such will be condemned by "those who are physically uncircumcised but keep the Law." Modern translations often render the prepositional

---

[13] I note here Song's attention to Paul's vocatives in the singular form, particularly of one taken as prisoner of war and sold as a slave (2004: 41). Ἄνθρωπε (Rom. 2:1-3) as with ἀνδραποδίστης is here a harsh, censuring expression (2004: 46, contra. Stowers 1981: 85). Barrett draws attention to the meaning of ἐριθεῖα in v. 7, derived from ἐριθευεῖν to act as an hireling (rather than from ἔρις strife), and this may involve a negative view by some critics (1962: 47).

phrase as a disjunctive, as in the RSV "You that have the written code and circumcision *but* break the law" as if this person were a transgressor *in spite of* his fulfillment of the circumcision commandment. But *what Paul actually wrote was that the interlocutor becomes a transgressor precisely through, not in spite of, his circumcision*. By undergoing circumcision, he violates the circumcision commandment (Novenson 2016: 148–9). Our reading here concludes that the nature and number of the questions and the expectation of an affirmative answer points rhetorically to a general challenge of breaking the specific command to circumcise on the eighth day, which thereby renders the accused guilty of breaking this commandment. This conclusion suggests that Paul does not fully recognize the self-designation of the "one calling oneself a Jew" as legitimate. He is not legitimately a Jew as yet, and therefore is not excluded from the Torah's judgment on ethnē, especially those seeking to justify a new self-understanding on the basis of their achievements.

> The judgmental pagan proselyte who considers himself a Jew, will himself be judged … whereas the "foreskinned" whose hearts are circumcised will be praised by God. The circumcision that Paul devalues then is proselyte circumcision … Proselyte circumcision, was like Ishmael's circumcision; it could not make him into Abraham's heir. (Fredriksen 2017: 157–8)

What Might Be Considered the Benefits of Calling Oneself a Jew?

As noted, Jewish tradition did receive some acknowledgement by the Romans because of its ancient traditions, and at times at least was allowed freedom of assembly as a legitimated association. At critical times of political unease, non-Jews such as Christ-followers might assemble with Jews, even without proselyte status, thus escaping the risk of possible punishment for membership of an unrecognized group. There is evidence that enough non-Jews did associate with Jews to result in the arousing of libels and criticism from philosophers and historians such as Juvenal (14:96-106), or Seneca.

One example I have found may offer a parallel in which claiming to be someone, or as taking on a certain status, could possibly have been practiced in Rome. There is some evidence that social performance according to this or that status or identity could in some cases be acknowledged as a legal qualification leading to the eventual acquisition of that actual status. In the reign of Claudius, we have the example of how a legal fiction was used to sort out the status of some of the Alpine tribes administratively subordinated to the Tridentini: "I so grant this benefit to them that whatever they have done or transacted as if they were Roman citizens, either with the Tridentini or with others, those things I order to be legally valid, and the names which they have previously had as if they were Roman citizens, I permit them to retain." Claudius here solves the ambiguity of names and status by confirming that those things that were done previously as if they were Roman citizens but prior to becoming such are confirmed exactly "as if they had been citizens at the time when they began their military service." Clifford Ando describes this incident as a case of social performance when social performance as interpreted by a conventional viewer was in imperial law taken as proof of status in suits for freedom in Roman law. Thus "in the crucial matter of one's identity as slave or free, the fact that others took you as one or the other was sufficient to prove as it were what you were, and the legal judgment that followed was taken to bring into harmony the legal and the social" (Ando 2019: 175–88). Recognizing that being socialized into a group's memories and thereby identifying with its collective past is a significant aspect of the process of acquiring social identity, it is intelligible and explicable that non-Jews for some perceived social advantages, might take upon themselves the performance of Jewish practice.

We note that since this is a situation involving diversity, we are dealing with the phenomenon of intergroup loyalty and conflict, particularly where Jews and Greeks are involved. Paul mentions the latter four times in all, culminating in 2:9-10. We may thus be facing issues of competition that may imply resonance with Paul's thematic utterance, "For it is not as if I were ashamed of the gospel" (1:16). This is another way of confessing pride in the message of Paul, which is regarded by some as somehow lacking? As Keck notes, "appeal to God's impartiality to validate one's own group's identity readily turns God's impartiality into partiality" (2005: 82). The existence of gentile groups, that is, of God-fearers in some connection with synagogue assemblies, perhaps as subgroups implies also, as we have noted, the existence of leaders from among such groups. Inevitably, this would sometimes involve pressure to conform to group norms as seems to be implied in 14:1–15:13 (Campbell 1995: 276–8). We need to keep this issue open as we continue to consider social groups in Rome.

Romans 2:1-24: Paul's Interlocutor and the Dynamics of Group Identity at Rome

Up to this point in his letter, Paul has stressed the universality of his gospel and likewise accountability before the judgment of God, which treats both Jew and non-Jew impartially. What then might be the context in which a "gentile" in Rome might wish to be recognized as a Jew who teaches non-Jews? The Jewish way of life as an ancient tradition did receive a certain recognition from successive Roman rulers, despite the fact that some Jews were, in times of crisis, exiled because of accusations of disturbing public order (as, e.g., Acts 18). The Jews' right of assembly was usually acknowledged, while other associations may have been liable to prosecution if they lacked authority to meet. Non-Jewish assemblies could enjoy shelter under the profile of Jewish assemblies as God-fearers, and proselytes, and groups of these did associate loosely with Jewish gatherings.

The entrance of non-Jews into full association with Jewish groups was partly hindered by the barrier of proselyte circumcision because of the stigma it often carried in non-Jewish societies. Also, Jews did not actively encourage non-Jews to proselytize, that is, to become a full participant as far as was possible in their communities (Goodman 2007: 91–116). Non-Jews who admired Jewish patterns of life but without undertaking circumcision were able to marginally participate as God-fearers in some aspects of synagogue life. But proselyte adherents did exist and need to be acknowledged. We might ask whether it is to these or, alternatively, to those who have not accepted circumcision, that Paul refers in the calling of oneself a Jew in 2:17. Since Paul does not himself make use of the term proselyte, we cannot be sure about the identity of the one wishing to be "called a Jew," but in light of the statement of 2:27, "you who have the written code and circumcision," it seems preferable to assume proselyte status.[14]

One fact is clear, we are not speaking only about an individual or group but about influence upon and the teaching of others. It is significant that in 1:32 the final criticism of wrong-doers is that though they know God's decree that those who practice such things as Paul has listed in the previous verses, "not only do them, but applaud others who are practicing them." This accused group, whom we will assume may or may not be led by an individual (since the vocative singular address may indicate a group of people as in 11:17), is gentile by birth but Jewish by persuasion. We are referring to *those* who teach other "gentiles," compare the citation from Isaiah 52:5 in 1:24, "The name of God is slandered among the 'ethnē' because of you." God's name here is slandered not by Israel, but among the "gentiles" because of Israel's enemies. We presume this negative outcome from Paul's reference to "you who teach others," in 2:21. Thorsteinsson concluded that Paul was not writing to "gentiles" at large, but "to a certain group of gentiles whose knowledge of Jewish writings and experience of Jewish ways of life was substantial. Every aspect of Paul's message in Romans must be read in light of this particular audience" (2003: 122). In addition, we learn from the argument about consistency in 2:25-29 that circumcision implies a certain pattern of life that honors God, and thus we can reasonably assume that those teaching have themselves already received circumcision, otherwise they would be in breach of this critique regarding consistency in life in relation to this honorable status. But what may be problematic in Paul's eyes is that the theme of the teaching seems to include the topic that we can provocatively label as teaching "Circumcision for the Nations."

An important question now needs to be more closely addressed—what is the identity of the "one who calls oneself a Jew" who teaches others? If "he" really is a born Jew who keeps Torah, then this would represent one of the passages most critical of Jews in the Pauline letters. The charge of breaking the Law indicates Paul's profound displeasure. If we are not to present a contradictory image of Paul, certainly at "face value" the content of this charge, that is, breaking the Law, would require some serious explanation, and this in turn becomes a pointer that this is a problematic reading. It is not in keeping with the self-image Paul projects in his view of Jewish tradition elsewhere throughout this letter.

In the first apostrophe, Paul, though he uses a rhetorical form of address, "o man whoever you are," nevertheless seems to be addressing real persons from 2:1 on. This is despite the fact that 2:17-24 is entirely hypothetical, the whole pericope being dependent on the introductory εἰ δέ pattern commenced in v. 17. But with Keck (2005: 81), we can read this not as "if" but "when," meaning that whenever non-Jews "do the things of the law," they are not entirely without law. But they become not *the law* or *a law* but "law unto themselves" as Käsemann puts it (1980: 64). The lens through which

---

[14] How much may be claimed from the fact that Paul does not use the term "proselyte" is unclear since Josephus also does not use the term.

I read Romans ch. 2 is that it seems that someone is encouraging non-Jews, probably God-fearers, to keep the Law rather than to seek acceptance with God through Christ according to Paul's message (cf. Rodriguez 2016: 60–1). From 2:26, it certainly might be inferred that, hypothetically, as Paul suggests, "if those who are not circumcised fulfil the requirements of the Law, will not their uncircumcision be regarded as circumcision?" It looks here as if someone is instructing non-Jews (cf. 2:18) as to how to become a Jewish proselyte. Indeed, it looks as if a "Jewish" mission to non-Jews is operating, but one that is in reality not Jewish in that this is being led by someone who is not a *recognized* Jew but who only claims to be so, "if you call yourself a Jew" (2:17). It is probable that this person had become a proselyte, but if we follow Philo's pattern, he would not yet be eligible to be a full member of the synagogue assembly and so should be considered a proselyte, not a Jew. Shaye D. Cohen has demonstrated the diversity of opinion about who constitutes a Jew at this period (1989: 13–33).

If the one teaching claims to be a Jew but is not fully recognized as such by others, it would seem that here we encounter a relatively new phenomenon in Rome, what Paul regards as a gentile-led mission that influences non-Jews to take up the Law as a way of life. What may be different in this context is that the leaders themselves do not as yet qualify to be accepted as full members of the synagogue assembly in that they are not the third generation in a proselyte family, as Philo would stipulate. This nonrecognition of the status of those teaching "circumcision for the nations" may also reflect Paul's own personal (past) experience of similarly "proclaiming circumcision" to the nations. "Claiming to be a Jew" is still significant in that it illustrates diversity in lifestyle and opinion at this period in Rome (Cohen 1994), and some confusion about ethnicity and identity possibly denoting mutual influence between Jewish groups and non-Jewish groups, some of whom may also be Christ-followers. We need to keep this issue in view as we continue to consider social groups in Rome.

Identifying Social Groups in Rome

Older interpretations seeking to avoid the binary presentation of reading 2:1 as already addressing Jews in succession to the gentile addressees in 1:19-32 distinguished another group in 2:1-11. Schniewind identified a group of (moral) philosophers here who regarded themselves as morally superior to ordinary sinners,[15] and certainly there is differentiation in Paul's discussion that distinguishes within the diverse moral/ethical behavior patterns of the gentile world. Paul does not say that all non-Jews are identically sinful. But this awareness makes it even more acute to find out what is the focus of his argument concerning the breaking of the Law. In older readings, Jews among the Christ-groups at Rome were simply presumed, so Jewish groups would have been posited alongside gentile Christ-followers of varying persuasions, implying

---

[15] Schniewind's readings of Romans were circulated privately among postgraduate students at Tübingen (cf. H. W. Bartsch 1968: 286, n3). Barrett used these to avoid the traditional exegesis of Rom. 2:1 as addressing Jews. Thus Barrett subdivides Rom. 1:18–2:29 into several sections, first "Judgment and the Gentile," second "Judgment and the Critic" 2:1-11, "Conscience" 2:12-16, and beginning only in v. 17 "Judgment and the Jew" 2:17-29.

it is Jews who break the Law. It is concerning the identity of the non-Jewish groups that our attention will focus.

One clear pointer toward group identity is found in 2:27, "then those who are physically uncircumcised but fulfil the Law will condemn you who through the letter and circumcision are a transgressor of the Law" (Novenson 2016: 139). This latter indicates that one group is typified as a proselyte group having both circumcision and Law adherence in which to boast (23). Paul can be even more precise and perhaps ironic—"you boast of your relation to God" and in knowledge of the Law so that you are able to discern what really matters because "you are instructed in the Law," κατηχούμενος (2:18). The somewhat exaggerated style of this section makes it difficult to discern Paul's precise stance. Is he using diatribal style to distance himself from the *persona* he describes? This group's profile and how Paul presents this, points us, as noted, toward the criticisms of judgmental behavior he will go on to make in 14:10; the link with the terminology of judging and distinguishing what things are permissible strengthens this probability. The "leader" is self-opinionated as Paul exemplifies him in the exaggerated form of an overconfident teacher of (would-be) proselytes. The language Paul uses in 2:17-24 looks like traditional language for guiding proselytes. But this group is being lead wrongly in Paul's opinion. It seems that we may have here glimpses of leaders among gentile God-fearers and proselytes possibly among those operating as a subgroup attached to a synagogue community. We will return to this issue.

Paul signals the outcome of God's judgment in a comparison with another group, that is, non-Jews, who by nature do not possess the Law, having been born and nurtured in a gentile *habitus*, but who yet do what the Law requires. The Law is written on their hearts, and they will judge those who are thus self-opinionated. As noted above, this group, because of their description as having what the Law requires written on their hearts, must be (normative) gentile Christ-followers possibly, though not necessarily, of *identical* persuasion to Paul. So, Paul is perhaps signaling here a debate that is going on in Rome about the virtue of non-Jews, possibly God-fearers, becoming proselytes to the Jewish way of life rather than only converts to the gospel.

Paul's criticisms appear as genuine challenges regarding consistency in teaching about behavior presented in question form from 2:21-24. First of all, as noted above, in vv. 17-20, Paul gives an exaggerated self-description of the (idealized) teacher based on the traditional image of the good Jewish teacher, "a guide to the blind, a light to those who sit in darkness, a tutor of the foolish, a teacher of children, having in the law the embodiment of knowledge and truth." The presumed answer of the teacher(s) to Paul's question must surely be "yes, of course I do," but this response is now in v. 23 met by a more serious inference, "You that boast in the Law, do you dishonor God by breaking the Law?" This is followed by noting its likely outcome or effect: "The name of God is slandered among the 'gentiles' because of you" (citing Isa. 45:2). Paul is speaking here through scriptural citation—his reasoning uses scriptural words in place of his own, and what the words say is affirmed by Paul as he reasons through scripture (cf. Ehrensperger 2004: 32–52).

As the scripture citation indicates, we take this reference to ethnē being led to slander as an indication that Paul is here potentially referring to the behavior of gentile leaders who are misleading those from their own ethnic group rather than Jews. How are we to interpret Paul's stance here? As commentators have noted, Paul does not argue in the vein, "if you break one commandment, you break them all" (e.g., Rodriguez 2016: 54–67). Even if Paul were addressing one or more leaders here, it is unlikely that he could accuse them of causing idolatry since he seems to be in line with the book of Judith that "Jews in the present day, do not worship idols" (Jud. 8:18) (Rainey 2018: 230).

To sum up our findings about the glimpses of differing groups we have identified earlier in this chapter, we concluded that those judging in 2:1-6 (Group 2) were differentiating themselves over against the foolish idolaters of 1:19-32 (Group 1).

To these we have now added two other identified groups: those who have the written code and circumcision but break the law (2:27b) (Group 3), and who will be judged by those who are physically uncircumcised but keep the law (2:27a) (Group 4). These groups at least display an in-group bias by negative out-group perception. They seem to be in competition as to who embodies the relation to the one God most appropriately (Tajfel 1978, Tajfel and Turner 1979, Turner 1975, see our discussion pp. 22–3).

The terminology Paul uses to describe the normative group "fulfilling the law" τὸν νόμον τελοῦσα indicates that these ethnē do so, not by observing the law, but fulfilling it through the Spirit as Paul will explain later in ch. 8. These are the normative group by which the other gentile groups will be judged according to Paul's gospel. Neutel comments on Paul's flexible use of terms "where he personifies ἀκροβυστία (uncircumcision) and imagines it keeps the Law and judges others" (2021: 64–6).

We have in the close reading of the text of Romans 2 discovered from our interrogation of Paul's text that he imagines the Roman context of the ethnē in Christ to be a context where diverse but mutually influencing groups of ethnē seek a distinct identity within the confusing options presented to them. One of these options, wrongly perceived according to Paul, is to take up the Jewish law and thus to be called a Jew. Paul sees this as misguided and requiring critical negation in that it is misleading the ethnē into a self-understanding that is deeply flawed both spiritually and ethnically (as he will show later, especially in Romans 7). Paul's problem is that he does not want to criticize Jewish tradition or its Law since the Roman ethnē are already leaning in that direction. Thus, he seeks to explain how both ethnically and spiritually the ethnē in Christ must perceive themselves as non-Jews who through Christ as the Messiah from Israel enables them to become Abraham's seed, part of the family of Abraham alongside Israel, in an aggregative rather than a supersessionist development.

One other factor needs to be noted as also relevant in Rome. Jews were strict in their opposition to perceived participation in the worship of idols. God-fearers attached to the synagogues, however, continued with idolatry as they were only marginal adherents. But the Pauline pattern was that Christ-followers must separate themselves completely from idol worship. Perhaps the Pauline challenge to disassociate from idolatrous practices rendered God-fearer status more readily acceptable than the Pauline pattern for ethnē in Christ. This implies that some God-fearers may follow a different pattern from that attributed to Paul; they dispute his authority, and hence there must have been debate about the proper pattern for ethnē in Christ to pursue. We need to decide whether the criticisms are caricatures of Paul's teaching by opponents in Rome and elsewhere, or serious misunderstandings of the gospel by Paul's supporters in Rome, or possibly both.

Romans 2:25-29: Paul and the Circumcision of Non-Jews

²⁵For circumcision confers benefit if you practice the law, but if you are a transgressor of the law, your circumcision becomes a foreskin. ²⁶If then a foreskin[ned person] keeps the regulations of the law, will not his foreskin be regarded as a circumcision? ²⁷And the natural-born foreskin[ned person] who completes the law will judge you who through the letter and circumcision are a transgressor of the law. ²⁸For he is a Jew who is not only (a Jew) in public, nor in the circumcision visible in the flesh, but (he is a Jew) who is also a Jew in secret, and in the circumcision of the heart in pneuma, not only in letter, whose praise (is) not from people but from God.

This section, 2:25-29, is more than just an argument against inconsistency, it is not against circumcision for those born Jews, nor even a redefinition of Jewish tradition itself as a spiritual entity. There are not many texts in Paul that offer clear evidence for an explicit redefinition of Jewish tradition, and this is not one of them. It is significant that Paul introduces into the discussion the term ἀκροβυστία, lit. foreskin, here clearly a synonym for non-Jews. An important clue may be found in that this section leads into a discussion of circumcision in 2:25-29, continued in slightly different form in 3:1-9. The term περιτομή that Paul uses can refer to the act itself (Gal. 5:11), to its result (Rom. 4:10), or to the person/group on which the operation was performed, that is, "the circumcision," as the Jews are thus designated in 3:30. The opposite term, ἀκροβυστία (usually rendered uncircumcision cf. Abraham in Rom. 4:12), indicates the state of not being circumcised, and the two terms were probably both sometimes used prejudicially in inter-ethnic disputes (Marcus 1989: 67–81).

Paul can refer to "the good news for the foreskin" in Gal. 2:7 or even to "foreskin by nature" in Rom. 2:27 (in order to distinguish natural foreskin from the metaphorical). He can even personilfy foreskin and imagine that it keeps the law (2.26). In this varied and almost playful passage, Paul's starting point is the positive connotation of περιτομή "circumcision," and ἀκροβυστία "foreskin" is not merely its opposite, but carries with it negative overtones since it is connected to violation of the law, even though both of these may be subverted. Ἀκροβυστία bears the stigma of a negative character, marked by distance from God (Neutel 2021). It denotes the ethnē as outsiders, from the perspective of the of περιτομή, the Jewish insiders. Paul seeks to challenge this perspective asking whether if the ἀκροβυστία keeps the law, might this not be equated to with circumcision (Neutel 2021: 65). Paul's dynamic question challenges the attribution of static stereotyping in both directions. "If you are a transgressor of the Law, your circumcision has become foreskin" and "If the foreskin keeps the requirements of the law, will not his foreskin be regarded as circumcision?" We will return to this discussion in Romans 4.

Circumcision, as Cohen (1989: 13–33), Thiessen (2016: 41–2), and others have alerted us, was not an exclusively Jewish phenomenon. "By distinguishing between

Ishmael's circumcision and that of Isaac's, Genesis 17 stresses the distance between the infant circumcision practiced by Israel and the pubescent or adult circumcision of all the other nations in the ancient Near East that practiced the rite" (Thiessen 2011: 39–42). Thus, it must be clear that circumcision as such does not make one a Jew, and this explains partly why Paul refers to someone who "calls himself a Jew"—he may do so, but it does not prove that he is what he claims. A non-Jew who is accepted as a proselyte by one community may not have been so regarded by another, and to *become a proselyte did not make one a Jew*, other factors were involved.

The significance and focus of Paul's statements emerge in 2:25. "Circumcision indeed confers benefit if you practice the law," but if you are a transgressor of the Law, "your circumcision has become foreskin." In 2:25-29, Paul gives a radical view of circumcision, the benefit of which is tied to keeping the Law, which concludes with the assertion that a Jew is not one on display as such. But he is a Jew who is one secretly rather than only publicly, "whose praise is not from people but from God." This statement should not be taken to mean that Paul regarded circumcision as purely spiritual, *or* that by this he is redefining Judaism (Novenson 2016: 160–2); like Philo he would have regarded it as including both the act itself and also what it signified. Also, there is no suggestion here that a single violation of the Law renders circumcision as uncircumcision, and thus nullifies its covenantal status and significance. As Rodriguez argues, Jer. 9:25 does not contradict this claim, since the reason why those of the house of Israel are described there as uncircumcised in hearts is because they have abandoned Torah altogether (2014: 57).

Matthew Thiessen has recently proposed that it is not the whole Law in its entirety that is broken here but rather the interlocutor is portrayed as a transgressor of the specific Law concerning the rite of circumcision (2011: 111–41). As Thiessen asserts,

> Eighth-day circumcision functioned to weave together Jewish practices with proper genealogical descent. In theory at least, only the [male]descendants of those who were themselves Jewish would be able to undergo this rite. The priestly writer of Genesis 17, the author of *Jubilees*, and Luke stress infant circumcision in order to distinguish between Jews and "gentiles," covenantal circumcision and non-covenantal circumcision. Not all circumcisions were created equal. Even in the Second Temple period, many Jews continued to define Jewishness in genealogical terms, refusing to view circumcision as a ritual remedy for the deficits of a Gentile identity. (2011: 143)

If, therefore, it is to the Law of circumcision that Paul directs his critical and challenging questions in Rom. 2:17-29, these would cohere and make sense from this perspective on circumcision now that these questions can be understood, not as anti-Jewish, but rather as anti-adult circumcision. In this view, Paul may be somewhat skeptical of the addressee's boast in the Law and in his Jewishness, especially when, with all the enthusiasm of the new convert, he also teaches others to proceed to follow his example. But, from this understanding of Paul's perspective, by assuming the rights and responsibilities of Torah, the proselyte has transgressed Torah, which was never intended for the ethnē in the first place. As a transgressor of Torah (παραβάτης νόμου), the interlocutor's circumcision has become foreskin (2:25). "The gentile proselyte, *in the very act of being circumcised*, transgresses Torah's commandment of circumcision" (Rodriguez 2014: 59–60). Thus, though we agree with Thiessen's reading that adult circumcision breaks the law of circumcision, we differ on the reason for coming to this conclusion. Ehrensperger maintains that it was not possible to become a full member of the people Israel not because this is *genealogically* impossible but because it is *ritually* impossible. She notes that Philo implies there is a process of joining Israel for non-Jews, but it is a three-generational process: only the grandson of the one who initiated the process will be a full member of the assembly of the people Israel, that is an Israelite, since he will be the son of a man who had been circumcised on the eighth day (*Virt*. 108) (Ehrensperger 2022b). We conclude that it seems (that) in most cases a proselyte in antiquity was not regarded as a full Jew. Only one who was born from someone who was circumcised on the eighth day could attain full Jewish status, this becoming possible only by the third generation. Moreover, in the new era since the coming of Christ, the taking on of proselyte status is not regarded by Paul as achieving the desired result of access to full sharing in Jewish heritage.

This explains Paul's somewhat exaggerated depictions of the "Jewish" teacher(s) of the ethnē in 2:17-29, and his own apparent leveling of ethnic differentiation by means of a judgment of works and divine impartiality in 2:1-16, while nonetheless continuing to speak in terms of Jew and ethnē. It is an inner-Jewish debate about the meaning and practice of circumcision in which non-Jews are involved in teaching "gentiles" interested in or committed to Jewish tradition, a sphere of work in which Paul sees himself as having priority in terms of both divine commission and wide experience. From Paul's stance on the matter, it seems apparent that he does not consider the interlocutor who calls himself a Jew to have yet achieved this full and proper status. At best, he can call himself a προήλυτος but not a Ἰουδαῖος. Worse still, Paul sees this person as misleading other non-Jews to seek circumcision, which Paul now thinks does not make one a full member of the Jewish people until the third generation and does not save them from the consequences of gentile sin.

We have only one text that explicitly suggests that Paul was ever involved in proselyte circumcision, but it is hard not to give it real significance, since it is part of an argument used by Paul himself that would be meaningless if he had not been actively involved in such activity. In Gal. 5:11, Paul argues, "Why am I being persecuted if I am still preaching circumcision?" This clearly implies the assumption that at one period in his life, Paul did preach circumcision. It might be a reason why he is so adamant that the Christ-followers in his communities should be severely warned against accepting circumcision after baptism. It is also in Galatians that Paul gives us the report that the assemblies of Judea that are in Christ only heard it said that "he who formerly was persecuting us is now proclaiming the trust he once tried to destroy" (Gal. 1:22-3). Here again we have a reference to Paul's involvement in persecution (διώκων). The question then arises, if the report of Paul's activities is true, did Paul cease his preaching of circumcision at the same time as he stopped persecuting? This suggestion would seem to carry some weight since otherwise it would be strange if Paul's call to be apostle to the nations did not alter his practice of preaching circumcision. But if Paul himself had changed, as we think he had, from being a preacher of circumcision to non-Jews to become an apostle of Christ, this meant for him a lasting opposition to those who still mistakenly practice a policy that he now regarded as no longer viable. This was because they had not followed due process in seeking to become proselytes, but also, most significantly, because the times had changed. We will note in our exegesis of Romans 11 that although Israel continues to reverence her God and his Torah, she is not convinced that the Christ-event is proof of the arrival of a new era, and thus new ways for the ethnē, at the dawn of Messianic Time.

Concluding Summary

Concerning the groups that are in view in chs. 1 and 2, we have concluded the following through our exegesis and analysis:

There are ethnē who confuse the created with the Creator, and are thus plainly idolators.

There are other ethnē who are aware of the Creator or "High God," but continue to worship the created instead of the Creator. These are those addressed in 2:1 as ἄνθρωπος.

Then there is the so-called Jew (2:17), a proselyte who has actually turned from idol worship and committed himself to exclusive loyalty to the one God. Nevertheless, this "gentile" is not a Jew in Paul's perspective because we have found no concept of a one-generation conversion at that time, so he remains, despite best intentions, a gentile breaker of the Law of circumcision, and still under the judgment of the Law as a "gentile."

There are also then those ethnē who turned away from idols and committed themselves to exclusive loyalty to the one God, not via the impossible attempt of becoming Jews but through trust in Christ.

And, of course, there are Jews (φύσει Ἰουδαῖοι), like Paul and others, who are not addressed here, although part of the wider picture of the inhabitants of Rome.

This discussion demonstrates that the ethnē had some difficulty understanding their status as ethnē in Christ, and thus associated with Jewish tradition and the Jewish people, but still not able to become Jews. This confirms our thesis that Paul is indirectly referring to various categories of ethnē in varied relation to Jewish traditions.

In our analysis of Romans 2, we have discovered various responses to Jewish traditions and to the message concerning the Christ, which of course preceded, but later included, Paul's "gospel." We seek to avoid being over-precise in our claims about "groups" of people who have emerged from our discussion of the text. This exercise was conducted mainly to draw attention to the diversity of options prevalent in Rome at the time of Paul's letter. This represents differing views on how to understand and argue for Christ-movement identity. Paul, in this context, seeks to present his perception of the corporate identity of ethnē in Christ. The diverse options noted here reveal the various responses that help to illuminate differing chapters of Romans, especially ch. 7, in which Paul depicts an imagined "gentile" struggling with the Law, without Christ, and without the Spirit. That ethnē imagined they could become Jews by observing the Law rather than through Christ is contrary to Paul's teaching, but this nevertheless demonstrates reverence for the Law.

What has emerged is that there are signs of ongoing interaction between Jews and the ethnē, one of which is certainly positive, though mistaken, that is, possibly an individual, but more likely a group of ethnē, calling themselves Jews. At minimum, Romans witnesses a certain fluidity in the interaction of diverse groups at this time, that is, 57–8 CE (cf. Wendt 2016).

We are left at this point with an as yet unanswered question: how did the ethnē regard Jewish practices and patterns of thought? Did they look upon these with animosity, antipathy, or with varied degrees of appreciation? Or were they possibly divided in attitude to Jews in that there is evidence that will emerge later of those who thought Israel had been rejected from the current purposes of God, and that the ethnē in Christ had replaced them?

Paul's response will demand clarification of the nature of ethnicity in relation to inclusion in the people of Israel and of Jewish Law in relation to the message concerning the Christ. This means he must also clarify his own view of the ongoing significance of circumcision within Jewish tradition, so that the ethnē in Christ can understand this adequately. Through his redescription of the ethnē as brothers of Christ (8:29), Paul will construct the way God solves the problem of the relation of the ethnē to Jewish tradition and the Jewish people.

Romans 3

Romans 3:1-2: The Advantage of the Jew and the Value of His Circumcision

¹Then what advantage has the Jew? Or what is the benefit of circumcision? ²Huge, in every respect. For in the first place the Jews were entrusted with the words of God.

Our approach to this section is guided by what we have established in ch. 2:1: the gentile address of 1:19-32 is continued, and thus the ἄνθρωπος addressed in 2:1-6, (16) cannot be a Jew. This reading has been strengthened further by the realization that in 2:17-29, the *persona* addressed is not a Jew, that is, the self-styled Jews are not φύσει Ἰουδαῖοι but only call themselves Jews. We have found no reason for reading back the address to the "one who calls himself a Jew" (2:17) into 2:1-16, something a live audience would be incapable of doing. This means addresses to actual Jews as such have not been identified. Moreover, our reading of 2:25-29 as a continuation of the gentile address means that these verses are a discussion of circumcision *for "gentiles"*, showing in fact that circumcision for non-Jews does not solve for them the problem of sin, judgment, and moral transformation. Also, our reading of 2:1-29 has enabled us to identify different gentile groups in Rome with related and differing attitudes to the Jewish heritage. These gentile groups identified as addressed in Romans 2 did not include Jews, but lived alongside Jewish groups and as such were mutually influenced and aware of each other's opinions to some extent. It is in this context that the benefit of circumcision for "gentiles" would be of interest.

This removal of an anti-Jewish address in Romans 1–2 has freed the interpretation of ch. 3 to relate it more adequately and meaningfully to chs. 1–2. Paul's emphasis upon the spiritual meaning of circumcision in 2:25-29 might suggest, as we have noted, that Paul views the outward rite as only of secondary significance. "(He is a Jew) who is a Jew also in secret" might seem to support this opinion. But in 3:1, Paul faces the issue directly, that is, the benefit of circumcision (cf. ὠφελεῖ in 2:25 and ὠφέλεια in 3:1), immediately giving a strongly positive answer concerning the value of circumcision for Jews, "Huge in every respect" (3:2a); he continues "for in the first place, the Jews were entrusted with the words of God." We note that Paul immediately connects circumcision with the Jews and their stewardship of the scriptures, so here the *topic is still circumcision but now, not for gentile proselytes, but in contrast, as practiced and perceived by Jews*. There is no hesitation or reserve in Paul's reply, circumcision is part of Jews being entrusted with the words of God; it is part of the covenant heritage that they enjoy. This strong affirmation leads away from questions about Jews to the character of their God in light of some of them proving to be unconvinced about the proclaimed dawning of Messianic Time, εἰ ἠπίστησάν τινες (3:3). These are questions emanating from non-Jews, from the ethnē, about Jewish covenantal relations with their God, *not questions asked by Jews or questions put to Jews*. 3:1-2 commenced with gentile questions about the benefit of being Jewish, and there is no syntactical or grammatical reason to infer a Jewish audience or interlocutor. Thus, 3:1-2 acts as a kind of heading for the discussion to follow. Our starting point is that possibly the best explanation of 3:1-2 is that in order to establish an identity for ethnē through Christ, Paul finds it necessary first to explain Israel's status and identity in the divine plan. As Israel was called via Abraham, so the ethnē are called through Christ. Hence, some of the (gentile) questions and inferences in 3:1-8 concern the people of Israel and God's relation to them.

Thus, as in 2:25-29 so in 3:1-2, this is not a general discussion of circumcision as such, but it leads into a diatribal style discussion punctuated with a series of questions, concluding with 3:9, which seems to relate closely to, perhaps even to reiterate, the content of 3:1-2 from a different perspective. The issues addressed in Romans 2 all focused on non-Jews and their attitude to Israel's God (Rodriguez 2016: 61). Paul was critical of non-eighth day circumcision, and thus argues that such circumcision was of no benefit for non-Jews. Here he clarifies his presentation of the issue, but now as far as Jews are concerned. Paul, as he initially makes clear, supports circumcision, but only for Jews—he views it as part of the trusted heritage included in "the words of God" τὰ λόγια τοῦ θεοῦ (3:2), which most likely means "God's covenantal promise to Israel" and all that this entails (Fitzmyer 1993: 326, Käsemann 1980: 262, Cranfield 1979: 473, Elliott 2007: 263).

But even though this question raises a Jewish issue and proceeds from a Jewish perspective, it remains a question from a gentile interlocutor about the advantage of "the Jew" (3:1). The question raised is "Is there any benefit in being a Jew?" But it is only non-Jews to whom this question could relate. As we have already noted at several points, it is not always Paul himself who asks questions or offers inferences arising from the discussion, but an imagined conversation partner normally referred to as an interlocutor. Rhetorically, this figure often serves as the voice for opinions that a writer would prefer not to state explicitly in his or her own person or that do not adequately represent the writer's considered attitude or opinion, but rather a point to be put in an ongoing discussion. In Romans, the interlocutor is a non-Jew even though the themes discussed may include questions about Jews, as here. Paul's designated audience in Rome is a gentile one, and it is therefore not a surprise that it is a gentile interlocutor that is used "to respond in advance to potential objections to what is being uttered in the letter." The interlocutor's "interruptions give voice to the potential thoughts of the intended audience"[1] (which is

---

[1] One of the advances resulting from Stowers's pioneering study, *The Diatribe and Paul's Letter to the Romans* (1981), and subsequent publications is that it has emerged, not initially, but in more recent study that Paul's interlocutor is always of gentile origin and presents his questions from this perspective (Thorsteinsson, Thiessen, and Rodriguez 2016: 19–20).

"gentile"). Keeping in mind that the interlocutor is consistently a non-Jew will greatly assist in identifying and interpreting Paul's dialogical style.

Romans 3.3-8: The Advantage of the Jew and God's Covenant Faithfulness—Gentile Reactions to Paul's Gospel

³*What, then, if some were unconvinced? Their failure to trust does not nullify God's trustworthiness, does it?* ⁴*Far from it! Although everyone is a liar, let God be proved true, just as it is written,*
"So that you may be vindicated by your words, and win when you are brought to trial"
⁵*So if our wrongdoing serves to confirm God's righteousness, what shall we say? God is not unjust for inflicting his wrath [on us], is he? [I speak in a human fashion]* ⁶*Far from it! For then how would God judge the world?* ⁷*But if the truth of God abounds to his glory by my falsifying, why am I still being condemned as a sinner?* ⁸*And isn't it likely that we should (as we are being slandered and as some people claim that we say such things) do bad things so that good may result? Their condemnation is well deserved!*

Further clarification may tentatively be offered concerning the above-noted potential thoughts of the intended audience. In this context, there is a real possibility, in view of the link back to the gospel in 1:16-17 noted in 2:16 ("according to my gospel"), and the reference to being slandered in 3:8, that the "potential thoughts of the Roman addressees" most likely concern Paul's mission and its significance, especially in its concentration on non-Jews. The significant introductory τί οὖν "what then" (vv. 1-2) continues the topic of circumcision from the end of the previous chapter, which serves as a springboard for further inferences, questions, or responses. Thus 3:1-20 consists of two units, 3:1-8 and 3:9-20 (with 3:21-31 providing the answer as to how ethnē can get righteoused). Verses 1-2 of ch. 3 continue the theme of 2:25-29 and also serve as a bridge to the remainder of the letter, which thus indicates 3:1-2 must have a certain thematic significance when taken alongside 3:3.

We will try to analyze the content of Paul's many questions in 3:1-8 in order to look for a pattern since they are obviously designed by Paul for a specific function. The opening question is, significantly, "then what advantage has the Jew?" introduced by τί οὖν "what then?," Paul and Epictetus's most favored term (Song 2004: 3). This links, as noted, back to 2.29, and the statement in 3:1 on the advantage of the Jew leads into the retort in the immediately following verse, "What then, if some were unconvinced? Their failure to trust does not nullify the trustworthiness of God, does it?" (3:3, cf. 3:31). Continuing the diatribal style, Paul responds with a strong rebuttal, μὴ γένοιτο, "far from it," which becomes his standard response to improbable or improper inferences from his statements, that is, the μὴ γένοιτο pattern first evidenced here in 3:4 is repeated ten times in total, that is, 3:4, 6, 31; 6:2, 15; 7:7, 13; 9:14; 11:1, 11. The fact that so many of Paul's responses are (initially) negative must be kept in mind in the assessment of the nature and function of the letter overall, and contributes to the (mistaken) view of Romans as polemical. The introduction of opponents imagined from the dialogical response pattern changes the entire tone of the letter and provides an occasion to include topics or themes to be rejected rather than discussions to be pursued.

Even though these questions/inferences are in the voice of a gentile interlocutor, this is how Paul introduces the topics he wishes to deal with, whether positively or negatively. And when we study the chapter divisions as, for example, 3:1, 4:1, 6:1, 11:1, and the major breaks within chapters, as for example, 3:31, 6:15, 7:7, 8:31, 9:14, 11:11, it becomes clear that Paul uses these questions and inferences as a pattern by which to structure chs. 2–11 of his letter. It may even be likely that 3:1-8 functions as a contents list in which he gives a preview in very condensed form of his envisaged topics (Campbell 1991 and 2021). If this is so, this means that these verses must occupy a significant place in Paul's construction of the letter.

Thus, the μὴ γένοιτο "far from it" formula normally operates not to mark the termination of an argument (except in the case of 3:31) but rather a transition (Malherbe 1989: 32–3). The extent of the diatribe is thereby lengthened into new sections of the letter, rather than simply (being) concluded at this point. Even though 11:11 is the last instance of μὴ γένοιτο in the letter, it leads into one of the most important sections of Romans. At this point, prior to continuing our analysis of 3:3-8, we will pause to consider Paul's pattern in using unwarranted inferences and their conclusions as a way to structure his letter.

Paul's Dialogical Pattern—Unwarranted Inferences Rejected and Unclear Conclusions Reformulated

Although possibly one of the more significant, the μὴ γένοιτο response is not the only rhetorical pattern Paul employs throughout this letter. (We considered these in more detail in Excursus I concluding with a discussion of Paul's use of Rhetorical Questions, which is recommended to be read at this point.) No less than eleven times in Romans, Paul interrupts himself with the rhetorical question τί οὖν ("What then?" 3:1, 9; 4:1; 6:1, 15, 7:7, 8:31, 9:14, 19, 30, 11:7). In five of these, he follows up with a strong negative exclamation, usually μὴ γένοιτο (6:2, 15; 7:7; 9:14; 11:7). As has been noted, the inference Paul introduces in the second part of the τί οὖν construction is usually false (Garroway 2012: 102–5); in 3:9 οὐ πάντως is a negative retort equivalent to μὴ γένοιτο. On possibly four occasions, however, the inference is correct. Garroway notes that Paul always indicates where falseness is definite, whereas when the inference is correct, he offers no dissent, as in Rom. 4:1 and 9:30 (Garroway 2012: 103–5, cf. also Rodriguez 2016: 193–4). In my view, this holds also for the questions in 3:1 and 8:31, which are not negated.

First, according to the pattern that we have just noted, Paul sets up through an interlocutor specific negative suggestions or responses and then (he) immediately rejects these with a recurring μὴ γένοιτο, "far from it."[2] By this means he introduces

---

[2] "By no means," "no way," even "absolutely not" are too weak as responses and do not sufficiently capture the strong element of abhorrence present in Paul's rejection μὴ γένοιτο. As Matera notes on

via the interlocutor the negative stances he wishes to address, and immediately makes clear that he rejects these, thereby exposing stances he does not hold, and about the denial of which, *particularly in relation to Israel*, he wants to make sure there can now be no ambivalence. The question of Israel necessarily involves the character of the God of Israel and the nature of the Law. But these latter issues, though of supreme importance in Romans, originate because of Israel and not vice versa. They derive from the issues surrounding Israel. Paul's chosen manner of indirect address in the voice of a fictitious non-Jewish interlocutor indicates his carefully considered form of address. He can indict the interlocutor sharply without offending his actual addressees until he has further clarified his own stance.

Second, in a more positive vein, rather than always giving a fierce response to an inference or objection as with the repeated use of μὴ γένοιτο ("far from it"), Paul in a subsidiary pattern of response, can also refine or revise interpretations of his message, repeating an explicatory introductory formula τί οὖν ἐροῦμεν "what then are we to say" (in light of the wrong inference) in order to prevent further misunderstanding. This subsidiary pattern of address thus indicates Paul's own response to the (per)versions of the gospel message with which he has been charged, especially where he does not wish to reject outright, but rather to refine stances or opinions, as for example, in 8:31 and 9:30c. He can also vary the introductory formula (τί οὖν ἐροῦμεν); for example, 3:1 and 6:15 begin only with τί οὖν, whereas 3:5 includes the ἐροῦμεν but omits the οὖν (cf. also 6:15 and 11:7 where Paul uses only the briefer form).

The normal pattern, τί οὖν ἐροῦμεν, occurs in six instances, that is, 4:1, 6:1, 7:7, 8:31, 9:14, and 9:30. The links between the gospel and the Law (3:31) and between the Law, and sin in 7:1, 7:13 are hereby indicated as significant, as derivatives of one of the two most important themes running throughout the letter (Dunn 1988a: lxiii). Another issue, "Of whom is Abraham father?" (4:1) is also likely to be one of the important topics Paul wishes to address (cf. 4:9). This can, however, be subsumed under the theme of Israel, linking also to 9:14, 9:30, 11:1, and 11:11 where issues about Israel dominate. The diatribal style, though variable, permeates Romans 1–14 and must be viewed as a significant element in how Paul chose to present himself and his gospel in any attempt to give an overview of the argument.[3]

Romans 3:3-8 Gentile Reactions to Paul's Gospel

As we have noted above on 3:3, the first (gentile) question refuted in the diatribe pattern of μὴ γένοιτο ("far from it") concerns the significance of the ἀπιστία, unpersuadedness, of some Jews. Will the resistance of some Jews to Paul's message nullify the covenantal advantages enjoyed by the Jews? The strong rejection of this negative inference is followed in 3:4 by the comment, "Although everyone is a liar, let God be proved true," and is supported in v. 4.b by a scriptural citation "So that you may be vindicated by your words, and win when you

---

3:5, "Paul responds to the question as strongly as he can" (2010: 82). The strong retort by Paul, which the Revised Version (RV) (1888) renders "God forbid," contains an element of emotion indicating how opposed Paul is to such suggestions or conclusions.

[3] We recommended earlier that our Excursus I should be read after our exegesis of Romans 1.

are brought to trial" (Rodriguez 2014: 62). This citation of Ps. 51:4, which is part of Paul's argument (rather than an adornment or proof), expresses David's acknowledgment that his sin merits God's negative verdict, and Paul has the interlocutor acknowledge with David that God's being true includes his just judgment on him. The function of this citation is to support the truth or vindication of God in his remaining true to his words and faithful to his covenant despite the negative response of some Jews (cf. 3:26).

The question concerning some Jews remaining unconvinced leads Paul in 3:5 into a discussion of divine justice. If our ἀδικία "confirms righteousness" δικαιοσύνην συνίστησιν, this indicates that God's character is in debate since, while human ἀδικία promotes his glory, he nevertheless condemns the sinners. In 3:7, the character of God is further questioned, reflecting in this instance a question about Paul's gentile mission (signaled in the use of ὑπερεπερίσσευσεν—abounds, cf. Rom. 5:20), that is, how can God be just to accept sinners, that is, non-Jews, since he inflicts wrath upon ἀδικία (according to 1:19-32)? This theme is developed in a reported slander of Paul included within a false inference in v. 8b, "Should we do bad things that good may result?" There can be little doubt that this denotes a critical judgment upon the acceptance of gentile sinners in a conversation in which God's dealing with unconvinced Jews also figures.

In my opinion, the use of the first-person plurals and diatribal style indicates a gentile source of this inference in v. 8. This contrasts with 3:3, where the subject matter was the conclusion *which "gentiles" have drawn concerning the lack of trust of some Jews*. The use of the terms ἀδικία (wrongdoing 3:5) and ἁμαρτωλός (sin 3:7) supports this (gentile) view as would the issue of the character of God in his relation to the idolatrous world of those from the nations so strongly condemned in 1:19-32. So also, would the third-person references to the Jews in 3:1-2. These questions/inferences indicate *gentile misunderstanding of Israel's calling and covenant in light of Paul's gospel*, and hence resultant questions concerning the character of the God of Israel. It is the interlocutor who asks the questions and Paul who responds or answers with another question in 3:7-8 (Matera 2010: 80). The focus of the questions on the character of God helps explain the strong theological emphasis of Romans. It appears that Paul's proclamation of the incoming of the nations may have had a reflex effect on the perception of Israel among non-Jews. Paul's proclamation of grace appears to compromise the character of Israel's God (Tobin 2004: 119).

To sum up our view of 3:1-8, it is a series of questions/inferences dealing with God's faithfulness to the Jewish people from the perspective of the rightness of God's judgments in relation to Paul's gentile mission. Since these questions originate from and concern the ethnē, Paul puts them, not in the voice of Jews (contra Beker 1980: 77), but in the voice of the imagined gentile interlocutor. This reflects gentile misunderstanding of the God of Israel's relation to the recent "incoming of the nations," that is, as uncircumcised adherents to the heritage of Israel. *How is the character of this God and the nature of his covenant with Israel to be viewed in light of these events?* These hypothetical ("what if?") questions, often followed by μὴ γένοιτο, will be taken up at points throughout the letter, but Paul lists them here to introduce his planned literary itinerary.[4]

---

[4] See also our list of Rhetorical Questions in Excursus I (pp. 44–8).

3:3 What if some were unconvinced, etc.?	9–11 11:1 and 11:11
3:5 What if our wrongdoing …?	7:7 and 7:13 9:14 There is no injustice on God's part, is there?
3:6 How could God judge the world? But if through my falsifying …	6:1 Should we continue in sin? 6:15 Should we sin because we are not under law but under grace—

Romans 3:9-20: Scriptural Reasoning—The Whole World Living under the Power of Sin

⁹What then? Are we excelled? No, not at all; for we have already charged that all, both Jews and Greeks, are under the power of sin, ¹⁰as it is written:
"There is none who is righteous, not even one;
¹¹   there is none who has understanding,
      there is none who seeks God.
¹² All have turned aside, together they have gone astray;
      there is none who practices kindness,
      there is not even one."
¹³ "Their throat is an open grave;
      they use their tongues to deceive."
    "The venom of vipers is under their lips."
¹⁴   "Their mouths are full of cursing and bitterness."
¹⁵ "Their feet are swift to shed blood;
¹⁶   ruin and misery are in their paths,
¹⁷ and the way of peace they have not known."
¹⁸   "There is no fear of God before their eyes."
¹⁹Now we know that what the law says to those who are in the law, it speaks in order that every mouth would be silenced, and the whole world would be brought to account before God. ²⁰For "no human being will be vindicated in his sight" by works of law, for through the law comes the knowledge of sin.

The material of 3:9-20 forms a second main unit in ch. 3, connecting to the diatribal questions and responses of 3:1-8 by means of the question in 3:9; "What then? Are we excelled?" This connects back to 3:1-2 and is responded to in 3:9b in Paul's assertion "far from it"[5] for we have already demonstrated that all both Jews and Greeks are under sin (the scriptural citations that follow function as a continuation of the response in

---

5   We take οὐ πάντως "no, not at all" here as an equivalent to μὴ γένοιτο (cf. Song 2004: 96).

3:9b). At first glance, 3:9 may appear to contradict the claimed advantage of the Jew in 3:1-2.

Romans 3:9

However, the tendency to view the first-person plural reference in 3:9 as relating to Israel has been almost universal, encouraged by the list of citations following in 3:10-20, and only somewhat hindered by the potential conflict with the specific affirmative content of 3:1-2, as the resultant textual variants and readings illustrate. Based on the accepted *traditional* presupposition that the question has a Jewish source, that is, that it is from a Jewish interlocutor, most commentators have rendered προεχόμεθα as an active verb despite the absence of such usage elsewhere. The Revised English Bible (REB) even gratuitously introduces a term not present in the Greek, "are we (Jews) any better off?" But, as we have demonstrated, the interlocutor is not Jewish, and προεχόμεθα is most naturally rendered in the passive voice, that is, "are we excelled" (pace Vulgate which takes this as middle) or "are we disadvantaged" by Jews, (cf. New Revised Standard Version [NRSV] marginal note).

Thus in 3:9, despite the varied options noted by Cranfield (1975: 187–9) and Dahl (1977), we follow the reading of the verb in the passive also strongly supported by Thiessen who claims that "placing προεχόμεθα in the mouth of a gentile accounts for both the context and the grammar felicitously" (2016: 33). The question "are we excelled" makes good sense as a gentile question arising from the apparent claim of 3:1-2 that Jews excel over "gentiles" in that they are entrusted with the words of God, τὰ λόγια τοῦ θεοῦ (although this should be read with Hultgren as "advantages without privileges" (2011: 141–3).

According to 3:1-2, there is an advantage in being a Jew and circumcision has value, but for a "gentile," there is no value in simply becoming a proselyte via circumcision, as Paul has already argued in ch. 2. Notable in 3:20 is Paul's emphasis on the present time, νῦν "now," indicating that he is writing from the perspective of the coming of Christ, that is, of Messianic Time, and the proclamation of the gospel, which radically alters the outlook for the gentile people. From the perspective of the gospel, the route for non-Jews to acceptance with God is now not by becoming a proselyte. Hence, the numerous citations that comprise 3:10-20 focus on the universal domination of sin affecting both Jews and Greeks. When scripture is cited, it is hard to omit some reference to Israel as its subject, but scripture in Paul is most frequently cited in relation to non-Jews, his normal target audience as apostle to the nations.

Romans 3:10-20

Beginning with the scriptural introduction, "as it is written" Paul cites mainly from the Psalms (with the exception of Isa. 59:7-8) to claim "there is no one who is righteous, not even one; there is no one who has understanding; there is no one who seeks God," concluding with 3:18, "There is no fear of God before their eyes." The traditional view of these listed citations is to read them as supposedly cited to prove the accusation with which all are charged, that the nations as well as Jews are all ὑφ' ἁμαρτίαν "under sin" (1:18-3:20), under the rule of sin with its historical consequences (Rodriguez 2016: 70).

Thus, the verb προαιτιάομαι, "we have already charged," is read as referring back sequentially to what Paul has stated previously. But it has been noted by scholars such as Thorsteinsson (2003: 235–6) and Ehrensperger (2019: 289–91) that this does not really summarize any of Paul's previous statements here. If Paul feels it necessary to offer a catena of citations as he is about to do, for something he has already regarded as proven *prior* to 3:9, this seems superfluous to his argument. With these scriptural verses, Paul rather demonstrates at this point that all are forced to live under sin. Helpful for this reading is Thorsteinsson's recognition that "Paul does not use the first person singular, 'I have already charged,' but the plural 'we have already charged.'" If the former had not been the case, the verb προαιτιάομαι would unquestionably have referred to something which Paul himself had uttered earlier (presumably in his letter). But the use of the first-person plural, "we," indicates as likewise the λέγομεν γάρ "for we say" in 4:9, that Paul is referring to scripture. As we have already noted in regard to Rom. 2:2, since Paul, following the conventions of the diatribe, is very self-conscious about his use of pronouns and does not casually move from singular to plural, his use of "we" in 3:9 must indicate a reference to scripture. This reading does not oppose the identity of Paul's interlocutor as "gentile" (Thorsteinsson 2003: 235–8).

The reference to προ here means "what has been demonstrated at an earlier period of time," exemplified in the citations that Paul is about to recite. This introduces a new sequence in the text rather than concluding a former one. These Psalm(s) are to be read more as a lamentation of the situation in which they all, Jews and the nations, victims and oppressors, live "under sin" though affected in differing ways, that is, under a sinful Roman regime in which, contrary to its claim of establishing peace and well-being for all, for many means to live under a regime of apparent and structural violence and oppressive power (cf. Ehrensperger 2019: 289). These texts should be read as lamentations of the oppressed, especially Israel, crying to God for help and vindication, rather than becoming proof of universal sin, that is, making Jews and the ethnē the same in their status vis-à vis sin (Thorsteinsson 2003: 191). The distinction is between Israel and those who have no fear of God (LXX Ps. 35:2). They are all affected by sin (under sin), but that does not mean that sin affects all in the same way. To deceive, spit venom, and shed blood are not the same as suffering under such behavior (LXX Pss. 5:10; 13:1-3; 35:2; 52:2-4; 9:28; Isa. 59:7-8). When these verses are analyzed contextually, their content clearly indicates that Paul's verdict is upon those who inflict evil, but the oppressed cannot escape it, even though crying to the righteous God for deliverance. None can escape the vicious cycle of sin and its consequences, and no human effort can get release from the power of sin.

The Psalms in the context of Israel represent the weak and the oppressed lamenting their situation but trusting themselves to God's righteousness and mercy. Ehrensperger criticizes Dunn who, though recognizing that the Psalms cited here refer to oppressed Israel's lamentations, crying to God for help and vindication, still regards them as universal indictment, and the Jew as the paradigm of the universal sinner (2019: 288–91). Moreover, these texts indicate not that Israel is unaware of sin, but rather that

Israel has learned from her scriptures that no one, whether oppressed or oppressor, can escape the power of sin.

As Rodrigo J. Morales points out, "that each of the texts in the chain resonates with broader themes in the letter suggests that Paul cites these in particular to emphasize not only human sin, but also, more subtly, God's righteousness and fidelity." Thus, though the majority of Psalm 14 is taken up with castigating the wicked for their evil ways, it "ends with a plea for God to deliver Israel" and "to restore the fortunes of his people" (2012: 114). Perhaps we read Paul's use of scripture in too precise literary fashion, in a more written-based culture, where we lose some of the nuances that Paul puts before us. Do we hear only the cry of Israel about her oppression and the arrogance of those in whom there is no fear of God, and overlook the fact that the righteous are in dialogue with their righteous God? As Morales claims, "That each of the texts in the chain resonates with broader themes in the letter suggests that Paul cites these in particular to emphasize … God's righteousness and fidelity" (2012: 115). It is surely significant that Paul's use of δικαιοσύνη, which he prepares for in 3:9-20 (cf. Pss. 5:9; 35:7) is not something without *positive* preparatory significance for what he will argue from 3:21 to 4:25.

This chain of texts about the wickedness of Israel's powerful enemies is Paul's attempt to demonstrate for his gentile readers the tragedy of living under sin, revealing the true nature of the *Pax Romana* as a system of violence contrary to its own claims for universal peace (cf. 3:25). When the Psalm citations Paul uses are read as scripture, demonstrating the impossibility of anyone, whether Jew or from the nations, escaping from the universal domination of sin, then they are seen to serve their proper function, not principally as indictment of Israel but as denying the gentile aspiration to escape from sin's domination by becoming proselytes (Ehrensperger 2019: 291, cf. also Thorsteinsson 2003: 233). This is an important issue in Romans. The interpretive tendency to see mainly Jews being judged by Paul at this point has meant that Paul's targeted gentile audience and their misdirected attempts through "works of law" to rectify themselves by becoming (law-observing) Jews, has been almost entirely overlooked.

Romans 3:19-20

This does not mean that oppressed Israel is free from sin or its domination any more than the ethnē, nor, on the other hand, does it mean that Israel is more guilty than others. Paul's use of οἴδαμεν δὲ, "now we know," to introduce this verse, reminds the ethnē of what he holds in common with them in the understanding of the function of the Law. If, as Elliott notes, we allow the indicative verb forms (λέγει, λαλεῖ, v. 19) to structure the sentence, the phrase τοῖς ἐν τῷ νόμῳ "those in the law" falls into place more naturally modifying the preceding λέγει rather than the following λαλεῖ. Thus, 3:19 should not be punctuated as in the RSV and other English translations "Now we know that what the Law says, it says to those who are under the Law …," putting the rhetorical weight upon the Jews. But if we follow Elliott's reordering, omitting the comma after "what the Law says" it now reads, "Now we know that what the Law says to those in the Law it speaks in order that every mouth may be stopped, and all the world be brought to account before God." We would render τοῖς ἐν τῷ νόμῳ as "those in the Law," that is, Jews. Read in this way, it is clear that though the Jews are entrusted with the Law, unlike the ethnē "without the Law," ἔθνη τὰ μὴ νόμον ἔχοντα, the Law applies to the entire world, and not only to the Jews (Elliott 2007: 145-7). Of course, the Law is Israel's but Paul here makes the claim that its scope is universal. Non-Jews though not having the Law still fall under the jurisdiction of the God of Israel. Only in light of this Law is pagan worship and distorted behavior following on from this (cf. 1:19-32) evident as sin. This is what is meant by "through the law comes the knowledge of sin" (3:20b). But the Law is not the cause of sin, it only registers this.

No one can avoid the inescapable oppression of violence and deprivation, but these texts should no longer be read simply as Paul's universal indictment against sinners, or by viewing the Jew as the paradigm of the universal sinner, but rather as Paul's clear statement to the ethnē in Rome that their switching of ethnic categories will not bring acceptance with God. If Paul wishes to illustrate the human condition, he necessarily has to use Israel's scriptures, but his reception of these must be read to reflect the context in Israel, and Israel's use of these in confession (rather than self-indictment), and in trust that the Lord will deliver.[6]

Israel, no less than the nations, lives under the power of sin as it is manifested in the world in which they live, even though Israel promotes the worship of her God and does not worship the gods of the nations. That all human beings are under the power of sin is clearly Paul's presupposition here, yet his argument does not imply that all humans are the same, but takes account of differing modes of sin, without the Law, under the Law, and so on. Thus, gentiles' core sin is idolatry, that is, distorted worship and part of their ethnic makeup. This is a deliberate, conscious act, because they could know and do otherwise (1:19-20). By this behavior, they have stored up God's wrath and there is nothing, no adherence to the Law that can redeem a non-Jew from this condition. God handed them over to distorted behavior as a collective punishment for their idolatry. By contrast, Israel corporately and Jews individually also sin in different ways, in that their sin is characterized as disobedience, but not by the particular problem of idolatry as in the case of the ethnē. Nickelsburg notes that "sins of violence ... are not attributed to Israel. The Israelites are victims of Gentile violence, which is usually punishment for another kind of sin committed by Israel ... this sin is caused by blindness and involves the flocks straying from the path that God had shown them" (Nickelsburg 2001: 355). Because Jews are in a covenantal and familial relationship with their God, they may disobey God, but this does not break his faithfulness to them. In as much as there is a difference between Jews and the ethnē concerning sin, so there is a difference also concerning judgment. Israel may be punished harshly for her disobedience but always is called to repentance and restoration by God's mercy. "Gentiles," however, apart from Christ, are in a permanent position of sinfulness, that is, "sinners" (Gal 2:16)—a disastrous situation because they are not in a covenant relationship with God. This implies that there is for them no means of repentance and atonement. Paul clearly makes this distinction when he emphasizes that "all who have sinned apart from the

---

[6] Keck's comment here is interesting. "Paul reads scripture through the lens of Christ, he does not criticize in the name of Christ" (2005: 112).

law will perish apart from the law, all who have sinned in the law will be judged by the law" (2:12).

Significantly also, Paul's concept of sin though it includes this, as noted above, is not limited to personal transgression but includes the corporate and universal dimensions of sin as a power in direct contrast and opposition to the power of God revealed in the gospel concerning the Christ (cf. 1:4, 1:16). It is this corporate and universal aspect of sin and oppression in 3:2-20 that is missed when primarily the failings of Israel are noted.

The strong emphasis upon the Law as bringing awareness of sin (3:20) and of the δικαιοσύνη of God in Christ being revealed χωρὶς νόμου "apart from [the] Law" (3:21) is Paul's response to those ethnē who mistakenly thought that by the aspiration of their taking on the demands of the Law this, rather than the gospel, would deliver them from judgment. It appears likely that it was in such a context as this that the phrase ἔργα νόμου ("works of law") (3:20) first emerged. It should not be taken to refer to the observance of the Law by Israelites, but instead to the observance of the Law by non-Jews seeking to achieve right standing in face of God by means of accepting circumcision and observing the requirements of the Law. It emerges from a misunderstanding of Jewish tradition as capable of enabling non-Jews to achieve a right standing with God in accordance with the demands of the Law. It is not Jewish tradition itself that Paul criticizes but a tradition for non-Jews that is ineffective against sin, hence his declaration that ἐξ ἔργων νόμου οὐ δικαιωθήσεται πᾶσα σάρξ ("For no human being will be vindicated in his sight by works of law," 3:20). When statements such as this are universalized to refer to Jews as well as non-Jews, Paul's original argument against non-Jews becoming proselytes rather than Christ-followers is overlooked, indicating the crucial significance of the identity of Paul's targeted audience. Similarly, the oft-cited opposition of Paul to "works of law" thereby on this reading renders Paul anti-Law and thus anti-Jewish.

As noted, the nations on account of their idolatry are sinners by nature, a condition that attracts upon itself justified punishment; they are sinners *by nature*—and nothing they do—no pattern of behavior can change that condition. Proselyte conversion, that is, following Torah as a non-Jew, does not remove this sinfulness. Ethnē bring with them also a (mis)understanding that performing rituals for the gods, initiated by them, would rectify their relation with these gods, and this doing "works of law," that is, circumcision and further Jewish practice, would rectify their sinful condition and thus also their relationship with the God of Israel. Thereby they would be safe at the eschatological judgment. This gentile misunderstanding is what Paul addresses.

Summary of 3:9-20

We must now summarize our conclusions from 3:9 to 3:20. First, these texts have suffered from being misread as the second part of an argument that is first set out in 1:19-32 describing the sins of the gentile world. In older traditions, due mainly to uncritical presuppositions that Paul is developing here a systematic or dogmatic theological argument to prove that all peoples are the same under the power of sin whether they are Jews or non-Jews, 3:1-20 has been read as the second part of this "proof," and the foundation for the view that there is not, nor can there be, any difference between Jew and non-Jew. This is not Paul's goal, nor is it his opinion.

Thus, rather than regarding the scriptural citations in 3:10-20 as having only a negative function in relation to what succeeds them, it now emerges that one of the reasons why Paul chose these Psalms to cite here is that they use the terms δικαιοσύνη, righteousness (LXX Ps. 5:9; 9:5-9; 14:2); and ἀλήθεια, truth/faithfulness, which Paul will cite frequently in his letter (Elliott 2007: 139, n1), indicating that he is aware of the wider context and not just the explicit content of the texts that he repeats. This wider context illustrates and presumes the trust of Israel's psalmist in her God. Thus, his character and the relation of trust that it inspires is remembered as well as the specific part of the Psalm or of Isaiah actually repeated. Moreover, it reminds the reader of the confidence that the use of scripture conveys, that is, that God in his righteousness and faithfulness will not desert his people Israel. This is where I entirely disagree with Dunn's reading of scripture against Israel. He refers to the catena of citations in 3:10-20 not as Jews crying to God for help under oppression by others but as a sequence of Psalm passages that formed the *Jewish* indictment of others (Dunn 1988a: 145–6, unfortunately followed here by Rodriguez 2014: 67–72).

We have sought to clarify the meaning of these verses by showing that Paul clearly distinguishes Jews and non-Jews both here and throughout the letter, particularly in recognizing the covenant and promises of God in relation to the people Israel. Significantly, here Paul reminds non-Jews that the Law is not just a Jewish peculiarity, but it applies universally, that is, to them also. We note again the universal claim of 3:19-20 that the Law, although it is God's gift to Israel, judges the whole world, so that the non-Jews, though not possessing the Law are nonetheless under its judgments that apply also to them. This gives more clarity to Paul's stress upon everyone being under the power of sin—the nations without the Law, as well as the Jews with their Law. Were it not for the Law, non-Jews would not know about God's judgment upon sin, but the Law reveals this, even though it cannot, of itself, offer the solution. Knowledge of the Law therefore brings responsibility for sin but does not, cannot, remove sin.

Romans 3:21-26: The Revelation of God's Rectifying Power in Christ

²¹But now, apart from the Law the righteousness of God attested by the Law and the prophets, has been revealed. ²²the righteousness of God [is being revealed] through the faithfulness of Jesus Christ to all who trust. For there is no discrimination, ²³since all have sinned and fall short of the glory of God; ²⁴they are now rectified by his grace as a gift, through the redemption that is in Christ Jesus, ²⁵whom God put forward as a hilasterion by his blood, effective through trust, to demonstrate his righteousness, because of the passing over through his forbearance of sinful actions previously committed; ²⁶to demonstrate his righteousness in the present time so that he himself is righteous and rectifies the one who is of the trust of Jesus.

It is significant that in 3:21 the verse begins with νυνὶ δέ, "but now," emphasizing the new era of the revelation of the righteousness of God χωρὶς νόμου "outside or apart from Torah" (cf. also 5:9, 11; 6:19, 22; 8:1; 11:30). This is now being revealed in light of the situation of the ethnē before and apart from the advent of Christ, denoted in 1:19-32. Paul's gentile interlocutor has, of course, not disappeared in this section, 3:21-26 (Stowers 1994: 202–6). Thus, the phrase "now being revealed apart from Torah" has particularly in mind the gentile group depicted in ch. 2, who were being taught to follow Torah as an alternative to Paul's gospel even though this action would not remove them from the sphere of the righteous judgment of God. Adhering to Torah's principles, in Paul's view, will not lead to righteousness for non-Jews since Torah was gifted to Israel, and Paul intends in Romans to show it will not and cannot bring blessing, but only judgment to non-Jews (Rodriguez 2014: 75). "Now," means now at this time, when the in-breaking of the Messianic Time has begun and God's revelation of righteousness in Christ has occurred (cf. 13:11). Paul views the acceptance of circumcision and the taking up of the requirements of the Law by non-Jews as a gentile misconception of the divine purpose, including the Law. For Paul, the gospel for non-Jews consists of trust in God's rescuing power through Christ, the core of a transformed social identity that could be installed in hearts and minds, not in a programmatic taking up of Jewish identity to become proselytes. It was not that Jews would have disagreed with this perspective. As Dunn has pointed out, Jewish Christianity shared Paul's belief that justification came not from covenant works but through trust (2005: 88–110). The typical first-century Jew would not have disagreed that trust was the essential first principle (cf. also Morgan 2017). But the problem historically is that what Paul criticized here as "works of law" has generally been read as representing the normative tradition of Jews rather than applying it in the first instance to the particular case of non-Jews (at the time of the in-breaking of Messianic Time), mistakenly seeking to perform the works of the Law as a means of attaining God's favor.

The most important and primary meaning of the term δικαιοσύνη θεοῦ—the rectifying power of God in Romans—is, in my view, "God's covenant fidelity to Israel" (because it is through this that God's faithfulness is demonstrated). But why should Paul feel it necessary to claim that God is δίκαιος, righteous? The critical questions raised in 3:1-8 would indicate that this affirmation is required in light of misunderstandings of "righteousness apart from the Law" as proclaimed in the gentile mission. As Elliott says, "Paul is less concerned here with soteriology per se than with vindicating the righteousness of the saving God" (2007: 148). We agree with Keck in his use of the term "rectify" rather than the traditional "justify" to translate the Greek verb δικαιόω (2005: 107–13). In English, "justify" unfortunately carries overtones of being proved to be right, whereas the covenantal context would demand a recognition of needing to be put right. As my teacher Anthony Hanson used to say in relation to the narrative of Job, man needs to "repent in sackcloth and ashes" as Job did when he saw the Lord (Job 42:1-6), since it is God alone who will be justified/vindicated. Rom. 3:26 gives two goals for the revelation of God's rectifying power, δικαιοσύνη, in Christ, the primary one being to show that he, God, himself is righteous, and the second being "that he rectifies the one who lives by the faithfulness of Christ." It is striking that "this is the only time Paul says that God is righteous," but he does so in order to emphasize that the righteousness that is manifested apart from the Law in no way compromises God's own rectitude and integrity (Keck 2005: 113). That Paul relates closely the faithfulness of God to Israel and the revelation of God's righteousness in Christ should ensure that Christ and his reconciliation should never be set in antithesis to Israel and the covenant, but rather that the one be viewed as the outcome and consequence of the other (as Rom. 3:21-26 and its continuation in ch. 5:1-11 would suggest).

The rectifying power of God is now manifested, πεφανέρωται, a perfect passive verb expressing the ongoing import of the Christ-event, a completed event in the past. This declaration in 3:21-26 relates back to 1:16-17 and forms part of the nucleus of Paul's explanation of the gospel, as distinct from other sections of Romans where the diatribal style is more evident (cf. Witherington 2012: 99). The connection of this declaration with the preceding verses is that it proclaims what the nations need but which, in accordance with Paul's gospel, cannot be acquired by non-Jews taking on the obligations of Torah. This explains the strong rejection in 3:20 of the possibility that any one will be "righteoused" (Sanders 1983: 21) by the works of the Law, ἐξ ἔργων νόμου. This phrase cannot refer to the doing of the Law by faithful Jews, otherwise Paul must often contradict himself (cf. e.g., 7:12-14). As our designated address of Romans as a letter to non-Jews requires, and as we will discuss further in relation to 7:7-25, the phrase "works of the law," ἔργον τὸν νόμον, is what non-Jews do in seeking to take on Jewish law, for example, in calling oneself a Jew in 2:17-29. But with the Law comes the knowledge of sin which the Law identifies and registers, but does not remove, 3:20.[7] That the Law is not in opposition to the gospel is further indicated by Paul in that he claims that the revelation of universal righteousness, that is, inclusive of non-Jews is "attested by the Law and the prophets" (v. 21). The fact that the revelation of God's righteousness is revealed outside or apart from the Law, χωρὶς νόμου, is significant in that it means that non-Jews can participate in the purpose of God; the route to righteousness for non-Jews is not via becoming Jews, and hence is open "to all who trust" "for there is no διαστολή, discrimination, in relation to sin" (3:22-23).

As we will demonstrate later, in 10:12, as also here, the emphasis is not on the qualities or ethnicity of those under discussion, but on the non-discriminatory and impartial acceptance of all by God. Hence, it would be wrong to read this phrase in an anti-ethnic, that is, universal *human-focused (anthropological)* way. It is not that those whom God calls are all the same with no distinction between them, but rather that *theologically* God's call is non-discriminatory because it is determined, not by humans but by God (Barclay 2015: 65). Thus, all can now be rectified (δικαιούμενοι) by his grace as a gift through the redemption διὰ τῆς ἀπολυτρώσεως (Keck 2005: 107). The word ἀπολύτρωσις is related to the term λύτρον; ransom and redemption/redeem are metaphors drawn from buying the freedom of slaves and captives, here probably intended as a link word pointing to Romans 6–8. In the book of Isaiah, the word "Redeemer" is frequently used for God as, for example, Isa. 41:14; 43:14; 59:20, but

---

[7] Cf. Ehrensperger 2021. We will return to this topic in relation to Rom. 7:7-35. Cf. also Nanos (2021: 75).

never in the New Testament does anyone actually call Christ, the Redeemer (Keck 2005: 107).

Righteousness here comes through trust, διὰ πίστεως Ἰησοῦ Χριστοῦ, literally through trust of Jesus Christ. In analogy with 3:26, τὸν ἐκ πίστεως Ἰησοῦ should not be translated as "those who have trust *in Jesus*," but must refer to the trustworthiness of Jesus, in parallel with 4:16 where ἐκ πίστεως Ἀβρααμ clearly refers to the trustworthiness of Abraham. This issue has been well discussed recently by Young who notably takes ethnic issues fully into account (2015: 30–521). We read this text as evidence that trust here means not through trust *in* Jesus Christ (objective genitive), but through the trust or trustworthiness *of* Jesus Christ (subjective genitive; cf. Markus Barth 1969: 363–70, 1974: 224, 347). The list of scholars who adhere to this understanding seems to be on the increase (cf. Longenecker 1964 and also 2011: 317–21). We remain open to the view that this reading need not exclude the notion of trust in Jesus Christ in other Pauline texts. In light of the diversity of opinion among Pauline scholars, Rodriguez's support for Wallace's proposal of a plenary genitive here is an interesting possibility that allows both the objective and subjective meanings simultaneously (Rodriguez 2014: 76, n11).

The reality of who God is and who he has revealed himself to be is central to this passage (3:21-26). As noted, *this is the only time that Paul says that God is righteous*. As Keck points out, "he does so in order to emphasize that the rectitude that is manifested apart from the Law in no way compromises God's own rectitude—God's integrity, God's trueness to God's nature and character—but expresses it definitively" (2005: 113). Paul is claiming here that God has revealed his rectifying power in the redemption that is available in Christ in which he (God) not only identifies and rewards/punishes whoever is right or wrong but "also makes right whoever is not right" (113). A similar definition of "righteousness" has been proposed by Victor Furnish, that is, "God's power to put things right" (2012: 187–202), or as "an appropriate way to refer to the righteousness of God" (Rodriguez 2014: 80, n24). This is achieved by God's action in Jesus Christ, "whom God put forward (προέθετο) as the ἱλαστήριον (possibly ransom) through his faithfulness" (3:19-20). It is best to leave ἱλαστήριον untranslated, for reasons set out below (Rodriguez 2014: 74). If the rectifying power of God in its most basic significance refers to the fidelity of God to his promises to Abraham and his descendants (cf. εἰς τὸ εἶναι αὐτὸν δίκαιον) then, in accordance with the divine integrity, this identifies it as covenantal loyalty to Israel. The meaning of ἱλαστήριον must be determined primarily in relation to this context. This means that the righteousness in view here is not an entirely new phenomenon, one that was previously unknown—by no means—"it was attested to by the Law and the prophets" (3:21b). According to this verse, the emphasis denotes specifically what is new, "But now, the rectifying power of God is being revealed *apart from Torah*." We misunderstand Paul if we translate this as "But now the righteousness of God apart from Torah is being revealed" (Rodriguez 2014: 77, n12). Neither God himself nor Torah is new, but the pattern of revealing "apart from Torah" is the new entity. Thus, χωρὶς νόμου (3:21) indicates a sphere of reality outside the realm of the Law, though not in opposition to it. Because of, and in keeping with, the newness of the revealing, Paul will need to find differing terminology to express his message to the ethnē. As noted above, since Paul closely relates the fidelity of God to Israel and the new revelation in Christ, this means that reconciliation in Christ must never be viewed in antithesis to Israel and the covenant just because the new redemptive act in Christ is outside or apart from the Law. It has to be thus so that the ethnē can participate in it. But both the faithfulness of God to Israel and God's redemptive act through Christ testify to the character of the God of Israel. It seems that the Roman ethnē in Christ were tempted to set the one in opposition to the other, leading them to doubt God's own righteousness so that for the only time in his letters here Paul has to assert that God himself is δίκαιος (righteous). This contrasted strongly with the perceived arbitrariness of the Roman deities, revealing another aspect of the Creator God of Israel.

Christ, the Gift of Reconciliation and Peace

Romans 3:25-26

How does the revelation of God's rectifying power, that is, his commitment, become effective? Keeping in view the specific (gentile) context here, we should preferably ask, "How is reconciliation to be achieved?" Paul continues to expand here (cf. also Rom. 5:1-11) the meaning of God's δικαιοσύνη, and since in 3:22 he does not restate the verb, it is best to add the phrase "is being revealed" (in parallel with 1:16-17) to give the reading "the righteousness of God is being revealed through the faithfulness of Jesus Christ for all who trust" (Rodriguez 2014: 78–9). Though the term ἱλαστήριον is a *hapax legomenon*, that is, unique in Paul's letters (used elsewhere only in Heb. 9:5, clearly referring to the lid or cover of the ark of the covenant, *kapporet*), it is a frequent term in the LXX. Here the term ἱλαστήριον occurs more than twenty times, in six separate passages (Exod. 25:16-21; Num. 7:89; Lev. 16:2-20; Ezek. 43:13-21; Amos. 9:1; 1 Chron. 28:11) where it always means "cover" or some related architectural term.[8] It can also metaphorically connote the place of revelation in terms of God's presence and the place where he speaks (e.g., Exod. 25:22). Rillera claims that "*hilasterion denotes the place of revelation both in terms of Divine presence and the place where God speaks.*"[9]

The interpretive tradition here sees a connection between sacrificial terminology and the death of Christ. However, ἱλαστήριον in the LXX does not refer to any sacrifice, and the link to Leviticus 16 and the ritual of atonement does not involve the death of the animal. The method of dealing with iniquities does not involve the goat being killed, but the Israelites' sins are placed upon the head of the goat, which is then sent into the wilderness. The blood sprinkled on the *kapporet* in the context of the Yom Kippur ritual has a purifying, rather than a sacrificial, function.

Stowers rightly suggests that "blood" refers to Jesus dying a martyr's death, and that this contention is more plausible than that of positing a traditional link with Leviticus

---

[8] This usage comes by virtue of the fact that ἱλαστήριον derives from the verb ἱλάσκομαι ("conciliate, seek the favor of"), which shares the same lexical root as the verb ἐχιλάσκομαι ("expiate"), employed to translate the Hebrew verb *kipper* ("wipe clean"), "perform rites of expiation" and sharing the same lexical root as the noun *kapporet*, the lid on the ark of the covenant (of the righteous judgment of God). Cf. Glaim (2014: 177–9).

[9] See Rillera 2021.

16 (1994: 210). Since neither ἀπολυτρώσις, redemption, nor λύτρον, ransom, appear in Leviticus 16, there is no verbal connection with 3:25 (21-26). What is telling is that Paul did not choose a word sequence that indicates a reference to Leviticus 16.

Also, Christ as ἱλαστήριον appears, as noted, only here in Paul—it is a unique reference—which, since it is a significant one, it is strange that it does not appear elsewhere, nor in a related scripture cited (Stowers 1994: 213). From this, we can assume that Paul did not consider his attributed meaning of ἱλαστήριον to be dependent on Leviticus 16. Since the *kapporet* was no longer a part of the cultic furniture of the Second Temple, Paul could only be making an *historical reference* to it here, and one that would not be very clear to his gentile audience who would require an allusion that would resonate with their own traditions or experience.

What must be noted is that the older view that Paul addressed a mixed audience of Jewish and non-Jewish Christ-followers gave more significance to a Leviticus connection than would be warranted if he were addressing here, as is stated, a gentile audience to whom he wishes to communicate *the meaning for them* of Christ's death. Given that Jewish tradition does not offer a viable connection at this point, it seems best to look to the context of the Greco-Roman world for analogies and explanations (Collins 2019: 273–86, 285). It should be noted that we are not here prioritizing Roman mythology over against scriptural allusion to Leviticus. Our stance is that Paul wished to give an explanation of Christ's faithfulness both in life and in death (Longenecker 2011: 322) that would illuminate the Roman ethnē's understanding, particularly of the role of the God of Israel.

Our perspective is thus dominated by the view that Paul is seeking to explain the meaning of the Christ to a gentile audience influenced by Roman imperial ideology, rather than linking back to the probable Jewish source of his own convictions. This reading does not mean a departure from Jewish traditions, but only a change in perspective in a process of cultural translation of these for the sake of the gospel. *We hold that Paul's language and discourse are decisively indebted to the Jewish Greek resistance discourse, a narrative tradition of belonging that frames and shapes all aspects of Paul's understanding of the Christ-event* (on this, see section "The Gospel as an Alternative to Roman Imperial Ideology" in the chapter "Romans 1"). Furthermore, we also agree that "rather than only emerging with the Christ-event, it has been argued that the understanding of the Christ-event actually emerges from this alternative tradition" (Ehrensperger 2013: 219). Here we have an example of Paul's ingenuity in translating an element emerging from Jewish Greek tradition into the cultural context of his Roman addressees. Paul clearly recognizes the foreignness of his message to Greeks and seeks a means to bridge the gap in understanding. How would the Greek-speaking Romans have heard the term ἱλαστήριον with which Paul sought to convey the meaning of the Christ-event is the important issue?

What becomes clear in cultural translation of a living tradition is that to repeat this in identical terminology or even simply in its grammatical equivalent is not necessarily to communicate the message that has to be transferred. Umberto Eco takes an example of translating Shakespeare's *Hamlet* from English into Italian. He notes that whereas in English, French, German, and Spanish the term "rat" refers to a small animal of which people are frightened, this is different in Italian. Thus, to translate "rat" with "ratto" would miss Shakespeare's point entirely, and hence to arrive at the same effect "rat" has to be "translated" as mouse "topo," the animal that would cause Italians to be frightened. Eco claims that the context as well as the actual term itself will help in the negotiation of the transfer of the intended meaning from one linguistic base to another in order to decide which part of the expressed content is strictly pertinent in that given context (Eco 2003: 32–4). Thus, Paul is concerned to convey the meaning of Christ's death in terms that his targeted audience, a gentile one, will understand without difficulty. It is not surprising, therefore, that the imagery of military operations such as warfare, weapons, truce, and the making of peace commends itself to him for use in his explanation. Some such thinking may lie behind his choice of presenting the Christ as a ἱλαστήριον.

"Conciliation" might be a possible rendering of Paul's thought, bearing in mind his gentile audience, and the enmity of the gentile world noted in 1:19-32. This would accord with Glaim's view that the ordinary Greek usage comes closest to Paul's use, giving the meaning of "conciliation," which, in his opinion, "fits the context and the wider Greek usage perfectly" (2014: 183–6). In relation to the latter, Daniel Bailey notes the occurrence of the term ἱλαστήριον on monuments, statues, stelae, and tripods dedicated to the gods and discusses Dio Chrysostom's reference to the Trojan horse as a ἱλαστήριον intended to conciliate the goddess Athena (2000: 151–8). Since the term ἱλαστήριον is unique in Paul's writing, it is difficult to be sure of the meaning he intended by its use in 3:25. But recent investigation of ἱλαστήριον in Greek inscriptions might suggest another resonance in Romans. Altars found at the Asian city of Metropolis in the 1990s probably refer to the altar (ὁ βωμός) of Octavian "Caesar, the bringer of reconciliation," *Kaisaros eilasteriou* (cf. Wilson 2017). It is possible that Paul deliberately chose to explain the role of Christ as bringer of (re)conciliation in contrast to the role ascribed publicly to the Caesar. So this might indicate that Jesus Christ represents for Paul both the presence of God and the gift of reconciliation.

Memories of the Maccabean martyrs and also of the Trojan horse episode, itself a tangible gesture of conciliation (although used deceptively), would assist the reception of Paul's message about God's action in Christ for his designated gentile audience. For Jews after the Maccabean period, there would be a resonance with the exemplars of noble deaths offered in service of their own people. But the martyr's death for others has here nothing to do with sacrifice or the Temple cult (Stowers 1994: 212, cf. also McMurray 2021: 212).

Recently, McMurray also argues convincingly that ἱλαστήριον is best understood in Greco-Roman usages, pointing to a conciliatory gift, and that this conciliation carries a strong ethnic dimension (2021: 67). More specifically, he argues that Paul's use of ἱλαστήριον refers to a conciliatory gift at the end of a conflict, meaning that Christ was set forth as conciliatory gift ἱλαστήριον in the truce of God. "This view of ἱλαστήριον— as revolving around the idea of cessation of conflict—fits with Paul's themes of cosmic conflict, the anger of God, and of course the opposite of conflict, namely the recurring theme of peace" (2021: 68). The presence of the words δωρεάν, gift, ἱλαστήριον, conciliation, and ἀνοχή, truce, in the same sentence strongly supports this reading of ἱλαστήριον as a conciliatory gift upon the cessation of conflict, that is, an amnesty as Tamez (1993) has suggested. The traditional rendering of ἀνοχή as "forbearance" is inadequate. This translation omits entirely its primary military dimension (McMurray 2021: 72, cf. also 47–50). The only occurrences of the term are here and in 2:4. The primary meaning of ἀνοχή relates to the holding back or to the stopping of hostilities; thus the terms armistice and truce are both indicated in this primary definition (2021: 68–9). It has been established in 1:19-32 that punishment is deserved but that God generously, and indeed as a revelatory act "to show his righteousness" (3:25), has called a truce between himself (God) and "gentiles," who are currently acting as slaves of sin. Paul also uses the word πάρεσις, letting go, or remission of debts. In 3:25, Paul states that God has let these preceding sins go, implying the sequence of already letting the preceding sins go, and then putting Jesus forward as a ἱλαστήριον, granting a truce or armistice. Christ is here recognized as a ransom, or price of release (cf. ἀπολύτρωσις, 3:24). The terminology here would easily conjure up for Paul's audience images of prisoners of war being ransomed or of slaves being set free.

Christ, in this perspective, is thus a ransom for the release of captives in the establishment of a truce or cessation of hostilities. For this purpose, he can be described as "handed over" (παρεδόθη, 4:25) to death for our trespasses … in a dynamic of prisoner ransom or exchange (contra Romans 1 where people were "handed over" to impurity and the passions whereas Jesus is handed over to death). God's actions here serve as illustration of his characteristics, that is, suggest a peace-making characteristic of God. In the latter, ἀνοχή refers clearly to a characteristic of God alongside kindness and patience. This conception fits well with the revelation of divine righteousness, and the idea of God granting an armistice fits appropriately here, as well as the idea of ransoming, or exchanging prisoners of war.

Thus, the term ἱλαστήριον resonates with a number of notions in a metaphorical way such as martyr's death, conciliatory gift, and ransom paid in release of prisoners of war. The context of these images in Greek and Roman tradition is a truce, that is, the end of enmity and beginning of peace. Paul evokes these images to explicate the meaning of the Christ event particularly for ethnē without providing one exclusive conceptualized meaning. This is the reason for our not translating this term.

This conciliation carries a strong ethnic implication in the sense that, as ethnē are conciliated to God through Christ, this means that ethnē do not mistakenly try to achieve righteousness through works of the Law, thereby maintaining ethnic distinction. Living in the Law is reserved for the Jews to whom it has been given as guidance that constitutes them as a people, and so they can respond in trust to the call of God.

Romans 3:27-31: Drawing Accurate Inferences from the Revelation of God's Rectifying Power in Christ

[27]Where then is boasting? It is excluded. By what (reading of the) law? That of works? No, through the law of trust. [28]For we reckon a person to be set right through trust apart from works of law. [29]Or is God the God of Jews only? No, the God of ethnē also, [30]since God is one; and he will set right the circumcision from trust and the foreskin through this trust. [31]Do we then neutralize the law by this trust? Far from it. On the contrary, we establish the law.

In view of Paul's emphatic argument in 3:21-26, that God's rectifying power through reconciliation in Christ is being revealed, the interlocutor introduces a question immediately succeeding Paul's declaration, "Where then is boasting?" And follows this with another, "By means of what reading of the Law? One of works?" Paul in his own voice gives the answer, "No, but by means of Torah understood through trust" (as Rodriguez translates). Paul continues, including himself in the response, "For we reckon a person is rectified by trust quite apart from works of Law" (3:28). The alternative would necessitate, in Paul's words, "Or is God [the God] of Jews only?" The interlocutor confirms the implied response to Paul's question, "No, [God] also of the nations." Paul affirms this and gives his rationale based on the Shema (Deut. 6:4-9), "since God is one, and will rectify the circumcision by trust and the foreskin through trust."[10] In view of Paul's statement, the interlocutor infers, "Do we, then, nullify the Law by our trust?" and Paul gives his typical categorical response, "Far from it" (μὴ γένοιτο) followed by his comment "on the contrary, we establish the Law." The strong patterned rejection of any suggestion that Paul opposes the Law is indicative in our opinion of some of the issues current in Rome about which he is informed. The conclusion possibly has been drawn, since Paul teaches that the ἀκροβυστία, the uncircumcision can be accepted by God "apart from the Law," that thus the Law itself has been rendered redundant (cf. καταργοῦμεν, 3:31). Some have wrongly inferred that the Law has been superseded. But Paul's sharp repudiation opens the way to ch. 4 in which it is asserted that instead of the Law being annulled by the gospel, its role is in fact, established, ἱστάνομεν, as Paul will demonstrate in the case of Abraham.

The main inference that can be drawn from 3:21-26 is that since acceptance of non-Jews by God is now possible through reconciliation by Christ apart from the Law, then for non-Jews to take on the yoke of the Law is both fruitless and misguided. Since reconciliation with God comes apart from "the Law," then for non-Jews to try to gain acceptance with God by doing the "works of the Law" in order to become Jews is a wrong route to their desired goal.

It is important to note that the reference to boasting links back to the apostrophe in 2:17-24 where the proselyte teacher boasts in the Law and in his knowledge of God. Paul's response was to affirm that while circumcision indeed is of value to Jews and represents the blessing of the covenant that offers this advantage, nevertheless the entire world lies under the power of sin. Now that Christ has come, what is required for non-Jews is not a program by which they could become Jews, but the reconciliation that God has achieved through Christ and trust in him. Crucial to Paul's gospel is that the deliberate and unatoned for sin of those from the nations cannot be overcome by taking on the yoke of the Law. This commitment has indeed the opposite effect in that the Law only brings judgment and condemnation despite gentile attempts to keep its guidance (as Paul will go on to demonstrate in 7:7-25). Only God's action in Christ Jesus can enable the rectifying power of God through trust to reach sinful ethnē and

---

[10] It is possible that the differing readings, "from trust" ἐκ πίστεως, for the circumcision, and "through trust" διὰ τῆς πίστεως, for the uncircumcision, are meant simply to avoid repetition of the same preposition, but it is also possible as Stowers suggests that Paul intends ongoing differentiation (1994: 241).

to enable the fulfillment in them of the δικαιῶμα, requirement, of the Law through the Spirit.

Paul's anti-boasting reading of the revealing of God's rectifying power thus seems to channel the discussion away from ethnic issues toward a repudiation of a boasting in human achievement, at least this is the typical post-Reformation reading of grace/faith versus works discourse. Rodriguez, however, rightly determines the meaning of boasting not from its normal negative English use but from a study of its use in the LXX, where he notes that the term boasting, καύχησις, bears a positive nuance in nine out of its ten occurrences indicating something like "glory" or "honor," especially in relation to the divine name. As Rodriguez notes, "So, when the interlocutor asks, Where, then, is boasting? he is asking a question about the positive benefits of observing Torah, i.e. 'Where, then, is the value, the beauty of me, a proselyte-observing Torah?'" (2016: 86). This is similar to "the boast" that Jews regard as legitimate, that is, boasting in God or the name of God. But the proselyte has not understood that he cannot boast in circumcision or in his keeping of the Law. The Jewish boast consists not in what they do as Jews, but in giving honor to the God of Israel who called Abraham and gave him promises. It is in the divine initiative that Israel boasts, not her response to this. But in the typical gentile (mis)understanding, the emphasis falls upon activities to please the gods in order to receive their blessing. In this, doing and giving precede the desired blessing, whereas in Jewish tradition the call of God is the foundation of all blessing and requires a positive response.

In Romans, as in any discussion where the distinctive ethnic qualities and cultures of differing people are in interaction, it would be quite easy to play off the cultural and social capital and traditions of each against the other. This would constitute boasting as the word is used in normal English today. But if we take into account the LXX emphasis of καύχησις as value, glory, and so on (cf. Rodriguez 201: 86-8), then it is possible to see another nuance here in that it can refer to what one brings to life of value from a particular group in society (2016: 86-8). In this respect, we need to review our understanding of how we interpret 3:1-2, the advantage of the Jew and the value of his circumcision. To acknowledge value is not equivalent to boasting as traditionally understood in English. However, the proselyte interlocutor of 2:17 misunderstands the value of being a Jew when he "calls [himself] a Jew, relies on the law and boasts of [his] relation to God." The social capital of Jewish tradition, that is, the social outcomes of living by God's law, easily comes to mind, and New Testament scholars have traditionally been alert to challenge any boasting about what might be thought to accrue some merit before God. But Paul's argument is that *nothing* we bring with us merits acceptance with God, acceptance with God comes *only by the call of God*, not by human meritorious qualities. The typical Roman boasting originates from emphasizing the works they had done to relate properly to the gods. Proper Jewish boasting, on the other hand, is boasting in the goodness of God in his grace rather than on what Jews have done in response. It is the God of Israel's qualities rather than those of his people that are to be acknowledged and honored. Thus, Paul traces the advantage of being a Jew back to the call of Abraham who was called by God and responded in trust to that call. Jewish tradition built upon that call is a fruit of faithfulness resulting from trust, not a pattern of Law-keeping to please the gods, but rather a thankful response to the

God of Israel's grace, his freely offered favor, and ongoing interaction in grace. For the ethnē, however, in Paul's gospel this can only happen through the grace of God now freely offered in Christ.

So the Reformation critique of works of law, though it has often been criticized for its anti-Jewish outcomes, was not entirely misguided. It was correct in its opposition to human achievements as the pathway to acceptance with God. But in Romans, it missed the targeting of Paul's critiques to the ethnē rather than to Jews. Due to the fact that this letter is addressed to non-Jews, its content cannot be transferred to Jews who are not addressed, especially as it thereby deflects attention away from the self-righteousing tendencies of the ethnē in Rome, including their boasting over Jews (11:17-24). What makes the exigency at Rome more complicated is the fact that some of the ethnē wrongly take up the Jewish pattern of life, not recognizing that the Law is the possession and obligation of the Jews only, and that they are not Jews. Moreover, the gentile person taking up Jewish patterns with a view to making themselves right with God is then open to the just condemnation of Paul that no one can be justified by works of Law (3:20) as these ethnē were seeking to do.

Conclusion to Romans 3:27-31

Paul appears here to refute a typical *gentile* misunderstanding that performing rituals achieves acceptance with the gods (cf. Josephus *Ap.* 2:247-249) and overcomes sinful status.[11] This may be the focus of the claim in 3:27, "But we hold that a person is rectified by trust apart from works of Law." The non-Jews in keeping with the pattern of relating to the gods, presumed they had to do something to please the gods, thus regarding their attempt to keep the Law as the way to please the God of Israel, and thus rectify their relation with him. It is in this performance of "works of law" that they boast and thus they failed to recognize that the Law was a gift to the people of Israel. The proselyte in 2:17 mistakenly boasts in circumcision and the Law, and other distinguishing Jewish attributes, (and) thereby shows his double misunderstanding. But it must be kept clearly before us that we are here referring to a proselyte's misunderstanding in a diatribal construction, not to Paul's own stated view of Jewish tradition. As Stowers comments (in relation to 2:17-29—the one who calls himself a Jew), "It is grossly misleading to generalize this fictitious address to a critique of Judaism" (1994: 144).

The traditional reading of 3:27-31 arises from the presupposition that the fundamental issue in the reception of Paul's letters is how a human being can find acceptance with God. The assumption is that Paul reacts against a Jewish view that righteousness is attainable by keeping the Law—hence good works. Whether to Jew or non-Jew, it is perfectly clear that Paul opposes any such mistaken perception. In our exegesis of Romans 1-3, we have found that the text itself offers no proper basis for such a conclusion concerning this mistakenly assumed view of Jewish practice. Instead, it opposes a proselyte view of attaining acceptance with God through teaching the ethnē to take on the obligations of keeping the Law, and thereby establish through their ἔργα,

---

[11] Philo warns that proselytes are at risk of using language and concepts that they had learned (and that are wrong) in relation to the one God (*Spec.* 1:53).

works, a relationship with God. For Jews by birth, the ἔργα are their response to God's grace by which he had called them to be his people. If it is misguided to teach non-Jews to take on the obligations of the Law, does this not necessitate the view that the Law is the exclusive possession of Jews, and the resultant question whether God is therefore the God of Jews only? and its sequel, "Is he not the God of ethnē also?" (3:29).

As we have noted, Paul responds to this question on the basis of the Shema, which affirms the oneness of the "God of Israel" who thus is also the God of the nations (Nanos 1996). He will go on to develop this explicitly in 4:9-22. So Paul's question is not one about human beings finding acceptance with God (though it includes this), but a particular issue, "If the God of Israel is truly God, is he not the God of both Jews and 'gentiles,' and how can this work in practice?" This is Paul's fundamental question, raised specifically by the revelation of God's rectifying power in Christ, and it is inherently and unavoidably ethnic as this discussion evidences and assumes; as Thiessen argues, only a miracle should transform the gentile person, a sinner by nature (Thiessen 2016: 149), which (nature) requires to be reconstructed through the Spirit (McMurray 2021: 159–68). If "gentiles" were to become Jews, God would be the God of Jews only; it is only by both maintaining their respective identity is it affirmed that God is God of Israel and the nations.

Romans 3:31 The Law Is Established When the Ethnē Trust in Christ

As noted above, one ethnic outcome emerges already in 3:31. Even though the revelation in Christ takes place "apart from the Law" (3:21), and the ethnē do not need and cannot successfully take up the Law in order to find acceptance with God, in acknowledging these factors Paul forcefully denies that the Law is thereby nullified or rendered meaningless. On the contrary, the function of the Law is confirmed when it is properly understood through trust. If Paul had stated that the Law died, it would be interpreted as constituting an anti-Jewish claim, even though he was writing only for non-Jews. Instead, he claims that the proper meaning and function of the Law is upheld by trust in Christ, a nuanced understanding of the role of Law in relation to non-Jews, which we hold is typical of his stance throughout Romans. By this we mean that though non-Jews are not required to practice the Law, what the Law requires can be fulfilled in them through faith in Christ and thus its role is established ἱστάνομεν (Rodriguez 2016: 88). Christ is instrumental to the fulfilling of the Law via the Spirit.

Paul's confirmation of the role of the Law has relevance in the Roman context (cf. 13:9). A wrong inference could have been drawn by ethnē assured that they do not need to accept circumcision or the yoke of the Law, that is, that the Law is dead and can be ignored without any inhibition. Paul probably knows via reports from his friends in Rome that some gentile Christ-followers are already prone to err in that direction, and he refuses to encourage that "lawless" tendency in any way (cf. 3:8, 4:7, and 6:19). His claim to uphold the Law indicates not only his own personal conviction but also his deep concern not to misrepresent the relation of his own tradition to the Christ-event and thus cause misunderstanding among his fellow Jews. Moreover, he is deeply concerned not to give gentile Christ-followers any cause for misunderstanding or criticizing Jewish life and traditions. Elliott considers that one of the "obstacles"

Romans is designed to address is "a perspective on the Torah as an ethnic peculiarity, at best an obsolete and irrelevant system of obligations, at worst a system for recording transgressions through which Israel has merited God's judgment" (2007: 279). Paul, himself a Pharisee, is very cautious in discussions concerning the Law in Romans, and he is careful not to allow the Law to be seen as temporary, or even as nullified, with a corresponding effect on the status of Jews and Jewish tradition.

What must not be overlooked is that the Law is given by God to guide his people Israel. It is revered as God's Law and Israel's particular guidance, part of their God-given self-understanding. In this sense, it thus constitutes a boundary issue between Israel and the nations. The Law, therefore, is both an ethnic and a theological issue since it belongs to Israel and not to the nations. But its scope is universal in that it is spiritual and reflects God's will for Israel and his creation. As such, it has a different meaning for Israel and the nations, respectively. Although to propose the reconciliation of the ethnē independently and apart from (χωρίς) the Law (3:21), as Paul has announced in 3:21-26, looks as if the boundary between Israel and the nations has been abolished, this is not so as he strongly denies μὴ γένοιτο, "far from it." The Law has neither been abolished for Israel, nor is it irrelevant for the ethnē. Through Christ it will be fulfilled in them through the Spirit. Hence Paul's gospel and gentile mission do not abolish, but rather establish the Law in 3:31. Reconciliation in Christ and the Law do not stand in opposition to each other.

Romans 4

Romans 4:1-8: Abraham, the Forefather "According to the Flesh" of Those Ἐν ἀκροβυστία?

¹*What then? Do we claim to have found Abraham [to be] our forefather according to the flesh?* ²*For if Abraham was justified by works, he would have a boast, but not before God.* ³*For what does the scripture say? "Abraham trusted God, and it was reckoned to him as righteousness."* ⁴*Now to the one who works, the pay is not reckoned as a gift but as something owed.* ⁵*But to the one who without works trusts him who sets right the impious, his trust is reckoned as righteousness.* ⁶*Just as also David pronounces the blessing upon the person to whom God reckons righteousness apart from works:* ⁷*Blessed are those whose iniquities are forgiven, and whose sins are covered;* ⁸*blessed is the one against whom the Lord will not reckon sin.*

Introduction

The framing of the question that introduces Romans 4 puts the emphasis on what "we," that is, Paul, his imagined gentile interlocutor, and the Roman audience, have found rather than on what Abraham himself discovered about God. The character of God is in view here in that Rom. 4:2 links back to the previous section, 3:27-31, via the theme of boasting. It is not a question as in historic debates about faith and works, about *how one may earn God's favor*; since God is one, boasting in God as the God of Jews only, as follows from the proselyte's stance (cf. 2:17-24), contrasts sharply with the affirmation that God is the God of the Jews but *now also of the nations.*

We have found that the diatribal pattern with dialogical elements emerges again in the questions and answers given after 3:26, and continues in ch. 4:1-2a (and 4:9-12). This is followed by Paul's supporting arguments in 4:2b-8, (Stowers, 1981: 171; cf. also Witherington 2004: 119, Song 2004: 97). Thus, after the declaratory argument in 3:21-26, which recapitulated the theme of 1:13-17, followed by the dialogical section in 3:27-29, where ethnic issues are central, Paul's interlocutor asks in 4:1 "What then shall we say?" τί οὖν ἐροῦμεν. "Have we ['gentiles'] found Abraham [to be] our forefather according to the flesh?"

I understand Paul to respond to this question by an answer in the negative (Hays 1985: 76–98; Grieb 2002: 46), which would normally be, μὴ γένοιτο, "far from it." But here the negation is not so explicit, "for if it had been on the basis of works, Abraham would have a boast *but not before God*" (4:2). The latter phrase indicates Paul's negative response introduced by ἀλλά (Stowers 1981: 165, n41). The response then continues, "For what does the scripture say?" proceeding to the relevant scriptural *exemplum* or proof (168–71).[1] Although I agree with Stowers generally, I disagree that the discussion here is with a fictitious Jewish teacher (Stowers 1994: 231–4), I hold that the interlocutor is consistent and non-Jewish throughout.

It has to be borne in mind that the "we" in Rom. 4:1 represents the gentile Christ-followers speaking via the interlocutor, continuing from 3:27-31. Stowers interprets 4:1-25 as the *exemplum* that ensued from Paul's argument (inclusive of the μὴ γένοιτο formula) in 3:27–4:2 (1981: 155–74). The identification of the speaker depends largely on how the opening question is interpreted. Following from the reading emanating from Theodor Zahn (1910: 212–19) and developed mainly by Hays, Grieb, and others, we take the question to be "Have we found Abraham (to be) our forefather according to the flesh?" We note that here the issue is not what Abraham himself found, but what, on the basis of scriptural exegesis, he has been found (εὑρηκέναι) to be. This claim is introduced (as are also chs. 3, 4, and 6 and with slight variation) with the characteristic τί οὖν ἐροῦμεν, "what then shall we say?" We have noted already that this formula occurs at major breaks between/within chapters at 4:1, 6:1, 7:7, 8:31, and 9:14. In the six instances in Romans in which the formula occurs (4:1, 6:1, 7:7, 8:31, 9:14, 9:30),[2] in every instance except at 8:31, this phrase stands alone as a complete sentence. Moreover, in every case the question posed is rhetorical, and in nearly every case, the follow-up question presents a false inference to which Paul explicitly objects (Hays 1985: 78–9, Garroway 2012: 103). The pattern is observed even when Paul uses the similar, abbreviated expression τί οὖν as, for example, in 3:9 and 6:15.

Romans 4:1

As already noted in 3:1-8, and in Excursus I, the recurring phrase τί οὖν ἐροῦμεν, "What then shall we say?" is indicative of major stages in the construction of Romans. This recurring summary response in question form to what precedes, in the form of another question, gives us some idea of Paul's argumentative process in the letter. As noted, this construction signals that Abraham's paternity is likely to be one of the significant issues at Rome (though the form of the actual question here is not typically Pauline). Rodriguez translates Rom. 4:1 as "What then? Shall we claim to have found Abraham (to be) our forefather according to the flesh?" (2014: 89, n51). He takes the first question to be τί οὖν, what then? This means that the following ἐροῦμεν "shall we say" is separated from the τί οὖν to begin the second question ("Shall we claim to have found …?"). On balance, though Rodriguez is in broad agreement, I prefer Richard B. Hays's translation because this fits better with Paul's rhetorical pattern

---

[1] In ancient rhetorical theory, the *paradeigma or exemplum* was treated as a kind of rhetorical proof (Stowers 1981: 171).
[2] Here we reiterate some of the arguments put forward in Excursus I, and also on "Paul's Dialogical Pattern" (Romans 3).

elsewhere in Romans (though τί οὖν is also possible, since it is Paul's normal way of introducing a false inference). In contrast to the RSV translation, Hays translates, "What then shall we say? Have we found Abraham [to be] our forefather according to the flesh?" (2005: 61–4; cf. Fredriksen 2017: 243, n42). Though Paul offers no answer to this question, Hays and Grieb insist it would have to be a repudiation. Even though the actual expression μὴ γένοιτο is missing here, I find this proposal fits my expectation of how Paul might respond (contra Garroway 2012: 101–10). The response given here is not as explicit as elsewhere, but the concluding phrase in 4:2, "but not before God" indicates Paul's negative stance.

Thus, despite their new Abrahamic lineage, the "father" who ultimately counts for these ethnē is not Abraham but "God" (Fredriksen 2017: 151). But this cannot mean that Abraham has not in some sense (i.e., through Christ and the Spirit) become the father of ethnē in Christ since they are now his σπέρμα. Paul could have reacted more sharply, but he seems to explore the issue in a balanced way. He avoids making a categorical statement that entirely denies the worth of any fleshly connection with Abraham, which for Paul as a Jew is absolutely essential. Opposing this connection would render him antithetical to Jewish tradition, and point the ethnē in an Israel-critical direction, which they are already too prone to pursue. Paul relates the gentile interlocutor to the heritage of Abraham, while simultaneously retaining positive recognition of the status of Abraham for Israel in Jewish tradition. The question that the interlocutor puts here in the first-person plural, representing Roman ethnē, would not anticipate an answer in the affirmative from Paul. In Paul's perspective, ethnē in Christ do not have a fleshly connection with Abraham (pace Garroway 2012: 83–6), though Paul does present Abraham as trusting in God "who rectifies the impious" (τὸν δικαιοῦντα τὸν ἀσεβῆ, 4:5). Thus, we take the course of the argument here to be that it is the interlocutor, representing the Roman ethnē, who asks the question in 4:1.

The implied inference of how non-Jews should relate to Abraham in 4:1 is one that Paul is going to refute. But for proselytes, or potential proselytes, circumcision did seem to offer a possible fleshly connection with the patriarch, who like them was circumcised as an adult, and so Abraham could be (somewhat surprisingly), presented as ungodly, that is, as a non-Jew. Paul's argument is that for both Jews and non-Jews, trust is the way. Thus, a negative response is required to the question whether Abraham is the forefather, *propater* (Metzger 1971: 450), of non-Jews κατὰ σάρκα "according to the flesh." He was considered to have been the first proselyte, but now that the revelation of God's rectifying power is revealed to include the nations as non-Jews, the fleshly connection with Abraham for ethnē would be contrary to this end-time revelation. Through the Spirit, it is God, not Abraham that these ethnē—like their older brother Jesus, and like ethnic Israel—can now call "Father." As Stowers states, "Paul's goal for his mainly gentile communities was to ground them in the heritage of Abraham not as Jews but as legitimate heirs of the promises" (1994: 249).

The manner in which Abraham is introduced here probably reflects contemporary debates about proselyte affiliation with Abraham rather than the value of eighth-day Jewish circumcision of sons. Thus, it is not an issue for Jews but specifically one for non-Jews. Stephen Young speaks of the "ethnic nature of this deity." The God of Abraham from the point of view of Paul's audience was "the Judean god," since Egyptians and others had their own ethnic god or gods. Young goes on to claim that "righteousness for Gentiles comes through Christ's πίστις, the faithfulness of a representative figure who causes others to participate in the Judean god's ethnically-coded eschatological blessings apart from the law." He describes this as "gentile inclusive law-authorized ethnic logic" (2015: 31, n3; 44; 51). The fact that for non-Jews in Rome this God would have been regarded as the God of the Jews alerts us to the interethnic implications of the Pauline gospel and apostleship to the nations.

For those non-Jews who followed the pattern of Abraham's turning from idols, a very serious issue was how Jewish these converts should become, especially with reference to avoidance of idolatry. To claim affiliation with the great forefather Abraham would have been inviting in terms of ascription of honor thus ennobling their particular identity in potential contrast with Aeneas (Esler 2003: 187, 189). But what actually constitutes a meaningful paternity in Abraham would be rather unclear, bearing in mind his status in Jewish tradition. Fredriksen reminds us that ethnicity included the gods who with people formed family groups, and the strange thing from a gentile point of view was that though having turned to the God of Israel, they are still *not* Israel, and thus not answerable to the Jewish Law (2017: 117–18). So, the question of how the gentile Christ-followers relate to Abraham is important, especially since Paul is adamant that they are not to be regarded as becoming Jews. Abraham cannot become their biological father, nor should it be anticipated that they could call him father. Abraham is presented as leaving his "father's house" in Genesis, and in this and other instances, it is God who takes the place of the lost parent. The Hebrew Bible assumes a unique dependence of the special people upon God (Levinson 2012: 213–14).

What then is the value of non-Jews claiming Abraham's paternity? Bearing in mind the mistaken understanding of the proselyte who boasts in the Law and in his relation to God (2:17), Paul wants to make sure that this "person" will not make the same mistake in boasting in Abrahamic connection. If the proselyte views Abraham as one who achieved great merit and was therefore accepted by God, this in Paul's view would be to completely misinterpret Abraham. Thus Paul continues the discussion against boasting begun in 3:27-31 as the immediate corollary of unmerited grace and does this to ensure that Abraham is not perceived by gentile Christ followers within a "payback system," a pattern of work and due reward (Harrison 2020: 167), but as the pioneer of trust (thus the inference in 4:1 is not one drawn from Paul's own position but is a continuation of the argument he wants to refute). Paul's argument is scripturally based—he cites a key text Gen. 15:6 (LXX): "Abraham trusted God, and it was reckoned to him for righteousness." The scriptural citation serves two functions, linking ethnē in Christ to the scriptures of Israel and providing authority for his arguments. Paul puts primary emphasis upon Abraham's trusting πιστεύω rather than his *working*—ἐργάζομαι.

The scriptural narrative demonstrates that it was not the case that Abraham's circumcision resulted in rectification, but rather that rectification was credited to him because he trusted in the one Creator God. Along with the Genesis narrative concerning Abraham, Paul further adds a Psalm citation concerning David, which provides him with a reference to how sin was dealt with in Jewish tradition. In Jewish scriptural interpretation, there was a common pattern called *gezerah shewah* in which two passages containing a particular word in common are placed alongside one another, the one aiding in the interpretation of the other. Paul is, especially, interested in the words, "Blessed are those whose iniquities are forgiven, and whose sins are covered; blessed is the one against whom the Lord will not reckon sin" (4:7-8). The verb λογίζομαι, to reckon, is a favorite term for Paul (he repeats it nine times in this passage). It typifies his argument that one either lives in a "work and wages" relation or, as Paul stresses, a "trust and credit" system. The latter is what Paul finds demonstrated in the case of Abraham. Thus, in his view, it is therefore a misapprehension to use Abraham primarily as indicative of how non-Jews can find acceptance with God by circumcision and living a Torah-guided pattern of life.

Romans 4:9-12: "Not Only but Also, οὐ μόνον ἄλλα καὶ" Paul's Inclusive Argument

⁹Is this blessing, then, upon the circumcision, or also upon the foreskin? For we say, "The trust was reckoned to Abraham as righteousness." ¹⁰How then was it reckoned? In circumcision? Or in foreskin? Not (in) circumcision but in foreskin. ¹¹And he received the sign of circumcision, a seal of the righteousness through trust while in the foreskin, that he might become the father of all who trust while in foreskin that righteousness might be reckoned to them, ¹²and the father of circumcision not only to those who are circumcised but who also follow in the steps of the trust that our ancestor Abraham had when he was in foreskin.

Because this chapter has traditionally been viewed as addressing both Jews and ethnē in Christ, the relative value of Jewish circumcision has been assumed to be an issue, but such a view is not supported in the text (the value of Jewish circumcision was confirmed in 3:1-2). This is clear when one notes the frequent occurrences of ἀκροβυστία, foreskin/uncircumcision, in 4:9-12. In the history of interpretation, the sequence of events in Abraham's life has been taken as demonstrating the relative value of circumcision in comparison with trust as if Paul were seeking to evaluate whether circumcision has any value or indeed any (universal) significance, that is, for anyone who trusts in the God of Israel. But Paul is not promoting an open debate about circumcision generally, but only about the significance of Abraham as an uncircumcised man of trust. Thus, 4:9-12 is not an open discussion about the value of circumcision for the abstract human, but rather a very specific discussion of the value of circumcision for non-Jewish Christ followers (as distinct from what could only be a retrospective evaluation of what was normal in the Jewish eighth-day circumcision pattern). As noted, the fact that Abraham's trust and circumcision are explicitly discussed here probably resonates with ongoing discussions in Rome, possibly concerning the issue of the validity and significance of proselyte conversion.

Thus, ἀκροβυστία *here* indicates a specific concern for those from the nations, an ethnic category that certainly is not neutral or a non-issue for Paul. Abraham was accepted by God as a non-Jew through his trust. He was justified when he was "in foreskin," so "foreskin" need not be a problem. However, the temporal reading (stressing the timing of Abraham's circumcision), and the presupposition that Paul is commenting on how circumcision relates to justification generally, seem to push this ethnic awareness into the background and cause scholarship that views ethnic issues as central to be regarded as peripheral. This has been encouraged by the mistaken emphasis that Paul's gospel is anti-ethnic, as if difference itself were the cause of sin. Dunn's (anti-)ethnic discourse of boundary markers fitted too easily into the discourse of anti-legalism, works of the law, and so on, and thus provided "reasons" for criticizing Judaism (Ehrensperger 2013: 189–214). Περιτομή and ἀκροβυστία are ethnic distinctions, but not only ethnic—for Paul they are inherently also theological. These marked the distinction between belonging to the realm of the one God of Israel and belonging to the realm of all the other gods. Thus, it is a false dichotomy to prefer theological issues and ignore the ethnic, since for Paul and the people of his time, the theological involves the ethnic and vice versa.

Yet non-Jews, as noted, do require a connection with Abraham. They need to be related to him, yet how? By declaring that the nations through the mediation of Christ have found access to the promise of blessing (μακαρισμός, 4:9) given to Abraham, Paul is able to claim that the God of Israel is the God of the nations also (3:29). It is this perspective that Paul develops in Romans 4. In Galatians, aspects of this same message had already been outlined, so there are some similarities between the two letters. In Galatians, the nations stand center stage, "that in Christ Jesus the blessing of Abraham might come upon the nations" (3:14), and this might give the impression of excluding or bypassing Israel (a view we will find evidenced in Rom. 11:19). It is characteristic of Romans that though it is addressed to those from the nations, in this letter, the nations have to share the stage in association with the people of Israel as distinct from Galatians. There the concern is that the ethnē must not become Israelites. Thus, in Romans 4 we can claim that though the nations are still of central significance, here they are an "also" in an inclusive argument—"To the Jew first and also to the Greek" (1:16, cf. 4-16). They have to share center stage with Abraham and his Israelite descendants. Though the ethnē in Christ are the sole addressees, the scope of Paul's thought includes Israel also; at every point in Romans, the heritage of Abraham and Israel are kept in focus. Paul does not forget about Israel when he addresses the ethnē, "Paul wants them to understand their security as gentiles in Christ apart from Judaism and yet to know their kinship to Abraham's lineage" (cf. Stowers 1994: 249).

We note that the main reason for the discussion of the figure of Abraham at this point is with reference to the question of who constitutes Abraham's σπέρμα, seed (4:16) (thus reframing older debates about justification/rectification). Continuing the theme of 3:29 on the oneness of God as being the God of both Jews and non-Jews, in 4:9-18 it will become clear that the focus is not upon the rectification of the ethnically unspecified individual, but on two groups, Jews and those from the nations, that is, "on whom is Abraham's blessing pronounced?" The issue is not which individuals, but which peoples, constitute the σπέρμα Abraham, who are his κληρονόμοι, heirs, how the God of Israel can be the God of both ethnically identified Jews and those from the nations now that Christ has come.

A vitally important aspect of Paul's argument in Romans 4 is that he does not argue in binary fashion—"Jew or Greek," but inclusively "not only the Jew but also the Greek." The "οὐ μόνον ἀλλὰ καί" construction appears in 4:12, 16, and 23-24. The repetition, nine times in the letter,[3] is significant in that this form of argument already rules out any suggestion of "Greeks only" or "Greeks as the norm" (and similarly with Jews) but ensures that the emphasis is in accord with Paul's theme "to the Jew first and also to the Greek" expressed already in 1:16 and reiterated also, similarly to here, in 2:9-10. Although it contains elements that would support this contention, Paul's strategy in Romans is not simply to equalize the status of Jews and non-Jews in Christ but rather to situate both groups together in association within the ongoing purpose of God (4:11-12). In this, according to Paul's perspective, the people of Israel play a decisive role, which, at this point in the letter, is simply assumed. This role is primarily relevant for ethnē to understand as their social identity is intrinsically linked to that of Jews. As Wengst notes, in 4:9 Paul's question concerning whether God's blessing falls upon the circumcised or upon the uncircumcised is not formulated in binary fashion, "Does the blessing come upon the Jew or upon the gentile?" (2014: 149–52). The question is first put in what has been interpreted as an exclusive form, "Is this blessing pronounced [only] upon the circumcision?" But the "only" is inferred. It is not denied that the blessing comes upon the circumcised, it is rather affirmed and extended in that it is not denied that it comes, as the first question suggested, "upon the circumcised" but, alongside this, the blessing for the nations is added, "also upon the uncircumcised." Since the Jew first is affirmed, and thus can be assumed, in this chapter the dominant interest is not so much Jew and non-Jew, or even their equality, but how can the ἀκροβυστία share in the inheritance with Israel? It is certainly mistaken to assert that "Paul uses Abraham to make the Gentile route to God the standard and rule" (contra Adams 1997: 63).[4]

Abraham entered the scene in Romans in a discussion in 4:1-8 that does include the traditional theme of faith and works, gift, and pay (v. 4) (Barclay 2015: 485–6). But this theme should not be read as an anti-circumcision argument. *As in the previous two chapters, in Romans 4 there is no repudiation of circumcision for Jews, or of Jewish tradition*; Paul addresses non-Jews in a city where the Christ-movement had a Jewish foundation, and where those he addresses live in contact with Jews, some of whom are Christ-followers, who may meet separately but share a messianic conviction. *Though he does not address these*, Paul clearly acknowledges Jewish people who also revere Abraham and live by their scriptures (cf. 4:23). The argument about "foreskin" assumes it is a problematic category where circumcision is the norm and where "foreskin" has to find justification (Neutel 2021: 62). We note that κατὰ σάρκα has no necessarily denigrating overtones in 1:3 or 9:5. Also, in 4:16b, οἱ ἐκ τοῦ νόμου meaning "those of the Law" or "adherents of the Law" has no pejorative overtones. To assert that the promise did not come by the Law is a factual, descriptive statement—not necessarily pejorative. This phrase, adherents of the Law, simply indicates a parallel

---

[3] Rom. 1:32; 4:12, 16, (23); 5:3, 11; 8:23; 9:10, 24; 13:5. Cf. also 3:29 and 4:23 (Jewett 2007: 797, n146).
[4] 'Paul's argument makes sense in a worldview in which περιτομή self-evidently belongs to God and ἀκροβυστία is a negative and problematic category, which, as we have seen, is the opposition Paul assumes. It was this opposition he is attempting to undermine by showing in Rom. 2:25-27, that under the right circumstances, foreskin can actually be regarded as circumcision (cf. Neutel 2021: 64).

group to οἱ ἐκ πίστεως Ἀβραάμ, "those of,/adherents of, the trust of Abraham." Thus "those of the Law" indicates a Jewish group whether Christ-followers or not in parallel to the gentile Christ-followers.

Romans 4:10

Here the term ἀκροβυστία is introduced into the discussion about Abraham. Thus, the argument begins with two entities, the περιτομή and the ἀκροβυστία, and the issue concerns how the blessedness pronounced upon Abraham was received. Here a common reading resorts to questions as to *when* this blessing was received, that is, before or after his circumcision. The NRSV translates 4:10, "how then was it reckoned to him? Was it before or after he had been circumcised? He received the sign of circumcision as a seal of the righteousness that he had by trust while he was still uncircumcised. It was not after, but before he was circumcised." But the words that refer to time in this translation, "before," "after," and "still" do not reflect direct equivalents in Greek. This is not Paul's emphasis. Rather than arguing about sequence of events, it is not a matter of what came first in the case of Abraham, his justification, or his circumcision. Paul puts the question: is "foreskin a problem?" The answer Paul indicates is "No, look at Abraham, he was justified when he was 'in foreskin,' so 'foreskin' need not be a problem" (Neutel 2021: 68). Hence, the passage is then concerned not with the necessity, or even value, of circumcision, but rather *what is required of "gentiles."* The fact that Abraham was justified ἐν ἀκροβυστίᾳ is not understood in most interpretations as a description of what Abraham was—"in foreskin, a gentile," but primarily of *what he was not:* circumcised. In this traditional reading, scholars do not see ἀκροβυστία as a specific quality of the outsider, but implicitly, as a characteristic of all peoples in the time before circumcision was introduced. In sharp contrast, Paul's interest is covenantal—the relation of the nations to Abraham, hence the question "Have we gentile Christ-followers found Abraham to be our forefather according to the flesh?" (4:1). This interlocutor's question is repudiated in Paul's demonstration that the nation's relation to Abraham is via Christ and ἐν ἀκροβυστίᾳ. He affirms that in Christ turning away from idols is now possible whilst remaining in the state of ἐν ἀκροβυστίᾳ.

Romans 4:11b-12

We have noted how this is formulated in two parallel sets of texts, indicating two distinct groups of people. "The purpose was to make him the father of all who trust without being circumcised and who thus have righteousness reckoned to them (Group 1), and likewise the father of the circumcised who are not merely circumcised but also follow in the footprints of the trust our father Abraham had before he was circumcised" (Group 2). This grouping of people points directly to Paul's goal, since in 4:12 he refers specifically to "our father Abraham," indicating that though ethnically different, and thus distinctive identifiable groups, as σπέρμα these groups *both have Abraham as father.* Similarly, in 4:16, Paul claims, "That is why it depends on trust, in order that the promise may rest on grace and be guaranteed to all his σπέρμα—not only to τῷ ἐκ τοῦ νόμου the adherents of the law (Group 1)" but also "to τῷ ἐκ πίστεως Ἀβραάμ, those who share the trust of Abraham" (Group 2).

It has been commonly assumed that Paul views both, nations and Jews, becoming heirs of Abraham on the same criterion of trust, usually understood to be trust in Christ Jesus. The tradition of interpretation has tended to "correct" the text of Rom. 4:12, removing what is considered to be an unintended dative article τοῖς "to those" located just after the correlative conjunction ἀλλὰ καί (but also) and just prior to the participle στοιχοῦσιν ("who walk"). As Livesey notes,

> The presence or absence of the article τοῖς significantly alters the meaning of Rom. 4.12. Without the τοῖς, Paul addresses a single group of circumcised Jews who demonstrate faithfulness similar to that of Abraham prior to his being circumcised; with it, Paul addresses two different ethnic groups: circumcised Jews and then a group of foreskinned gentiles who demonstrate this Abrahamic faithfulness. (Livesey 2012: 275)

"Abraham is father, πατήρ, first to the circumcised (τοῖς ἐκ περιτομῆς) ... and then to the foreskinned, as noted by the second τοῖς ... and the final elongated phrase of the unit"(Livesey 2012: 284). Of specific interest in relation to Livesey's conclusions is that her work is based both on grammatical insights and on the role that sound plays in conveying meaning (cf. the sound map of Rom. 4:9-12, 2012: 279).

The repetition of the two differing descriptions of the groups of whom Abraham is father in 4:11-12 and 4:16 demonstrates and also confirms the view that there is more than one group of people described in both places. The problem with reading these verses as describing Abraham as the father of only one group is that this reading disregards the apparent introduction of another group in v. 12b denoted by the recurrence of the second dative article τοῖς. It must be noted that Abraham's fatherhood of groups is mentioned in both vv. 11 and 12, connected by "likewise" and by "and" in most English translations. As indicated by the presence of the "and," καὶ, along with the repetition of τοῖς "to those" in 4:12, two groups with differing specific identities are presumed in the discussion, not one group who share the trust that Abraham evidenced as a non-Jew. As Tucker notes, "It is more likely that Paul has two groups in view here, and thus Abraham continues to be the 'father of the circumcision,' understood as non-Christ-following Jews, and of those who have followed in the footsteps of Abraham's faith" (Tucker 2018: 70–1).

But this reasonable conclusion concerning two distinct groups who both have Abraham as father is much disputed based mainly on whether the second dative article τοῖς is original and legitimate. Without the presence of this disputed τοῖς, there would be no emphasis on another group. Thus, Sanday and Headlam claim, "He (Paul) is speaking of Jews who are both circumcised and believe" (1895: 108). Surprisingly, Cranfield, despite acknowledging that it is risky to emend a text where there is no manuscript to support the change, nevertheless claims that the τοῖς should be "ruled out grammatically by the position of the previous definite article in the Greek in relation to the words represented by 'not' and 'only'" (1985: 89). Cranfield is representative of many commentators who for various reasons, ideological, theological, and so on, dismiss or ignore this grammatical evidence.⁵ But his claim that the second τοῖς is ruled out grammatically because of word order in the Greek, which Dunn also supports because the syntax is awkward, cannot be substantiated, especially in a letter where Paul may place words in a certain order to draw attention to what he is saying. This is in spite of the amazing list of official biblical translations that ignore Paul's "not only but also" argument that demands two groups (Livesey 2012: 276–7).

Thus, it is clear from Paul's argument that Abraham is meant to be an inclusive figure *who represents and links both Jews, and Jewish and non-Jewish followers of Christ*. Despite the emphasis upon the incoming of those from the nations, there is no evidence here that Paul intends to bypass or nullify the special role of the Jews. As I recall, the first time that I became aware of this exegetical stance was in conversation with Markus Barth.⁶ If, in fact, Paul were concerned only to stress the incoming of the nations, he did not need to repeat his emphasis on two ethnic groups at each point in vv. 11-16. Paul deliberately presents Abraham as the father of two distinct groups from Jews and from the nations, obviously with a view to underlining the significance of their common connection to the patriarch. His argument proceeds from an unqualified "not only to the adherents of the Law" (4:16). This statement could have been written differently limiting it to those Jews who were Christ-followers, but it is left open. There is no argument or presupposition here that Christ-following Jews would not still remain adherents of the Law or that Paul means to eliminate non-persuaded Jews from this argument about Abraham's fatherhood, a most un-Pauline suggestion. Thus, as we have argued earlier, and above, Jewish heritage is presupposed, even though its full significance is not developed until chs. 9–11.

So even though Abraham, as we have noted, in one respect seems primarily to represent the pattern of non-Jewish trust, this does not displace Jews who exemplify the trust of Abraham. Rather, what heretofore belonged only to Israel has come also to the "gentiles." In fact, Paul presents the receipt of blessing on those from the nations so as to stress that the blessings to which through Christ they now have access, are blessings that are available only through sharing with Jews. Abraham as presented in Romans 4 is primarily a uniting figure rather than a divisive, and this suggests that Paul is seeking for harmony amongst the various Jewish and non-Jewish groups at Rome, something that will have relevance in the forthcoming discussion of issues in Romans 14–15 (of which the Romans' audience as yet know nothing since they can only operate in real time and cannot refer forwards in the text being read; Livesey 2012: 273, n3). But Paul's presentation of his gospel and gentile mission in Romans is indicative of more than peace and harmony between differing groups at Rome, though it does develop from this basis.

The fact that even in a letter to those from the nations Paul does not allow any conception of the ethnē worshipping God on their own without reference and relation

---

⁵ This requires in Greek the omission of the article τοῖς "to those" before στοιχοῦσιν, which is found in all existing manuscripts. Westcott and Hort suppose that τοῖς may be the remains of original αὐτοῖς (1881: 108). We may think that Tertius made a slip of the pen and that this remained uncorrected. If the slip was made by Tertius himself, it must have been made in some very early copy (Livesey 2012: 276–7). Livesey lists some eleven commentators who read thus (2012: 276, n9).

⁶ These views developed in his commentary on Ephesians (1974). I became acquainted with Barth at the SNTS Annual Meeting in Durham, 1979, and later at the SNTS Annual Meeting in Basel, 1984, where he was my host.

to Israel is very significant. There is no place in Paul's perspective for a gentile mission that is built upon the complete failure of Israel or a final, permanent rejection of Israel. Historically, the latter perspective has tended to be part of the presupposed story of the "gentile church," that is, that it exists because Israel failed to hear God's message, and the nations responded in trust.[7] But Paul's scenario for Jews and the nations now that Christ has come is not predicated upon the presupposition that Israel has been cast off. As we shall discover later in Romans 9–11, Paul repudiates any suggestion that Israel has been bypassed. Quite the opposite, Paul's scenario is built upon hope of the restoration of Israel and a rejoicing of the nations with God's people. In view of this, Abraham must remain the one to whom the promise was given that he would become the father of many nations. Thus, he remains unique and irreplaceable by any other figure, and he cannot be reduced to being primarily the model for gentile trust in the God of Israel. As we hope to demonstrate later in Romans 9–11 particularly, Abraham is confirmed as the father of many peoples, in and through him shall all the families of the earth be blessed. Thus, to designate him father *only* of either Jews or of the nations is drastically to diminish his role and significance. But there can be no debate that the designation as "our father Abraham" is a strong confirmation of ethnē in Christ identity. With Jews they share the fatherhood of Abraham to whom the promise was first given. Alongside this commonality comes the qualification that though this renders them joint heirs of the same promise, it denies them any existence separate from Israel since they must now and always share the inheritance *with Israel*.

Romans 4:13-18: Abraham, the Promise, and the Inheritance

[13]For it was not through a law that the promise that he would inherit the kosmos [came] to Abraham or to his descendants but through righteousness of trusting. [14]If (only) those of the law are the heirs, the trust is null and the promise is void. [15]For the law produces wrath; but where there is no law, neither is there transgression. [16]Because of this [it is] by trust, in order that according to grace the promise might be guaranteed to all his descendants, not only to those of the law but also to those of the trust of Abraham who is the father of us all.

In order to guarantee the promise to the nations as well as to the Jews, Paul stresses that the inheritance to Abraham did not come via the Law, but via the promise. The Law is not a conduit for the promise to the ethnē, but for these it produces wrath (4:15), shorthand for the wrath of God (cf. 5:9, 12:19). This claim links back to the previous chapters where the wrath of God is declared to be revealed in and with the revelation of God's righteousness and power. This refers specifically to those from the nations, for whom the only release from the wrath of God comes through divine reconciliation through the Christ (3:21-26).

---

[7] Paul does present the gentile mission as somehow related, possibly sequentially, to the limited response of the Jews, but this is presented as God's specific plan, which includes a restored Israel as its consummation.

Thus, we are dealing here with the promise to Abraham as it is experienced by the ethnē in Christ. The promise to Abraham included the incoming of the ethnē, which, as we have noted above, has sometimes been interpreted as exclusively referring to the ethnē only, superseding the original recipients of the promise. The promise did extend to the nations through its confirmation through Christ via the Jewish people. But it did not do so in a supersessionist manner at the expense of the people of Israel. As noted above, we emphasized that Paul used the "not only but also" form of argument no less than nine times in ch. 4. This is particularly salient in relation to Israel and the nations—not only the circumcised but also the uncircumcised, and so on (Tucker 2018: 68–71).

What has not been sufficiently noted, however, is that it is inconsistent to stress the continuing inclusion of the people of Israel within the divine purpose, and yet ignore another aspect of that same promise, that is, the promise of the land. The biblical covenant contains promises of land, progeny, a great name, and divine blessing as well as that element of it most frequently celebrated, the incoming of the nations (Gregerman 2018: 137–58). The covenant began with the singular people of Israel, which was its original locus even if its history extends to the whole of humanity. Paul's "not only but also" form of argument demands that the affirmation, βεβαίαν (v. 16) of that same promise should include some affirmation of land within it. But there must be a qualification here since Romans addressees the ethnē, not Israel, though some chapters (e.g., 9–11) focus upon the future of Israel in relation to the promise. Paul does not claim all the inheritance of Israel for the ethnē in Christ. The language here is language of confirmation, not fulfillment (cf. 15:8); indeed 4:16 is a summary verse about whose content there need be little dispute. If we reject the concept of certain elements being transcended in relation to the covenant as a whole, we must be consistent and cannot allow a similar perspective to operate in respect of the inheritance including the land. As Walter Brueggemann insists, "The Abraham imagery apart from the land is an empty form. No matter how it is spiritualized, transcendentalized, or existentialized, it has its primary focus undeniably on land" (1977: 170).

This means that it must be acknowledged that a specific land was promised by God to Israel. This satisfies the genuine desire of every human group to inhabit territory in a permanent manner and the correlate concern not to be a stranger or a refugee (Zacharias 2020). This is not dependent on what the people do. It is God who owns the land, so the inheritance of Israel is therefore a grant or a gift from God (Forman 2011: 67). The promise is unconditional and irrevocable. Though the people can be punished with exile for disobedience, they cannot entirely lose their connection to the land promised to the patriarchs (Gregerman 2018: 52–4). Even the harshest prophetic denunciations leave open a way to return to the Promised Land (Amos 9:11-15, Micah 5:6-7, Jer. 12:15, and Ezek. 36:24-28).

The Promise of the Land and the Incoming of the Nations: Inheriting the Kosmos

Romans 4:13

But if Paul is addressing only the ethnē in Christ in Romans, how does Abraham's inheriting the land relate to them. Some link with non-Jews may be found in Paul's reference in 4:13 to inheriting the world, κόσμος. Since at no stage in the Hebrew Bible/LXX is the phrase "inherit the world" explicitly used or put in such bold, expansive terms, there is a consensus amongst Paul's interpreters that in using the expanded version of the promise, Paul is drawing on Jewish interpretative traditions of the Second Temple period, such as, for example, the *Book of Jubilees*, which has three direct references to the inheritance of Israel (Forman 2011: 80–5). If the Abrahamic promise includes the nations, this wider reference is only to be expected since these ethnē also would require a place in which to live and flourish in sharing in the promise and blessing with the people of Israel. If Abraham's progeny are to be numerous and flourish, they will occupy a larger space. On the other hand, if we stress the extension of the promise to the whole world, through the inclusion of the nations, then it may be legitimate to consider that here we must be envisaging the time when the Messiah will rule the world in righteousness and peace. The use of cosmological language such as κόσμος and κτίσις point to this (Adams 2000: 169). This would not deny the promise of a particular land to a particular people but rather extend this hope to all the nations through the Messiah. But even as we stress this expansion of the promise, it must be recognized that everything that the ethnē have comes only in and through Christ and is shared with the inheritance of Israel. So, we are not reflecting on a promise of land for the ethnē in Christ, but only on how these might possibly share in Israel's promise of land, that is, space to live.

The language of inheritance carries expectations as to who inherits the land and how land (and by extension, power, control, and sovereignty) should be distributed and managed in society (Forman 2011: 20). Thus, Paul needs to show his awareness of the contradictory ideals and disparity promoted by Roman ideology in contrast to the extreme conditions for many people living in Rome at this period (Forman 2011: 53–5). Paul may be claiming that it is not the Romans, favored by the gods, who determine the distribution of land. The Romans were aware of the world beyond their jurisdiction, that is, they could not claim more than the one known οἰκουμένη, but they could claim to fit into the order of the cosmic destiny. Whether they were under the protection of, or they held a covenant with, the gods, their rule was divinely sanctioned. Indeed, they became therefore an element, or the guarantee, of world order (Forman 2011: 32). But the Roman people and its rulers looked for no less than sovereignty over the earth, which Augustus and the Julian family were anticipated to achieve (2011: 33), but it is the Creator God who makes promises regarding inheritance, establishes covenants, and keeps his promises to provide a land, that is, living space, for his people. A link between royal figures such as a (Davidic) Messiah and the final realization of the land promise is a stable feature of Second Temple discourse. Thus, if Paul asserts that the Messiah, Jesus, has enabled trusting Jews and non-Jews to share in the eschatological inheritance of the whole earth, this can be identified as a recognizably messianic or royal claim with its corresponding anticipated outcomes for both land and people.

The emphasis in Rom. 4:13-18 is not only on the fact of the promise but also on its content. There is evidence that already in Paul's time, some Jews thought of the content of the promise as having universal relevance, although this is not always the case in all discussions of "the final realization of the land promises." These may "transcend" the boundaries of the original land promise (McCaulley 2019: 52). The invasion of

Jerusalem in 63 BCE prompted the writing of the collection of *Psalms of Solomon*. In *Psalms of Solomon* 17, the excessive suffering caused by Pompey leads the author to predict the coming of the Davidic Messiah who would liberate the people and the land. The restoration in *Psalms of Solomon* 17 is not limited to Israel—the author envisions a king whose rule would extend throughout the known world. "He shall judge peoples and nations … he shall have the peoples of the nations to be subject to him under his yoke" (*Pss. Sol.* 17:29-30). In this pivotal text, the land is restored to its people through a Davidic king who defeats the foreigners and regathers the people. They will live in a land cleansed of enemies, in the inheritance promised to them. But the Davidic king in this text would do more than restore Israel to the land promised to them. He would assume a worldwide rule that brings blessings to the world. What is of much significance in *Psalms of Solomon* 17 is that here God's faithfulness to the covenant takes the form of raising up a Davidic king to restore Israel to its inheritance (Hester 1968: 69, 88).[8] What is also to be noted is that since this author, drawing on language with its roots in the Abrahamic promises and referring to the land as Israel's inheritance, witnesses that it is the Davidic Messiah who would bring about the final realization of the Abrahamic promises in the context of a worldwide kingdom (McCaulley 2019: 55–6). So, the gentile sharing in the inheritance of the κόσμος, was not Paul's invention but preceded him and his claims of the incoming of the nations. It is not surprising that Paul includes this perception in Romans 4, so soon after proclaiming the divine truce and reconciliation through Christ the Messiah in ch. 3:21-31. The extension of the promise of land to a promise through the Messiah of worldwide blessing is an appropriate extension of Paul's thought that takes account of the gentile incoming and the confirmation of the promise, even if it is still in the process of being formulated.

Another valid reason for Paul's including the κόσμος in his thought here may be the context, which he is addressing in Rome. The promise to Abraham that he "would inherit the world" bears an intriguing likeness to the phrase "lords of the world" as used in the *Aeneid* 1:281-282 (Forman 2011: 41). Destined by the gods, Rome claimed to be the center of the world, the city being the focus of all things under Roman rule. Reality revolved around the imperial city. Thus, Roman claims extended to determining who lived in which land and under what conditions. Rome's imperialistic view of the future envisioned prosperity and victory for Rome in a golden era; there was an expectation and a claim that Roman rule would bring peace, stability, order, abundance, and tranquility (Forman 2011: 25, Rock 2012: 52–65). Virgil's *Aeneid* anticipates that Rome will take on leadership and rule without limits of any kind, be it time or space, the gift of empire without end, destined to rule earth's peoples (*Aeneid* 6:756-854). However, in striking contrast to this vision, many of the people under Rome were undernourished and struggling with abject poverty, inflicted to a great extent by Rome's taxation policies for non-citizens and immigrants. Thus, the imperial boasts in the language of unlimited inheritance and power may have jarred and clashed with the actuality of subjugation experienced under Rome, not least in the promise of a peace, that is made possible by an ideology of war, victory, and military dominance (Forman 2011: 29–30).

---

[8] Thus, McCaulley uses the term "final realization" rather than "restoration of what was lost" (2019: 47).

In face of this, Paul offers an alternative vision for the Roman ethnē in Christ based on the promise of land, but extended to allow for the incoming of the nations alongside Israel, a real peace resulting from reconciliation between peoples. Can it be that in the narrative of Abraham Paul offers an alternative vision for the ethnē in Christ in order to boost their self-understanding in competition with the all-pervasive ideology of the *Aeneid*? They too have a glorious ancestor, the father of worldwide peoples.

Abraham as the Recipient of the Promise of Blessing for the "Gentiles"

Another reading of Abraham has to be considered at this point. Abraham, as noted, has frequently been read from Paul's presentation here as the supreme exemplar of "trust in contrast to works." However, as the *Book of Jubilees* depicts him, Abraham forsakes all idolatry and steps out in trust *in response to the call of God*. The rejection of idolatry is the ultimate criterion for those who are faithful to the God of Israel, and a main reason why Paul refers to Abraham here in an address to non-Jews. In his function as father of all those who exclusively relate to the one God, he is unique, and cannot be paralleled. The rewriting of Gen. 12:1-3 in *Jubilees* chs. 11–12 significantly depicts Abraham's departure from his father's house and homeland as representing his departure from the impure world of the nations—from idolatry (Mühling 2011: 343–69). Some such tradition may underlie the presentation of Abraham in Romans ch. 4. Adams has argued that Abraham tradition depicted him as a former idolator who reasoned from the creation (back) to the Creator in contrast to the failure of the idolators in 1:18-32 (1997: 47–66). This suggests that the worship of the one God and separation from idolatry characterized Abraham as God's own in Jewish traditions at the time of Paul's writing. Abraham was significant as the one to whom the Creator God offered to be his God, to be with him and to bless him and his seed. What distinguished him was his turning away from idolatry and exclusively worshipping this God; significantly, this happened while he was in a state of ἀκροβυστία, uncircumcision—this is emphasized three times in 4:11-12.

Paul emphasizes the fact that only Abraham received the promise (singular) that in his seed the nations will be blessed (Gen. 12:3). Paul does refer to promises in the plural elsewhere (in 15:8 and 9:4) but his emphasis in Romans 4 is upon the promise to the nations, assuming the promises to Israel as already in operation (Stowers 1994: 133). In Paul's delineation, Abraham is the first of the faithful to whom the promise was initially given (cf. 4:13, 14, 16, 20, 21), and thus, as Käsemann rightly emphasized, the bearer of the promise per se who is not replaceable by any other figure (1971: 98).

In that respect Abraham's unique status cannot be replicated. As Paul will note later in again discussing Abraham's σπέρμα in Romans 9, Abraham is the "father" of Isaac and Jacob, the lineage of *promise* that constitutes the people of Israel; thus, to separate Abraham as an individual from Isaac and Jacob and the traditions of Israel is unwarranted. In Exodus 3, God reveals himself as God of Abraham, Isaac, and Jacob/Israel. It is the term σπέρμα/seed (4:16) that is key to Paul's seeing in Abraham the father of two differing groups, Jews and the ethnē in Christ. By differing routes, these two groups are both constituted as σπέρμα of Abraham, the one by promise and natural descent, κατὰ σάρκα, the other becomes seed by incorporation into Christ. But although it might seem from the discussion above that Abraham is primarily the father of gentile Christ-followers, and that henceforth *only* this gentile pattern should be normative, this would be a mistaken conclusion. We have argued already that Paul sees the nations as an "also" in relation to participation in God's purpose which historically has given a specific role to Israel as his people. *There are no grounds in Paul's letters for considering the nations as the primary recipients of God's grace in analogy to Abraham's call in foreskin.* Indeed, arguing in this fashion could result in an inference that to follow Abraham's "example" fully would legitimize "circumcision after calling" as the pattern for all the nations, something Paul strongly opposes. Focusing on Abraham's turning away from the gods of his fathers, and his refusal to worship the gods of the nations makes him *only in this respect* a model for gentile Christ-followers who like Jews worship only the God of Israel. Israel's call comes via the call of Abraham, and the call of the nations through Christ follows that pattern, that is, those of us whom he has called, "not from the Jews only but also from the 'gentiles'" (9:24).

Abraham—Not a Prototype for the Ethnē

Although he is forefather of other groups of people, some of whom also practice circumcision and receive promises of descendants and blessing, Abraham for Paul is primarily the forefather of Israel, as well as being the one who received the promise of blessing for non-Jews, making him much more than an exemplar. As Keck states, "Abraham's justification/rectification is *not* exemplary, it is defining" (2005: 126). Keck's terminology is correct here as stated for the ethnē in Christ, but his designation of Abraham as prototype of both groups, Jews and non-Jews, is problematic. We will note some issues here, but return again to these later in this chapter.

Abraham can be the prototype in one respect—all his seed both Jews and ethnē in Christ share his pattern of trust when he was called. This they undeniably have in common.

But not the succeeding patterns of life thereafter, which differed necessarily once the Law was given, and this did not apply to the nations who were outside the sphere of the covenant until the new revelation in Christ. Thus, Abraham is really only a prototype for Jews, in that he trusted God and then accepted circumcision as the sign of the unconditional covenant God had granted him and his seed. To make him the prototype of trust universally has the effect of perceiving Abraham's circumcision as irrelevant, thus excluding the Jews as Jews by disregarding their Jewish identity. To make Abraham not just the first of the faithful, but *the only exemplar of* trust until Christ, is not only to ignore but worse still, to deny and paganize, the entire history of Israel. That is a deplorable arrogance, given that someone like Philo can discern and proclaim a great future for Israel (*Praem.* 158). To proceed directly from Abraham to Christ requires an arrogance that judges the past as mistaken in its entire attribution of value. Such a negative perception of the scriptural tradition claims a perspective that requires a vantage point not actually available to most human beings, an overwhelming arrogance that has no connection with Christ but more with gentile cultural arrogance.

It is not justifiable to claim revelation in Christ as the vantage point that provides such a perspective. Which texts in Paul, if any, can be precisely identified as a basis for this opinion? Again, this negative perspective is not justified because others have wrongly attributed revelation to human history itself making it a Heilsgeschichte—salvation history rather than a history of human failures and compromises, and so on (cf. Käsemann 1980: 255–6). To exaggerate and thus to pervert the understanding of divine action in history does not justify a denial, (making Abraham a unique exception) of all such divine action, that is, of God's covenant with Israel. I recognize that some scholars note that there is not much specific reference to covenant in Romans 4. Esler, rightly, is critical of terms such as "fulfillment" and "climax," neither of which I hold (2003: 189). I speak in terms of "confirmation" of the promises rather than of "climax" in order to avoid encouraging an overrealized eschatology (Campbell 2018: 299–333).

But Abraham is not a unique individual whose understanding of God dwarfs or diminishes the prophets, he is rather the first of the people of Israel and of their interaction with their God throughout history. He cannot be separated out from Israel as a special individual or regarded as a pinnacle of revelation that is explicable apart from Israel and her traditions. To thus imagine Abraham as the only human who truly understood God's ways until Christ is, in my opinion, much more difficult than to conceive of God working in and through Israel, her prophets, scriptures, and so on. As Käsemann has argued, "If the experience of the righteousness of God is limited to the post-resurrection period, and prior to that related to Abraham exclusively, both the exclusiveness and the choice of Abraham are absurd … Marcion should then be followed" (1980: 116–17). Käsemann was opposing Klein (1963: 424–47) who maintained that the history of Israel has been "radically de-secularized and paganized," which Käsemann perceived as rendering the "whole appeal to the Old Testament as meaningless." Thus, we confidently affirm God's activity in history, though we do not specify precisely how this is to be understood, since it cannot be entirely discontinuous, and thus some explanation of the continuity is required (Campbell 2013: 161–81). It is significant that Paul who emphasizes Abraham as the first of the faithful, in Rom. 4:6 also proceeds to explain Abraham's insights with the help of scriptures attributed to David. It is in this respect that we designate Abraham as father first of all to the Jews and only then to those from the nations. Abraham is a good exemplar (Witherington 2012: 116) but only so when ethnic distinctions are not disregarded and he remains the father, not only of one, but of two ethnically distinguished groups who nevertheless hold much in common in their links with him (see Introduction, p. 27, Neufeld and Schmitt).

Paul affirms God's grace to the ethnē, not separately to ethnē only, but rather to ethnē also as noted above. Indeed, the only place where Abraham figures as example in a proper sense is, as we shall see in 4:19, where Paul claims that "he did not weaken in trust when he considered his own body." As such, Abraham is not fully delineated if he is not depicted as primarily father of Israel, as well as of gentile Christ-followers (even though others also descend from him who are not part of Israel) (Jipp 2016: 190–1). Abraham is indeed a good *model* from the past, and in this sense only is Paul rhetorically correct to so present him. Yet he is not presented by Paul as the father only of a non-ethnic trust, this is a post-Pauline creation. For Paul, he is much more (Young 2015: 43–4)—the father of Israel, the recipient of the promise for the ethnē, a prototypical Israelite, a paradigm for the future.

Abraham and Ethnicity—a Uniting Figure for Those ἐν ἀκροβυστίᾳ and Those ἐν περιτομῇ

We have already argued that Paul's use of Abraham in Romans cannot legitimately be read as indicating that Abraham is primarily the father of non-Jews. We have shown that the status of Jews as those within God's covenant is assumed even though the incoming of the nations is stressed. We have also demonstrated that theological and ethnic issues must not be considered in isolation from one another. A main theme of Romans 4 focuses upon who actually constitute Abraham's σπέρμα, and how they are constituted (Forman 2011: 60), thereby linking the references to Abraham in both chs. 4 and 9, which thus focus on this common theme. Hermeneutically, this moves the figure of Abraham from a theological discussion of trust and works to an ethnic and theological discussion of the relation of Jews and those from the nations, from which the binary of divine choice versus human achievement can still rightly be derived, though as a secondary rather than as a main point of Paul's argument here. Abraham's significance cannot be limited to Christian debates about justification. It was, in fact, Paul's view of the relation of Israel to the "gentiles" that shaped his view of justification, and not vice versa (Dahl 1977: 156). The discussion on who constitute Abraham's σπέρμα originates from the issues raised by the incoming of the nations through the reconciliation in Christ outlined particularly in 3:21-26. So even though two groups of people, Jews and the nations, figure in the discussions throughout, the burning issue is the place of the nations in relation to Abraham and Israel. This is not in opposition to or inconsistent with a view of Abraham as a uniting figure for Jews and ethnē in Christ, since the integrity of each group must be safe-guarded in any over-arching common in group identity.

The traditional reading, which emphasized justification, suffered from the presentation of this in an anti-works, anti-legalism argument that encouraged the retention of a reading of Romans where circumcision and Jewish tradition were critiqued from the perspective of the Reformation, which unfortunately had a blind spot in relation to Romans 9–11 (Käsemann 1980: 253–6). The net result of reading Romans as only or mainly a theological document was to consider the elect in Christ as safely justified at the end of Romans 8, with 9–11 being regarded as a postscript or digression. But neither the Reformation nor subsequent theology demands or supports such a conclusion. As we have asserted, Romans is written *only* to those from the nations and does not address Jews.

Note should be taken at the outset of this discussion that Paul emphasizes here not Jews and ethnē, as such, but chooses very specific equivalent terms drawn from the Jewish symbolic universe. The terminology of περιτομή and ἀκροβυστία are terms that cannot avoid reference to ethnicity in the explication of their meaning. Thus, Neutel claims that Paul is driving home the point that, like circumcised Jews, foreskinned "gentiles" can become righteous heirs of Abraham (2021: 65). From a slightly different perspective and despite being critical of the frequent misunderstanding of ἀκροβυστία, Neutel still notes that though "the term refers primarily to a physical reality," she goes on to state "and beyond that to an ethnic and religious group marked by this physical reality" (2021: 64). As Neutel notes, to omit ethnic issues in this discussion is to render it inadequate, if not sometimes explicitly misleading. It is clear that ἀκροβυστία is viewed "through the lens of circumcision" so that "its main feature is the feature that is and should be removed through circumcision" (2021: 65). In Livesey's reading, περιτομή rightly becomes "circumcised Jews" and ἀκροβυστία "foreskinned 'gentiles'." The fact is, as noted above, that Paul stresses ἀκροβυστία, foreskin, repeating it six times in the four verses in 4:9-12, a central passage in this chapter. "The lexeme ἀκροβυστία is prominent throughout with its placement at the end of nearly every breath unit or colon of the structural unit" (Livesey 2012: 285).[9] Ἀκροβυστία denotes not merely the absence of circumcision but, following the LXX and Philo, and in some cases in Paul, refers directly to the part of the body that is cut in circumcision, so that "foreskin" seems the primary meaning and most appropriate translation. This indicates, since ἀκροβυστία is a gentile-only property, that the issue under discussion in these verses is non-Jewish, but arises in a context where circumcision is part of the intellectual furniture. If we claim that Abraham was rectified "in a state of foreskin," that is, as a "gentile" or non-Jew, this correctly describes his status and necessarily involves ethnic and theological issues intertwined.

This is partly because it is usually presumed that Paul is here discussing *the issue of circumcision generally*, that is, potentially for all people whether it is necessary or valuable, and so on and that his specified audience includes Jews. This is a particularly problematic case of universalizing Paul's contextually grounded statements on specific issues and is encouraged by insufficient attention to the particularity of address of Paul's letters in context. But if we follow the nations-only address of Romans, Paul's argument here can be expressed as "foreskin a problem?" And the response, "No, look at Abraham, he was justified when he was 'in foreskin,' so foreskin need not be a problem." As Neutel notes

> that Abraham was reckoned as righteous while "in foreskin" is presented as a surprising fact, which disrupts not what circumcision stands for, but rather what being "in foreskin" is thought to entail. The surprising possibility of being justified through πίστις while having the negative characteristic of being "in foreskin" ἐν ἀκροβυστίᾳ is relevant to the larger question of who the possible recipients of God's blessing are. (2021: 68)

Abraham responded in trust in the state of ἀκοβυστία, and thus received the promise that in him all the nations will be blessed (Gen. 12:4). Here the non-Jewish nations are clearly in view. The subsequent confirmation of this in the covenant in Gen. 17, however, does not include non-Jews as covenant partners, nor are they included in any covenant renewal, be this with Isaac or Jacob or at Sinai. The covenant and the covenantal sign, circumcision, are with and for Israel. The nations are only associated through the promised blessing. The goal of Paul's argument is not principally to affirm the incoming of the nations as non-Jews. This has already been affirmed. It is to demonstrate that Abraham is the father of two peoples both of whom are his seed and

---

[9] Livesey's research is based upon the insights of orality studies on the role sound plays in conveying meaning and upon a sound mapping tool developed by Lee and Scot in particular. She convincingly demonstrates how ancient auditors would likely have heard the structural unit in Rom. 4:9-12 in order to discern the identity of the group involved in the last phrase of 4:12.

therefore his heirs. They are equal in status and also kin by virtue of both being seed of Abraham. The concentration of the argument is upon the foreskin since, as noted, Abraham's fatherhood of Israel, and thus her covenantal status, is assumed, Israel's priority remains. But the negativity associated with ἀκοβυστία should be annulled since through Christ the nations have been reconciled (Neutel 2021: 65–7). The nations are now through Christ also within God's purpose, but only so in their relationship with Israel, not separately or by themselves. They join Israel in their becoming seed of Abraham but *not by becoming Israelites* because pluralism is inherent to the terms of the promise.

God was described in 3:29 as the God of Jews and non-Jews, not of one of these only or of either of these in isolation. In order for the God of Israel to be God of both Jews and ethnē, he cannot be the god of the περιτομή alone or of the ἀκοβυστία alone. Here with continuing emphasis upon the nations being called in Christ, and the assumption of God's grace first to Israel, which this presumes, Paul's aim is to present Abraham as the father of two distinct peoples both of whom are Abraham's seed. The one is called via Abraham—as Israel was called—the other through Christ in whom and by whom the nations are now also called.

There were most likely indications at Rome that the ethnē in Christ were not sufficiently aware that since Abraham is father of both Jewish and non-Jewish σπέρμα in the families of God, they ought to accept one another as fellow-members of one family rather than boasting in opposition to one another. Paul in SIT terms mounts a challenge against competitive group behavior. Also, there should be no pressure on the ἀκοβυστία to accept circumcision.

We note that Paul does not seek for the two groups to become identical—this was not possible. Paul's vision was not that there would be only one uniform group of Jews and ethnē in Christ at Rome. Some ethnē were already mistakenly seeking to follow Jewish patterns of law-keeping, which might have eventually produced a uniform group of people. A similar goal could have been followed if a group could unite on the postulate that the Jewish people and their traditions had been bypassed and that a gentile pattern of life for everyone would result. Paul saw neither of these as the solution. This was not so much a rethinking of identity as a reenvisioning of identities as Jews within the covenant, or as "gentiles" in Christ. Changing identity as Jew or "gentile" would not provide the answer since ethnicity as such was not the problem.

The order of Paul's argumentation concerning the family/ies of God seems to proceed from reconciliation in ch. 3, to becoming seed of Abraham alongside Israel in Rom. 4:1-16, to adoption through the Spirit and thereby becoming brothers of Christ in Romans 8, so that Christ becomes the firstborn of many brothers (8:29). Thus, one of the peoples, the ethnē, of whom Abraham is father is here being described, and their status constructed. Attention to the other family of whom he is already father will be devoted in chs. 9–11. This reading allows us to avoid repeating the discussion in 3:1-2 of circumcision as an advantage and a value to "the Jew," and to view the topic here as being concerned only with what is required of non-Jews. Paul in Romans is seeking to construct an identity for the ethnē in Christ for which Israel may be a template. But it is not an identity that makes them Israelites, or displaces Israelites, but one that situates them as a satellite people alongside the people of Israel, with Abraham in differing ways, the father of both.

Paul promotes Abraham as the forefather of many peoples (Bakhos 2014: 51–3, 90, 103) but first of Israel. Alongside this, as we have argued above, he presents Abraham as father also of those from the nations who share the trust of the patriarch. Paul's argument centers on the fact that in the scriptural tradition, Abraham's greatness did not result from his circumcision but from his trust in God. This continues the ethnic issues in relation to the oneness of God, discussed already in 3:29. Such trusting while ἐν ἀκροβυστίᾳ, in a state of foreskin, as scholars have noted, makes Abraham a paradigm, especially for non-Jews who likewise put trust in God without being circumcised (Michel 1978: 14). His circumcision did not produce (ἐργάζομαι) rectification; instead this was credited to him through his trust in God. It might even be argued that the narrative of Genesis 17 makes Abraham *primarily* the father of non-Jews, but this would be in tension with Paul's stance in relation to the Jew first (cf. Thiessen 2016: 83).

If Abraham was rectified in a state of foreskin—ἐν τῇ ἀκροβυστίᾳ—this can be seen as proof that circumcision is not necessary for non-Jews. But that is not exactly what Paul is stressing. The repetition of ἀκροβυστία in 4:9-12 in each of these four verses indicates it is central to Paul's argument. The issue is upon whom is the blessing of Abraham reckoned—upon περιτομή, the circumcised, Jews, or upon the ἀκροβυστία, the uncircumcised, that is, those from the nations bearing in mind that we have claimed that his trust was reckoned to him as rectification. The dialogue with its very brief questions might be read as originating as a question from the interlocutor "upon whom is the blessing reckoned—upon the περιτομή the circumcision?" To which comes Paul's response, "also upon the ἀκροβυστία—the foreskin?" His comment continues (for) "we say trust was reckoned to Abraham as righteousness. It was reckoned to him as righteousness (while) ἐν τῇ ἀκροβυστίᾳ i.e., as a non-Jew." It seems Paul uses ἀκροβυστία in a novel way, uniquely dividing people into περιτομή and ἀκροβυστία (Rom. 3:30, 4:9, cf. Gal. 2:7, Livesey 2012: 14). Paul sees in this the purpose of God—εἰς τὸ εἶναι—so as to be the father of all those ἐν περιτομῇ or ἐν ἀκροβυστίᾳ who share the trust that Abraham had (while) ἐν ἀκροβυστίᾳ. As noted, this argument would support the view that Abraham is primarily the father of non-Jews, the ἀκροβυστία. But a closer look at Paul's statements indicates other than this. The actual presentation of Abraham makes a clear argument that the non-Jews are now rectified through Christ following the pattern of Abraham rectified ἐν ἀκροβυστίᾳ. Paul's argument includes certain assumptions, one of which is that Abraham is the first of the faithful, the father of the Jewish people. So even though he is discussing the requirements for non-Jewish Christ-followers, *the presupposition of the discussion is that Abraham and Israel already exist as people of God*. What needs to be taken seriously into account is, as we have noted already, that Paul's οὐ μόνον ἀλλὰ καὶ "not only but also" form of argument assumes the acceptance already of Jews through trust and (that) this makes the rectification of non-Jews an also, not a separate, or independent entity, or the one and only goal of Paul's argument. They cannot appear on the scene as the only people of God since he is already the God of the people Israel, hence the significance of Paul's "not only but also" aggregative form of argument.

Paul affirms the grace of God to the ethnē not separately but "to ethnē also" as noted above. In Paul's view, Abraham was called as a non-Jew, and thus his call involves ethnic issues. The primary contrast is not "faith or works" but rather "works versus the call of God" (9:11). Thus, for Paul, writing in a first-century context, acceptance with God depends primarily upon whom God calls in his grace, and this in Paul is both a theological and an ethnic issue (Young 2015: 30–51; McMurray 2021: 239–43). Thus, grace is always prior to works. This is so in God calling his people Israel into being (before Christ), with the Torah being the gift given to them to guide them in their life as God's people. Such a gracious call is now extended to non-Jews through Christ. Paul's conviction is that for non-Jews, in contrast to the pattern that existed prior to the coming of Christ, "now the rectifying power of God has been manifested apart from Law, the rectifying power of God through the faithfulness of Jesus Christ, to everyone who trusts" (3:21-22). Access to the promises, though not to the covenant itself, has now been opened up to non-Jews, so both Jews and those from the nations can find blessing. Not only the Jews have been called—in the reconciliation in Christ the nations also are called, and it is this confidence that leads Paul to present Abraham as father now of both Jews and non-Jews who have trust like that of Abraham. We note again here Paul's inclusive form of argument.

Romans 4:17-25: Abraham, the Forefather of Israel, and Father of Many Nations

[17]Just as it is written "I have appointed you to be a father of many nations," in light of this he trusted God who gives life to the dead and calls that which does not exist into existence. [18]In hope beyond hope that he should become a father of many nations as he had been told "So shall your descendants be." [19]Also not having weakened in trust when he considered his own body already dead [for he was about a hundred years old], and also the nekrosis of Sarah's womb. [20]With regard to the promise of God no distrust made him waver, but he was empowered in his trust giving glory to God, [21]and fully convinced that the One who had promised is capable also to do [it]. [22]For this reason "it was reckoned to him as righteousness." [23]But it was not written, "it was reckoned to him," for his sake alone, [24]but for our sake also, for whom it will be reckoned, we who trust in him who raised Jesus our Lord from the dead, [25]who was handed over to death for our transgressions and was raised for our rectification.

In this section of the chapter, Abraham's trust is exemplified. The narrative is certainly expressed in a format that particularly relates to the nations. Abraham trusted God to make him the father of many nations despite, in his old age, not having a son to further his line of descent. The God in whom he put his trust, who called him to leave his homeland and to entrust himself to him, is described as the one "who gives life to the dead and calls into existence things that do not exist" (4:17). He is a God of resurrection and new creation, even as he is described as the (fore)father of Israel. The context in ch. 4 must be kept in mind—Abraham has already been presented as the first of the faithful, the father of both Israel and the nations. What is stated here builds upon and develops this image of Abraham; it does not deny it or overlook it, it is presupposed, even though it is ethnē who are addressed. Indeed, it is entirely unwarranted to read 4:17-25 as if it were not preceded by vv. 1-16, which rule out, in my opinion, a Hegelian kind of conception of God as one who acts mainly in antithesis to his previous revelation. In my view, it is likewise unwarranted to posit a divine activity that disregards or annuls previous activity.

Thus, it is not warranted to present the God of Abraham in 4:17-25 as a God *only* of radical new creation and resurrection in contrast to the image of the Creator God of Israel as the God of an historical people who leads them out of Egypt (Campbell 2018: 338–42). The God who creates things out of nothing (4:17b) is not unknown prior to New Testament times, but, as Rom. 9:1-13 demonstrates, in the beginning he called Israel, creating a people for himself, so they are "new creation." Similar action now takes place with the incoming of the nations through Christ as Rom. 4:17 reminds us. The nature and character of God were matters of discussion in Rome, and here Paul presents God specifically as the God of the nations also, indicating this without denying but rather keeping in view his relation to Israel. Thus, Abraham and Sarah are given a son, whom Paul views as a product of Abraham's trust. Here Abraham is presented as trusting that God would do as he had promised, that is, to make him the father of many nations. Although the audience in Rome, listening to Paul's letter being read, would not have access to this information until later, we can recognize resonances here with "the weak" and "the strong" that are not introduced until Romans 14–15. But if Paul's depictions of Abraham ring true, what is discussed in Rom. 14:1–15:6 would not be an entirely new topic. Abraham did not "weaken in trust" when he considered his own and Sarah's deteriorating body (4:19). There is repetition of the same theme in v. 19, "he did not weaken in trust concerning the promise of God, but he grew strong in his trust as he gave glory to God, being fully convinced that God was able to do what he had promised."

Our image of the God of Israel and of Christ is not that of a god who tires of human sin and idolatry, who discards these failing peoples and starts all over again with the creation of new peoples (Isa. 54:9-10). Such an image of God would be flawed in its readiness to envisage a God who easily casts off one people and replaces them with another, a God of power and principle, but not of transforming love. God, in the New Testament, does not give up on his people, nor displace them with another people, but he is faithful to his people and to his previous interaction with them throughout history, this is his covenant commitment, his δικαιοσύνη. Any "new people" *do not bypass Israel but share in the promises previously made to this people*, and so, in that sense, the *"new people" are always an associate people* linked to those that preceded them in the divine purpose, but never the only exclusive people.

Paul's hortatory repetition is already preparing to influence those wavering in trust. The fact that the promise of God is singular in 4:13, 14, 16, 20, 21 is again indicative that it is the promise that concerns the nations upon which Paul bases his thought (Stowers 1994: 133). In view of Abraham's trust in the promise, those from the nations should not doubt their inclusion as ethnē alongside the people of Israel. But although Rom. 4:17-25 is commonly viewed as describing the personal trust of Abraham, this is an incomplete, individualistic perspective. Abraham trusted that God was able to do what he had promised, and this, as we have noted above, included "descendants," "land," and being a "great nation," that is, "inheriting the world." This is supported by the strong possibility that Paul echoes Isa. 54:1-3 in Rom. 4:13-21, indicated among other things by the inherit word group κληρονομέω used twice in both Isa. 54:3 and Rom. 4:13-14. This suggests that the original intent of the promise to Abraham—that one day the people of God would become a populous nation and inherit the world—is beginning to be fulfilled (4:13-18).[10]

In the last few verses of the chapter, in vv. 23-25, Paul speaks again of "us," to emphasize that what was true of Abraham's trust also applies to the Roman gentile Christ-followers. "Thus, just as Abraham's trust was reckoned to him as righteousness," since the scriptural narrative was not written "for his sake alone, but for ours also who trust in him who raised Jesus from the dead," then it will be reckoned to us also. Here the paradigm that was glimpsed in 4:17 is repeated—non-Jews trust in the God who raised our Lord Jesus from the dead. The pattern of trust in God as equivalent to the non-reckoning of sin as in the narrative of Abraham is repeated in the lives of gentile Christ-followers. A history of divine mercy becomes recognizable (Barclay 2015: 558). The phrase, "but for us also" (ἀλλὰ καὶ δι' ἡμᾶς) (4:24) here refers to Paul and the Romans he addresses, and does not include Jews. These would have to be read into the address at this point, but this perspective results from a mistaken assumption that in Romans, because of its universal inclusion of Jews and "gentiles" in God's purpose, Paul must always address both of these. In view of Paul's differentiation of Jew and non-Jew up to this point, to read 4:23-25 as an ethnically undefined "us" represents not so much a summary of Paul's intentions as a repudiation. An additional point is emphasized, that is, that the gentile Christ-followers should have access to the scriptures of Israel because they were written *not for Abraham's sake alone* (and his descendants) but for these ethnē also. Paul's "not only but also" inclusive pattern is repeated for emphasis. "It was reckoned as rectification" applies also to gentile trust in Christ. But thus, it also necessarily applies to their sharing in the realization of the promise, indicating that Paul's vision here is ultimately on the messianic hope about all the seed of Abraham and their sharing in the world to come. In the final verse, 4:25, Paul links back to 3:21-26 and forward to 5.1-11 with a brief reference to Christ's reconciling work as the basis for the next step in his argument.

Conclusion to Romans 4

From our exegesis of Romans 1-4, the presence of differing groups of ethnē in Christ and other non-Jews in various diverse relations to Jewish tradition and the message about the Christ has been identified. We note in summary Paul's inclusive, non-competitive presentation of such groups in his formulaic pattern, "not only but also." Contrary to some readings of these chapters, Paul does not divide the world into only

---

[10] The fact that the inheritance word group, κληρονομέω, is not used in Genesis 17 allows Forman to maintain that when Paul appropriates the story of Sarah and Abraham in Romans 4, he must have both the Genesis 17 context and its interpretation in Isaiah 54 in mind (2011: 90–2). Cf. Zacharias (2020).

the trusting "human" and the unpersuaded "human," but into ethnically differentiated groups under the one God of Jews and non-Jews. Paul's goal is to affirm those ethnē in Christ in their new identity, but not to do this to the detriment of the Jewish people. Paul argues aggregatively and not in a binary fashion as if the divine mercy were limited, and either Jew or non-Jew were the only option. The acceptance of the ethnē cannot be seen to depend on the exclusion of Israel.

To the contrary, although the ethnē were seeking an identity as those in Christ, a desirable goal and necessary ambition, Paul seeks to guide them away from the separatist understanding they are envisaging (as we will see in 11:13-24) to one that presupposes the existence of God's people Israel. Beginning with Abraham, he has construed an identity for them as also lineage (σπέρμα) of Abraham, in conjunction with the σπέρμα from Abraham, Isaac, and Jacob. Paul's repeated use of the aggregative formula "not only but also" underlines this common ancestry to Abraham, especially how this is achieved for the ethnē through union with Christ. Through him they were ransomed according to 3:21-26, and now in ch. 4, Paul has elaborated the outcome of this ransoming in the ethnē's new relation, not only in union with Christ, but through him to the other σπέρμα of their common father, Abraham. Christ is the linchpin that supplies the affiliation in this new familial construction. But only in 8:14 (sonship) and 8:29 (brotherhood) and eventually in 12-15 (a new charter for the ethnē without the Law but with ἀγάπη) will Paul develop more fully his conception of the familial relation into which the ethnē have been introduced through Christ (McMurray 2021: 157–9). This is an important element of the social identity that ethnē derive from belonging to the Christ-movement. And the basis for this construction will be developed in Romans 9–11when the meaning and promised future of Israel in 11:29 (election) on whom the entire lineage introduced in ch. 4 fundamentally depends. But since we are interpreting Romans in a sequential and progressive reading (Casson 2019: 192–5), we cannot preempt the content of Paul's progressive text, in keeping with his Roman audience who could not do otherwise.

We noted in our "Introduction" chapter that recent developments in SIT have stressed the non-conflictual model of the emergence of groups, and that thus the mere fact of group-belonging does not necessitate opposition to other groups. The Roman ethnē in Christ were debating how Abrahamic paternity could be established for their group. They tended to see their inclusion as the necessary cause of Israel's posited exclusion. But Paul so presents Abraham as to make him the father of both Jews and also of non-Jews in Christ. Paul thus confirms the identity of Jews and of non-Jews in his use of Abraham tradition. Any threat to a group's identity is likely to result in opposition and hostility to others, and conversely the affirmation of group identity can lead to mutual acceptance and peace (Wenzel, Mummendey, and Waldzus 2007: 333). Paul uses Abraham to affirm the identity of two peoples who both need Abraham for self-identification.

He does not dismiss the identity of the Jewish groups in Rome or elsewhere but so presents Abraham as father of both circumcised Jews and of uncircumcised ethnē as to promote mutual acceptance. The recently emerged ethnē in Christ must not make the mistake of assuming that their gentile identity is the norm or the common in-group identity for all God's peoples. Nor must these ethnē be forced to accept circumcision and to keep the Law as if Jewish patterns of life must be common to ethnē in Christ. It is only when mutual acceptance of differing groups in their ethnic difference is practiced with a common in-group identity under the God of Israel that the reconciliation of Christ will be made manifest. In the relation of differing subgroups under a superordinate, that is, common in-group identity, there may be asymmetry in the exercise of power, but equality in the certainty of belonging (Neufeld and Schmitt 2019).

We do not know the relative numerical strength of the ethnē in Christ and their presumed Jewish neighbors in Rome, but Paul's emphasis is inclusive and total. Note the emphasis on "all who trust" in 4:24. By affirming the paternity of Abraham for both Jewish and non-Jewish groups, Paul does not deny either group's identity or encourage arrogant competition as to who best represents the "people" of the one God of Israel. Both circumcision and foreskin are accepted, and peace must be maintained as Paul is about to reason in ch. 5. What is notably entirely absent from Romans 4, despite the emphasis upon the family of Abraham, is the concept of all the people of God as one identical, non-differentiated people.

Romans 5

Romans 5:1-11: "Now That We Have Been Reconciled, Let Us Enjoy Peace"

¹Therefore, having been rectified by trust, let us have peace with God through our Lord Jesus Christ, ²through whom we also have obtained access to this grace in which we stand; let us also boast in our hope of sharing the glory of God. ³And not only that, let us also boast in our afflictions, knowing that this affliction produces endurance, ⁴and endurance produces character, and character produces hope, ⁵and hope does not cause shame, because God's love has been poured into our hearts through the Holy Spirit that has been given to us. ⁶For while we were still weak, at that time Christ died for the impious. ⁷Indeed, rarely will anyone die for a righteous person—though perhaps for a good person someone might actually dare to die. ⁸But God demonstrates his own love for us in that while we still were sinners Christ died for us. ⁹Much more surely then, now that we have been put right by his blood, will we be saved through him from the wrath. ¹⁰For if while we were enemies, we were reconciled to God through the death of his Son, much more surely, having been reconciled, will we be saved by his life. ¹¹But not only that, we even boast in God through our Lord Jesus Christ, through whom we have now received this reconciliation.

With this section of Romans, Paul moves into a discourse in chs. 5–8 where the diatribal questions and inferences appear at first glance to be less obvious, especially in 5:1-11 (Jewett 2007: 346, Rodriguez 2016: 110). Despite this Porter notes other features such as dialogical mode, rhetorical questions, and the characteristic flow of the argument that point toward the diatribe (1991: 666–7). We note that in Romans 5 there are no dialogues with the second-person singular, nor μὴ γένοιτο rejection, nor the characteristic vocatives (Song 2004: 72). The οὖν, therefore, connects back to 4:25 showing that here we are dealing with the outcome of the δικαίωσις, rectification, first announced in 1:16-17 and developed particularly in 3:21-26. Rom. 5:1-11 is reminiscent of 3:21-26 in various ways. "These passages share the language of sin, the glory of God, righteousness, grace and blood, and they also share a soteriological logic: sinful human beings are made right with God through Jesus's blood" (Jackson 2018: 300). Instead of recurring, challenging diatribal questions, here the emphasis is upon the declaration of what is enjoyed through Christ. The first-person plural continues from 4:23 where the reckoning of πίστις as righteousness, it is noted, was not written for Abraham's sake alone but for ours also. Thus, at the end of Romans 4, we have a distinction between Abraham and gentile Christ-followers, but Paul includes himself in the "we," and in chs. 5–8, nevertheless, a clear distinction between Paul and his gentile addressees will continue to be observed.

As already discussed at several points, Paul in Romans addresses ethnē only, and the careful regard to his use of singular and plural pronouns and verbs strongly confirms this perspective (Rodriguez 2016: 101–31). Thus in 5:1-11, the concentrated use throughout the pericope of first-person plural "we" indicates that Paul wishes to draw attention to the de facto unity that exists between himself and his readers on the basis of the experience of righteousness and reconciliation in Christ (Jewett 2007: 347). Esler notes that 5:1-11 contains eighteen first-person plurals and that only vv. 4 and 7 lack a reference to "us" (2003: 196). In view of the slanderous reports concerning Paul's gentile mission, Paul is concerned not only to differentiate himself from mistaken reports but also to link closely his views and mission with those of the Roman gentile Christ-followers wherever possible. The basis of the commonality is their joint participation in the blessings they share through Christ, and this includes Paul as their representative apostle even though he is not part of the ethnē. In social identity terms, Paul seeks to exercise leadership in relation to the ethnē in Christ at Rome as apostle to the ethnē under whose apostolic sphere of influence they are included. He expresses and elaborates the implications of the Christ event for them, that is, their shared vital group convictions, and as such strengthens their transformed social identity as Christ-followers. In this perspective, this means emphasizing their common goals, binding them together as one entity despite difference. Here there are frequent first-person plural "we" constructions, rather than addresses to "you." Thus, Paul stresses his oneness with them since this is the way he can have influence as the leader who embodies all the aims they share together. This resonates with Daniel Bar-Tal's emphasis on the social nature of shared beliefs (1990). Shared beliefs play a crucial role in the construction of a corporate identity, in terms of both individual and collective self understanding. Bar-Tal claims that "sharing beliefs is one of the basic elements for the expression of common social identity, because beliefs with particular contents prototypically define a group" (2000: 4). If Paul succeeds in convincing the Romans that he shares their central values, then he will be recognized as their apostle and will have power and influence among them. This is not in the sense of an individual leader who imposes his own (possibly) alien values upon those he leads, but as the one who upholds or best represents the core values of this group. In view of his goal to be their recognized leader, it is of importance that Paul succeeds in convincing the Romans that he shares much of their perspective. As Steffens states, "successful leaders mobilize followers to the extent that they successfully manage a group identity that they share with followers" (Steffens et al. 2015: 181). From this perspective, "the ability to lead depends on the ability to represent a group consensus that itself is produced by a shared identity" (Esler 2021a: 57). Thus, Paul's letter, whatever else it is destined to achieve, is intent on molding the identity of the Romans as a coherent group of Christ-followers led by the apostle to the ethnē. Romans 5, therefore, becomes a charter for this gentile group, and it begins by encouraging them to live peaceably together, "let us have peace with God through our Lord Jesus Christ."[1]

As non-Jews the Romans have now received access, προσαγωγήν, "through our Lord Jesus Christ" to this grace, the new status in which they stand. By emphasizing their new status as ethnē in Christ, Paul is excluding other options that may seem still to be open to them. Since προσαγωγή was a stock term for approaching the altar of sacrifice, this must mean that the ethnē now have access to God's presence (a reversal of 1:13, and of 3:23, Jackson 2018: 300). This access terminology is repeated elsewhere in the New Testament only in Eph. 2:18 and 3:12. It probably is particularly significant in Rome where Paul confirms the *new status* (access to God's presence) that those from the nations receive through Christ. But we need to be careful how we describe what it is that the nations have received. There is no claim that the differences between Jews and the nations have been dissolved through the reconciliation in Christ. The Law that distinguishes and thus separates Jews and non-Jews has not been abolished, but established in achieving its proper function in relation to each.

Since in their ascribed identity they are not designated Israelites, the ethnē, though they do have access to the presence of God are yet not included in the covenant, but rather they have access to the grace promised through Abraham and actualized through Christ. The ethnē in Christ cannot become Israelites because, in order for the promise to be realized in them and for the God of Israel to be demonstrated to be the God of both Jews and those from the nations, it is absolutely essential that they continue as ethnē and must not seek to become Jews. The God of Israel cannot be limited to being the god of only one ethnic group, since he is Lord of all—the Abrahamic promise even requires plurality (Nanos 1996, McMurray 2021: 189). The obligation of the covenant in terms of the Torah is the prerogative of Israel and differentiates them from the nations whose sharing in the promises comes only through the mediation of Christ; note the recurrence of the phrase "through our Lord Jesus Christ" (5:1, 5:11, cf. also 5:21). Since ethnē in Christ are not included in the covenant as are Israelites, they are totally dependent on Christ for their participation in the grace and blessings of God—everything they have or enjoy comes through Christ as Lord, and this enables non-Jews to have access to God's peace and other blessings. Paul is rejoicing that the ethnē have everything they need through Christ. In Christ, they lack nothing that is essential—everything is gifted to them (8:32). If they have everything they need in allegiance to God through trust in Christ, this is another way of claiming that they do not need to become proselytes or call themselves Jews since this is God's way of including the nations within his purpose.

Paul, in the first part of this chapter, describes the outcome of access to the promised blessings as "peace with God" and points to a new stage in his argument. Here we move to the language of reconciliation after estrangement. This "peace" stands in antithetical relation to the "wrath of God" revealed against idolatry and wickedness (1:18) and presupposes the conciliatory work of Christ. But now the truce terminology of 3:21-26 is expressed in reconciliation terminology, which allows emphasis upon a cessation

---

[1] The explicit concern with peace will be more fully developed here but will also reemerge in 14:17.

of hostility and its replacement by peace with God. Reconciliation seems to be Paul's favorite language for describing the result of ethnē turning to God (Martin 1981: 148, 152). This term is important in Paul's mission in that it allows Paul to emphasize reconciliation with fellow human beings as in 2 Cor. 5:18-20 and also with the whole world (Rom. 11:15). He views himself and his co-workers as being "entrusted with the ministry (διακονία) of reconciliation" (2. Cor. 5:19). Beale concludes that both in 2 Corinthians, Ephesians, and most likely also in Romans, "the emphasis is upon … the reconciliation of alienated people to God" (Beale1989).

Here Paul stresses that it is through the death of Christ that "we" have received reconciliation (5:11). The reconciliation terms may have originated from the emphasis upon the nations as Israel's enemies. As a former persecutor of Christ-followers, Paul can use this language meaningfully from personal experience. Probably elements of both of these are involved. It is to be noted how easily Paul moves from differing images of God's redemptive activity through Christ particularly in Rom 3:21-26, where conciliation after conflict was implicit, to an explicit reconciliation idiom in Romans 5–11. Paul is writing here in 5:6-11 in explanatory, reassuring terms focusing upon the difference in status and context between formerly, when "we were still weak, i.e., idolators," "while we still were sinners," "while we were enemies," and "now": "now that we have been justified through his blood" and "having been reconciled" or "through whom we have now received the reconciliation." Paul takes such "through Christ" language seriously, "For him, Christ is not a symbol of the power of self-giving (a Christ-figure) but *the* God-involving event—indeed, the redefining eschatological event" (Keck 2005: 142). The repetition of νῦν, now, in 5:9-11 corresponds to the "now" in 3:21 denoting the transfer of non-Jews from the era prior to 3:21 to the present era after the reconciling work of Christ. The fact that he is addressing those from the nations influenced Paul's choice of reconciliation terminology. We note here the diversity in Paul's theological vocabulary. In "Romans, God is theocentric but christomorphic—focused on God as understood in light of Christ. Christ is the means through which we have peace with God, access to grace, justification, reconciliation, salvation from wrath, all of which are God's doing by means of Christ" (Keck 2005. 140–1).

But the change in terminology does not mean that here we have simply a repetition of rectification language only now in terms of reconciliation. There is an advance in Paul's argument in Romans 5 from Rom. 3:21-26. Rectification with God applies to being set within a right relationship with God in spite of sin/estrangement. But in reconciliation a risk is involved in that if one of the parties takes the initiative to restore the relationship, the initiative can be rejected by the other party. Paul declares here that it is God who is the one who has taken the initiative. Hence, this metaphor of reconciliation enables Paul to stress his own role, though he does not do so here in the explicit manner he does in 2 Cor. 5:20, "we are ambassadors for Christ, since God is making his appeal through us; we entreat you, be reconciled to God." The emphasis in Romans 5 is on the receipt of reconciliation now, as in 5:11 "we have now received reconciliation." Here Paul joins with the Roman ethnē in Christ to stress their participation rather than separately stressing his own apostolic mandate. But there is another aspect to Paul's use of reconciliation terminology.

Breytenbach has shown that Paul drew this terminology from the political sphere of creating peace between warring parties in the sphere of diplomacy (1989: 40–104). Jewett has emphasized Paul's diplomacy in terms of an ambassador for Christ. It is likely that Paul is here creating a radical paradigm in which he contrasts enmity with another in everyday life, where the normal pattern would be that it is the offending party who must take the first step toward peace. Here it is God, the one who has been wronged, who takes the initiative in reconciliation (Fitzgerald 1989: 241–62). From his own experience, Paul knows that it is God who took the initiative to reconcile an enemy to himself. It is we who are reconciled to God, not God to us. Reconciliation is the proper antidote for being enemies (Keck 2005: 141). Paul is undertaking a diplomatic role as apostle to the nations on behalf of God toward all those ethnē who have turned to Christ. And he wishes to see this reconciliation working effectively between the differing groups apparent in Romans 2, and whom he will address later in chs. 12–15.

Of course, the different metaphors reinforce one another to a great extent (Campbell 2018: 302–5), but if we read with Jewett, following the variant reading, the more strongly supported subjunctive, "let us have peace" then we can see that Paul is moving his hearers forward to the obligations following from acceptance with God. Similarly, the duplication of καυχώμεθα in 2b and 3a, correlated with the subjunctive reading "let us have peace," as proposed here, supports emphasis upon what the ethnē are called to do rather than on only what they presently enjoy. Some scholars, for example, Michael Wolter (1978: 99–102; 2014: 55–69) tend to restrict peace to the relationship with God, but peace here should have a comprehensive implication that "includes the relationship with God as well as the rest of creation, including one's fellow humans" (Jewett 2007: 349). Peace, εἰρήνη is with or toward God, but also something to be maintained and aimed at, rather than simply celebrated. It includes the social dimension, a necessary social correlate that we shall see is explicit in 14:19 where peace refers directly to difficulties within the assemblies. As Jewett has stressed, following the variant reading, "The first-person plural includes all the members of Paul's audience as well as Paul and his colleagues in a common obligation. The theme of obligation carries through when the exhortative subjunctive ἔχομεν in 5:1 is translated in similar ways in vv. 2, 3 and 11" (2007: 348). And this call to peace is not entirely to be unexpected in that in the next chapter, ch. 6, Paul uses the imperative in giving guidance to the ethnē (v. 13).

The need for reassurance for the non-Jewish Christ-followers must be strong for Paul to so concentrate here on the change in status effected by trust in Christ. It is likely that Paul also seeks to reinforce the relationship between himself and his Roman audience, to overcome any alienation that may exist between them. There is some misunderstanding of his teaching and of his failure to visit them, so Paul cannot explicitly urge reconciliation as he did in 2 Corinthians 5. Instead, he hopes that by joining himself with them in celebrating the outcome of Christ's reconciliation with God, there may be peace also between the Roman ethnē and himself.

Paul's διακονία includes all the ἐκκλησίαι of the nations, even those that he has not founded as here in Rome. Paul's message is for the nations to be reconciled to God. The enmity of the gentile world against the Creator God resulted in their not perceiving him as just, righteous, and loving so that even those who had turned away from idolatry to Christ had great difficulty in relating what they had heard of the Christ message to their preunderstanding of their gods. They have difficulty relating the Christ story to common enculturated conceptions of how to relate to the gods, and probably in understanding a concept such as the love of the Creator God. This tendency that we note as a real possibility here became more pronounced as the Christ-movement extended into the gentile world.

So, although the emphasis here is upon Christ and the outcome of his death for sinners, the underlying rationale is that Christ reveals the love of God. It is through the activity of Christ that the love of the Creator God is known—his own love—that is, the character or nature of the "high God," who can be trusted because of this love. The Christological emphasis thus serves the function of revealing the theological underpinning of Paul's argument, which is based upon the revelation of God, perceived through the gospel message about the Christ.

The Christological rationale for peace and hope is provided in vv. 6-11. This is expressed in terms of the death of Christ ἀποθνῄσκω (die) vv. 6, 7, and καταλάσσω—καταλλαγή (reconcile) in vv. 10-11. The creedal-like statement—"Christ died on our behalf"—has parallels in 14:15 "one for whom Christ died" (cf. also similarly 1 Cor. 15:3, 1 Thess. 5:9-10, 1 Cor. 8:11, and 2 Cor. 5:14). As noted above, the important point Paul makes here is that Christ's death for sinners expresses God's "own love" (v. 8) that is being demonstrated and proved (συνίστημι). Thus, it seems likely that Paul cites a well-established formula at the end of v. 8 integrating it into his argument that Christ died on our behalf to thereby convey a sense of participationism and solidarity such as would accompany the repetition of these words at the shared meals in the ἐκκλησίαι (Jewett 2007: 362).

It appears from the preponderance of emphasis upon the good death, that is, death for others that the Romans had difficulty in linking properly the death of Christ with the love of God. In order to explain the meaning of Christ's death in terms that non-Jews could understand, an example is given, possibly by Paul, though it could be an interlocutor's interruption in the diatribe style. In everyday life, heroic benefactors may die for good causes even for another's sake, but it is unprecedented to die for unworthy people, as Christ did (5:7). This un-Pauline interruption in 5:6-7 might help to explain the text-critical evidence that has led some to find a gloss here. Keck offers a helpful understanding of the issues including the strange use of "weak" in relation to human existence and the use of a human parallel in the dying of someone on behalf of another to help interpret the unparalleled death of Christ. In 5:8, Paul will state that the law was weakened, not persons. Keck considers that here we have a marginal note that has crept into the text (2005: 139–40). I am sympathetic to the view that diatribal responses by an interlocutor might also be indicated. The basis of the argument here, which may reflect an early creedal formula (Jewett 2007: 359), is that "Christ died" on behalf of sinners ἁμαρτωλός (cf. 5:6 ὑπὲρ ἀσεβῶν) thus evidencing the love of God, a phrase found introduced only here, in 8:39, and 2 Cor. 13:13. The use of "sinners" here is virtually synonymous with ἀσεβής (impious) and reminds us that Paul is addressing non-Jews in language reminiscent of 1:19-32. The love of God Paul claims has been poured into our hearts (5:5) by the Holy Spirit acting as the agent of God to influence Christ-followers in their inmost being or self (as people would describe themselves today, but which in Paul's day was perceived as the heart Jer. 31:33). It is significant that Paul expresses his message in experiential language, relating to present realities (Witherington 2004: 139–40), possibly indicating an awareness of the needy condition of some of the Roman Christ-followers.

Paul will expand on the theme of the love of God at the end of ch. 8, but he develops its significance further by using a common argument, the *qal wahomer*, πολλῷ μᾶλλον, meaning "much more," which proceeds from the lesser to the greater.

Romans 5:8-10 (15-17) *Qal Wahomer* Arguments

The basis of Paul's argument is that if, while these Roman ethnē were still sinners, Christ died on their behalf, now that they have been justified by his death, *how much more* will they be saved from the wrath. What Paul is doing here through this form of argument is to communicate to the ethnē how much the sharing in this trust strengthens their social identity and mutual bonding as a group (Bar-Tal 2000). In Greco-Roman rhetoric, this is the *a minore ad maius*, "from lesser to greater" inference, which is equivalent to the Hebrew *qal wahomer*, "light and heavy" argument. It is a form of enthymeme in which the premise is provided in what has already been accepted as true and the inference is drawn to what has not yet been accepted as true. This form of argument was highly developed by Jewish scholars and became one of the seven exegetical rules of Hillel. It is evidence for Paul's Jewish education, though the mode of argument indicates ongoing Jewish appropriation and development of Hellenistic rhetoric (Black 1974). This passage links 1:16-17, 1:18-29, and 3:21-26 to ch. 5. The *qal wahomer*, "how much more," form of argument was a distinctive element of Paul's Christological argumentation—he uses it four times here in 5:8-10 and 5:15-17. He will go on to use it again and, significantly, in 11:12 and 11:24 (Grieb 2002: 61).

From Paul's earlier use of this form of argument in 2 Cor. 3:7-11, we learn that Paul looked at the world through the lens of Christ's redemptive work in *a teleological view of God's activity*. By this we mean that Paul uses this form of comparison in a positive sense where there has to be an element of continuity between the two items compared—here this is easy to see in that the basic premise is the death of Christ. If Christ died for the ethnē while they were sinners, how much more secure must they be now that they have been reconciled. Obviously, this *qal wahomer* form of argument was a very amenable one for Paul in expressing his teleological, Christological hope. It is based on an optimistic view of the world as an outcome of God's activity through Abraham and Moses and finally through reconciliation in Christ (cf. Campbell 2018: 309 22). The "how much more" element resonates with Paul's understanding of grace through Christ, which always seems to be associated with an element of superabundance, perhaps even of superfluity (cf. ἐπερίσσευσεν "abounded" in 5:15, and the rare noun περισσεία, "abundance, excess" in 5:17, where χάρις, "grace," and "the gift of righteousness," δωρεά τῆς δικαιοσύνης, are included in this excess of blessing) as "the superabundant fullness of the time of salvation" now inaugurated (Jewett 2007: 383, n175), but still to be consumated (cf. 2 Cor. 9:12-14).

Paul's focus here is essentially on a powerful contrast between two eras as inaugurated by two figures, Adam and Christ. The second, and the era associated with him, is so presented as to magnify the work of Christ in contrast to Adam whose failure to hearken (hear positively) the voice of God brought the reign of sin and death to have universal dominion. The surprising aspect of Paul's fourth use of the "how much more" argument in 5:17 is that the "how much more" relates to the subject rather than to Christ—it is those who trust who will reign through the one, Jesus Christ. This is the ultimate goal and outcome that will finally overcome the failure of Adam, but Paul's interest is not at this point on a detailed eschatological program, but only on magnifying the reconciliation achieved in Christ for whom Adam and his transgression are the foil and presupposition. The parallelism and dissonance between Adam and Christ noted throughout this chapter serve the purpose of magnifying the reconciliation God achieved through Christ, particularly in its effect as experienced by those who trust. The use of theological argumentation here has an anthropological outcome as its goal, as will become more obvious in the next chapter.

A New Kind of Boasting—Rejoicing in God through Christ

Paul apparently viewed life in Christ as an ongoing conflict leading to victory over the gods and other powers worshipped as gods, and resulting in the final consummation and revelation of the glory of God. The Romans are being reassured that they are part of God's work through Christ and that what has been begun in them will result in their hope of sharing in the glory of God (5:2). This can be their (new) boast. Instead of boasting over "others" apparently "broken," this boast is inclusive that is, rejoicing together. But this may include suffering together as the route to glory, as Paul sets out in a concise, spiraling rhetorical construction in vv. 3-5 (Talbert 2002: 135). Suffering, endurance, and hope enable Christ-followers to rejoice in "our hope of the glory of God" (5:2). Edwin Judge has contrasted Paul's emphasis here with the prevailing Stoic estimate of the cult of glory among the Roman nobility (1966: 32–45). The winning of glory was the only adequate reward for merit in public life and the only effective assurance of immortality (Barton 2001: 2032–5). Self-magnification thus became a feature of Hellenistic higher education. Jewett notes how the entire system of honor and shame was reversed by Paul in proclaiming the glory of God in and of itself as the highest possible good (2007: 352). The definite article preceding "afflictions" may mean *the afflictions* known to the Roman audience, and also to Paul—hence "our afflictions" (5:3). It appears that Paul acknowledges that he is aware that the Roman gentile Christ-followers know the meaning of suffering and affliction. Boasting in God and in the suffering that his call may require is the glory to which these Romans can rightly aspire.

The narrative moves from the description of the wrath of God coming upon the gentile world, to the ransoming by Christ in 3:21-26, to the reconciliation of sinners in ch. 5:1-11. The comparison of the beginning of the story to its outcome at this point leads Paul to argue in the vein of "how much more." It seems that though deliverance from the wrath of God through Christ was part of the teaching (διδαχή) that the Roman addressees had received, Paul thought they needed "reminding" (15:15). If Christ died for them while they were still idolatrous and sinful, then now that they have heard the call of God, they need not doubt that they will in the future be σωθησόμεθα from the wrath (5:9), that is, the last judgment. For if it was possible for reconciliation to have happened (κατηλλάγημεν), past tense (aorist middle indicative, "we were reconciled") even when we "gentiles" were hostile to God, now that reconciliation has taken place (καταλλαγέντες), past tense (aorist passive participle), "having been reconciled," it is self-evident that salvation will follow (future tense, σωθησόμεθα, we shall be saved) (Hultgren 2011: 212).

Paul ends the first section of ch. 5 linking back to the theme of boasting, but this includes a new form of boasting—boasting in our sufferings; the effect of suffering is to produce endurance, which in turn produces character, which produces hope. And hope does not lead to disappointment because the Spirit pours God's love "into our hearts." He concludes by stating that the gentile Christ-followers can even boast in God through Christ (5:11). It is not a boasting in "gentile" over Jew, or in the qualities of any ethnic group as such, nor in human achievement of any kind but in the love of God, and hope of the glory of God resulting not in an inflated self-estimate, but in sober judgment (12:3). Here as elsewhere Paul continues to move attention away from emphasis on human achievement of glory to rejoice instead in hope of the glory of God. "The glory of God exchanged in 1:23, and lacked in 3:23, is the same glory hoped for in 5:1-2" (Jackson 2018: 300). As Jewett notes, it is significant that Paul does not refer to the hope of salvation but to "the hope of God's glory," which draws attention away from the status of one's self or one's group (2007: 352). Although, as Jewett has concluded, Paul's reversal of the Roman system of seeking glory in an honor and shame culture offers a clear reading of Rom. 5:1-11, we must add a necessary clarification. Although Paul sets differing goals for Roman ethnē, he does not deny them the focus upon glory, but only a differing kind of glory, the glorification of God. This conclusion is typical of Paul who so often denies one form of action and replaces it with another, showing that he is not countercultural, but offers an alternative pattern of life that uses the language of his addressees while pointing to a differing set of values. This reflects the developed Jewish policy in relation to civic life and authorities of "playing and not playing" the game of acculturation.

Romans 5:12-21: The Rule of Grace through Christ Overcomes the Rule of Sin and Death

¹²Therefore, just as sin came into the world through one man, and death came through sin, and so death spread to all because all have sinned—¹³sin was indeed in the world prior to the law, but sin is not reckoned where there is no law. ¹⁴Yet death exercised dominion from Adam to Moses, even over those whose sins were not like the transgression of Adam, who is a type of the one who was to come. ¹⁵And is not the free gift just like the transgression? For if the many died through the one man's transgression, much more surely have the grace of God and the free gift in the grace of the one man, Jesus Christ, abounded for the many. ¹⁶And did not the free gift abound in the same way as sin abounded by the one who sinned? Yes. For on the one hand, judgment abounded from the one man to the point of condemnation.

> *For the judgment following one transgression brought condemnation, but the free gift following many transgressions brings rectification. ¹⁷If, because of the one man's transgression, death exercised dominion through that one, much more surely will those who receive the abundance of grace and the free gift of righteousness exercise dominion in life through the one man, Jesus Christ. ¹⁸Therefore just as one man's transgression led to condemnation for all, so one man's act of setting right leads to rectification and life for all. ¹⁹For just as by the one man's disobedience the many were made sinners, so by the one man's righteousness the many will be made righteous. ²⁰But law came in, with the result that the transgression multiplied; but where sin increased, grace abounded all the more, ²¹so that, just as sin reigned in death, so grace might also reign through righteousness [leading to] eternal life through Jesus Christ our Lord.*

The second section of Romans 5 links with the διὰ τοῦτο, "on account of this," directly to 5:11 and possibly as far back as to 1:18-32. It differs in many respects from what precedes most obviously in the absence of the first-person plural so frequent in 5:1-11. There is some evidence of diatribal style, particularly in v. 16a (Porter 1991) and "lesser to greater" constructions feature strongly in 5:17 as already in 5:8-10. We encounter here a carefully structured syllogistic argument—for if A then B, followed sometimes by *argumentative* links, therefore, just as, so then, and so on. Key biblical figures such as Adam or Moses in comparison with Christ help structure the narrative; and death and sin rule as personified powers while grace and righteousness rule through Christ. Law also enters the narrative from v. 13, particularly in its relation to and connection with sin and death. The new dimension that emergences here is the focus on the supraindividual powers that determine human destiny—negatively Adam, sin, and death; and positively Christ. The discussion of sin and death, grace, and the link with the Law in 5:13 and 20 obviously are in preparation for the themes on which the discussion will focus in chs. 6–8. The basic contrast is between the effects of Adam's trespass, enslavement, and so on and the hearkening of Christ, which results in grace through which the righteous, no longer enslaved, will reign with Christ (v. 17). But, as noted above, there is no direct address to an audience, in strong contrast to 5:1-11.

The outcome of the reconciliation through Christ is presented as the result of his ὑπακοή—hearing in trust that we designate, hearkening to God's voice (Ehrensperger 2009: 166–78), indicating Paul's goal as a teacher who intends to bring out the lessons that ought to be learned through a review of Christ's behavior in relation to God and to sin. Our assumption is that a number of the gentile Christ-followers at Rome would have received instruction first of all in (their) earlier association with Jewish tradition and catechesis on their first turning to Christ. It is difficult to be certain about the extent of their knowledge, but Paul seems to assume that Adam and Moses need no introduction, and only those with a certain degree of education in Jewish tradition would be able to get a good understanding of Paul's complicated argument, including his reference to Adam (5:14). The interlocutor boasts that he is instructed in the Law (2:18). This probably indicates a high level of competence on the part of some, accompanied by a need for guidance on the part of others. The other areas of expertise available in Rome among the Jewish community, some of whom are Christ-followers, must not be overlooked.[2] Thus, although we view Romans as addressed only to non-Jews, we regard them as living in a context where there were a significant number of Jews, some of whom were Christ-followers.

Paul points to the entry of sin into the world through Adam and emphasizes that death reigned even in the period prior to the giving of the Law when sin was not registered. This indicates a preliminary, partial negative response to the question "Is the Law sin?" (7:7). It also may indicate that the Roman ethnē may have associated the Jewish Law as the source of sin and death in that as Paul states, "Sin is not reckoned where there is no Law" (5:13). Since death reigned in the period from Adam to Moses, and since sin entered the world with Adam, prior to the giving of the Law, Paul may be saying that sin and its consequences cannot be attributable to the Law, whatever its dangerous outcome, especially for non-Jews. The main tendency of 5:12-21 is, in various ways, to argue the incompatibility between grace and continuing in sin. Via the themes of hearkening and refusing to hear with their corresponding outcomes, as well as by the references to Adam, Moses, and Christ, Paul seeks to locate the ethnē in Christ in the realm of God's grace, which he designates as the opposite realm to that of sin and death.

As noted, specific evidence for the continuance of diatribal style in 5:12-21 can be found in 15a and 16a where Rodriguez (2014: 106) follows Jewett, Caragounis (1985: 142-8), and Porter (1991: 655-77) in recognizing a rhetorical question anticipating a positive response. Jewett sees v. 15a as Paul's question which he put to his audience. Yet, Rodriguez convincingly argues for the question as coming from Paul's interlocutor, "But isn't the gift just like the transgression?" with the implied answer "Yes, it is." An answer in the affirmative derives from αλλ'οὐχ ("but not"), which is a typical opening for a rhetorical question in a diatribe (Porter 1991: 674). This reading of 15a changes the translation of the verse to the opposite of the common translation (as we will note later with reference to 9:6b). Thus, in contrast to the NRSV rendering: "But the free gift is not like the trespass" Rodriguez translates 16a "and didn't the gift abound in the same way as sin abounded by the one who sinned?" (2014: 106-7). The affirmative answer agrees on the similarities between the outcomes of the action of two very different characters in differing regimes, treated in stark, binary terms. Adam's legacy was the "reign of death" through sin, whereas Jesus's legacy was the "reign of life" through his faithfulness. The contrast is clear, Adam's sin was that he did not hearken to God's voice, Jesus was faithful and willing to "hear" that is, respond positively to the call of God. Here we note again the continuation and application of the truce brought by Christ on behalf of sinners in 3:21-26.

As commentators note, taking 5:15a as a rhetorical question resolves the tension inherent in viewing 15a as a negative comparison between the results of Adam and Christ, but set within a lesser to greater argument in 15c, which requires an argument of similarity. The role of the Law is noted as resulting in the increase of παράπτωμα, transgression in that where Torah exists sin is registered and the severity of sin thus increases in the presence of the Law. The point Paul wishes to stress is that the coming

---

[2] Cf. Tal Ilan (2009) notes the library facilities that may have been available in the Jewish communities in Rome.

of the Law registers idolatry as sin like Adam's, refusal to listen, whereas it was by obedient hearing that Christ brought reconciliation. It is interesting how Paul uses arguments about the life of Christ as well as about his death in teaching the Romans (cf. 5:10). This emphasis would be particularly relevant in a community of gentile Christ-followers where "sinning in order that grace may abound" was viewed as somehow a reasonable option.

In this particular context, where sinning so that grace may abound was cited as an option, Adam's refusal to listen in his failure to hearken to God's voice is contrasted with Christ's willing consent. The contrasted entities are not trust and "obedience" as necessarily opposites, but faithful hearing as a sign of trust, the "obedience" of trust that Paul intends to bring about in Rome, cf. ὑπακοὴ πίστεως (1:5). Here we get a glimpse of Paul's application of reconciliation through Christ for non-Jews, and how it relates to righteous or unrighteous behavior. Being rectified through trust does not point to a dichotomy between gentile reconciliation with God and the Law; their pattern of behavior, which includes the δικαίωμα of the Law being fulfilled in them, demonstrates that "the 'obedience' that trust produces" (1:5) is in conformity with the pattern of life to which the Law also points. Without denigrating the Law, Paul demonstrates that its effect, far from removing the consequences of sin, actually works with sin to produce judgment. In this respect, taking on the yoke of the Law does not, in fact cannot, solve the problem of gentile sinfulness.

It seems that Paul intends to polarize Christ and sin, in association with the emphasis upon sin and "obedience." Adam's failure to hear and to obey had disastrous consequences for all, indicating that Christ's way of trust and "obedience" to God must be exemplified in the paradigmatic life-giving response of those who follow him; grace does not demand otherwise. The grace of God is based upon a trusting relation to him, not in a forced compliance with his demands. But it does demand a positive response, a voluntary giving of oneself to God through Christ. The clearly enunciated outcomes of "obedience" and disobedience and the role of the Law are obviously meant to give guidance to Roman "gentiles" confused about the relation of sin and grace and of God's reconciling character as indicated in his welcoming of the ethnē through Christ.

Paul thus talks here of "obedience" and "disobedience" whether by Christ or Adam. But it is primarily "obedience" to God though Christ. It is not enough to hear the word of God but, as noted, to return to a rather archaic term, one needs to "hearken" to God's word, that is, to listen to it, and then to hear it positively, to put it into practice. The term Paul uses here is ὑπακοή, normally translated as "obedience," and παρακοή its opposite (5:19). Many differing theological stances have been created from the reading of this verse in its context and differing understandings of ὑπακοή have resulted (Ehrensperger 2009: 155–78). What Paul is stressing is the hearing in trust or "hearkening," that he wishes to stress as typified by the whole-hearted response of Jesus to the voice of God. The opposite response Paul finds typified in the scriptural narrative of the failure of Adam to positively hearken to the voice of God that resulted in the entry into the world of sin and human's enslavement to its alien power.

It must be stressed at this point that Paul's argumentation here is principally developed for the purpose of arguing that keeping the Law as ethnē will not be effective as a route toward pleasing God. In 7:7-25, Paul will demonstrate that the Law actually acts in conjunction with gentile transgression to allow the good guidance it provides in its precepts to become instruments of sin's power. It does not work, it is not effective because by ethnē performing it they seek to earn God's favor through what they do. This mistaken route to divine favor came, as we have noted, to be described as doing "works of law." These are thus described because they are not performed out of a positive response to God's grace as Jews were called to respond. This problem cannot be overcome by ethnē beginning to live as Jews or even calling themselves so. The truth that the ethnē need to understand is that the Law was given to Israel, it was never meant for non-Jews. Paul knows that this fundamental aspect of the Law is not fully or generally understood at Rome, otherwise there would not exist the differing groups we have noted in our analysis of Romans 2. The Law as such is not the problem, but rather the problem is that it is Israel's Law, gifted to her but not to the ethnē.

The respective reigns of sin and of grace indicate how reconciled "gentiles" should show their allegiance in loyalty to God through Christ. In this section, Paul relates sin and the Law to different periods in the divine economy giving thereby a sense of progression from one period of history to another—from the period before the Law to the time of Moses who introduced the Law, to the time of Christ who reconciled the nations to God. The ethnē in Christ at Rome are depicted as engaged in a drama in which they are facing powerful forces that lead to their enslavement and from which only the life and death of Christ and the operation of the Holy Spirit can free them.

Paul produces a certain dichotomy in his depiction of the ethnē in Christ as being subject to differing powers. Human beings, in Paul's perspective, are never autonomous—they are either under the rule of Christ, the realm of God's grace, or the rule of sin. With Christ they enter a new sphere of operation in which his Lordship overcomes the power of sin. If the ethnē have turned to follow Christ, they are no longer subjects of sin's rule, but subjects of Christ's rule. Here sin and death are presented as powers that dominate human life in opposition to God, they represent the sphere of disobedience, not listening to the voice of God, in contrast to those who hearken to his voice through the Lordship of Christ.

Chapter 5 reaches a climax in the reign of grace through rectification in contrast to the reign of sin in death (v. 14). The term βασιλεύω ("be king, reign") appears here for the first of five times with the sense of "dominion" exercised by death as a cosmic power. Paul introduces the figure of Adam here but only for limited purposes in relation to disobedience and as a contrast with the life and death of Christ. Adam features only in the discussion of how sin entered the world. The all-pervading power of sin was surpassed by the superabundance of grace; the effects of the "obedience" of Christ exceed by far the results of Adam's sin. As the one by whom sin entered the world, a parallel is found in Wis. 2:24 in the phrase "death entered the world," εἰς τὸν κόσμον εἰσῆλθεν. But Paul does not follow the tradition in which Adam is perceived as the "first father of Israel" (Scroggs 1966: 22–3). It is not surprising that in an address to non-Jews, Paul uses Adam in ways that differ from those that relate him to Israel.

The precise meaning of Paul's mentioning the entry of sin and death into the κόσμος has been much disputed, but it essentially depicts Adam's act of rebellion as allowing cosmic forces such as sin and death to bring all people into bondage.[3] It also helps to explain to non-Jews why it is that seeking to keep the Law outside the covenant cannot bring rescue. Paul does not speculate further as was customary in much intertestamental thought. Speculation concerning the devil's wiles, angelic corruption of Eve, her seduction of Adam, or her descendants, or the perverse heart of Adam are missing (Brandenburger 1962: 22–3).

The outcome of Adam's "disobedience" in the lives of his descendants remains a disputed topic partly fueled on the meaning of ἐφ' ᾧ πάντες ἥμαρτον, usually translated "because all sinned." Cranfield lists several options in interpreting this final clause, raising questions concerning the rationale for the outcome of universal human sinning. Was it because of involuntary participation in Adam's sin, due to their inheriting his corrupt nature, to their being imputed sinful because their representative Adam, sinned, or simply because of independent human actions following the example of Adam? (Cranfield 1975: 277). As far as Paul's own understanding of this issue can be discerned, he will go on to argue in the chapters succeeding this, that the person is never entirely free but always living under or subject to, some power, that is, the power of sin and death or the power of Christ (Harding 2016, 2017). This view will be developed further in the next chapter for which Paul lays the groundwork by demonstrating his own understanding of grace, χάρις, and righteousness, δικαιοσύνη, already contrasted with sin and death in 5:15-17. The subjects of the two clauses of the concluding verse in 5:21 are "sin" on the one hand and "grace" on the other. By placing them in contrast to one another, Paul once more emphasizes their incompatibility (Tobin 2004: 187).

The aorist tense of ἐπερίσσευσεν (it abounded) indicates that the new age inaugurated by Christ has already begun. It may be assumed from Paul's vocabulary of limitless grace, especially when accompanied by this verb, περισσεύω (v. 20) that the earliest form of the post-Easter messianic movement among the ethnē was strongly charismatic (Käsemann 1971: 122–37). This is confirmed rather than negated by the inference "shall we continue in sin that grace may abound" in 6:1, where the same wording πλεονάσῃ "abound" reappears. Similarly, see 3:7 where the verb ἐπερίσσευσεν occurs in relation to grace in a slander against Paul's gospel, which he will take up again in ch. 6. Overflowing grace to "the many" (15b) though theologically not exact equivalents, parallels "the many" who died because of Adam's trespass. Paul makes a link between Adam and Christ, viewing Adam as a τύπος (type) of the one who was to come (v. 14). The full force of Paul's "lesser to greater" reasoning is achieved in his argument comparing Christ and Adam. By enhancing the parallelism and dissonance between Adam and Christ, Paul renders his argument more effective (Jewett 2007: 384–5).

In thus relating Adam as a τύπος to Christ, Paul indicates that God had a purpose that encompassed both, thereby providing some explanation of the reign of sin and of Christ's relation to this. Here the God of Israel is brought into relation with the

---

[3] Jewett notes that there does not seem to be much differentiation in Paul's use here of παράπτωμα and παράβασις since the former is the dominant term for Adam's deed in 5:12-21. He suggests the use may vary for rhetorical reasons—παράπτωμα would resonate with similar endings here: χάρισμα, δώρημα, κρίμα, δικαίωμα, to provide homoiouteleuton (2007: 379).

world of sin and death in contrast to the hopes of a new age that were currently being advanced in Rome. An explanation is given for the origin and domination of sin in the created world. Adam's failure to listen to God underlines the sin of the gentile world in 1:19-32 in their mishearing (παρακοή) the word of the Lord, and thus failing to worship the Creator God and to give him glory. The Law revealed and registered that worship of the gods is opposition and denial of the Creator God of Israel. The death/life antithesis anticipates the notion that Paul's gentile addressees have died with Christ, and like newly born infants, they are now part of the new age, inaugurated by the death of Christ. Paul will elaborate on this in chs. 6 and 8 in more detail. From our study of Roman gentile attitudes thus far, we have noted a lack of understanding of the God of Israel, of his righteousness, of his relation to the created world, including his purported love for human beings, and of the meaning of grace in relation to sin. In a context where worship of the gods and their representatives was endemic, it must have been difficult to worship an invisible god and to ignore the pattern of enculturated life that was oriented around the gods' assumed control. There seems to have been some difficulty for Roman gentile Christ-followers to harmonize their view of the message of the Christ-movement with the Jewish and their own enculturated view of the world. It was proving difficult to valorize their identity as Christ-followers given the power of the various social identities they derived from the other groups they belonged to in their sociocultural settings. They were in the process of transforming their social identity, which they derived from belonging to this messianic group, and which was shaped by future-oriented hopes involving specific beliefs. As ethnē on the fringes of Jewish life, recently incorporated into the messianic movement in Rome, the development of a new self-understanding was proving a very challenging process for these Christ-followers.

Romans 6

Romans 6:1-14: "Should We Continue in Sin in Order That Grace Might Proliferate?"

¹What then are we to say? Should we continue in sin in order that grace may proliferate? ²Far from it! How can we who died to sin go on living in it? ³Do you not know that as many of us as were baptized into Christ Jesus were baptized into his death? ⁴We were therefore co-buried with him by baptism into death, so that, just as Christ was raised from [the] dead by the glory of the Father, so also, we might walk in newness of life. ⁵For if we have become identified with him in a death like his, we will certainly [be identified] with him in a resurrection like his. ⁶For we know this that our old self is crucified with him so that the body of sin might be rendered idle, in order that we no longer serve as sin's slave. ⁷For the one who died is declared free from sin. ⁸But if we died with Christ, we trust that we will also co-live with him. ⁹Knowing that Christ, being raised from the dead, [he] no longer dies; death no longer has dominion over him. ¹⁰With respect to that he died, he died to sin once but in respect to that he lives, he lives to God. ¹¹So you also must reckon yourselves on the one hand dead to sin but on the other alive to God in Christ Jesus. ¹²Therefore, do not let sin rule in your mortal bodies, to make you yield to its desires. ¹³No longer present any part(s) [of your body] to sin as instruments of wrong-doing, instead present yourselves to God as those who have been brought from death to life, and present your bodies to God as instruments for doing right. ¹⁴For sin will no longer rule over you, since you are not under law but under grace.

The controlling metaphor in this section of ch. 6 is baptism, which in the second half of the chapter is succeeded by the socio-political metaphor of slavery and lordship. It offers itself as a vehicle of self-understanding for ethnē in Christ since the practice of baptism seems to have been a crucial identity transforming ritual for them, and thus constitutive of the ethos of the ἐκκλησίαι (Bar-Tal 1990).

This chapter opens with a clear example of diatribe pattern, the τί οὖν ἐροῦμεν, "what then shall we say" followed by a false inference from the interlocutor, "Let us continue in sin" and Paul's normal response with the μὴ γένοιτο rejection, "far from it." "How can we who died to sin go on living in it?" Here we have a response to the slanderous report in 3:8 that Paul encourages the doing of evil so that good may come. The interlocutor's inference follows on from Paul's claim in 5:20 that "where sin proliferated, grace abounded all the more." But though it resumes the themes of sin (and therefore death), it is an absurd conclusion to draw from Paul's argument as his response makes clear. Of course, we must keep in mind that Paul writes this letter and that it is he who introduces the absurd inference in order to rapidly refute it. In diatribal style, this wrong inference need not indicate any actual exigency but might introduce only a hypothetical issue. But here we have a theme in relation to which Paul will later use the imperative in direct address in 6:11-13, thus demonstrating the dominant epistolary function of this letter, including even those sections where elements of specific diatribal style are visible. This epistolary function of Romans as a letter addressed to the ethnē in Rome showing them the proper path for their approach to the God of Israel is further evidenced by the fact that, after this question, the discussion switches to second-person plural address for the rest of the pericope (Jewett 2007: 391). "Or do you not know" (ἢ ἀγνοεῖτε) implies common teaching or catechesis that all ethnē in Christ ought to know; similarly, we note the repeated stress on "knowing" in vv. 6 and 9 (cf. also v. 17 and 7:1).

As Rodriguez has pointed out, this verb (ἀγνοεῖτε) is the only second-person plural verb in Rom. 6:1-10. Its significance is that here Paul uses second-person plural rhetoric to exclude himself from the rhetorical space of his audience, and their somewhat surprising ignorance of the meaning of baptism (Rodriguez 2016: 111). The implication is that "do you not know that as many of us as were baptized into Christ, were co-buried with him by baptism into his death?" (v. 3). Paul assumes that the ethnē whom he addresses had come to trust in God through Christ and had been baptized (presumably after some teaching about its meaning). It is significant that this is the first time Paul emphasizes that baptism is a dying with Christ to sin (Tobin 2004: 101). Paul interprets baptism metaphorically as immersion into Christ but, more significantly into his death. "'Baptism into' someone makes one a participant in that person's significance by entering into it, by sharing it, and accepting it as the meaning for one's own life" (Keck 2005: 159, cf. also Jewett 2007: 399). For Paul, in Romans, participation in Christ means to share in his death by dying to sin's power. In this "death," the body is rendered idle, so that sin in the form of the passions has nothing to work with, that is, has no base of operation (7:8). Here we encounter one of the most important emphases of Paul's understanding of the relation of the ethnē to Christ (Gorman 2019). Corporately and individually, they participate in one body in their being "in Christ" (and not merely as a collective of isolated, distinct individuals, separately connected to Christ). What was true of him must also become true for them. They are joined to him and to one another in a common relationship, which we will learn in ch. 8 is effected through the Spirit, and later in ch. 12 through new familial membership.

The analogy of baptism suggests that going under the water is similar to being buried, dying to the domination of sin, and rising from the water symbolizes renewal, the commencement of a "new" (renewed) creation in contrast to one's previous existence when "you" were gentile sinners. We note how the meaning of baptism is interpreted: "as Christ was raised from the dead by the glory of the Father, so we too might walk in newness of life" (v. 4; ἠγέρθη, cf. 13: 11, where this verb is applied to the ethnē themselves). Sin ruled ἐβασίλευσεν in death (5:21); participation in Christ means dying to sin, and thus moving from the sphere of its power through his lordship. Since sin is still alive and active, the only way to escape is for those baptized to die, not literally, but ritually so that the baptized now reckon themselves as "dead to sin" (6:11), as having been crucified with Christ, which precludes continuing to live in sin (Keck 2005: 158–9). Now that this consequence is properly enunciated, Paul joins in the corporate understanding, "we," and includes himself with his addressees in a unity/union that he locates "in Christ Jesus" (6:3), more particularly in his death (3-8), which should almost certainly have included, as here, some teaching, διδαχή (v. 17) to facilitate that goal. If some of the Roman ethnē were converts who had migrated to Rome from elsewhere, they may have been catechized previously, and those who came to Christ in Rome may have been taught in a differing pattern from that which was normal for Paul and his co-workers in his ἐκκλησίαι. Thus, Paul would here be confirming his agreement with the form of teaching they had previously been taught, that is, affirming their previous foundation rather than starting an ἐκκλησία in his own pattern.

We might summarize the focus on the death and resurrection life of Christ, which we have noted in this chapter, under the rubric of "having been united (co-planted, σύμφυτοι) with him" (6:5). The focus is not so much on baptism itself as a rite. The focus is on identification with, and participation in Christ, his death and resurrection life; it is indicated by the number of verbs with the prefix συν (co-), "we were co-buried with him"' (συνετάφημεν, v. 4), "co-crucified with him" (συνεσταυρώθη, v. 6),[1] "we co-live with him" (συζήσομεν, v. 8) (Wasserman 2008). This pattern of linking his followers with Christ and his destiny is typical of Paul's thought, but definitively so of the overarching theme termed "participation in Christ" expressed most frequently as being "in Christ." Paul had already introduced the Roman ethnē to the inheritance in which they gain a share of Abraham's blessing (cf. κληρονόμοι, 4:14, and with a *sun prefix* joint heirs, cf. 8:17).

It is interesting how Paul uses participation with/in Christ here as a teaching tool that sets out a fresh interpretation of baptism by connecting it more closely to the death of Christ. Paul's previous experience and what has been reported to him of the situation at Rome led Paul to stress an obedient response as the only adequate reaction to the call of Christ (15:16). In the context of the empire, a slave's life was entirely dependent on his master. The slave's life was inextricably linked with that of his master who held the power of life or death. The fate of the master could determine that of his slave. In the event of the master being subjected to capital punishment, the slave could share in his fate (Lewis 2016: 121–2). Also, where slaves died a pauper's death, the prospect of co-burial with other unknown paupers was a sad but real prospect; συνθάπτω normally refers literally to being buried in a shared grave (Lewis 2016: 119). An ordinary Jew of antiquity expected to be buried in the family tomb. He expected to "lie down with his fathers." "Choosing to be buried at Qumran was a renunciation of the biological family tie. It meant preferring to rest for eternity with one's sectarian family, no small matter" (Baumgarten 2021: 4). Sabou has made a convincing case that

---

[1] This term co-crucified, a hapax legomenon, was possibly Paul's own creation in his teaching about being "in Christ" (Lewis 2016: 119).

this *sun* language indicates very clearly belonging to the same family as the one with whom one is buried (2005: 90-3, 143-4).

Though he includes here, "being buried with Christ," it must be noted that Paul does not precisely follow through the identification of "dying with Christ" to "having been raised *with* him" as in Col. 3:1; Eph. 2:6. Rather, here Paul uses future tense verbs, "so that we will be united with him in a resurrection like his," cf. v. 8 "we trust that we will also live συζήσομεν with him." Not only so but Paul uses the future tense verb κυριεύσει (will/shall reign as lord) with an imperatival force as indicating a genuine future reality yet to be realized. The resurrection of the ethnē in Christ will be achieved through fraternal identification with the resurrected Christ (McMurray 2021: 155-9). The context with its preponderance of imperatival verbs supports this reading of v. 14 (Rodriguez 2014: 116) and the imperatives combine to establish the view that here Paul's apostolic intention is to influence, to teach the gentile addressees at Rome. In the structure of Romans, we find that, surprisingly, Paul has not yet properly introduced the Spirit. Instead, he speaks rather of the dominion of the risen Christ over those baptized, who must appropriate in their conduct what Christ has done for them (Fitzmyer 1993: 445). The Spirit (Romans 8) and what we might term "divine family dynamics" (8:28-11:33) are still to come. This draws attention to an important feature of Romans—Paul's exposition is layered—Romans 6 is linked with Romans 12, but is preliminary to it. As the teaching on the Spirit will not be fully presented until ch. 8, so not until ch. 12 will Paul explain how the ethnē will achieve newness of life, transformation, and so on, that is, appropriate λατρεία, leading to resurrection of life without following the Law. But the route from Romans 6 to Romans 12 proceeds via ch. 8 (the Spirit, etc.) and chs. 9-11 (affiliation with the people of Israel). This gradual escalation in thought enables Paul to fill out the meaning of identification with Christ, and its ethical outcome in familial connections within the aggregatively extended "family" of God.

Romans 6:11-14 Pauline Imperatives and Identification with Christ

"The second half of Romans 6 presents us with an important transition in Paul's rhetoric. Beginning in Rom. 6:10, Paul addresses his audience directly, which he has not done since the opening of the letter" (Rodriguez 2016: 115). The verb λογίζεσθε (v. 11) is certainly an imperative, a command or instruction (reckon yourselves) rather than simply an indicative statement of fact as Jewett holds (2007: 408). It relates to the transformation of the mind (νοῦς, φρονέω, etc.). These imperatives and their significance will remain important for our reading of the remainder of Romans. Paul takes care in this call to "reckon yourselves" dead to sin and "alive to God" (cf. Rom. 12:1) so that his concept of freedom will not be misinterpreted as license (Fitzmyer 1993: 450-1). Here we note an important issue with regard to diatribal style, in which ch. 6 begins (v. 1) and continues to be structured (6:15) (see Excursus I). We have already argued that there is a pattern in Paul's structuring of Romans, clearly demonstrated here in 6:1-2 (cf. 6:15) and including μὴ γένοιτο. There can be no doubt that ch. 6:1-10 demonstrates diatribal style, and that is why scholars like Jewett prefer to take the imperative as an indicative statement of fact ("you consider yourselves" rather than "consider yourselves"). He himself notes, however, that the words οὕτως καὶ ὑμεῖς (so also you) (v. 11) are argumentative, explicitly drawing inferences from Christ to Christ-followers. And as noted above, "the preponderance of imperatival verbs in the immediate context makes it all the more likely that at least *some* imperatival force attaches to the future-tense verb, κυριεύσει" (Rodriguez 2014: 116).

Ought we to decide that Paul has temporarily overlooked his (indirect) manner of address to the interlocutor, and slipped into normal epistolary language? The evidence here suggests that Paul intends to directly influence the behavior of the Roman ethnē despite using diatribal forms of address in 6:1 and 6:15. Perhaps there is a transition as Rodriguez claims from the diatribal style after 6:10. In v. 11, Paul turns to address his audience as if he had interrupted for the moment his diatribal style of address. If this is granted, it would very much support our approach in which we claim that though Paul uses diatribal style at certain points in the letter, Romans cannot properly be designated a diatribe. This style is subordinate to the epistolary goals of the apostle. From this, we conclude that though Paul is conversant with, and competent in, the use of diatribal style, his hortatory epistolary objectives take priority at important places in the construction of the letter. This ambivalence about how Paul will relate to the ethnē in Rome was visible already in 1:11-12, where he modifies his stated intent to "share some spiritual gift to strengthen you" to "rather that we may be mutually encouraged." Empowerment of the ethnē through participation in Christ, rather than via the Law, is a key dynamic throughout the letter (16:25).

Paul analyses the meaning of the baptism, which all have shared with the intention of drawing out its significance and consequence for living—to "strengthen" them.[2] Here again we meet Paul the teacher linking his addressees with their experience of baptism and its obligations, and reminding them of their commitment (6:14-15, Streett 2018). Just as in 5:12-21, Paul focused on the fact that Christ died for us, so now the implications of that death are explained. And thus, οὕτως καὶ (v. 11), those united with Christ in baptism have died with him, and ought as adopted "sons" to begin to live a transformed life in hope of a future resurrection life. One of the outcomes of this co-crucifixion with Christ is that the old self ὁ παλαιὸς ἡμῶν ἄνθρωπος, that is, the person in the condition of life prior to 'conversion' (Dunn 1988a: 318), has also been crucified "in a death like his" (Christ's), so that the body as slave of sin is dead (τὸ σῶμα τῆς ἁμαρτίας), that "we might no longer be enslaved to sin" (v. 6). Similar to what he will assert in respect of the Law in 7:1-6, Paul argues that death brings freedom from sin (6:7). He reasons that "if we have died with Christ in baptism, we trust that we will also live with him" (v. 8). Christ died to sin once ἐφάπαξ (6:10), and so Paul wants to stress turning to Christ as a complete change of life, the end of old affiliations and the start of a new belonging, of participation in Christ.

Thus, in Paul's perspective, the powers of sin and death had complete dominion over ethnē prior to their being ransomed and turning to Christ, but now that these have become Christ-followers, they are freed from that slavery to sin and death and released to live for Christ. We note here the echo of 4:3, Abraham trusted God and

---

[2] This theme, we will note later, recurs in chs. 8 and 14–15.

"it was reckoned to him as righteousness." Just as trust means the non-reckoning of transgressions, so continuing trust in Christ means a correlative self-understanding, reckoning oneself as "dead to sin" and alive to righteousness (v. 11). Reckoning (λογίζομαι) is a key term in Romans (cf. previously in 3:28 and predominantly in ch. 4) closely linked with the new self-understanding in trust, by which the gentile sinner continues to live in a sinful world but perceives himself as exemplifying a renewed creation, whose sins are not reckoned against them.

In v. 12, Paul exhorts bodily control to avoid letting sin force Christ-followers to obey its passions. In this sense, we can speak of Pauline asceticism. The reference to the mortal body (θνητῷ) resonates with the theme of sin and death as dominating powers over humans (5:12-21) (Beker 1980: 288–9). No longer should the limbs of one's body be at the disposal of sin resulting in wickedness, but instead the ethnē should present (παραστήσατε cf. 12:1) their bodies as an offering to God, as instruments/weapons for righteousness (v. 13) (Fitzmyer 1993: 528). This theme will be more fully elaborated as a significant focus of the letter in 12:1-2 in which it introduces a major stage in Paul's letter where the cultic or sacrificial meaning will dominate. Concrete, respons-able action is the anticipated outcome of being united with Christ. Instead of idolatry and giving over their bodies in the worship (ἐλάτρευσαν 1:25) of other gods, the ethnē must offer them to God to be used for his glory—"what people did with their bodies was eschatologically instrumental" (McMurray 2021: 133). In this way, Paul concludes, sin will not "lord (it) over" κυριεύσει the *ethnē*, for "you are not under Law, but under grace" (v. 14).

Romans 6:14 "You 'Gentiles' Are Not under the Law but under Grace"

We need to bear in mind that this somewhat surprising summing up is a specific address only to the ethnē in Christ. Paul does *not* say "we are (ἔσμεν) not under the Law but under grace," but "you are (ἐστε) not under the Law but under grace." "Paul creates a rhetorical space in 6:14; let us call that space 'not under Torah'. He does not himself occupy that rhetorical space, despite the fact that he also understands himself as 'under grace' (see 1:5, 5:2, 12:3, 15:15)" (Rodriguez 2016: 117). As gentile followers of Christ, they are not under the Law. The Law is for the Jewish people (9:4), and taking on the yoke of the Law does not and will not solve the problem of gentile transgressions. Paul has shown decisively, and will continue to demonstrate later, that living by the Law does not work for non-Jews. For these it is not empowering and transformative—as we will learn from chs. 7 and 8, only the Spirit ratified by adoption can achieve this. Paul addresses the problem of ethnē who may be turning to the Torah to structure their relation to Israel's God (Rodriguez 2016: 117). Paul guides them negatively by showing that what some of them are presently considering does not work (7:7-25), and positively, by indicating the appropriate path through liberation, transformative adoption through Christ, and reception of the Spirit (8:1-17). Thus the fact that Paul is addressing those from the nations explains what seems to be an anti-Torah inference here, setting Torah in opposition to grace, ὑπὸ νόμον versus ὑπὸ χάριν (v. 14). "*You*, ethnē who have turned to Christ (emphasis added)" (who perhaps had been wrongly advised to take up living by Torah as well as turning to Christ), "are not under law but under grace." It is neither necessary, nor accurate, to generalize being under the Law, ὑπὸ νόμον, to refer to Jews as well as "gentiles," or to the old epoch of Adam. It is only ethnē who, by virtue of their non-Jewish origins did not have the Law through birth, but had an option to choose to be ὑπὸ νόμον, whereas Jews live in the Law ἐν νομῷ *from birth*.[3] This differentiation is the main reason for Paul's change from first- to second-person plural language at v. 11; though sin and death have ruled over *you* gentile Christ-followers in your previous existence, just as death had no more power over Christ (who will never die again), so too *you* must reckon/perceive yourselves οὕτως καὶ ὑμεῖς λογίζεσθε dead to sin and alive to God in Christ Jesus (6:11).

In summary, as we have noted, we have encountered here an important transition in Paul's rhetoric in that he addresses his audience directly in the second-person plural ("you" not "we," cf. Rodriguez 2016: 115). Starting from 6:3 and through 6:8-9, Paul has used first-person plural verbs and pronouns, and also possibly includes himself at some points within that "we." This is decisive for the understanding of Paul in relation to his gentile addressees. It is not that Paul includes other Jews as well as himself in this. Nor does this "we" refer to a mixed group of Jews and ethnē, but only to Paul and his gentile addressees. The same grouping will recur in the direct address ἀδέλφοι in 7:1, and in the first-person plural address of 7:6: it will recommence after the speech-in-character of 7:7-25 and continue in its application to the "you" plural at 8:12, "So then ἀδέλφοι, we are not in the flesh ..." and eventually reaching its consummation in 12:1.

Only at 6:6 there may be what appears to be an exception to this differentiating pattern. Continuing his emphasis upon what "we know" τοῦτο γινώσκοντες, Paul includes in this knowledge that "our old self," ὁ παλαιὸς ἡμῶν ἄνθρωπος, was "co-crucified with Christ." Paul, by this terminology regarding the "old self," means to describe (only) the former life of *gentile* Christ-followers (Rodriguez 2016: 114), and this description is in harmony with what we envisage as Paul's normative pattern of differentiating Jew and non-Jew. But if this pattern is not otherwise indicated, it might seem warranted to read this verse as an exception where Paul is inconsistent, "a singular phenomenon" according to Lewis (2016: ch. 5). This would mean that the label "slaves to sin," an otherwise thoroughly gentile marker of identity would include a Jew (Paul) within the category "slaves to sin" (Rodriguez 2016: 114–15). But if there is indication, which we think there is, in that the text from 6:1-10 is marked as diatribal (cf. 6:1, 3) (Song 2004: 98–102), we could insist that the "we" thus represents the voice of the interlocutor, which we maintain is consistently gentile throughout. In a letter addressed to non-Jews and referring to their sinful past, this seems to be the stronger reading. This reading makes for clarification of 6:6b where Paul does not include himself in the "we" who "might no longer be enslaved to sin," since this language resonates particularly with gentile ethnicity, but reminds us of 1:1 where Paul introduces himself as a slave of Jesus Christ.

---

[3] Cf. Johnson Hodge who rightly argues that the phrase ὑπὸ νόμον refers to "gentiles," not to Jews (2007: 124–5, 198–9). She also makes the point (on 9:4) that since slavery as a status did not apply to Jews, a transfer from slave to son can only apply to "non-Jews" (2007: 71).

This is consistent with 6:14 where Paul does not include himself and focuses narrowly on his gentile readers, "For you are not under the Law but under grace." Paul is a Jew, and is under grace like the ethnē in Rome (cf. 1:5, 5:2). But he is a Law-abiding Jew who normally would not put Law and grace in opposite spheres. Ὑπὸ νόμον in Paul's use must refer here not to Jews but to judaizing "gentiles," where the nuance of someone in transit moving from another jurisdiction to coming "under" the Law's authority is primary. It was particularly appropriate to describe non-Jews tempted to adopt Torah observance "to structure their relationship to Israel's God," possibly to become Jewish proselytes, but it did not apply to Paul as his use of second person illustrates (Rodriguez 2014: 117). His denial of himself not being under Law, μὴ ὢν αὐτὸς ὑπὸ νόμον, but being ἔννομος Χριστοῦ in 1 Cor. 9: 19-22 accords with this reading in that Paul was law-abiding even as a Christ-follower, and would otherwise be in contradiction with himself if he were to deny that. Surprisingly, it is the first time in any of his letters that Paul writes of the holiness of the Law (Tobin 2004: 101). What is also to be noted is that Paul draws a distinction between his audience—the gentile Christ-followers in Rome as distinct from those ἐν νόμῳ (Jews). This denotes, as he clearly indicates elsewhere in this letter, that he does not write to Jews in Rome but only to the nations.

We might speculate on why there should have been an apparent failure to understand the meaning of baptism. Did the emphasis center on the entrance into a new life with corresponding neglect of leaving behind the former connections with idolatry? "Do you not know" in 11:2b will denote the introduction of a scriptural citation. Here it similarly implies something they ought to have known, which in turn implies not hearing and not performing what they had been taught in undergoing baptism (cf. 6:16, 7:1). It is significant that Paul writes to the Romans as a teacher telling them that they ought not to continue in the practice of sin. As Käsemann notes on 6:14a ("For sin should not rule over you"), "The future … permanently equates the command and the promise" (1980: 179). Here the epistolary aspect of Paul's communication is primary, and he appears to be sufficiently well informed about Rome to give specific teaching based on the pattern of baptism.

We have noted also the use of imperatives[4] alongside diatribal patterns such as μὴ γένοιτο in 6:2 and 6:15, οὐκ οἴδατε in 6:16, and ἀγνοεῖτε in 6:3. According to our previous discussion of 3:8, and so on, we have determined that Paul takes specific issue with the slanderous reports that were circulating concerning his gentile mission. This is one of the places where we find ourselves unable, despite the evidence for diatribal patterns, to view Romans as a diatribe. This is not inconsistent with the fact that we have continued to find evidence of diatribal style in most chapters up to this point and certainly support Stowers's thesis that the style of the diatribe is deliberate—central to the letter's message (1981: 178).

---

[4] Note also Robert J. Karris's discussion of imperatives in Rom. 14:1–15:3 (1991: 68) and Donfried's listing of rhetorical devices in Romans (1991: 117). Cf. also Furnish who includes the four exhortations (6:11-13, 19b) that stand within what he terms the expository section of the letter (2012: 187–202).

Theology and Ethics in Romans 6

In traditional interpretive patterns, theology and ethics are normally separated so that it is only from 12:1ff that we should anticipate ethical outcomes. Paul encourages his audience to follow or turn from certain forms of behavior, that is, norms that are shared in this group (Esler 2014). However, in view of the imperatival constructions, observable especially in 6:11-13, Victor Furnish has suggested that the respective labels of theology and ethics and their location in Romans ought to be revised. Other than ignoring Paul's grammar and translating imperative statements as normal present tense, there is no reason for not recognizing imperative statements at this point in Romans 6. But this is not straightforward due to Paul's use of diatribal style in this chapter.

Here we differ from Song's conclusions (2004: 90–117). Song's work is careful, and he gives some evidence for his view that Romans originated as a diatribe that thus, in his opinion, discloses no information about the Roman "church" (2004: 46). But Paul's teaching, in this chapter in particular, is decisive for regarding Romans in its present form as a letter to Rome. Support for this has emerged in Paul's direct address to his audience (the first since 1:6-15) beginning at 6:10 but clearly enunciated in 6:11 "so you must also reckon yourselves dead to sin." If scholars wish to pay attention to diatribal style as I have done, it is essential for them to follow not some general theory on how little or how much information concerning the exigency can legitimately be gleaned from the rhetoric in Romans. Our present knowledge of diatribe and its uses does not allow us to envisage some common pattern to whose constraints an author such as Paul must always comply by the mere fact that he favors this style of presentation (Song 2004: 90–117).

To the contrary, we cannot entirely subject Paul's letter, which uses diatribal rhetoric for pastoral and educational purposes, to other typical patterns of diatribe not evidenced to us in Paul's own writing. Where there may be parallels, however, as in Epictetus, we can learn from such by setting Pauline patterns in the context of those available elsewhere. This enables some viable comparison by which we may proceed from the known to the unknown rather than simply speculating from a mass of material. Song notes that both Epictetus and Romans share what many scholars regard as the most typical diatribe markers, that is, vivid dialogues, especially with fictitious interlocutors, the emergence of an imaginary second-person singular: characteristic rejection phrases such as μὴ γένοιτο both in Romans and Epictetus's *Discourses* characteristic apostrophic vocatives, for example, ὦ ἄνθρωπε (2004: 16, 90–111). It is significant that in the next pericope continuity with 6:1-11 is indicated by the repetition of τί οὖν and μὴ γένοιτο (6:15) while the οὐκ οἴδατε (6:16) resonates with ἀγνοεῖτε of 6:3.

The resulting question cannot be bypassed—if ch. 6 begins in diatribal style, evidenced again at 6:15, is it obligatory to rule out any possible imperatives (such as 6:12-13) as not necessarily indicating that Paul exhorts the ethnē to do certain things? This is because these are possibly, in the first instance, addressed to the interlocutor. We have tentatively suggested that the chosen form of address to the Romans has something to do with Paul's being misreported in Rome, and the resultant problems of his leadership there. This issue must not be overlooked, and it may demand disciplined use of Paul's statements, but through this, Paul does vividly inform the interlocutor of his own stated position—at least the ethnē should know better than to claim Paul promotes "sinning that grace may abound" (6:1). This question may encapsulate Paul's own response to the issue and may thus indicate what they should expect to hear him say. This in turn might lead us to infer that the diatribal questions here are designed to give Paul the chance to voice his own reactions to misreported claims concerning him and his gospel. With Elliott we can claim "that we are convinced that the category of paraenesis, understood, functionally (as an instrument for the reinforcement or modification of values), is valuable for understanding the character of Romans" (2007: 99). Thus, although ch. 6 exhibits indirect diatribal style of speech, it remains a valid option to view Paul as guiding the Romans already in ch. 6 in preparation for what he will go on to elaborate in ch. 12 concerning the use of the body. Already in Romans 6 special use is made of the concept of "presentation" (παρίστημι) that occurs five times in the chapter (vv. 13 twice, 16, 19 twice). So, when Paul will introduce the appeal in chs. 12–15 to thus present their bodies as a living sacrifice, as spiritual worship, "the appeals made already in chapter 6 are not simply being recapitulated and reemphasized" (Furnish 1968: 103). True, there is both ethical and theological continuity and consistency between these chapters. But Paul's argumentation is structured and layered. As well as continuity, there is hugely significant development so that the ethnē in Christ become part of a new family through brotherhood with Christ (8:29) and alongside Israel (9–11).

Romans 6:15-23: You Are Slaves to Whom You Obey— Putting Your Bodies at God's Disposal

[15] What then? Should we sin because we are not under law but under grace? Far from it! [16] Do you not know that to whatever you yield yourselves in "obedience"[5] as slaves, you are slaves to it, either to sin, resulting in death, or to "obedience," resulting in righteousness? [17] But thanks be to God that you, having been slaves to sin, responded from the heart to the imprint of the teaching to which you were committed, [18] and that you, having been set free from sin, were enslaved to righteousness. [19] I am speaking in human terms because of the weakness of your flesh. For just as you once presented your members as slaves to impurity and to lawlessness resulting in anarchy, so now yield your members in the same way as slaves to righteousness making for a holy life. [20] For when you were slaves of sin, you were free from righteousness. [21] So what fruit did you then get from the things of which you now are ashamed [for their end is death]. [22] But now that having been set free from sin and enslaved to God, the fruit you get is holiness and the outcome is eternal life. [23] For the wages of sin is death, but the free gift of God is eternal life in Christ Jesus our Lord.

---

[5] Normally I translate ‛υπακοή and related terms with terminology expressing listening trust. Here, Paul contrasts what is expected of slaves (obedience to their masters) with the trustful relation of Christ-followers to God, hence I retain the term obedience but in quotation marks.

Paul's argument starts from the presupposition that those in Christ have been freed from sin's domination, but he does not end at this point. Since they have been freed from something, it might logically be presumed that they can then be regarded as free persons. This is clearly not so since these verses are laden with hortatory language. Ethnē in Christ are rather *freed* from sin but *for* God; they are *freed* persons and not then simply free persons (cf. 1 Cor. 7:22). Their freedom is "Freedom for Commitment," as Fitzmyer titles 6:12-23 (1993: 443–4). He sees Paul's teaching on ἐλευθερία "freedom" emerging in vv. 18, 20, and 22. The contrast between slavery and freedom is drawn from the Greco-Roman world. In this context, freedom denoted the privileged condition or social status of citizens in a *polis* or *municipium*. The Roman ethnē in Christ must be aware of their new status as slaves to a great ruler, so that having died to sin, they must no longer let it hold sway over them, but live as enslaved persons bound to righteousness and to God himself. They are not free from all obligation but they now serve a new master in a new way.

Though Paul lives within the reality of Roman slavery, and uses its imagery in his teaching, it must be asked whether this teaching is drawn only from his contemporary empire context, or whether it ought not to reflect the Exodus tradition in accordance with his Jewish symbolic universe. Scholars such as Richard Horsley have claimed that Paul's thought emerges out of historic Israelite traditions rather than simply from the everyday slavery system of the contemporary Roman world. Horsley's stance represents a strong stream of scholarship that views the source of the most foundational elements of Paul's thought on slavery as his Jewish roots. This was influenced dramatically by the transmitted memories of the Exodus from slavery in Egypt and revived and activated across the centuries by countless challenges from hostile nations (cf. Horsley 1998: 153–200, Goodrich 2013: 509–30). Albert Harrill, on the other hand, views Paul's exhortations to his addressees as embedded in his Roman cultural milieu (2012). We will introduce the substance of the debate about the sources of Paul's thought on slavery in our Excursus on this (prior to ch. 7) and will only summarize these here in passing.

Paul's argument turns on the fact that if one serves a particular master, whether that be the (personified) powers of sin and death or righteousness, "you are slaves to whomever you obey" (6:16). As we have noted, the dominant context in which Paul operates is the Roman empire, particularly Italy where the phenomenon of mass slavery was most visibly practiced (Hezser 2005: 10). But Paul also speaks corporately out of his Israelite brotherhood allegiance (Rom. 9:3-5), and not necessarily as a typical Roman of the first century. Hezser seeks to show that though slaves of Jewish origin were certainly held by Jewish masters in antiquity, rabbis considered enslavement a reversal of the Exodus experience (2005. 9–11). However, Dale Martin claims that "Jewishness had little if any relevance for the structure of slavery among Jews ... The relevant factors for slave structures and the existence of slavery itself had little if anything to do with ethnicity or religion" (Martin 1993: 113).

Paul's immediate reference to Christ-followers as being no longer "under Law" (6:15) does not mean that the Christ-follower stands aloof from the divine claim expressed in the Law, which can only be met through the Spirit (8:4). What Paul means therefore by "freedom from the Law" cannot mean autonomy with regard to the demand of righteousness expressed in the Law, for, as Elliott asserts, "outside of the fulfilment of that demand there is only death" (2004: 248–9). Tobin neatly describes the content of 6:15-23 as "Freed from sin but Slaves to Righteousness" (2004: 208). Thus, slaves to sin, introduced already in 6:6, identifies the rhetorical space that Paul's gentile audience used to inhabit prior to their turning to Christ. Paul does not equate Jews and ethnē in this respect; hence, he does not include himself but directly addresses the Christ-followers in Rome in the second-person plural (v. 11) as noted above.[6]

Again, in v. 17, Paul refers to the period prior to turning to Christ as when "having been slaves of sin," *you* have become obedient from the heart to the τύπον διδαχῆς—pattern of teaching "to which you were committed" (παρεδόθητε). Παραδίδωμι is a key verb in Romans (cf. 1:24, 26, 28; 4:25) in that it denotes or involves the action of God. This indicates that the Roman Christ-followers were certainly ethnē, not Jews who, as noted above, Paul would not normally refer to as "slaves of sin." Indeed, slavery could have been for many such a horrible experience that to compare it in any form to being joined with Christ could be challenged. But it is to be noted that Paul still retains the vocabulary of slavery only this time with reference to righteousness (v. 18). Paul apologizes for arguing analogically, "speaking in human terms" of slavery but nevertheless again continues the analogy of being freed from sin to being "enslaved to God" (δουλωθέντες, v. 22). At this point, we must remember that one aspect of slavery was that it could provide some status to its victims. To be the slave of a powerful master would give benefits to his slaves, so that within that category, there would be differentiation, but still within an enslaved life. Paul will return to the form of relationship Christ's followers enjoy with him in 8:15 where he will stress that "you have not received a spirit of slavery" πνεῦμα δουλείας to fall back into fear. He, thus, will connect the debate between slavery and freedom with that of the Spirit and family membership.

In 6:18, Paul's focus is more on the outcomes rather than on the relationship, but he presses home an important point. Ethnē in his perspective, ἐλευθερωθέντες having been freed, are only free in relation to God—they are bound to him through Christ (cf. καρπόν and τέλος leading to eternal life (ζωὴν αἰώνιον, v. 22), otherwise they are slaves of sin with very differing experiences and outcomes. Käsemann is correct in observing the vast difference between this view of Paul and the idealistic traditions of Western thought, which assume that human freedom is basic. In Paul, in contrast to this, a person belongs constitutively to a world and lies under lordship, either to God or evil powers (1980: 179, Harding 2017). There are no pockets of neutral independence, no "freedom" (ἐλευθερία) "from one that is not immediately and necessarily fealty to the other" (Elliott 2004: 251, cf. also Jewett 2007: 416–17). This reading of Paul is crucial for distinguishing Paul's own views, which are centrally Christological, from some modern views, influenced to some extent by Paul's thought, but which are not governed by it, yet use it so as to give elements of his thought an independence from

---

[6] Scholars do not agree on which parts of Romans are diatribal (Song 2004: 5). Song is open to the view that a shorter version of Romans that is known from textual studies to have existed may have been a diatribe that was later appropriated as a letter (122).

the apostle that allows themes like "no distinction" or "free from Law" to take on a decontextualized, ideological life of their own.

The reference to freedom in relation to slavery would resonate with the sociopolitical background of Paul's addressees. In Epictetus's *Discourses*, the concept of freedom and slavery were very important such that δοῦλος and its cognates occur almost a hundred times (Song 2004: 41). The same language was employed by Pausanias in referring to the Corinthians having been set free from the Macedonians (Jewett 2007: 418). Paul's terminology of "enslavement to righteousness" reflects this milieu as does Josephus's report that the Israelites were enslaved (ἐδουλώθη) by the Persians (*Ant.* 11:300). "In the highly politicized context of Rome, where military conquest was so crucial a provider of slaves and victims for theatres, this language was unmistakable" (Jewett 2007: 418). We note here, however, these cited references appear to resonate with freedom or captivity of peoples, the political dimension, rather than with the commercial world of domestic slavery that Goodrich has documented (2013: 509–30).

The reason for Paul's choice of slave language may be possibly because Paul knew that many of the Christ-followers in Rome may still have, or previously may have had, a connection with slavery. It was indeed not uncommon in the Roman empire for desperate people to volunteer to become slaves because in many cases it gave them and their families a more secure living than they would have otherwise (Witherington 2004: 170). But the analogy of slavery was invaluable primarily for expressing the total authority and control over one's body that slavery constituted. As Harrill states, "Slavery is less a static institution of property law than a dynamic process of total domination, an absolute kind of mastery that denies the slave access to autonomous relations outside the master's sphere of influence—in effect, reducing the slave to an alienated outsider, socially 'dead' to the free population" (2016: 304). Similarly, Luise Schrottoff was one of the first to note a close analogy in Paul between sin's complete domination of humanity and the reality of slavery as a structural entity (1979: 497–510). Harrill is right to stress the total domination of slavery and its social effects (2016: 304–6).[7] He notes that Paul nowhere in his undisputed letters remarks about slavery's direct and insidious violence with the attention and zeal that the Deutero-Pauline material does (Eph. 6:5-9; 1 Tim. 2:9-10; cf. 1 Pet. 2:18-25).

Those slaves denied autonomous relations outside of their owner's sphere of influence need freedom in order to have some choice about their life. Paul's point is that only through identification with Christ can these be empowered to achieve self-mastery, rather than being forced to be the slave of sinful passions without a real possibility of self-control. A new self-understanding and identity as well as a new sense of security under divine protection is now available to those who had experienced that they had no control over their life and its outcome. They must reckon themselves "socially dead" in respect of sin. Thus, irrespective of whether one remains a slave of an earthly master, freedom as Christ's freed person (ἀπελεύθερος) is available to all (1 Cor. 7:22). Paul wishes to stress via the medium of slavery language the exclusive

---

[7] These have been well represented in a recent publication by John Bodel and Walter Scheidel (2017). This volume includes essays by Bodel, "Death and Social Death in Ancient Rome" (81–108) and Orlando Patterson, "Revisiting Slavery, Property, and Social Death" (265–95).

lordship of Christ and the undivided loyalty this demands. He will go on in ch. 7 to demonstrate that the Law cannot solve the problem of sin in the life of non-Jews. The choice lies between faithful service to Christ as his enslaved people, on the one hand, and the contrasting bondage to sin, on the other, in which even seeking to keep the Law cannot bring freedom. Thus, gentile slaves of Christ cannot serve the Law as their master, since for them it will not bring freedom but, due to the power of sin, a continuation of bondage. As Paul will demonstrate later in chs. 12–15, even gentile Christ-followers are not without connection to the Law, but this relation will also be governed by the Lordship of Christ.

"Dead to Sin but Alive to Righteousness"—Continuing Obligations and Affiliations for Ethnē in Christ

Paul calls upon the ethnē in Christ to reckon yourselves (λογίζεσθε, 6:11) as socially dead to sin and alive to righteousness. This could be understood as the social death resulting from turning from previous worship of the gods and associated cultural patterns. It might be interpreted to imply complete discontinuity with all their previous existence and, if converts have truly died, then they are ethnically neutralized, and can in future leave previous ethnicity behind. But Paul's metaphor of dying with Christ is based upon trust in Christ, a reckoning or trust stance derived from being in Christ. We must be careful not to overinterpret what is in fact a metaphorical image, thus implying a complete dichotomy between the pre-call person and the new life in Christ, as if radical grace in Christ should negate all that precedes it (Campbell 2006: 143–7).

Paul does indicate a complete transformation; it is not a replacement but a transformation of a living person though not, at this point, the resurrection of a dead body. It is true that a person's death normally implies the termination of all previous obligations but the death resulting from being buried with Christ and reckoning oneself dead to sin cannot imply the end of all previous obligations, otherwise the Christ-movement could rightly be accused of breaking up marriages and families. Paul confirms previous obligations in advising the continuance of marriage so long as the "unbelieving" partner is willing to remain in the marriage (1 Cor. 7:7 16). In fact, Paul makes a rule for all the assemblies that each person "should remain in the calling (including the ethnicity) in which you were called" (1 Cor. 7:20, Campbell 2008: 91–3). The ethnē in Christ die to the power and control of sin that has enslaved them. By dying to sin's power and demands through trust in Christ, these ethnē now have the opportunity to realize their full potential as human beings no longer enslaved but freed to serve God through Christ.

Radical discontinuity with the past is possible depending on the context, but not universal. It is a misuse of the metaphor of dying with Christ, to interpret this as dying to all previous obligations to which one was previously obligated. Dying to sin enables the person to undertake previous moral obligations in a transformed manner, not to negate them so much as to fulfill them. This can be better explained in that the gentile convert must die to their former way of life—as far as worship of the gods and related practices are concerned, this person has died. In that sense their previous life has ended—it is given over to God through response to Christ. But the paradox of dying with Christ is that the life that is thus offered, that is, given over to God, is then gifted back to the one offering to be used voluntarily in the service (λατρεία) of God (12:1-6).

Here I disagree with those who view radical grace as "a reality distinct from every human institution" (Barclay 2015: 362). The Christ-event cannot be isolated from both human and divine activity in history, especially from human institutions of worth (Campbell 2018: 142–3). The paradox of the person thus committing their life is that he or she has not lost the life that was offered, but that life has been given back to their control for social action under Christ's lordship—this is why Paul can claim "for freedom Christ has set us free" (Gal. 5:1).

In Corinthians, particularly, we have a recognition of previously existing obligations including both marital and ethnic affiliations, not their discontinuance, as in the worship of the gods. The presentation of the gospel message to ethnē might seem to suggest that dying with Christ, that is, the new life in Christ, brings an end to all existing affiliations and commitments; but life in Christ is not discontinuous with *all* previous patterns and obligations. What Paul advocates is not a replacement of the pre-call person within the same body, a factual impossibility, but rather a transformation of this same person through relation with Christ. This correlates with what we have noted elsewhere in Paul's theological statements that his pattern is not to replace or annul the past so much as the transformation of their entire relational network in Christ.

As noted in our discussion of Romans ch. 2, there are some indications that the ethnē were unclear about their status in that some seem willing to consider circumcision as an option and also seem not to realize that the Law brings wrath to those outside the covenant. But in Paul's view, "gentiles" in Christ remain "gentiles" even in Christ and therefore must continue to differentiate themselves in relation to the Jewish law that applies specifically to Israel. With respect to the Law, its demands differentiate Jew and non-Jew since the Law, as we shall note in ch. 7, has not died or been abolished; hence one needs to be clear about its sphere of application, about who comes under its jurisdiction *and how*.

Romans 6:17 The (Previous) Pattern of Teaching to Which You Were Committed

We now need to return to reconsider Paul's meaning in 6:17 in relation to his intentions to visit Rome. Jewett has drawn attention to several problems with 6:17, which has sometimes been regarded as a gloss, for example, by Bultmann. He considers that all of the irregularities would be removed if the original text lacked v. 17b (2007: 417). Jewett's concern arises mainly on the basis that to take the most widely accepted meaning of this verse as "obedience to the pattern of teaching to which you were handed over" is to accept "obedience" to a "form of teaching" that conflicts with the central Pauline emphasis on the Lordship of Christ (in contrast to the post-Pauline emphasis on commitment to or assent to sound doctrine). I am, however, reluctant to accept his detailed argument on this point, despite having sympathy with his stance (Jewett 2007: 417–19). The reference to the διδαχή to which they have been committed (handed over) fits very well my understanding of Romans, and the emphasis upon "obedience," better expressed as hearing in trust, or hearing by doing since ὑπακοή and ἀκοή are, in this respect, identical (Ehrensperger 2007: 167). The Roman Christ-followers were not without teaching, διδαχή, prior to Paul's letter, as he makes quite plain in addressing them. The interlocutor in 2:18 refers to being instructed in the Law, and some of the Roman addressees, even though non-Jews, would probably have received the Christ message from Jews, and would have had some contact with Jewish patterns of teaching, at least in the earliest period (Campbell 2015: 176–80). It must not be overlooked that the Christ-message had already been known in Rome for some years—note Paul's long-standing intention to visit—and thus there would have been time for different expressions of the gospel concerning Christ to have influenced the gentile Christ-followers there (see "Introduction" chapter).

Possibly the best reading of this text is Gagnon's proposal (1993: 667–87),[8] taken up by Jewett in his rendering of τύπον διδαχῆς as "the imprint stamped by teaching" (Jewett 2007: 413). Thus, when Paul refers to the Romans' commitment to "the imprint stamped by teaching" to which they had earlier been committed, he is simply acknowledging its validity from his perspective, confirming his recognition that the Romans had responded to, and received a lasting impression from, the gospel that had arrived earlier in Rome, long prior to his visit (cf. Rom. 1:12 and 15:14-15). He is not comparing the details of his gospel with that which the Romans had accepted, but recognizing their status as being faithful Christ-followers. To compare his gospel with their traditions would not have proved very effective in that it was questions about the nature of his gospel that had already raised significant issues at Rome (cf. 3:8).

The use of παρεδόθητε in relation to τύπον διδαχῆς implies, in my view, no more than that the Romans had received the gospel and accepted it gladly possibly a decade earlier. The difficulty arises because παραδίδομαι "hand over" is the classic verb for "handing on" a traditional teaching, and so could be taken to mean that the baptized had become obedient to teaching associated with baptism that imparts a certain form or pattern of life marked by tradition (Fitzmyer 1993: 449–50). It might be implied that this previous διδαχή differs from Paul's own pattern, but even if this is so, Paul has no difficulty in acknowledging its consistency with his teaching. Clearly, the issue behind this is how we envisage that the first Christ-followers at Rome had been introduced to the gospel, that is, was it to a Jewish Christ following pattern to which they were first handed over, that is, committed? Then if so, Paul may be indicating his awareness of its differing pattern and still acknowledging them *now* as competent and faithful Christ-followers. Yet this acknowledgement does not mean that Paul does not add to or develop the gospel specifically in its application to ethnē in Christ. If Paul worked almost exclusively among the ethnē, then his gospel would be what he expounds in Romans, that is, how the ethnē should live in relation to the God of Israel, relate to the Law, and so on. The commitment to this gospel is for ethnē only, but as we insist throughout our exegesis of Romans, concentration upon the ethnē need not imply

---

[8] Gagnon convincingly argues "that *tupos* possibly refers to the imprint made on the mind by divine teaching following Philo's idea that Moses stamped upon their minds as with a seal, deep imprints of understanding, and that at creation the invisible deity stamped on the invisible soul the imprints of itself" (1993: 686–7).

an opposition to Jews, and vice versa. Differentiation and distinction need not imply discrimination or antagonism against the "other."

In any case, we cannot be sure of the history of the Christ-message in Rome, and how that history developed. But we do not hold that being committed to a form of teaching implies that a person's relation to Christ is determined by the nature of his doctrinal beliefs. Exclusive commitment to Christ is primary for Paul, but he is able to recognize Peter as a fellow apostle despite differences (Galatians 2).

Conclusion to Romans 6

In this chapter, Paul has compared not only the "lords" under whose rule one is an enslaved person but particularly the differing outcomes of the relationships involved—"things of which you are now ashamed" (v. 21), or holiness, the *telos*, goal of which is eternal life (v. 22). Paul's summary conclusion of ch. 6 reflects the stark opposites he has laid before the Romans, death that has been deserved as the appropriate wage, or eternal life that is the free gift of God through Jesus Christ, our Lord (v. 23). It is fitting that "Lord" should be the last word in this chapter that has moved through the experience of slavery and death, to the gift and promise of eternal life through Christ.[9] This confirms Jewett's claim that at many points in Romans the issue comes down to which lord or master one serves. This has brought us to note how in many differing contexts, including links with 3:8, and especially in the use of the imperative, Paul develops the thesis on the τέλος or goal of the body in the service of God or of sin. Loyalty to Christ is clearly demonstrated "in our mortal bodies" in 6:12. This theme will be elaborated, especially in 12:1-2, the connection with which is indicated by the shared terminology of παρίστημι (to offer, present) thereby linking with the several occurrences of this verb in 6:12-23.

The claim that Paul has presented here is that the gifts and grace of God are only available in total commitment to Christ as Lord. This commitment includes the concrete dedication of the physical body, its limbs and energies, its total activities in the service of righteousness, coupled with a death to slavery to the passions and all the counterclaims of competing loyalties. Loyalty to Christ for non-Jews is not an additional claim to be included alongside gentile attempts to keep the requirements of the Law or added to the claims of cultic loyalties. It has to be an exclusive commitment to Christ expressed in what might be termed the ascetic use of the body.

---

[9] Cf. Barclay (2015: 457–8). It is to Barclay's credit that the title of his book so clearly epitomizes his intended focus (upon grace).

EXCURSUS III

Slavery to God

There can be no doubt that Paul (among other metaphors) views Christ-followers as enslaved people, whether as formerly "slaves to sin" or, as presently, "slaves to righteousness" (6:17-18). He looks back to the previous state of the Roman gentile Christ-followers and contrasts their former life as slavery to sin, whereas now (νυνί), having been freed from sin, ἐλευθερωθέντες, they have become "enslaved to God" (δουλωθέντες δὲ τῷ θεῷ, v. 22). The modern consensus seems to be that Paul's δοῦλος metaphors should be interpreted through the particular lens of the most common form of slavery, that is, Greco-Roman chattel slavery. Thus, "when Paul exhorted Christians that slavery was the proper relationship of the believer to God, his words were embedded in [his] Roman cultural milieu" (Harrill 2016: 334). But because of the unflattering associations of slavery terminology in relation to voluntary service to God, many scholars have sought to reduce the emphasis on forced obedience and have looked for other biblical models that might explain the content Paul wishes to convey in Romans chs. 6–8 in particular. Richard Horsley, despite his well-known attention to images of military might and conquest in Paul's symbolic universe, nevertheless insists that Paul's δοῦλος metaphors depict the worldview of the free (rather than enforced) service of the Jewish people to the God of Israel. Horsley grants that "slave of Christ" was a favored self-designation of Paul's, and that he considered all Christ-followers similarly to be "slaves of righteousness," but strongly objects that Paul refers to these generally as "slaves of Christ"—this does not adequately portray the God/Christ–human relationship, which in Romans 6 cannot be limited to, nor fully represented by, the relations between master and slave in the household.

With Horsley, I recognize that Jewish authors such as Paul were coming from a subjugated society with social relations and cultural traditions to some extent different from those of the dominant imperial society. Hence, "we need to take into account the discourse of Israelite-Jewish tradition (even after its translation into Greek terms) which originated in and was shaped by ancient Near Eastern political-economic-religious patterns" (Horsley 1998: 167). It is clear, in my view, that the δοῦλος metaphor in Romans 6 occurs in a context where the dominant imagery is not merely that of the household but of political rule and domination by such superhuman forces as sin and death versus the rule of God (βασιλεύειν 6:12, κυριεύειν 6:9, 14; 7:10). The imagery fits better that of the broader Roman imperial conquest, subjugation, and enslavement of peoples such as the Jews, especially the latter's current experience of subjection to the overwhelming military might of Rome. Though the Israelites had previously often been subjected to foreign powers until liberated by their God, in Paul's time the complete domination by Rome, and their experience of this, must have reawakened narratives of bondage in Egypt and hope of divine deliverance.

There is some justification, therefore, to contextualize slavery to God not primarily in the domestic context but rather in that of the enslavement of peoples by a dominating power. Thus, John Byron has argued that the episode in Egypt is not about the manumission of Israel but a change of masters, "the conflict is between two competing kings over who will be the king of Israel and whom Israel will serve" (2003: 48). The cult of the ubiquitous divine Caesar could offer a first-century-related context in which the challenge arises to give homage to a master other than the God of Israel (Jeffers 2002: 138). Adolf Deissmann found parallels to the acquisition of freedom through a slave's devotion to a deity in the famous Delphi inscriptions, particularly in the reports of masters freeing their slaves to the god Apollo by way of a trust sale. He saw in Paul's portrayal of Christ-followers, as people freed from sin and enslaved to God, analogies to the Hellenistic practice of sacral manumission (1910: 326). Thus, though the former slave was no longer in bondage to his master, he may still have owed indentured service (παραμονή) to the deity as his freedman (Westermann 1955: 55–64).

Byron seeks to show how the language of slavery became separated from the institution in which it initially developed to operate separately from its historical roots to describe situations and relationships in which subordinates showed obedience to an authority figure, whether voluntarily or by force. He thus explains while still retaining his emphasis on Israel's post-Exodus enslavement to God how Paul's slavery language is more amenable to influence from contemporary use of Roman slave terminology. This is a possible explanation that fits Paul's flexible vocabulary and its use. I am not sure that I would go so far as to suggest that the Exodus narrative could ever entirely lose its nuances or relevance in relation to themes such as Paul raises in Romans 6. In a sense, one's stance on this issue is closely related to and influenced by how one interprets Paul's own relation to his Jewish background and upbringing. Because I have always stressed his positive and abiding appreciation of this, I am inclined to give more weight to Paul's Jewish heritage as a strong component of his identity formation and theological thought. It would seem incumbent on scholars from this perspective to see a living impact from Paul's Jewish cultural traditions as informing his thinking on the action of God in freeing and vindicating Israel in face of other nations and conquerors. It is therefore not gratuitous to claim that Paul's statements here are in keeping with and influenced by Israelite traditions concerning slavery (and freedom from it) since these were a living part of Paul's symbolic universe. However, we must be aware as Brooten has claimed, "Throughout most of their histories, Jews and Christians have tolerated slavery in a way that reflects their surrounding societies" (Brooten 2021). While not regarding the Jews as completely conformist in relation to contemporary society, there is some evidence that they did not always or universally differ from it in relation to slavery.

Recently, John Goodrich has proposed that rather than deny the influence of Jewish traditions in Paul's slavery metaphors in Romans 6, it is better to recognize that Paul's δοῦλος metaphor qualifies to meet all the requirements of being a scriptural concept as Ciampa and others have argued (Ciampa 2008: 48). Goodrich affirms Byron's conclusion that though we cannot claim that Paul necessarily had the Exodus in mind when he wrote Romans 6, we can claim that "his understanding of enslavement to God was naturally shaped through the prism of the Exodus" (Goodrich 2013: 517, n26). Thus Paul, however close he lived to the everyday world of Roman practice of slavery, nevertheless included in his perception of servitude the Jewish tradition of a God who delivered his people from Egypt and who is still with them. This perspective cannot but have influence in Paul's thinking, and in his overall attitude to slaves and servitude, a dimension not available in the contemporary perceptions of Roman domination. Paul wishes to inform his hearers not only about the horrific conditions of contemporary slavery, with which they would have some familiarity, but also about the grand narratives of God's deliverance of his people, and the subsequent results of this in the history of his people. Yet, as Goodrich demonstrates by his consideration in 6:1-23 of the nouns κάρπος, τέλος, and ὀψώνιον, terms with financial connotations resonating with the commercial language of first-century Rome, the context of 6:16–7:6 suggests not military service but domestic slavery, and that Paul's employment of terms for slave productivity and perks indicates that Paul's δοῦλος metaphors in Romans 6 and elsewhere should be interpreted in the contexts of *both* Judaism *and* Hellenism (Goodrich 2013: 530).

It is on this point that we must be careful not to exaggerate the power of the language of the conquerors to change the thought of those subjected to their control. In Paul's use of slavery language as slavery to righteousness we see a positive appropriation of this language that defined the lives of the Roman ethnē as slaves whether in the Roman households or the Empire. But in so doing Paul is reclaiming and reworking this language to promote an orientation that fundamentally subverts the ideology of the empire. Tessa Rajak has demonstrated the peculiar use of language when it is used in cultural resistance. In the translation of the Septuagint, "absorption into the world of Greek expression was a fact which the 'consumers' of the translation pragmatically took on board but around which they also drew lines" (2009: 152–61). Thus, Rajak is able to assert, "The translation language they forged worked and survived because it did a job. Inscribed within the language itself is an assertion of communal independence which made it possible for the translations to serve as vehicle for quiet cultural resistance" (2009: 156). This was the biblical language Paul used with his ἐκκλησίαι and in which he operated throughout.

Another feature of language translation in differing cultures is that it can justifiably be argued that the vehicle of transmission, that is, the language itself, does not entirely determine the content it transmits. Ehrensperger has insisted that even in the use of English as *lingua franca*, the language is not simply a neutral or merely utilitarian means of communication, but "reflects the values and interests of its speakers who come from different linguistic and cultural backgrounds" (2013: 60–1). Bilinguals, or multilinguals, of which Paul was one, are aware of the fact that there is more than one way of seeing the world and experiencing life. This is particularly relevant in contexts where a dominating power attempts to impose not only its military strength but also its perception of the world, that is, its ideological justification of the military domination, on those dominated. "The Pauline discourse which is seen as shaped and rooted in a linguistic and cultural-/social and symbolic universe … provides a clear alternative to Roman ideology" (2013: 62). If Ehrensperger's conclusions, based on recent empirical research are valid, then even though Paul uses the language and terminology of the empire, the meaning he gives in his expression of his thought is the one determined by him as a Greek-speaking Jew.

This is not to deny or overlook the contribution of Benjamin Wright. He has argued that in the preponderance of uses of δοῦλος in Josephus and Philo together with the intimate knowledge these authors possessed of Greco-Roman slave systems, this suggests that they conceptualized the various modes of service mentioned in the Jewish scriptures in the same way as they perceived the chattel slavery they knew firsthand (1998: 83–111). Thus, he asserts that the term δοῦλος conveyed to the Greek reader in a later period "something different from what the word *ebed* did earlier" (1998: 84). In Romans, however, we are dealing with Paul's thought forms and patterns, not with Philo or Josephus who differ considerably from Paul at this point. This approach would allow Paul to give the meaning he desires to the terms he uses, but a problem then arises as to how the message would be received, and Paul will have to deal with that. However, Ehrensperger's stance is one that is also embedded in the contexts of speech— rather than giving a fixed interpretation of language irrespective of localized contexts following on the research of Farzad Sharifian (2011). This concerned the use of English by Aborigine communities in Australia, demonstrating that the language is adapted by a community to serve its needs and to express meanings specific to the community and particular situations. "English as a lingua franca is thus far from being unitary and monolithic but due to the diversity of its speakers always heterogeneous and locally appropriated" (2013: 60). Thus, Paul's mission to the nations is attempting, particularly in Romans, to relate gentile Christ-followers positively to the scriptural narrative of Israel, a dynamic that highlights the dominant traditions such as the Exodus narrative. It is unlikely, therefore, that Paul's speech in such a context would not resonate with the great symbolic events of Israelite history. But even when considering such, we ought to exercise care in talking about such concepts as "freedom" in relation to slavery in that it is difficult not to read into these conceptions from more recent Western thought, by which we are influenced, but which were not available to Paul. Paul still tells the Corinthians, "You are not your own, you were bought with a price" (1 Cor. 6:19-20). Freedom for Paul is freedom from one master in order to be free to serve another (Exod. 10:3).

In light of the emphases of Horsley, Harrill, Byron, Wright, and particularly Goodrich's comprehensive and detailed argument (2013: 526), it is justified to conclude that Paul's metaphors in Romans 6 and elsewhere are shaped *both* by Jewish tradition *and* Greco-Roman perceptions, though I would not wish to limit the latter *only* to domestic slavery, since Paul's thought encompasses much more. Yet Jewish slavery ideas, like other Jewish conceptions could not escape the influence of Greek thought, as Harrill and Wright have demonstrated and while this is true, it points to a modification or enlargement of conceptions rather than a takeover particularly where traditions about Israel's God, his character, and posited activities were concerned. Paul's letters do contain references to domestic slavery, for example, Rom. 14:4 (where the term is οἰκέτης, house slave), but the horizons of his thought in Romans are not limited to the household, but deal with the rule of God, of Caesar, and of the powers of sin and death. These also play their part in constructing what he means by slavery and freedom. If Paul, in his own self-presentation in the first verse of Romans depicts himself in a way that, without doubt, resonates with the Hebrew *ebed*, we must presume he has not forgotten such, six chapters later.

Romans 7

Romans 7:1-6: "You 'Gentiles' Have Died to the Law So That You May Belong to Another"

¹Do you not know, brothers—for I am speaking to those who know the law—that the law rules over a person only during that person's lifetime? ²For a married woman is bound by law to her husband as long as he lives; but if the husband dies, she is discharged from the law concerning the husband. ³Accordingly while the husband is alive, she will be called an adulteress if she lives with another husband. But if the husband dies, she is released from that law, and as a result she is not an adulteress if she marries another man. ⁴So then, my brothers you were put to death to the law through the body of Christ, so that you may belong to another, to him who has been raised from the dead in order that we might bear fruit for God. ⁵For when we were in the flesh, the sinful passions, that were identified by the law, were at work in our members so that we bore fruit for death. ⁶But now we are released from the law, [since] we have died to that which held us captive, so that we might serve in newness of Spirit, not in oldness of letter.

Paul has just argued in ch. 6 that gentile Christ-followers have been freed from being slaves to sin to become slaves of God through Christ. But what this means in relation to the Law needs also to be clarified. Thus 7:1-6 is a continuation of the arguments in ch. 6, this time not principally through the analogy of slavery but rather of marriage.

In this short section Paul, having in the previous chapter depicted his addressees as no longer enslaved by sin, further portrays their status in Christ through the image of death, already introduced in ch. 5. Those freed from sin are now reminded that freedom from sin is not an end in itself, a state of vacuous non-commitment (if that were possible, since for Paul, the self is never truly autonomous) but rather an occasion to belong to another (Keck 2005: 200). Paul has chosen the image of a married woman who, on the death of her husband, is then free to marry another (7:2). This is a very specific analogy chosen for a limited purpose and must not be read allegorically as if every detail had an exact parallel in Paul's thought. We need to be cautious in subjecting Paul's use of terms such as covenant to rigid conceptual distinctions (Avemarie 2014: 61). The main point Paul wishes to underline is that the death of the husband leaves his wife free to belong to another. In Paul's analogy, the fact that *the bereaved wife is free* from the legal obligation she previously owed to her husband is the main point. This was is in force only during his lifetime, and the Law applies to the wife only during his lifetime. Death cancels legal marital obligation. The gentile Christ-followers are discharged from the judgment of the Law, not because the Law has died, this is not what Paul says, but because in and through Christ, they have died (6:4-6), and the Law has no valid claim on someone who is deceased. Since this passage is not meant to be read allegorically, there is no need at this point to raise related issues concerning the relation of ethnē to the Law as, for example, if they were not given the Law, how can they require removal from its jurisdiction? Or is Paul a weak thinker because he should have stated that the Law died, or the "wife of the husband"? Paul has used the analogy to make only one point, the husband's death gives freedom for the wife from the legal obligation to the husband, not to argue that the Law has been annulled or terminated for ethnē in Christ, nor indeed to offer his complete theology of the Law. Paul's ethnic agenda is to discourage the ethnē from following the Law.

Significantly, Paul addresses the Romans here and again in 7:4 as ἀδέλφοι, brothers, which he has not done since the letter's opening in 1:13. This keeps alive the progress of Paul's argument on brotherhood, which will proceed via 8:12, 8:29, and 9:3 to its culmination in 12:1. Not only this, but he further describes them as "those who know the Law." But there is no change of audience; the audience addressed is still the same gentile one explicitly indicated in 1:5-7, 13-15; 11:17, and 15:17. These are non-Jews some of whom have come to know the Law most likely by association with the synagogues as God-fearers or perhaps as proselytes. Significantly, Paul does not use first-person plural here to address the Roman ethnē, thereby clearly excluding himself. It would have been tautologous to refer to a Jew like himself as one who knows the Law. Paul simply states that he speaks to those "who know the Law." It is their relation to the Law that is worthy of note, not his. There would have been no reason for him to add this observation to an address to Jews, since no Jew would not have "known the Law" (Thorsteinsson 2003: 119). The fact that these ethnē "know the Law" does not tell us anything precisely about their perception of the Law, except that they probably thought it worthy of respect in some sense. Here, as noted, Paul addresses the Romans as "brothers" not once but again a second time in 7:1 in the space of four verses. Why this emphasis here? In ch. 9, Paul will refer to (but not address) his Jewish kin according to the flesh as brothers. Because he is speaking here to "those who know the Law," it could be erroneously concluded that Paul speaks here to his Jewish ἀδέλφοι, so in order to stress that his audience is non-Jewish, Paul addresses his audience directly and intimately so that it is clear he addresses only them and them alone until 7:6. He will talk about, but not to, his Jewish brothers, separately and in detail in chs. 9–11. Here he uses a legal analogy to make clear to the Romans their relation as non-Jews to the Jewish Law and its verdict upon gentile sinners (cf. ἀνομία 6:19). We keep in mind here the universal applicability of the Law emphasized in 3:19-20 (Elliott 2007: 145–7).

Paul's theological perspective here is that through the death of Christ, literally the body—σῶμα of Christ—his followers have been executed with him (Christ) as denoted by the recurrence of συν compounds in chs. 6 and 8 (Rodriguez 2014: 126). Paul claims "you 'gentiles' were set free so that you can belong to another," "to him who has been raised from the dead." We note that here again Paul uses the normal "you" plural form of address, "you" not "we," since Paul does not include himself in the description of gentiles' sinful past. But with the concluding clause of 7:4, Paul includes himself in the desired outcome of the new belonging to Christ "so that we might bear fruit for God" (1:13). The specifically gentile problem Paul had introduced in Romans 2 was that turning to the Law did not give non-Jews the power to defeat sin, but they were (still) enslaved by sin, because they were living in the flesh without the power of the Spirit (7:5). Even taking on the yoke of the Law did not enable their emancipation from sin's slavery, because as born "gentiles" they were "by nature" sinners; we note the three references to nature in 1:26-27 (cf. 11:24), in analogy to their Jewish counterparts, who were Jews by nature φύσει Ἰουδαῖοι (Gal. 2:15). Only beginning from 12:1 on will Paul demonstrate the reconstruction of gentile nature through the Spirit in a new family brotherhood (McMurray 2021: 154–7).

Here Paul distinguishes Jews and non-Jews by their differing ethnic origins, but it is not simply biology or genes that Paul is indicating, but nurture as a Jew or non-Jew is also primary. The born-Jew receives a different upbringing that includes for males not only circumcision but also what circumcision indicated, living as belonging to the God of Israel. Being brought up in a Jewish family home, and nurtured in the "way of the Lord," would create a very different ethos resulting in very distinct characteristics in the groups of those involved. We take Paul's meaning of Jews or "gentiles" "by nature" as including enculturation from childhood into the values and life patterns of their parents and ethnic groups. By this we recognize the *habitus* that is developed in them, how they are formed from birth into distinctive patterns of behavior and of values.[1] Normativity is central to social identity (Esler 2014). To be brought up as a child within the Abrahamic covenantal pattern of life resulted in a very different pattern of life to that of the ethnē with very different cultural patterns.

This is why we do not read "I was alive once apart from the Law" (7:9) as a reference to some earlier stage of Paul's life or his childhood. When Paul speaks of the weakness of the flesh, he includes the individual's incorporation into the practices and life patterns, both good and bad, of the family group into which he or she has been born. The Jewish child has the "advantage" of life within the covenant, its practices and values, and nurturing in the exclusive ways of the God of Israel. This benefit is not to be confused with favoritism by God (Hultgren 2011: 141–3). From the point of view of the people of Israel, their advantage is one that accrues from being born as children of promise, which necessitates the acquisition of certain practices and values appropriate to those called by God to be a holy people who serve no other god. But the child in a gentile family is lacking in these particular values and patterns. They are raised to relate to the gods of the families and peoples, practices that are considered idolatrous from a Jewish perspective and are irreversibly polluting those practicing these things.

The latter may not be recognized as of primary significance, but this is a mistaken view that fails to acknowledge that "the child is father of the man," and that many of the most crucial influences on later development occur in very early childhood. The learning of a language is one of the most instructive examples here. Children learn

---

[1] Cf. Barclay's title "Under Grace: The Construction of a Christian *Habitus*" (2013: 59–76).

their language from their primary carers, in most cases their mother; hence, "mother tongue," and the thinking and speaking of the growing person is forever imprinted with the characteristics of that language and the associated culture that it transmits. In later life, the maturing adult may react against the childhood cultural patterns he or she inherited, but that reaction is still influenced even as a reaction to that against which he or she rebels. (The learning of another language simultaneously in a multilingual household will nuance the above claims but does not contradict them.)

No child, whether Jewish or non-Jewish, can escape the power of the nurture he or she has received. This patterning from birth will influence them positively or negatively throughout their life, producing a powerful *habitus* that links them inevitably to their social context and traditions. This *habitus*, in turn, may determine or at least influence their reception or rejection of the opportunities they encounter in life, in that the *habitus* precedes, and therefore influences, the decisions that they seem freely and independently to make. Again, this recognition of cultural influences is not in opposition to the new life and character that proceeds in Paul's view from the new familial membership that is so transformative in 12:1–15:13. Rather, it is consistent with it in that in both instances, the individual is formed and transformed in community.

Nurture and practice within Jewish patterns of life, as noted, include circumcision and other Jewish traditions, varied contextually as these may be. Where this becomes significant is in the evaluation of eighth-day circumcision. Only the latter is the mark and seal of the covenant including the male child in the covenant people Israel, as a φύσει Ἰουδαῖος and not a gentile sinner (Fredriksen 2017: 113–17).[2] Of course, nurture is relevant, but a Jew remains a Jew even as a transgressor.

The fact that Paul stresses his audience thus at this point indicates their specificity—they are non-Jews, but they also "know the Law." And since we have already demonstrated in the previous chapters that Paul's addressees are usually identified as ethnic-specific, he does not address humans in general, then those "who know the Law" would be an unlikely description of those who were born-Jews. As noted it would be a tautology to add to the designation Jews, the epithet "those who know the Law." Thus, although the addressees here are "brothers," that is, Christ followers who "know the Law," they know it not from childhood but after being enculturated as "gentiles." These, we noted, differ considerably from those born into a Jewish family. Moreover, even if a non-Jew seeks to do the Law perfectly, he can never do it in response to God's call to Israel, but only as a means of earning favor from God. This is particularly evident in the ineffectiveness of circumcision for adults. Adult circumcision is not the sign of the covenant in Paul's view.

From this (Jewish) foundation, being brought up as a child within the covenant predisposed the adult to live in the patterns of thought and behavior transmitted to them from childhood, and, as noted, these differ radically between Jew and non-Jew. If Paul adheres to the view that worship of idols rather than of the Creator God of Israel, results necessarily in pollution, corruption of values, and the degradation of

---

[2] I avoid reference here to religion because at this period of history it is anachronistic to deal with religion as separate from ethnicity (see, e.g., Nongbri 2013).

society, this would suggest that although all are under the power of sin, the non-Jews experience this more intensely, and that therefore the distinction between Jew and non-Jew in their socializing and enculturation are vital factors that cannot be ignored. Since one cannot escape pollution through idolatry nor the *habitus* formed in and by the developing adult, nurture within the covenant is a great advantage in contrast to those accustomed to the world of idolatry. These do not easily change their life pattern even when they desire to follow the Law. In Paul's language, perhaps he might suggest that "keeping the Law" is unnatural for the non-Jew, and therefore not easily successfully undertaken. In relation to this, it is interesting to note Philo's comments concerning proselytes. One should not use slanderous language about other gods, since they might mistakenly then in return use "impious language against the true and holy God … by reason of their having from their infancy learnt to look upon what was false as if it had been true, and having been brought up with it, they would be likely to err" (*Spec.* 1:53).

Later in this chapter, in 7:7-25, Paul will devote attention to this very issue, that is, of non-Jews seeking to take on the yoke of Torah, and the difficulties that ensue from this. It is quite clear in view of his own explicit statements on the holiness of the Law that Paul would not refer to the specifically Jewish adherence to the Law as to "the old written code" παλαιότητι γράμματος (7:6). Addressing the ethnē, this can refer only to the Law adhered to by the non-Jew in a slavish manner, and not in response to God's call of Israel, which of course only encompasses Jews. Thus, a non-Jew doing the Law inherently tries to thereby establish or earn his relationship with God, which amounts to works righteousness. This holds the *persona* captive, and from it discharge must be sought (cf. 7:24-25). Slaves under "the old written code" (NRSV) could never, in Paul's perspective here, apply to Jews though, theoretically, our translation, "oldness of letter" and "newness of Spirit," could apply to any group reading the scriptures. It is hard to avoid traditional law-critical nuances, but Paul's presentation of the Law here is designed to get the ethnē to follow their ethnically appropriate route via trust in Christ and subsequent support through the Spirit. The basic image consists in a contrast concerning how the Torah is perceived or adhered to—either as a proselyte without Christ and without the empowerment of the Spirit, signified as "in oldness of letter," or with Christ and through the Spirit, denoted as "in newness of spirit" (Rodriguez 2014: 126). "Letter and Spirit" through Paul took on a hermeneutical significance of their own, but here the meaning must derive from the context of non-Jews seeking to live by the Law, and without the Spirit (Campbell 2016: 150).

Now, through belonging to Christ, "we are discharged, κατηργήθημεν, from the Law, dead to that which held us captive, so that we might serve in newness of the Spirit not in oldness of letter" (7.6). Essentially, what Paul is indicating here is a change of master. The Law here has not died, but the ethnē through union with the resurrected Christ have been removed from its jurisdiction over gentile sinners, and so are free to live to bear fruit for God. Neither the Law nor the wife has died, but the one to whom she was legally committed, the husband, dies leaving his wife free from legal obligation to him, and free for commitment, that is, marriage to another.

It may be interesting to consider Paul's strategy in thus addressing former God-fearers and possibly proselytes. In his portrayal of the Law, as noted, he does not make any claim that the Law has been annulled, or that it is terminated. This would have led to repercussions from Jews and Jewish Christ-followers, but Paul does not encounter this problem because he removes the gentile Christ-followers from the sphere of the Law's jurisdiction over gentile sinners, that is, idolators, by their own dying with Christ, and thus becoming dead to sin's domination. We noted in ch. 6 that, for the first time in his letters, Paul claimed that Christ-followers died with Christ and were buried together with him. This point must therefore have specific relevance for the Romans whom he addresses here. A main aim of the letter is to get ethnē to focus upon their relation to Christ rather than on the Law, because it is only though Christ and the Spirit that the Law can be fulfilled. Ethnē in Christ have died with Christ and have been buried with him, so that they should reckon themselves dead to sin, freed from its domination, serving a different master. Again, it is apparent that Paul does not offer here any comments or conclusions on the role of the Torah in relation to Jews. Our arguments about being a born-Jew, and Jewish upbringing presume the value of the Law for Jews as in 3:1-2.

Now through Christ, God's grace is extended to the ethnē. They now can live as non-Jews in relation to God, and through the Spirit they have power to allow the Law to be written on their hearts, their new lives of love, fulfilling the Law as ethnē in Christ. But this means "we have died to that in which we were confined/held captive" (7:6). The verdict of the Law holds the ethnē in captivity to sin through the judgment of the Law upon sin, in which the Law is complicit. But the ethnē in Christ do not follow the Law as other non-Jews apart from Christ would do, because through Christ they have died to the Law, so are not within the sphere of its legitimate jurisdiction over gentile sinners.

The mode of serving the Law (rather than the Law itself) seems to be the import of 7:6, "so that we serve not in oldness of letter, but in newness of the Spirit." By "oldness of letter" rather than "old written code," Paul seems to be describing the Law in written form but as read by non-Jews without the aid of the Spirit. Paul cites the scriptures, the scriptures of Israel, reasoning with and through them so frequently throughout Romans, that "oldness of letter" here is unlikely to refer primarily to a Jewish reading of scripture. In a sense, the issue described here is rather artificial in that this begins the preparation for his argument in Romans 8 that the Law on its own is inadequate but requires the presence of the Spirit to be effective. Paul is explaining why ethnē, non-Jews who are also non-Christ-followers, cannot find righteousness simply by seeking to observe the Law. Without empowerment by God's grace, the Law cannot be fulfilled. This is why Paul first introduces the Spirit in 7:6 to prepare for his argument concerning the Spirit's absence in 7:7-25 and its effusive presence in Romans 8 (prior to its full expression in gifts of grace in 12:6-8).

The summary conclusion to this first section of Romans 7 reads like a hermeneutical key to Paul's theologizing about serving God in a new pattern ἐν καινότητι πνεύματος "in newness of Spirit" rather than καὶ οὐ παλαιότητι γράμματος "in oldness of letter." Paul deliberately offers a summary of his teaching on reading the Law, that is, the scriptures in the right way, that is, with or without the Spirit. Similar statements occur in 2 Cor. 3:6 (Campbell 2016: 120–50) in connection with the covenant, which allows us to conclude that in 7:6 Paul is speaking hypothetically, not about himself or other

Jews, but of a non-Jew reading the Law without the aid of the Spirit, that is, without having turned to Christ. This is illustrated in that through the remainder of this chapter, the Spirit is completely absent until 8:2. Romans 7 is thus somewhat artificial in that it does not reflect the Roman ethnē who had already turned to Christ but rather the interlocutor's questions about whether the Law is actually identical with sin. Paul's response is to exonerate the Law and to implicate sin. Paul uses speech-in-character to offer a hypothetical example of a non-Jew attempting to read the scriptures/do the Law without the aid of the Spirit.

Romans 7:7-25: Paul's Use of Speech-in-Character to Represent the Confused "Gentile"

Chapter 7 begins with a false deduction from what Paul previously claimed. Perhaps it would be better for non-Jews if they had never encountered the Law and its teaching, since with the coming of the Law comes knowledge of sin. Might it not be better to have remained in gentile ignorance? Beginning with the denial of the false inference in 7:7 that the Law is identical with sin, Paul continues in 7:12 to affirm clearly that he regards the Law as the inheritance of the Jewish people. This apology is continued in the affirmation of 7:14 "for we know that the Law is spiritual." This denotes its divine origin, but leaves Paul still with the problem of why a spiritual Law is nevertheless ineffective against sin, "so then the good became death to me, did it not?" (7:7) Paul is seeking to explain to non-Jews, the meaning of the Law for them. But he has a problem in that he grew up within the practice of the Law, he even became expert in its teachings and so knowledgeable that he could claim to be blameless as far as its practice was concerned (Phil. 3:6). So how can he imagine what it is like for a non-Jew without the experience of Jewish nurture and years of its practice to understand the effect of the Law upon the ethnē?

Paul's solution is one that is intelligible in light of his pattern of teaching in the earlier chapters of Romans. Here he has used the diatribal style of airing opinions with the aid of an imaginary speech partner who obligingly responds in ways that assist Paul in the progression of his argument. In this non-polemical address to non-Jews, Paul does not use the interlocutor to criticize Jews as such, rather he imagines a gentile interlocutor who voices in the first-person singular the likely response of non-Jews to his gospel and teaching. It is just such a non-Jewish conversation partner whom Paul introduces again in 7:7-25. As Stowers notes, "[Given] the representations of the gentiles in ch. 1, the descriptions of the audience's past lives, and several comments about their dilemma under the law, the imaginary speaker can only be a gentile describing his struggle to live by works of the law" (1994: 39). The diatribal pattern was often associated with imaginary interlocutors not just in short series of statements, but could be expressed in a longer sequence in a discussion termed "speech-in-character" to facilitate a fuller exposition of a topic. In this mode, an author or rhetor could elaborate a stance or viewpoint that he did not share or that was not autobiographical. Like an assumed character in a drama, in order to present himself or herself convincingly, the actor or author must literally "don the mantle" or *persona* of the designated character in a convincing dialogue. Here Paul takes on the *persona* of a gentile person who reads the Law and seeks to be guided by it, but without being a Christ-follower and thus without the illumination of the Holy Spirit.

In contrast to the spirituality of the Law, Paul prompts the *persona* to confess "but I am fleshly, sold as a slave to sin." "For I do not understand my own actions. For I do not do what I want, but I do the very thing I hate" (7:15). The whole of 7:7-25 is highly rhetorical (Tobin 2004: 243), and we must be careful therefore not to interpret it as if Paul himself were autobiographically simply reporting his own (Jewish) experience. The characteristically diatribal use of the second-person singular address, first encountered in the judging character of 2:1-5, and correlating with the you (σε) of 2:17, is already suggestive that the "I" of Romans 7 need not necessarily be Paul speaking about his own experience (Song 2004: 16). Such experience would necessarily be different from that of a non-Jew, and this is one significant reason why Paul speaks in 7:7-25 in the voice of a gentile *persona*.

"Paul does not say that, although he knows what is good and what he ought to do, he, Paul of Tarsus finds that he cannot do it and instead does the evil that he knows he ought not to do" (Rodriguez 2014: 139). Paul must indeed be speaking in 7:7-25 as a rhetorically portrayed character and not in his own voice, otherwise he contradicts what he has clearly stated earlier, for example, 6:3-8 where he includes himself among those who have died to sin. And even if it is allowed that Paul may sometimes contradict his own statements or claims, it would be very strange if someone so capable of writing so much coherent and competent teaching as Romans displays, would at this point contradict his own clear "biographical" statements within the course of two chapters.

Subsection A

Romans 7:7-12: The "Gentile" on His Own with the Law and without the Spirit

⁷What then should we say? The law is [the source of] sin, is it not? Far from it! Yet, if it had not been for the law, I would not have known what sin is. I would not have known what it is to covet if the law had not said, "You shall not covet." ⁸But finding an opportunity through the commandment, sin working in me produced every manner of covetousness. Apart from the law sin was dead. ⁹I once lived apart from the law, but when the commandment came, sin came to life again ¹⁰so I died, and the commandment that was for life for me was for death. ¹¹For sin took advantage of the occasion afforded through the commandment, deceived me and through it killed me. ¹²So the law is holy, and the commandment is holy and righteous and good.

In the heading of this section, I have deliberately used "gentile" without further detail since the "I" ἐγώ of Rom. 7:9 could be a God-fearer or possibly a proselyte. Paul's use of ethnē is always in the plural except where he cites Deut. 32:21 in Rom. 10:19 (the not-nation)—"gentile" is rather a marker of collective identity (cf. Lopez 2008: 22).

In 7:7, Paul switches from direct address in 7:1-6 in his own voice to the voice of an imagined interlocutor and speech-in-character. This section opens with the characteristic formula τί οὖν ἐροῦμεν (4:1, 6:1) "what then shall we say" in reaction to the previous arguments. As noted, in this pattern Paul often repudiates a false inference with an emotionally charged μὴ γένοιτο, "far from it!" or, more colloquially, "God forbid!" (RV). From Paul's references to the function, purpose, and effect of the Law, someone wrongly concludes by equating νόμος with ἁμαρτία that it is the Law itself that is the problem, "the Law is the source of sin, is it not?" (7:7). For Paul, this is a blasphemous slander, hence an emphatic response such as "far from it," but he gives some acknowledgment that the Law does serve a function in relation to sin. "Yet, if it had not been for the Law, I would not have known sin." The fact that Paul switches here in 7:7 from the first-person plural "we" of 7:5-6 to the first-person singular signals, in keeping with the accompanying formula "what then shall we say?" τί οὖν ἐροῦμεν, that he proceeds now in diatribal mode, to another significant topic and that the speaker, the "I," here is not Paul himself but a gentile interlocutor. Paul cannot include a footnote as easily as we can in our contemporary context, but orators must guide their audience, and Paul as an expert communicator in his own right, offers explicit grammatical clues to indicate a change of speaker. Yet this has not prevented many debates about the identity of the "I" at this point. In my view, in the history of Western Christianity since Augustine there has been too much preoccupation with the self and its struggles, that is, anthropological issues not typical of Jewish life or of Paul's robust conscience (Stendahl 1976: 78–96). Kümmel (1929) was one of the first to show that the discussion in Romans 7 is more about the Law itself than the identity of the "ἐγώ." Hultgren gives a good overview of the various options proposed in recent interpretation (2011: 681–91).

Who is this interlocutor? The "I" here was alive once apart from the Law, so that must mean that this *persona* was not a born-Jew (and thus cannot be Paul himself speaking). In addition, we learn that "the commandment came," marking a (point of) beginning of life with the Law, so that the gentile (*persona*) who now speaks must speak in the *persona* of a God-fearer or proselyte since it is only to these that the "the commandment came" at some period in adult life. Here Paul's view of non-Jewish observance of the Law emerges in similarity with our earlier discussion of Romans 2. The problem is for Paul that though the Law promises life, gentile practitioners are unable to achieve this without the Spirit, "The commandment that promised life, proved to be death to me" (7:10). The explanation given for this is that "sin took an opportunity, and through the commandment, deceived me and through it killed me" (7:11). This claim is designed to accuse sin as the agent, but to vindicate the Law in the process. Paul is now able to conclude "So the Law is holy, and the commandment is holy, just and good" (7:12). This is a powerful and critical claim that challenges all those who wish to view Paul in opposition to the Jewish Law. We have noted earlier that this is the first time in all of his letters that Paul writes of the holiness of the Law, so its significance here cannot be exaggerated. It arises from gentile misunderstandings of Israel's Torah, but is to be welcomed here in clarifying that it is not the Law that is the problem, but the ethnic failure of non-Jews to recognize that the Law is for the Jews and cannot be understood or effectively fulfilled by ethnē without the Spirit. This points to a central focus in Romans on how the ethnē there addressed are going to get the Spirit in order to fulfil the Law.

Paul's explanation of the function of the Law in relation to sin, is that the *persona* here, the "I," would have been ignorant of what it is to covet if, through the Law he had not been made conscious that this is sin. Sin used the good Law as an opportunity to arouse all "kinds of covetousness" in this *persona*. The Law is not to blame for the outcome, since it is holy, just, and good. Paul has absolved the Law and incriminated sin. This opens the door to another of the leading diatribal questions that form the underlying structure of Romans, "the good then, brought death to me, did it not?" (7:13), followed by Paul's stylized negative response, "far from it!" Paul's argument puts the blame squarely back on sin, "It was sin, working death in me through what is good, in order that sin might be shown to be sin, and through the commandment might become sinful beyond measure" (7:13). Paul does not want the ethnē in Rome to view the Law as a means to right relations with God through self-mastery, that is by doing ἔργα νόμου, works of Law, but he is extremely careful not to indict the Law itself in the process (as they may have done). The nearest he gets to implicating the Law is when he speaks of "you that have the written code" (2:27, cf. 7:6). The phrase "the written code" (NRSV) has been used as a critique of Judaism's misconception of the gospel concerning the Christ (cf. Käsemann 1971: 138–66). It is too simple to allow "spirit" to be identified with those in the new era, that is, Christ-followers and "letter" with those in the old (Campbell 2016: 120–150). Essentially, the phrase "the old written code" signifies the Law minus the Spirit's illuminating power—the absence of the Spirit is the key. This defines what the Law constitutes for non-Jews seeking to observe it without the Spirit. Thus, having answered that question whether the Law is possibly the source of sin (7:7), he is faced with a second question, "the good, then, brought death to me, did it not?" These two related questions, typical of Paul's diatribal style, in which these often occur in pairs, as for example, 6:1, 15; 11:1, 11 (Stowers 1981: 134) point to the Romans' probable familiarity with teaching that the Law brings death to non-Jews through the power of sin. There is some confusion about how a good, spiritual Law can be an accomplice in the outcome of death, and this may reflect the uncertainty among some non-Jews "who know the Law" concerning the actual value of the Law.

Although sin used the Law to lead the gentile *persona* to be more aware of covetousness and so resulted in judgment, the Law itself is not to be accused in that it was functioning properly in registering sin (without the Law covetousness would not be recognized as sin). Yet, even though the Law has been vigorously defended, its function in arousing sinful passions is noted by Paul as one of the reasons why non-Jews with the Law and without the Spirit are unable to achieve a right relationship with God. In this context, Paul teaches that the Law actually brings judgment to non-Jews who try to keep it. The Law was not intended for those from the nations, and to follow it as a non-Jew is ineffective in that the problem of sin is not dealt with, since as non-Jews they are by nature sinners. To explain why this is so, Paul gives a complicated argument that has functioned as a somewhat convoluted Christian anthropology. Keck provides a neat summary of the issues (although from a more universalistic perspective).

In contending that the law is neither the problem nor the solution for the problem, Paul exposes two kinds of naivete—the one assumes that intuitive ("natural") goodness would flourish were it not for the Law's (culturally conditioned) prescriptions and prohibitions; the other is confident that by "doing the right thing" persistently, human wickedness can be overcome eventually. From Paul's angle, the former is naïve about human capacity, the latter naïve about the already-mentioned character of human existence that one assimilates in society. Neither one reckons seriously with the reality of that heinous power that Paul calls "sin" because each regard it as a wrong that one *does* rather than a reality that wrongs the doer and the deed alike. (2005: 184–5)

It appears that Paul regards the Law as ineffective for non-Jews because of the "handing over" to the influence of sin due to misdirected λάτρεια (Rom. 1:24-28). Thus non-Jews even with the Law are unable to overcome the power of sin, and instead of becoming enemies of sin, they are enslaved in its service, by what was meant to guide to righteousness (as we note in the case of the tenth commandment in which the actual goal of the commandment to prohibit desire was perverted by sin so as to bring about every kind of desire, cf. 7:7-8).This is not meant by Paul as a critique of Jewish keeping of the Law, but is specifically directed against non-Jews seeking to achieve self-control by means of the Law. It is an argument only against non-Jews mistakenly seeking in the Law a way to acceptance with God. (Contra Wolter who argues that the I is a Jewish or an Adamic I, 2015: 361).

What distinguishes Jews from the ethnē is that the Jews have been called by God and given a covenantal relationship as Israel (cf. Isa. 41:8), "But you Israel, my servant, Jacob whom I have chosen, the seed of Abraham my friend." This distinguishes them from the ethnē "We ourselves who are Jews by birth and not gentile sinners" (Gal. 2:15). The promise (Rom. 4:13) is transmitted to all the heirs of Abraham across the generations. But it did not extend to the nations, as they are *outside the covenant with Israel*. Those within the covenant keep the Law not to earn God's acceptance—they are already accepted since the covenant is to "you and to your children" as a gift of God's grace. These respond by giving honor and thanks to the God who called Abraham and gave him promises for the future. But the nations outside the covenant, though not outside the purpose of God, are regarded as sinners, not simply because of their licentious (or otherwise) pattern of life, but because they perversely worship beings that are not God (cf. Rom 1:18-25). It is impossible for these, in Paul's Jewish perspective, to become Jews by adherence to the Law. The pollution of idolatry cannot be so easily removed. The "handing over" must be reversed through adoption. Only through Christ and his call (cf. παρακαλέω 12:1 and 9:24) can the ethnē fulfill the Law by the Spirit.

This may seem strange since the Law promises life to those who live by it. But the Law is a result of God's call of Israel, not the cause of it. What it signifies is God's favor toward Israel, a favor already offered and received. For the nations not thus called, who do not enjoy this bestowed favor of God, it is impossible to work their way into God's free grace. To do so even through commitment to the Law does not work for ethnē. This is because God's grace cannot be earned—acceptance with God cannot be achieved by any good works even following the guidance of the Law. If favor with God can be merited, then God is not the God of grace but only the one who is obligated to accept all those who achieve a certain standard. He is then not the one who "decides" on those who will comprise his people. But God freely decides that his favor will rest on Israel and on those who are included in the promise for Abraham to be father of many nations. The inheritance that the people of Israel enjoy is patrilineal, passed from father to son—in this respect it cannot be earned (even if it can be rejected). As Runesson notes, "Salvation is ultimately dependent on ancestry (the promises to the Patriarchs) and can therefore only be inherited, κληρονομέω, never earned" (2016: 441). But the nations without the promise are born outside the covenant and need a different form of relation to the Creator God. Since they cannot earn God's favor, without contradicting the nature of the gracious calling that would enable entrance into God's people, they remain sinners. Hence, the importance of adoption through Christ. It was considered possible by some for non-Jews to become proselytes through immersion and male circumcision, but some of Paul's contemporaries rejected this as not a viable option for adults, since the Law of circumcision requires circumcision on the eighth day in order to be valid. We have earlier noted that Philo regards proselyte circumcision as viable but, in his view, full membership of the synagogue is only valid for the third generation, that is, not for the son of a proselyte but only for the son of someone born a Jew, a Jew by nature, that is, circumcised on the eighth day. I am doubtful that Paul regards circumcised adults as full members of the Jewish people; for him they still constitute "gentiles" (even though they may "call themselves a Jew") because they try to earn God's grace by doing the Law. Also from Paul's Christological perspective, whatever view he held about becoming a proselyte prior to Christ's coming, once Christ has come, for non-Jews to seek circumcision constitutes in essence a refusal of the ethnē to hear God's call to follow Christ without the requirement of circumcision or becoming Jewish (Fredriksen 2017: 157). They not only do not need to get circumcised, in fact they must not.

This way of thinking must lie behind Paul's arguments in Rom. 7:7-25. In summary, the *persona* here is not a Jewish person seeking to keep the Law, nor a Christ-follower but one who seeks to do the Law as a non-Jew with a view to self-mastery and setting up a right relationship with God. This attempt, made without the Spirit, is doomed to failure.

Subsection B

Romans 7:13-25: The Conflicted Self—The Good, then, Brought Death to Me, Did It Not?

13The good, then, brought death to me, did it not? Far from it! It was sin, working death in me through what is good, in order that sin might be shown to be sin, and through the commandment might become sinful beyond measure. 14For we know that the law is spiritual; but I am of the flesh, sold into slavery under sin. 15I do not know what I bring about. For what I do not want this I practice, but what I hate I do. 16Now if I do what I do not want, I agree with the law that it is good. 17But in fact it is no longer I that do it, but the sin that resides in me. ¹⁸For I know that the good does not reside in me, that is, in my flesh. I can will what is right, but I cannot do it. ¹⁹For I do not do the good I want, but the bad I do not want is what I practice. ²⁰Now if I do what I do not want to do, I am no longer the one doing it, but sin that resides in me. ²¹So I discover that while my will is directed to the law in order to do what is good the evil lies close at hand. ²²For I delight in the law of God in my inmost self, ²³but I see in my members another law at war with the law of my mind, captivating me by the law of sin that resides in my members. ²⁴How wretched a person am I! Who will rescue me from this body of death? ²⁵Thanks be to God through Jesus Christ our Lord! So then, left to myself, I am a slave to God's law in my mind, but in my flesh I am a slave to sin's law.

In this passage, Paul seeks to explain why the ethnē with the Law but apart from Christ (and therefore the Spirit) cannot succeed in doing the Law that they have chosen to follow. This is not the proper route for ethnē in Christ. Paul's explanation concerns the nature of the person, the "I," (ἐγώ) who seeks to obey the Law. The entire person including the body itself is central to Paul's conceptualization here. For the first time in his letters, Paul argues persuasively that the Law itself is spiritual (πνευματικός), and thus again must have this unique specific reference to the exigency at Rome. The spirituality of the Law contrasts vividly with the ἐγώ, the self, seeking to keep it, who is fleshly (σάρκινος), who thus becomes, as we will see, an unwilling accomplice in his own resultant fatal condition. In 7:5, Paul spoke of living "in the flesh" as in a domain of power, a controlling field of force, and here to be "fleshly," σάρκινος means to be controlled by one's fleshly existence when it inappropriately exercises power.

Paul understands the human body as a vehicle by which the service of God or the slavery of sin is promoted. The body itself is flesh but not necessarily sinful because of its fleshly character. When used in God's service it can be πνευματικός, spiritual, but when it is ruled by sin, it becomes σάρκινος, controlled by sinful desires. As Keck notes, if Paul had meant to depict living in a body as the problem, he would have used the term σῶμα rather than σάρξ.

Paul's solution is not the total annihilation of the body but its transformation through its sacrifice to God (as we will discover more fully when we come to Romans 12, where the life given to God is returned to those in Christ to be lived in a transforming community of brothers).

Σάρκινος refers to the person being ruled not by physicality but governed by fleshly desires, rather than those relating to the Spirit. In this context, fleshliness manifests itself in desire, when one's physicality becomes "fleshliness" and inordinately defines the self and controls it through desire. As Keck notes, "It is not bodily existence as such, but the phenomenal, functioning as inordinate power that determines the self" (2005: 186). The resulting condition is bondage, sold under sin (v. 14). The solution Paul will announce in Romans 12, is to "present your bodies as a living sacrifice to God."

Paul's argument here focusses on weakness, the will is unable to actualize itself in the deed proposed and thus reveals the self's slavery, focusing on achievement, whether positive or negative (cf. κατεργάζομαι vv. 15, 17, 18, 20). Human beings' inability to achieve intended goals was a common complaint, not unique to Paul's interlocutor, but for Paul the problem is more precise. It lies neither in ignorance of the good nor even the lack of will to do it, but the inability to do the willed good that is known through the Law (Keck 2005: 188-9). This is identified as what is holy, just, and good (7:12). But this "good" is not what dwells in this person's flesh—"the good does not reside in me"—it is "sin (that) resides (οἰκέω) in me" (7:18-19). The *persona* delights in the Law of God in the inward person (ἔσω ἄνθρωπον), but finds himself in conflict with a different power—the law of sin in my outward self, that is, the body as expressing the action of the person. The "law of my mind" is another form of the inner self, which agrees with God's Law, though it does not succeed in achieving it (7:22-23). The "good" the *persona* wishes to do is not in response to God's call, and thus constitutes an attempt at earning God's grace, which is an impossibility.

Romans 7:7-25 Paul's Explanation of the Law's Powerlessness for Ethnē without Christ

Since Paul in this section focuses on the Law throughout it is important for the sake of coherence to look at it as a whole to understand his argument. The imagery of being sold as a slave links back to Romans 1, and more closely to 6:20, "When you were slaves of sin, you were free in regard to righteousness." Being a slave of sin belongs to the period prior to that when the Christ-follower first turned to Christ. Therefore, this is a clear indication that the *persona* who speaks here in ch. 7 is neither Paul himself nor a Christ-follower, since this *persona remains* a slave of sin from which one would otherwise have already been transferred to Christ. The "I" here is still "under sin," and must refer to a non-Jew not yet transferred from being "under the Law" to being "under grace" according to 6:14-15. This *persona* cannot be the same one who in 6:22 had been "freed from sin and enslaved to God."

Rodriguez has clearly enumerated the contradictions in which Paul would be involved were he (Paul) speaking biographically out of his own experience (2014: 133-8). This view is strengthened by the fact of the Spirit's absence after 7:6. If life in Christ in any form were under discussion in 7:7-25, mention of the Spirit could not have been omitted (Das 2007: 207). The absence of the Spirit here and the contrasting abundant references in ch. 8 (nineteen times in total) are clear evidence that Paul through his speech-in-character is reflecting a very specific stance, not his own, rather than presenting a normal pattern of existence in Christ (with the Spirit) as he does in Romans 8 and elsewhere.

Let us be quite clear that as interpreters, we are not simply inventing clever devices for avoiding what Paul himself says. Rather it is Paul in the text who raises these issues by introducing a character who, unlike Paul, was born without the Law—"I was once alive apart from the Law" (7:9) but who later took up the yoke of the Law, "but when the commandment came" (7:9); who then found it could not free him from his enslavement to sin, "I died" (7:10). Since this *persona* is still speaking, he is not physically dead, but only metaphorically. This indicates that the same interlocutor/conversation partner already encountered in chs. 2-3 is still salient. As was the case there, although knowing the Law, the interlocutor was accused of being a transgressor of the Law who would be judged by those non-Jews who had the Law written on their hearts. Paul continues to speak in the *persona* already adopted, of someone such as a

God-fearer or proselyte who once did not observe the commandments of the Law but who now does them or tries to do them. Even the fact that Paul uses the first-person singular, ἐμοί means not that he himself is speaking but rather that he maintains the *persona* adopted from 7:7 (and earlier, cf. Tobin 2004: 241).

From 7:7 onward, Paul begins the speech-in-character clearly signaled, as is normal in the introduction of a new character or of a new voice, by the move to the first person singular, and also from 7:13 on *the speaker, the "I," describes his situation*, not Paul's. This emerges from the events described in 7:9-10, after the *persona* has begun to observe the Mosaic Law. But it is most likely that the "character" speaking here describes the situation that Paul envisages as epitomized in some of the Roman ethnē. This is not then an entirely new "situation" just introduced here in the speech-in-character of Romans 7, but links back to Romans 2, especially from 2:17-29, where the inner man is linked with the circumcision of the heart as connected positively with the Law. Here, as there, Law is portrayed "in utterly positive terms"—the problem lies in the well-intentioned "gentile's" use of the Torah, God's covenant with his people Israel, as a means for self-mastery (Rodriguez 2014: 138). One significant quality of the Law is its educational effect in that it provides knowledge of what is right and wrong in light of God's calling so that all are thus accountable (3:20), and so that the exceeding extent of sin is revealed in its true nature (7:13).

What is telling is that the issue of the Law has not gone away; it has been present in every chapter and is still very much part of the discussion, for example, in 4:15, 5:20, even after the declaration that righteousness apart from the Law has been disclosed (3:21). The varied use of νόμος and its frequent occurrence (sixteen times in ch. 7) only tends to emphasize that the Law in various settings and manifestations is still a central theme. This will be further mentioned in Romans 13 in relation to the language of fulfillment. As such it deserves, as we noted earlier in this chapter (on "Paul's Dialogical Pattern"), to be viewed as one of the major themes of the letter. As it is presented here, the discussion reveals a good awareness of how the function of the Law was reinterpreted in the categories of Greco-Roman ethics. This indicates that Paul knows or presupposes that the Roman Christ-followers lived in and were familiar with a milieu in which these issues were popular. Both Greek and Jewish writers were concerned with the topos of self-mastery (Rodriguez 2014: 120–1). Thus, empowerment to fulfill the Law though differing from self-mastery terminology was not necessarily in opposition. Jewish writers were accustomed to view slavery to the passions as typical of "gentiles." The "slave to the passions" in ancient literature was typically the ethnic "other" or barbarian (Stowers 1994: 58–65). In Jewish terminology, the Law is involved in a struggle with sin and death, but in popular Greek and Roman culture, another struggle, that of knowing but being weak and unable to perform what is right was well known, and elements of both traditions probably explain the creativity present in Paul's speech-in-character (Matera 2010: 66).

Stowers maintains that "all Paul's rhetoric … makes sense if we suppose that Paul's literary audience represents something like those who have traditionally been called God-fearers in modern scholarship. From beginning to end, Romans presupposes an audience that consists of gentiles who had or still have a lively interest in Judaism" (1994: 277). The questions raised about the Law are not Paul's personal questions either before or after his call to Christ. Paul continued to observe the Law and to regard it as God's gift to Israel (9:4). The issues about the Law represent issues concerning its application or relevance to non-Jews arising from the mission to the nations rather than from Paul himself—they are not questions to which he personally is seeking an answer.

We noted that already in 7:1, Paul makes it clear that he knows that the Roman gentile Christ-followers have been taught about the Law and its significance. Several times he refers explicitly to what these non-Jews know in terms of the Law and its teaching. These are gentile Christ-followers who have experience and contact with Jewish teaching concerning the Law. This may also be supported by the terms κατηχούμενος, taught from the law (2:18) and τύπον διδαχῆς, pattern of teaching (6:17). They know "the will," that is, the will of God, how to discern what is best and are capable of making informed judgments. The rhetorical "I" of Romans 7:7-25 represents the gentile proselyte or God-fearer "who agrees with Jews that Torah deserves to be highly regarded, but has found it powerless to deliver what he truly seeks: freedom from death and sin" (Rodriguez 2014: 137). Not only do these addressees have acquaintance with the teaching of the Law, but it seems to have elicited differing responses from some of them, probably not deriving from the Law itself, but rather from its reception in a context where the message about Christ and other innovative messages were struggling to be heard.

The speech-in-character continues to the end of ch. 7 in that there it is no neutral observer who will speak from outside, but only the "I" as the one who is experiencing the dilemma, a "wretched man" who cries for deliverance from the body of this death (7:24), that is, the body as the slave of sin preventing the realization of the good as defined in the Law. Because of the power of sin within them and in the world around them, ethnē in their fleshly existence cannot achieve the good that they see attractive in the Law but only "works of law." This will lead into Romans 8 in which Paul will argue that for a non-Jew the Law can only be fulfilled through the Spirit, as a gift from God. In this chapter, Paul thus describes the plight of non-Jews in relation to the Law prior to their experience of Christ. Likewise, he provides his solution for non-Jews through the extension of God's gracious call also to the nations via Christ. As we will see, Paul in ch. 8 demonstrates the decisive role of the Spirit in this process.

Romans 8

Romans 8:1-11: The Law of the Spirit of Life in Christ Jesus

¹For there is now no condemnation for those in Christ Jesus. ²For the law of the Spirit of life in Christ Jesus has set you free from the law of sin and of death. ³For the law being powerless in that it was weak on account of the flesh: God having sent his own Son in the likeness of sinful flesh, and to deal with sin, condemned sin in the flesh, ⁴in order that the righteous requirement of the law might be fulfilled among us, who do not walk according to flesh but according to Spirit. ⁵For those who exist according to flesh set their minds on the things of the flesh, but those who exist according to Spirit set their minds on the things of the Spirit ⁶For the mind of the flesh is death, but the mind of the Spirit is life and peace. ⁷Because the mind of the flesh is hostile to God; for it does not submit to the law of God—indeed it cannot, ⁸and those who exist in the flesh cannot please God. ⁹But you, you do not exist in flesh but in Spirit, since the Spirit of God resides among you. But if someone does not have Christ's Spirit that one is not his. ¹⁰But if Christ is among you, though the body is dead because of sin, the Spirit is life because of righteousness. ¹¹But if the Spirit of the one who raised Jesus from the dead resides among you, he who raised Christ from the dead will also give life to your mortal bodies through his Spirit that resides among you.

Romans 8:1-2 The Transition from Romans 7:7-25

With ch. 8, a transition is signaled by the move from first-person singular of the speech-in-character of ch. 7 and its *persona* in bondage. The γάρ "for" in 8:1-2 indicates procedural strengthening, raising expectations that the information that follows will be linked to what has just preceded (Casson 2019: 72–4). Thus, we read this as inferring that Paul's teaching about the Spirit is here related to the desperate deficiency described in 7:7-25. The variant readings of 8:2 (με) point to this. Now, apart from this potential brief backward reference (in the variant) to the interlocutor, Paul resorts to his authorial voice. If he had been speaking in his own voice (i.e., as himself), in 7:7-25 (i.e., as Paul the apostle), then the pathetic, conflicted person would have been a defeated apostle overcome by sin, but this reading would put Paul in contradiction with what he says in the space of two chapters and would suggest that he was unclear about the gospel.

Paul the apostle to the nations glorifies his ministry (11:13). We remember that Paul had already said in 6:11-13, "So you also must reckon yourselves on the one hand dead to sin but on the other alive to God in Christ Jesus. 12 Therefore, do not let sin rule in your mortal bodies, to make you yield to its desires. 13 No longer present any part(s) [of your body] to sin as instruments of wrong-doing, instead present yourselves to God as those who have been brought from death to life, and present your bodies to God as instruments for doing right" (cf. 1:26-27). These verses alone make it clear that the Paul speaking in 6:11-13, and similarly the triumphant person of 8:1-2, cannot be the same person who speaks in 7:7-25 as a person still defeated by sin.

Paul's common mode of address is to speak to his addressees as a group, that is, "you" plural. So it is somewhat surprising to find that an impressive list of manuscripts[1] of Romans 8 offer ἠλευθέρωσέν σε—"you" singular—as their reading of 8:2, that is, "he freed you" instead of the anticipated normal ἠλευθέρωσέν ὑμᾶς "he freed you" plural. A smaller number of manuscripts read "he freed me" ἠλευθέρωσέν με, which, Rodriguez points out, fits better with a *mis*reading of Romans 7 in assuming the same person is still speaking as in 7:24-25. This reading, as demonstrated above, would involve Paul in severe self-contradiction. Alternatively, the second-person pronoun σε (singular you) fits better with a reading that recognizes Paul's speech-in-character (as I have done) and his *persona* as depicting a gentile God-fearer or proselyte to the Jewish way of life.

It is therefore better to read "you" rather than "me" in 8:2, since here Paul returns briefly for a (final) address directly to his gentile interlocutor, σε (you singular, cf. Rodriguez 2016: 157). Paul uses the singular pronoun σε "you" to indicate he is telling his gentile audience in diatribal style that the interlocutor (you singular) of ch. 7 has been shown the way out of his dilemma through Christ and the Spirit. Paul does not and cannot include himself in the defeated *persona* of the previous chapter (as he would be doing if he used με to refer to himself). Paul was never a "gentile" who tried to achieve righteousness by following the Law without the Spirit. So, the singular "you" indicates the final address to the character imagined in 7:7-25. With the transition from ch. 7, Paul also now changes his vocabulary to the language of Spirit—from the predominance of νόμος, (fifteen times in 7.7-25, and five times in 8.1-7, but there is no further reference to νόμος in this chapter after 8:7. In ch. 8, πνεῦμα becomes dominant, twenty-seven times). With this change comes also a change in tone from the depressed *persona* in bondage to sin in 7:24 to the triumphant tone of one who expresses the experience of liberation (and adoption) in Romans 8. This is because the love of God is poured out in the hearts of Christ-followers through the πνεῦμα given to them (5:5, cf. 12:9-11).

The link with the conclusion to ch. 7 also appears immediately in the inclusion of the term κατάκριμα, condemnation, in 8:1. The inclusion also of νῦν "now" links

---

[1] Sinaiticus (ℵ) and Vaticanus (B) read "he freed you" (sing.). This is the best supported reading, but a number of manuscripts (A D and a large number of miniscules and Fathers read "he freed me"). Bruce Metzger thinks that the first-person pronoun με harmonizes better with his reading of Romans 7, which, in agreement with Rodriguez, we reject as a misreading since it was not Paul himself but his imagined interlocutor who was speaking as a defeated sinner (Rodriguez 2016: 157, n25).

back to 3:21 and 5:9, indicating that Paul speaks here from the new perspective of the revelation of righteousness in Christ. Paul does not offer an anthropological critique of the Law's inadequacy for "gentiles," it is rather a view from a different perspective. It is not the view of the gentile *persona* alone with the Law, but now a perspective of ethnē in Christ, empowered by the experience of the Spirit. "The wretched man" of 7:24 has found deliverance through the Spirit of Christ. Rather than proclaiming the weakness (and hence possibly the redundancy) of the Law, the Law through the presence of the Spirit becomes reinterpreted christologically, so that here the theme is no longer "the 'gentile' on his own with the Law," but it is now "ethnē with the Law and with the Spirit" (8:2). This confirms Paul's argument that it was not the Torah itself that was overpowered by sin, or Paul himself, but the gentile *persona* portrayed in 7:7-25. This brings Paul to stress the eschatological moment of the true response now made possible by Christ's arrival. But in Romans, when it is read sequentially, as we think it should, the full articulation of the life in the Spirit announced and explicated in ch. 8, is in fact only fully developed after 12:1. This is evidenced and articulated in the transformation empowered by life in the context of a new brotherhood after adoption into a new family (McMurray 2021: 4).

Romans 8:3-11 "God Has Done What the Law Could Not Do"—Ethnē in Christ with the Spirit

The Law no longer operates on its own as weakened because of the flesh,[2] but the Spirit comes to reside amongst the ethnē (8:9a), in each and all of them, pointing to a collective rather than to an individual "you" (Rodriguez 2014: 157). Thus Paul, now in his own voice, can focus on a positive link between the Law and the Spirit, and can associate both of these with life in Christ Jesus (8:2). The inability of the Law has been overcome through the advent of the Spirit, so that what the Law, weakened by human existence under sin (flesh), could not do, God has done by sending his own son in the likeness of sinful flesh. McMurray views the Spirit as bringing the ethnē into coherence with the Law (2021: 84). Thus, through Christ, the ethnē both come to fulfill the Law and to escape the negative consequences of the Law for ethnē.

That this is valid is further indicated by striking combinations such as "the Law of the Spirit" (the Law with the Spirit of Romans 8) contrasting directly (as between two dominions or differing legal systems) with "the Law of sin" (the Law without the Spirit of 7:25). Because the Law did not die, but ethnē die to the Law through Christ to escape its judgment, then we have the situation where devout Jews like Paul continue to live according to Torah, which does not apply to ethnē in Christ in the same way as it applies to Jews. Moreover, the "pattern of life" of the ethnē who are not under Torah, but slaves of God and led by the Spirit, is not contradictory to the Law, but consistent with it (cf. 13:8-10). Otherwise, Paul could not claim that what the Law requires may

---

[2] As Jewett notes, it would be a unique occurrence if Paul attributed weakness to the Torah itself (2007: 493). However, it is not a theoretical view of the Law that Paul discusses but the Law in a world where Sin dominates universally, so there is no place where the weakness due to Sin's influence is not experienced, that is, no place where a theoretical view of the Law might be possible.

be fulfilled by the Spirit in the lives of ethnē in Christ (8:4). Some such interpretation of the Law for Christ-following ethnē is required to explain Paul's novel constructions such as "the law of the Spirit of life in Christ Jesus has set you free from the Law of sin and death" (8:2). We note that the Law is the subject and therefore the agent here and is bound up with other key Pauline concepts such as Spirit, life, and Christ. The Law in the empirical reality of everyday ethical life is never the Law by itself in isolation, but the Law either with the Spirit or as used by sin with corresponding outcomes in death or in life. In Paul's understanding, as he demonstrated in Romans 7, non-Jews seeking to observe the Law without Christ encounter the Law only as an instrument of bondage to sin and death. This is why he asserts οἱ δὲ ἐν σαρκὶ ὄντες θεῷ ἀρέσαι οὐ δύνανται—"but those who are in the flesh cannot please God" (8:8). Paul does not mean here that some ethnē err in allowing the flesh to determine their behavior while others do not. Ἐν σαρκί, ("in the flesh") here must refer to all non-Jews without Christ in toto. In contrast, we note that Paul in Romans 12 will use the terms εὐάρεστον and ἀρέσκω when referring to the sacrifice of the body to God. As Paul makes clear in 8:9, "But you—ethnē in Christ—are not in the flesh ἐν σαρκί, since the Spirit of God resides among you." Any non-Jew "who does not have the Spirit of Christ does not belong to him." Without the Spirit, the δικαίωμα of the Law cannot be fulfilled in them, and their enmity to God is not cancelled. Once freed from the power of sin through Christ, the requirements of the Law are fulfilled in them, not by the ethnē's own attempts to make themselves right with God, but only through Christ and the gift of the Spirit. Only thus, and only then, can the δικαίωμα of the Law be fulfilled in them, thus constituting this actualization or fulfilment as δικαιοσύνη.

Hence, Paul concludes, it is now possible that what the Law pointed to may be fulfilled in the ethnē, who walk not under the control of the flesh, but under the guidance of the Spirit (8:4). Rom. 6:1–8:13 is more than an exposition of "life in Christ." It qualifies "freedom from the Law" as *obligation* to the righteousness required by the Law, which is possible only in the sphere of the Spirit (8:1-13, Elliott 2007: 271). We note that the verb is in the passive, πληρωθῇ "might be fulfilled"—it is God's Spirit who is the agent who actualizes the δικαίωμα "in us," so it is also activity done "by us." Rodriguez translates δικαίωμα, as Torah's acquittal of sinners—the outcome of the verdict of the Torah being realized (2014: 153). It is interesting that Paul uses the verb πληρόω, fulfilled, here, which again indicates not the result of human effort or achievement, but rather the outcome of the indwelling work of the Spirit (Campbell 2019). As Tobin states, "by fulfil, he (Paul) must mean something other than observe" (2004: 69). What the Law really intended (for ethnē) is now made possible in the life of the ethnē in Christ. It is possible to distinguish here between different meanings of the δικαίωμα τοῦ νόμου as the verdict that the Law announces (as, e.g., Wright 2002: 577, and Kirk 2007: 790). Kirk regards the reference here as meaning the legal requirement of death met in the death of Christ. I take the emphasis here to be more on the positive side of what the Law required, that is, the possibility of the Law being fulfilled in the ethnē in Christ (Campbell 2019). This means that what the Law intended was that ethnē also turned to God, which is now possible through (brotherhood with) Christ, this intention thus being fulfilled.

To summarize our understanding of the just requirement of the Law, we need to keep the content of 7:7-25 before us. To non-Jews who had not accepted the call of

Christ but were instead seeking to become right with God by doing what the Law requires, Paul insisted that this would only lead to judgment from the Law rather than blessing. This is because these ethnē were seeking to rectify their sinful status by their own actions, as was the pattern of relationship to the divine realm in their Roman context. In Paul's view, non-Jews are still in a status of enmity with God. The observing of the Law cannot overcome their status as sinners by nature. Only by the intervention of God through Christ can they be liberated from sin, and thus their status in relation to God be changed by the Spirit to a status of holiness (cf. 7:25), resulting from their adoption into the divine family.[3] They will then be empowered by the Spirit to have fulfilled in them the just requirement of the Law as an expression of God's will, that is, Israel's Torah (Rodriguez, 2016: 152, n15), even while still ethnē but, decisively, as ethnē in Christ. Thus, there is an anticipated response to the call to ethnē through Christ. Though they must not seek to initiate themselves into divine favor by observing the Law as ethnē, once they enjoy the blessing of the Spirit in their lives, an appropriate active response to God's call is required, and they must actively respond to the leading of the Spirit. In this they respond to God's call in Christ to the ethnē and, through this, offer their bodies in thanks to God as slaves to righteousness rather than sin, 6:19b (cf. 12:1-2). Only when the ethnē offer their bodies as a living sacrifice will transformation through the empowerment of the Spirit be realized.

Traditionally Paul is perceived here as describing differing modes of behavior, that is, "living under the control of the flesh" or "living under the guidance of the Spirit" (8:5-7). These may represent alternative consecutive modes of gentile behavior, living as formerly, as a "gentile" without Christ or living as now, with Christ and with the Spirit's guidance. The best way to formulate this pattern of life is not to translate misleadingly as "sinful *nature*" (NIV) or "live on the *level* of the old nature" (REB) because Paul is not contrasting "natures" or "levels" but "sovereignties that govern one's life" (Keck 2005: 202). It is through Christ and the Spirit that the δικαίωμα of the Law is fulfilled or realized in the life of the ethnē and not by their own attempts to make themselves right with God.

But Paul states here that this does not mean that there is no obligation of any kind on ethnē in Christ, they will still owe the obligation to love (13:8). They are not merely passive, but their obligation is stated in terms of love. They have heard God's call and have positively responded. Just as they have been called and have responded affirmatively to that call (so) now that they are in Christ and his Spirit *resides* (οἰκεῖ) among them, as a stable way of life (Jervis 2012: 143), so too they must positively respond to the Spirit's guidance in their everyday ethical choices. They can continue to live as formerly—"gentiles in the flesh," and governed by its desires, or they can live by the pattern of the Spirit—that is, of transformed ethnē in Christ—the choice is theirs. They who would serve God are called to "set their minds φρονεῖν (v. 5) on the things of the Spirit," and not on "the things of the flesh" (8:5-6). The related noun φρόνημα

---

[3] Israel as a nation was that people God set apart for himself. Israel was "separated" ἅγιος, a "holy" nation (e.g., Exod. 19:6). Cf. Fredriksen (2017: 153–4). For Paul, the "gentile nations were inherently *koinos* common, not distinguished from one another in the way that Israel, through descent and through God's *torah* 'teaching,' was set apart from all of them."

(mindset) "indicates more than cogitation; it includes also an avowed stance, a life-shaping attitude … it is the mentality that determines what one lives by; it shapes one's existence" (Keck 2005: 202). The mindset ruled by the Spirit means life and peace, but the mindset ruled by the flesh is hostile to God because it does not submit to his rule, in that it continues the misguided λατρεία of non-gods. The reference here not only to life, but to peace, keeps in view the reconciliation to God through Christ, emphasized in the truce (ἀνοχή) of 3:21-26, elaborated in ch. 5, repeated in ch. 8:6, 12:18, and which will reappear particularly in 14:17 in association with the kingdom of God. The reconciliation achieved through Christ not only brings peace with God but, through the Spirit, may become a creative agent of peace with all, particularly among those within the families of God.

Following on from this explanation of differing modes of being, Paul turns again directly to the Roman ethnē themselves reminding them in second-person plural, "But you are not in the flesh," that is, no longer indebted to the flesh, indicating the transition to being in Christ, so no longer living in hostile opposition to God, but "you are in the Spirit" since the Spirit of God resides among you (8:9). In ch. 7:17, Paul's chosen *persona* confessed that "nothing good resides in me," and also that "sin resides within me." Here it is the Spirit that "resides in you" (οἰκεῖ ἐν ὑμῖν. 8:9). Paul views the Spirit as the essential link between God's liberating act in Christ and the individual person living in community with other Christ-followers. The Spirit residing in you, ὑμῖν demands a plural "you" in English, referring to all the Christ-followers addressed. This should be understood both communally and individually, and can be translated as "among you," rather than only as "in you," It is when Christ-followers gather together in community as his people that the presence and power of God is fully experienced. Earlier in ch. 8, Paul had introduced the term "life," ζωή in contrast to death θάνατος, which has featured strongly since the beginning of ch. 5 (eighteen references in chs. 5–7). The outcome of living under the rule of the Spirit is life and peace (8:5). Paul's anthropological claims assert that if Christ resides in people, although the body is dead because of sin, the Spirit brings life because of righteousness. He develops this thesis further, "If the Spirit of him who raised Jesus from the dead resides among you, he who raised Christ from the dead will give life to your mortal bodies through his Spirit that dwells among you" (8:11, cf. 12:1). Thus, it is clear that the coming of the Spirit represents the coming of the Spirit of the resurrected Christ.

Romans 8:12-17: A New Identity—Adopted into the "Family of God" as Those from the Nations

[12]So then, brothers, we are obligated ones not to the flesh, to live according to flesh— [13]for if you live according to flesh, you are going to die; but if according to Spirit you put to death the practices of the body, you will live. [14]For all those who are being led by God's Spirit these are sons of God. [15]For you did not receive a spirit of slavery resulting again in fear, but rather you received a spirit of sonship by which we cry out, "Abba! Father!" [16]It is the Spirit itself that bears witness with our spirit that we are God's children, [17]and if children, then also heirs, on the one hand heirs of God,

and on the other, co-heirs with Christ since we are suffering with him so that we will also be glorified with him.

Paul begins with the standard inferential construction ἄρα οὖν "so then" that concludes one section and transitions to what lies ahead. In the previous paragraph, Paul made a strict distinction between flesh and Spirit, but develops this by pointing out that the brothers (ἀδελφοί) are in debt "not to the flesh" but to the Spirit. The term ὀφειλέτης debtor resonates with the Roman Imperial system where debt and obligation went together (cf. 13:8). Paul gave a radical introduction to the theme in 1:14 where he asserted his indebtedness to all people whether Greek or barbarian in a vivid reversal of the social obligations of the Greco-Roman world (Jewett 2007: 493). In 8:12, Paul's addressees are the debtors whose debts are released.

In 8:12, Paul repeats his direct form of address, ἀδελφοί, brothers (and sisters),[4] as previously in 1:13 and 7:2-4. Paul concludes that instead of being controlled by the former pattern of life without the Spirit, the consequence of his argument in chs. 6 and 7 is that Christ-followers should now regard themselves as obligated to live under the guidance of the Spirit (8:12). The Spirit opposes the practices proceeding from the σάρξ, which are leading toward death (8:13). Σάρξ is translated as "flesh," but this translation does not mean that flesh is inherently sinful. Flesh can be used as the instrument of sin. For Paul, what people do with the body is instrumental in terms of creating the outcome of life (McMurray 2021: 142–52). Thus, Paul states that "if you live according to the flesh, you will die but if by the Spirit you put to death the deeds of the body, you will live" (8:12). The possibilities refer to life without Christ and under obligation to Roman deities, or alternatively, life under obligation to the Spirit of God. People are never free from obligation to some ruling power whether from the Creator God through Christ, or from the powers of sin and death. It is difficult to perceive the full import of Paul's stark contrast between the old life under the control of the flesh, that is, life under obligation to the Roman deities (cf. Romans 1) and the new life in Christ, that is, life with the empowerment of the Spirit. But the outcome of living by the Spirit is a new life of confidence rather than of fear because of being adopted as ethnē through Christ into God's "family." The Holy Spirit responds to the human spirit signaling that ethnē as non-Jews have been adopted into "the family of God." There is already a people of God, that is, Israel, yet non-Jews are not adopted into Israel, but into the gentile branch of the "family of God." Since they do not replace Israel, they must share the blessings of Abraham, not as Jews and Jewish Christ-followers, but as gentile representatives of the nations, *an associate people*, through Christ, alongside Israel.

In Paul's perspective, this family is constituted by the Spirit through adoption. This scenario lies behind Paul's analogy of sons by adoption, probably influenced by Roman practice.

---

[4] Although we noted initially that we would use the ancient terminology "brothers," we repeat the inclusive form here just to remind readers that we are not simply ignoring modern social patterns but remain acutely aware of the danger of anachronism in simply repeating ancient patterns without qualification.

Roman legal culture had long availed itself of adoption as fictive kinship—sons not begotten but made—as a way to settle and to stabilize the next generation of "family" both for issues of ancestry/continuation of patrilineal cult. The new son was thereafter responsible to and for his "new" paternal ancestors and to and for the *genius* (inherited *numen*) of his new father and family (*gens*) (Fredriksen 2017: 148, cf. 37).

We note here in particular that the nations have been adopted, not *into the family of Christ, but into the family of God, through and with Christ*. Not only do the nations receive acceptance with God through Christ, but they become joint heirs συνκληρονόμοι with him, a very important indicator of status. In Romans 4, Paul depicted Abraham as heir κληρονόμον to the world. Here Christ is heir of God and those who follow him are described as joint heirs with him. It is Christ through the Spirit who is the basis for entering a new family. Thus, Christ is the firstborn of a family of many brothers (8:29), the latter (brotherhood) being a new image that Paul first introduces here in Romans.[5] "With Christ" these ethnē form a new collective entity with a new (gentile) identity. As we have emphasized already, these ethnē are not depicted simply as a number of individuals who trust in Christ, but as a collective entity they comprise the representatives of the nations within the divine purpose for the world.

It should be noted that Paul does not speak of τέκνα Ἀβραάμ but τέκνα θεοῦ. He has now reached a desired point in his argument for Roman gentile Christ-followers. They too can become sons or children of God since they did not receive a spirit of slavery, to fall back into fear, but have received a "spirit of adoption."[6] This enables them to call God "Abba," father. Paul interprets what seems to have been an echo of Christ-followers' prayers in worship as the Spirit within Christ-followers confirming that they really are children of God (8:17). As noted above, it seems that Paul regards human beings as either led by the Spirit or governed by the flesh, which is their physical existence devoid of God's Spirit, not living in exclusive loyalty to the one God. "But if by the Spirit you put to death the practices of the body, you will live, for all who are led by the Spirit of God are sons of God" (8:13-14, cf. τέκνα-children in 8:16, 17, 21). It is interesting that the only other instance of this verb in Romans is 2:4, "Do you not realize that God's kindness is meant to lead (ἄγει σε) you to repentance?"

Paul uses the adoption image in 8:15, "spirit of sonship," reflecting his indebtedness both to Roman patterns of adoption, and contrasting with the Roman practice of slavery. In being adopted as sons, they did not receive a spirit of slavery, πνεῦμα δουλείας leading them back into a life of fear. The fear noted here not only is likely related to the analogy of slavery but also reflects the experience of the Roman Christ-followers in another way—the fear of not being able to live out the demands of the Law, which it seems some of them had been erroneously advised to do. Only through

---

[5] The significance of the new brotherhood with Christ is very well developed by McMurray (2021: 159–88).
[6] This imagery signals specifically a gentile audience, cf. Johnson Hodge, "the whole analogy, in which 'slaves' become adopted sons of God, makes no sense for Jews, who already enjoy this status (Rom. 9.4)" (2007: 71). Cf. also Fredriksen (2017: 150–1).

release from the demands of the Law can the ethnē find security through the Spirit and a new confidence. The spirit of fear reminiscent of life as a slave resonates with what seems to be echoes of baptismal rites in which the participants confidently, even enthusiastically, cry out "Abba, father" (Käsemann 1980: 229). This confident cry contrasts vividly with the fearful response of the enslaved person. It denotes the confidence given in and with the experience of the Spirit, which Paul regards as confirming the radical change of status into the family of God. Possibly the initiates cried out using the traditional Aramaic word combined with its translation as Father. The verb κράζειν denoted crying out in prayer and suggests corporate worship—it is a technical term of acclamation in which the congregation spontaneously call upon God as their father, both in Aramaic, *Abba,* and Greek terminology ὁ πατήρ. Fitzmyer explains this phenomenon thus; when the original *abba* was taken up in Greek-speaking communities, it was not translated by the vocative πατήρ as it should have been but was retained and ὁ πατήρ was added, thus becoming a liturgical formula in Greek-speaking Christian communities (1993: 500).

A New Social Identity: Gentile Children Who Can Call God Father

In 8:16, Paul changes to the image of τέκνα, children, but in 8:19, reverts again to υἱοί, sons.[7] In Galatians, Paul had argued, "For in Christ Jesus you are all sons of God υἱοί through trust" (3:26). If they are τέκνα, children (8:17), then this means that Christ-followers from the nations become "heirs of God, and joint-heirs with Christ," provided they share in suffering with him as well as in inheritance, so that they may also share in his glory—note the συν verbal forms in 8:16-18. To these, as noted already in ch. 6, we may add συνετάφημεν "we were buried with" (6:4) following Sabou's illuminating thesis that this burial language emphasizes belonging to the same family/dynasty of the person with whom one is buried. "'Joint heirs', belongs with a group of at least fourteen συν compounds" used by Paul to express 'with Christ' language (Jewett 2007: 502). It is particularly interesting that Paul in Romans extends his συν compounds to make a link for the Romans with Christ's burial, thus emphasizing the extent of their identification with him. They are truly part of his "house" in life and in death. Thus, the presence of the verb συμπάσχειν, "to suffer with" or "sympathize with" is not unexpected here, denoting the full participation in Christ of his gentile followers. Only those who share Christ's sufferings can anticipate sharing his glory (Käsemann 1980: 229).

But it is noteworthy that despite Paul's high view of Abraham already outlined in Romans 4, "it is God, not Abraham, whom these ethnē—like their older brother Jesus, and like ethnic Israel—can now call 'Father'... God's new sons call him *Abba*, addressing Israel's God by his 'Jewish' family name" (Fredriksen 2017: 151). By this family genealogy, Paul reminds his hearers/readers that the gentile Christ-followers as a whole and by themselves now constitute part of the totality of God's "family," but only one "branch" of this "family," *an associate family, a brotherhood with Christ, alongside*

---

[7] It seems that Paul at this point equates υἱοί and τέκνα. This may be to indicate that he will use τέκνα again in chs. 9–11 (cf. 9:8) and, as is his pattern, gives notice earlier or in passing, that he has still a particular term or topic in mind.

Israel. Perhaps it might therefore be more appropriate to speak of families or peoples of God, plural rather than singular, but while this pattern would preserve the diversity, it might likewise obscure the unity within these. Careful use of terms relating to God's family is essential for clarity regarding status, the image should not be casually used as a "hold all" term designating various imprecise groups. The ethnē in Christ are no longer outside the "family of God," they have become part of the family. In Paul's perspective, the ethnē in Christ are an associate people alongside Israel.

But, on the other hand, all differentiation within that family has not disappeared, and Paul does not confuse ethnē in Christ with Israel. In Paul's address, he pointedly tells the ethnē in Christ how things have changed for them in terms that indicate his ongoing awareness of and sensitivity toward ethnic issues. Rather than including himself, a Jewish Christ-follower, as one of them, up until 8:12-13, he continues to use the second person distinguishing their incoming as "gentiles." He thereby maintains his own distinct identity as a Jewish follower of Christ whose history differs from that of the non-Jews even though he serves them in the role of "apostle to the ethnē" (11:13). The conditional "if" you live according to the flesh speaks to *the ethnē only without Paul's inclusion*. "You (ethnē) did not receive a spirit of slavery to fall back into fear, but you have received a spirit of adoption." Adoption signified a transfer to a new family usually of a higher or more prosperous level, and slaves would seldom be adopted. The reason for Roman adoption was primarily to secure the continuity of the family line and fortune (Fredriksen 2017: 37, 148). Because of the practice of adoption in powerful families in Rome, adoption as such would have resonated with Paul's Roman audience. In 8:15, Paul offers a parallelism "you did not receive a spirit of slavery (to fall back) into fear, you have received a spirit of adoption," thus making the comparison very precise.

The spirit of adoption resonates with its opposite, the servitude of slavery that Paul described at length in 1:24-28, and especially chs. 6–7. The missing element in 7:7-25 was the Spirit of God, which Paul powerfully introduces after a preliminary mention in 7:6. Paul possibly includes the whole cultural encyclopedia of slavery in his thinking here, but my impression is that "sons of God," the new status that the ethnē enjoy by adoption through Christ and the Spirit, is where the emphasis lies, and the adoption analogy is briefly introduced for one purpose, to elaborate and illustrate the change of status. As Fredriksen notes, at this point, Paul's thought is at one and the same time at its most Roman, at its most traditionally *Jewish*, and at its most *ancient* (2017: 148). As noted, in Roman perception, the new son was thereafter responsible to and for his "new" paternal ancestors and to and for the *genius* (inherited *numen*) of his new father and family (*gens*). In Paul's use, it is the immersion and conferral of Spirit that binds the Christ-following ethnē into a new family, so that they, too, can inherit and can enjoy blessing.

We note again particularly the transition proceeding from slaves in 6:17 to adopted sons in 8:15. Lewis has suggested that the juxtaposition of the adoption analogy would have resonated with Paul's Roman audience to evoke back to the practice of imperial succession, particularly the adoption of Octavian by Julius Caesar; "every person in Rome was acquainted with the 'spirit of adoption' that had come upon Octavian at his official adoption. Octavian had in fact used this image as a way of solidifying his position. Upon his adoption, Octavian had received the spirit of Julius Caesar's genius as his own" (Lewis 2016: 191–2). It may be that it was this association of spirit with adoption that led Paul to offer an echo of this well-known adoption narrative in Rome so that his mainly poverty-stricken, gentile audience would see clearly the explicit transfer that occurred in turning to Christ and its outcome in the gift of the Spirit. Paul is presenting these ethnē in Christ with a sign or evidence that they need not fear the anger of the gods they had deserted. The adoption of Octavian had dramatic consequences—a new name, a new fortune, a new power, and, most significantly, for Paul's purposes in Rom. 8:15, a new spirit or *genius*. The *genius* and *lares* of a family required care and attention not to mention the strict observance of ritual. "The primary function of an adopted member of the family was to secure the estate and facilitate the religious rites of the family in order to guarantee the blessing of the family by the family spirits" (Lewis 2016: 183). In Paul's perspective, the incoming of the nations is essential to ensure the fulfillment of the ethnic plurality demanded by the promise.

With the transfer through the Spirit, the ethnē in Christ are released from all obligation to the desires of the flesh—they no longer need to be concerned to follow these, but should follow the leading of the Spirit. In Roman society, the large numbers of freed slaves were not freed from all obligation to their former masters—they still had to fulfill some of these. But Paul's argument is that the ethnē, though formerly bound as slaves to sin, having been freed through Christ via the Spirit, are freed from the power of sin operating through the flesh. The gentile Christ-followers are not under any obligation to yield to the demands of the flesh (including the social constraints of their former way of life reverencing the gods), which was put to death through Christ, and to which they must now regard themselves, that is, their bodies, as dead. If the body is regarded as having been put to death or idle (καταργέω 7:2, 6), then sin has nothing to control, having lost its base of operations. This is the outworking of the imagery of 7:1-6 where it was not the Law that died, but those over whom it exercised dominion. Now, having died to sin and (thus to the Law's verdict), these ethnē are freed from being debtors and from all the obligations of such slavery. They are called and led by the Spirit according to God's purpose, obligated only to God through Christ. As non-Jews, they also experience another freedom from obligation—that of the honoring and worship of the Roman gods, to which we will return below.

The above discussion about obligations linked to revering Roman deities was clearly addressing ethnē, indicated by the consistent use of second-person plural in vv. 1-15a. But with 8:15b, Paul switches to first-person plural, "we" and after that never uses the second-person plural "you" in the rest of this long chapter (cf. Rodriguez 2016: 157, n26).[8] The switch is evidenced in 8:15. "For *you* did not receive a spirit of slavery again unto fear, but *you* received a Spirit of adoption by which we cry out, *Abba* Father." Paul's emphasis emerges in the contrasting of "spirit of adoption" and "spirit of slavery" (and the ongoing fear that accompanies this).

---

[8] The change to first-person plural does not indicate that both ethnē and Jewish Christ-followers are now described as one entity. Romans addresses only the ethnē, and it is not until 15:7-13 that Paul will call upon the ethnē to expand their reconciliation with one another to include reconciliation with God's people Israel (contra Rodriguez 2016: 160).

As noted, a key aspect of adoption is the securing of the right to inheritance. But this needs to be clarified. It is significant that Paul does not argue that the ethnē in Christ have become co-heirs with Israel, but rather co-heirs with Christ, so that although they share in the promised inheritance, they do not attain this by becoming the same as Israel, or by becoming part of Israel—Israelites, but rather by sharing in this inheritance through Christ. The label of Israelite is notably not applied to the ethnē by Paul—they are not incorporated into the people of Israel (contra Keesmaat 1994: 29–56). This is another argument against viewing gentile Christ-followers as Israel. They are differentiated from Israel in this way at a point in Romans where close undifferentiated affinity between gentile Christ-followers and Israel in reception history might have been strongly anticipated in advance of chs. 9–11. But this is not what Paul had in mind. And, in adoption, the adopted remain distinct as in all human adoption (Fredriksen 2017: 149). They are adopted as ethnē, as representatives of the nations, not as potential Israelites.

The Roman ethnē in Christ are a people, a new people alongside Israel, *an associate people-of-God with Israel, but not a λαός instead of Israel*. This gives them a self-consciousness with a new corporate social identity in Christ, which it seems they lacked previously as indicated by some ethnē discussing circumcision and proselyte status and, negatively, by presuming they had displaced a rejected Israel. As noted in the "Introduction" chapter, Paul wishes the ethnē in Christ to be clear that together as a group they have a specific status in Christ, not dependent upon their becoming Jews (which would be misperceived for ethnē in Christ). But Paul does not combine this differentiated identity with arguments against association with Jews or the synagogue (as ethnē in Christ). Nor does he allow that the presence of ethnē in Christ and the gentile mission signify the bypassing of Israel in the divine purpose. The narrative of Abraham in Romans 4 and continued in Romans 9–11 will clarify both their own (ethnic) status in relation to Abraham and the destiny of Israel. The ethnē through Christ are to become the brothers of the Jews. Paul uses adoption language in the political context of Rome where memory of the adoption of Octavian by Augustus was probably still vivid, to stress the reality of the new status and new family into which the ethnē in Christ have been adopted as children of God. They could not possibly continue to live as if their acquired status into a new family, a new name, and a new protecting Spirit had not been realized. Moral empowerment for Paul proceeds out of family membership that then leads to transformation.

Thus, the image we are discussing here is the transfer from one family to another as illustrated by the analogy of adoption with which the populace of Rome would have been conversant from examples in prominent Roman families. The concept of transfer from one Roman family to another is basic. The ethnē have transferred to a new household (cf. οἴκος linked with οἰκέω). But it is Roman ethnē whom Paul addresses, not "Christ followers" in general, and thus a break is implied with the household deities and public worship of the gods whose protection was regarded as essential. Paul made it obligatory that his gentile Christ-followers discontinued all idolatrous worship having turned to Christ. In keeping with the pattern when a person was adopted in Roman republican times, he had to denounce the religious duties of his old *gens* and assume those of the new.

The *genius* and *lares* of a family required careful and strict attention to ritual in order to avoid the serious consequences that would otherwise ensue (Flower 2017: 40–75, 78–144). Here we get a glimpse of devotion to the gods as practiced in the houses and on the streets of Rome. This reflects normal everyday Roman life— the life from which the ethnē in Christ have transferred in a change of status, and *points implicitly to the change in divinities that has occurred in their turning to Christ.* This may include aspects of emperor worship. The humble image of Augustus's *genius* does nothing to conceal the notion that he enjoyed divine powers, "This is evident in the statuettes of his Genius which were worshipped all over in public and private shrines" (Lewis 2016: 183). Commenting further on this phenomenon, Lewis notes,

> Add to that the compital shrines to the *lares* and the *genius Augusti* in Rome, and it seems probable that every person in Rome would have been familiar with the idea of Augustus's family spirit and, therefore, of Augustus's reception of that spirit by way of his adoption by Julius Caesar. (2016: 183)

But Paul's advice for ethnē in Christ to cease all participation in idolatrous activities would have created a real challenge in that "not to participate in cultic practices in the house, at the street corner, or at the frequent festivals in a *polis* or *colonia* separated these Christ-followers from the nations from their 'normal' ways and means of finding meaning in life, protection and reassurance in risks and dangers" (Ehrensperger 2019: 345).

Paul finds an analogy in the experience of the Christ-following ethnē having been adopted into the family of God as ethnē through the Christ. The new children of God have been granted the right to cry Abba, Father/ἄββα ὁ πατήρ, thereby participating in the worship of the Jewish God, most likely repeating Jewish liturgy but also appropriating the key honorific title given to Augustus and his successors (Lewis 2016: 184). The stress upon security via the Spirit's presence may reflect the uneasiness some ethnē have experienced in their cessation of traditional piety toward the gods. Some may have felt vulnerable because of forsaking the gods. Have they possibly been disowned by their own families because of ceasing to worship the Roman gods? The reassurance is that in the new family to which they have been adopted, the Spirit of Christ will reside in and among them. The gentile children/sons of God, though having turned from their traditional gods, are not bereft of comfort and security, the Spirit of Christ will protect the ethnē in Christ not the *genius Augusti*, which is not required (Lewis 2018: 282). In the new status in the gentile branch of God's family, the Spirit undertakes the total care, protection, and guidance of the ethnē in Christ, rather than numerous deities.

Romans 8:18-30: The Creation Waits for the Revealing of the Children of God

[18]For I reckon that the sufferings of this present time cannot compare with the coming glory to be revealed to us. [19]For the creation waits with eager longing for the revealing of the sons of God; [20]for the creation was subjected to futility, not voluntarily but

> *rather by the will of the one who subjected it, in hope* ²¹*because the creation itself will be set free from its enslavement to corruption for the freedom of the glory of children of God.* ²²*For we know that up to the present the whole creation has been groaning and suffering in labor pains;* ²³*and not only the creation, even we ourselves, who have the first fruits of the Spirit, groan within ourselves as we wait adoption, that is, the redemption of our body.* ²⁴*For in this hope we were saved. Now a hope that is seen is not hope. For who hopes for what is seen?* ²⁵*But if we hope in what we do not see, we wait with perseverance.* ²⁶*In a similar way the Spirit lends assistance in our weakness; for we do not know how to pray as we ought, but that very Spirit intercedes with unspeakable groans.* ²⁷*And the one searching the hearts, knows what the intention of the Spirit is, that, according to God's will he intercedes on account of the saints.* ²⁸*For we know that in all things it cooperates for good for those who love God [those who are called according to a purpose].* ²⁹*Because those whom he foreknew he also predestined to be conformed to the image of his Son, in order that he might be the firstborn among many brothers.* ³⁰*And those whom he predestined he also called; and those whom he called he also rectified; and those whom he rectified he also glorified.*

With the imagery of adoption and the mention of future glory for those who share Christ's sufferings, Paul seems to have moved away from present sinful reality, that is, 8:18 "the sufferings of this present time, τοῦ νῦν καιροῦ." It is not only the children of God who face a struggle of life or death, in the flesh or in the Spirit, but the creation itself is enslaved, having been subjected to bondage to decay, and needs to be set free. Paul uses the image of childbirth to describe the state of the creation as in pain similar to the pangs of childbirth. Thus, it is important to acknowledge that new creation language in Paul is not limited to new self-understandings on the part of Christ-followers but implies literally complete redemption of bodies and of the entire created κόσμος as well as a renewal of spiritual hope. "The metaphor has a cosmic-universal dimension—it is not an individual matter but the redemption of the whole body of the created order" (Beker 1980: 289). Jewett is one of the few scholars who have linked the hope of redemption with the acknowledgment of the corruption and need for redemption of creation in light of the future of the planet (2004: 25–46, 2007: 508–12). In apocalyptic thought, the transition from a world in slavery to sin to the world of new creation is never smooth or without conflict, and Paul in this respect is no exception.

There is much in Romans about the use and control of the body, but presupposed in this is the hope of a new bodily existence beyond death. Paul's view of the body includes its redemption (1 Corinthians 15).

Here, in 8:19, 23, 25, Paul introduces the imagery of waiting. There is a new hope for those in Christ, an anticipation of release from bondage, but it is not yet actualized in full. Paul stresses the "not yet" of hope, "who hopes for what is seen? But if we hope for what we do not see, we wait with perseverance" (8:25). Paul has earlier announced the great new event of the revelation in Christ of the righteousness of God and gone on to stress its significance, especially for the ethnē. What he has written up to this point presupposes the good news, the εὐαγγέλιον of the revelation noted in 3:21. But now he points out that "in hope we were saved," (8:24), which indicates the non-arrival as yet of the *fulfillment* of hope. Paul, in the coming chapters, will indicate that God's plans for Israel have not yet reached fruition. Nor have these plans failed or been annulled. Present lack of fulfillment does not denote failure or annulment, rather it denotes the need to wait in eager expectation (8:19). So, in anticipation of this future reality, he reminds the Christ-followers that they need to wait for the further unveiling of God's purpose (8:28), that is, that in fact *they were saved only in hope*, so they need to continue in that hope. But this hope is not without suffering and opposition. Here Paul extends the image of the creation in birth pangs to include the Roman gentile Christ-followers themselves, "not only the creation, but we ourselves, who have the first-fruits of the Spirit, groan inwardly while we wait for adoption, the redemption of our bodies" (8:23). Even though they have experienced the first installment and thus the guarantee, of the divine harvest of the Spirit, the ethnē in Christ are subject to sharing in the imperfections of the sinful world even as they await their full redemption. Sin has not disappeared, neither have its effects, even though the hope of glory is already a present experience.

A new dimension to their hope is introduced with the inclusion of the whole of creation within the scope of Paul's gospel. Since Romans 4 in the story of Abraham, and the narrative of sin's introduction into the world in Romans 5–7, the narrative into which Paul's gentile Christ-followers had been introduced by the gospel has continued to unfold, it is difficult to discover exactly why this discourse on waiting in hope should have been written by Paul, if there were not specific circumstances in Rome to warrant this. The perversion of Paul's gospel about grace in relation to sin might suggest that there was lack of clarity about the meaning of death for those called through the gospel, possibly even an expectation of escape from persecution in a kingdom already presumed to have arrived. Realized eschatology in the understanding of grace may be symptomatic of other imbalances, that is, concerning the supposition that Israel had been rejected in favor of those from the nations (cf. 11:19).

The likelihood is that reports concerning the gentile Christ-followers in Rome had suggested to Paul that guidance in this area was needed. The presupposition here is that Paul, even here, was giving instruction because it was needed, rather than just providing useful teaching without a specific target, this being a possibility we will return to in relation to chs. 12–15. It might be argued that in 8:18, Paul commences with a formulaic phrase, "the sufferings of this present time," which refers to the apocalyptic expectation that the end time would involve severe suffering for the righteous. Thus, Paul may be simply teaching a general expectation of persecution from which the Roman Christ-followers will not be exempt. If, as we think was the case, Paul was writing to Rome from Corinth, he could not avoid being cognizant of gentile over-realized enthusiasm, as Käsemann has stressed. The correlative of over-realized eschatology for one group often has the effect of a parallel over-realized conception of judgment for the "other" in their context. Indeed, the pessimistic view of the future of Israel in Rome may have emerged from, or been encouraged by, an overoptimistic scenario of gentile Christ-followers extrapolating on their miraculous experience of the arrival of grace to them through the gospel. This would also help to explain some aspects of the "high-mindedness" of these non-Jews when combined with Roman imperial cultural presumption. Thus, we may posit from the clues in texts such as Rom. 3:8, 6:1–7:6, and

11:19 that there may have existed, first, some form of realized eschatology among the gentile Christ-followers in Rome that reflected negatively on the Jewish people, one of the defeated nations that Rome had subdued. Also, second, Paul may have thought that the prevailing optimism about Rome's role in the world was misplaced when the suffering that Rome's subjugation of peoples often caused was noted.

The choice of topic (the corrupt state of the created world) may also emerge from the fact that Paul needs to provide some teaching concerning the creation itself and its involvement in decay and suffering in association with its deliverance from corruption. His addressees need to know about these things, and how to address their effects. Thus 8:26 brings in another development in terms of empowerment. "The Spirit helps us in our weakness." This seems to relate, among other things, to not knowing how to pray, "the Spirit intercedes for the saints according to the will of God" (8:27, cf. 8:34). It appears that those former God-fearers felt isolated and insecure, having had to leave behind cultic allegiance designed to ensure the protection of the gods. In its place, Paul offers the protection of being within the will of God. But it is protection not for the proud and overconfident, but for the persecuted and distressed.

If, as seems likely, many of the gentile Christ-followers in Rome were in extreme poverty, and at risk to all kinds of dangers to their health and well-being, overcoming the power of death, and stressing the future hope for the resurrected body may have been Paul's comfort and encouragement for them. Rather than looking to the promised idealistic renewal of the world in Roman ideology, Paul offers even to those facing the challenges of life and death a hope of victory through Christ, not merely inward salvation but a renewed cosmos, devoid of the power of sin. This hope includes the transformation of the body, including "putting to death" (θανατοῦτε) the deeds of the body, not the entire body itself[9] through the Spirit as the way to life. The transformed body is very much part of Paul's eschatological vision.

The purpose of God who chose ("foreknew") those called was that these were predestined to be conformed to the image of Christ that he might become the firstborn of many brothers. It is surprising that the introduction of such a hugely important new concept as brotherhood with Christ (8:29) has not attracted more scholarly attention in the past. The danger of human pride and vanity misreading the significance of this has probably contributed to its neglect. But gentile brotherhood with Christ a son of David is a vital element in Paul's attempt in Romans to construct a meaningful social identity for the ethnē as a part of the household of God. It connects them intrinsically to the Jewish tradition of the Messiah and his achievement, but as ethnē, rather than pseudo-Jews. Instead of Christ being claimed as hero for non-Jews, in contrast to the poor reception of his messianic significance by Jews, the Christ is here intrinsically related to "gentiles" who trust the God of Israel. Rather than viewing Israel as being bypassed in God's purpose, and as being entirely alienated from the ethnē in Christ, Paul has constructed a family affiliation in which the latter are intrinsically related to the Jewish people via their Messiah. A bridge is thereby constructed in this conception

---

[9] Somewhat surprisingly, Paul does not say "deeds of the flesh" as might have been anticipated following on from ch. 7. Τὰς πράξεις τοῦ σώματος (8:14) is possibly used in view of the fact that Paul wishes to move toward the hope of redemption of Christ followers' bodies later in this chapter.

of a new familial connection that affirms both their identity as ethnē and their affinity (not sameness) with the people of Israel.

Although his letter's audience in Rome are not as yet aware of it at this point in his letter, Paul here seeks to undermine any attempt to by-pass the Jews in the claim that "branches were broken so that I could be grafted in" (11:19). The gentile misunderstanding of the role of the Law for ethnē, which we have glimpsed in Romans 2 and Romans 7 (including probably circumcision), points to an insecure identity for ethnē in Christ at Rome particularly in their relation to Jews and Jewish patterns of behavior. They have learned from reports of Paul to differentiate themselves from Jews, but they have misinterpreted this to mean antagonistic competition in relation to Christ. Differentiation, as demonstrated in the "Introduction" chapter, must not mean an antagonistic displacement of the "other" but an acceptance of them in their difference—a "sharing in the riches of the olive tree" (11:17).

This teaching, that all gentile Christ-followers share a similar destiny patterned on that of Christ, offered a secure destiny including foreknowledge, calling, justification, and glorification provided they continue in his kindness (11:22). Whatever protection previous idolators may feel they may have lost in turning away from idolatry, Paul seeks to demonstrate, has been more than compensated for in their being called and protected within the gentile associate family of God (8:29, McMurray 2021: 106–110).

Thus, Paul does not speak in terms of survival or even of deliverance, but of conquerors, super-conquerors (ὑπερνικῶμεν, 8:37, Fitzmyer 1993: 534). If ever a word resonated with the Roman context, it is this. Significantly, the vocabulary of νίκος will recur again at the end of ch. 12 (v. 21), following upon a reference to peace in 12:18. The Romans were super-conquerors both in their own eyes and that of others (Reasoner 2019: 71–90). Paul did not need to present Christ-followers through this parallel to Roman victories, but he chose to do so, not simply to oppose Rome's domination, but to offer the greatest possible image of victory. The Christ-followers at Rome need not be overawed by Rome's power, however great, because through Christ they can be victorious over all powers or forces. Here those who belonged to the vanquished nations not only survive the vicissitudes of the present eschatological crisis but also prove themselves through, and with Christ, to be super-conquerors, more than equivalents to Rome in the process. Christ is not only the Son of David, a cosmic warrior or super-conqueror (Fredriksen 2017: 140) of a different kind in his providing reconciliation through a truce, but still active on behalf of his people at God's right hand, interceding for his people (8:34). This security not only replaces but will exceed by far the lost protection of the gods, and this hope marks Israel, and the nations, as an associate people alongside Israel, as the people destined for glory. Indeed, "The critical features of the narrative of God's covenant have been applied to the ethnē" (Lewis 2016: 192). Ethnē in Christ becoming members of God's family reads like a parallel to God's care of Israel in his covenant, and *Paul here is seeking to reassure former idolators of divine protection in analogy to Israel*, but without these seeking to become Israelites, or to displace Israel. "Who will bring any charge against God's elect?" (8:33). We will return to this theme later.

Romans 8:31-39: "If God Is for Us, Who Is Against Us?"

³¹*What then are we to say in view of these things? If God is for us, who (is) against us?* ³²*He who did not spare his own Son, but gave him up for all of us; will he not then freely give all things to those who are with him?* ³³*Who will bring any charge against God's elect? It is God who rectifies.* ³⁴*Who is the one who judges? Christ [Jesus], who died, who moreover was raised, and is at the right hand of God, who also intercedes for us.* ³⁵*Who will separate us from the love of the Christ? Affliction, or distress, or persecution, or famine, or nakedness, or danger, or sword?* ³⁶*As it is written,*

"For your sake we are being killed all day long; we are accounted as sheep for slaughter."

³⁷*But, in all these things we are super-conquerors through him who loved us.* ³⁸*For I have become convinced that neither death, nor life, angels, rulers, things present, or things to come, nor powers,* ³⁹*nor height, nor depth, nor anything else in all creation, will have power to separate us from the love of God in Christ Jesus our Lord.*

At the start of this section, we note that both the Spirit (8:27) and Christ Jesus intercede for the saints according to the will of God, "It is Christ Jesus ... who indeed intercedes for us" (Rom. 8:34). The progress of the text from 8:17 on becomes increasingly interspersed with terminology that relates to the sufferings associated with this present time (8:18), culminating in the catalogue of persecution-related experiences beginning to be narrated in 8:35. Starting with the question concerning who could possibly separate Christ-followers from the love of God, these dangers include hardship, distress, persecution, famine, nakedness, peril, or sword. With the exception of the latter, that is, sword, all of these afflictions had been experienced by Paul himself. They are supported by the citation, "For your sake we are being killed all day long; we are accounted as sheep to be slaughtered" (Ps. 43:23 LXX).

In 8:31, Paul begins as he has frequently done (cf. 4:1, 6:1, 7:7) with the retrospective question, Τί οὖν ἐροῦμεν, "What then are we to say (in response to these things)?" It seems he is reaching a significant stage in his argument in Romans—the gentile Christ-followers have now been included as representatives of the nations as an associate "family of God," and they must wait in hope for the redemption of their bodies. At this stage, he pauses to ask a question, which we paraphrase as (having pursued our argument up to this point), "where do we go from here?" that is, here toward the end of our eighth chapter, "a chapter in which Paul directly contradicts the propaganda of the Roman Empire" (Reasoner 2019: 72, Wasserman 2018: 170). Paul has by no means finished with the topic of the future of the ethnē, but he (also) prepares for what has sometimes been viewed as a digression, concerning the future of Israel, to which he will turn in chs. 9–11. But, as we have already noted, Rom. 3:1-9 indicated that Israel would be central to Paul's agenda in this letter. Therefore, from this perspective, chs. 9–11 can never be secondary since these concern both, the misunderstood identity of the Roman ethnē as replacing Israel, and Paul's newly constructed social identity for these ethnē as brothers of Christ.

What Paul here envisages for these ethnē in Christ seems to be patient endurance in face of hardship of many possible kinds. He is aware of "our weaknesses" (8:26). This section may represent a continuation of the sufferings "of this present time" (18) but whatever they are precisely, Paul seems to be seriously alarmed at the vulnerability of the Roman Christ-followers. If the extent of their vulnerability is to be measured by the strength of the assurances and support that Paul offers, their situation must be critical. Whether it is already so, or beginning to deteriorate and likely to get worse, either way, Paul views them as in great need of support. The emphasis is not only warning about coming dangers, the tone is also very supportive, to reassure those who feel under threat, whether through social harassment from neighbors, severe punishment by the civic authorities, or other forces normally perceived as being kept under the control of the gods (Flower 2017: 251–2). Wasserman views Paul's varied references to other gods and powers as indicating a type of political thinking that "implicitly reclassifies other gods so that they are imagined as subordinates to the Jewish God" (2018: 171).

What should be remembered is that the call to the ethnē to forsake the worship of the gods and all things associated with this would have caused an enormous cultural break for non-Jews. The gods were very much part of everyday life in a city like Rome. The offering of sacrifices to ensure the people's protection was customary—not to practice this might put the entire city at risk of suffering the anger of the gods. Those foolish enough to risk angering the gods would be regarded by others and probably also by themselves as vulnerable. The protection attributed to the gods could not be taken for granted, but required zealous and appropriate action, particularly on the part of those most vulnerable. Thus, Paul's catalogue of dangers from which to be saved in 8:37-39 is not hypothetical but something from which his addressees might certainly feel the need for protection. Obviously, the Roman gentile Christ-followers did feel vulnerable to issues of life and death, in the present or future or to other hostile forces in the whole of creation. Paul follows this with an appropriate scriptural citation, chosen possibly among other reasons, because of its inclusion of ἐλογίσθημεν, "we are reckoned as sheep to be slaughtered" a term that is key in Paul's vocabulary for the rectification of non-Jews. The long history of conflict and suffering when Israel was dominated by stronger, more powerful neighbors was doubtless vividly remembered by Jews in Rome, but it may be that Paul envisages suffering as a real and immediate threat to which Jews and Christ-following ethnē may be particularly subject. The questions began here with the possibility of separation from the love of Christ to which Paul will respond with the prospect of a new familial belonging as brothers of Christ. For Paul, it is this familial membership that brings effective transformation. This is Paul's formulation of the issue, but it may not be impossible to envisage the possibility of having to separate from another group of Christ-followers, or from other groups; if such had happened or could be envisaged as a future possibility, this may have suggested to Paul this formulation of the danger they face.

But another likely separation envisaged is the separation from communal worship of the Roman gods. Paul's pattern for former God-fearers is that they should separate from all association with the worship of the gods, an enormous step for those accustomed to this pattern of living. The issue may have been, if Christ-followers separate from idolatry, will they be separated from the protection of the gods, and thus left isolated and vulnerable to all the forces of evil from which the gods had guaranteed protection? As Reasoner notes, "The Romans worshipped their gods for very practical reasons—they perceived that their gods could bring specific, assessable qualities and conditions to the Roman people" (2019: 88). But the reverse of this was also true, failure to maintain the worship of the gods would leave the people vulnerable, worse, even liable to all kinds of hardships from which previously they had protection (Fredriksen 2017: 89–90).

If Paul's advice to them will lead possibly to more isolation and persecution, then he wants the Romans to be prepared for the coming conflict. Strong reassurance emerges in the rhetoric that Paul employs in these verses. The conditional (enthymeme) "if God is for us," which sets the pattern of thought, is followed by alluding to God in the language of Abraham's willingness to sacrifice Isaac, God, like Abraham, "did not spare (οὐκ ἐφείσατο) his own son," but ὑπὲρ ἡμῶν πάντων παρέδωκεν αὐτόν, "gave him up for us all." This is the basis on which Paul builds his confidence that "God is for us," that is, by a parallel of God's familial connections and those of Abraham. Paul's powerful reasoning is explicit—"if God has already done all this for us," how can we doubt his beneficence and providential care? If God has already given his son for us, will he not also with him give us all things? Now Paul also is included in the "us," the recipients of the divine giving. If God gave up his own son on our behalf, Paul reasons, "Will he not then freely give (χαρίσεται) all things to those who are with him?" (8:32). This resonates with key aspects of Roman ideology about *Victoria Augusta*, as Reasoner (following Fears) argues, "In this system of Roman values, Victoria Augusta is the linchpin … Once *Victoria* was in place, other significant virtues which the Roman state had also deified, were guaranteed" (2081: 73). The deified virtue *Victoria* was the key virtue of the Roman state. "By his triumphant actions the emperor ensured for the world those blessed conditions explicit in such abstractions as Pax, Concordia, Libertas, Spes, Abundantia, Securitas, Iustitia, Clementia, Felicitas and Aequitas." (2081: 73). Even in Constantine's time, *Victoria* continued its Augustan role as the guarantor of all other imperial benefits. Clearly, there is an analogy with Paul's words, "How shall he not with him also freely give all things?" Paul's presupposition is that God's victory in the reconciliation, not through Augustus but through Christ, is the foundation of all the Christ-followers' hope. In and through God's gift of conciliation in Christ, all other benefactions must follow. Using the image of a court of law, here the divine court, Paul asks, "Who will bring any charge against God's elect?" First, Paul's reassuring of the Roman Christ-followers, those called and chosen by God, ἐκλεκτοί θεοῦ, resonates with the theme of Israel as God's chosen people, but it is not here meant to indicate a people chosen *instead* of Israel, but an associate people—chosen alongside Israel as the representatives of the nations. On the other hand, the resonance with the election of Israel is salient in two senses. First, it refers to the action of the God of creation toward the ethnē, those originally outside the sphere of the covenant with Israel, and second, it is a reminder that the election terminology had its original referent to Israel. A victorious triumphalism could be aimed at affirming the calling of the ethnē but in such a way as to draw attention to the paradoxical condition of Israel in covenant with God but presently unpersuaded by the outcome of the Christ-event.

Paul is deliberately drawing an analogy with Israel as he prepares to discuss the election of Israel and its significance in chs. 9–11. Paul may actually be referring to accusations against God's elect made in Rome against the people of Israel, which we will meet in 11:1, 11:11, and 11:19. But here he is putting these questions to the ethnē in Rome concerning their security in the divine plan. No one will lay any charge because God has accepted these ethnē also through the work of Christ, who is depicted as victorious, raised from the dead, seated at God's right hand, and who intercedes for us (8:34). What is significant here is that the election language, normally reserved for the people of Israel, is here explicitly applied and thus extended via adoption and Spirit terminology, to those from the nations, thus possibly resonating simultaneously with Rome's claims to be favored by the gods and the object of divine predestination.

In many other places in Paul's letters, there are texts that with some justification can be read as referring to all God's people whether Jewish or from the nations. However, here I see Paul drawing a deliberate analogy between gentile Christ-followers and the people of Israel. In analogy, a parallel is drawn between two items that are not equated but that remain separate and distinct. It is these ethnē in Christ who are predestined to be conformed to the image of God's Son that he might become the firstborn of many ἀδέλφοι (8:29). A careful look at Romans 8 and its vocabulary reveals parallels that Paul draws between the gentile Christ-followers and Israel. Calling, sonship, adoption, children of God, foreknowledge, election, and glory are only some elements of the shared inheritance that Paul highlights here. An important question that must be put at this point is what is missing in the lives of these representatives of the nations that requires this new ascription of identity in analogy to Israel to fill the gap? (Campbell 2018: 23–46).

There are innumerable questions in Romans, and with the spiraling crescendo that concludes the first eight chapters, Paul asks several more: the inaugural question "Who is against us?" elicits only an unstated "No one" (8:31). In 8:33-36, Paul returns to the theme of opposition by asking three more questions as if in a court room, "who will accuse God's elect?" "who will condemn?" and "who will separate us from the love of the Christ?" Paul lists seven forms of suffering that might separate ethnē from the love of the Christ—affliction, distress, persecution, hunger, nakedness, peril, or sword (Jewett 2007: 531). Keck notes it is better to read these as "who will bring any charge…? God who justifies" with the implied answer, "impossible." Paul's diatribal style offers the short snappy exchange of a dialogue as in a court of law (here possibly the divine court)" (Keck 2005: 220–1). Paul's strategy at this point seems to suggest that, as he comes near to the end of a main section of the letter, that is, Romans 5–8, he briefly enumerates all fearsome options that might endanger the ethnē in Christ, and draws them all together in order to claim that, nevertheless, the Spirit of God who resides among them will co-operate in all things for their good (8:28). The fact that the diatribal style permeates the second part of this chapter is difficult to evaluate with any precision without too much speculation, except as a way to summarize briefly in conclusion. One conclusion may reasonably be drawn—that Paul is claiming that the new life of the Spirit "who intercedes for us" (27) is more than equal to any protection previously anticipated from the Roman deities, and ultimately superior. If the ethnē feel vulnerable because they may no longer participate in honoring the gods, they are reassured by God being "for us" (31b).

To illustrate the dangers that Paul perceives as facing the Christ-followers, he cites from Ps. 43:43 LXX, "For your sake we are being killed all the day long: we are accounted as sheep to be slaughtered." Whatever details Paul may have had reported to him, he seems reasonably confident that severe sufferings are a very real possibility for Roman Christ-followers in the future. But these are not limited to earthly powers alone, they are cosmic in scope as 8:38-39 demonstrate. In the list of forces that Paul offers, ten forms of adverse power in all (Jewett 2007: 533), all possibilities seem to be listed. Paul is seeking to exhaust all possible options in order to claim that absolutely "nothing else in all creation can separate us from the love of God in Christ Jesus our Lord" (8:39). Such a conclusion confirms our insight that the ethnē in Christ at Rome are in dire need of reassurance. They are deeply insecure, and the fact that cosmic forces δυνάμεις (v. 38) are included shows that the break from traditional Roman religion is causing deep anxiety.

Certain other factors may have led to the ethnē in Christ being insecure in their own self-understanding. If God's plan for Israel has not come to fruition as expected, if one election can fail, so too can another. If God's promise to Israel has not succeeded, and we ethnē are only in God's plan by virtue of Israel's unpersuadedness of the Christ-event how can we be sure that God will be on our side? If we forsake the worship of our ancestral gentile gods, who will take care of us? It seems that the ethnē in Christ at Rome tended to reason in a binary form of argument. One people can be replaced by another in the favor of the gods. This can lead to two different conclusions—just as Rome has been victorious over all the 'weaker' nations because their destiny is assured by the gods, so they have replaced other empires. Israel is part of the subjugated nations, perhaps Israel is being replaced by a new gentile people who will not have to suffer the judgments of Israel's law, which we heard Paul believes brings only death and judgment for ethnē without Christ. Perhaps it is better to separate from Israel's patterns of life and continue our gentile traditions of recognizing the gods who have formerly protected us? As noted already in our reading of Romans 4, Paul's pattern of thought is not binary but aggregative and inclusive, not only but also, and Paul will proceed now to apply this form of reasoning to Israel itself and the ethnē.

Paul's response to these questions was to seek to provide a secure social identity and status for those from the nations who, like Abraham, had forsaken all to follow God's call. He sought to do this by linking these positively to Abraham's seed and inheritance, but in such a way as not to nullify, but to affirm the promises to Israel that require ethnic plurality. For non-Jews, this would not mean their becoming part of Israel, and so losing all aspects of gentile identity, or even opposing Israel and seeking to take Israel's place in the divine purpose. For Paul, it is not Aeneas but Abraham who can provide a secure destiny for the nations. It is through Jesus Christ that the promise of blessing to those from the nations is transmitted by their becoming an associate people alongside Israel, differentiated but related. They too are part of God's purposeful plan—they are his children τέκνα θεοῦ (8:16).

Thus, ethnē in Christ are secure because they are destined by God to be linked through Christ as an associate people to Israel. The ethnē as a new people cannot and must not take Israel's place, because God's plan for Israel is still operating—in fact, for the nations to have a secure destiny, Israel's destiny must also be secured. What seems not to have been recognized was that God's promise to Abraham cannot be separated from Israel to be claimed by another group of people. The best and in fact, the only, option available to the ethnē in Christ is to *share* in God's blessings first gifted to Israel.

In the repetition of οἴδαμεν, "we know," Paul speaks in concert with transmitted early tradition in which there is a clear assurance that God through the Spirit works in all things for the ultimate good of all in God's creation, "for those who love God and are called according to his purpose" (8:28). There is some ambivalence about the character of Israel in Rome. If God can separate his providence from Israel, might he not do the same to ethnē in Christ? The judgment of God upon sin, and Israel's failure (to be convinced by the Christ-event) seem to have made a strong impression in Rome. The character of the God of Israel is under discussion, so Paul stresses on the basis of God's reconciliation through Christ that God loves and cares for those who love him and that he is completely trustworthy, he is "for us." Probably, while deliberately focusing on the theme "God being for his people," Paul knew he would indirectly raise the question, "if God through Christ is granting such blessings to the nations, where do the people of Israel now stand in relation to his promised blessings? This question will reappear in chs. 9–11, where Paul will address the question of God's faithfulness to his covenant with Israel in light of the incoming of the nations.

Romans 8:30-39: The Transition to Chapters 9–11

Paul's use of second-person constructions that separate or isolate the apostle from his addressees, and the inclusion of himself with gentile Christ-followers in an inclusive first-person plural from 8:15b to the end of the chapter, are indications of stages in his argumentation. There is a developing climax in the theme of the Spirit's association with the Christ-followers that, taken in association with the progress in the narrative content from foreknowledge to glory, has encouraged and supported a major division after 8:39, and also the view that the content of chs. 9–11 may be somewhat of a digression.

On the other hand, both rhetoric and content indicate that other formulations of the structure of Romans as a letter are possible. Elliott has presented good arguments in favor of a break after the argument of 6:1–8:13 so that there is no "artificial boundary" that occurs at 9:1.[10]

> The sudden shift in Rom. 9.1 marks neither the beginning of a separate essay on a distinct theme nor an unguarded effluence of personal feeling. It rather capitalizes on the rapturous doxology to the divine will in 8.17-39 in such a way as to reshape and redirect the sympathy of Paul's audience. (Elliott 2007: 261)

---

[10] Elliott takes the argumentative unit to be 6:1–8:13, succeeded by a second unit 8:14–11:36 (2007: 250–3).

Romans 9–11 is an intrinsic part of the letter and its opening is destined to arouse sympathy in Paul's audience for the Jewish people. The important outcome of Elliott's proposal is that "Rom. 9:1-5 transforms the assurances of 8.31-39, based as they are in the unshakable divine purpose, into an awed compassion for the people to whom these assurances pre-eminently belong" (2007: 263). This is in contrast to a reading that exults in the divine blessings assured at the end of ch. 8 for ethnē in Christ whilst relegating what succeeds it to a digression or subordinate theme.

However, while favoring the excellent insights Elliott's proposal offers, not least into the argumentative structures of the letter, I have sought to use these without accepting a break at 8:14 as the commencement of a new section concluding at 11:36. The proposed division at 8:13 is, in my view, not as distinct as Elliott's proposal requires. But I am in whole-hearted agreement already noted throughout our discussions in this chapter that "connections of vocabulary and themes from 8:14-39 to chapters 9-11 show that the latter chapters are not an appendage to the theological 'core' of the letter, but represent a climax towards which the preceding argumentation builds" (2007: 253). These chapters are the basis on which Paul will expound the pattern of life for ethnē leading to the conclusion in 15:7-13 of association with Israel.

Romans 9

Romans 9:1-5: Sorrow for Israel and Israel's Heritage

¹I am telling the truth in Christ—I am not lying; my conscience confirms by the Holy Spirit—²that I have great sorrow and unceasing anguish in my heart. ³For I used to even pray that I myself be accursed and cut off from the Christ for the sake of my brothers, my kinsfolk by natural descent. ⁴They are Israelites, and to them belong the sonship, the glory of the divine presence, the covenants, the giving of the law, the temple worship, and the promises; ⁵to them belong the patriarchs, and from them comes the Messiah by natural descent, who is over all, God blessed forever. Amen.

In Rom. 8:22, Paul portrayed all creation writhing in labor pains, "groaning and suffering (συνωδίνει) until now." He makes a link with this in Rom. 9:2 to describe his unceasing distress(ὀδύνη) for his fellow Israelites (Tomson 2019; Rodriguez 2016: 171). This section contrasts with the glorious conclusion of the narrative of election, calling, love of God, and glory in ch. 8:26-39 where nothing can separate us ethnē from the love of God, which is in Christ Jesus our Lord. Paul deplores the state of God's people Israel who as a majority, despite their inheritance, have not been persuaded that the new Messianic Time had dawned in the Christ-event. Paul does not tell us precisely why he is so concerned about Israel, just that he is. He experiences great sorrow and strong emotional upset in his heart. He would be willing to become anathema—to become accursed and cut off from Christ—were it possible that he could take their place. At least that is how the normal reading of 9:3 proceeds. But Paul does not say that his brothers, his kinsmen according to the flesh, are in the same particular state that he would be willing to enter into in their stead for their restoration. This is presumed and developed by lively imagination. We must not read in here psychological perspectives on Paul's grieving such as Stendahl deplored in relation to the Western introspective conscience (1976) nor use Paul's publicly exposed grief as a reason for pessimism about Israel's future. It is to be kept in view that it is not Israel's failings alone, whatever they may be, but Israel's plight among the conquered nations dominated cruelly by Rome that constitute Israel's condition about which Paul is so concerned. To separate Israel's spiritual condition from her social and political situation is to misunderstand Paul.

We note that everything here is about Paul, his deep concern and passionate feelings toward Israel. This is underlined by Paul swearing on oath that he is not lying, his conscience in light of the Holy Spirit bearing witness that "I have great sorrow and unceasing anguish in my heart." It is possible that Paul is drawing attention that here he is speaking in his own voice and genuinely from the depths of his heart. The depth of Paul's concern is primary, not the details of Israel's plight whatever that may be. The oath and the way the concern is expressed is so strong that it seems necessary to presuppose that Paul needed to convince his addressees that he is not an enemy of Israel, but genuine in his passion for her welfare. Paul even wishes like Moses, and Israelite heroes of old, that he could sacrifice himself—become cut off from Christ (ἀνάθεμα) on behalf of Israel (Exod. 32:32; Num. 11:15). Paul could not make his own personal commitment to Israel more explicit than he does here. This suggests that an image of Paul and his gentile mission was circulating in Rome that put Paul on the side of Israel's opponents rather than being pro-Israelite. If there was animosity between Jew and "gentile" at this period in Rome, as we posit there may have been, it may have appeared that Paul had become a traitor against Israel by choosing "gentiles" in her place and ignoring Israel as if she were a *former* people of God. Inferences from Paul's gentile mission activity in concentrating on those from the nations, non-Israelites, and reports of what Paul had said or not said about Israel in his letter to the Galatians may have combined to give a certain radical view of Paul's posited relation to his native Israel. Jin Yong Kim has noted that Wright (2002: 689) for example, uses Paul's grief as evidence to support his view that Paul expected the destruction of unbelieving Jews—"if that were not so, 9:1-5 is sham and 10:1 a mere formality" (2021: 2).

Kim, however, offers a more critical and probable rationale for Paul's emphasis on his grief for his own people at the very beginning of his discussion in chs. 9–11. She recognizes that though the scholarly climate is now more open to optimism about Israel's future, the function of Paul's grief can still continue to be used negatively in respect of his view of Israel. Paul's grief actually functions here not to depict him as unable to control his grief, but rather as a wise man who experiences grief for his kinsfolk's present status, yet who controls it through a logical understanding of God's logos (cf. 9:6a). Grief functions as an indispensable element of Paul's argumentation, and Paul uses it in the course of his discussion in chs. 9–11 "to transform the gentile misunderstanding and boasting over Israel into a correct understanding, 'sober judgment of themselves' (12.3) and proper pathos of fear and hope" (2021. 10). This perspective on Paul's lamentation over Israel's grief allows it a positive, instrumental function in which Paul as an apostle uses his pain as part of his persuasion of the ethnē in Rome not to negatively prejudge Israel until he has finished his narrative.

What is difficult to determine is whether the ethnē in Christ at Rome were criticizing Paul among themselves for his supposed anti-Israel stance. Were they less or more pro-Israel than the apostle? Were they identifying with a reported "pro-gentile" Paul and thereby seeking confirmation of their own skewed perception of "Paul"? In terms of SIT, it appears that they understood Paul's pro-gentile stance in his gospel in an antagonistic way implying that a positive group identity demands by necessity a negative stance over against another group. However, Paul clearly advocates the opposite, namely, that although the groups remain different, this by no means leads to or demands a negative self-definition over against the other (as noted in the "Introduction" chapter, pp. 23–5.). It is this pro-gentile, anti-Israel image that Paul emphatically denies in 9:1-5. This is Paul speaking passionately in his own authentic voice directly to the Romans not just about his own emotions but about his identity and his positive relation to the identity of Israel, "my own people, my kinsfolk by natural descent." Although this introduces here a new chapter in Paul's argument, Israel and her future is not an entirely new topic. As we noted, this is present particularly in relation to 3:1-2.

To elaborate on his personal view of Israel and her inheritance, Paul resumes a list of the advantages of being a Jew that he had commenced but not completed in the πρῶτον of 3:2. Paul asserts his own people's singular, enduring identity. "They are Israelites, and to them belong (present tense), the sonship, the glory of the divine presence, the covenants, the giving of the Law, the temple worship and the promises; to them belong the patriarchs, and from them comes the Messiah by natural descent" (9:4-5). As Fredriksen asserts,

> Ethnic Israelites, quite apart from Christ already have sonship *huiothesia* (cf. Exod 4.22, Israel is my first-born son); they already are in a family relation with Christ (Rom. 9.5, the Christ is from Israel *kata sarka*)—the redeemed nations rejoice with God's people, his *laos*, Israel. (Rom. 11.1, 15.10; Deut. 32.43, 2017: 150)

In this comprehensive account of Israel's heritage, Paul makes it plain that he identifies with the people of Israel (cf. "I myself am an Israelite," 11:1), and that he confirms the continuing promises that God has given them. We do not read Rom. 9:1-5 as indicating that Paul was maintaining a space between himself and those features (of Israel), including ἡ λατρεία, the Temple service, mentioned at 9:1-5 (contra. Esler 2021a: 230–1). Because he is writing to ethnē in Christ, Paul stresses his natural link with Israel, and if there is any distance intended here, it is the distance between these ethnē in Christ and the Jewish people who remain temporarily unpersuaded; so even though Paul does not use the inclusive "we" (which here would separate him from the ethnē whom he addresses) but appropriately "they," his differentiation includes more than solidarity with Israel, as he clearly affirms in 11:1b. There is no doubt that there is positive approbation of Israel in the features listed here, despite their being unpersuaded.[1]

However, he himself may have been reported, whether positively or negatively in relation to his own people Israel, Paul here adamantly rejects a negative view of Israel. If Israel is being despised by some, and perceived as being bypassed, it is the word of God to Israel that is being despised, and Paul does not anticipate that the word that initially called Israel into being and to blessing has failed or is likely to fail. It is worth noting that Paul's list of Israel's blessings includes the glory, and the worship, the latter including the worship of God in the temple (which was still standing) and God's enduring presence amid his people. Not only so but the patriarchs are also part of Israel's glorious legacy that includes, by natural descent from the seed of David, the Messiah, God's eschatological champion. These together form part of the identity of Israel (Keck 2005: 230).

---

[1] My reading here coheres with but is not dependent on "Paul within Judaism" scholarship, which it precedes by at least two decades.

Thus, if the Roman ethnē in Christ have somehow separated God's history with the people of Israel from their own experience of trust in Christ, Paul gently reminds them that the Christ in whom they have trusted is none other than the promised Messiah of Israel. Likewise, he uses his own grief to call upon these ethnē to share with him his deep concern for Israel, and with him to further consider that God would never forsake those with whom he remains in covenant.

Romans 9:6-13: But It Is Not as Though the Word of God (to Israel) Has Failed

⁶It cannot be that the word of God has failed. For all those from Israel are Israel are they not? ⁷"It is not so that all the children [of Abraham] are seed of Abraham but [rather] it is through Isaac that seed will be named for you." ⁸This means, the children of the flesh these are not the children of God, but the children of the promise are reckoned as seed. ⁹For this is the word of the promise, "About this time I will return and Sarah shall have a son." ¹⁰And not only this; but Rebecca out of one intercourse conceived [children] by our ancestor Isaac. ¹¹Even before they had been born or had done anything good or bad so that God's purpose in election might prevail, ¹²not on the basis of works but on the basis of the one who calls she was told, "The elder shall serve the younger." ¹³As it is written, "I have loved Jacob, but I have hated Esau."

After such an exalted description of the heritage of Israel, one would not anticipate that Paul would immediately dilute or diminish what he has now so fully elaborated and in which his own commitment to Israel is included. This factor is further emphasized by the very next verse, 9:6a, which the RSV translates as "But it is not as though the word of God has failed." Thus, first we have a full list of Israel's advantages, followed by a denial that God's promise to Israel has failed, that is, the singular "word of God" (ὁ λόγος τοῦ θεοῦ) refers back to and incorporates the gifts of God's grace previously noted in 3:2 and elaborated in 9:4-5 (Wengst 2008: 294–5). We disagree with Jewett's view in his identification of ὁ λόγος with the gospel (2007: 573–4). Paul lists the spiritual credits of Israel, trying to build up the honor rating of the Jews in light of his gentile addressees (Witherington 2004: 250). This includes the traditions of Israel in the scriptures, which we would summarize as God's spoken promises. Keck thinks that the word "entrusted" (*episteuthēsan*) gives a clue to which promise is meant. The Jews are entrusted by God with the promise to Abraham that envisages the nations being blessed through him and his descendants (Gen. 12:1-3; 22:16-18). "This is precisely the point of being a Jew in a gentile world, being a steward of God's promise" (Keck 2005: 90). As Sam K. Williams has argued, τὰ λογία τοῦ θεοῦ in 3:2 means specifically the promise given to Abraham that God would bless the gentile peoples through Abraham's seed (Christ) (1980: 294–5). While we agree with Keck and Williams in focusing attention on Israel's role as a light to the nations, we would not wish to interpret this role in a narrow sense, that is, purely functionally, since her role included, but was not limited only to, this (cf. Kaminsky and Reasoner 2019: 421–46). We take the plural, covenants, διαθῆκαι, and promises ἐπαγγελίαι (9:4) to signify God's ongoing covenantal relationship with Israel, that is, Israel is God's beloved—"his servant in whom God will be glorified" (Isa. 49:3). It would be most inconsistent and surprising if, immediately following on *this* introduction to the chapter, for Paul then to begin immediately to retract on the claims he has just so positively advanced.

But this (retraction) is exactly what we are asked to believe if we read 9:6b with, for example, the RSV as a statement, "For not all who are descended from Israel belong to Israel." If this is what Paul knew he was going to write in this verse, it seems he chose a very poor preface as it does not in any way prepare for the partial denial of Israel's call by the sudden introduction of what amounts to a redefinition of Israel (Schnelle 2005: 380) that actually contradicts much of what he has just so strongly emphasized. Following on from 9:4-5, we would anticipate that Paul would be tending to argue in the opposite direction, that is, that the nonacceptance by (part of) Israel of the message about Jesus as the Christ does not mean that God's grace-gifts to Israel have been nullified. Thus, in terms of consistency, it would seem more likely that Paul would here be arguing for the ongoing validity of God's election of Israel rather than redefining Israel or denying her election. And, if the word of God has not failed (9:6a), then we would expect v. 6b, if it is presumed, as it normally is, to oppose the positive content of v. 6a, to start with an adversative ἀλλά, "but," or even with a μὴ γένοιτο ("far from it") exclamation. However, Paul continues with γάρ—"for"—a connective particle which suggests that the thought of the first part of the verse is being further elaborated rather than negated as Casson (2019) has proposed. As Michel perceptively noted, "Schwierigkeiten macht die logische Verbindung zwischen v. 6a und 6b: statt des γάρ wäre eigentlich ein ἀλλά zu erwarten" (1978: 300).

Most translations render 9:6b as affirmation that God's word has not failed on the presumed reading "all Israel are not Israel." But if Israel is not in some sense Israel, then all the attributes of Israel so clearly enumerated in 9:4-5 are almost completely devalued if Paul immediately juggles with the definition of "Israel" (Hübner 1984: 17). Moreover, this is not any less problematic if, according to some readings, those from the nations are also included within the term "Israel," because if the content of the title "Israel" can be changed in one direction, it is thus open to change in others (cf. Stegemann 2012).

What then are we to make of the *apparent* contradiction, or at least hiatus in Paul's statements concerning Israel following the normal translations of these verses? It would seem that what is claimed in vv. 4f—that Israel according to the flesh was designated bearer of the promise and the recipient of sonship—is, in vv. 6b-7 partly and, following on from this in v. 8, fundamentally, disputed (Käsemann 1980: 251). Those following closely Paul's train of thought would have anticipated that here in vv. 6b-7, Paul would have positively added to or developed his immediately preceding affirmation of Israel's election and blessing. But astonishingly, what we seem to find is not affirmation but denial, or at least qualification of an extreme kind—the "Israel" first presented here is in fact not the real Israel; only a part is truly "Israel."

It seems as if Paul suddenly realized the problem of what he had just claimed, God's word to Israel has not failed, and yet Israel has not accepted his estimate of Christ.

The solution since Justin in the second century[2] has been to solve the problem by a redefinition of the term "Israel," so that it is now erroneously taken to mean that Jewish tradition has no validity apart from Christ since on this reading it has been superseded. From this perspective, at maximum, only a part of Israel is actually Israel. But this suggested solution gives a poor image of Pauline rhetoric if it were Paul himself who supposedly would have created this dissonant discussion in the space of a few verses. Even if he is dealing with a topic that is incredibly difficult, Paul could have introduced it better.[3]

Romans 9:6b "For All Those from Israel Are Israel, Are They Not?"

In struggling to find a coherent and consistent interpretation of Romans 9, I had decided that part of the problem lies in the fact that Paul is really concentrating in the first half of the chapter on how Israel came into being, on Israel's initial call. Thus 9:6b-13 is really a discussion that could precede 9:1-5 in that it defines who Israel is and how she was created. The explanations based upon the distinction between descendants as τέκνα or as σπέρμα explained for me the limitation within Abraham's progeny that first constituted Israel. But it was only later when I found Klaus Wengst's proposal that 9:6b-7 be read as a rhetorical question, not as a redefining statement, that I was able to develop a coherent reading such as presented here. Since the traditional reading of 9:6b as a negative statement about Israel is so inconsistent with, and therefore inappropriate to, its context, can another, more satisfactory reading be found? As has been noted variously as characteristic of diatribal style, questions, especially rhetorical questions, are unusually frequent in Romans (see Excursus I, pp. 44–8). Tobin lists some twenty examples of rhetorical questions in Romans 9–11 (2004: 300), but these rhetorical questions also permeate most of the rest of the previous chapters.

A significant feature concerning Paul's use of rhetorical questions is that these tend to occur in Romans where Israel is a topic of discussion (as in Rom. 3:3, 9:6b, and 11:1). In light of this frequency and in light of (its) content as well as (its) context, one possible option is that 9:6b can be read not as a (conceptual) statement "For not all who are descended from Israel belong to Israel" but rather as another rhetorical question expecting an affirmative answer—οὐ γὰρ πάντες οἱ ἐξ Ἰσραὴλ οὗτοι Ἰσραήλ "For all those from Israel are Israel are they not?" This rhetorical question points to an anticipated positive outcome, "Yes, it is true that all those from Israel are Israel." But then in v. 7, Paul changes the subject somewhat in that he now speaks not of Israel's descendants "οἱ ἐξ Ἰσραήλ" but of Abraham's children τέκνα/σπέρμα. This move in Paul's argument is missed by many interpreters, who fail to see that Paul's real question here concerns not so much Israel's present response to Paul's gospel, as Jewett thinks (2007: 573–4). But rather "How did Israel first become Israel? What makes Israel distinctive?" It appears that Paul now sets out to explain in detail how Israel became Israel, and thus is and remains Israel. Our tentative proposal is that where Israel is discussed in Romans, Paul may ask a rhetorical question as a way to keep the conversation open rather than

---

[2] On Justin's life, see Lampe (2003: 272–84). On Justin's views about Jews, see Remus (1986: 293–340).
[3] Wengst's reading is "Sind denn nicht alle aus Israel eben Israel?" cf. Wengst (2008: 293–340).

risking premature closure by being too explicit. Paul's discussion of issues about Israel in Romans 9–11 should be seen as a refutation (*refutatio*) of misunderstandings by gentile Christ-followers of the heritage of Israel (Witherington 2004: 17). This proposal should be extended throughout the letter.

Reading 9:6b as a rhetorical question does in fact cohere well with diatribal style, and such questions are to be anticipated in association with this (diatribal) style that Paul uses frequently throughout Romans. We have already noted how reading 5:15a as a rhetorical question changes the translation of the verse to its opposite, a similar possibility to our suggestion here (Porter 1991: 655–77). The translation and identification of rhetorical questions have become an issue of some interest among recent interpreters of Romans as, for example, Caragounis (1985) Porter (1991), Jewett (2007), and Rodriguez (2014) demonstrate.

Paul clarifies his understanding by noting that it is within Abraham's descendants (not Israel's) there is a selection. "But rather, ἀλλά not all of Abraham's children, τέκνα, are his seed, σπέρμα" (v. 7).[4] Moreover, it is also stated that it is (only) through the line of Isaac that the promises continue, "in Isaac shall your σπέρμα be named," citing Gen. 21:12 (LXX). Then this line of thought is consistently developed and explained in v. 8, "This means that it is not the children of the flesh (fleshly descent only) who are the children of God, but it is the children of promise who are reckoned as σπέρμα." Reading 6b not as a negating statement, "for not all those from Israel are Israel" but as a rhetorical question "For all those from Israel are Israel, are they not?" makes a serious difference in interpretation. A rhetorical question, expecting an affirmative answer, does in fact, continue the positive presentation of Israel from vv. 4-5, and the qualification and limitation regarding Abraham's descendants introduced in v. 7, does not contradict the *affirmation of Israel*. Unlike the traditional reading of these verses, an alternative reading is thereby rendered that does not contradict what precedes, and that likewise resonates well with what succeeds.

Not only does this reading avoid the contradiction with the vivid, positive depiction of "Israelites" and their heritage in 9:4-5, and what immediately succeeds it, but it coheres well with the differentiation Paul goes on to stress in 9:8-13 that Abraham's descendants were not all included in Israel, the people of the covenant, but were according to Gen. 18:10 and 21:12 limited to those within the lineage of Isaac (v. 8). We note here that this reading is a differentiation *within* Abraham's descendants—*it is thus that Israel originated*. So this differentiation, since it draws a distinction between τέκνα and σπέρμα *within* the descendants of Abraham, cannot be read as eliminating Israelites, the descendants through Isaac of Jacob, from the people of promise, nor is it a repudiation of normal human descent, but rather a limitation within this. Failure to note the change of subject from descendants of Israel in 9:6b to descendants of Abraham in 9:7 has led to confusion (cf. Wengst 2008: 298–9). The binary opposition here is not σάρξ, flesh, and πνεῦμα, spirit, but rather σάρξ and ἐπαγγελία (promise). Physical descent alone does not determine membership of Abraham's lineage, but only

---

[4] There is a selection within the descendants of Abraham, but *not* within the descendants of Isaac and Jacob. Wengst shows that his reading here is supported by a reading of a similar construction using οὐδέ (v. 7) in Heb. 9:25 (contrary to Walter Bauer, *Wörterbuch*, 1196, vgl BDR 445, 2).

both descent and promise. But there is no denigration of physical descent at this point since Paul is referring to ethnic Israel to signal positive relation to Israelite corporate identity (Esler 2003: 185–94).

Paul here differentiates τέκνα, children, to refer to Abraham's descendants generally but limits his use of σπέρμα, seed of promise, only through the descendants of Isaac to Jacob. Thus, v. 7 does not follow smoothly as an addition to the thought of v. 6b but is to be taken antithetically "but rather, not all are σπέρμα of Abraham (just) because they are his τέκνα; it is only the children of the promise who are reckoned as σπέρμα." Thus, it does not refer to a selection *within Israel*, nor does it suggest that there will be any selection *of this kind* in future among the people Israel whom God first chose to be his own. This refers to a *unique calling* in which God first *chooses Israel from among Abraham's other descendants* for his own purposes.

Thus, when Paul proceeds to develop his argument in vv. 8-13, he demonstrates through the example of Isaac, the promised son to aged parents (rather than Ishmael), and Jacob (rather than Esau despite being twins) that Israel is constituted by people of descent *and promise*, rather than simply by those of fleshly descent from Abraham. Paul draws a distinction between "the children of flesh," τὰ τέκνα τῆς σαρκὸς and "the children of promise," τὰ τέκνα τῆς ἐπαγγελίας (v. 8). As noted earlier, in Paul's theology of reckoning, it is not the children of fleshly descent alone but the children both of fleshly descent and of promise who are reckoned as σπέρμα (v. 8).

But we note here that Paul is speaking in terms of groups, not just individuals. The discussion began with the issue of the origin of corporate Israel, and Abraham, Isaac, and Jacob together indicate Israel as a people, not merely three individuals. The patriarchal tradition supports the kind of distinctions that Paul wishes to draw between the various sons of Abraham. Jews of the Second Temple period were accustomed to having to distinguish Abraham's children from Abraham's σπέρμα. Jewish exegesis claimed that it was the lineage of Abraham, Isaac, and Jacob, not just Isaac or Jacob individually that received the promised inheritance. Thus, for example, in Exod. 3, God reveals himself as God of Abraham, Isaac, and Jacob (Mühling 2011: 343–69). Paul's citation of Gen. 21:12 in v. 7 indicates his first source, which distinguishes Isaac, the son of Sarah, from Ishmael, the son of Hagar, Sarah's maid. According to *Jubilees* 14–15, despite Abraham's intercession on behalf of Ishmael, the Lord insisted that the promise to Abraham will be fulfilled through Isaac (Rodriguez 2014: 174–6).

The decisive example of *the divine purpose in the lineage of promise* that Paul offers as proof here is the story of Rebecca's twins. In the previous example, it could have been argued that the reason for Isaac's choice was that he was preferred because Ishmael was the son of the maid, rather than of Sarah, Abraham's wife. But in the case of Rebecca, the only reason that could be given was that God's purpose ἡ κατ' ἐκλογὴν πρόθεσις might continue (μένῃ) to be according to election (Keck 2005: 231), citing the scriptural support from Mal. 1:2-3, "I have loved Jacob but I have hated Esau" (v. 13). Thus, for Paul, Ishmael and Isaac, and Jacob and Esau, demonstrate the difference between physical descent and heirs of promise, giving a binary opposition between Jacob and Esau. These figures must not be read as individuals but rather as the ancestors of differing peoples, and their role in the narrative of Israel and the nations. Further, the items Paul sets in contrast are not works and trust, as might have been anticipated, but rather human works and God's call; it is these that constitute the foundation of the historic "faith versus works" dichotomy. Thus, Paul is stressing that those who are related to Abraham *only* by physical descent are not his σπέρμα. What is more, no amount of human achievement or works can bring a people into or within the sphere of heirs of promise since this is constituted, not by human worth or works, but by the call of God (cf. 12:1). There is a real likelihood that the discussion of Israel here originated from ongoing discussions about proselytes, God-fearers, and ethnē in Christ at Rome.

Thus, here Paul continues the narrative of Israel and the nations in their role within God's historical purpose. Israel's (Jacob's) unique origin and status has been affirmed, but what of Esau? If Jacob represents the collective identity of Israel, which nation is Esau? Here our reading is based upon the premise that chs. 9–11 point to the destiny of nations and not primarily to the procurement by individuals of salvation (Rock 2012: 290; also, Leenhardt 1961: 249–50). There is some evidence that sometime during the first century the eponomous use of Esau/Edom (the Edomites were the descendants of Esau) was thought to refer to Israel's enemies. Feldman maintains that sometime around 100 CE, literary evidence of the equation of (the) Romans = Esau was seen in 4 Ezra 6:8-9. This speaks of Esau as "the end of this age" and Jacob as "the beginning of the age that follows." Feldman identifies R. Akiba as the first to equate the two (1993: 493–4, n57). But already in the *Book of Jubilees*, the tension between the Jews and the Idumeans is expressed in the eponymous use of Jacob and Esau in a contest between two guardian angels in which Jacob's guardian is mightier than Esau's (*Jub.* 38:2-3).

On the premise that Paul views Israel as oppressed by her enemies, in Paul's time the Romans, it seems a likely inference that the Romans could easily fit into the binary grouping of Israel's enemies represented as Esau (Gaston 1982: 400–23).[5] In the face of Roman claims of eternal rule and of claims that Israel has been cast off, Paul confirms that God's choice of that nation through which his purpose of election will flow is Israel, and not Rome. It is important to stress that here the topic Paul addresses is not the destinies of these nations, but rather their function in the history of salvation (Rock 2010: 291).

How Israel Was Called from among the Nations: Linking the Call of Israel and the Call of the Nations

In 9:1-13, Paul is formulating Israel's identity, what makes Israel distinctive, how Israel was called, how the Lord created Israel. In order to discuss his people Israel as he does in Romans 9, *Paul starts with his concern for Israel, that is, with the assumption of Israel as already existing*. But to account for her earliest origin, he has to go back to the narrative of this people's beginnings. So, in 9:6-13 Paul is setting out what makes Israel distinctive, how Israel was first called. As we have noted, 9:6-13 could have preceded

---

[5] Cf. Bertholet (2016) and Bertholet (2021: 345).

9:1-5, in that the origin of Israel, where Israel came from, and who Israel is, her identity, necessarily precedes how Paul thinks about her as a people, her particular attributes. She is called by a selection from among the descendants of Abraham to be the recipient of the promise, and thus Jacob (Gen. 28:13-16) is called to be the bearer of this promise in accordance with the divine "purpose of election" (9:11). It is the choice by God to make Jacob/Israel the bearer of the promise that makes her distinctive. Once Israel is identified, she is differentiated from other groups who are descendants of Abraham. Thus, there is only one Israel here, and not an Israel within Israel—Paul's reading precludes such a perception. Also since there is no mention of the calling of non-Jews until 9:24-29, there can be no question of a displacement of Jews by non-Jews. Paul will go on in 11:7 to draw a distinction between a remnant and the rest of Israel. This is not the same distinction as that of the traditional reading of Rom. 9:6-13 where Paul's distinction between Israel, οἱ ἐξ Ἰσραὴλ (6b), and Abraham's τέκνα is often overlooked. Paul's concern in 9:6-13 is not how Israel survives—continues to be Israel—but rather how Israel first originated.

We have maintained above that the primary issue in Rom. 9:1-13 is how Israel came to be Israel. Jon D. Levinson has shown that there are differing narratives of how Israel became the chosen people. In Genesis, the new people comes into existence only through God's promise to Abram, a childless man with a barren wife, so that the new people are not a nation like any other. Israel never had an identity unconnected with the God who called it into existence in the beginning (Levinson 2012: 22-3). The variant tradition of Ezekiel draws attention to the fact that the difference between the chosen people and the rest of humanity is not genetic in that it features an adopted child abandoned by her parents, and adopted by the God of Israel who eventually marries her. The prophet suggests that the people emerged from the adoption of an existing child of undistinguished, even shameful origins. For the sake of emphasis, we include here the words of Levinson: "In Ezekiel, the chosen people who probably represents the whole chosen people ... has emerged from two idolatrous peoples whom Israel supplanted long ago." Similarly, as Genesis claims, "the childless man from whom the promised nation will emerge is one of three brothers: like them and every other human being, he is descended not from the gods ... but from Noah and his wife and from Adam and Eve before them" (Levinson 2012: 22–3). It is interesting that Paul, in Romans 9–15 echoes yet another version of Israel's origins based on the narrative of Deuteronomy, possibly indicating diversity of opinion on this at Rome.

Because Israel's election was being challenged by some gentile Christ-followers in Rome, Paul returned to the traditions concerning Israel's claim to be a people chosen by her God. In Paul's perception, these appear to be illuminated particularly by Deuteronomy generally and Deuteronomy 32 in particular, which is echoed in (9:14), 10:19, 12:19, 13:11-12, and 15:10 and which is thus demonstrated to hold some significance for Paul's own understanding of Israel's origins and peculiar status. The specific context in relation to which Paul reflects on Israel's becoming Israel is here the city of Rome itself, including the situation of the Christ-followers there, (and) this must be recognized as the salient context in view. Because Paul has not yet, at the time of writing, visited Rome, the Roman context of the addressees has not been adequately taken into account by most scholars. Yet this is significant for understanding Paul's argument in the letter and not only at this point but throughout.[6] Here our interest is on why Paul should consider that the Romans' challenge to Israel's election resonates with Deuteronomy 32.

The Exigency at Rome Illuminated by Deuteronomy 32

Several scholars from differing perspectives have considerably illuminated Paul's use of Deuteronomy 32 in Romans, particularly in relation to chs. 9–11 (e.g., Bell 1994, Wagner 2003, Rock 2010 and 2012, Harrison 2020). Bell claims that "Paul's Heilsgeschichte was similar to that of the Song of Deut. 32:1-43 and of Deuteronomy as a whole" (1994: 201, 285). Bell goes on to suggest that Paul's meditation on the Song may have inspired his own proposal concerning the mystery of the final salvation of Israel in Rom. 11:25-27. Both Wagner (2003: 165, 187) and Rock (2012: 64–72) view Deuteronomy 32 as foundational for understanding Paul's thinking in Romans 9–11. Rock's drawing of parallels with Virgil's Aeneid illumines Roman contextual elements that may suggest that Paul's view of Israel's future role may be formulated in sharp contrast to Roman imperial ideology (cf., e.g., *Aeneid* 1:257-296). These may even have originated from a subcultural reading of the *Aeneid* (2012: 78). Wagner reads Deut. 32:1-43 in conjunction with Isa. 65:1-2. This is determined by his conviction that he "cannot do justice to Paul's use of Isaiah 65:1-2 without closely examining his quotation of Deut. 32.21" because "their words are so closely conjoined in Rom. 10:19-21" (2003: 189–91). He concludes that Paul probably interpreted each of these texts in light of the other in order to understand the outworking of God's redemptive plan in his own day in the context of honoring other gods, that is, idolatry.[7] David Lincicum in his survey of the content of the Song similarly concludes that it was the storyline Paul found in the Song that served to good purpose in his argument in Romans (2010: 161–7). The Song tells of Israel's election, unfaithfulness, punishment, and vindication and is about what is to take place "in the end of days" when Yahweh will vindicate his people (Deut. 31:29, cf. also 32:20). Significantly, Deut. 32:8 includes a reference to the integrity and righteousness of the Most High (NRSV).

> When the Most High apportioned the nations
> when he divided humankind,
> He fixed the boundaries of the peoples
> According to the number of the gods.

The Song continues in 32:9-43 to affirm that

---

[6] My research has always stressed the reading of Romans as a letter to Rome, that is, "Why Did Paul Write Romans?" (Campbell 1991: 14–24). This emphasis has recently also been stressed by James Harrison (e.g., 2020: 6–9).

[7] One of the parallels noted by Wagner is that both Isa. 65:3 and the *Song of Moses* speak of Israel sacrificing to *demons*—language that appears elsewhere in the LXX only in Ps. 105:37 and *Bar.* 4:7, and both explicitly deny that these false gods are at all comparable to Israel's God. Also Isa. 65:3 and Deut. 32:21 agree that Israel's gods are no-gods.

the Lord's own portion is His people
Jacob his allotted share. (v. 9)

The Song narrates how Israel's God—the Most High—found Israel in a desert region (Rock 2012: 298–300), watched over him like an eagle over its nestlings, even carrying them on its wings. This was the work of the Lord alone, no alien god was at his side (32:12).

This narrative tells in poetic form how Israel became Israel by being found and then protected by the Lord. But it is a narrative that also tells how Israel rebelled and forsook the Lord "who made him" (32:15). In spite of the blessings enjoyed from God's favor, Israel became "a people void of sense, lacking in all discernment," and the Lord might have destroyed them since "they incensed him with alien things, vexed him with abominations, they sacrificed to demons, no-gods" (32:16-17). But despite his anger at Israel's idolatrous behavior, and lest Israel's enemies boast over Israel's demise and the Lord's name is dishonored, "the Lord will vindicate His people" (32:36). Lincicum's conclusion is that "the vindication of his people will be, in turn, the Lord's own vindication (cf. 32:39 with 32:26-27). In other words, the salvation of Israel after judgment is a part of God's vindication as the faithful covenant Lord" (2010: 160).

The poetic narrative of Israel's beginnings recounts the call and eventual idolatry of Israel in a context of other gods or demons. In the Roman context, there is a real possibility that such discussions were salient in the debate about the status of God-fearers and proselytes. The narrative's resonance in Romans 10–11 has a reference to oppression by Israel's enemies, and here it may potentially include Rome if Rome treats Israel as an enemy. Although Deut. 32:28-33 speaks of God's judgment, it is not due to the Lord's weakness that Israel suffers but rather his using Israel's enemies for his own purposes; they can only cruelly treat Israel because God has temporarily removed his presence, "hid his face" from Israel (32:20). (Wagner 2003: 198–201).

From Deuteronomy 32, we derive three principles concerning God's activity which Paul enumerates:

(1) Essentially the Song of Deuteronomy 32 affirms the powerful sovereignty of the God of Israel over the destiny of nations, who are expected to do obeisance to Israel's God along with Israel (15:10). Israel's God has not failed.
(2) Israel and the nations serve differing functions at differing times and contexts. Their role is determined by the Lord's use of them in his ongoing purpose which is the constant factor.
(3) Despite failure, and the possibility of rejection from God's purpose, Israel retains a central role. How the nations react to this purpose of God of which Israel is a central element determines their success or failure—a warning to the ethnē in Christ at Rome?

In Deuteronomic terms, on a number of occasions it appeared as if Israel must be cast off because of her failure to do the Lord's will. But it is noteworthy that despite Israel's rebellion, the Lord does not reject her from his purposes but retains her in a central role within them, a significant nuance as Paul works his path through Romans 9–11.

But what is the reasoning behind God's faithfulness to unfaithful Israel? This is part of Paul's theological agenda.

In Romans, the integrity and justice of Israel's God is disputed in 3:1-8, and in 11:1 it is asked, "God did not cast off his people, did he?" We take the combination of questions/responses to denote issues salient in Rome concerning the righteousness/integrity of God arising from the claim that those from the nations now have access through Christ, to the God of Israel while remaining non-Jews. As already noted, it seems that the inclusion of non-Jews in sharing in the promises to Abraham, raised questions about the nature of this God, about how he had first chosen Israel, and whether this commitment still continues after the advent of Christ and the incoming of the nations. It is some such exigency at Rome that is required to explain Paul's argumentation (including his use of Deuteronomy) in Romans 9–11.

Deuteronomy 32 is interesting in that it narrates what seems to be a description of a heavenly council among the gods about their peoples in which Israel is kept by the Most High as his own chosen nation, whom he will vindicate (32:36).[8] This reminds us of the thinking about nations and their gods contemporary with Paul. Gods and peoples were closely related:

> The fact that ancient gods ran in the blood meant that people were born into their obligations to particular deities—family gods, civic gods, and (a special case) imperial gods. If these pagans became Christ-followers, ceasing to honor their gods with cult, they risked alienating heaven and thereby endangered their city. (Fredriksen 2017: 89–90)

When this link between human families and their gods is taken into account, the proclaimed transfer of those from the nations to worship Israel's God can be seen as likely to create dissension from gentile neighbors whose welfare and that of their city thus appeared to be threatened. As noted already in relation to Romans ch. 8, the insecurity and possibility of suffering were responded to by Paul with emphasis upon the security supplied by the Spirit (8:26-27), by Christ (8:34) and by the love of God (8:28, 39). Paul knows how insecure non-Jews separated from their traditional allegiances could feel. Something of the risk of angering the gods by failing to honor them lies behind some of Paul's arguments/statements in Romans. The Deuteronomic scripture gives confidence in that it claims that the gods of the nations are as nothing compared with the God of Israel. "I am He; there is no god beside me" (Deut. 32:39)—a text that does not necessarily mean that the gods of the nations no longer exist but rather that they have no power compared with the God of Israel.

Paul wants to confirm Israel's irrevocable call (Rom. 11:29), in that the God of Israel does not recall/rescind the gifts he has given, but Paul also wants to stress that the call

---

[8] Rock notes, "The Deuteronomic ideology therefore establishes that world order begins not on earth, but in heaven under the supreme God of Israel and of the universe (the Most High—Deut. 32:8); it is a story about the divine creation of Israel. Israel is the property of God and owes her total existence as a protected and prosperous people to the Lord alone. It therefore follows that God intervenes in the affairs of Israel in times of distress" (2010: 83).

does not constitute favoritism. This call is determined by the righteous character of Israel's God—the probing questions raised in Rom. 3:1-8 indicate the saliency of these issues in Rome as we have shown earlier and also the intrinsic relationship between 3:1-8 and chs. 9–11. These demonstrate that Israel's disputed status among the gods as noted here is a matter of discussion/debate but not of general consensus in the gossip[9] of the Roman neighborhoods (Flower 2017: 162–74). Our assumption here is that there would have been social irritation with those who would not conform to popular expected patterns of honoring the gods, and resulting ideological disparagement of these who were different. The incoming of the nations in some affiliation with Israel has disturbed accepted presuppositions related to Israel's status among the gods. If the allocation of the nations to the protection and patronage of "the gods" constituted the agenda of the heavenly council noted above, this would help to explain Paul's interest in how Israel had first been chosen by her God. The allocation of the nations to the protection and patronage of the gods constituted the agenda for the heavenly council. Thus "I will have mercy on whom I will (have mercy)" would resonate with this narrative (Rock 2012: 302–8).

The use of the Deuteronomic pattern of righteousness and judgment in its wider context may be part of the reason for this text being chosen for citation. It is not limited to issues between Jews and the incoming of the nations but links back to the fundamental question of the righteous character of Israel's God. This factor helps explain part of the content of these chapters, particularly the theme of jealousy in chs. 10–11. In Romans 9–11, Paul not only affirms the call of Israel and seeks to justify this in relation to the nations, but he does so by pointing out that Israel has experienced God's righteous discipline/judgment as evidence of his grace so that a remnant rather than the entire people is currently responding affirmatively to Paul's gospel. But as noted, the salvation of Israel after judgment is a part of God's vindication as the faithful covenant Lord—the vindication of his people is bound up with the Lord's own vindication (Lincicum 2010: 161).

Romans 9:14–29: The Sovereign Creator, the God of Israel—"I Will Have Mercy on Whom I Will"

[14] What then are we to say? There is no injustice on God's part, is there? Far from it! [15] For he says to Moses, "I will have mercy on whomever I have mercy, and I will have compassion on whomever I have compassion." [16] So then it depends not on the one who wills, nor on the one running, but on God who shows mercy. [17] For the scripture says to Pharaoh, "I have raised you up for the very purpose of showing my power in you, so that my name may be proclaimed in all the earth." [18] So then he has mercy on whomever he chooses, and he hardens the heart of whomever he chooses. [19] You will say to me then, "Why then does he still find fault? For no one can

---

[9] Elliott refers to "the scurrilous generalizations likely to be heard on the Roman streets about the returning exiles as unworthy beneficiaries of Nero's clemency" (2008: 106).

resist his will?" ²⁰Nay rather who are you, a human being, to answer back to God? Will what is molded say to the one who molds it, "Why have you made me like this?" ²¹Surely the potter has power over the clay, to make out of the same lump one treasured and one ordinary vessel? ²²What if God, desiring to put his wrath on display and to make his power known, has endured with much patience the vessels of wrath that are ripe for destruction; ²³and what if he has done so in order to make known the riches of his glory for the vessels of mercy, which he has prepared beforehand for glory—²⁴including us whom he has called, not from the Jews only but also from the nations? ²⁵As indeed he says in Hosea, "Those who were not not 'my people' I will call 'my people,' and 'the-not-beloved' (I will call) 'beloved.'" ²⁶"And in the very place where it was said to them, 'You are not my people,' there they shall be called sons of the living God." ²⁷And Isaiah cries out concerning Israel, "If the Israelites be countless as the sand of the sea, the remnant of them will be saved; ²⁸for the Lord will execute his sentence on the earth quickly and decisively." ²⁹And as Isaiah predicted, "If the Lord of hosts had not left us seed, we would have fared like Sodom and been made like Gomorrah."

That a significant stage in Paul's argumentation has been reached is indicated by the τί οὖν ἐροῦμεν "what then shall we say" formula, succeeded by the anticipated repudiation. The false inference μὴ ἀδικία παρὰ τῷ θεῷ ("There is no injustice with God, is there?") represents the interlocutor's wrong inference, which is to be categorically rejected. The content of the question links back to what seem to be rather arbitrary choices by the God of Israel in choosing who will participate in his election purpose as described in 9:6-13. There is some doubt in the mind of the interlocutor, representing voices in Rome, whether the God of the Jews, the Judean God as he may have been perceived from an etic perspective, is just and fair in his dealings with people. That this issue is important is indicated, as we have argued above, by the introductory formula, "what then shall we say" succeeded by the μὴ γένοιτο response. Together these repeated formulae point to this, that is, the character of Israel's God, a topic to be reverently discussed as being a significant issue in Paul's agenda for his letter. We bear in mind here that gentile Christ-followers did not have knowledge of the God of Israel from birth, and that their cultural repertoire included inherited and cultivated notions of the gods that differed in many respects from Jewish teaching. These gods differed in their attributed justice, anger, and impartiality. In light of this, the doubt about Israel's God is not such an outrageous inference as it might first seem, even though it is a very serious one since it touches on the gods and their attitude to differing peoples. The question is how the deity of a subjugated people could have the power to bestow blessings on a foreign people (cf. Young 2015: 30). Clearly for Paul, this "Judean" God is not the localized God of Judea but the God of all Creation.

Why or why not, and on what terms should those from the nations share in the heritage of Israel? Paul has already argued that Abraham is destined to become the father of both Jews and non-Jews. By this means, that is, trust in Christ, Paul represents Abraham as offering and providing Abrahamic descent through Christ to non-Jews. Significantly, this access is not on the normal terms of having to adopt the Law, the ancestral pattern of Jewish life (for Jews), but through trust in the Creator God of

Israel, through Christ's work of reconciliation. The integrity of God may well be seen as threatened if it appears that the gentile newcomers to Abraham's kinship are, with Paul's advocacy, introducing incompatible life patterns that must necessarily conflict with the traditions of Israel.

What becomes apparent as we study the progress of Paul's argument here is that it has to do with God's compassion, and that compassion as directed particularly to the people of Israel. Even Pharaoh fits this analysis since through him as well as through Israel, God's power and glory are manifested. As Paul's cited texts (Mal. 1:2-3 and Exod. 33:19) indicate, God's purpose of election has to do with divine compassion to Israel. These are not an explanation of predestination as a systematic presentation about God's choice and rejection of individuals as was expounded several centuries ago (cf. Sievers 2000: 127–73). The interlocutor's question sets the agenda, rather than a balanced presentation of God's justice in human terms. The key text for Paul is Exodus 32–34 from which he cites; it is the theme for the ensuing discussion "I will have mercy/show compassion on whom I will have mercy." Other texts and allusions will enter the scene, but all are to be read in light of the divine compassion. An analysis of Paul's use of texts demonstrates that Paul sets out primary texts almost as headings, which point toward and, to some extent determine, the meaning of lesser, secondary texts within his narrative. Not all cited texts have equal significance in the narrative, some serving a primary rhetorical function but others only a secondary role in this context. Here Exodus 32–34 denotes the primary text for Paul (Campbell 1979).

This overarching theme of compassion applies first to the use of the terms "love" and "hate" in relation to God in the citation of Mal. 1:2-3. These are technical terms for describing God's choice in relation to the covenant, not to be confused with emotional reactions to others. The Hebrew root *sana* of the Greek verb μισέω is not an exact equivalent to the English word "hate," God does not hate Ishmael or Isaac; it is better to read "I did not prefer" or "I did not choose" because the context is choice for a particular purpose. But if God's compassion is thus presented as Israel-oriented, one may question why this should be. The fuller explanation requires an exploration of God's covenant with Israel and through her to the nations, but there is a given, the fact of God's choice to make one vessel for a special purpose and another for a menial task, as Paul will suggest in 9:21-24. Earlier exegetes focused on Paul's arguments to explain the incoming of the nations, and the problem of finding equality for them with their Jewish brothers. But here in Romans, the context has changed and the issues have been reversed in that now the problem is why should Israel be chosen, especially since she is not persuaded that Jesus is the Messiah. One imperfect solution that could be proposed is that Israel has now been cast off and the nations chosen "in her place" (as 11:17 is erroneously translated in the RSV, and surprisingly still in the NRSV, but now corrected in the NRSVUE). But this solution, however amenable to translation scholars who ought to be better informed, is rejected more than once by Paul in Romans 9–11 as well as in earlier chapters. This is because Paul's understanding of the divine righteousness does not create a binary either/or argument in contrasting it with posited divine justice and impartiality. In this righteous purpose of God in history, his purpose includes Jews as well as the nations, and their role in relation to each other is determined by this purpose, not by favoritism, or by human achievement in which the strong must have the advantage.

As Paul hints, the divine purpose does not necessarily accord with normal human patterns and values, as in his inversion of the role of siblings—the elder will serve the younger, and in this instance, one twin brother will be preferred before the other. In earlier debates since the Reformation, the interpretation has often got stuck in intricate debates about elected individuals such as whether Tom, Dick, or Harry will inherit the kingdom or be cast out. But this is to read modern individualism into Paul in a manner that fails to understand historical development or to distinguish Paul's era from Augustine's and ours. Nothing could be clearer in reading Paul's letters that he has an important place for individual persons within the body of those who together are "in Christ," and in the final judgment from which no individual can be omitted. But the individuals' social identity is derived from the collective of which they are part and has no independent existence in isolation. The universal scope of Paul's gospel accentuates this. And in Romans Paul deals with larger issues, especially the relation of Jews, whether in Christ or not, the nations and the gospel. Individuals are not ignored but they appear in their association and inclusion with the larger groupings from which their social identity derives (Tajfel 1978). The point of emphasis is not upon individuals *as such* but on chosen leaders like, for example, Moses and a remnant to secure the future of the entire people Israel. Romans focuses not on individuals and their final destiny but on God's purpose for Israel and the nations within history (Leenhardt 1961: 249–50, cf. also Stowers 1994: 229).

The sovereign Creator, the God who revealed himself to Israel, has the freedom to achieve his purposes within history in ways that are appropriate to his character. But we must be careful not to generalize or to read more into Paul's statements than he intended. Although, in the initial call of people, one son is chosen in preference to another, this pattern of selection involving Israel and the nations will not continue once Israel is chosen and constituted. At this point, the story of Israel's call does not terminate with the choice of Isaac but continues in the choice of Jacob, and with that choice (i.e., of Jacob), Israel has been constituted, and no such selection will occur thereafter in the Israel whom God has called. That is because "the differentiation into Israel and the nations is made only after Jacob becomes Israel (Gen. 32:28)" (Ehrensperger 2019: 240–1, n35). This is the reason why I have stressed that the theme of 9:6-13 is "how Israel was called"—how Israel became Israel.

So, Paul is not dealing with speculative questions about what the gods might do, though these lie behind some of the questions, but he is dealing with the traditions of Israel, and how this God reveals himself in history. His presupposition is that the answers to questions about how God acts or will act are to be found in Israel's scriptures. As noted, the God of Israel includes Pharaoh within his narrative in Exod. 9:16 in that Pharaoh can be used to serve the divine purpose as well as Israelites,[10] so that he too can be a participant in the purpose to reveal the God of Israel's power and to proclaim his name (9:17). "God's action upon Pharaoh was part of the means, not only of rescuing Israel from slavery, but of declaring God's name to the world" (Wright 2002: 639). The

---

[10] Jewett in a careful comparison of Paul's text with that of Exod. 9:16 notes how Paul adjusts the text to state "for this very purpose I have raised you up" in order to place more emphasis upon divine action and intentionality through repetition (2007: 84).

sovereign God of Israel is the one who determines—this is based not on human will or achievements, but on God who shows mercy. This is the God of Exodus 32-34 who was revealed to Moses whom Paul is expounding and whose ruling characteristic is compassion and mercy. Thus, Wengst entitles 9:19-23 as "Das Übergewicht von Gottes Erbarmen," "The Preponderance of God's Mercy" (2008: 305). As Jewett asserts, "Paul applies the widely shared teaching about Pharaoh's hardening in order to make the much more controversial case that God's mercy is sovereign" (2007: 586). If the hardening of Pharaoh's heart resulted (from what we can know of this), from his own unwillingness to submit to the Creator God, then it is possible to see in the hardening of Pharaoh's heart an expression of God's love and compassion for Israel (Rodriguez 2014: 183).

As noted, the underlying issue in Rom. 9:14-29, is not whether God's compassion should extend to the nations, but rather, now that it has reached the nations whether that compassion still includes the people of Israel. *It is probably significant that Paul insists here that God has the right to harden whom he wills which we will later discover includes Israel also, for the sake of the nations.* It would be most unlikely if the calling of the nations alongside Israel did not raise significant issues, since Israel's history and claims in relation to her God were well known. One of the resultant questions concerns the source of these questions—are they raised by Israelites or by those from the nations? The reception history would tend to indicate Jews but I think it is more likely from an overview of the text that these emanated from a gentile source in Rome.

The first reference to the (gentile) nations in chs. 9–11 only appears in 9:24, the significance of which is frequently exaggerated when the nations are considered as becoming part of Israel through Christ rather than a separate group of people. The choice of Israel is primary, but alongside this Paul is keeping in mind Romans ch. 4 where he demonstrated that the nations now also have Abraham as their father, by means of the promise actualized. The incoming of the "nations" is never far from the horizon of this discussion. So, Paul in 9:25 turns to the prophetic words of Hosea 1-2 "Those who were not my people, I will call 'my people,' and her who was not beloved, I will call my beloved." As Dodd states, "It is rather strange that Paul has not observed that this prophecy referred to Israel, rejected for its sins, but destined to be restored." But it was Dodd's further comment that caused me to check, "strange because it would have fitted so admirably the doctrine of the restoration of Israel which he is to expound in ch. 11" (Dodd 1932: 160). The original referent for these verses was not the gentile peoples as Paul knows very well, and the nations are not the focus of his narrative. The reference to the nations comes in almost as an aside, and Paul does not stop to pay attention to their "incoming" but pushes on with the argument.

I maintain therefore that Paul does not use the Hosea citations primarily with reference to "gentiles" since this was not the original reference, and since it is immediately followed by two other scriptural citations that have the same point of reference, that is, Israel. "Rejected Israel," like the northern tribes, will be restored. This is Paul's primary thesis in keeping with the Hosea context, but in and with the restoration, another non-people, the ethnē, will also be blessed. Paul does apply the Hosea citations from 2:23 and 2:1 (LXX) in a secondary sense, typologically, to "gentiles" also, but only after he has first used these appropriately to refer to Israel (Campbell 2000: 187–211). In light of the divine freedom to have compassion on whom he wills, even the non-peoples, the nations, as Paul has shown, can be chosen. But here Paul's emphasis is Israel-oriented, so the incoming of non-people ("gentiles") points also to the restoration of Israel who continues to trust in God *but not in Christ*. In light of this, perhaps it would be better to think in terms of God's activity, God's action whether in relation to Israel or to the nations in that this can encompass both groups and involve both judgment and blessing. Thus, Wengst appropriately titles 9:1-33 as "God's Electing Activity on Behalf of Israel and the Nations" (2008: 287, cf. Fitzmyer 1993: 571).

Romans 9:22-29 A Hypothesis—What If God Were to Act in This Way?

Paul's openness to a positive future for both "foolish ethnē" and, by analogy, presently unpersuaded Israel is indicated in an incomplete sentence starting in 9:22. It seems like a reaction to the stark assertion in 9:18 that God can have mercy upon or harden whom he wills. The interlocutor responds, "Then why does he still find fault? For who can resist his will?" The diatribal answer, as also in 2:1, "O man, who are you to argue with God?" is a retort rather than an adequate response. But the beginnings of an answer appear in Paul's image of the potter forming and re-forming the clay, not casting it away but shaping it into a specialized vessel while another portion is for menial tasks (9:20-21). The emphasis here seems to be on the differing uses to which the pots are put, and there is no sign of the vessels created being thrown away. The hypothetical "what if" continues the shaping of an answer, even though it remains incomplete—an anacoluthon. This is not an assertion but a tentative hypothesis, "What if God, desiring to show his wrath and to make known his power, has endured with much patience the objects of wrath ripe for destruction?" Barrett's rendering is suggestive "What if, as is the case …?" (1962: 189). Paul's hypothetical question asks, what is the problem if God is too patient with rebellious people, that is, primarily the world of gentile sinners? This possibly here also has a bearing upon discussions about the future of Israel. What if God is more compassionate than they deserve or than we would expect him to be? This open-ended and incomplete sentence resonates with the pattern of rhetorical questions frequently used in Romans (see listing of rhetorical questions in Excursus I, pp. 44–8). These typically make a suggestion arising in the sequence of a discussion as a possible inference but followed by a question, so that a conclusion is only tentatively proposed as something to be considered as a possible reading of divine activity in relation to human response.

This hypothesis represents a similar process of reasoning—a voicing of possible responses or courses of action. This response implies a complaint against God's compassion, hence the earlier reference to Exodus 32–34. The Malachi 1 citation might be taken to imply that God can equally as easily reject as elect, as the interlocutor's retort in 9:20 indicates, but Paul's hypothesis invites consideration of the suggestion that God's purposes are determined only by his all-encompassing mercy (Dunn 1988b: 553). The hypothesis is elaborated to give more precise information, "and what if he has done so in order to make known the riches of his glory for the objects of mercy, which he has prepared beforehand (8:29-30) for glory[11]—including us whom

---

[11] There is resonance here with the string of verbs of divine action: foreknew, predestined, called, justified, and glorified, listed in 8:28-30. The first two words in this chain, προέγνω and προώρισεν,

he has called, not from the Jews only but also from the nations?" (9:24). The potter image shows that Paul's line of thought here proceeds along a trajectory of reusing and remodeling the clay with which he works, its first nuance is transformation rather than casting off, although the sovereignty of assigning to a particular function is also present in Paul's reading.

In 9:24, we note that Paul uses Jews rather than Israel. "Us whom he has called, not from the Jews only but also from the 'gentiles'." But the term Jews has no negative overtones. Paul is talking here primarily in ethnic terms—he wants to stress the incoming of the nations alongside the inclusion of Israel. The inclusive terminology in 9:24 "not from the Jews only" has been (mis)interpreted to mean that Israel now comprises both Jews and the nations since both are explicitly identified within the goal of God's saving calling. But Paul does not state that the nations, that is, ethnē in Christ, are part of Israel. There can be no doubt that both are included in God's saving purpose, it necessarily includes both of these. But both these are included as two different entities not as one. Israel and the nations remain the differing categories of Paul's symbolic universe, and Israel as Paul understood her, was only one of these. The content of 9:24 does not warrant, and cannot support the weight of, an assertion that this text demonstrates the inclusion of gentile Christ-followers in Israel. It states only that the "us whom God has called" includes Jews *as Jews* as well as "gentiles" as "gentiles" among those called. It denies equally, "not from the Jews only" and "not from the ethnē only," meaning that both are represented but not as de-ethnicized humans, and the one at the expense of replacing the other. That Israel may be constituted of both Jews and non-Jews is a major step that requires more substantiation than is available in this text or any other elsewhere in Romans. If, as we shall discover later, Jews and non-Jews do reappear in this text, that is, in Romans, should this hypothesized change in content (of the term "Israel") not be more visibly and strongly nuanced than appears in the remainder of Romans 9–11. The image of the olive tree where non-Jews are still called "a wild olive shoot," and the claim that rescue has come to the nations to make "Israel" jealous do not give any adequate rationale for changing the meaning of the term "Israel" (Campbell 2018: 233–6, 244–6, Ehrensperger 2019: 229–46).

Paul's extended hypothesis suggests that in this apostle's view, the God of Israel is more patient than he is expected to be. The terminology, vessels of wrath, and vessels of mercy imply his using nations for different functions in his sovereign purpose. It presupposes that the God of Israel is operating with a purpose within the world which he has created. But everything in these verses is hypothetical—so Paul is not affirming a known purpose of God, so much as inferring as to how this purpose might be described. What is important is that *for Paul the overarching purpose of God is one of compassion for both the nations and also for Israel*. The God of Israel's actions differ radically from the ascribed patterns of behavior of the pagan gods previously worshipped by the nations. So, Paul's hypothesis is to ask whether it might not be the case that God's patience will allow the non-people, the nations who were not chosen as was Israel, access to grace through Christ. Similarly, might this same God not also be

feature the προ prefix that appears also in 9:23 (προητοίμασεν), "prepared in advance" (Rodriguez 2014: 186, n54).

patient with presently unconvinced Israel to restore her to himself? Might not the God who made access possible through Christ for the nations, not also restore his rebellious people to himself? Paul then continues in 9:27 his discussion concerning the possible compassion of God to both Israel and the nations by citing further reassuring texts, this time from Isaiah confirming that after the actualization of God's word (λόγον συντελῶν) his mercy ensures that a remnant will be saved to continue God's purposes for Israel.

In v. 27, LXX Isa. 10:22 is cited, "Though the number of the children of Israel were like the sand of the sea a remnant will be saved." The emphasis lies on the fact that a remnant will be saved from the people. In the context of judgment, it is affirmed that a remnant will still be saved—the "only" in v. 27 is gratuitous commentary (cf., e.g., the Zurich Bible). The remnant presupposes judgment having been executed and, because of that, the fact of a remnant is always a sign of hope—that God has not completed his work through that people, who therefore still have a future (and to use the terminology of "rejected" in relation to Israel with its note of finality in English is premature and therefore inappropriate). It does not pay sufficient heed to the scriptures' potential reversal of punishment (cf. Reasoner 2014: 388–404).

Again, a conditional note is struck in a second citation, this time from Isa. 10, "If the Lord of hosts had not left σπέρμα to us, we would have fared like Gomorrah and been made like Sodom" (9:29). This text again denotes the patience and mercy of the Lord. The references to Sodom and Gomorrah are reminiscent of the nations described in 1:18-32 (Esler 2003: 51–63), but the remnant theme relates first to Israel. As we noted in relation to ch. 8, Christ-followers from the nations have received adoption, not into Israel, but into the larger "family" of God, so it is more probable that it is Israel in the first instance that the Hosea citations in 9:25-26 are meant to indicate. When we look closely at their content this confirms our application. While it is very appropriate to describe the "ethnē" as a non-people, in ch. 8 they have already been called through Christ as representatives of the nations alongside Israel. Hosea's children's naming and renaming signify the process whereby Israel is first of all "rejected," but then the "rejection" is reversed and Israel's status as "children of the living God" restored (Ehrensperger 2005). One of the problems of reading Romans as a whole as Paul's argument for the nations' equal access with Jews to the promises of God is that the gentile connection and incoming receives too much attention, and the positive reversal of judgment through the remnant for Israel far too little. Thus, as Rodriguez rightly notes, by reading 9:25-26 as references to the "gentiles" Jewett, Morales, and Wright focus attention on the latter rather than on *Israel's* reversal of fortunes (Rodriguez 2014: 188, n61).

Romans 10

Romans 9:30–10:3: Israel Stumbling but Still in the Race

³⁰*What then are we to say? Shall we say that ethnē who were not striving for righteousness, have attained it, that is, righteousness through trust;* ³¹*but that Israel, who did strive for the law of righteousness, did not achieve that law.* ³²*Why so? Because it (is) not from trust, but as if from works. They have stumbled over the stumbling stone,* ³³*as it is written, "See, I am laying in Zion a stumbling stone, even a rock of offense, and he who trusts in it will not be put to shame."*

10 ¹*Brothers, my heart's desire and prayer to God for them is for their restoration.* ²*I can testify that they have a zeal for God, but not in accordance with knowledge.* ³*For, being ignorant of the righteousness of God, and trying to establish (it) for themselves, they have not submitted to God's righteousness.*

Rom. 9:30 is both an introduction to a new section and a summing up of the previous section. With v. 30, we reach another stage in the argumentation signified by the presence of the τί οὖν ἐροῦμεν "what then shall we say," formula, but without the common accompanying μὴ γένοιτο. We concur here with Garroway (2012: 103–5) and Rodriguez (2014: 94–5) that this is one of a very few occasions that Paul may actually agree with his interlocutor since he offers no dissent and since the content of the verse is not in opposition to Paul's thought. This is possibly how some Roman Christ-followers may have viewed the arrival of the gentile mission. The nations seem to have "stumbled" almost accidentally upon the righteousness through Christ, since they were not striving (διώκων) for it, whereas Israel even though she sought Torah, failing to understand her own Torah, stumbled over God's action in Christ. It is possible though he does not as yet say so, that Paul sees Christ as the goal that Israel missed, and thus he became the stone over which she stumbled.

It is most important to identify precisely what Paul diagnoses here as the reason for Israel's "stumbling." He refers to Israel in the third person, "They have stumbled over the stumbling stone," as it is written "See, I am laying in Zion a stumbling stone, even a rock of offense, and whoever trusts in it shall not be put to shame" (9:32-33, citing Isa. 8:14; 28:16). Notice that Paul does not simply equate Jews and the nations here as both being sinners. He depicts the nations as not even striving for righteousness, but qualifies it by stating he means the righteousness of trust. He distinguishes the two entities, and it is particularly important to consider his diagnosis of where he thinks Israel and the ethnē may have gone astray.

The dominant imagery here is of runners in a race, one of whom stumbles. The citation in 9:33 comes from Isa. 28:16, and Paul will inform us in 11:11 that though Israel stumbled, she did not fall. This will prove significant, since Paul obviously thinks that Israel has not dropped out of the race, while the nations have actually found righteousness through Christ. The nations have received gratuitously that which they did not pursue, but Israel has failed to reach this goal, despite her social capital—her illustrious heritage of the Torah and the prophets, and so on. Rodriguez makes a decisive clarification here. What Israel did not attain in seeking a valid target, righteousness according to the Torah, was Torah itself (2014: 194). Paul's diagnosis of the reasons for Israel's not achieving Torah are based on earlier traditions that have already identified Christ as the stone of stumbling from Isaiah.

In light of Israel's resistance to recognizing the arrival of Messianic Time, the faithful remnant who were already fully persuaded identified Jesus Christ as the stone over which Israel stumbled, and confirmed this in their rereading of the scriptures, especially of Isaiah. The fact that Isa. 28:16 (LXX) states, "Look, I myself am putting in place, as the foundations of Zion, a stone both valuable and chosen, a precious cornerstone, as her foundations, and whoever puts his trust in it will certainly not be put to shame" resonated with their convictions about Jesus as the Christ.[1] Paul indicates this reading of scripture by setting Isa. 8:14 in association with Isa. 28:16 (Wagner 2003: 131–4, Davis 2002: 120–30). The Hebrew text of the former sets out God's oracle of judgment against both houses of Israel, which we noted above would have been totally consuming had it not been for divine intervention in retaining a righteous remnant to ensure a future for his people. But the combined citation of Isa. 8:14 with 28:16 enables Paul to emphasize not only judgment but trust ὁ πιστεύων—a vindication of those who, as we shall see, recognize the arrival of Messianic Time. We note in passing that Paul identifies Christ-following Jews as the remnant, and in correlation with this, those Jews not recognizing the dawning of Messianic Time as not hearing and consenting to the word of the gospel. Those who do hear and consent comprise the righteous remnant, but this does not necessarily mean a tiny number as is often casually assumed; it could have been quite significant, especially in the earliest days of the Christ-movement before this became more gentile-oriented. Stark is surely correct to claim that the explanation of the rapid growth of Christianity after 150 CE requires the positing of large numbers of Jews responding positively to the Christ-message (1986: 314–29).

Continuing the interlocutory style, Paul asks simply "why" (διὰ δί, v. 32). If our reading of this verse is correct, it is Paul's conversation partner who explains Israel's misstep as "Because not out of trust but as if out of works." Most likely this means that they could not see that now the nations could get access to God through trust in Christ rather than by doing ἔργα νόμου. This clearly could have been the words of Paul

---

[1] On the textual difficulties and other issues involved in the Isaiah passages for further details, see Jewett (2007: 612–14), Wengst (2008: 319–27), Rodriguez (2014: 195–7).

himself, but in any case, Paul approves it and expands on it in v. 32c-33. He confirms, "They stumbled upon the stumbling stone" and gives scriptural support in v. 33, as we have noted above.

Up to this point, we have more or less followed traditional readings of 9:30–10:13, which presume that Paul is here analyzing why Israel as a whole did not respond positively to the message concerning the arrival of Messianic Time in Christ. In 10:2, Paul acknowledges that Israel does have zeal for God but is misinformed. Not a word is spoken against zeal itself. Paul does not criticize zeal but rather zeal for a wrong cause.[2] Israel's response does not consist only in not being persuaded that the Messiah is Jesus, but she lacks the specific understanding of the implications of the Christ-event, that is, the changes for Jews and ethnē that necessarily proceed from this. Paul claims that Israel did not see the arrival of God's way of righteousness in Christ (which included the incoming of the nations, as nations, i.e., without becoming Jews). Failing to comprehend this, Jews sought to maintain (στῆσαι) their own previous pattern of righteousness, that is, a righteousness limited by the observance of the Law, and therefore exclusive to Jews alone. Thus, they did not acknowledge the mission to the nations as God's new way of rectifying the ethnē, and its radical implications for their own understanding of the God of Israel.

The diagnosis of Paul that the Jews did not submit to God's righteousness does not entail that the Jews were opposed to God's righteousness as such—they could not see, and hence did not recognize, God's activity in the Christ-event, especially in the acceptance of the ethnē as ethnē. Prior to the coming of Christ, the only way open for "gentiles" to relate to the God of Israel had been to become a proselyte or remain a God-fearer on the margins of Jewish life. Being ignorant of the righteousness that now comes from God becomes here a reason for Israel's failure to recognize the gospel particularly the incoming of the ethnē apart from observing the Law. That God's righteousness has been revealed apart from the Law, allowing the ethnē to follow Christ and to worship the God of Israel without having to keep the Law, was not recognized by the majority of Israel. That of which they were ignorant was that, in the coming of Christ, God's way of rectifying the unrighteous nations had been revealed. They did not see that for the nations God had now acted to provide a way to be right with him without having to become Jews and thus to observe the Law.

To explain his understanding of Israel's failure to understand God's revelation in Christ, Paul turned again to the scriptures for illumination. Thus, he found in a powerful image of runners running in a race in which some stumble, as depicted in Isa. 8:14 and 28:16, an explanation for Israel's present non-acceptance of the Christ-message. Israel could not understand how the ethnē could be accepted by trust apart from the Law. So, the stumbling stone in 9:33 includes the arrival of Christ as Messiah, but it consisted also in the inability of some Jews to recognize the divine acceptance

---

[2] Ehrensperger (2022b) sees a continuity in Paul's concern with the distinction between profane and holy in his earlier persecution of Christ-followers (due to their association in an ἐκκλησία with ethnē who would have attracted impurity through continuing in polytheistic cult practices), and his work as apostle to the ethnē who, having turned away from idols, could attain a status of holiness through purification in Christ. Throughout his life, Paul was still concerned with the holiness of God and his people.

of Christ-following ethnē apart from the yoke of the Law (Meyer 1980: 59–78). Thus, although the recognition of Christ as Messiah of Israel was central to this new movement, according to Paul, the stumbling had a gentile dimension to it as well (Gaston 1987: 129).[3] It was the entire Christ-event with its opening of access to ethnē apart from commitment to the Law that Israel did not perceive as a new revelation of God. In the two biblical passages Paul combined to explicate his message, these both referred to God's action and trust in it. So, it might be more accurate here to claim that not all Jews were able to discern God's righteous activity in Christ, including especially in the eschatological pathway for non-Jews. It was this gentile outcome of the Christ-event that they stumbled over—though in the end the obstacle was theological rather than Christological, God-centered rather than Christ-centered. They were not opposed to differing conceptions of messianic scenarios, to which they were accustomed, but they did not see God's hand in the Christ-event leading to the gentile mission. Many of them could accept and appreciate the former even where they differed. The righteousness of God was fundamental to Jewish convictions. But with the increase in numbers in the gentile response and the claim of a new revelation of righteousness that involved the nations, the latter claim could not find acceptance among many Jews.

One of several reasons was a Jewish skepticism about gentiles' ability to separate themselves from idolatry and all its cultural manifestations. To be a Jew required no less than eighth-day circumcision and commitment to the familial life-long obligations into which the child was thus introduced. A second reason for a negative response from Jews to Paul's gentile gospel in its social manifestation was a fear of political trouble between Jews and non-Jews that might irrupt when Paul's converts ceased reverencing their Roman gods. In the past, the Jews had often got into disputes with civic authorities through hostile interactions arising substantially from gentile neighbors, and they would wish to avoid such at all costs. Of course, the fact that ethnē in Christ as non-Jews were counseled not to observe the Law, and the repercussions of this pattern for Jews with whom they were in contact was an important consideration that also had strong influence. What we note is that it is too simplistic to regard the proclamation of Jesus as the Messiah, though decisively important, as of itself the deciding factor that hindered the majority of Jews from joining in the Christ Movement or recognizing the Pauline pattern of the mission to non-Jews.

As previously at the beginning of Romans 9, and as he will repeat at the beginning of ch. 11, Paul commences by stressing his concern for "them," his own people Israel. In 10:2-3, he witnesses concerning his view of Israel's response to the message about Christ which, as we have shown above, demonstrates that Israel had heard "they have a zeal for God" but are "ignorant of the righteousness of God." Israel had heard the proclamation of a new time *but did not fully comprehend in that she did not discern God's action in Christ as now requiring the in-bringing of the ethnē as ethnē, and without the Law.* It was not that the ethnē were *not* to be related in some way to the God of Israel, but rather how, that is, on what terms the ethnē were to be included, that

---

[3] Stephan Davis thinks Paul is deliberately ambiguous, and that the stone is a polyvalent symbol of the law, the Messiah and the "gentiles" (2002: 142–5). This is somewhat similar to Wayne Meeks (1991: 105–24).

caused Israel's tripping up. Nanos has greatly illuminated this image of Israel's reaction to the righteousness of God in Christ, which, though Paul depicts it as "stumbling," has tended to be read as a final falling out of a race rather than as a temporary, and therefore recoverable, stumbling (2018: 114–20). Years of ill-considered anti-Jewish New Testament readings and of Paul in particular have facilitated this exaggeration of Jewish "failure" as a terminal fall.

What Paul asserts metaphorically is that Israel stumbled as a runner might do in a race. A majority within Israel has tripped over the understanding of Christ as opening the door to ethnē apart from the Law. But Israel is still in the race. Later we will hear from Paul that, despite stumbling, and thus being delayed, Israel has not fallen out of the race (11:11). As noted above, we are dealing here with metaphorical descriptions of historical realities, and so we must be careful not to read more into these than may be intended. Surprisingly, the ethnē are responding positively to the message concerning the Christ, but a majority of the Jewish people are not. The order of events is not, in this new Messianic Time, "the Jews first and also the ethnē" as anticipated, but ethnē first, a surprising new revelation of God's grace.

A greater obstacle to positive Jewish response to this messianic message emerged when this incoming of the nations was misperceived by some of the Roman ethnē as "ethnē first and Israel not at all" (11:17-19). This pessimism regarding Israel probably emerged in analogy with the Roman perception of the gods transferring their protection from one nation to another, as indicated by success or failure in conflict. In the image of stumbling, Paul holds out hope for Israel, even more than hope, confidence that Israel, though delayed, will eventually be restored since he has just argued in ch. 9 that all Israel still belong to Israel (9:6). This was signaled particularly in Paul's severe lament in 9:2-3.and is also evidenced in our new reading of 9:6b as a rhetorical question. In Paul's denial that the word of God regarding Israel has fallen or failed ἐκπέπτωκεν (9:6a), he was able to affirm that "all those from Israel are Israel" (Nanos 2018: 116–20). This fits our analysis of Deut. 32 concerning the God of Israel's relations with his people, there is little place for Israel's "falling out of the race" in Paul's reading of Deuteronomy.

Romans 10:4: For the Goal of the Law Is Christ

⁴For the goal of the law is Christ so that there may be righteousness for everyone who trusts.

Rom. 10:4 is an important verse, not only because of its content, though this is significant in that it relates Law and Christ, possibly pointing to a potential Christological interpretation of the Law. This verse has been compressed, and seriously distorted into the slogan, "Christ is the end of the Law" (Keck 2005: 250). This tells us something of the anti-Jewish reception history (Campbell 2018: 51–77) that preferred this reading, and that has persisted over a long period so as to contravene the most natural meaning of the statement Paul makes here after having presented an entirely positive view of the Law in Romans 7–8. The New English Bible (NEB) reading even changes the Greek noun to a verb and translates "For Christ ends the law," making for a more forceful and one-sided statement. While it is hard for gentile scholars to understand fully the depth of loathing of Jews faced with ideas concerning the possible termination of the Law, for example, 7:7, more sensitivity could have been anticipated. This could have included how morality in Christianity could have been more involved with issues concerning how the ethical demands of the Law are to be fulfilled. Other English readings as in the Authorized Version (AV), Revised Version (RV), and New Revised Standard Version (NRSV) translate τέλος as "end," which can include both termination and goal within the scope of its meaning rather than termination only.

To take end in the sense of termination is a one-sided reading not warranted by the term τέλος.[4] In the past decades, it was difficult sometimes to get a fair hearing if one held to any kind of positive link between the Law and Christ. Charles Cranfield was a notable exception and checking the proofs for the second volume of his International Critical Commentary (ICC) commentary gave me ample opportunity to become acquainted with his positive stance on law in particular. Despite Sanders's opposition to the twin pillars of election and covenant in Paul, his research, particularly in his *Paul and Palestinian Judaism* (1977), helped turn the tide of opinion about Judaism as a legalistic religion and highlighted the bias against a positive meaning for the Law inherent in much mainline interpretation of Paul. Sanders helped swing the emphasis in the scholarly interpretation of Paul away from "contrast with" toward "comparison with" Judaism even if the patterns of religion were different. Zeal for the Law was often linked by scholars, for example Hengel, with a posited Jewish nationalism of which aspects of Paul seemed indicative (Ehrensperger 2022b). The relatively recent scholarly trend commonly labeled as "Paul within Judaism" is fully intelligible only in a post-Sanders interpretive community.[5] My own contribution to this perspective on Paul is that my research on gentile identity originated from the conviction that Paul would not oppose the continuation of keeping the Law by Christ-following Jews. I developed an interest in gentile Christ-followers' identity because I wanted to apply the same rules to all Christ-followers as for the ethnē in Christ (Campbell 2006: 93–6). This led me to affirm the ongoing validity of Jewish Christ-followers continuing to keep the Law.

That a positive statement concerning the Law and Christ is to be anticipated is indicated by phrases such as the Law of trust (3:27), the Law of the Spirit of life in Christ Jesus (8:2), and the Law of righteousness (9:31). At many points in Romans, Paul brings in references to the Law even where we would not expect these, or in strange combinations, for example, the law of works (3:27), or "the law of sin and death" (8:3). But the total impact of his use of νόμος, even taking these into account, must be guided by his fullest treatment of the topic in ch. 7 where his positive statement is incontrovertible, "So the Law is holy, and the commandment is holy, just and good" (7:12). Of course, Paul's presentation of problems in ch. 7 are to be viewed via the solution offered for ethnē in 8:1-17 where the Law through the power of the Spirit is

---

[4] When a student in Otto Michel's exegesis class in Tübingen, I remember him claiming that up to four historic churches part company in their reading of Rom. 10:4.
[5] Though Sanders himself as an interpreter of Paul is in some respects still representative of Paulinism (cf., e.g., Ehrensperger 2020). Note that Longenecker credits W. D. Davies with turning the tide in New Testament study in relation to Paul's rootedness in Judaism (2011: 326).

the route both to moral transformation and to final rescue. What we are noting here is that on the macro-level, Rom. 10:4 sits in a context bracketed on one side by Rom. 7:12 and on the other by Rom. 13:10.b, "love is the fulfilling of the Law," which put severe limits to the options for interpreting 10:4 negatively.

This indicates that even when addressing non-Jews, Paul does not view the Law when properly understood as in opposition to, or in competition with, the claims of Christ. Indeed, it has been asserted by Badenas, correctly in my view, in his useful study, *Christ, the End of the Law*, that all references to the Law in Romans 9–11 are positive (1985: 104). Our conclusion is that from a balanced overview of the evidence, the very negative view of the Law requiring its termination in Christ is less guided by Paul's letter to Rome than by a one-sided enculturated reception that reads Paul, not in *comparison* with, but under the influence of a widespread consensus in "Paulinism," in *contrast to Judaism*. Meeks is very critical of "Dunn's tortuous exegesis" in the attempt to prove that the righteousness promised in the law is the ἰδία δικαιοσύνη not the righteousness of God itself (10:3) (1991: 115, n31). Meeks offers a more positive view of the significance of the Law:

> Paul's surprising choice of words (in 9.31) proclaims that the righteousness promised in the law but unattained is not the ἰδία δικαιοσύνη that stands in opposition to the righteousness of God (10.3) but is God's righteousness itself, to which Torah and Prophets bear witness, even though it is manifested finally χωρὶς νόμου (3.21) (1991: 115).

Because the Torah genuinely did promise God's righteousness, and because God sent his son "that the δικαίωμα τοῦ νομοῦ be fulfilled among us" (8.3-4), 10.4 can only be understood as saying that for ethnē "Christ is the goal and completion of the law."

In fairness to these interpreters, the scene has now changed radically in that since 1990 it has become more common to view Romans as a letter addressed to the ethnē. This view originated with Munck (1959) whom I followed and, in the last two decades strongly advocated by Stowers (1994, cf. Nanos 2017: 285), as a letter addressed *only* to ethnē in Christ. The significance of this is that the link between Christ and the Law must now be considered not in how and whether the Law, since the coming of Christ, has any validity for the Jewish people (since in Romans these are not addressed). Rather the topic here must be the significance of Christ as the τέλος of the Law for gentile Christ-followers. It is to these that Paul affirms that Christ is the goal of the Law. It could be the case that Paul is attempting to explain to ethnē in Christ why Israel was not convinced that a new day had dawned in the Creator God of Israel's purpose for the world. But the ethnē are still the actual addressees and what is said here must have primary reference to them.

The fact that Paul begins this section (10:1) by referring to his addressees as brothers is significant. Only four times previously in this letter (1:13; 7:1, 4; 8:12) has Paul directly addressed them as "brothers" (ἀδελφοί). This direct reference indicates, therefore, that Paul is saying something of importance at this point that should resonate both with his own perspective and that of the tradition of the Roman ethnē. Thus whereas in 9:3, he called the people of Israel his brothers, ἀδελφοί κατὰ σάρκα, thereby distinguishing himself from his ethnē in Christ addressees, here he specifically identifies himself with the former as his brothers, even though the subject he is exploring is the theme of Israel's Law. Proceeding from the discussion concerning the stumbling of Israel with the connecting γάρ (for) Paul asserts in a brief but profound statement "for the τέλος of the law is Christ." Commentators have spent much effort in analyzing the content of what appears as a somewhat enigmatic statement, and as many as seven possible legitimate translations of this text (τέλος γάρ νόμου Χριστός) have been listed by Keck (2005: 249) and by Rodriguez (2014: 199). The principal ones are, in my opinion:

1. For Christ is the end of the Law
2. For Christ is the completion of the Law
3. For Christ is the fulfillment of the Law
4. For Christ is the goal of the Law

The merit of the traditional rendering as "end" is that it carries overtones of both end-as-termination and end-as-goal rather than only one of these. Thus, Leenhardt claims that Christ puts an end to the Law for the Law finds in him its goal and its crown (1961: 266). The second and third renderings have the merit of stressing the achievement of something, or the fulfilling of some function, by the Law. Thus, the NRSV translates as "For Christ is the end of the law *so that there may be righteousness for everyone who trusts*" [emphasis mine]. Karl Barth interprets τέλος, presuming that behind it lies the rabbinic concept of the *kelal*, as a comprehensive formula for the manifold content of the Law. He reads it in the sense of *anakephalaiosis*, the sum or totality of all that the Law stood for (*Church Dogmatics*, II, 2, 1957: 245). C. F. D. Moule possibly voices the concern of some Christian theologians that the goal of the Law is Christ might suggest that Christ is somehow equated with the Law, whereas the claim that God has acted in a new way in Christ requires that Christ should be greater than the Law (1967/68: 301).

But the context and Paul's presentation of this passage as well as the text itself indicates in my view that interpreting τέλος as goal is by far the most preferable sense of the term in this context. We read this in the sense that Christ is the goal of the Law with respect to God's plan to redeem the nations (Stowers 1994: 308). This implies that it is the function of both the Law and Christ in relation to the nations that is the primary issue.

Here, as often in Romans, Paul's aim is explanatory rather than polemical. That v. 4 is explained in vv. 5-13 is shown by the fact that Paul's interpretation in these verses picks up all the key terms in v. 4 except τέλος itself: law, righteousness, all, trust, Christ. The γάρ "for" with which v. 5 commences should thus offer a reinforcing of prior contentions rather than a negation of these. Casson takes issue particularly with Dunn's negative reading of 10:4 according to which "Christ is the termination of the law as a means of righteousness for all who have trust" (2019: 193). Casson's reading accords with our understanding of Rom. 7:7-25 that it is the gentile Christ-followers who die through Christ rather than that the Law has died or is terminated. If Paul were going to claim that the Law is terminated in Rom. 10:4, it seems strange that he would affirm its nature as "holy just and good" in ch. 7. It is not typical of Paul to claim the termination of one entity and its replacement by another so much as the transformation of one into the other through the Spirit. Thus a "termination" reading of 10:4 stands in vivid contrast within the context of 10:1-8, which preferences a "goal or fulfilment" reading. The use of τέλος in the common theological term "teleological" indicates that one, if not the dominant, use of τέλος cannot avoid some such emphasis as "goal," a significant factor in seeking to formulate a theology of Paul. Goal is now the preferred rendering of many commentators (e.g., Cranfield 1979, Fitzmyer 1993, Badenas 1985, Hays 1985, Keck 2005, Nanos 1996, and Rodriguez 2014, cf. also Casson 2019: 193). This is the consistent meaning of the word τέλος in ancient Greek as exemplified in a line from Plutarch's *Amatorius* 75E that is an exact parallel to Paul's expression, including the word order and lack of verb and article—τέλος γὰρ ἐπιθυμίας ἡδονή. This ought not to be translated to mean that pleasure is the termination of desire, but rather that the object or goal of desire is pleasure (Badenas 1985: 46–7). The central emphasis is a link between the Law and Christ that ensures that now there may be righteousness for *everyone who trusts*. No one will be excluded because they are ethnē. As Keck states, "To specify the law's telos as Christ is to assert that its purpose, its intent, the goal toward which it is oriented, that in which its inherent character is actualized, is an event called Christ" (Keck 2005: 250).

By concentrating on the possible meanings of 10:4a, we have in fact not yet given due weight to 10:4b, which explains the significance of Paul's viewing the goal of the Law as Christ. The purpose of Christ being the goal of the Law is so that (εἰς) there may be righteousness for everyone (παντί) who trusts. Here the posited link proposed between the Law and Christ is so that the ethnē may find righteousness. The ethnē do not have the Law, and even if they seek to observe the Law, because of sin they must fail to achieve this as shown already in ch. 7. So ethnē, without Christ and without the Spirit, cannot be δίκαιος.

But, according to Paul, a revelation of righteousness *for everyone*, both Jews and the nations, has been revealed in the coming of Christ. Paul's stress on all, πᾶς, is striking throughout Romans (occurring seventy times). It is particularly noteworthy here in Romans 10 where the universal appeal of Christ's work is mentioned. Paul added πᾶς to his citation in 10:11 of Isa. 28:16 LXX. "All" in Paul certainly resonates here with the "incoming" of the nations. It would be somewhat surprising to assume that Paul, having linked Christ and the Law as together pointing toward some single goal, would immediately *contrast* this with the covenantal pattern of Law observance. As we noted already in connection with 9:6, such readings present Paul as a bad rhetor and a worse teacher if he contradicts his immediately prior conclusions. Yet, in a general sense, this is precisely what has tended to be the consensus regarding the relation of 10:5-13 with what precedes.

Romans 10:5-10: How Christ Is the Goal of the Law

⁵*For Moses writes concerning the righteousness revealed by the law, that "the person who does these things will live by them." ⁶and the righteousness revealed through trust says, "Do not say in your heart, "Who will ascend into heaven?" [i.e., to bring*

Christ down] ⁷*or "Who will descend into the abyss?" [i.e., to bring Christ up from the dead].* ⁸*But what does it say? "The word is near you, on your lips and in your heart" [i.e., the word of trust that we proclaim]* ⁹*because if you confess with your lips that Jesus is Lord and trust in your heart that God raised him from the dead, you will be saved.* ¹⁰*For with the heart it is trusted unto righteousness and so one is rectified, and with the mouth it is confessed unto (your) rescue.*

As he already did in 9:1-5, Paul emphasizes in 10:1 his concern for Israel, "my heart's desire and prayer for them is for their restoration." It is significant that each of the verses, after Paul emphasizes in 10:1 his concern for his Israelite brothers, all begin with γάρ ("for") implying a continuation and further support for the content of the preceding verse. It reads like a continuous, consecutive train of thought. However, the γάρ ("for") in v. 5 and the δέ ("and") in v. 6 have traditionally been regarded as plainly denoting a contrast between law-righteousness and the righteousness of trust, following on from a negative reading of τέλος as termination of the Law in 10:4. But our reading is confirmed by the fact that Paul did not write the usual word ἀλλά, "but," rather he uses instead δέ, which can combine continuation with distinction *without making a strong contrast*. In 10:5, Paul compares the pattern of righteousness through the Law with the new pattern of righteousness for ethnē through trust in Christ, which has now been revealed.

So, when 10:4 is read as goal without the negative sense of termination, then we are able to avoid having to force δέ and γάρ into an artificial sense of contrast. This allows the γάρ of 10:5 to be read as indicating *how* Christ is the goal of the Law. Thus, we are not reading the argument of 10:5-13 as adversative, the δέ of v. 6 has only a normal *connective* or explanatory function (Stowers 1994: 309). Instead of setting out a contrast between law-righteousness (v. 5) and trust-righteousness (v. 6), Paul intends both citations to support his claim that the righteousness now realized in Christ is that to which Moses also pointed (Badenas 1985: 118–25). The hermeneutical significance of reading v. 6 in continuity with v. 5 is to avoid an adversative reading of v. 6 as if, in Paul's view, Moses should be read in opposition to the righteousness of trust. But Rom. 10:6-8 complements and supports 10:5, rather than opposing it (Stowers 1994: 308).

In the normal pattern of Jews following the Mosaic Torah, life was promised to those who kept Torah. Here Paul turns to Lev. 18:4-5, which states that "the person who does these things will live by them," that is, Moses promises that one will find life by doing the Law. This promise became a standard component in Jewish thought (cf. Ezek. 20:11, 13, 21). Similarly, Philo quotes Lev. 18:5 and adds, "So then the true life is the life of him who walks in the judgments and ordinances of God" (*Congr.* 16). In Rom. 7:10-11, Paul himself referred to "the very commandment that promised life" though he then explained that "it proved death to me," that is, we must remember that the "me" in 7:7-25 is not Paul of Tarsus speaking but the imagined gentile interlocutor (mistakenly) seeking to do works of Law by observing the Law without trust in Christ and thus apart from the Spirit. Cranfield interprets 10:4ff as indicating that Christ is the doer of the law who receives life, a view supported by Stowers but rejected by Keck (2005: 251). There is no critique here in 10:5-13 of Jews who observe Torah, but only an implied criticism of those who reject Christ and the new pattern of worshipping the God of Israel as ethnē.

Rather than criticizing Moses and faithful law-keeping, as a stereotypical reading of these verses (as) denoting a presupposed "Jewish legalism" might lead us to expect, Paul *continues* his explanatory argument in v. 6. It is unlikely if we agree that the goal of the Law is Christ, that Paul within the next two verses, would set righteousness from the Law, τὴν δικαιοσύνην τὴν ἐκ τοῦ νόμου, in opposition to the righteousness of trust, ἡ δὲ ἐκ πίστεως δικαιοσύνη, that is, the righteousness that the nations attained. Here, following the common pattern of moralists of personifying abstract concepts, Paul introduces a form of *prosōpopoiia*, speech-in-character, and personifies Righteousness by Faith, the righteousness that comes from trust in God (Jewett 2007: 631). After citing Moses on the promise of life that comes from doing the Law, Paul continues his same line of thought with the connecting word "δε," which should, as we have argued above, be translated as "and," providing a second citation concerning righteousness that supports and complements the first in v. 5 (Stowers 1994: 308–9). Casson's recent study on *Textual Signposts in the Study of Romans* is particularly relevant to the meaning of 10:4-5. She shows that Dunn's reading according to which "Christ is the termination of the law as a means to righteousness for all who have trust," is undermined by a procedural reading of the two instances of γάρ in these verses. She also asserts that the signposting role of γάρ within the immediate literary context of 10:1-8 preferences a goal or fulfillment reading (Casson 2019: 192–5).

Paul cites only a few lines from Deut. 30:11-14, but he probably has the entire passage in view where Moses (before promising that "if you obey the commandments … then you shall live and become numerous" [v. 16]), insists that the Law is not too difficult to put into practice (the italicized words below are used by Paul):

Surely, this commandment … is not too hard for you, nor is it too far away. It is not in heaven, that you should say, "*Who will go up to heaven* for us, and get it for us so that we may hear it and observe it [lit., to do it]?" Neither is it beyond the sea, that you should say, "Who will cross to the other side of the sea for us, and get it for us so that we may hear it [LXX 'and make it audible for us'] and observe it [lit., to do it]?" No, the word is very near to you; it is in your mouth and in your heart [LXX inserts "and in your hands"] for you to observe [lit., to do it]. (Keck 2005: 251).

Paul makes some changes to the Deuteronomic text, replacing "crossing the sea" of the LXX version with "who will descend into the abyss?" This came to mean the name for the netherworld or Tartarus (Ps. 71:20, Job 41:23-24) (cf. Fitzmyer 1993: 590, cf. also Lk. 8:31, and Rev. 9:1 2, 11) with reference to the underworld. It seems Paul sees in this reference an allusion to Christ's resurrection from the dead enabling him to point to the Christ-event as a whole (of which Christ as Messiah is a central part).

To understand Deuteronomy 30, we must recognize that it refers to a significant change in the people's relationship with the God of Israel. This text promises that the people would no longer require an intermediary like Moses ("Who will go up for us?"). The word of God would be directly available to the people by means of the written Torah, the oracles of God (3:2) (Hanson 1974). Rodriguez notes the significance of

Paul's interpretation of the "word, ῥῆμα, of the covenant." In Deuteronomy, the ῥῆμα refers to "this commandment, which I am commanding you today"—the singular term ἐντολή (commandment) referring to Torah as a whole rather than to any single instruction. So, in Deuteronomy the person who ascends into heaven or descends into the abyss would be seeking the commandment (Torah) of the Lord. But for Paul it is the ῥῆμα of trust that has a strong Christological dimension here, most likely meaning God's revelation of righteousness in the entire Christ-event (1:16-17, 3:21-26), particularly as it affected the nations.

In having trust-grounded Righteousness speak, Paul implies that this Righteousness has actually arrived. Since this is the Righteousness that the nations attain, it proclaims that the Christ-event has already happened. If Christ has already come down, as Paul seems to assert, he must have in mind a descent–ascent pattern such as in Phil. 2:6-11 or John 6:2. This would mean that Paul has here the entire Christ-event in view, not merely, as we noted above, that Jesus is the Messiah. We include within this, of course, the incoming of the nations, which is proof that a new era—Messianic Time—has dawned—the goal of the Law has been realized in God's sending Christ and raising him from the dead. As a result, the "doing" that Moses calls for in Lev. 18:5 is identified as the response of trust that Paul proclaims. Wagner claims as a result of a careful comparison of LXX Deut. 30:11-14 with Rom. 10:6-8 that "doing the commandment"' has been replaced (for the ethnē) with the story of Christ (2003: 164).

Stowers, and earlier, Cranfield, follow the view that Christ fulfilled the Law. Stowers notes that Paul retains ἄνθρωπος in 10:5 as he did not do in the same citation in Gal. 3:12, because he wants to point to the messianic faithfulness[6] of the one man (1994: 308). Such a view resonates with the Christological link Paul appears to create between the Law and Christ, and would provide a greater rationale for Paul's use of the biblical citations used here. The total context of 10:4-13 offers a Christological link with the Law as the focal point for Christ being the key to the new revelation of God's righteousness that opens rescue to the nations without becoming Jews.

Thus, the crucial point Paul makes here is in an allusive, intertextual comparison between the situation of ancient Israel and his own time. In order to assert that Christ has come and that a new option has been opened up for the nations, Paul does this by the combination of two texts, Deut. 8:17 ("do not say in your heart") and Deut. 9:4 ("my might and the strength of my hand have gotten me this great power"). But this new option comes with a warning against pride as self-congratulation, as the combined force of these Deuteronomy citations demonstrates (Stowers 1994: 309). When hostile gentile peoples are overcome by the power of the Lord, it should not be presumed with Deuteronomy that it was Israel's virtue or power that caused this. So too, at the present time, by the application of an Israelite narrative to the ethnē in Rome, Paul warns the ethnē not to think that God's grace-gifts were due to their achievement or were owing to their righteousness. Paul is able

---

[6] I prefer the term faithfulness or trustworthiness rather than obedience with reference to Christ's life and death (Longenecker 2011: 322–3).

to infer this from Jewish Wisdom theology, which provided the conceptual basis for his reading Deut. 30:11-14 Christologically (Keck 2005: 253). This rereading of Deuteronomy is not one that separates Paul from his Jewish milieu, but is "set in a chronological chain of Jewish encounters with the end of the Pentateuch." It is "not a crass Christological hermeneutic that seeks to find Jesus behind every verse" though by means of it, Paul is able to make some striking statements about the identity of Christ (Lincicum 2010: 168). The Christ-event enables the nearness Moses inferred from the givenness of the Law, "on your lips" and so forth, to be proclaimed as now realized in the revelation of righteousness "the word of trust" τὸ ῥῆμα τῆς πίστεως, "which we proclaim" (10:8). Of course, Christ as Messiah is foundational for Paul's argument for the arrival of Messianic Time, but for Paul it is Christ and the effects of claiming Christ as Messiah that were set in motion by his coming, that constitute the revelation of God's righteousness. "The *rhema* of God's covenant, the trust-revealed righteousness, and Christ all bridge the distance separating the people from God" (Rodriguez 2014: 204).

As already noted (Livesey 2010: 8), here this revelation of righteousness has an ethnic dimension; it includes the incoming of the nations. Because Christ has been faithful to God, gentile Christ-followers can now through Christ and through the Spirit fulfill the Law. They do not become Israel but remain an associate people who, through Christ the firstborn of many brothers (8:29), are linked to Israel and the heritage of Abraham. Dunn is typical of those scholars who stress the incoming of the Greeks alongside Israel. But this inclusion has already been thoroughly expounded in chs. 1–8. Rodriguez criticizes Dunn (1988b: 617–18) for putting all the stress here upon the inclusion of Greeks rather than upon the continued inclusion of (at least some of) the Jews (2014: 207, n46). As we noted already in the "Introduction" chapter, such a stress has sometimes been visible in SIT where the affirmation of one group's social identity is sometimes wrongly presumed to indicate a necessary correlative antagonism toward groups who differ.

In 10:9-11, Paul elaborates on the word of trust that he and his co-workers proclaim, following Deut. 30 on the use of one's body in the response, centering on the heart—"trust in your heart"—and confession—"with the mouth." The "heart" refers in Hebrew thought to the center of humans where the deepest convictions are held. Paul does not mention hands as does the LXX, but the focus is on a complete commitment of one's self to Christ as Lord. This does not imply only belief about Christ's status, but loyal response and active commitment to Christ as Lord, even though these are not explicitly noted. As Jewett notes, the active verbs for believing and confessing used in most translations are not typical of Paul in that these thereby place the emphasis entirely on the human response, although it is presupposed. So, in line with verses such as 15:18-19 ("what Christ has accomplished through me"), he translates these more appropriately as "trust is evoked" and "confession is evoked" (Jewett 2007: 630). For those from the nations, loyalty to this Lord demands a rejection of the worship of idols and the pattern of life that this involves, hence the confession "Jesus as Lord" is widely regarded as an early Christian confession used in baptism (cf. 1 Cor. 12:3).

Romans 10:11-13: For with God There Is No Discrimination

¹¹The scripture says, "Everyone one who trusts in him will not be put to shame." ¹²For there is no discrimination [with God] of Jew and Greek; for the same is Lord of all, generous to all who call on him. ¹³For, "Everyone who calls on the name of the Lord shall be saved."

In 10:11, Paul repeats the scripture text LXX Isa. 28:16 now with the addition of πας, everyone, which he had already cited in 9:33 ("whoever trusts in him [or it] will not be put to shame"), so that it now reads, "everyone who puts his trust in God will be vindicated," that is, will receive a positive verdict at the Last Judgment. We follow Meeks who holds that Paul does not necessarily intend a single referent here: "Thus we do not need to choose whether it is Torah, Christ, or God himself that is signified in the verse about a rock that is both obstacle and reliable foundation, as if one excluded the others" (1991: 115). Keck similarly observes that Paul does not need to decide whether the reference is to God or Christ "because the status of the resurrected and exalted Jesus as Lord does not compete with the lordship of the one God, but expresses it" (2005: 255). These are distinguishable, but not separable since God's lordship is now exercised through the lordship of Christ.

The emphasis here is inclusive—everyone, that is, inclusive of Jew and Greek. From this v. 12 draws the conclusion, "(For) there is no διαστολή—discrimination between Jew and Greek." This conclusion emerges from the fact that "the same Lord is Lord of all and is generous to all who call upon him." Since the Lord accepts all, Jew and Greek, who call upon him, there is no favoritism for or prejudice against Jew or Greek in God's dealing with people. The nations in this respect are the same as the Jewish people. But the text does not say that all who call on the Lord are the same, that is, ethnically identical, or ethnically undifferentiated. The "all who call" are either Jew or Greek, they are not just humans in the abstract.

Non-English native speakers may need to be aware that the vocabulary of differentiating may include the confusing use of the term "discriminating." This term, that is, "discriminating" may have a positive or neutral sense as, for example, discriminating taste, which means not poor or biased taste, but finely discerning taste, the ability to make fine differentiation. However, in this Pauline context, where distinctions between Jew and gentile continue, οὐ γάρ ἐστιν διαστολή "there is no discrimination," refers to biased discrimination so that what Paul is stating is that while distinctions continue to be made, "there is no discrimination against anyone." Thus, in this recurring use of πᾶς "all" means the inclusive "all" that now includes the ethnē in Christ as well as God's people Israel, and so, in keeping with the fact that Romans addresses the nations, we must state that the great new event in Paul's perspective is the "Christ event" in its totality but especially as enabling also the calling of the nations. But this celebration of the arrival of good news for the nations, as Paul seeks to demonstrate, includes the continuing recognition of the reality of God's call to the family of Israel/Jacob. The universality of God's call affirmed and realized in the Christ-event, as the Romans must all recognize, is truly a call to "whosoever calls upon the name of the Lord" as Joel announced (LXX 3:5). No one can be discriminated against, and especially not those whom God first called, the people of Israel. God will ensure that Jew and non-Jew will be included, for there is no διαστολή, that is, discrimination *on his part*. But it is significant that in 10:9 Paul states "because if you confess" not using the first-person plural "we," that includes himself, but the second person, "you" (ethnē), indicating this ethnic difference still remains. If no διαστολή is translated as "no distinction," Paul ought surely to have been inclusive of Jew and non-Jew at this crucial point. Differentiation abides even in Christ despite the popular and misleading use of the mistaken slogan, "no distinction," which at best can only have a limited application within biblical exposition.

Rom. 10:12 (and to a lesser extent 3:22) has been used to create an anti-ethnic Paul as if he still saw the need to argue at this point in his letter what has already been demonstrated in the earlier chapters, that is, that all those in Christ whether ethnē or Jews are of equal status. And according to this view of a proposed non-ethnic Paul, they are not only equal in status, but if Paul is perceived as abolishing ethnic differences, then all in Christ are not only one but "one and the same." Some scholars mistakenly hold that part of Paul's mission was to annul the difference between Jew and non-Jew. I have discussed this at length in my book *The Nations in the Divine Economy* (2018: 129–52), so I will not repeat my arguments but only add to what I demonstrated there. When 10:12 is rendered as "no distinction is made," it is assumed that though distinction is possible, it is not being made in this instance. The basic meaning of διαστολή in the LXX is about people or animals being categorized for specific purposes rather than on their nature or qualities. Thus, διαστολή refers to what God does or does not do with reference to ethnic differences; the phrase οὐ γάρ ἐστιν διαστολή is anti-discriminatory rather than anti-ethnic. God, in dealing with humans, does not "put difference between," that is, show favoritism in differentiating between them (Campbell 2018: 144–6).

The whole of Romans presupposes the abiding difference between Jew and non-Jew because of God's ongoing covenant with Israel. In the Romans 10 context, the emphasis is theological, about God and his actions, not anthropological about the state of human beings. Thus, οὐ γάρ ἐστιν διαστολή can and should be read as "for there is no discrimination"—indicating that a God who has been claimed to be impartial in Romans 2, cannot here be presented as partial or discriminating against any people, Jew or non-Jew, but as generous to all who call upon him. I put strong emphasis on Fitzmyer's reading "for no distinction is made," (1993: 587), which I take to mean, "for there is no discrimination with God." This means that we do not translate Rom. 10:12 as "For there is no distinction" as if there were any strong evidence that διαστολή should mean "(no) distinction" rather than as I think is clear here "(no) discrimination."

Since the publication of my book noted above, I have been alerted to a text in the *Letter of Aristeas* that strongly supports my reading. Josephus labels the latter a βίβλιον, probably a book that may have been known to Paul as it is generally dated to the second-century BCE (Doering 2012: 217–32). "For the strength of our whole body and its activity depend upon our shoulders and limbs. Therefore, he compels us to recognize that we must perform all our actions with *discrimination* according to the standard of righteousness—more especially because we have been *distinctly separated from the rest of mankind.*"[7] I have put emphasis upon two factors that are to be noted in this text. It is stressing careful performance, that is, differentiating/discriminating activity, and, second, the context is confirming distinctions, not abolishing them, "we have been separated from the rest of mankind." Significantly, this text uses both the noun διαστολή and the verbal form διαστέλλω of the term, both confirming the reading I suggested. So it is clear that "for there is no discrimination" is the best reading of Rom. 10:12 and does not support but denies the abolition of distinctions among those in Christ. Distinctions remain, and there is no discrimination against anyone.

It is evident that group differentiation is clearly affirmed. There is no call to become the same in order to be in Christ. "The Lord is the same for all" (v. 12b), but they (πᾶς) encompass Jews and Greeks in their difference. Difference is marked, and distinctions drawn but not in negative terms. The fact that the groups are different is not accompanied by negative evaluation or antagonism against each other. This is an example of positive evaluation of difference and along with it goes a recognition of commonality that needs to be distinguished from sameness as has been demonstrated by recent SIT research. Rather than assuming that recognition of difference must be accompanied by antagonism against the out-group, we have shown (see "Introduction," pp. 24–5) that this is not necessarily so. Since there is no inherent connection between positive in-group perception and negative out-group perception, these aspects may but do not need to be interconnected. Different groups can coexist in a mutual recognition under some superordinate collective identity, in this case "both belonging to the same Lord."

Romans 10:14-21: "His Hands Are Stretched Out Still"

[14]But how are they to call on one whom they have not trusted? And how are they to trust in one of whom they have never heard? And how are they to hear except someone proclaims him? [15]And how are they to proclaim him unless they are sent? As scripture says, "How welcome are the feet of messengers who bring good news!" [16]But not all have responded in trust to the good news; for Isaiah says, "Lord, who has trusted our message?" [17]So then trust does come from what is heard, and hearing comes through the word of Christ. [18]But do I really say that they did not hear? Nay rather "Into all the earth their voice has gone out, and to the ends of the world their words." [19]But do I really say that Israel did not (come to) understand first? Moses says, "I will make you jealous of those who are not a nation, with a foolish nation I will provoke you." [20]And Isaiah is so bold as to say, "I have been found by those who were not looking for me; I was revealed to those who did not ask for me." [21]And to Israel he says, "All day long I have held out my hands to an unpersuaded and obstinate people."

---

[7] Aristeas 151, ἡ γὰρ ἰσχὺς τῶν ὅλων σωμάτων μετ' ἐνεργείας ἀπέρεισιν ἐπὶ τοὺς ὤμους ἔχει καὶ τὰ σκέλη. μετὰ διαστολῆς οὖν ἅπαντα ἐπιτελεῖν πρὸς δικαιοσύνην ἀναγκάζει τὸ σημειοῦσθαι διὰ τούτων· ἔτι δὲ καὶ διότι παρὰ πάντας ἀνθρώπους διεστάλμεθα.

The question inevitably arises as to whether Paul is here speaking to the Roman ethnē in Christ (who have already confessed Christ's name) or possibly moving forward, continuing the discussion of Israel's response. This issue is also important for the next section of this chapter prior to moving on in ch. 11 to consider the future of Israel.

In this second half of the chapter, we often find among interpreters terms such as "excuses" or "accusations" used in relation to Israel's negative response to the events that together denote the arrival of a new era—what we have designated, Messianic Time. For example, Keck states, "In verses 18-21, 'Paul relies on the diatribal style to voice two *excuses* for Israel's refusal …'" (2005: 260). My suggestion is that in order to appreciate how Paul argues, it might be more fruitful, to speak of explanations rather than excuses. Although I do not intend to criticize Keck's balanced and perceptive scholarship, in my opinion, there has been too much interest in scholarship in ensuring that Israel is shown to be guilty and worthy of punishment. This arises from my conviction that here Paul is seeking to understand and explain Israel's encounter with the Christ-event, rather than to pronounce a verdict of any kind. The citation "All day long I have stretched out my hands to an unpersuaded and obstinate people," is proof of God's continuing fidelity to Israel despite her temporary obstinacy. There is no question of God giving up stretching out his hands to Israel. He is patient, and he does not grow tired of his people (Campbell 2000: 199).

The questions in vv. 14-15 with which Paul begins are not to do so much with the refusal of the message but with how it can be heard—the process of hearing. If Paul were soliciting help from the Romans for a future mission in Spain, this might be in his mind, that is, the gospel spreading out to the ends of the earth was still in process (cf. Aus 1979). Thus, we disagree with those interpreters who see in vv. 14-21, Paul's reading of Israel's failure to be convinced that with the event of Christ, a new messianic age was arriving. Thus, for example, Keck sees vv. 14-17 as indicating "how trust is elicited," but in contrast subsequently claims, "Only in vv. 18-21 is there a connection with the latter in that these are viewed as offering two (inadequate) excuses for Israel's refusal" (2005: 256). It is possible that the interlocutor's questions are seeking to excuse Israel by asking whether Israel did not understand what she has heard. But if we bear in mind, it is Paul who puts the words into the interlocutor's mouth, then this tells us that Paul himself is seriously asking the question put by the interlocutor. If we take up "how trust is elicited" as the potential theme here, we could take vv. 14-15 as Paul's analysis of the conditions necessary for "calling on the Lord." These are enumerated by a series of questions proceeding in reverse order back from the actual call in the rhetorical pattern of *klimax* (cf. 8:29-30). The self-evident answer to each question is, "They cannot." Thus, "they cannot call on the name if they do not trust; they cannot trust unless they hear; they cannot hear if there is no proclaimer (or herald); they cannot proclaim unless they are sent (to do so)" (Keck 2005: 256-61). After clearly enumerating the conditions for calling upon the Lord, Paul somewhat surprisingly observes, "But not all have responded (ὑπακοή) to the gospel—τὸ εὐαγγέλιον," which indicates that the "they" is most likely the Jewish people as emphasized by Paul at the beginning of the three chapters of Romans 9-11 (Zahn 1910: 489).

Paul's tone in relation to Israel here is reserved, almost apologetic. "Not all" is usually read as "not many," though perhaps, as earlier noted, the positive response to the gospel message among Jews must have been greater than normally acknowledged.

Stark rightly maintains that in light of the rapid rise of Christianity after 150 CE, the traditional perception of an early and ongoing negative response of Jews to the gospel is not necessarily required (1986: 314-29). Paul then cites Isa. 52:7, which celebrates the end of Israel's Babylonian captivity as return to Zion (Jerusalem) ending with the words "all the ends of the earth shall see the salvation of our God." But what is clearly indicated here is that the messengers who bring the good news have arrived, and thus the conditions necessary for calling on the Lord have been fulfilled. If we read this in relation to Israel, it could mean that the only missing factor is a positive response on Israel's part—that is, presuming that all the conditions have really been fulfilled.

This brings us back to the two rhetorical questions (Excursus I) that have been read as inadequate excuses for Israel's negative response. We do not agree that the questions in 10:18-19 concerning whether Israel heard and whether she then understood ought both to be read as similar and demand a similar answer, that is, that Israel both heard and understood what she had heard. This is presupposition and not necessarily what Paul actually says. I have dealt at length with these presuppositions under the heading "The Hermeneutics of Antithesis" (2018: 51-77).

In vv. 18-21, Paul returns to the diatribal style to introduce these two questions that have been variously interpreted. He links back to the "but 'not all' responded to the gospel" in v. 16 by asking a rhetorical question, "But do I really say that Israel did not hear?" Since the sentence begins with the particle μή, this indicates a negative reply is expected. Paul's response at this point is probably a denial, (μενοῦνγε) of the suggestion that Israel has not heard[8] using the words from Ps. 19:5 (LXX 18:4) indicating the universal preaching of the message about Christ, "To all the earth their voice has gone out, and to the ends of the world their words."

The second rhetorical question, suggests that[9] "Israel did not come to understand, (γινώσκω) what was heard." At least this reflects the normal translation, but it leaves the next sentence beginning with an improbable πρῶτος, first, to which no "second" is provided in the subsequent verses. Theodor Zahn a distinguished German commentator, provides a better proposal (1910: 490-1). He suggests the isolated "first" should be attached to the preceding sentence providing my preferred reading, "But do I really say that Israel did not come to understand first?" This rendering of the text would move the force of the question from whether or not Israel accepted the message, to the anticipated order of σωτηρία, that is, Israel was expected to respond to the call of God first (1:16), and then become a light to the nations. There seems to be no strong grammatical or textual reason to oppose this reading, which, as Cranfield notes, was first proposed by Richard Bentley.[10] It would offer a more likely cause for dispute among Christ-followers in Rome, than the posited rejection of Israel, as such.

---

[8] Jewett notes the possibility that this response may indicate an ironic comment (mentioning Schmidt and Michel) and Zahn's critique of the same. It cannot be viewed by itself as a full response (2007: 643, n85), cf. also Keck (2005: 260).

[9] "But do I really say" indicates not Paul's voice, but that of the interlocutor (Keck 2005: 260-61, Song 2004: 103). The teacher's responses here resort to an authority, to Scripture. (Song 2004: 103).

[10] Although he gives no strong reasons for rejecting it, Cranfield (1979: 539) does not follow Bentley's proposal. The adverbial use of πρῶτος would be required in both readings and the only solid reason he offers is that the traditional rendering maintains a more exact parallelism between vv. 18 and 19.

That this reading is to be preferred is confirmed by the two citations Paul offers in support of his claims. The first, "I will make you jealous of those who are not a nation; with a foolish nation I will provoke you" (Deut. 32:21), envisages Israel reacting in jealousy (Aletti 2011: 244) to provocation from a non-people, an unenlightened people. This, in accordance with Paul's use of terms in Romans 9, must indicate that the non-people are the nations. Further support is found in Paul's second citation, this time from Isaiah, "I have been found by those who did not seek me, I have shown myself to those who did not ask for me." This citation makes clear that the foolish, non-people really are the nations who despite their status or condition have responded to the message proclaimed.

Here we discover that Paul's conception of the divine plan of σωτηρία is that the coming to trust in Christ by those from the nations would, in turn, provoke Israel to jealousy to respond positively to the Christ-event, thereby reversing previous conceptions. This is then evidence for Paul and hopefully, also for the Roman Christ-followers, that according to the divine purpose, the nations rather than Israel will respond first. The fact that Israel remains unconvinced that the Messianic Time has dawned is in accord with Paul's reading of scripture. By contrast, Israel (v. 21) is depicted as an unpersuaded and rebellious people to whom God has held out his hands in appeal and welcome "all day long" (Isa. 65:2). This image, despite clarity, has been misread because of inherited or culturally induced predisposition to suggest that God has become exhausted by holding out his hands, that is, with the effort to save Israel, and has turned to the nations instead (Tucker 2018). The result is a supersessionist ideology[11] that is an affront to the mercy of God, who is thereby depicted as less than an earthly parent imploring a rebellious child (Witherington 2004: 265).

But Paul's words in 9:1-5, and in the remainder of chs. 9–11, give no basis either for a casting off of Israel by God, or a replacement of Israel by ethnē in Christ. At this stage in Paul's narrative, what we have is an affirmation that God's word to Israel has not failed (9:6a), that Israel in our new reading of 9:6b has not been divided despite God's choice of the family of Isaac and Jacob from among the descendants of Abraham, that the goal of the Law is Christ (10:4), and now, in 10:21 that God's hands are still stretched out toward Israel despite her failure to be persuaded of the new Messianic Time in God's purposes revealed in Christ. There is one new element that has been added to the conversation, which is that the nations are being used by God to make Israel jealous (10:19b). Paul wishes to move the Roman ethnē to caring concern for Israel, rather than continuing animosity (contra Jewett 2007: 646, 679). This implies, that by living a transformed life in Christ, fulfilling the Law through love, the ethnē demonstrate to Israel that God's grace is effective also in them and not inconsistent or in opposition to his grace and love for Israel. As such they are not threatening or antagonistic in any way to God's first love, Israel, whether in Christ or not, but should be agents of peace and reconciliation between all those who in their difference belong to God's family.

How may the contribution of ch. 10 to the entire letter be evaluated? The previous chapter concluded with the image of runners in a race, one of whom, Israel, stumbled but

---

[11] On this see our Excursus IV after the conclusion of our exegesis of Romans 11.

did not fall out of the race. Our investigation showed that Paul acknowledges that Israel does have a zeal for God, but has failed to see the righteousness of God revealed in the Christ-event, which enabled the nations to find righteousness through Christ yet without becoming Jews. Israel did not understand that Christ is not in opposition to the Law but he is in fact the goal to which the Law pointed for the nations. Thus, the Law has not been annulled, even though because of sin, it cannot become the way to righteousness for non-Jews. Non-Jews do not need to observe the Law, but this is not because the Law has died or been annulled but because they as non-Jews die to its rule through Christ. It is in this way that the nations find a righteousness through trust that does not make them Israelites, but only brothers of Israel, in the sense of a parallel lineage of Abraham through Christ, an associate people. They do not become Jews but are linked to Israel and her traditions through Christ, and must recognize this as an unbreakable link which has social and ethical consequences. Because a majority of the people Israel cannot understand God's action in Christ, which enables the ethnē to become his brothers, they remain opposed to the message of trust that Paul proclaims. The focus of Israel's doubts about the arrival of righteousness concerns her inability to see in the Christ-event a way for the nations to be righteous without keeping the Law as Israelites do.

Did Israel not Hear?

As noted, Israel cannot see that a new Time in God's revelation has dawned—it is not so much Christ himself that Israel rejects as the interpretation of the meaning of his life and its effects in relation to the nations. Paul acknowledges that Israel has heard the good news of the gospel, but he seems to think it possible that she has never understood it (10:19). According to the pattern of σωτηρία previously anticipated, Israel would be restored prior to the nations responding, and therefore the time cannot yet have arrived for the incoming of the nations. So there is some evidence that might partly excuse the ethnē in Christ at Rome who thought that Israel had been bypassed. Traditional wisdom had generally taught that the ethnē would only come to trust *after* Israel had first responded in trust. But since, despite all the conditions for the hearing of the good news of Messianic Time had been activated, and Israel had not yet given her anticipated positive response, she must have been bypassed in God's purpose. It is possible that there were debates about whether it was justified to continue to expect a positive response by Israel, that is, Israel should have known that Messianic Time had already dawned, and since she has not responded positively, the time for expecting such response has already passed. Contrary to this, Paul argues in 10:18-19 that Israel was not meant to recognize the dawning of Messianic Time first, that is, prior to or even simultaneously with the ethnē, since the scripture says through Moses and Isaiah that God would provoke Israel because of the ethnē who now worship God as a result of the gentile mission. Whether this reaction is caused by jealousy, or positive emulation is unclear—the essential point is that there is interaction with Israel as a result of the gentile mission.[12] What will be the outcome of this is not yet evident. Paul

---

[12] Contra Bell (1994: 106) we prefer to translate παροργίζω as provoke (a reaction) possibly through emulation rather than anger.

seeks to reduce any hostility between ethnē in Christ and the Jewish people, hence he seeks a positive influence of the ethnē upon Israel. The ethnē cannot force Israel into recognition of the new Time, but they can hinder this if God's grace is not visible in them. The mutual interaction that Paul hopes for does not require any continuation of animosity (Lincicum 2010: 166).

It is probable that in the early days of the Christ-movement, it was anticipated that non-Jews who joined the movement would accept circumcision and keep the Law. But when it became clear that this was not (going to be) the normal route for the nations, then some Jewish Christ-followers may have reacted strongly because they were faced with gentile leaders who thought not only that the Law was not applicable to non-Jews but that it had been annulled so that it was inapplicable for Jews in the Christ movement. Later in Acts this is one of the accusations Paul has to refute. Thus, a threat to the Law was perceived by the incoming of those from the nations, which had a knock-on effect for Jews (Aletti 2011: 262–4). So, the fact of gentile Christ-followers worshipping the God of Israel without keeping the Law presented a challenge to the practice of the Law itself in that it indicated a potential opposition between the recognition of Christ and the Law. Later in the history of the church, the ethnē in Christ pattern was universalized to apply to Jews as well, thus combining the Law itself, as well as following Christ, into one huge stumbling stone over which Jews must necessarily stumble.

What needs to be recognized is that Jesus and other would-be/potential messiahs did not necessarily present such a major challenge to the Jewish way of life. In the early centuries of the Christ-movement, it was Law-keeping, not Jesus as Messiah, that separated groups who could still live relatively amicably together, even sharing each other's major festivals. As Reed as demonstrated, in the Pseudo Clementines, it is the practice of the Law that is the dividing line (2014: 23–62, cf. also Zetterholm 2019).

The question remains that if Israel continues to be unpersuaded that the Messianic Time has dawned, and that ethnē can worship God alongside the people of Israel, does this not mean that Israel has been bypassed and hence cast off from God's purpose? However, another interpretation is possible. The present misconception of God's purpose by Israel may be only a temporary delay in her full restoration in line with God's purpose. This is the theme of ch. 11.

Romans 11

Romans 11:1-10: "God Didn't Cast Off His People, Did He?"

¹I say, then, God didn't cast off his people, did he? Far from it! For I myself am an Israelite, from the seed of Abraham, a member of the tribe of Benjamin. ²God did not cast off his people whom he foreknew. Or do you not know what the scripture says of Elijah, as he appeals to God against Israel? ³"Lord, they killed your prophets, they have demolished your altars; I alone am left, and they are seeking my life." ⁴But what is the divine oracle to him? "I have kept for myself seven thousand men, men who have not bowed their knee to Baal." ⁵So too at the present time there is also a remnant, chosen by grace. ⁶But if it is by grace, then consequently not on the basis of works, for otherwise grace would then not be grace.
⁷What then? That which Israel sought it did not obtain. But the elect did obtain it. But the rest were hardened, ⁸as it is written,
"God gave them a sluggish spirit,
eyes that would not see
and ears that would not hear,
down to this very day."
⁹And David says,
"Let their table become a snare and a trap,
a stumbling block and a retribution against them;
¹⁰let their eyes be darkened so that they cannot see,
and keep their backs severely bent."

This chapter opens in the style to which we have become accustomed, with a question or inference arising from previous discussion. The stress on Israel's failure to be persuaded by the gospel led the interlocutor to ask concerning its meaning, "I say then"(λέγω οὖν), continuing in the same vein as 10:18-19, and with a similar topic, the negative response of Israel to the message proclaimed about the Christ event. The extremely unlikely and alarming possibility is that God might have rejected his people, "Therefore I say, God did not cast off his people, did he?" This emerges as a rhetorical question rejected with the customary μὴ γένοιτο. The term ἀπώσατο, reject, that Paul uses here has legal significance in relation to adoption practice. In a fourth-century document, there is a prohibition of rejecting (ἀπωθέω) an adopted son or of selling him into slavery. Thus, it seems that this term ἀπώσατο would resonate with the Romans who would have been familiar with adoption terminology and laws. As Saller has pointed out,

> The Romans considered the bonds of family and kinship to be biologically based but not biologically determined ... Roman law, to be sure, offered citizens a flexibility in restructuring their kinship bonds that was remarkable by later European standards: not only were divorce and remarriage easy in the classical period, but adoption permitted change of filiation. (Saller 1994: 25, 43)

Paul has mentioned the sonship, υἱοθεσία, of Israel in 9:4. Israel was adopted as God's son, and legally this means that the one who adopted is bound by the adoption law that cannot simply be dismissed—Israel cannot easily be cast off by God who contracted to adopt her (Krahn 2018, ref. to *Oxy.* 9:1206).

The first evidence Paul provides for the non-rejection of Israel is in fact himself, though he is not thinking here in terms of individuals, so much as in ethnic groups, Jews, and the nations. If he himself, a loyal member of the tribe of Benjamin, has not been rejected as is obviously the case, then "God cannot have cast off *his people* whom he called and interacted with across the centuries, whom he foreknew" (προέγνω 2a, cf. 8:30 in relation to Christ). As a second witness against Israel's being cast off, Paul offers the example of Elijah. The prophet is, in fact, a negative witness in that he pleads with God *against Israel*. According to 1 Kings 19, having slain the prophets of Baal, Elijah, fleeing from their patron, Jezebel who had vowed to kill him, in a moment of despair claims that "they have killed your prophets, they have demolished your altars: I alone am left and they are seeking my life (v. 14)."

Contrary to Elijah's pessimistic assessment of the people of Israel, the divine oracle reveals, "I have kept for myself seven thousand who have not bowed the knee to Baal" (based on LXX 1 Kgdms 19:18). The number symbolism of this passage indicates that contrary to Elijah's skeptical perspective, a considerable number within Israel had refused idol worship (Hanson 1972–3: 300). The contrast between God's perspective and assessment with that of Elijah suggests that there may be differing views about Israel's loyalty or lack of it, and that not only at the time of Elijah but now also here in Rome at the present time. Paul reminds his hearers that he is speaking in the "now," ἐν τῷ νῦν καιρῷ (cf. also 3:21, 26; 5:9; 8:18; 11:30-31), the time of the present revelation of God's righteousness. Paul goes on to announce that just as there were faithful Israelites in Elijah's day, "so too at the present (Messianic) Time, there is a remnant chosen by grace" (11:5). The remnant is not what just happens to be left over, as in a fabric shop, but is a positive result of gracious election. Paul changes what we know as the LXX text to emphasize divine initiative, from "you will keep seven thousand" to "I have kept for myself seven thousand" (Keck 2005: 24–65). The remnant theme in prophetic thought combines an announcement of divine judgment with a promise of a remnant that will survive the judgment and lead to future deliverance. There is no mention here of the size of the remnant, only the fact of it. The number of "seven thousand" (11:4) probably denotes the number of completeness, the full number. Paul underlines that the fact of a remnant is due not to merit but to the grace of God, κατ' ἐκλογὴν χάριτος, as has already emerged at different points in this letter. He again emphasizes the exclusivity of the way of grace and the way of works, ἐξ ἔργων (v. 6, cf. 3:27).

In 11:7, the interlocutor seeks to sum up the implications of Paul's claims. In the regular pattern, he asks "what then (τί οὖν), Israel failed to obtain what she was seeking." Paul gives his view in the second half of the verse, "the elect obtained it but the rest were hardened." Here we have a division within Israel, "the elect" and "the rest," corresponding to the reality revealed by the preaching of the Christ message. "The remnant" is interpreted as those who accepted the message, and "the rest" as those who rejected it. The division here comes from the proclamation of the Christ-event—it is a result of Christ being preached, so it describes what has been happening and what still continues in the present—Paul's eschatological/Messianic Time.

What is clear here is that however small or great may be the extent of the remnant, Paul's assumption is that Israel as a majority can be represented as rejecting the Christ-event, refusing to see in the incoming of the nations, the new act of God claimed by Paul and others. This becomes explicit in vv. 8-10 where Paul again expresses and supports his viewpoint in biblical statements. What must be emphasized is that Paul's citations demonstrate that he does not perceive resistant Israel as acting alone but rather sees Israel's God as the activator of the events described. Using portions of several biblical passages, which report divine interaction with Israel in Isa. 29:10, Deut. 29:3, and Isa. 6:10, *Paul presents God's activity in and through Israel rather than reporting these as the actions of Israel alone.* As previously noted, we anticipate that Paul has in mind the entire context from which his citations are drawn. The first text (Isa. 29:10) is clear about God's action, "The Lord has made you drink with *a spirit of stupor*, and he will close their eyes (emphasis added)." The second, Deut. 29:3 reports God's action in saying what he did not do, "The Lord did not give you a heart to understand, and *eyes* to see and *ears* to hear *until this day*." The third citation (Isa. 6:10) lists the body parts necessary for a full response to the call of God. "The heart of this people has been made dull, and their *ears* have become hard of hearing, and they have closed their *eyes*, lest they see with their *eyes* and *hear* with their *ears* and understand with their heart and turn, and I will heal them" (Keck 2005: 266-7).

The three citations that Paul puts together here witness in their combined import to Israel's failure to give a positive response to the new revelation in Christ. But more than this, they also offer evidence that it was not Israel's actions alone that produced this reaction, but the activity of the God of Israel who was active in and through her refusal. The Lord is explicitly denoted as the agent in the first two citations, and the passive tense of the third is just another way of indicating divine agency. Reading through Romans, it becomes increasingly clear that the call of God does not depend on human activity or "works" but only on divine grace and mercy. So too here the negative response of Israel to the claim of a new activity of God in opening the door to the nations is viewed as due to the activity of her God. It is not as though Israel has no responsibility for her refusal. Human beings in Pauline perspective are never mere robots performing the divine will, but on the other hand, neither are they able to be entirely free agents in control of their own destiny. Thus, it is now clear that when Paul says that "the rest were hardened," he meant that the Lord intended this hardening to enable the incoming of the nations. So, when Israel reveals a 'hardened' heart, in Paul's terms, it is Israel's fault, but it may also denote the activity of God.

Paul's use of παράπτωμα in 11:11-12 should be read in the context of the race metaphor introduced in 9:30-33. It was the common term both for both the misstep of a runner in a race and for a transgression against God (Stowers 1994: 313). To put too much emphasis upon the latter misses the metaphorical language of motion implicit here. I prefer "stumbling" (contra Cranfield 1979: 555–6) in view of Paul's metaphorical use of this image in 11:9, 11:11, and so on, and his general use of tripping over an obstacle while engaged in running a race (Nanos 2018: 118, n16). Thus, it points to the misstep or tripping of a runner in a foot race. The structure of Paul's story echoes Homer's tale of the footrace in the funeral games. But in the latter race, there were three contestants, not two as in Paul, Israel and the nations. In Homer's race too, a god trips a runner: Ajax is in the lead and Odysseus prays to Athena who gives him greater speed but also causes Ajax to slip and fall. The outcome was that Odysseus gets first prize while Ajax manages to get up and finish the race before the third contestant.

What is significant is that Paul uses the footrace imagery, implying the competitive spirit of Jew and non-Jew in ancient Rome, but also softening the criticism of Israel's misstep. The impact of Homer's footrace imagery suggests a good outcome even for the one who tripped up. Interestingly, the gods of non-Jews are here again within the context of the discussion, not surprising considering Homer's basic role in education (παιδεία). But Keck notes that by calling the non-acceptance of the gospel "their trespass," Paul restates the refusal to "submit" to God's righteousness (10:3) (Keck 2005: 268). Even if it was a mistaken or false step, it is still described as Israel's responsibility. Israel missed her step, but Paul will go on to deny that this was a fall that put Israel out of the race entirely. A runner could trip or stumble without being so far behind that they had no longer any chance of success.

Paul uses two further images in speaking of Israel's misstep. Linking back to 11:1-7, Paul asks whether Israel's stumbling caused a final fall after which there could be no success (Song 2004: 104–5). That a final rejection of Israel by God is not ruled out by some interpreters is shown by the translation of Ps. 69 as cited in 11:10. Cranfield alerted me in personal conversation to the relatively recent tendency to translate διὰ παντός as "for ever" (as, e.g., RSV, NRSV, NIV, Barrett, NEB), which is, he thought, "surely mistaken." The emphasis is on the intensity of the servitude rather than its perceived duration (1979: 552). This gratuitous imposition of unending suffering for Israel reflects the anti-Judaism inherent in much traditional Pauline scholarship prior to the 1970s and, in some instances, continuing until the present. Thus, Keck refers to the mistranslation of διὰ παντός as "for ever" (implying that God's action in Paul's time continues endlessly into the future) as "an inference that has legitimated the pernicious notion that Jews are perpetually suffering because they did not become Christians" (2005: 267–8). But precisely the point denied by this mistranslation is what Paul wishes to affirm, that is, that Israel's 'hardening' is not final and not "for ever." Whatever the source of this pernicious suggestion that Israel has been cast off, it is precisely on this issue that a difference between the Roman deities and the God of Israel emerges. The Roman gods could remove their protection from peoples at will but the God of Israel is faithful to his covenant and his people.

Romans 11:11-16: Israel's Stumbling: The Kindness and Severity of God

¹¹So I say, they have not stumbled so as to fall, have they? Far from it! But through their stumbling rescue has come to the ethnē so as to make Israel jealous. ¹²Now if their stumbling means riches for the world, and if their lagging behind means riches for ethnē, how much more will their fullness mean!

¹³So I am speaking to you ethnē. Then notwithstanding that I am an apostle to the ethnē, I glorify my ministry ¹⁴in order to make my own people jealous, and thus heal some of them. ¹⁵For if their deprivation is the reconciliation of the kosmos, what will their acceptance be but life from the dead! ¹⁶If the portion offered as first fruits is holy, then the whole batch is holy; and if the root is holy, then the branches also are holy.

Repeating the λέγω οὖν of 11:1, a similar interlocutory inference is put, which by Song is translated "when they stumbled was their fall final?" (2004: 104–5). Paul gives the final instance of his typical response, μὴ γένοιτο, which must indicate we are coming toward the end of this section of Paul's long letter. Paul absolutely denies that Israel's stumble has any final (negative) significance for Israel and notes accordingly that the result of it has meant that "rescue" has come to the nations (11b), so as to make Israel jealous. This purpose clause in itself points to a goal (to make Israel jealous) that the nations must serve as a consequence of Israel's stumbling, thus indicating that the stumbling was not the conclusion of the narrative, but at most penultimate. By the term σωτηρία, Paul means the acceptance of ethnē in Christ as full and equal participants in the outcome of the Christ-event. But this σωτηρία does not include their becoming Israelites, this is not required. Σωτηρία includes both Israel and the nations each in their abiding distinctive difference under the commonality of the worship of the one God of Israel.

The series of scriptural citations Paul introduced in 11:8-10, demonstrating the πώρωσις 'hardening' of Israel, produced such an effect that the interlocutor feels forced to ask whether this 'hardening' was evidence of Israel's final rejection, that is, not merely a single misstep, but a 'hardening' leading to a final fall, ἔπαισαν ἵνα πέσωσιν (11:11). This Paul strongly denies. In his theologizing, the concept of πώρωσις serves to explain how and why Israel did not respond positively to the Christ-event as might have been expected. Moreover, a temporary πώρωσις of Israel has not been understood, but has been interpreted in terms of rejection by the gods. Nanos's translation of πώρωσις in terms of the forming of a protective callus on a branch of a tree has the merit of suggesting the protection rather than the "rejection" of the tree, which is obviously still growing. This indicates some of the difficulty in translating metaphors into reality (conceptual speech, Esler 2003; Nanos 2018: 153–78). The thorough investigation that Nanos has pursued of the metaphors that Paul used almost always indicates negative over-interpretation of the imagery under discussion (1996; 2018). 'Hardening' is no exception and indicates that all that is done by the keeper of the olive tree, removal of branches, cutting down of dead trees, and the grafting in of new shoots is done for the good health and production of fruit of the entire olive tree orchard. We will return to these metaphors throughout this chapter, but to remember their overarching historical context is crucial. We accept that the image of "callused" carries more historical realism and hence explanatory power than the traditional term "hardening," and that the latter's negative overtones are a hindrance to understanding (Nanos 2018: 155–6). The same difficulties in understanding the imagery of a divinely planned ("the rest were hardened," 11:7), but humanly responsible resistance to the Christ-event faced Paul in Rome and were multiplied in subsequent translation. Thus, Jewett reads πώρωσις as "obtuseness—a failure to discern and to see what was simultaneously a willful act and divine punishment" (2007: 694, 699–700). The primary issue remains—what was Paul seeking to transmit to the Roman ethnē by his horticultural imagery concerning both Israel and themselves?

Romans 11:11-12

In structural terms, relating 11:11 to 11:1 is interesting. The latter seems almost a repeat, but this is to underestimate the force of 11:11 and Paul's use of hardening imagery. The repeated μὴ γένοιτο pattern in the letter would suggest that 11:11 is parallel and equal in significance to 11:1. The ascending verdict from stumbling to final "putting away" or rejection serves to clarify the meaning of what Paul said and did not say in 11:1. Without this explicit denial of Israel's final rejection at this point, his hearers might have allowed the serious judgments noted in the cited passages in 11:8-10 to carry more negative impact than Paul intended.[1] It is as if he said, "yes, I did say that Israel has been 'hardened' but I did not mean this as God's rejection of Israel." Paul did not suggest that this 'hardening' means Israel is not still within God's care and protection, that he has no more plans for her. Amazingly, it means quite the opposite, so he then proceeds to mention these plans again. What is significant here is that Paul does not speak of Israel's destiny as if this were an isolated entity but of Israel's future as intertwined with that of the nations. Paul points out that Israel's stumbling, παράπτωμα, was not an indication of final rejection, but this stumbling has served a purpose to allow rescue to come to the nations, and this will in turn have the result, εἰς τὸ παραζηλῶσαι αὐτούς "so as to make them (Israel) jealous," that is, have a salvatory effect on Israel. Consummation cannot unfold until God's promises are fulfilled, because they must be fulfilled. The "gentiles" coming in, to fulfill the promise (many nations), is therefore an essential condition to the unfolding of the eschaton.

This is Paul's confident argument. If God was involved in Israel's negative response to the Christ-event, then he must have intended some positive outcome by it. Paul, after much reflection and no doubt also soul-searching, has come to the conclusion that the divine purpose for which Israel was 'hardened' was none other than to allow

---

[1] The earliest proclamation of the gospel necessitated some reference to its rejection by many Jews so that the concept of Israel as being bypassed or cast off gained a hearing. It may also demonstrate knowledge of a presupposition that Israel would accept the message first, and only then would gentiles have an opportunity. If Israel has not responded first, this might suggest that Israel has now been bypassed—she has missed her opportunity (Nanos 2018: 153–78).

the incoming of the nations. This is Paul's own perspective on the poor response of Israel to the good news of the Christ-event. If Paul was accustomed to view Israel and the nations as reacting in mutual response to the actions of God, then it is not surprising that the solution he begins to formulate here relates to the both of them (i.e., Israel and the nations). God achieves his purposes in the world by the interaction of Israel and the nations, whether in friendship or enmity. Paul is part of an explanatory Jewish framework in which both the present misfortune and the future restoration of the Jewish people is related to the present good fortune and future punishment of the nations who gloated over Jewish misfortune (Tobin 2004: 366).

Paul continues his step-by-step argument in 11:11, "So I say, they have not stumbled so as to fall, have they? Far from it. But through their stumbling salvation has come to the ethnē, so as to make Israel jealous." These verses, 11:11-12, could be related to the previous discussion in 11:1-10, as an extension of that argument indicated by the repetition of the μὴ γένοιτο construction. But this pattern can equally well introduce a new section of the argument. Thus, Paul continues the discussion based on the scriptural citations that conclude in 11:10. The new emphasis that emerges in this extension of the argument is the function of Israel's "resistance and hardening" and its outcome in allowing the incoming of the nations. This is presumed as having been discussed in 11:1-10, but an additional outcome is stressed in 11:11-12 as making Israel jealous and so, in turn, contributing to God's ongoing purpose of σωτηρία. The narrative has already moved on from the fact of Israel's "resistance and hardening" to its effect and outcome; the new section should begin in 11:11-16 and continue to 11:24.

Jewett proposes, on rhetorical and argumentative grounds, a logical organization of this pericope (11:11-24) with a thesis in 11:11, followed by a logical enthymeme in vv. 12-15 and an allegorical enthymeme in vv. 16-22, with a rhetorically effective conclusion in vv. 22-24 (2007: 668). Bracketed by the absence of scriptural citations, 11:11-24 overcompensates, as noted above, with a great variety of forms of argumentation. Another diatribal section begins in 11:11 (itself parallel to, but not simply a repeat of, 11:1) with a rhetorical question from the imaginary interlocutor and continues to 11:24. Attention should be drawn to the parallel series of chain-link references that connect vv. 12-15 with what follows. Paul, accordingly, reasons concerning Israel's future, using as previously in ch. 5:10, 15, 17, an argument from the lesser to the greater—if X is true (as it certainly is) then how much more is Y true. The presupposition of the argument is, as just noted, that God has "hardened," that is, delayed Israel's positive response to bring rescue to the nations. Then, on this basis Paul builds a cumulative argument extending from 11:11 to 11:24.

If, as is the case, God has "hardened" Israel and her παράπτωμα, stumbling (in not accepting the Christ message as the arrival of Messianic Time) has brought riches for the κόσμος, and Israel's ἥττημα,[2] deprivation, has brought riches for the nations, "how much more will their πλήρωμα, full inclusion, mean?" (11:12, cf. Keck 2005: 269).

This looks forward to the time when the divide within Israel between the remnant and "the rest" of Israel resulting from the Christ-event will no longer exist. As just

---

[2] Though the term can mean "defeat," in parallel to "riches" Keck prefers "loss" (Keck 2005: 269). I prefer "deprivation" since the passive indicates it is not all Israel's doing.

noted, the first εἰ "if" in 11:12, as also in 11:15 and 24, employs the *a minore ad maius* (from lesser to greater) argument, and the two "if" clauses in 11:16 establish an "argument from similarity" scheme. Jewett sees a perfect parallelism between the two, each including an "if" clause and an inference clause introduced by "so also." He also notes that the extensive argument of the olive tree employs three more "if" clauses in vv. 17-24, giving a total of ten "if" clauses in this pericope (2007: 670).

This analysis of the rhetorical structure of vv. 11-24, particularly vv. 17-24, shows that this is rhetorically and logically very carefully constructed. The fact that scriptural citations do not appear is, in my opinion, due to the fact that here Paul reasons on the basis of Israel's stumbling, interpreted as a divine purpose intended to bring rescue to the nations. All the conditional clauses derive from 11:11b, "but through their stumbling rescue has come to the ethnē so as to make Israel jealous." This is Paul's "hopeful" and optimistic interpretation of Israel's stumbling as part of the sequence that results in the opportunity for the ethnē to *understand first*. Since this is his own distinctive reading of this happening, and there were no easy answers available in the scriptures then, as noted, he relies on his own reasoning to explain and make it plausible to the ethnē in Christ at Rome (so also Tobin 2012: 366). Paul had to rethink, reinterpret what was happening in light of the fact that God's call to Israel is irrevocable.

Despite the fact that the theme in chs. 9–11 has centered on the meaning of, and problems resulting from, Israel's failing to be convinced that the Messianic Time had arrived with the Christ-event, Paul nevertheless interprets this series of events optimistically. Whatever blessing has already come to Israel in the Christ-event, the future will by far exceed the past. The repetition of the *qal wahomer* form of argument in itself, in Paul's use of it, denotes an optimism in which the powers of this world are overcome by the action of God through Christ (Campbell 2018: 160–2). It is based on Paul's conviction that the Messianic Time has dawned, and that this revelation of righteousness is the guarantee that thus God's plans for the world will come to full fruition/consummation. This optimism can also be expressed in other typically Pauline texts such as "where sin increased, grace abounded all the more" (5:20).

Other terms like πλοῦτος, riches, and πλήρωμα, full number, presuppose this enrichment (cf. 11.12). It is this form of reasoning that enables Paul to infer from the Christ-event (3:21-24), the realization of what he has described already as "the full number" of Israel, what he will later indicate means the restoration of "all Israel" (11:26). We might regard this as "hopeful or optimistic argumentation," but Paul regards it as the appropriate and therefore legitimate and reasonable conclusion from a full understanding of the Christ-event and God's purpose as revealed therein. But it tells us that even from the beginning of the writing of Romans, Paul already had in mind the positive outcome of the narrative he was engaged in writing.

Romans 11:13-24 It Is You Ethnē That I Am Addressing

There are two issues here needing to be clarified, the first relating to the addressees and the second to the nature of Paul's address. Paul emphasizes that he speaks to his addressees specifically as ethnē. That this is an ethnic issue could not be clearer. Paul indicates that he is addressing his Roman audience as those from the nations, not as

Jews, or as a mixed audience of both Jews and non-Jews. The translation of v. 13, "now, I am speaking to you 'gentiles'" (NRSV) is not good in that it may suggest (wrongly) that previously in this letter (or elsewhere) Paul may have been speaking to Jews. Competent public speakers cannot suddenly change the audience addressed without serious problems, nor does it help if they switch from addressing one group after the other. If a new group is addressed, can the others switch off from the speaker, and how would they know when to focus attention again? But it is clear from v. 13 that Paul is explicitly reminding the Roman gentile Christ-followers that it is to them that he is addressing his remarks, and that thus they are the previous and only addressees.

And yet in v. 17 it is to be noted that this audience may be further defined, now as a personified wild olive shoot. The question is, ought vv. 17-24 to be read as bracketed within an address in 11:13-25 to "you ethnē," so that though the diatribal section of vv. 17-24 addresses the audience only indirectly it does so within an existing form of direct address already specified as to non-Jews? The problem Paul has apparently created here is that after addressing his audience emphatically and directly as those from the nations, at a crucial point (v. 17) he resorts to an apostrophe in which he chooses to address them only indirectly. This seems to be the best understanding of Paul's strategy. At a critical stage in his argument, he seeks, as he has done earlier in Romans, to avoid direct criticism, but puts his argument in a diatribal form, so that its force is indirect though nonetheless powerful. Thus, there need be no confusion if these parameters are observed—since the diatribal style occurs in a passage specifically and pointedly addressed to the Romans as ethnē (11:13-25), the impact of the diatribal style, though indirect, is nevertheless targeted at them. As in other parts of this letter, careful attention must be paid both to the fact of diatribal style as well as its limits.

We note again that they are addressed as ethnē, though with no explicit reference in the address here that they are Christ-followers. This may mean that Paul is thinking both of their status as ethnē and of their calling in Christ (which is implied). The focus is their situation as non-Jews living in a non-Jewish, that is, pagan, environment. This draws attention to their gentile location as well as their ethnic identity, but, more precisely, it focuses also on the influence of that context. (Elliott 2008: 20). Only a few commentators have noted the significance of Roman pagan influence on the attitudes of the gentile Christ-followers in relation to prejudicial perspectives of Jews. Elliott perceptively notes that

> one of the most puzzling ironies in Romans scholarship is this determination on the part of scholars like Kümmel, Schmithals and Beker, who recognize Paul's warning against Gentile-Christian arrogance ... not only to deny this warning more than a peripheral role in the apostle's purposes, but to go on to hypothesize a Gentile-Christian audience quite inconsistent with this warning. (2007: 41)

Credit should be given to earlier pioneers such as Wilhelm Lütgert, *Der Römerbrief als historisches Problem* (1913); Hans Werner Bartsch, "Die antisemitischen Gegner des Paulus im Römerbrief" in *Antijudaismus im NeuenTestament* (1967); and Lloyd Gaston, *Paul and the Torah* (1987), and so on for being open-minded and courageous enough to offer differing readings of Romans from mainstream Paulinism at this point (Elliott 2007: 41).

Jewett rightly asserts that if it had no basis in the current behavior of the audience, the wild olive imagery would have proved insulting, and thus takes this action as clear evidence of residual antisemitism within the Roman "churches" (2007: 686). Elliott is one of the most ideologically aware in this respect. He notes the varied political treatment of Jews in Rome and the continuation of anti-Judean slanders among the Roman aristocracy and in the streets. He holds that Paul in Romans "confronts both the 'boast' of supremacy over Israel and, by necessity, the attitudes in the wider cultural environment that nourished that boast" (2008: 20). Paul makes it clear that he does not share this arrogant perception with his audience. In this Paul perceives them as influenced by pressures of imperial ideology (Elliott 2008: 15, 110). From this perspective, it appears that Paul shares a counternarrative (not necessarily countercultural) with Philo and other Jewish writings. This was due to the fact that

> Roman rule could not only cause problems for Jews at the socio-political level, but the claim to be the people divinely ordained to rule the world forever, clashed diametrically with Jewish perceptions of the world as God's, and of their specific role within the purpose of their God. This tradition was prone not to buy into Roman ideology and constituted by its mere existence an implicit counter-narrative to Roman claims. (Ehrensperger 2019b: 152–53)

This "wider cultural environment" is what I think Paul has in mind when he addresses the Christ-followers not explicitly as adherents of Christ but as part of the cultural context of a gentile city, a cultural ethos in many respects antagonistic to the claims of Christ. Thus, Tobin may be correct in pointing out that "the identity of the Gentiles whom Paul is addressing needs to be understood rather broadly" (2004: 363), but not as he proposes by drawing in information from other contexts and thus reducing the significance of Rome.

The repetition in 11:13 that Paul addresses non-Jews is another reminder that there is absolutely no evidence for Paul addressing Jews in Romans. The gospel Paul proclaims is a universal message that omits no one, but his call gave him a specific task, to be apostle to the nations, as he constantly reminds everyone (Rom. 1:1; 1 Cor. 1:1; 4:9; 9:1-2; 15:9; 2 Cor. 1:1; 11:5; 12:11-12; Gal. 1:1, 17; 1 Thess. 2:6). Paul rejoices in the task, διακονία, which he has been assigned, using himself as an *exemplum*, "I am indeed an apostle to the nations" but sees it, notwithstanding, as having a goal beyond that of his assigned addressees (Jewett 2007: 666; Aletti 2015: 264) "to make my own people jealous, and thus save some of them" (11:14). Rather than having left behind in ch. 8, the separate address as "you 'gentiles,'" to combine, henceforth, all Christ-followers into one group of "believers," that is, Israel (contra. Rodriguez 2014: 158–9, n30), Paul not only addresses himself in 11:13 to ethnē but continues in the next verse to speak of "my own people," obviously Jews. This usage indicates beyond doubt that ethnicity did not disappear in theological discourse with the advent of Christ but that Paul, throughout his career, still thought and reasoned in the real world where ethnicity no less than theology/ideology plays a dominant role (McMurray 2021: 2–6, 95–133).

Paul might be viewed as lacking vision or ambition in making here a unique claim that he hopes to make his own people jealous "and thus save some of them" (11:14). Yet Paul's apostleship is to the nations, not his own people Israel as he here strongly underlines. His work is in the Diaspora, among, and addressed to, those from the nations. What we can and should infer from this is not that Paul is opposed to presenting the Christ message and its claims to his own people (Aletti 2015: 261–4), but merely that that is not his sphere of work because it has been assigned to Peter and others. Of course, if an individual or group of Jewish birth wished to discuss Christ and his significance with Paul, if time allowed, he would certainly do so. But this could not be his first priority, since this was not what God had called him to do. Thus, the "saving" (healing them from their error or stumbling) of a few Jewish people is presented as an almost incidental by-product of Paul's work among the nations—he himself is more than fully occupied with his call to the nations. It should be noted, however, that despite the cautious and almost veiled way Paul speaks of Israel's response in Rom. 9:6 and 10:16, τίνες "some" of them must not be supposed to refer to only quite a small number of Jews (Munck 1954: 46, Stark 1996). But alongside that Paul also hopes that God will eventually save "all Israel." Paul's immediate role is embedded in a larger plan that will lead to the salvation of all Israel (Tobin 2004: 315).

As noted above, Paul has great confidence that God's power will bring about the restoration of Israel, arguing again in the lesser to greater pattern, "For, if their deprivation is the reconciliation of the world, what will be their acceptance but life from the dead" (11:15). It is interesting that when he refers to the incoming of the nations, Paul uses reconciliation terminology confirming our understanding of 3:21-26. It is also significant that Paul, here, refers to the resurrection of the dead in a context where the acceptance of Israel is mentioned as if there were a logical link between the two. In Paul's mind, I think there was. Paul reinforces his argument by a second strand, this time using the image of the dough offered as first-fruits. According to Num. 15:17-21, a portion of each lump of dough to be prepared for baking should be dedicated to God as a holy offering that would render holy the entire batch of bread. These first-fruits of the dough become a burnt offering whose smoke/aroma is pleasing to the Lord. The same principle pertains with reference to the harvest. Here it applies throughout the analogy of the olive tree up to 11:24 (Tobin 2004: 363). In its immediate application, the imagery from the firstfruits of the dough requires that if the firstfruits are holy, then so is the whole of Israel. This argument reappears with the analogy of the root to insist that "if the root is holy, then the branches are also holy" (11:16). For Paul, the whole is identified with the parts, and the holiness of the remnant extends to the whole of Israel, who therefore still play a role in God's purpose (Cranfield 1979: 548–52).

In 11:17-24, a basic fact underlies the narrative, that is, the distinction between a cultivated and a wild olive tree. The olive tree, the ἐλαία of 11:17, belongs to the species *Olea europaea* L., and is usually divided into two subspecies: *Olea europaea sativa* (which includes the cultivated, the καλλιέλαιος of 11:24) and *Olea europaea oleaster* (the wild olive, the ἀγριέλαιος of 11:17). The existence of these two subspecies, and the imagery and symbolism associated respectively with each, underlies Paul's discussion in 11:17-24.

As already noted, the hypothetical form of argument, εἰ δέ, "but if," in 11:12-24, meaning here probably "as is the case," indicates in another analogy, the damage of a part of Israel, "the rest," in relation to the life-giving connection of branches to the fatness of the olive tree. In the analogy, the branches are broken, implying a damaged connection to, but not necessarily, except where stated, a complete severance from, the sap of the parent tree, or root (Nanos 2018: 112–52, 130). It is after all, only an analogy, but we must not ignore its import by reading more into the image than it offers. It is an extended metaphor, not an allegory in which every small point would function as an equivalent to something else (Tobin 2004: 363, Anderson 1999: 237). Nanos also uses the term "extended metaphor" following Esler (2003: 106–07, 112, 140). The hypothesis is put in an extended metaphorical address to the wild olive shoot beginning in 11:17 (this is indicated by the discourse of "you" as opposed to "they," which begins at this point and continues to the end of the pericope). The "they" here must be the majority of Israel that has thus far not accepted the Christ message and its implications.

Since Paul addresses the nations here, not Jews, he stresses the significance of this fact in creating a diatribal discussion with a representative gentile Christ-follower as interlocutor, depicted unflatteringly here as a wild olive shoot. The wild olive shoot, grafted contrary to nature, implies a whole cultural encyclopedia of Jew/gentile differentiation (Rainey 2018: 233–5). The choice in 11:17 of the second-person singular address σὺ δέ (cf. also 11:18 and 11:19) in the emphatic position has "a lively, exemplary effect that makes a potentially deprecatory allusion acceptable to the audience" (Jewett 2007: 683). It is to be noted that the playful, humorous quality of this speech-in-character discourse avoids polemic with the audience. But to be personified and addressed very pointedly as "you, a wild olive shoot," a small scraggy bush was not complimentary. Jewett claims that Stowers gives up on the attempt to claim diatribe is unpolemical discourse and that Paul severely criticizes the Romans in 11:18 (2007: 686). But as Tobin observes, Paul only addresses the interlocutor in a non-polemical manner (2004: 363). I would suggest rather that this avoids *direct* polemic with the audience in that the audience is still indirectly addressed but is not thereby rendered mere spectators in a drama. The diatribal style ends at 11:24, so there can be no uncertainty about whom Paul directly addresses in 11:25-35, and the content of this section fits clearly with the diatribal reading of 11:13-24. There the wild olive shoot is depicted as interpreting Israel's negative response to the gospel about Christ as meaning that "you were broken so that I could be grafted in," and 11:25 continues the theme of "Israel's hardening" in relation to the nations. The continuity in theme thus requires that the content of both sections (11:13-24 and 11:25-35) should address, though in differing modes, the same audience (on the same topic). In this conclusion, full recognition is given to the diatribal nature of 11:13-24, but also to its function in the chapter as well as in relation to the argument of the entire letter. It addresses neither a different audience nor implies a different attitude than the diatribe suggests—there is no reason to propose Paul uses the rhetorical conventions of the diatribe differently here. As Jewett usefully describes the process of speech-in-character, it "allows Paul to speak with an imaginary interlocutor whose traits are sufficiently exaggerated that the audience does not feel attacked, but sufficiently analogous that the audience can grasp the allegorical relevance" (2007: 684). (I would replace allegorical in this citation with "analogical.")

Romans 11:17-24: "You Were Grafted In"—an Apostrophe Reprimanding the Wild Olive Shoot

[17] But if some of the branches were broken, and you, a wild olive shoot, were grafted in amongst the branches to share the rich root of the olive tree, [18] do not boast over the branches. If you do boast, remember that it is not you that support the root, but the root that supports you. [19] You will say, "Branches were broken so that I might be grafted in." [20] That is true. They were broken because of their lack of trust, but you stand only through trust. So do not think proudly, but be fearful. [21] For if God did not spare the natural branches, in no way will he spare you. [22] Note then the kindness and the severity of God: severity toward those who fell but God's kindness toward you, provided you remain in this kindness; otherwise, you indeed will be cut off. [23] And even they, if they do not persist in lack of trust, will be grafted in, for God has the power to graft them in again. [24] For if you have been cut from what is by nature a wild olive tree and grafted, contrary to nature, into a cultivated olive tree, how much more will these natural branches be grafted back into their own olive tree.

Reading from the image of broken branches, it is important to state that the image does not necessarily denote a complete severance from the parent tree. Many trees can survive damage that can be described as resulting in broken branches, but branches cannot survive if they are entirely separated. From certain types of trees, some broken branches that still have some connection to their tree and if they are touching the ground, can survive long enough to grow a fresh root system that enables them to flourish long-term alongside the parent tree. What becomes obvious is that this discussion seems to presume, as do most of the commentaries, that we have in mind here large branches, not small twigs or shoots such as might be used for grafting purposes, that is, we are presuming that we are dealing with a large limb of a tree, which might constitute a substantial proportion of the tree were it to break away. But this assumption seems unlikely in this case. In harvesting fruit, normally a certain amount of damage can be anticipated due to the weight of the fruit, and the fruit-pickers or their ladders, and so on. Only occasionally would large branches be broken, as this results in lasting damage to the tree itself. So, it seems preferable to think here in terms of somewhat smaller branches rather than huge boughs, which, in any case, could not be grafted in again. Theophrastus normally used κλάδος/οι to refer to a branch or a twig in distinction to the larger branches or boughs from which these grow. He distinguishes "the annual shoot" (κλάδος/οι), coming as a single whole, from the ἀκρεμόνες (main branches), and similarly from κλῶνες (slips) or suckers (πτόρθοι). This distinction indicates that Paul is referring to small branches sustained by the main branches rather than larger (Nanos 2018: 133, n48). As noted above, the "gentiles" are usually thought of as being grafted into Israel, which is represented by the main trunk or tree. But Nanos interestingly holds that the Israelites are also but small branches in the tree sustained by the main branches and trunk (2018: 133).

The main point is that the grafted-in wild olive is totally dependent on the parent tree from which its sustenance derives. This is not a totally improbable scenario that Paul describes, but not the most common practice. Paul is aware of this, as his "contrary to nature" indicates (v. 24). The imagery of the olive and the way it is used does not reveal any deficiency in Paul's knowledge of oleiculture, if we do not read more into the text than warranted when read in context. Branches would be broken off in pruning or by accident in harvest, and wild olives were used in the propagation of cultivated trees because they had more vigor due to a better root system (Esler 2003: 302). As a life-long gardener, my own experience of grafting does not lead me to question Paul's knowledge of oleiculture. Wild root stocks are still grown for the grafting on of roses to ensure stronger growth. As Theophrastus states, "That is why people recommend that one should first plant wild olive trees and graft in buds or branches later, for the grafts hold better to the younger stock, and by attracting more nourishment, the tree bears rich fruit."[3] The branches of the tree on which the graft is placed are not, in Paul's image, completely broken, and there are other branches still standing, otherwise he could not speak of being grafted ἐν αὐτοῖς among them, not "in their place" (NRSV still following RSV). The intrusive "in their place" is not to be explained (a) in terms of grammar—this is not what the Greek text says, or (b) in terms of oleiculture—the other branches need not be removed to make space for the (tiny) in-grafted shoot, or (c) in terms of Pauline theology since this concept of replacement theology—supersessionism[4]—ironically is precisely what Paul intends his olive tree grafting image to deny (Esler 2003: 103–24, Tucker 2018).

What becomes clear is that the olive tree image serves the purpose of Pauline theology and not vice versa, the theological content is not determined by what olive-growers can do (Keck 2005: 276). A binary either/or perspective is reflected in the wild olive shoot's assertion, "branches were broken so that I could be grafted in" (11:19). But it seems clear there is no necessity in terms of oleiculture that in order to graft in a shoot, other branches must be displaced. It does not require the cutting of several branches to accommodate only one grafted-in shoot, but this shoot does require space to grow, which Nanos secures by referring to branches being bent aside (2018: 132). This scenario, reflected in the speech of the wild olive, is where Paul applies normal olive tree husbandry to suit his literary/theological purpose, which in turn is based on news of actual discussions reported as already arising in Rome. In that respect, the text mirrors reality, not in the sense of normal oleiculture but of the early Messianic movement. It should not be forced into an allegory at every point since the concept of extended metaphor seems adequate to account for the narrative (contra Klauck 1998: 305–6; Jewett 2007: 693). Thus, it must not be forgotten that

---

[3] Translation of Theophrastus *De causis plantarum* from Esler (2003: 302). As Esler notes, Theophrastus is aware of the possibility of grafting wild olives shoots into a cultivated tree, but rejects it since it will not produce fine fruit.

[4] Stegemann already claimed in 1980 that with Romans Paul tried to encourage the addressees to resist the antisemitism prevalent in Rome and stand in solidarity with the Jews. In that sense, it is the earliest witness against a gentile theological anti-Judaism (now in 2005: 39).

Paul's main aim in using the olive tree image is not, at this point, a concern with the broken branches, though they are essential to the story frame, but a concern to correct the arrogance of the wild olive shoot. This is where a balanced overview of the olive tree analogy is essential in order to pay attention to the main point of the narrative rather than unfruitfully concerning oneself with the marginal details. There is a form of grafting of fruit trees such as plums or apples in which the main stem or branch of the tree to be grafted is cut off at a particular point. Then the stem is split in two and grafts inserted in the space where the stem is split. In this case, the original stem or branches are necessarily removed to give space to accommodate the new shoot. Perhaps a parallel with this contemporary form of grafting encouraged the erroneous replacement theology of the NRSV's translation, "in their place," a phrase without any basis whatsoever in the text of Romans.

Earlier interpreters, following on the views of Sir William Ramsey, and patterns of ancient oleiculture known from Columella (*De re rustica* 5:9-16), considered that the rejuvenating of ancient trees to make them more fruitful by the in-grafting of wild olive shoots may have been in Paul's mind when choosing this metaphor, but this appears to be incidental (Esler 2003: 301–2). A by-product of grafting in wild shoots to old trees would be to give more life to the aged tree, and therefore have an Israel reference, but Paul's attention is focused on the wild olive shoot.

Paul's metaphor has the purpose of humbling the arrogant "gentiles" who were foolishly boasting over what they perceived to be the fate of Israel. Thus, Paul's use of the olive tree image is not to seek to rejuvenate Israel, as one might a tired and possibly no longer productive tree. Moreover, in Romans 11, the emphasis is not on the tree and making it more fruitful, but on the boasting of the engrafted gentile shoot. The wild olive could produce little good quality fruit. Paul puts emphasis on the fact that the engrafted shoot is borne by the native olive tree to which it has been attached. The verb βαστάζειν, to bear or support, will be used again in 15:1 where the strong are told they must bear with the weaknesses of the weak, and not please themselves. It is therefore illogical for the totally dependent "shoot" to boast as if it was responsible for its own destiny. It could not survive on its own. It is not self-sustaining in the sense that its existence could be meaningful apart from its "roots" in Israel and Israelite traditions. Applied to gentile life in Christ, this image represents a necessary and permanent reminder of gentile incompleteness without acknowledgement of and connection to Israel.

Bragging over the Broken Branches

In 11:18, Paul uses in the only example in his letters, the term κατακαυχᾶσθαι. This, when followed by a noun in the genitive, has the connotation of boasting or bragging over against others. It refers to an entirely inappropriate boasting, acceptable or even required in the competitive atmosphere of the Roman world, but illegitimate within the community of grace, though possibly exemplified in Rome. In diatribal style, Paul sharply repudiates this boasting over others with the imperative in v. 18, and in v. 20 adds weight with an alternative imperative "So do not think proudly but be fearful." This might indicate that the diatribal style has served its purpose and that now at this point in the letter, Paul addresses the Romans directly, using his apostolic authority over the nations to call them to voluntary response to the pattern of Christ. But it is more complicated than this in that the "you" singular σε, the wild olive shoot of v. 17 continues through vv. 22-24. (It is only in 11:25-36 that Paul returns to addressing the ethnē directly as ἀδέλφοι.) It could be maintained that the imperatives in 18-21 within a rhetorical form of address, as here, do not address the Romans directly at all and, therefore, have nothing significant to say to them, but this is not so. Jewett thinks this passage is unpolemical, but nevertheless, the impact of this diatribal address is deliberate and framed to impact indirectly but nevertheless powerfully upon the listening audience. Paul is limited by his irregular relation to the Roman Christ-followers so that he cannot speak to them in the direct pattern of his own ἐκκλησίαι, but the diatribal form of address is nevertheless powerful, as good rhetoric always is, however, presented. The fact of broken branches to which the ethnē drew attention in the case of Israel, should cause the ethnē to be less arrogant and to acknowledge that they "stand" only by trust. There is no room for pride, "for if God did not spare the natural branches, in no way will he spare you" (v. 21). Far from using a non-ethnic language of sameness, Paul continues to stress ongoing ethnic difference in repeating the terminology of natural and wild olive branches. Thus, the view that Israel has been rejected, irrespective of its truth and results for Israel, is deemed by Paul to have a dangerous outcome for the ethnē who are thereby encouraged toward an uncritical pride and ethnic self-confidence over against Israel that is in diametrical opposition to their trust and standing in Christ.

At this point, a clear distinction needs to be noted between Paul's use of the verb ἐκκλάω, which can mean broken rather than broken off (vv. 17 and 18), compared with his later use in vv. 22-24 of ἐκκόπτω, which does mean "cut off" (Nanos 2018: 189–93). Nanos suggests that the use of ἐκκλάω in relation to Israel corresponds to the stumbling image used in chs. 9–10, which would support the image of broken rather than broken off, as this is more akin to what Paul asserts, that is, that Israel has stumbled but not actually fallen. Thus, the second verb Paul uses has perhaps a deliberately more extreme function, to warn those whom Christ has received by trust that this dependence leaves no space for them to boast over those who are "broken" because they stumbled. Those who are boasting over Israel's stumbling are warned that they are in danger, not of stumbling and being broken, but of being completely severed from the people of God. This would account for Paul's dual emphasis that includes both kindness and severity, a pattern fully illustrated in Israel's history and from which "wild olive shoots" must learn.[5] This is a severe warning that the graftee lives only by trust; therefore, the grafted shoot must "continue in the kindness, otherwise you also will be cut off." As Keck notes, "Paul could hardly have emphasized more strongly the believers' continued reliance on God's kindness. In v. 23, the same point is made with regard to the broken branches: if they cease their ἀπιστία, God has the power to graft them into the tree" (Keck 2005: 275–6; Reasoner 2014: 388–404).

---

[5] The history of Israel, though it gave rise to conceptions of "salvation history," was nevertheless a history that included slavery and exile, and Paul's grief in Rom. 9:1-4 is sufficiently real so that if Israel can suffer in this way, it must be a pattern from which "wild-olives" such as ethnē in Christ cannot be excluded. But see Reasoner (2014: 388–404).

Romans 11:25-36: Israel Will Be Restored but only after the Fullness of the Nations

*²⁵I want you to understand this mystery so that you do not keep thinking how wise you are, brothers, a hardening has come upon part of Israel, until the fullness of the nations has come in. ²⁶And so all Israel will be restored; as it is written,
"Out of Zion will come the Deliverer;
he will banish impiety from Jacob."
²⁷"And this is my covenant with them,
when I take away their sins."
²⁸As regards the gospel they are enemies for your sake; but as regards election they are beloved, for the sake of their ancestors; ²⁹for the gifts and the calling of God are irrevocable. ³⁰Just as you were once unpersuaded but have now received mercy because of their unpersuadedness, ³¹so these have now been unpersuaded in order that, by the mercy shown to you, they too may now receive mercy. ³²For God has joined everyone in a state of doubt so that he might show everyone mercy.
³³O the depth of the riches and wisdom and knowledge of God! How unsearchable are his judgments and how inscrutable his ways!
³⁴"For who has known the mind of the Lord?
Or who has been his counsellor?"
³⁵"Or who has given something to him,
so God has to give something in return?"
³⁶For from him and through him and to him are all things. To him be the glory eternally. Amen.*

To the Jew First?

It was the great achievement of Johannes Munck that he recognized that the earliest apostolic proclamation held to the assumption that the nations would hear the gospel message but only after the Jews. "Mark's gospel starts from the assumption that the Gentiles are to hear the Gospel after the Jews: and it is left open to debate whether that sequence can be departed from" (1959: 262–3). Based on the story of the Canaanite woman in both Matt. 15:21-28 and Mark 7:24-30, Munck notes that Matthew's version starts from the assumption that Jesus is sent only to the house of Israel (15:24) and that Jesus only reluctantly agrees to the woman's request for help, after having first stated that it is not fair to take the children's bread and give it to the dogs. In Mark 7, however, the passage is introduced by the words, "let the children first be fed," putting the emphasis not on whether the "dogs" may share the children's food, but rather on the order of eating. Paul also refers "to the Jew first and also to the Greek" (Rom. 1:16; 2:9f.). He also is reported as saying in Acts 13:46, to the Jews of Pisidian Antioch, "It was necessary that the word of God should be spoken *first* to you. Since you thrust it from you … behold we turn to the 'gentiles.'" "It is quite clear that the problem behind Matthew's version is the authorizing of the mission to the gentiles, not, as in Mark, the time of its beginning. The implication of Matthew's version is that it would not be right to break off the mission to the Jews in order to carry on a mission to the gentiles" (as there is not enough time for both before Christ's return, Munck 1959: 262–3).

From Munck's discussion here, we get an introduction to the context of the messianic movement shortly after the time of Paul's writing to the Romans. In Munck's perspective, there are two missions, one of which, that to the Jews, may have been regarded by some as completed, but not in missionary terms very successfully. This conclusion was not a new realization, but one which had gradually become evident. The problem facing the respective leaders of the Christ-movement was that of where should one's priorities lie; with Paul's relatively successful mission to the nations, or with the faltering mission of Peter to his own people? This issue was further complicated by the strength of the tradition that only when Israel is restored will it be right to take the Gospel to the "gentiles."

As we have argued in the previous chapter, evidence for discussion concerning the priority of mission to the "gentiles" or to the Jews is found in Rom. 10:19. The πρῶτος, which in traditional translations begins v. 19b, giving the reading, "First, Moses says" is not very satisfactory in that there is no second to succeed it. But if it were taken with the preceding sentence (v. 19a), then it would read as a rhetorical question (expecting a negative reply) "Israel did not come to understand first, did they?" Thus, it would have the sense—should not Israel have trusted prior to the worldwide proclamation to the nations described in 10:18? As the form of the rhetorical question indicates, Paul's reply is, "No it is not the case that Israel should come to know first" because, as the scriptures state "I will provoke you to jealousy by means of those who are not a nation, I will enrage you by means of a nation that lacks understanding" (Deut. 32:21). Paul would read the reference to "not a people" or to "a nation that lacks understanding" as certainly a reference to the nations. The Isaiah citation would be read similarly, as indicating that the nations find the Lord though not seeking, that is, prior to Israel (cf. Paul's scenario in Romans 9–11 of the stumbling of the Jews). Thus, the tradition that Paul knows and cites has not found verification in the developments originating in the Christ-event, and it is likely that the answer to the question about Israel being restored prior to the nations arises out of Paul's own experience and reflection. The answer emerges from reading the scriptures in light of current events as was also a pattern of the Qumran community (VanderKam 2012. 156–62). It is in light of such discussions that the pessimism of the Roman ethnē toward Israel can be contextualized.

Paul, in spite of the new events resulting in the coming in of the nations, and the anticipated restoration of Israel, still awaits with confidence the eventual coming to understanding of Israel. Unlike the Roman ethnē who seem to have concluded, on the basis of a generally negative response from Israel, accompanied by a surprising embrace of the gospel by those from the nations, that what Paul interpreted as Israel's stumbling was, in their eyes, evidence of Israel's rejection of the gospel, and a corresponding casting off of the Jews by their God.

In the penultimate section of Romans 9–11, Paul underlines a point he wishes to put to the Romans by means of a stylized disclosure formula and direct address as ἀδελφοί, brothers,[6] indicating he is about to say something of extreme importance

---

[6] Brothers is not frequently used in Romans 1–13 but, as here, occurs at strategic points (cf. 1:13; 7:1, 4; 8:12, 29; 9:3; 10:1; 11:25; 12:1).

for his audience, and his reason for writing to them. The pericope contains two major parts: a disclosure of the mystery with scriptural support, 11:25-27, and a theological explanation of its significance for God's purpose, 11:28-32 (Jewett 2007: 695). Strangely, this concerns not something specifically relating to their own identity as nations, but instead, and somewhat surprisingly, what is to be disclosed concerns *Israel*. Paul also gives a motivation for this disclosure. "I want you to understand this mystery, brothers, so that you do not keep thinking how wise you are." Nanos translates the second part of this verse as follows "because for a while a callus/shield has formed around Israel, making her unresponsive until the fullness of the nations shall commence" (2018: 291).

It is to be noted that here Paul is possibly echoing Prov. 3:7—"do not be wise in your own eyes" as he informs the ethnē in Christ at Rome about something that concerns their own self-understanding, ignorance of which may make them unduly conceited, wise in your own eyes παρ' ἑαυτοῖς φρόνιμοι,. The use of the verb φρόνειν is significant in Rom. 11:20–12:3. In 11:17-24, the group cultural superiority of the nations is repudiated (cf. also in 12:3 and 12:16).

Not only is there an inward, that is, insider effect within the Christ group from this grandiose self-conceit, but it equally seriously also affects the gentile Christ-followers' perspective on Israel whom they appear to consider in a binary relation to themselves. It is evident that the risk of the Romans becoming self-opinionated somehow relates to Israel. The content of the mystery revealed then, not—surprisingly, relates to Israel. The mystery revealed is that for a while a callus/shield has formed for Israel until the fullness of the nations shall commence (v. 25) (Nanos 2018: 153–78). This information about Israel is considered by Paul as essential to avoid an elevated self-estimate on the part of the Romans. If we take the address to the wild olive as a starting point, it appears that this would help solve the problem as to how the self-understanding of the Romans is influenced by the condition of Israel. "Branches were broken so that I could be grafted in," wrongly implies a binary relation between the two entities, Israel and the nations. The diatribal exchange of 11:19 is based on an either/or antithesis—either Jew or non-Jew—which implies that Israel had to be rejected in order that the nations might enter. The premise on which is based the view that Israel has been rejected is wrong, and so the conclusion is also necessarily impaired. But the discussions that led to this binary perspective, possibly reflected in the diatribal questions, indicate that issues originating from Israel's resistance to the acknowledgement of the new era were alive in Rome and elsewhere. Thus, Ehrensperger proposes that it can be assumed that their (the Roman gentiles') understanding of belonging to Christ was at risk of following a separatist and dualistic pattern that linked God's mercy in a causal and conditional way to "being in Christ." Jews who did not respond to the message of the gospel may be perceived as having forfeited God's mercy (2019: 324). In response to these, Paul reveals a divine mystery. The μυστήριον

> thus serves the purpose of communicating to them in a cautious way that, although lacking in certain knowledge and understanding, they are not being blamed for, or exposed in their ignorance by Paul. The μυστήριον has a supportive function for establishing a positive relationship with a community he has not founded,

and thus for a positive reception of the explanation of the μυστήριον that follows. (2019: 319–37, 324)

Paul, in offering this mystery to the Romans, is claiming to tell them something they should have known, an aspect of their call, in which they are deficient. In that sense, he is exercising his apostolic authority over them, but in a somewhat reserved manner. He did not teach them previously, nor was he the first to bring to them the message about the Christ. So, he cannot attribute blame, nor does he take on the stance of a seer or a mystic that would allow him claim to a superior form of insight, not available to them. He does not describe the content of his message here as a "teaching" διδαχή, or an admonition (παράκλησις). Revelation language is absent as is any reference to unveiling a secret, because the μυστήριον is not secret, but based on the scriptures rather than ecstatic experience. This μυστήριον existed in the scriptures but required investigation and discovery in light of contemporary events, that is, particularly Jewish failure to embrace the Christ-event (Ehrensperger 2019: 326–7). The scripturally based argument throughout chs. 9–11 demonstrates the source of Paul's authority. It does carry an authority claim but not in an exclusivist manner via the means of a unique charisma, but via the sharing of the scriptures that mediate and regulate the relationship to the God of Israel (Rom. 4:23, 15:14). Even here as he claims scriptural authority, Paul limits his claim to the understanding of this particular mystery, and even as he does so, he is creating a bond that consists in the sharing of knowledge related to the Divine with those in Rome, a development in understanding of the character of God that differentiates this God from the Roman gods (Ehrensperger 2019: 331–2). The God of Israel must not be interpreted through the lens of Roman deities, but by the traditions of Israel. As we have noted several times previously in earlier chapters, the character of the God of Israel in its difference from Roman cultural patterns and deities is a serious issue for the Romans.

The problem noted above has resulted in ethnē boasting over unconvinced Jews. Christ-following Jews would be unlikely to share this perspective, so the main thrust of Paul's scripturally based reasoning aims at changing or preventing gentile boasting or supermindedness primarily as these affect unpersuaded Jews. This implies contact or communal interaction with Jews, otherwise it would be difficult to explain the presence of such attitudes and opinions (cf. "Introduction" chapter). As in Romans 2, we have evidence here of differing groups in various relations to Judaism and the Christ-movement, but this is one of the more significant references since here unpersuaded Jews are an essential element in the emerging narrative of Paul's address to the Romans. These Jews, of course, are not addressed. Their literary presence points to the social context in which Paul refers to one of the several groups, which is a necessary supposition for a full understanding of communal relations in Rome. If Nanos is correct in his assumption of ongoing connection of ethnē in Christ with Roman synagogues (1996: 13, 163), this would offer a scenario where such contacts might take place, at least temporarily.

The mystery Paul wishes to disclose to the Romans is not just that a "hardening" has come upon Israel, but that this is only "for a while," that is, temporary not permanent. Ἀπὸ μέρους is best read, not as referring to part of Israel, but as a time limit, defined as ending with (ἄχρι) until the incoming of the fullness of the nations. It is similar in meaning to 15:24 where Paul states that he will stay in Rome ἀπὸ μέρους for a while before he heads for Spain (Nanos 2018: 170–3). This reading is supported by Paul's cited scriptural texts in 11:26-27 that substantiate the mystery he seeks to disclose. These do not refer to part of Israel, but to a temporary stage in Israel's history.

In my opinion, elements of Paul's and other Christ-followers' proclamation of the Christ-event must have been known to the gentile Christ-followers in Rome. It is not that they knew little or nothing of the message of Christ to the nations, but what they did know was accompanied by its reflex, the refusal of many Jews to be convinced by it. A partial knowledge of Israel's history was known to the ethnē, but not well understood. The God of Israel was the Creator God, Lord of all peoples, not just of Israel. But the possibility that he would behave toward some as a capricious and unpredictable god who might easily replace one favored nation by another was not ruled out. Gentile Christ-followers may have known something of narratives such as 2 Macc. 7:33 but have difficulty with stories that suggest "that the anger of the living God will last only for a short time, just enough to shock and educate his people and then it will cease." As Rajak states, this "is in keeping with the Hebrew prophets' conception of a finite process of chastisement set in motion by terrifying but temporally limited divine displeasure. The tyrant's (Antiochus's) anger is explicitly contrasted with that kind of anger that operates in association with justice *dikē*" (Rajak 2009: 193). Gentile Christ-followers, even those trained and taught about the coming of Christ and its implications in relation to differing groups of people, were prone to misunderstanding of such narratives (Rajak 2009: 207). The Hebrew Scriptures in their Greek translation would be cited, and the story of the great acts of God in relation to Abraham or Moses and the prophets would also be reported. But the translation of the thought-world of the scriptures into Greek culture—was not easy, as Rajak points out, "this literature denies easy access by virtue of its intertextuality. Any one text is only completely understood in terms of multiple allusions and resonances" (2009: 193–4). It was a huge transition for non-Jews to enter the Jewish symbolic universe with its very particular nuances and commitments, so it is no surprise that in an environment where differences between Jew, Greek, and barbarian were explicit and where conflicts of interest arose in relation to their differing values, there should have been debate about the relative status and consistency of the Creator God of Israel in relation to the family of Abraham, and his new people, the nations.

From what they knew of God's judgment upon or disciplining of Israel by the use of other powerful nations, the ethnē in Rome had concluded that the Jews as a people subject to Rome, as were many others, had been judged by their God. But the concept of God disciplining his people *temporarily* seemed foreign to them. God's judgment on Israel in their perception meant that she no longer enjoyed divine favor and that she had been displaced by another people. The narrative of God's ways with Israel, perhaps something like Stephen's speech in Acts ch. 7, was probably somewhat familiar to the ethnē in Rome. But the concept of God's people, and especially the nature of the God of Israel's dealings with people were not well understood. Such a concept as πώρωσις was difficult to comprehend. This was rendered more so in light of the earliest traditions in which it was firmly established that Israel was destined to come to blessing prior to those from the nations. When Israel was not easily persuaded that the Messianic Time had dawned, then it appeared to many ethnē in Christ that Israel must have been cast off only to be replaced by a favored other in the pattern of the Roman gods. Paul wants the Roman ethnē to distinguish *appearance from reality and also* the *present from the future*. They must disassociate the present as the apparent failed realization of God's promises from the future as the complete realization of God's purposes in history, since the full revelation of God's justice is yet to come (Elliott 2008: 107, cf. also 108–9).

The gods were either for you or against you, not temporarily judging or disciplining you. So Paul's mystery is to inform the Romans not only that Israel has been rendered incapable of hearing and understanding the message of the gospel (so that this message would now reach the nations) but also that Israel's lack of understanding has an *appointed time limit*. It is temporarily limited, Israel's God still has future plans for the world, and Israel is part of these. She has not been rejected or divorced by her God, whose plan is that "the whole of Israel will be saved."[7] But though it is basic to this narrative, as in Paul's theological thought, *that* God will restore Israel, it is still unclear *precisely how* and exactly when this will happen.

The καὶ οὕτως of v. 26 means "and thus" or "in this way." It does not read "and then" καὶ τότε, which indicates that the issue is not "when" but rather "how" all Israel will be restored.

Paul's wrestling with the incoming of the nations alongside the limited response of Israel did not lead him to find a binary solution, that is, either the nations or Israel, but an inclusive solution, the nations in the Christ-movement, and then all Israel.[8] It seems Paul's assumption led him to start with the fact of a successful gentile mission, and then to proceed to argue from that how God, who could not possibly finally reject his own people Israel (because "the gifts and call of God are irrevocable" (Rom. 11:29), could solve this paradox.

Paul could not bring himself to deny either the gentile mission, or that God must be faithful to Israel, he felt fully obligated to affirm both. His solution was to see each of these entities, not as in competition with each other, nor the one as an alternative to the other, but as each mutually reinforcing the image of the God of Israel in his working in and through the Christ-event.

Only in this scenario of the rescue of the nations contributing positively to the future restoration of Israel could the nations themselves be prevented from becoming self-opinionated and proud, boasting as if they could possibly ever replace Israel in God's purposes. Paul wants to emphasize the dependence, even the causal nexus between the two. "The partial hardening of Israel and the entry of the full number of the Gentiles are the way through which 'all Israel shall be saved.'" "The real mystery of God's plan is a paradoxical relationship: all Israel depends on the entry of the full

---

[7] Wolter indicates that "Paulus nicht einfach nur eine chronologische Abfolge beschreiben, sondern den Zusammenhang zwischen den vor und hinter καὶ οὕτως stehenden Ereignissen aufweisen will. Die Aufhebung der 'Verhärtung' der nichtchristlichen Mehrheit Israels nach dem 'Reinkommen' der 'Vollzahl der Heiden' wäre dann die Voraussetzung dafür, dass 'ganz Israel' gerettet wird" (2018:129).

[8] For the debate of this issue, see Zoccali (2008), cf. also Tucker's discussion (2018: 190–2).

number of the Gentiles" (Tobin 2004: 371). Rather than being mutually exclusive, the rescue of the nations and the restoration of Israel are interdependent; they need each other in the divine plan.

One of the characteristics of Romans is that in it to a greater extent than in any other of Paul's letters, he deals corporately with the nations as nations rather than as a grouping of individuals. "All Israel" is a common concept in the Hebrew scriptures,[9] and it is fitting (that) in a letter where a "remnant" has been discussed, and Israel's potential rejection has been voiced, that it is Israel *as a whole* whose restoration is assured. Thus Paul expects the division symbolized by "the remnant of Israel" and "the rest of Israel" to be a temporary phenomenon the termination of which will be signaled by the restoration of "all Israel."[10] This emphasis also is very much in keeping with our reading of 9:6b, as a rhetorical question rather than a redefinition of Israel as being internally divided into an Israel within Israel.[11] Her restoration, "being made safe" (Nanos 2018: 287) is, as Paul clearly demonstrates, "in accordance with scripture."

As evidence Paul cites from Isa. 59:20-21 (combined with Isa. 27:9), "Out of Zion will come the Deliverer; he will banish impiety (ἀσεβείας) from Jacob." Wolter lists the small handful of texts in the "Old Testament" and in the literature of early Judaism where the expression ἐκ Σιών is found. This always concerns the salvation of Israel—"from Zion" Israel can expect nothing but salvation. Moreover, Israel's God is the only one who lives in Zion. Wolter also notes that the actors in this part of Romans 9–11 are exclusively God and his people Israel (2018: 131–3).

It is noteworthy here that the two verbs in 11:26 are both in the future tense. The Deliverer (ὁ ῥυόμενος) may possibly be thought by Paul to be Christ "the one who delivers (τὸν ῥυόμενον) us from the wrath to come" (1 Thess. 1:10). But since there are only two references to Christ in Romans 9–11 (i.e., 9:5 and 10:17), and since nothing in the citation in 11:26-27 clearly refers to Christ, it is more likely that in keeping with the original citation, the Deliverer is God himself since it is God who is the central figure throughout. This emphasis is important in deciding who will bring about the ultimate final restoration of Israel. Paul obviously combined what he viewed as two similar citations both spoken by God, both refer to a future event, and both have parallel formulations (Tobin 2004: 373-4). The second Isaiah citation, modifies LXX 27:9: "Therefore the sin of Jacob will be taken away" to read "when I take away their sins." This may be significant for Paul in that it reads as God speaking, active rather than passive.

It seems that Paul intends to describe the action of God himself in "my very own covenant" ἡ παρ' ἐμοῦ διαθήκη, which Jewett (following Behm) views as "in contrast to the plural form in 9:4, that refers to the various covenants made between God and

---

[9] In the Jewish scriptures it is used approximately one hundred and fifty times, and it always designates historic ethnic Israel was a whole (Tobin 2004: 372).

[10] As Wolter argues, "Es ist nicht nur der judenchristliche 'Rest' Israels, der gerettet wird, sondern auch seine nichtchristliche Mehrheit." In this salvation, Paul's prayers in Rom. 10:1 will find their answer (2018: 126).

[11] We differ from Keck, who, having noted that though Paul began the whole discussion with 9:6 declaring that it is not the case that all who are of Israel actually *are* Israel, then has to ask "Does he (Paul) now say in effect that all who are of Israel are Israel?" (2005: 279–80).

the patriarchs in the past, this implies a final and ultimate covenant to be enacted in the future." I can see Jewett's reasoning, but I am not persuaded that the restoration of all Israel involves another (new) covenant or that such a *contrast* between past and future is intended. I am all too aware, as I have argued at some length, of the historic tendency to read Paul in *contrast* rather than in *comparison* to Judaism.[12] Verses 28-32 seem to emphasize not a totally new covenant in the future, but rather the confirmation of the election of Israel. Since the covenant had been renewed through Christ, this new covenant is not a future event, even though the action of God, which it describes toward Israel, is still to come. But that future activity will be initiated by the action of God, which is the expression of his original calling of Israel, and confirmed in the Christ-event.[13] In terms of the gospel proclamation, some Jews are opposed to the proclamation of the gospel to the nations without these ethnē being obliged to live by the Law on the same terms as Israel. These Jews are not, as the RSV amazingly depicts, "enemies of God for your sake" (11:28). To thus describe Jews as "enemies of God," when there is no noun or other term that might justify depicting the Jews as enemies *of God* requires an unacceptable liberty with the text. This translation is all the more reprehensible when it occurs in a sentence that goes on to describe the same people in vividly contrasting terms "as regards election they are beloved for the sake of the patriarchs," ἀγαπητοὶ διὰ τοὺς πατέρας. The connecting γάρ gives the reason for Israel's status. It is due to the faithful character of God.

And as if the reference to election were insufficient, Paul makes a solemn claim that is entirely unqualified in any way—"for irrevocable ἀμεταμέλητα are the gifts and calling of God" (11:29) (with irrevocable in the place of emphasis). We translate ἀμεταμέλητα as irrevocable because the English stem retains a link with calling, implying a legal axiom that cannot be repealed, though Jewett follows the basic emphasis of ἀμεταμέλητος "without regret" (cf. 2 Cor. 7:10). The point Paul wishes to underline is that God does not revoke the calling of Israel, he has no regrets that would cause him to change his mind. This might be termed a description of the content of election—the gifts or begracements, χάρισματα, and the calling κλῆσις of God are what constitute what God has given in his grace to Israel (9:4-5) (Jewett 2007: 708). Unlike the gods of Greece and Rome, the God of Israel is limited in what he would choose to do, or not do, by the limitation of his own δικαιοσύνη. But this means he is limited only by his own freedom, he is faithful to himself and to his commitments in covenants

---

[12] See Campbell (2018: ch. 2 and part of ch. 3), where I demonstrate that F. C. Baur was heir to a tradition of interpretation stemming from the English Deists, Thomas Morgan and John Toland and others, which together with Hegelian influence, lead him to view universalism and particularism as necessarily in diametrical opposition, Judaism being relegated historically to the latter (negative category), and thus necessarily the antithesis of Christianity (2018: 51–2, 79–82).

[13] As Wolter emphasizes, Paul is certain that God will save Israel, but he is unclear precisely how. The "that" is clear, the "how" remains an open question. Wolter cites Otfried Hofius and Neil Elliott as two contrasting scenarios of how God will save Israel, Hofius by their acceptance of the gospel from the returning Christ, and Elliott stressing the Jewish recognition of the fulfillment of Deutero-Isaiah's promises when God leads an entourage of Gentile converts to Jerusalem (2019: 135–6).

that are necessarily determined by his own righteousness, δικαιοσύνη (Rom. 3:26).[14] The God of Israel in Paul's perspective combines both freedom and faithfulness. The God and Father of Israel and of Jesus Christ has demonstrated his freedom to act in a new way in the Christ-event, but in a way that does not eject Israel from his purposes. Because the Lord is free, he is free to bring in the nations as brothers of Israel through Jesus Christ, but because he is bound only by his own righteousness, he is free to retain Israel in his purpose. In this purpose, revealed in the Christ-event, God covenants himself to continue to be δίκαιος to Israel and now also to the nations. This means that Christology has to be consistent with the revelation of God in the scriptures of Israel. God proves his faithfulness not by the Christ-event on its own but by the Christ-event interpreted through the scriptures of Israel. Only thus can it be seen that God is consistent with himself, that is, with his self-revelation.

The only possible grounds for finding a scriptural basis for God's casting off of Israel could be those places where God is reported as changing his mind, or destroying the world that he has made (as, e.g., Gen. 8:20-22, 9:1-17). The foundation of Israel's confidence in her God was based on his making covenants with her (as, e.g., the covenant made with Noah). The God of Israel is not arbitrary in his decisions—he is faithful—he remembers his promises and can be relied upon to keep them. Thus, Israel can be confident in her election—she is "beloved on account of the fathers" (11:28).[15] This is the point at which Paul differs sharply from the perspective of some of the ethnē in Rome in that he views the God of Israel as being fully committed to Israel despite her "stumbling." More than this, Paul thinks he has found a clue, perhaps *the* clue, to understanding God's ways. Despite the fact of Israel's not being persuaded by the gospel, God is using her hostility to the mission to the nations as the route he will use to restore his people to himself and his purposes. "Hostility" perhaps toward some aspects of the gentile mission, and "estrangement on your behalf," but not "hostility to God," or "enemies of God" (cf. Nanos 2018: 286). Jews continued to worship God, but had great difficulty in being persuaded that the new Messianic Time that allowed the nations entry to the promises had dawned.

So confident is Paul in his vision of God's unfolding purpose that he finds a real comparability in how the nations and Israel have been treated. "Just as you (ethnē) were once unpersuaded but have now received mercy because of their (Israel's) unpersuadedness, so these have now been unpersuaded in order that, by the mercy shown to you, they too may now receive mercy" (11:31). The reason why there is such comparability between the narratives of the two differing peoples is that Paul sees a divine principle at work in both—"for God joined everyone in a state of doubt,

---

[14] Cf. Zeller (1976: 200). As Jewett points out, it was Joseph Sievers who drew attention to the decisive contribution of Karl Barth in overturning the consensus that the "believers" were the sole heirs of these promises. Barth argued that Rom. 11:29 expresses the abiding commitment to the Jewish people, whether they trust the gospel or not (noted by Sievers 1997: 338). Daniel Harrington continues this emerging consensus of Roman Catholic exegesis in affirming, that this verse "is Paul's endorsement of the continuing nature of God's election of Israel, even of those Israelites who have refused to accept the gospel" (1992: 64).

[15] God's love for the patriarchs is an important theme (e.g., Deut. 10:15; 33:12; Isa. 41:8), and similarly for Israel as a whole (e.g., Deut. 7:7, 9-13; Ps. 127:2; Isa. 63:9; Hos. 11:1; 14:4, Prov. 3:12).

ἀπείθειαν, so that he might show everyone mercy" (11:32).¹⁶ It seems that though he continued to stress the difference between Israel and the nations in keeping with the narrative of Israel's history, Paul felt most confident when he was able to align his theology of differentiated peoples with a commonality of status determined by the electing purpose of God. This, nevertheless, illustrates that *God uses each of these within a purpose of σωτηρία that includes them both.* This purpose is, as was claimed earlier in 9:15, "I will have mercy." The recipients of divine mercy are not determinative, what is primary for Paul is that—God "should be merciful to all," 11:32. No clearer response to this pessimistic view of God's dealings with Israel (of which Paul implied he had heard reports in Rome) could be given than that God's purpose is determined by his mercy, not by the caprice of the gods, and that God's character including his anger is just and works in all things for good for those who love him.

What must be noted, however, is that at this climactic stage in Paul's argumentation, "all" is not an undefined, generalized abstraction, that is, the universal individual human condition of individuals in Christ but groups specifically still designated as Jews or as ethnē. These designations abide as determined by God's purpose and are symbolized by the specific relation of Jews and "gentiles" who are united with Christ. It is interesting to note that when Jewett summarizes 11:32, he states, "Nowhere in the ancient world, outside of this text, was mercy granted in so indiscriminate and impartial a manner" (2007: 711). His summary demonstrates what I have claimed is the proper understanding of διασολή in 3:22 and 10:12, that is, indiscriminate and impartial granting of mercy and judgments (or making of distinctions).¹⁷

It has been a long and difficult route that Paul has traversed from Rom. 1:1 to Rom. 11:32, and at this point it is not surprising that he should marvel at the pattern of God's revelation of righteousness in the Christ-event. But there is no specific reference to Christ, "the passage resolutely concentrates on God" (Keck 2005: 287). Thus, in v. 33 Paul makes awesome claims, "O the depth of the riches and wisdom and knowledge of God. How unsearchable are his judgments/decisions and how inscrutable his ways." It is significant which aspects of the divine nature Paul lists here—riches, wisdom, knowledge, God's decisions/judgments, and his ways. The emphasis is primarily on wisdom, knowledge, and a (presumed) justice and righteousness in God's actions, which we take to be included under the terms κρίματα, judgments, and ὁδοί, ways. In keeping with the rhetorical pattern of Romans, Paul, rather than making assertions praising God, asks probing questions to uncover the divine majesty. The claims of v. 33 are related to the succeeding three questions by a connecting γάρ "for", indicating that they function as the warrant for these claims.

The implied answer to all three questions is "no one!" The first two questions focus on knowledge, "Who has known the mind of the Lord? Or who has been his counsellor?"

---

[16] Nanos's translation (2018: 288). Jewett cites Hans Wilhelm Schmidt's claim (1963: 201) that there are no New Testament allusions to enemies as hated by God (Jewett 2007: 707). Schmidt makes it plain that the idea that Paul intended a fusion between hating God and being hated by God is unsupportable.

[17] Jewett claims, 'The reduplication of πᾶς (all i.e. all persons) is the climactic expression of one of the most important themes of the letter, salvation for all, found in 1:5, 7, 8, 16, 18; 2:10; 3:9, 12, 19, 20, 22, 23; 4:11, 16; 5:12, 18; 6:3; 8:14; 9:5, 6, 7, 17; 10:10-13, 18, 26" (2007: 711).

Clearly, the pattern of God's dealings, especially with respect to the incoming of the nations in relation to the stumbling of Israel, had caused major questions for the ethnē in Rome. Paul has wrestled with these issues, and he cannot but give praise for what in his thinking looks like a majestic solution to the σωτηρία of gentile and Jew, in that in this each contributes positively to the σωτηρία of the other, as Godet has perceptively stressed (1977: 415).

The third question also anticipates a negative response in that it rejects the notion of "exchange" or recompense between God and the worshipper as expressed in the well-known Roman concept that the relation between immortals and mortals was based on the exchange of gifts and countergifts (Scheid 2003: 99). It is significant that at the climax of his argumentation here, Paul reiterates a core theme of his argument about grace and calling. Human beings cannot enter into a bargaining system with God, which would force him to operate in human systems of "wages due for work done," which would restrict his freedom and put him under obligation to them (Barclay 2015: 25–50). "Who has given something to him to receive something in return" epitomizes Paul's doctrine of the freedom of God and indicates that the nature of the God of Israel may still be a "stumbling block" for those ethnē in Christ hitherto accustomed to the rituals of Roman and other non-Jewish religious traditions. The final verse does not speak specifically about God as the Creator of all that is but in his use of wisdom theology here, Paul admits that God is a mysterious God, and even when humans try to describe his actions toward, and ways with, the world our explanations are incomplete and imperfect because our task is not to explain God so much as to worship him and give him the honor due to him. Paul's all-encompassing summary has Stoic parallels, "All things are from him, through him, and to him are all things" (11:36). But Paul does not specifically mention Christ as the mediator of creation as he does in 1 Cor. 8:6, "For us there is one God, the Father, from whom are all things and for whom we exist, one Lord Jesus Christ, through whom are all things and through whom we exist." Paul wishes to end on a note of mysterious wisdom. Having indicated already that it is not good "to keep thinking how wise you are" (wise in your own self-understanding) (11:25), he needs to set an example of humility and awe before God for the Christ-followers at Rome.

Having earlier misguidedly persecuted the ἐκκλησίαι of Christ, and having now realized that Israel will accept God's saving action only after the incoming of the nations, Paul has learned to be more humble. By ending on this note, Paul gives a clear signal that he himself cannot grasp fully the mystery of God's ways with the unpersuaded majority of Israel (Wolter 2018: 132–42, 141), but he can still give praise for this God's mercy.

EXCURSUS IV

Supersessionism at Rome

Do the Ethnē in Christ Have a Connection to Any of the Synagogues at Rome?

This question needs to be answered before entering fully into the debate about potential supersessionism at Rome. Socially, the threat of supersessionism implies an existing or former connection with the Jews over whom one posits supersession, thus necessarily involving relations with synagogues. Doubtless there was variety in the style of Jewish synagogues in Rome, not least in their perception of Paul's mission, and there may also have been corresponding variety in the meetings of gentile Christ-followers residing in Rome. It is interesting that Paul mentions in ch. 16 those who seem to be leaders of groups in Rome whom he apparently has not met. Paul makes it clear *that he is the apostle to* the nations, both over those residing elsewhere, and also in Rome. But how would he (Paul), relate to local leaders of groups who did not affiliate closely with his network of mission workers? Could Paul's apostleship to the nations justify his undisputed leadership over such people without meeting similar problems resulting from outside interference as noted in 2 Corinthians? It is obvious that Paul would not command much authority if he did not stress the ethnicity factor that distinguishes his mission. On the other hand, he must now construct an identity for these ethnē that coheres with his ascribed apostolic authority. It is interesting in this respect that a common feature of the people addressed in ch. 16 consists in some association with Paul and his gentile mission. Thus, Paul by writing to the Romans as those from the nations, to some extent, inevitably strengthens their identity-consciousness as ethnē. This holds good even if some of them, at least, still continue relations with synagogues. But, properly understood, identity consciousness need not mean separation from association. Ethnē in Christ may not already have been distinctive as a group, but only as a subgroup and so inherently linked to Jews. But even a distinct identity need not demand separation from those who identify themselves otherwise. Paul is not demanding separation but constructing meaningful genealogies that include both Israelites and ethnē in Christ, a major function of Romans 9–11. There are identity issues in relation to "judaizing" these gentiles (Fredriksen 2010, Runesson 2022: 207–26), but Paul's leadership here is to lead them from separateness to links with Israel, interpreting distinctiveness not as separation-but as distinction without opposition. A synagogue building was essentially an "umbrella" context under which many varied activities, though all of the groups Paul addresses in Romans 16, need not meet in designated buildings, but possibly could meet in the homes of their masters or less formal settings. If the Christ-movement had a Jewish foundation at Rome, then we need to posit a point at which the ethnē in Christ would separate from this—if not ejected by Jews, they would probably just continue rather than adopt a new pattern. In which instance, Paul would have to be very cautious to avoid appearing to interfere in an area outside his apostolic commission.

Paul's intentions in Romans seem to include maintaining association with Israel outside of the Christ-movement. This is one of the ways in which he opposes any proposed takeover of Israel's heritage by ethnē in Christ in which there may have been a tendency to interpret the Christ in the vein of a Roman conqueror whom the ethnē alone have recognized.

Romans is Paul's attempt to counteract the effects of imperial ideology within the Roman congregation not least anti-Jewish tendencies (Elliott 2008: 158, Stegemann 2010: 5). As Elliott notes, it is necessary to "situate the rhetoric of Romans in a complex field of discourses in which the themes and tropes of imperial ideology were both abundant and powerful" (2008: 21).

Supersessionism at Rome? The Influence of Roman Imperial Ethos among the Ethnē in Rome

What requires attention at this point is the advent of a new messianic movement in Rome that included non-Jews turning to the God of Israel. This meant a drastic reconfiguration in how to think of one's relation to the Roman gods. The Jewish people and their God were understood to some extent by the Romans, but when a Jewish rooted movement began to influence people beyond its normal affiliates, then this represented a radical questioning of traditional ways of viewing one's relation to the gods. Christ-followers from the nations inevitably found themselves in a liminal space since their place of belonging, individually and collectively, was unclear when considered in light of the maps of belonging prevalent at the time. Via genealogical reasoning, Paul tries to place them into the lineage of belonging to the God of Israel, not in place of, but alongside of this people of Israel (Ehrensperger, "Abraham Our Father and Herakles Our Cousin," 2022a). The uncertainty and hence insecurity of the ethnē in Christ at Rome concerning their new social identity had to be answered in terms of identity construction. Paul does this by means of genealogical or familial narratives of belonging in Romans 4 and 9–11. People at this period of history expressed who they were in relation to those to whom they were related—collective identity is relational if considered in terms of genealogical narratives. Not only does this relational dimension mean that one differentiates oneself from others, but it can express commonality as well as difference in a dialectical process. The narratives of Abraham, Isaac, and Jacob express the specific relation and commitment of God to this lineage. The promise and call constitutive of Abraham and his σπέρμα, however, though unique to them, does not involve supersessionism of others. Supersessionism implies that a group and their identity and characteristics are taken over and replaced by another. But nowhere in these narratives do Abraham and his σπέρμα replace any other people to whom God would have made the same promise (Ehrensperger 2023). Israel used kinship narratives to express their identity in such a way that it did not involve assimilation but rather "commonality with difference" in accordance with our use of a positive understanding of social identity as already noted in the "Introduction" chapter and elsewhere in our exegesis. We view these genealogical narratives as designed to situate these ethnē in a meaningful kinship relation to Israel in contrast to their posited displacement of Israel. New questions about these relationships would inevitably arise, particularly concerning the God of Israel, his relation to the Jewish people and to the created world.

Evidence of the concept of "Jewish rejection" is clear from Rom. 11:1, 11. The same theme emerges in two instances, "Has God cast off his people," "Have they stumbled so as to fall?" (was their fall final?). These questions correlate with the diatribal claims of the wild olive shoot: "Branches were broken so that I could be grafted in" (Rom. 11:19). That some people came to the conclusion that Israel had been bypassed in the divine purpose seems clear from Rom. 11:17 where a more careful report is given in contrast to the challenging diatribal version in 11:19. Here, the syllogistic reasoning allows that, hypothetically, it may be asserted that some branches had been broken and others grafted in among them. This view may be open to several interpretations, which we must clearly distinguish where possible. But one of these is entirely rejected by Paul in the diatribal image of the olive shoot. It is noteworthy that it is only in this diatribal challenge in v. 19 that actual replacement theology emerges (if we ignore the mistranslation of the RSV, NRSV incorporating the words "in their place").

The latter reference makes it plain that it is not simply the rejection of the Jews by God that is being claimed but much more—their replacement by another people, the ethnē in Christ, even if this judgment comes in a diatribal retort. One aspect of the Roman gentile Christ-followers' mindset that is specifically critiqued by Paul is a certain high-mindedness, a super-mindedness that is hard to explain (cf. Rom. 11:17-24; 12:3, 16; ch. 14). One explanation seems reasonable—the ethnē in Christ have learned from the Roman conquering mentality that the Jews are part of the subjugated peoples, and as such can be despised. But alongside this is another aspect difficult to explain—how do Christ-following ethnē become proud and over self-opinioned? I think this attitude was born from the view that the Jews, as a majority had not been convinced that Messianic Time had dawned with the Christ-event and the incoming of the nations. As a result, they (the Jews) could be considered to have been cast off by God from his ongoing purpose, which would continue now via the ethnē in Christ. Also, since the ethnē in Christ had accepted the good news that many Jews rejected, this may have led to a sense of superiority on their part. This could have been a common theological conviction among at least some of the followers of the Christ, probably enhanced by the banishment of some Jews from Rome at various times for varied reasons.

Also, as we have noted, it includes aspects of biblical perspectives on refusal to respond positively to the call of God, which must have been known to the Roman ethnē from the proclamation of the gospel. If not to acknowledge the Christ-event as the activity of God could be regarded as failure and, correspondingly, acceptance of this good news, as success, then a rationale could be found to affirm gentile Christ-followers as those superior people who were chosen for the divine purpose in place of the rejecting Jews. However, this sense of superiority was in opposition to the gospel that puts trust in Christ in binary opposition to human achievement, as set out clearly in Paul's letter. Roman ideology would suggest that those who failed to succeed deserved no better. Their rejection was just. But it was an outcome of the proclamation of the gospel message about the initial reception of the "good news" combined with a variation or development of this that sprang into view in Rome—that is, that the Jews had been replaced in God's purposes by the new gentile Christ-following people of God. It was this stance combined with a residual or general perception of Romans as conquerors that provided the ideology for gentile supersessionism and overconfidence. In other words, we are considering a possible link between two seemingly unrelated ideologies—Roman imperialist ethos and supersessionism over against Jews, originating as a by-product of the proclamation about the Christ-event in popular perception (cf. Stegemann 2005: 39).

We do not know the actual effects of this perception other than what can be gleaned from Paul's letter, which is necessarily carefully expressed, and possibly involves understatement at certain points. We cannot presume too much from the fact that Paul addresses only non-Jews at Rome since this is his normal pattern in his letters except that in some of his other letters scholars presume (as many also still do in the case of Romans) that he also addresses a minority of Jewish Christ-followers. Since Munck's explicit claim over half a century ago that Paul addresses only those from the nations in his letters, there should be no problem in acknowledging an exclusively gentile audience, at least as a possibility. On the other hand, we have no solid detailed information concerning Jewish Christ-followers as a group in Rome. One credible option would be that these continued to participate in the life of one of the various synagogues of which there is evidence. In which case we do not need to be precise about how we think these Jews might relate, if at all, to gentile Christ-followers. The potential relations between these groups would be determined by the structures in or around which they lived their corporate existence. Synagogue meeting places might not have differed much in this respect from household assemblies/tabernae/associations, and these may not have been mutually exclusive. Small gatherings of people from these groups may have been located across the city of Rome.

A major issue concerning such gatherings would have been their right to meet. Did they claim a right historically as Jews or did they exist as separate groups, for example, associations/collegia that would not have any connection with synagogues or with Jews as Jews? Although not formally recognized as associations, they may still have had structural similarities to such but without severing their connections with synagogues. I am inclined to take the view that connections with synagogues would enable Christ-followers to "hide" under this "umbrella," and thereby avoid drawing attention to themselves, thus rendering a synagogue connection functionally useful and socially beneficial. As we have noted in the "Introduction" chapter, the possibility is that all Christ-groups initially originated via synagogues and only later became separated. Variations probably existed where slaves followed the Christ-allegiance of their masters, and, alternatively, of slaves whose masters did not share their trust in

Christ. Doubtless there were many gentile Christ-followers who still retained their historic affiliation with a synagogue when Romans was written, and it is probable that varieties of patterns of behavior existed among these, despite possible interruption at times of crisis.

In light of this possibility, how serious would it be for gentile Christ-followers to posit the view that Israel had been cast off? First, it would mean that separation from non-Christ-following Jews would soon prove unavoidable and that relations with Christ-followers would be adversely affected. Is there any evidence for this from Romans? In earlier readings of this letter when chs. 14–15 were frequently read as involving a dispute between Jewish and gentile Christ-followers, "the weak" tended often to be read as of Jewish origin, and the issues about eating meat, drinking wine, or observing days (were) interpreted as indicating Jewish patterns. When Romans is read as a letter to ethnē only, the evidence concerning Jewish views or presence can no longer be registered in precisely this way. If Paul is aware that there is, in the near future, a possibility of non-Jews in Rome separating from synagogal affiliation, he may see this as a politically dangerous move that may well draw attention to ethnē in Christ as not having any recognized legal right to exist.

Another possibility exists, that is, that the "weak" who in my view cannot be other than of gentile ethnicity nevertheless, include those who still associate with Jews, out of shared convictions. It is noteworthy that Paul upholds these people and though he does not call himself "weak" here; he nevertheless revises his depiction of "the strong" in 15:1-6 to identify those strong enough to associate with "the weak." Paul effectively re-categorizes "the strong" to enable himself to be associated both with them and the so-called "weak." What we mean by this is that in 14:1-23 Paul gives broad hints as to those patterns he shares with those calling themselves "the strong," but until 15:1 he does not explicitly include himself. He does this only by giving a description of "the strong" as those able and willing to bear the burdens of "the weak," and who are capable of accommodating his perspective. From this perspective, it emerges that if "the weak" are those who, from shared convictions, continue to associate with Jews, then we can see that the division, though it is an inner-gentile one, does by implication shed some light on Jew-gentile relations at Rome. Some Christ-followers such as Paul can feel free to eat meat, drink wine, or observe certain days so long as these actions do not damage those who conscientiously act otherwise. Such a group is not necessarily of only either Jewish or gentile composition but cuts across ethnic origins in the practices they conscientiously adopt. Where they differ is in the attitude to inherited Jewish patterns. Paul reveres these but is flexible where non-Jews are concerned. He is knowledgeable as to what is permissible and what not. Some Jews may or may not eat meat. Some non-Jews may or may not observe the Sabbath, or drink wine. Paul follows no fixed pattern other than love of the weaker brother and the conscience of those involved (which may explain some of the criticisms he encountered).

It is noteworthy that Paul forces no one to act against their "convictions" (conscience) (13:9). So he cannot be anti-Jewish or recommend the rejection by gentile Christ-followers of certain patterns of behavior that they ("the weak") wish to follow. In supporting such "weak" people, Paul shows his sympathies lie with those gentile Christ-followers who are sympathetic to their experience as synagogue-related

God-fearers and who possibly wish to maintain such links. This may include ongoing links with synagogues in this capacity, and Paul does not counsel otherwise but advises worshipping God "with his people," even though this would have been as a gentile subgroup (Nanos 1999: 283–304, 2012:12–16).

If we take 15:10b literally, as I think we must and, as we shall see when we reach ch. 15, the context demands "Rejoice O 'Gentiles' with his people" must mean "maintain links with the synagogues i.e. with the Jewish people?"

This means for ethnē in Christ actual ongoing contact with Jewish people and their activities is to a certain extent encouraged by Paul in Rome. At minimum, we can affirm his opposition to those who would promote a way of life that would make it difficult or impossible to have any association with Jews, especially those who also are Christ-followers. If the Christ-following Jews are not a distinctly identifiable group, then it is Jews as a whole who must be considered. There may even be groups of Jews who are still undecided whether Jesus may be the Christ. Paul does not ask for, at this point, a clear demarcation, nor does he here demand such between Christ-followers and other Jews, he has no authority over synagogue life and practice. At most he may have some influence over those gentile Christ-followers who join in certain synagogue activities. Also, his knowledge of Roman life is only what is reported to him by others. So, Paul gives no encouragement for his gentile addressees to separate from the synagogue if they still adhered to its activities to any extent (Campbell 1990: 122–31). His counsel is to "rejoice with his people" (15:10). We will consider further the implications of this section when we come to ch. 15.

Romans 12

Romans 12:1-2: Offer Your Bodies as a Living Sacrifice—a Distinctive Ethos

¹I appeal to you therefore, brothers, by the compassion of God, to present your bodies as a sacrifice, living, holy, and acceptable to God—your reasonable worship. ²And do not be conformed to this aeon, rather be transformed by the renewing of your mind, so that you may discern what is the will of God—the good and acceptable and perfect.

That Paul has arrived at a significant stage in his letter is indicated both by the cessation of the dialogical exchanges of "questions, inferences, and retorts" featuring the phrase μὴ γένοιτο construction so prominent in chs. 3–11, and by the now-dominant use of imperatives; this change facilitates the claim based partly on the use of παρακαλῶ that 12:1-2 is the structural center of Romans (Thorsteinsson 2003: 53–4). What must be noted is that this is the first use of παρακαλέω in Paul's normal letter pattern in that in 1:12 the term used was συμπαρακληθῆναι so that there it was a joint appeal including the addressees together with Paul. In the past, I have argued that Romans 9-11 is the climax of the argument of chs. 1–11, and I see this as confirmed by the argumentative structures throughout these chapters (cf. also Elliott 2007: 67). Moreover, chs. 12–15, rather than comprising a general list of added-on instructions, are the inherent resultant implications of Paul's argumentation in the letter and as such its culmination. McMurray's view is similar except that he sees 12–13 as the culmination of the letter (cf. McMurray 2021: 154). The main adjustment to his view, which I would propose, is that 14:1–15:13 be included along with chs. 12–13 in this summing up, denoting the coherence of Paul's paraenesis here. In this view, the climax of the socio-theological argumentation in 9–11 is nicely distinguished from the applied guidance of 12–15.

This chapter (12) is viewed by some scholars as demonstrating a specific connection with Romans 1 as the reversal of the idolatrous worship of the ethnē in 1:19-32.[1] There are significant parallels between 1:16-32 and 12:1-2. In particular, the correspondence in vocabulary and theme between Romans 1 and 12 is striking. In 12:1-2, Paul is

---

[1] Cf. Furnish (1968: 103), Stowers (1994: 317–18), Elliott (2007: 97–8), and McMurray (2021: 169–71).

calling the "brothers" to a new life exactly the opposite to that which he has previously described (Furnish 1968: 103–6). Rom. 12:1-2 is but a restatement in hortatory mode of 1:16-17, and in Romans 12–15 the appeals introduced already in ch. 6 are being recapitulated and reemphasized. It needs to be noted, however, that the teaching in Romans 12–15 is grounded in a sustained enthymematic argumentation in chs. 1–11 (Elliott 2007: 291). An immediate link to chs. 9–11 is indicated by the recurrence of the term οἰκτιρμός in 9.15 and 12.1. The rationale for Paul's exhortation is given simply as "by the compassion of God" διὰ τῶν οἰκτιρμῶν, which can be considered as including the self-revelation of God in the scriptures of Israel and in the revelation in Christ. Having constructed in Romans 1–11 a long but coherent argument responding to criticisms and inferences concerning the gentile mission and its implications for the people of Israel, Paul's goal is to modify the self-understanding of the ethnē in Christ as a corporate entity. This is primarily to make them aware of their own identity as ethnē in Christ. They are not simply a loosely connected group of individuals influenced by a powerful leader, executed by the Romans. Corporately, they represent the earthly "body of Christ," something that not only includes them but also exceeds through their mutual interaction with Christ and one another their individual powers and capabilities to make them potentially a powerful united and transforming force for God. In addition, in the process of this common belonging with Christ and with each other, they will be morally transformed by the influence of the Spirit residing among them. But the powerful impulse of this new affection has been misinterpreted by some of these ethnē. It has emerged particularly from 11:13-24 that they are mistakenly assuming that a positive social identity as Christ-followers requires an antagonistic response to other groups with differing commitments, especially Jews unconvinced about the salvatory significance of the Christ-event. Thus, to avert the danger of gentile Christ-followers becoming conceited in boasting over Israel (Elliott 2007: 291), and misconstruing their own identity in God's family, Paul explicitly now constructs their newly adopted status as brothers of Christ. He thus locates them aggregatively within the "family" of God as a parallel entity alongside Israel, rather than in an antagonistic opposition to, or displacing of Israel. This goal significantly is manifest in the macrostructure of the whole letter, a cumulative ongoing argumentation connected, for example, by the particle γάρ at major intersections of the discussion (Casson 2019: 27–60). The introductory heading of 12:1-2 corresponds to the concluding summary of 13:8-14 (love as fulfillment of the Law) (Käsemann 1980: 323). We will consider the content of 12:1-2 as prelude to the exegesis of 12:3–15:13.

Paul now sets out how the proper worship of God should be expressed by the gentile ἀδελφοί as a corporate entity, the worship of the ethnē corresponding to the λατρεία of Israel in 9:4. Chapters 12–15 illustrate how the ethnē are to be transformed by the sacrificial giving of their bodies as public worship of the One God. This is how they can replace the worship of the Roman deities. The vacuum left by the cessation of their sacrificial worship is to be filled by giving over their limbs to God's service in grateful response to his grace through Christ. The Lord will more than replace the protection and blessing in childbirth, illness, and of crops and so on that the gods were previously thought to provide. Christ will intercede for them through the Spirit (Rom. 8:34).

As is customary, Paul appeals, παρακαλῶ, to the Romans as brothers ἀδελφοί. His request formula, 12:1-2, indicates the significance Paul attaches to this appeal.[2] Paul's appeal, grounded on the entire merciful activity of God, is that they offer their bodies as a sacrifice living, holy, and pleasing to God (McMurray 2021: 155-68, Tucker 2014). Romans differs somewhat from Paul's other letters in that this παρακαλῶ "I appeal" comes somewhat later than usual in this letter. Request formulas could occupy a central position and function in ancient letters, serving in some instances, as their sole or main occasion and purpose. The positioning of the request here may be explained by the fact that Paul has not yet been in Rome, and that he cannot, prior to this point, make a specific appeal until after he has explained some aspects of his gospel about which there is dispute or misunderstanding in Rome. Until he has offered some gift to them (i.e., this letter), he cannot expect anything from them (as we argued in ch. 1 above). But the οὖν, therefore, shows that by 12:1, Paul has a basis for appeal, that is, his teaching, including theology as well as its relevance for the ethnē (i.e., the content in chs. 1–11). That Paul can base all his appeal at this point on the content of all that precedes demonstrates the acute significance Paul attributes to his letter. This is his gift to them from which he anticipates a correlative response. The weight Paul attributes to his letter likewise indicates the significance of the response he anticipates to its contents (Thorsteinsson 2003: 53–4).

Thus, we do not make an absolute distinction between theology and ethics at this point as if there were no ethics in 1–11 and no theological teaching in 12–15. Our exegesis confirms Paul more as a teacher (rather than as an evangelist in our modern understanding) who concentrates on the maintenance and support of gentile Christ-followers within the ἐκκλησίαι. Thus, Romans is argumentative, offering reasoned rhetorical arguments, including diatribal stylistic devices, concerning the status and moral behavior of gentile Christ-followers particularly in chs. 1–11. Chapters 12–15 differ only in that here the outcomes of the arguments in 1–11 are applied specifically to moral issues in the Roman context. Individual sections of the letter may not relate obviously or directly to its argumentative pattern but contribute support for the conviction resulting from the entire argument. The traditional understanding of paraenesis is not helpful here. In parallel with Hellenistic moral teaching, New Testament paraenesis has been regarded as ultimately general in content and application. Paul's pattern of particular paraenesis with a connection to the exigency addressed in each letter suffered particularly from this approach. It is not that there are not real parallels between Paul and his contemporary moralists as Meeks (1983, 1986), Malherbe (1986, 1987), and others have demonstrated. Abraham Malherbe and Leo G. Perdue sought to modify Martin Dibelius's formal approach to paraenesis as normally general to include a more functional understanding of paraenesis as the activity of moral exhortation (Elliott 2007: 100). More recent research on Paul's letters, especially on Romans, gives weight to our claim that Paul, despite close parallels at points, has a differing agenda

---

[2] If the basis of the request formula in 12:1-2 consists in the preceding discourse as a whole following the οὖν, the audience could not have failed to perceive the weight that Paul attributed to his letter as well as the significant response it demanded (Thorsteinsson 2003: 53–4).

and is distinctive from, contemporary moralists influenced partly by his calling to be an apostle to the nations in continuity with the pattern of the prophets of Israel. In the calling to be God's people, moral guidance and a call to righteous living played a central role. This was in line with the perceived character of Israel's God to "be holy as I am holy" (Lev. 11:44, 19:2, 20:26). Again, the voluntary response of a grateful people determined the expectations of this hermeneutical approach (Muilenberg 1969). It was not framed as an absolute demand so much as an expected outcome of a familial and cultic relation—"you will be holy as I am holy." This is how some of Paul's hortatory statements can be read—not as straightforward imperatives but as participles in the present or imperfect tense illustrating the pattern of ongoing anticipated behavior, for example, 12:9-21 (Rodriguez 2014: 240). These participles may be read as having imperatival force, but must be read in accord with Paul's voluntarist perspective.

Brothers with Christ: Constructing the Identity of the Ethnē in Christ Group

Paul's address of the Romans as ἀδελφοί is significant in that he has used this terminology only at distinctive points in the letter. The first of these, as is to be expected comes early (i.e., in 1:13). The term is not used again until 7:1 and 7:4, where he addresses these specifically in direct address prior to turning to speech-in-character in 7:7-25 in the *persona* of a non-Jew seeking to follow the Law, but without the Spirit. Then in 8:12, he returns to the mode of direct address to stress their (gentile) status as non-Jews being adopted into the family of God. In 9:1-5, he indicates a family connection with his own people with explicit use of the term, ἀδελφοί. He elaborates this by adding τῶν συγγενῶν μου κατὰ σάρκα "my kinsmen according to the flesh." In 10:1, he begins with ἀδελφοί and concludes this section (i.e., 9–11) with the same term in 11:25. The ἀδελφοί of 1:13, 7:1, 7:4, 8:14, 10:1, and 11:25 (we will deal with later the several instances in 12:1–16:27) consists of the ethnē in Christ at Rome, whereas the other instance in 9:3 is related to Paul as the brother of his family kinsfolk, the Jews. Paul has family connections in two directions—to his people Israel to whom he is related by natural connections (birth and upbringing) and to the Christ-following ethnē as a brother and apostle in Christ. We need at some future point (in ch. 15) to continue to explore the relationship denoted by this diverse affiliation, particularly the plural example of 8:29 in which Christ is presented as becoming the firstborn of a large family of brothers.

Paul's appeal is very specific—παραστῆσαι "present your bodies as a sacrifice to God." Paul stresses corporeality as the characteristic sphere of worship (Käsemann 1980: 329). This passage resonates with 1:25 where the nations instead of honoring, thanking, and worshipping God exchanged the truth of God for a lie, and worshipped the created rather than the Creator also emphasizing the corporeal dimension. As just noted, the link of 12:1-2 with 1:19-32 comes via 6:12-23, where Paul asks the question "What fruit did you get from the things of which you are now ashamed?" This illustrates the typical Pauline pattern in its "once" but "now" contrast.

These former worshippers of "other" gods are ashamed of their previous way of life that Paul vividly presented in 1:19-32 and summarized again in 6:15-23, as "when you were slaves of sin" (6:20). Instead of putting your bodies at the disposal of sin, "present your bodies to God as instruments for doing right" (v. 13b), or "as slaves to righteousness" (v. 19b). Paul thus links chs. 6 and 12 via the verb παριστήμι used five times in 6:13-19 and repeated in 12:1-2. Again, 12:1-2 via 6:13-19 resonates with 1:19-32 as the reversal through Christ's reconciliation of the practice of idolatrous worship to its opposite, reasonable, appropriate worship (contrast the λατρεία of 1:25 with the λατρεία of 12:1-2) (McMurray 2021: 3–4). Whereas the idolators of 1:19-32 worshipped (λατρεύω) the created rather than the Creator, the λατρεία that Paul envisages in 12:1-2 resonates with the proper λατρεία worship characteristic of Israel according to 9:4-5, which Paul views as a gift from God.

The priority of honoring and worshipping God as the only God, the Creator of the world, is central to Romans. The emphasis upon the misdirected worship of the nations and its reversal here in terms of a living sacrifice, holy and acceptable to God, indicates that both the appropriate (λογική) worship of God and its opposite play an important role in this letter. But we must remember that our exegesis of 1:19-32 demonstrated that Paul's extended critique of mistaken λατρεία, stemming from idolatry, serves the function of informing the Romans in an indirect way about the Supreme God of the cosmos, the Creator God of Israel. The failure to honor God as God is a main reason for the Jewish critique of gentile life. But, by virtue of God's gift of reconciliation through Christ, the non-Jews are now able to worship the Creator God of Israel in accordance with his nature and character. Set alongside λατρεύω, λατρεία in association with θυσία and παρίστημι, it is clear that Paul indicates cultic service—the appropriate sacrificial service that is in keeping with the new status of the ethnē in Christ as adopted children of God (cf. McMurray 2021: 168–71).

Paul's exhortation to the Romans is to offer themselves to God: the four descriptors he lists are living (ζῶσαν), holy (ἅγον), pleasing to God (εὐάρεστον τῷ θεῷ), and your reasonable act of worship (τὴν λογικὴν λατρείαν ὑμῶν). The verb θύω carried the meaning of sacrificial offering in cult contexts, which is what Paul has in mind here (in the LXX, it could refer to a cereal offering as well as an animal offering). Unlike animals offered for sacrifice, which are killed when offered, Christ-followers continue to live for God and must use their bodies to serve and worship him. They were called to be holy (κλητοῖς ἁγίοις, 1:7), and now they must live in the new social identity given them in God's call, that is, as those called to die with Christ they are dedicated to God. But this giving of oneself to God by dying with Christ is not the end but only the beginning of what may be termed "walking with God through Christ." The life dedicated to God is given back by God and endowed with charismatic gifts empowering them to live their lives transformed as ethnē in Christ. But these divine blessings of the bodies dedicated to God and given back to the Christ-followers can only be realized and shared collectively in a new community. The third descriptor Paul offers to describe the Romans' self-sacrifice is "pleasing to God," which reminds the worshipper of the quality required of sacrifices that will be pleasing and acceptable to God (cf. 14:18). Only the best could be offered to God. The other descriptor Paul uses in relation to the self-offering of the ethnē is "your reasonable act of worship." We take λογική as logical or reasonable to indicate an appropriate response in contrast to the misguided worship of those who "became fools" μωραίνω (Rom. 1:21). This eschatological worship of the ethnē recognizes appropriately the God of Israel as he has been revealed in the Christ-event.

The worship described here is not a non-ethnic, universal worship in contrast to the Temple. Non-Jews could access the Temple only as far as the court of the nations upon the pain of death, so they need to have a worship suitable to their calling as non-Jews. The new λατρεία will function in parallel to and in tandem with the λατρεία of their new brothers, the Israelites (9:4). This is in keeping with Isa. 56:7-8, which speaks of "foreigners joining themselves to the Lord" (not as Israelites but as foreigners). God states, "Their sacrifices will be sacrificed on my altar: for my house will be called a house of prayer for all peoples (ἔθνη)." Thus, following this example, Paul sees the ethnē as offering an appropriate worship to God in the offering of their own bodies as living sacrifices. The full extent of this will become evident at the conclusion of the argument of the letter in 15:7-13.

Furnish notes Paul's tendency to relate life and death in explicating the meaning of the Christ-event—life frequently follows upon death (Furnish 2012: 194).[3] We note particularly the striking, almost contradictory, image of "living sacrifice" here. What must be noted, however, is that though Paul recognizes that life proceeds from death; his formulation here is significant. He does not say that the offered self simply dies when offered as a sacrifice. "The selves to be put at God's disposal in the world are precisely those which, having been brought from death to life (Rom. 6:13) are indwelt by the life-giving Spirit (8:1-13) and are alive to God in Christ Jesus (6:11)" (Furnish 2012: 194). The giving of oneself to God sets in motion a new life of service for God. What is given to God is given back again to be used in his service (Campbell 2018: 331–62). As noted above, the language of θυσία, sacrifice, indicates a cultic context (i.e., the sacrificial system). Λατρεία (act of worship) is also a cultic term. In the LXX, λατρεία refers to the Passover service (Exod. 12:25-26; 13:5), to the temple service in general (1 Chron. 28:13), to sacrificial systems more generally (Josh. 22:27), or even to the entire system of corporate Jewish religious practice (1 Macc. 2:19, 22; Rodriguez 2014: 235–6).

Paul follows the positive request to present their bodies τὰ σώματα to God with a negative exhortation: "Be not conformed μὴ συσχηματίζεσθε to this age, but be μεταμορφοῦσθε transformed through the ἀνακαινώσει τοῦ θεοῦ "renewing of your mind." In the koine Greek, at this time, the words μορφή and σχῆμα lose their classical sense of shape or form—they here designate the total nature of existence. Hence to refuse to conform and to be transformed both characterize the totality of the change from the old to the new aeon. Both body and mind as part of one indissoluble but distinguishable self are affected by being in Christ and should not be flattened to a cipher for the person (Käsemann 1980: 327). Most likely, we are dealing here with typical baptismal exhortation as demonstrated by the use of terms such as "this age" ἀιὼν οὗτος, rebirth, ἀνακαινώσις τοῦ νοός, and the specifying of God's will as the norm of conduct. As Michel claims, the renewal of the minds is a baptismal act of the gifting with the Spirit of God (Michel 1978: 371; cf. Furnish 1968: 105, Käsemann 1980: 327–9). The term ἀνακαινώσις (renewal) appears in this verse for the first time

---

[3] Furnish recognizes the parallels between Romans 6 and Romans 12 and challenges the traditional dichotomy between doctrine and exhortation, followed by Rodriguez (2016: 235). Cf. also Käsemann (1980: 324) and Elliott (2007: 290–9).

in Greek literature (Jewett 2007: 733). Even though Paul can speak in terms of "new creation" (2 Cor. 5:17), there as here, it means the renewing of the mind in keeping with the "new covenant" understood as the "renewed covenant"[4] to denote continuity in God's revelation and action.

The focus here is on group decision-making. Individuals are not left to wander on their own, but are called to conduct that is worthy of their Lord and his earthly community. "The Spirit lays demands upon each individual completely and concretely in his particular relationships and makes him capable of a new manner of life. He does this in such a way that the individual shows himself thereby to be a member of the community" (Käsemann 1980: 324). In contrast to the ἀδόκιμον νοῦν (1:28) through the renewed mind, the Christ-following ethnē working as a group will together be able to discern δοκιμάζειν the will θέλημα of God, what is good, acceptable, and perfect. τέλειον, in accordance with the meaning of τέλος as goal in 10:4, means perfect in the sense of what is appropriate in keeping with the coming consummation of God's purpose. We note here how Paul's statements resonate with Greco-Roman and Jewish ethical thought. Similarly, the adjective ἀγαθόν, good, and its corresponding noun significantly appear a number of times in Romans beginning with, for example, 12:1. Michel rightly notes the proximity to Stoic popular ethics in the expressions τὸ ἀγαθὸν εὐάρεστον (the acceptable good) and τὸ τέλειον ἀγαθόν (the perfect good) (1978: 372, n24).

Paul Promotes a Distinctive Ethos for the Ethnē in Christ in Romans 12–15

Here we must inquire whether and to what extent, Paul consciously negotiates within the ethical systems of his time, even as he speaks of the transforming values of the coming kingdom of Christ. The ethnē in Rome did not live in a vacuum sealed off from the influences and debates of the wider world, and neither did Paul. To the extent that early Christ assemblies shared and fostered an ethos distinct from their environment, paraenesis served to establish social boundaries and to maintain them in the life of the group (Elliott 2007: 101). In Romans 12–15, Paul is specifically seeking to provide a charter for ethnē in Christ. But though ethnē in Christ are a new people, an associate people living alongside the Jews, the fact that they are an associate people demands commonality with Jews as well as differentiation. Paul nowhere describes ethnē in Christ as "Israelites." They are Christ's brothers (Rom. 8:29), the latter term implying both commonality and difference (as well exemplified in the narrative of brothers in Israel's history). They will, therefore, offer not the same λατρεία as that of Israel (9.4), and Rom. 12:1-2 demonstrates how the new response of the ethnē appropriately respects but differs from the λατρεία of Israel. It is only through Christ, and with Christ and the Spirit, that this worship may be achieved. In 12:1, the θυσία *and* λατρεία is offered to God by ethnē and as ethnē. If the sacrifice to which the ethnē are called is to be recognized, it demands that the worshipping of the ethnē alongside Israel has transforming consequences. In fact, Paul uses the language of sacrifice to negotiate and

---

[4] Cf. Ulrich Barth on 2 Cor. 4:16 argues against reading ἀνακαινοῦνται as *creatio ex nihilo*; it signifies rather continuity and affirmation—"re-newal" rather than "new" (2021: 401–2).

define the relationship between Israel and the ethnē. Sacrifice paired with acceptance of brotherhood will ratify the new kinship of adoption through Christ (McMurray 2021: 171). So, the call of Paul to the ethnē is to accept the new status of kinship into which in and with the Christ of Israel they are called. Recognizing Christ as proceeding from the people of promise means recognizing a new relation for ethnē with Israel. This involves accepting that God's purposes with Israel are still continuing as Paul argued in chs. 9–11. Honor and respect are therefore due to the people of Israel as God's people through whom his purpose is being continued. For ethnē to ratify through the sacrifice of their bodies to God their response to Christ means simultaneously to recognize also God's promises to Israel.[5] They cannot affirm their new brotherhood with Christ without acknowledging brotherhood with Israel if they are to praise the God of Israel together (with Israel) *while remaining ethnē. Paul creatively develops in Romans for the first time a new theological/genealogical conception of gentile brotherhood with Israel through the Christ.* Rather than denying God's continuing purposes through Israel, they are to acknowledge these and thus likewise acknowledge a new familial brotherhood constructed via the promises. Paul will return to this theme in his conclusion in 15:7-13. But commonality is not limited only to what is shared with Israel.

Commonality is also shared with the gentile "outsiders" who are neither followers of Christ nor Jewish. The call to be transformed implies the existence of contemporary social values perceived as not entirely fitting for the coming kingdom of God. Here we glimpse Paul negotiating with the normal conceptions of "the good" prevalent in Greco-Roman society (cf. "your good" 14:16). His use of the term λογική suggests genuine negotiation with contemporary values as does his emphasis on the renewal of the mind along with the sacrifice of the body. As regards the apostle's own social perspective, he appears to be speaking as a cultural transformer rather than counter-culturally.

We need to be careful here not to claim more for the Christ-movement than is warranted. This calls for clarification and differentiation between actual ideals acknowledged and practiced and ideal activities as yet only envisaged. What does emerge with some clarity, as we have noted, is that the Pauline ideals and actual promoted practices were not counter-cultural. He did not recommend total denial of this world but rather a transformation of life in this world. Although the imagery of life and death are abundant in Paul's letters, the dominant image is of transformation in contrast to conformity to the normal social pattern—"be not conformed but be transformed." The "person" that is beginning to be transformed dies—is crucified with Christ—but yet still lives on (Romans 6). As Alan Segal has noted, "the one expression that Paul uses most comprehensively in his own writing to describe this experience is transformation" (1990: 73, Campbell 2009: 338). Meeks is impressed by "the way in which Paul can mix together commonplaces of Greek and Roman moral rhetoric, arguments from Jewish scripture, and beliefs and rules peculiar to the Christian sect and then use these to describe 'the company of the holy ones'" (1983: 151).

Paul's envisaged scenario seems to comprise a picture of an ideal network in which both he and his associates are the significant leaders and focus of the activity.

---

[5] 'The conceptualization of the body as a temple as, for example, in 1 Cor. 6:19 and of the Spirit residing in people complements that of Jerusalem rather than superseding it (McMurray 2021: 171).

The ongoing activity in which Paul and his associate workers in the gentile mission are primarily involved is the creation of alternative culture from the perspective of messianic renewal. Romans 12–15 is a charter for such a project and represents community tools as a part of the story of the development of emergent "Christian" cultures. The culture of the ethnē in Christ is a form of alternative culture, whether this is lived in some relation to one of the synagogue communities in Rome or as part of *collegia* or community associations.[6]

But we must take into account Esler's assertion that none of the thousands of voluntary associations with which the Christ-groups were broadly comparable (Kloppenborg 2019) used Paul's term ἐκκλησία as a group designation (Park 2015: 56–9, Korner 2017: 52–76, Esler 2021b: 121). The Christ-group was unique in using this word as a group designation. Esler views the shared kiss as a frequent feature of Pauline letter endings, which may have reminded the Christ-followers at Corinth that they were part of a translocal movement and conveyed that this was an unusual form of voluntary association (Esler 2021a: 370–1). What must be noted as significant is that Jews chose to refer to their group meetings as ἐκκλησία (e.g., Philo, *Leg.* 3:81, *Her.* 251), and Paul followed this pattern for his ethnē in Christ. Thus, for Paul and his gentile followers, ἐκκλησία is how they see themselves, even if outsiders may have viewed them as some kind of associations.

The shared life in community of the ethnē in Christ cannot escape being part of the majority imperial Greek and Roman culture, which like other cultures of the ancient Mediterranean was a collectivist rather than an individualistic culture. This culture gave priority to the goals of their in-groups rather than to personal goals. But it differs from this in two respects. The Christ-followers generally as a group, as far as can be discerned, were originally almost all of Jewish extraction. Like a majority of Jews, they would have followed the Jewish pattern of conforming and yet not conforming to Roman ideals. As more ethnē joined the Christ movement, more influence from outsider patterns of behavior could not be avoided, but the influence of Jewish alternative cultural patterns of "conformity with resistance," would still continue to be followed, at least for some time, probably by a majority of ethnē in Christ.

The ethnē would be distinctive in another respect. Unlike God-fearers, the ideal of the Pauline communities was avoidance of all perceived idolatry. Jews, of course, were adamant about this stance. But it was, however, particularly challenging for Pauline Christ-followers and offered them parallels with Jews rather than commonality with the wider culture. Thus, paraenesis for the ethnē represents secondary socialization "by which an individual is introduced to the group's or role's social knowledge, including especially norms and values pertaining to group or role behavior; the individual internalizes this knowledge, and makes it the basis for both behavior and the meaning system by which he interprets and orders his world" (Perdue 1981: 251). It is not perhaps sufficiently emphasized that paraenesis in Paul was designed not for initial entry to a group but more to maintain membership within the group, that is,

---

[6] See, for example, Ricker (2021: 143). The possible relationship between, parallels with, and differences from, associations and assemblies (ἐκκλησίαι) of Christ-followers, especially of non-Jews, is a fascinating area of research.

διδαχή rather than κηρύγμα. To evangelize in a Pauline sense is more akin to restore to memory rather than to win to new allegiance (Dahl 1976: 18–19). It is not only the content of paraenesis that ensures its effectiveness but the social world in which it is experienced and in which the paraenetic activity makes cognitive and affective sense. If Jews may be regarded as offering a viable alternative culture, then in some respects the ethnē in Christ similarly inhabited an alternative culture.

A major issue is whether in fact they did continue to do so as subgroups of the synagogue communities that normally had permission to legally exist and to meet. We are less certain concerning the status of associations that functioned to serve various needs and were often linked with particular trade guilds. It is conceivable that gentile Christ-followers, as distinct from those of Jewish origin and conviction, would meet in an association of some kind—Ricker gives the subtitle to his recent monograph on Romans 12–15: *Ancient Epistolary Association Culture and the Purpose of Romans* (2021). In such a context, they would likely have had issues of eating food that could possibly, for various reasons, be perceived as tainted by association with idolatry (which will be discussed in relation to Romans 14). Since, as far as we are aware, there was no identifiable opposition between associations as such and affiliation with a synagogue, could it have been possible that particular individuals or groups might participate in both? There are identifiable patterns of behavior that could apply equally in associations as in (gentile) synagogue subgroups within the synagogues at Rome (as Nanos has envisaged the ethnē in Christ at Rome (1996: 283–304; 2012: 12–16). These are not such different social groups that they follow entirely different patterns of social behavior (Esler 2021a: 371).

At the moment we are unable to answer this question of overlapping affiliation. We presume that if synagogal connection existed, that it would continue to do so until problems might arise. We do have evidence from Paul's letters that there were no impenetrable barriers between his "converts" and the outside world. Passers-by can drop in and see what is happening (1 Cor. 14:23), and the same pattern probably allowed ongoing connections with synagogue groups.

So, to what extent are the issues addressed in Romans 12–15 actual depictions of ongoing interaction among the ethnē in Christ at Rome or purely envisaged scenarios of such issues as may have existed elsewhere as in Corinth but which here serve as fodder for theoretical discussions needed to guide a community as yet unknown to Paul? Thus, Esler has been criticized for construing actual addressees in Romans with very specific issues, indeed, more specific than the evidence justifies. His "reconstructions produce problems of their own in reconstructing an original audience and a purpose for Rom 12–15" (Ricker 2021 84–5).[7] But is the concept of an ideal network any better than Esler's proposals? It is one thing to allow that Esler's understanding may be more precise than the information will sustain, but it is quite another to move from the given fragments of historical evidence almost entirely to an envisaged ideal scenario. Ricker claims that

---

[7] Ricker claims concerning Esler, "I think it is better to avoid guesswork like his about the precise authorial intention of Paul, or about any putative positive, accurate knowledge on Paul's part concerning real tensions between real identifiable groups in Rome" (Ricker 2021: 111).

the epistolary paraenesis of Rom. 12–15 [read within the wider context of the letter's epistolary frame and the even wider context of comparable ancient letters] shows that "the purpose of Romans" involves offering ideal addressees the opportunity to feel and act like insiders belonging to an ideal functional, global community network. (2021: 78)

He sees this view as warranted by reading through a SIT lens. However, the argument for general paraenesis has been made on the basis of Greek and Roman general patterns of admonitions, and the use of SIT here is not required to arrive at this conclusion advocated by earlier scholars. We must be critical in assessing the evidence, but not so negative that we give hardly any weight to the actual text before us that is historically well attested and, in this respect, compares favorably with contemporary extrabiblical texts. Paul has not yet visited the Christ-following ethnē at Rome, but the fact that he writes a long letter required a minimum of knowledge of its addressees. Also, the fact that he has been in contact with them for many years, even if it is only in his prayers on their behalf, implies a certain acquired amount of information.

If we want to locate Paul as a leader in a wide first-century network, we already have committed ourselves to accepting a certain amount of information in Romans 12–15 as amenable to certain forms of construction of a probable community scenario, even if its precise contours defy precision. A notice on a church noticeboard, which I saw many years ago when a student, continues to guide me at points such as this. It read, "Don't let the things you don't know destroy the things you do know." Much remains hidden from us concerning the exigency among the ethnē in Christ to which Paul addressed Romans, but much is also revealed and provides enough to offer foundations or at least skeletal outlines around which to generate consistent conclusions. Romans, like other ancient letters, offers a text to be critically taken into account as specific evidence closely related to, even if not precisely determined by, factors known to Paul variously communicated to him in advance. It is a long letter that thus includes much information of all kinds giving clues as to its composition and to its purposes even though these may not always be easily uncovered. Closer scrutiny in many instances of its interpretation as circular or general in nature might have yielded more substantial results, rather than undue emphasis on its difference from other Pauline letters, or on the fact that Paul had not yet visited Rome. To give only one example, the address of Romans as limited to ethnē in Christ is demonstrated not only by the several explicit statements to addressees in chs. 1, 11, and 15 but also in innumerable pointers in terminology as regards the ethnē and the Jewish people, in indications in grammatical argument, especially in the use of terms in first- and second-person singular and plural (Thorsteinsson, Rodriguez, and Thiessen 2016).

Also, Paul writes to ethnē in Rome who have been Christ-followers for some years and who are already acquainted with at least some of the content of the gospel message, even if Paul is not identical in his message with other apostles. So the ethic Paul presents is neither entirely new in its content, nor entirely untried as a way of life. It is this that permits the apostle to claim that he has written "most boldly by way of reminder" (15:15). Even if it is specifically targeted at local issues that may sometimes be peculiar to a certain location, many of the exigencies have parallels that allow Paul, without denying his own pattern of teaching, to teach certain things common to "all the ἐκκλησίαι of the 'gentiles'" (1 Cor. 7:17b). We conclude, therefore, that Paul is self-consciously dealing with renewal ἀμακαινώσις, common to the Christ-movement, and that even though his ideals are by no means limited to a known conceptualized future, they are never purely idealistic. Here we write also in awareness of the "socio-rhetorical observation that structures of identity and authority are not in fact givens" (Ricker 2021: 81).

As the priest in the priestly service of the gospel of God who guides the nations as to how to discern τὸ θέλεμα τοῦ θεοῦ, the will of God, Paul gives in 12:1-2, as noted, a summary of his guidance, both positive "present your bodies as a living sacrifice" and negative "do not be conformed to this world." The envisaged outcome of "the renewing of your minds" is to be achieved via response to a further imperative "but be transformed by the renewing of your mind." Paul will proceed to develop and clarify his guidance but it begins with very specific exhortation in the call to self-offering specifically of the mind (cognitive) and of the body (sacrificial). Even though the adjective λογικός is reminiscent of the stoic prioritization of reason, Barclay views the Christian *habitus* as self-consciously at odds with the prevailing logics of contemporary society. He sees the "criteria of reason as newly defined by the act of God in Christ," a renewed rationality (2015: 509). McMurray sees the ethnē's λογικὴ λατρεία as "their eschatologically appropriate and proper λατρεία, its reasonableness contrasting with the misguided λατρεία of Romans 1, the stupidity of Romans 1 contrasting with the reasonableness of Romans 12" (2021: 170). The way to transformation is via self-sacrifice not by thinking more highly of oneself than one ought to think (12:3). It is noteworthy that though Paul's exhortation includes a transformed mind, this transformation is registered via the concrete offering of one's body. There has been a number of significant references to the body throughout this letter, which are now drawn together around this self-giving presentation (cf. McMurray (2021: 154–7).

Though Paul is not counter-cultural, neither is he simply following a selected version of wider cultural practices somehow negotiated to offer distinction from society as a whole. Rather we see Paul as continuing the Jewish pattern of "playing and not playing the game" of the majority culture. This was not measured in a listing of the continuities and discontinuities between this and the Christ-movement, but distinctive in the ethos created and carefully sustained in a networking by Paul and his colleagues, which promoted a distinctive alternative way of life centered around the Christ-event and the numerous widely distributed cells of its adherents (Meeks 1983: 104).

Romans 12:3-8: The Alternative Pattern of Life for a Community in Process of Transformation

³For by the grace given to me I say to everyone among you do not be super-minded above what you ought to be minded, but set your mind on being sober-minded, each according to the measure of trust that God has assigned. ⁴For as in one body we have many members, and not all the members have the same function, ⁵so we, the many, are one body in Christ, and together we are members one of another. ⁶We have gifts that differ according to the grace given to us: prophecy, in proportion to trust; ⁷ministry, in ministering; the teacher, in teaching; ⁸the encourager, in encouragement; the giver, in generosity; the leader, in diligence; the compassionate, in cheerfulness.

Paul continues his emphasis on the mind in 12:3. The wordplay on φρονεῖν stresses the significance of Paul's exhortations.[8] The link back to 11:20 is important in that there he warned against a proud mind μὴ ὑψηλὰ φρόνει. Jewett has captured well Paul's clever use of terms, "Paul tells his readers not to be 'super-minded' above what one ought to be minded, but (to) set your mind on being sober-minded" (1982: 66). In his commentary, he translates ὑπερφρονεῖν as "uppity-minded" (2007: 666). This followed on from the negated boast in 11:18-19, where the *persona* of the wild olive shoot boasts that the wild olives, the nations, were grafted in which was considered to render them superior to the people of Israel. What is negated here is a very specific kind of boast and all the more serious because of that. Thus 12:3 is quite explicit. Paul speaks as apostle to the nations in accordance with God's grace to him—"do not be super-minded" but think wisely—"be sober-minded"-in your self-estimate (as non-Jews dependent on the Messiah of Israel). It must have been evident to Paul from what had been reported to him that these gentile Christ-followers had an arrogant set of mind exemplified, especially in relation to Israel; we will return to this later. Thus, it seems that Paul follows a line of thought beginning in 8:7-8 through 11:20 to 12:3. The mind is never neutral, but with the body is either operating according to the flesh or according to the Spirit. The clear emphasis in this line of thought culminating in 12:3 is that Christ-followers should not be arrogant or despise those who are confused. A humble attitude of mind, not proud self-confidence, is demanded of those who formerly were gentile sinners, and who now are slaves of God; no boasting of one group over another can be acceptable. In this respect, Käsemann's stress upon concrete obedience that arises from trust captures the proper use of mind and body as one entity to be used for the everyday service of God (Käsemann 1980: 330).[9]

That Paul addresses the Roman ethnē in Christ as a charismatic leader becomes clear, especially in 12:3, thus the content of these verses originates primarily from Paul's own experience. Here as the charismatic leader Paul links back to his calling as apostle to the nations noted most recently in 11:13 and gives guidance on adaptability in light of the diversity of gifts. Paul's calling rests on the χάρις, grace given to him by God, and each one of the Christ-followers has also been given a "measure of trust" (μέτρον πίστεως) by God. As Paul has previously stated in 1 Cor. 12, varieties of charismatic gifts have been gifted to individuals by the Spirit for the benefit of the ἐκκλησία. But here the emphasis appears to be on the function of individuals as determined by their gifts without specific explicit reference to the Spirit at this point, except in the brief reference in v. 11 (the Spirit will reappear in 14:17 and 15:16). Contrasting with the similar themes in 1 Cor., it is χάρις, grace, that is referenced here as the source of

---

[8] Cf. Stone (1988: 122). Stone notes that Paul is apprehensive in Rom. 11, lest gentiles would become proud and no longer respect the Jews in their midst.
[9] Cf. also Käsemann's challenging essay, "Worship in Everyday Life: A Note on Romans 12" (1969: 189–95).

the charismata, rather than the Holy Spirit. Paul's goal here seems to be to refer to grace as related to self-estimate—it is an anti-pride reference so that those who exercise particular roles do not think too highly of their own status. Paul asserts the God-given nature of gifts in order to work against human inflated self-estimate. He does so by reminding the Romans of the divine nature of these gifts, that the ēthne in Christ all form one body in Christ, and that thus they all belong to one another (12:5).

There are two important emphases in 12:3-8—the diversity of gifts within the body and the oneness of all members within this diversity. Paul will not spend so much time here on the body metaphor as he did in 1 Corinthians. So, although he will tell the Romans to accept one another (15:7), there does not seem to be the same factional groups in Rome as in Corinth. The emphasis lies upon each performing the function (12:4) that their charismatic endowment enables them. Each of his audience must display their various gifts "in accordance with the grace that was given to us" (12:6). The exhortation to humility is intended to resist pride and over self-confidence and to encourage mutual acceptance amid diversity. It is highly likely that the Roman Christ-followers came from different geographical backgrounds, spoke various languages, and were culturally diverse. Paul's focus is on making them into a corporate body of gentile Christ-followers by stressing what they have in common, grace through trust, the gifts of God's grace, and solidarity with one another. Where they differ is not so important in contrast to what they share in common, that is, trust in Christ. Paul's guidance here is not to seek to overcome diversity among the house assemblies and tenement buildings in Rome but to stress unity and commonality so that the diversity can continue within the Christ groups rather than forcing them apart.

The differing χαρίσματα charismatic gifts are listed beginning in 12:6. Since Paul in 12:3 has already specifically addressed "everyone among you," each share in the gifts that God has given. By listing these activities as gifts from God, this might remove grounds for boasting in their acquisition as due to some inherent characteristic or achievement by their bearers. Since they are all gifts from God, those who exercise these are equally indebted and equally have no grounds for personal boasting. What comes to man from God as a gift of grace can never be a ground for boasting. Paul lists a number of the gifts implying that the proper response to God, the Giver of these gifts, is to exhibit the various gifts in accordance with what has been given. "At the center stands an idea of social interrelation in which each person in the community maintains a social identity partly constituted by her or his abilities to benefit others" (Stowers 1994: 319). This is an ethic that balances individual difference and social unity. Whether it is prophecy, ministry, teaching, exhortation, charitable giving, leadership, or comforting those in need, those who have thus been gifted must allow God to work through the grace that he has distributed among them (12:6-8). There seems to be some sense of God giving a certain proportion (measure) of trust that is determinative of how the gift is to be exercised, implying that it is God who gives and therefore is the one who determines the significance of the gift, not those thus endowed.[10] Also, since the diversity of gifts comes from God, their appropriation and appreciation should be determined by their

---

[10] Käsemann (1969: 741–42). Cf. Jewett (1982a: 59–67). Here Jewett argues that

point of origin, not by one member making their form of expression of trust a norm for others (Käsemann 1980: 34–5). The nature and form of one's own charisma should prevent anyone attempting to force a brother to adopt his particular pattern of life. Similarly, this should not warrant a refusal to recognize the gifts exercised by others that God has given.

These gifts are notably corporate in their exercise, rather than merely individual; exercised together they will demonstrate the proper presentation of bodies as living sacrifices to God. However, there is also a specifically individual application. Jewett has argued that each individual has a unique μέτρον πίστεως, a measuring rod, a norm provided for each in the appropriation of the grace of God (12:3). His reading is supported by the emphatic position of ἑκάστῳ, "each" and Paul's choice of the verb μερίζω, "to deal out or distribute." What is important in this emphasis is that it allows for differentiation within the trust of those who follow Christ; they are not forced into a mold determined by the needs of other groups, and the individual's unique appropriation is bounded by incorporation into a community of Christ-followers, who together comprise the body of Christ and who grow together as they share their differentiated transforming trust.

We may presume that the exercise of a diversity of gifts such as these, though they might apply to some Pauline congregations as in Corinth, do exist to some extent in Rome also otherwise it would seem unwarranted for Paul to mention them. And if this is so, it might indicate that there were already a significant number of gentile Christ-followers in Rome. If the actual number of addressees were very small, it would seem not to warrant Paul's drawing attention to such great diversity.

Romans 12:9-21: The Response of Trust—Overcome Evil by the Good

⁹This love (is) without pretense; abhorring evil, holding fast to the good; ¹⁰having affection for one another in brotherly love, taking the lead in honoring one another, ¹¹not flagging in diligence, ardent in spirit, serving the Lord ¹²rejoicing in hope, persevering in affliction, persisting in prayer ¹³sharing in the needs of the saints, pursuing hospitality to strangers. ¹⁴Bless those who persecute you; bless and do not curse them. ¹⁵Rejoice with those who rejoice, weep with those who weep. ¹⁶Being of the same mind with one another; do not be super-minded, but identify with the lowly; do not keep thinking how wise you are.¹⁷Do not pay back evil for evil, concentrate on things that all consider honorable. ¹⁸If possible, so far as it depends on you, live peaceably with all persons. ¹⁹ Not avenging yourselves, beloved, but leave space for the wrath; for it is written, "Vindication is mine, I will pay back, says the

> faith in Christ has pluralistic possibilities—each person has a unique norm of faith that should be maintained in integrity. Faith consists in the individual appropriation of grace, but there are political, ideological, racial and temperamental components that are legitimately connected with faith thus comprising the peculiar "measuring rod" that each person has been given. (1982a: 62-3)

Lord." ²⁰*But, "if your enemy is hungry, feed him; if he is thirsty, give him drink; for by doing this you will heap burning coals on his head." ²¹Do not be conquered by evil, but conquer the evil with the good.*

As often happens, Paul's varied individual exhortations and imperatives can at first glance give the impression that these are merely a catalog of useful instructions that Paul composes to give general advice to congregations. Whatever their origin, these should be viewed corporately as community guidance for Christ-group identity formation (Esler 2021a: 34). The individuals that comprise the community are not merely an ad hoc group of isolated individuals, but together form a new entity, the body of Christ in a particular location with a unity and identity more than the numerical quantity of its constituents. Esler views Rom. 12:9-21 from the perspective of social identity: In Rom. 12:9-21, Paul sets out a long sequence of characteristics of Christ-movement identity—which can appropriately be designated "identity-descriptors"—beginning with ἀγάπη, the characteristic love of the Christ-movement, in which the prominence of aural effects, such as alliteration, assonance, and even rhyme, which likely had a mnemonic function, suggests that this is a precious fragment of Paul's oral proclamation (Esler 2003: 317–19). The first "identity descriptor" (Esler 2021a: 34) concerns love, the preeminent communal virtue. "Let love be genuine"— ἀνυπόκριτος without hypocrisy (12:9).[11] These "identity descriptors" are not simply the creation of Paul and all the ἐκκλησίαι of the "gentiles." They represent a kind of prototypicality in general, applied now to the gentile Christ-groups originating from Jewish groups (including the qualities of righteousness and mercy). The characteristics of Christ-movement identity described above can be supplemented by Jesus as the greatest exemplar, or Paul as his λειτουργός, or others already noted such as Abraham, those who actually embody the features so described. Barentsen views these visions of great leaders as painting a verbal picture of the desired social identity (2011: 56).

The key characteristics of the social identity of those in Christ, ἀγάπη is not part of the *do ut des* payback system typical of Roman ethics, so the person acting in love can do so without giving thought to whether or not the recipient will reciprocate. Love can thus be sincere without looking for love in return (Rodriguez 2016: 241). This positive aspect of identity can also be negatively defined by its opposite in the prohibition, "hate what is evil." The extent of agape is further emphasized—"Love one another with mutual affection: outdo one another in showing honor" (12:10). The latter phrase in the NRSV, although it gives the general sense to some extent, is better expressed in Jewett's translation, "taking the lead in honoring one another" (2007: 761). This indicates that love takes the initiative in a proper appreciation of one another, no matter how great the difference. We note here almost a sense of competition in the exercise of God-given gifts, evidence no doubt of cultural influence. The repetition in v. 10 of ἀλλήλους "one another" (cf. also v. 16) after φιλαδελφία as well as the

---

[11] Chapter 12:9-21 includes a series of participles that, with Rodriguez (2014: 240), I regard as probably carrying imperatival force, particularly as they lead into actual imperative verbs in 12:14 that continue the second-person singular (interlocutor) through to 12:21.

exhortation to "brotherly love" itself all focus on communal belonging and *reciprocal*, harmonious relations. "Live in harmony with one another" (12:16) is preceded by the imperative "bless and do not curse" (those who persecute you). As McMurray has noted, it leads into a section on divine repayment of evil and a further stress on non-retaliation in vv. 18-21 (2021: 181–5). In 12:11, πνεύματι ζέοντες can be read as a reference to the human spirit, that is, meaning "ardent in spirit." But since this is the only reference to the Spirit here, for this reason alone it is likely that Paul means to "be aglow with the Holy Spirit" meaning to be stirred up emotionally, implying that Christ-followers are stirred to activity through the life-giving Spirit (Hultgren 2011: 455).

In v. 16b, the reference to "do not be proud but identify with the lowly" is significantly followed by "do not keep thinking how wise you are" linking back to the specific warning against being "super-minded" with the words μὴ τὰ ὑψηλὰ φρονοῦντες. These references taken together with this imperative indicate a combined diatribal corrective against inflated self-estimate. Thus, we have a link from 11:20 via 12:3 to 12:16 focusing on pride and over self-confidence, and not merely gentile arrogance generally but a specific arrogance arising from comparison with Israel. We have reached this conclusion from the fact that Paul makes a link between preventing the Romans thinking "how wise they are," and the proposed understanding of the 'hardening' of Israel in 11:25. If the proper understanding of Israel's 'hardening' that Paul proposes somehow prevents boasting over Israel, then this issue must be part of the failing thus prevented as Paul's linking of these suggests. This arrogance by the ethnē in Christ particularly over against Israel is therefore not a minor issue or one that can be overemphasized. It is amazing how little attention in commentaries on Romans has been devoted to gentile boasting and arrogance in view of how Jews, as Jews, have been regularly stereotyped as prone to boasting. Gentile arrogance has emerged as a vital factor in Paul's argument in chs. 9–11 and demonstrates an ongoing issue that will surface again in chs. 14–15. What we have here is a clear indication of an antipathy on the part of gentile Christ-followers toward others that reveals itself in an inflated self-confidence, which is fueled in part by a negative attitude toward Israel. The emphasis on peace, repudiation of violence, and divine vindication is not without relevance to Roman imperial attitudes toward the Jews in particular.

Roman imperial arrogance toward the subjugated seems to have had a corrosive effect on social relations in which malicious gossip, stereotyping, and suchlike dominate the attitude toward those socially weak.[12] As some scholars have noted, it was not surprising that the Roman imperial attitude toward the subjugated would be replicated in the lower echelons of the social pyramid (Flower 2017: 255–46). Thus, Jews subjugated and continuing to be in some respects frustratingly different from the popular gentile social norms of honoring the gods would often be subject because of this to malicious stereotyping and misrepresentation. Though the link is not always noted, Paul is not opposing here "high-mindedness" in general, but a specific "boasting"

---

[12] Cf. on Roman neighborhoods, particularly Flower (2017, chs 2 and 4).

over against Jews. Here attitudes of ethnē in Christ toward Jews as rejecting their estimate of the Christ possibly contributed to the(ir) depiction of Roman Jews as being cast off from the on-going purpose of God. It is this perception of claiming to know the future of the Jews that Paul designates as "continuing to think how wise you are" (16b). But if the God of Israel has the power to use nations for honorable purposes as well as common (9:21), it is only he who can determine the future of peoples for his righteous purposes. If the Jews in the majority did not see in the "Christ-event" a revelation of God's righteousness toward the nations, while a minority from these nations did see this valorization, this reading of the sequence of the differing responses to the Christ-event evidences not the rejection of Israel but only a delay, since the God of Israel will not fail to keep covenant with her.

The advice to be patient in suffering is followed by the instruction in v. 14 to "bless those who persecute you, bless and do not curse." Sharing in the needs and sadness of others is further evidence of communal solidarity. Paul advises, as far as it is possible live at peace with all, meaning first of all those within the Christ-following community but clearly inclusive of opposition from a variety of outside sources. This emphasis upon non-retaliation and peace will be continued more precisely in ch. 14, but here in v. 19 it is given a particular focus by the citation of scripture from Deut. 32:35 and Prov. 25:21-22. "Judgment is mine; I will repay," says the Lord. As noted already in relation to Rom. 9:14, and 10:19 here again we see Paul's thought resonating with the narrative of Israel in the scriptures, particularly in Deuteronomy (as Rock has shown in detail, 2010: 80–5). The temptation in responses to evil is to think only in terms of individual responses, but the context here continues from ch. 11 where it is Israel as a whole that is perceived as cast off by some Christ-followers in Rome whether socially, politically, or otherwise. The fact that Deuteronomy continues to be used by Paul sets the scene with rebellious Israel facing her enemies in a hostile world.

Responding to the need of food or drink of one's enemies is all that is required, judgment is God's prerogative. So, vindication is also God's prerogative, and since it is God's, it means we cannot have it—it cannot be ours (Miller 1990: 234–5). Paul specifically advocates and forbids in relation to opposition. Using imperative verbs for the first time since 12:1-2, he will give a number of instructions that seem to focus on how to respond. Those who belong to Christ are only obligated to overcome evil with good, not by repaying evil deeds with evil. Nor are they required to seek to resist evil by self-mastery or strength of will. God will morally transform the ethnē by creating for them a new familial, brotherhood—by making them good (McMurray 2021: 12–14). It is God who will repay evil, not those who are victims of wrongdoing. In 12:14-21, Paul picks up the second-person singular from Proverbs 25 and continues it through the final verses of Romans 12 indicating that Paul still imagines himself addressing his interlocutor to highlight the proper response to opposition and how to overcome it (Rodriguez 2014: 239–40). This reflects both the lack of social power and influence of those in the Christ-movement and the spirit of the sermon on the plain. It is clear that living together in peace and humility was the anticipated pattern for the Christ-followers in Rome, and the fact that it is stressed here points to the possibility that this was not being realized as Paul would have expected. It is tempting to imagine the precise influences at Rome, but we will find further evidence as we proceed to chs. 13–15 that include negative reactions to Israel, ill-treatment particularly from outsiders,[13] that were combined with divisions among the ethnē in Christ.

The Song of Moses was earlier noted as significant for Paul in relation to the understanding of Israel's security and future. Moses's contention is that despite the divine faithfulness in dealing with Israel, Israel will prove faithless, but this does not mean that the covenant is annulled and that Israel will be destroyed. The contrast between Israel and her righteous God does not mean the destruction of the covenant. In the allocation of the nations of the world and the division of human beings in accordance with the number of the gods, God retained Israel for himself. Israel is the property of God, and she owes her total existence as a protected and prosperous people to the Lord alone (Rock 2012: 297–8). The theme of Deut. 32:28-33 is God's use of the nations as instruments of his wrath against Israel. The nameless nation, now defeated, was too arrogant to realize that the victory over Israel was allowed by God, who had withdrawn his protection over Israel, so that the victory was not due to the dominance of the other nation or its superior might, but only through God's will. The Song of Moses assumes that the difficulties that had befallen Israel are due to God's *temporarily* abandoning the people because of its unfaithfulness, but God's favorable intervention is sure. The gods of the nations can do nothing to help their allotted nations, but these gods cannot be compared to the God of Israel, and her enemies will be revealed as fools.

The repeat of citations from the Song of Moses indicates the background of Paul's thought from Romans 9–15 and the conclusions that ought to be drawn from this. The rejection of Israel theme haunts the narrative, but with resonance from the narrative of Israel's choice by her God. Just as Rom. 9:1-13 commenced with the story of how Israel was first formed out of the descendants of Abraham, so too this narrative continues this with the protection of Israel by her Creator God, despite her enemies and her failings.

---

[13] Thus, although the dialogical "question and response" exchanges of diatribal style, common through most of Romans 1–11, are no longer so visible, some diatribal elements remain.

Romans 13

Romans 13:1-7: "Pay All, What Is Due to Them"

¹Let every person subject himself to the governing authorities; for there is no authority except that by God, and those authorities that exist have been instituted by God. ²Therefore the one who resists this authority resists what God has instituted, and those who resist will incur judgment. ³For rulers are not (a cause) of fear to the good deed, but to the bad. So, you [sg] want to have no fear of the authority, do you? Practice the good, and you [sg] will receive its approval; ⁴for it is God's agent for you to attain the good. But if you [sg] do practice what is wrong, be afraid, for it does not bear the sword to no purpose! For it is God's agent to execute wrath on the wrong-doer. ⁵Therefore it is mandatory to submit, not only because of wrath but also because of perception. ⁶For this same reason you [pl] should also pay taxes, for the authorities are God's administrators, busy with this very thing. ⁷Pay to all what is due to them—taxes to whom taxes are due, revenue to whom revenue is due, fear to whom fear is due, honor to whom honor is due.

The theme of non-retaliation from the end of ch. 12 continues here. It is important not to miss this theme, connecting what may seem to be, an incidental collection of sayings in ch. 12. At several points, we have resisted the view that Paul's teaching may be perceived as general, not specifically related to a particular context. Thus Jewett, though he normally seeks to interpret Paul's statements in relation to the letter context, notes that ch. 13 "joins directly to the gnomic collection of sayings that conclude chapter 12" (2007: 781). But our perspective is that if Paul in order to support or even to constitute an argument links together a series of texts or ideas with a common theme, this indicates selection of contents in relation to the situation addressed, contextually related even though the words or phrases are not all Paul's own or newly formulated. When we consider Paul's statements here as a whole, we find that these sayings focus around the response to violence and lead via ch. 12 into ch. 13 in which submission to the authorities is central. This focus begins with 12:14, "Bless those who persecute you" and continues with the summary advice, "Do not be overcome with evil, but overcome evil with good" in 12:21. Paul obviously envisages a conflict situation that may involve the Roman authorities, to which he now turns with regard to the specifics of the constraints.

I follow the majority of commentators who see 13:1-7 as a genuine, integral part of the letter rather than as an interpolation. As Tobin states,

> Although clearly distinct, Rom. 13.1-7 does exhibit connections both with what precedes and what follows. It is a continuation of the theme of conduct towards outsiders in 12.17-18, especially the command as far as possible to be at peace with all human beings in 12.18. There are also verbal links both with what precedes and with what follows ... [T]he most obvious is the contrast between "good" (ἀγαθόν) and "evil" (κακόν) which runs through this entire section of the letter [i.e., 13:1-7]. (2004: 396–7)

The presence of diatribal elements such as the second-person singular form of address in 13:3-5 and the rhetorical question in 13:3 indicate that Paul is here indirectly addressing his Roman audience. Moreover, Jonathan Draper (1988: 35) has noted that "Romans 13:1-7 is located within Paul's teaching on love as the mark of the Christian life and the fulfilment of the law (12:3-21–13:8-14)" (cf. also McMurray 2021: 188–91). Käsemann is perceptive in that he notes that Paul does not offer here a universal doctrine of "church" and "state," but "he has in view very different local and regional authorities ... It deals with that circle of bearers of power with whom the common man may come in contact and behind which he sees the regional or central administration" (1980: 354).

My view is that Paul addresses here specific issues arising for subjugated peoples, particularly Christ-followers, living under Roman power in the first century in Rome (Lim 2014: 39–49). He appeals to give to each official what is legitimate, what is their due. This would include the Roman emperor, whether Claudius or Nero. But "Paul never provides a systematic or comprehensive critique of the emperor (whom he never names) or of the empire as such. The empire as such is never his direct target; his goal is to lay a claim on the allegiance of his listeners with which the rival claims of empire inevitably interfered" (Elliott 2008). This would have included giving to the gods the honor traditionally due to them, since only thus could the populace be protected from bad harvests, disease, childlessness, and so on.[1] This is categorically ruled out for Christ-followers, so there may be a qualification inherent in the understanding of "what is due." The emperor or other authority should not be given what is due to God alone. Conversely, the God who gave his son, with him will also provide all things needed in life and in death (Rom. 8:32).

This chapter presents a call for every person to be subject ὑποτασσέσθω to the authorities, that is, actual persons, ἐξουσίαι, which in vv. 2-3 soon gives way to the (singular) "authority" as both person and political agency (Hultgren 2011: 471).

What must be noted is that Paul here in 13:3b-5 uses the second-person singular form of address to the Romans, and not the second-person plural as would be normal. But Paul is not addressing only a single individual here. As Rodriguez's concludes, "The second-person language provides a continuity across the entire letter (rather

---

[1] Thus, the victory by Octavian at Actium was perceived as a gift from the gods (cf. Rock 2012: 179).

than that Paul introduces a second, and different dialogue partner in (and for) this pericope" (2016: 248, n35).[2] In 13:1, Paul began by referring to "every person," and 13:2a continues in the same vein of "the one resisting authority," and he turns in 2b to the third-person plural "They will receive judgment." But from 13:3b-5, Paul turns to diatribal style to challenge the interlocutor—"If you (singular) wish to avoid fear of the authority, then do what is good, and you will receive its approval" (Jewett 2007: 781). It seems clear that Paul is here indirectly commending the performance of that respect and honor that is due to the civic powers. In 13:1-2, "every person" is to be subject to the governing authorities ἐξουσίαι, probably indicating diverse levels of power and administration as experienced at the local level, as noted above, but carrying also the power of life and death as indicated by the reference to the sword in v. 4. Also Paul is not saying that civil authorities reward those citizens who live morally upright lives, who fulfill all familial duties and do their work conscientiously—he is only stating that people are rewarded (not for being morally upright) but for exhibiting what is regarded as civic duty by those in power (Rodriguez 2016: 249). We do not share Cranfield's confidence that "in one way or another, 'the power will praise the good work and punish the evil'" (1979: 245). It is only when he comes to 13:7 that Paul explicates what civil submission entails, that is, giving to all "what is due," whether tax, revenue, respect, or honor.

There is evidence that heavy taxation at the period of Paul's writing this letter (i.e., 57–58 CE) may have caused some unrest. These taxes were very onerous and were difficult for many to pay (Rock 2012: 112–13). It is likely that many of Paul's addressees were immigrants to Rome and thus would face pressure, and likely also force, from greedy tax-farmers who were a main cause of unrest in the early part of Nero's reign, as Tacitus reported (Tobin 2004: 399). We will return to this later. Nero did introduce a number of reforms in order to make the collection of taxes fairer and the prosecution of the excesses of tax-farmers easier (Tobin 2004: 399). Paul's advice in 13:7 is that the Christ-followers do their civic duty, give respect, and pay taxes where due. But it should be noted that "what is due" includes in Paul's mind also, primarily what is due to God, recognition, worship, and the highest honor. But what should the ethnē do when Caesar demands, not what is due to him, but what is due to God alone? Thus Paul, writing in this context, does not offer any support for a tax revolt or tax avoidance, but he may be leaving open the possibility of a different perspective in which there is a strong hint that the demands of Caesar may not always be compatible with loyalty to the God of Israel. This view in relation to gentile overlords was not peculiar to the Christ-movement, it was typical of an alternative way of life—of Jews living in the world of the Diaspora. An arrangement between Jews and Rome had been negotiated, which exempted the Jews from worshipping emperors and Roman deities, acknowledging Roman rule by offering a sacrifice for the well-being of the imperial family to their God in their Temple in Jerusalem. Paul, in keeping with this perspective, views these rulers as not to be honored as deities but as having received

---

[2] On this, see Excursus I. The use of the rhetorical question with the singular θέλεις, you wish (v. 3), and σοί, you (v. 4), denote a shift to the diatribe, which Jewett also notes but points out that here "its argumentative function has not been clarified" (2007: 793).

their power from the Creator God of Israel, rather than, as they claimed, from Jupiter, Juno, Minerva, or any other of the numerous deities.

It is difficult for us to conceive the enormity of this claim. Such a claim would appear ludicrous to every Roman citizen, except the tiny minority that represented Israel/Jerusalem on the world stage of the empire.[3] But, since the rulers do receive their authority and power to rule from God, these rulers must be held in respect—give them their due, nothing less, but also nothing more. Josephus holds that Jews hold the emperor and the Roman people in such honor as is second only to that paid to God. There is even a bit of irony in 13:4 where twice it is stated that the one in authority is God's servant διάκονος (Hultgren 2011: 472). What Paul says about payment of taxes is framed by Jewish apocalyptic theology that all power is granted, not permanently or absolutely, but *only temporarily and in a limited capacity* by the God of Israel, as freshly understood by the life and death of Jesus as the Christ (Portier-Young 2013: 9, 37, 44). The main thing is that people should recognize the governing authorities and their function to exact taxes for the time being. The Christ-followers should continue to pay their taxes, Paul is reinforcing that. There is no obligation to develop a servile pattern of behavior, since we must bear in mind that reference to taxes would have carried overtones of subjugation, forced exaction, and domination by foreign powers (Hultgren 2011: 471, Coleman 1997: 309).

Two different taxes are in view here: direct taxes (φόρος, *tributa*) and indirect taxes (τέλος, *vestigalia*). Thomas Coleman has shown that immigrants to Rome were being compelled by the Neronic administration to pay a tribute tax as immigrants, that is, people of the status of *peregrini* (who may have comprised a significant proportion of the members of the Christ-movement). These may have been seeking to avoid paying the heavy tax. Those who had been temporarily expelled from Rome would be liable, on their return, to taxation as immigrants (Jewett 2007: 798–9). Also, Paul's associates Priscilla and Aquila would remember the emergency when they and others were expelled from Rome several years previously and would not be willing to risk conflict with the authorities (cf. Acts 18). Jewett holds that there were high-ranking Roman administrators in the Roman house "churches" according to ch. 16 and that Paul's concern for his planned mission to Spain means that he will make extreme efforts, as evident in 13:1-7, to prove that his mission will not lead to unrest of the kind that had led to some Jewish leaders being expelled from Rome by Claudius. Paul is writing in the early part of Nero's reign, which, as noted above, began promisingly in 54 CE, and Nero did later abolish certain taxes, partly in response to civil unrest and possibly on Seneca's advice (Tacitus, *Ann.* 13:50-51). He was prevented from reducing taxes further because of its likely political and economic effect. Taxes are referenced only in 13:6-7. This could, but does not necessarily, indicate that taxation is not important. On the other hand, in 13:6-7, Paul reverts to addressing the Romans directly in the second-person plural, rather than in diatribal mode (Tobin 2004: 396), which means that it is addressed as one issue among others indicating real discontent in Rome. Even though

---

[3] "By me [God] kings reign, and rulers decree what is just" (Prov. 8:15). Similarly, cf. LXX Jer. 34:5-7; Isa. 45:1-3; Dan. 2:21, 36-38; and Sir. 10:4. Other Hellenistic Jewish texts reflect similar attitudes (*Arist.* 45; Philo, *Legat.* 157; Josephus, *War.* 2:197; *Ap.* 2:76-77) (Tobin: 2004, 397–8).

it is difficult to determine its extent, unrest against Roman domination was increasing at this period in Judea, and it would continue to do so until the outbreak of the Jewish–Roman war in 66 CE.

This may have had already some impact on Jews in Rome (Ehrensperger 2022b: 289–305). How Paul's gentile mission was perceived in this context is again difficult to assess. But certainly, Paul would not have wanted to encourage public resistance to Rome in that this, apart from its futility, in his mind, would not have enabled the restoration of Israel. This he regarded as being somehow intrinsically related to the success of his gentile mission, since "vindication is mine" (Rom. 12:19), that is, vindication lies with God rather than in the hope of military victory.

But in keeping with Jewish conceptions of rulers as being divinely instituted, Paul's recognition of those who rule is, as already noted, not unqualified. Paul advocates submission out of loyalty to God under whose sovereignty Nero has temporary authority. It is due to military might that Rome rules and everyone must subordinate themselves to this out of response to God rather than to the emperor who is God's servant to punish and to execute God's wrath—the subordinated have a divine duty out of loyalty to God to submit to this temporary authority. Here we follow those scholars who claim on the strength of the γάρ "for" that introduces Rom. 13:6, that τελεῖτε must be taken as an indicative—"this is also the reason you pay taxes," rather than an imperative "for this reason you must pay taxes" (Rock 2012: 313). What is legally due is to be rendered to every ruler, that is, the minimum requirement. Yet, the authority that the emperor wields is not without its limits. Every person is under the authority of the emperor, but in Paul's perspective Caesar is also under authority. Rome, being subordinate to the God of Israel, must be obedient to his rule. The one who is the most powerful person in Roman rule is twice described somewhat ironically as the διάκονος (servant) of another (i.e., the God of Israel). "In its ancient context, the term means that the one in authority is not divine, but subject to God" (Hultgren 2011: 472).

The governing authority itself is agent of God "for your good." It may be that there is an implied qualification here—it should be "for your good," not "for your harm" (13:4). But in any case, the authority Paul acknowledges for those who govern is not autonomous or independent government, even Caesar rules as an agent (διάκονος) of God (13:4). The authorities are God's administrators, λειτουργοί (13:6).[4] This may mean they may be the instruments of his wrath (Rock 2012: 313). These titles refer to offices or functions in a situation of authority/administration where those acting are not functioning on their own behalf but are under obligation to do the work allocated to them by their overlord. So, they are not all-powerful, but both they and their work are determined by one to whom they are subject and to whom they must eventually answer. Caesar is not Lord of the conscience (13:5). Like Pharaoh in 9:17, rulers are seen as being raised up or put down by the God of Israel, whose purpose is determinative in history (cf. πρόθεσις, 9:11). This suggests, as James C. Scott has demonstrated, that public discourse can include hidden transcripts and that what appears to be confirmed

---

[4] Paul applies both of these terms to himself (in Romans), cf. also Christ as διάκονος περιτομῆς "servant of the circumcision" in 15:8.

on one level can be undermined on another (1985, 1990). Paul in Rom. 13:1-7 appears to argue in this particular fashion.

As noted already earlier, Jewish traditions had for centuries been exposed to foreign rule and had developed ways to relate to such while maintaining their own traditions, their identity, and their own perception of the "world" and events.

> Intrinsic to this was their refusal to consider their defeat or conquest as evidence of the defeat of their God. The Jews maintained that their God continued to be the supreme ruler of the cosmos, the Creator of the universe to whom all and everything was subject. Hence any equivalent claim, whoever might have raised it, was inherently refuted. The outcome of this Jewish confidence in their God, is that this led to a relativization of any and all power-claims over the Jews and a critical distancing from these whatever their source. (Ehrensperger 2019b: 152)

This meant that they re-claimed agency and the power of self-perception over against the powerlessness attributed to them as subjugated people (Mermelstein 2021). The destiny of Rome according to Virgil was to rule as an eternal kingdom (cf. Rock 2012: 52-64). But although the Romans claimed divine appointment and eternal power, important strands of Jewish thought regarded earthly rulers as temporarily circumscribed with limits to their sovereignty fixed by the God of Israel, whose purpose and fame rulers like Pharaoh and the Roman emperor are destined to serve. Informed by Berthelot, Ehrensperger points out that "Even Philo, who to some extent accepted Roman rule, never affirms Roman claims that their rule was the result of Divine providence."[5] Divine providence in Philo does operate but only on behalf of Israel when endangered by the Romans (*Legat.* 220). Divine providence (πρόνοια) is cited only with reference to Israel but never cited in respect of the Romans themselves, "Divine providence rather sustains, and provides for the functioning of the universe, caring especially for the well-being of the Jews" (Ehrensperger 2019b: 152).

Rome's claim to be the people divinely ordained to rule the world eternally clashed diametrically with Jewish perceptions of the world as God's creation and of their role within it. Rome may rightly be perceived as an instrument of God's wrath, but Rome's status in this respect is temporary "contrary to Virgil's assertion that Rome had been ordained to eternal rule. Israel (Jacob) and not Rome (Esau) is still preferred; the election is irrevocable" (Rock 2010: 88). Louis H. Feldman earlier had noted a parallelism between the two nations, Israel and Rome.

> [These] peoples may well have been enhanced by their common view that they had been divinely chosen for a unique destiny, as the Bible, on the one hand, and Livy and Virgil, on the other hand, emphasize. Each was said to have engaged, after great suffering, in a massive national exodus to a promised land, the Israelites

---

[5] Philo says that what the Romans achieved was granted to them by Fortuna *Tyche*. Like some Greek authors, Philo implies that there is no intrinsic value to what has been granted to her—what has been granted by Fortuna has nothing to do with God's will. Fortuna has nothing to do with the Law of Moses, which operates in accordance with nature, see Berthelot (2011: 179–80).

from Egypt to Canaan, the Romans from Troy to Rome. Each had a great leader, Moses and Aeneas respectively, who had a very special relationship to the divinity. Moreover, both the Bible and Virgil have an apocalyptic technique that looks forward to a kind of salvation. (Feldman as cited in Rock 2012: 317)

According to Paul's perspective, the power to punish wrong-doers and reward the good is legitimately borne by the Roman authorities. Israel's God disciplines Israel and judges the nations in the exercise of the power entrusted temporarily to them. The Romans may sometimes be used as the instruments for exercising God's wrath. God through them will punish evil-doers and support the good, "vindication is mine, I will repay" says the scripture (12:19). What should not be overlooked is that the Jews considered they were under the protection of their God and that those who persecuted them would receive their just punishment. The punishment of the nations who had oppressed the Jews is certainly in view in Philonic writings and in 1 Enoch (Ehrensperger 2019c: 153). Paul appears to share this view of Roman government. He certainly shares the tendency not to buy into Roman ideology thereby constituting an implicit shared counter-narrative with Philo and others. This established a function for Roman rule as given by the God of Israel (not the Roman deities), thereby providing a rationale for subjection to Rome but with the possibility of a limit to the obedience subjects were required to give and to the obedience the Romans could legitimately demand. Indeed, Paul's use of terminology reflects a clear distinction between allegiance to God and subjection to the Roman authorities. Thus, we note that πιστός and εὐσέβεια are never used by Philo in relation to the rulers or those in power, only in relation to Israel's God (Eyl 2021). As Stegemann has noted,

> It is revealing that Paul applies the word πιστ-stem only in relation to relationships between humans and the God of Israel or Christ, and probably also between Jesus [Christ] and God … A [Roman] ruler, however, is not characterized as πιστός [faithful] and he does not deserve *fides* [faithfulness] either. According to Romans 13, he only deserves obedience, fear and honour. (Stegemann 2010: 20–21)

This counter-narrative of Jewish eschatological expectations (Ehrensperger 2019b) is glimpsed somewhat unexpectedly from the works of Josephus who writing after the end of the Jewish Roman War (*Ant.* 10:210) still seems to hold on to Jewish expectations about the final vindication of Israel (Berthelot 2011). In this passage, Josephus refers somewhat reticently to Dan. 2:44-45 about "hidden things which are to come." Here he described how God would set up a kingdom that would last forever and would crush all other kingdoms. In the context of Daniel, this eternal kingdom was obviously Israel, so it is striking that residing in Rome after the defeat of the Jews, Josephus still attests to these Jewish eschatological expectations yet to be fulfilled. It is significant that though Josephus in the Jewish Roman war deserted the rebel forces to turn to Rome because he thought God sided with the Romans at that point, yet he still did not think that God had abandoned his people or that Jewish history had come to an end. Divine providence, πρόνοια, preserves the Jewish people from destruction. The fact that God had used the Romans to punish the Jews implies that God will one day change sides and punish the Romans (Rajak 1991: 132).

Josephus did not speak only of the rise of Rome to a vast empire, which he acknowledged could not have happened without God's aid (*War* 2. 390). He also spoke, albeit allusively and cautiously, of the future fall of the empire (Spilsbury 2002: 317). Paul likewise is aware that, as with other great world empires, Rome's rule has a termination point. So he never says that submission is obligatory when the authorities in power do not support justice but rule unjustly persecuting the righteous.

The implication is that there is a limit to the submission that is due in such a context. This age will continue for only a limited period, so it is bounded by that fact. Nevertheless, the view that the Roman authorities have a function to perform given them by God means also they are responsible to God, that is, subject to him, and that in extreme circumstances where there is conflict, one must obey God rather than men. Thus, throughout the centuries there have been Christians like Calvinists, Huguenots, Scots Presbyterians, and many others who, based on Paul's teaching in Romans 13, have conscientiously resisted what they perceived to be unjust ruling powers.[6] And so also Jews have chosen forms of resistance where possible, often under violent pressure to forsake their loyalty to their God and way of life, in the form of migration, or hidden loyalty as, for example, Crypto-Jews. The fact that the Roman authorities are themselves subjects, that is, designated as God's διάκονοι and λειτουργοί, has relativized the extent of the submission required to them, since they themselves are not only instituted τεταγμέναι by God, but are also subject to him (Stegemann 2010: 6). All authorities, even the Roman emperor, reign at the good pleasure of Israel's God (Rodriguez 2014: 244). This means their rule is qualified—it is certainly not to be regarded as absolute.

Since there is no authority except from God (13:1b), the legitimation of those in power comes from God to whom they must be faithful if they are to use this authorization. "What Paul is advocating here is a subversive call for the Christians living under the Roman hegemony to examine whether respect and honor should be conferred on those who have failed to discharge their divinely appointed duties, resulting for example in oppression and injustice" (Lim 2014: 47). Paul's exhortation could be taken as advice to practice the arts of resistance but in ways that would not threaten the community and the nation. Paul may have sounded compliant/obedient, but he noticeably commands the giving of nothing to the empire except what is due, and "his apparent advice about loyalty is couched in language teaching how to survive in an environment hostile to the Christian minority" (2014: 47).

In any case, claims to eternal domination of the whole οἰκουμένη by Rome were relativized by the ongoing contact between Jews East (in the Sassanid empire) and West, since totalizing claims to power were evidently wrong according to the sociopolitical map and actual conditions. On the ground these claims were revealed to

---

[6] To illustrate what an alternative culture may involve, we may widen the context to draw attention also to Jews and Muslims in European countries, for example, in Germany or France today. Unlike pop culture these groups are not merely a sub-culture, but an alternative culture because at significant points they feel obligated to differentiate themselves radically from the dominant ethos and yet still seek to be conscientious citizens.

be ideological postulations rather than facts in that the empire had boundaries in the East and beyond (Ehrensperger 2022b: 296).

We cannot be confident whether or to what extent the ethnē in Christ at Rome affirmed positive hopes about Israel's future, but certainly Paul's Jewish friends greeted in ch. 16 would be likely to support these as would those Jews whether Christ-followers or not whom we know were present in Rome (Rock 2012: 321). Josephus would hardly have cited from Daniel (*War* 6:312-14) if this represented only a minority opinion in Rome, so this may indicate that the Jews in Rome shared Josephus's opinion (cf. Tobin 2004: 260) even if Josephus considered that it was Vespasian who was meant in the oracle as the one from their country who would rule the world. I do not see the views of the Romans as "more of a piece with those of the Roman Jewish community than were Paul's views" (contra. Tobin 2004: 262). It is significant that Paul in his final reference to φόρος tax in v. 7 returns to the theme of submission called for in 13:1. Here with the second-person plural imperative, ἀπόδοτε, he gives direct advice to the Romans in relation to the authorities. What needs to be noted is Paul's use of terminology. He never uses ταγ-related terms (e.g. ὑποτασσέσθαι), with reference to the gospel, but for him this rather denotes issues concerning "order" in the communities or here in relation to political authorities (Ehrensperger 2009: 172–4). It advocates submission to the rulers of this world allowed to rule for a limited time. It seems clear that Paul did not want to leave any doubt about the subjection of the gentile Christ-followers to the governing authorities. But, as has been noted (Rodriguez 2016: 252), this call for demonstration of submission comes alongside Paul's warning that the civil authorities are themselves under God's authority, accountable to God, and that if they do not act justly as servants or administrators, they will be subject to the wrath (ὀργή 13:5, 1:18). Paul appeals to the Romans to discharge their obligations (τὰς ὀφειλάς) to everyone whether these concern taxes, revenue, respect, or honor, the latter being properly due only to God. As noted above, Jews like Philo were careful not to offer fidelity to those in power since this was unto death, for example, the oath of loyalty taken by Romans and non-Romans in Paphalogonia to the Caesarean house (Rock 2012: 195).

Romans 13:8-14: The Link between the Law and Ἀγάπη—Love Fulfills the Law

⁸Owe no one anything, except to love one another; for the one who loves the other has fulfilled the law. ⁹For "You shall not commit adultery; You shall not murder; You shall not steal; You shall not covet"; and any other commandment, are summed up in this word, "Love your neighbor as yourself." ¹⁰This love does no wrong to a neighbor; therefore, this love is the fulfilment of the law. ¹¹Besides this, knowing the time, that it is now the hour for you to wake up from sleep. For rescue is nearer to us now than when we came to trust; ¹²the night is far gone, the day is near. Let us then lay aside the works of darkness and put on the armor of light; ¹³let us walk decently as if in the day, not in raving and drunkenness, not in sexual immorality and licentiousness, not in quarrelling and jealousy. ¹⁴Instead, put on the Lord Jesus Christ, and make no provision for the flesh, to gratify its desires.

Harrison notes, "Perhaps it is in Rom. 13.8-10 that we see the most incisive interaction of Paul with the expectation of obligation in antiquity ... The four governmental obligations mentioned in v. 7 reciprocate the service of the Roman ruler to his subjects mentioned in Romans 13.4" (2020: 165). The language of indebtedness, first announced in Rom. 1:14, is regularly returned to throughout the epistle and features strongly toward the conclusion (15:27). Paul was indeed an astute observer of ancient social relations, and he could hardly avoid endorsing and engaging the rituals of recompense embedded in the Greco-Roman "payback" system in a variety of contexts. However, in light of the unconditioned grace of God revealed in Christ, Paul inverts the social operations of the "payback" system in challenging ways (e.g., 3:27-28, 4:4, 11:6). Like Cicero in *De Officiis* 1:15, Paul can stress giving to everyone what is due, but this is a minimum and is surpassed by ἀγάπη unconditional love inspired by the Spirit (Harrison 2020: 163). "It is the universalism, open-endedness, and perpetuity of Paul's social construct of 'indebtedness' in Rom. 13.8-10 that would have been surprising and challenging for Roman auditors of his letter" (Harrison 2020: 166–7). The last reference to νόμος Law occurred in 10:4-5 where Paul made the distinctive theological link that the goal of the Law is Christ. Now he makes another significant theological link involving a corresponding claim that "the one who loves the other has fulfilled Torah" (Rodriguez 2016: 252). In contrast to the exhortation to pay taxes that can and should be paid, Paul states, "Owe no one anything" (13:8); here Paul refers in a surprising reversal of the dynamics of indebtedness, to the duty to love the other as a duty that can never be completely discharged—it is an abiding debt (ὀφείλω) always due (13:8).

The link between the Law and love indicates that love has the power to actualize for "gentiles" (πεπλήρωκεν) the duty of loving the other. Instead of setting the Law in opposition to the gospel, or the Law in opposition to Christ, Paul sees God's purpose as being confirmed in the doing of the Law through the love that arises through the power of the Spirit. The Law is not rejected by something else taking its place (as in replacement theology) but is fulfilled in the sense of being done, adhered to, so that Law and love are both constituents within God's historic purpose inaugurated in Christ. Thus, a careful investigation of Paul's use of fulfillment terminology shows that Paul does not frequently use the verb πληρόω to fulfill. Also, I do not find "fulfillment" a fruitful translation in that many contemporary users of the term use it in the sense that something is partially fulfilled simultaneously with some part of it being rejected; thus "fulfillment" can cover up a partial rejection of the past, that is, of scripture, Law, or Judaism, while appearing to be confirming it. In my perception of Paul's use of πληρόω, the termination of something is not included (Campbell 2019b).

The δικαίωμα of the Law (Rom. 8:4) is not fulfilled by us but in and through us. As Keck notes, "The text does not replace the law with love. It claims that the law is actualized in love" (2005: 200, 328–9). The Law is done by putting it into practice in the community, it is not terminated by this action. Paul's use of terminology indicates that he prefers teleological rather than fulfillment terminology as, for example, Rom. 10:4; cf. also 2 Cor. 1:20 where the promises are actualized in Christ (since the consummation of God's promises still awaits its revelation). As Beker claims, for Paul, "Christ is not so much the fulfilment of God's promises as the guarantee or confirmation of these promises" (1980: 345).

A line of thought concerning the Law continues, sometimes unobtrusively, throughout Romans. The Law is discussed both positively and negatively in relation to trust, to sin, to grace, to the promise, to the Spirit, and to Christ. So, Paul's statement that the one who loves the other has fulfilled the Law indicates a kind of summary conclusion to this line of thought. "The virtue of love epitomizes the whole ethic. When the readers exercise the virtue of love, they will actually be doing what the law requires of gentiles" (Sanders 1994: 40–1). The Law and love both relate to human behavior; love does no wrong to the other who is and remains different. In the case of ethnē in Christ as is the case here, these have been warned not to take on the obligation of Law as Jews naturally do, and that for non-Jews, apart from Christ, the Law brings only judgment. But they also need to know that the Law is not in opposition to Christ, and that the Law can be fulfilled through love (Fredriksen 2017: 117–18). Thus, the Law is not limited to being merely a Jewish pattern of conduct but has positive links with allegiance to Christ. It is this understanding of the Law that Paul wishes to promote in Rome and which he will discuss further in Romans 14–15. Paul has no objection to commandments as such, but their significance is summed up in loving your neighbor as yourself. The summary of the Law in the Decalogue for Paul is not without serious significance for ethnē in Christ (Fredriksen 2014: 801–8). As Sanders asserts, "The twin pillars on which the Rabbis' understanding of salvation rested were election and atonement. God chose Israel by his grace 'for his own sake.' As a consequence of the election and in his role as King, God gave the Israelites commandments to obey—not as a means of salvation, but as man's proper response to the covenant" (1977: 180).

Does Paul need to stress the relation between the Law and love because he had been reported as being opposed to the Law? Or does Paul link Law and love positively because the Roman ethnē have failed to do so? In 13:9-10, Paul sets out the horizontal person-to-person commandments (you shall not commit adultery, you shall not murder, you shall not steal, you shall not covet, Rom. 13:9) to demonstrate the content of the citation of Lev. 19:18 "You shall love your neighbor as yourself." Love here is not merely a sentiment but relates to behavior, that is, action in relation to the neighbor. In contrast to the indebtedness underlying Roman *caritas*, which is hierarchical and status-ridden, the communal, covenantal ethics of Leviticus includes a concern for the weak and the poor, the hired man, those with disabilities, the resident alien. In the ancient Greco-Roman "payback" system, obligation was first to be extended "to country and parents, then to children and family and, last to kinsmen" (Cicero *Off.* 1.58). Paul's unqualified obligation to the barbarian would be inconceivable in this closed system of moral responsibility" (Harrison 2020: 167). The self-conscious cultural superiority of Greeks toward the barbarian tribes as well as the boastful arrogance of Romans to both groups is relativized in Paul's mutual obligation to each group (Harrison 2020: 161). Thus, Paul redefines the operation of reciprocity in unconventional and unexpected ways in light of God's covenantal revelation to Israel and its confirmation in Christ (Harrison 2020: 164). Care must be exercised in comparisons such as we have indicated here. Comparisons can be odious, and it is only too easy to extol the virtues of one system/ideology over another as, for example, Greco-Roman ethics versus Leviticus, or Pauline ethics over both of these. Paul negotiates the cultural worlds of all involved, Greek, barbarian, and Jewish, rather than simply presenting a counter-cultural ethos.

There could have been no more explicit evidence that Paul sees no contradiction between following Christ and the Law than his statement, that these commandments (and any other such that there might be) are all summed up, ἀνακεφαλαιοῦται, in "loving one's neighbor as oneself." The Decalogue concerns the relationship between Israel and Israel's God, but the relation to this God achieved through Jesus Christ brings the non-Jews also into a relationship to the Law, not the same as for Jews, but not in opposition and certainly not in antithesis to the Law or to Jewish patterns of its practice. In keeping with Paul's most recent and positive reference to the Law in Rom. 10:4, it would be surprising if Paul confirmed here what he had claimed was supposedly terminated there. Indeed, here he links love and the Law inextricably by claiming the former as a summing up of the latter (Campbell 2019c, McMurray 2021: 189–90). A radical opposition between Jewish traditions and Christ-related convictions such as introduced by Marcion is here categorically repudiated, but not in such a way as to diminish the emphasis upon the gospel of grace, but rather to strengthen its roots in the narrative of God's ways with Israel (Muilenberg 1961; Brueggemann 1997: 413–49, Wagner 2003: 191). Paul stresses the negative aspect of love as well—"Love does not result in evil to a neighbor therefore love is the fulfilling of the Law" (13:10). The use of the verb ἐργάζεται, accomplish or do, links 13:10 back to 2:9 (κατεργάζεται) under the theme of the doing of the Law (cf. Rodriguez 2014: 256, n59). We take πλήρωμα here as the full measure of the Law, not as a partial affirmation and partial rejection, but as an affirmation of its purpose as willed by God.

It is noteworthy that the line of thought concerning the Law that proceeds slowly but unerringly throughout Romans finds its goal (cf. 10:4) in this explanation. In Romans 2, Paul referred to ethnē in Christ as "doers of Torah," that is, those who really keep the Law—worshipping the Creator rather than the created gods of the ethnē. Just as the failure to honor God resulted in the catalog of gentile anti-social behavior listed in 1:29-31, the proper recognition of the relationship between God, as Creator, and the work of his hands must lead to pro-social behavior. Paul depicts the fulfillment of Torah in terms of both worship of the Creator God and right relationship with others (i.e., ἀγάπη). This link between the Law as encapsulated in the Decalogue as Torah's epitome is sustained by citing the love command from Leviticus, "even if there is any other commandment, it is summed up in this saying, (*en tō logō*) 'You shall love your neighbor (*ton plesion sou*) as yourself' (Rom. 13.9, citing Lev. 19.18)" (Rodriguez 2014: 255). This emphasis on Law as fulfilled in love indicates the link between the way of life for ethnē in Christ and the way of life for Israel. In that sense, Paul's gospel is Israel-centered or Israel-oriented. An alternative designation might be to state that Paul's gospel is covenant-oriented (Campbell 1991: 162–3). Paul reaches a climax to his argument in his affirmation, "Therefore love is the full measure (*plerōma*) of Torah" (13:10), and fully consistent with the Decalogue (Rodriguez 2014: 256). Further demanding implications of "the Law of love" will be developed in 14:1–15:6, when Paul turns to the relation between differing groups in Rome.

Paul concludes this chapter with a specific reminder that the Roman ethnē in Christ know what time it is in God's eschatological calendar. A major difference between Paul and some of his Jewish compatriots was that they were not persuaded that the Messianic Time had been inaugurated with the Christ-event. The form of Christ's death and the claims for his having been raised from the dead were not persuasive for some. So, while Paul and those "unpersuaded" agreed on many things, they differed on the consequences following on the interpretation of the Christ-event, that is, of non-Jews following Christ and being accepted as ethnē into God's kingdom as a satellite community. It was the timing of the proclamation of Jesus's Messiahship and its significance for the nations that was decisive for differing reactions. Here Paul adds another emphasis based on the image of the coming of rescue, which he claims is now "nearer than when we first trusted in Christ." Applying this image, Paul argues that it is time to "wake up from sleep" (13:11). "The night" the present sinful age "is far gone and daybreak is near." To respond appropriately to this Messianic Time, it is essential to "lay aside the works of darkness and put on the armor of light" (13:12). The "put off," "put on" imagery reflects baptismal patterns of new life replacing the former ways of ethnē before they turned to Christ. As is fitting in the new day, old patterns of behavior must cease and new ways of life be embraced. Not living with excess food or drink, or in quarrelling or jealousy but making no provision for fleshly living, to gratify its desires, instead of all these "put on the Lord Jesus Christ." Via the imagery of old and new dress, Paul stresses the transition that the ethnē in Christ have or should have experienced through trusting in Christ. It echoes the negative aspects of the sins of the nations underlined in 1:19-32 in a clear-cut contrast with life in Christ. The response of offering one's body as a living sacrifice means a rejection of all that is evil in relation to the other and an embracing of all that is good as defined by ἀγάπη enabled through the Spirit.

Romans 14:1–15:6

As we have demonstrated throughout the previous chapters, Paul's addressees are the ethnē in Christ at Rome. Since there is no explicit grammatical or rhetorical indication, it would be surprising if Paul would turn at the end of the letter to address an audience other than the one that supposedly followed his long and detailed argument up to this point. Where Romans differs is in its style of presentation (in how it is presented), *not in its nature as address*. As noted in Excursus I, to acknowledge the use of a certain style does not in itself require that only a certain content is transmissible by such a style. Rather, as Donfried, Stowers, and others have successfully argued, *the recognition of diatribal style throughout Romans does not rule out the option or the obligation to read it as is done here, as a letter of Paul to Rome.*

Already in our exegesis of earlier chapters, especially of chs. 4, 7, and 9–11, we have demonstrated that although, at certain points, the Jewish content of the argument and the discussion of, or reference to, actual Jews might suggest that Jews may be among the audience addressed, this has not been evidenced. The careful reading of such passages points only to a gentile audience, which unsurprisingly continues to be addressed in chs. 14–15. Jewish-related issues do not demand Jews among the addressees, and audience cannot confidently be derived from content alone. The findings of our exegesis of Romans 1–11 support and point toward the conclusion that also in 14:1–15:6 no Jews are addressed. The closest we come to acknowledging related issues among Jews in the Roman context is only to recognize that some issues that Paul raises concerning non-Jews may possibly parallel or reflect similar discussions among Jewish groups. And this suggests that it is not an *ethnic issue as such* that here differentiates the stances between "the weak" and "the strong."

Romans 14:1-4: Welcome "The Weak"—Paul's Measure of Strength

[1] Welcome the one who is weak in trust, but not for quarreling over disputed matters. [2] The one is confident in eating anything, while the weak eats vegetables. [3] The one who eats must not despise the one who does not eat, and one who does not eat must not pass judgment on the one who eats, for God has welcomed him. [4] You, who are

you to pass judgment on someone else's household slave? He stands or falls before his own lord. And he will be made to stand, for the Lord has the power to enable him to stand.

In the Roman context, whether that was an assembly based around the home, tenement dwelling, or private association,[1] there were disputed issues threatening to cause serious division among the Christ-followers. If this were not so, it would be offensive for Paul to warn against it. Where differing practices were followed, whose conscience should be determinative? We discern the labels of "weak" (and, with refocusing, also of the "strong" in ch. 15) as those emanating from among the Romans themselves, rather than from Paul's choice of terminology (cf. Jewett 2007: 836). In order to enter meaningfully into the debate, Paul had to use recognizable labels for the disputants in order to make a contribution that would be intelligible to his audience, so most likely he uses the labels that the Romans have created. "Weak" is hardly complimentary, but Paul though he does not include himself in the category, offers no criticism of it (Rodriguez 2016: 264). It is significant that it is only from 15:1 that he will include himself along with "the strong" though this does not mean he shares fully the stance of the, probably, self-styled "strong."[2] We designate those who despise or pain "the weak" in ch. 14 as self-designated, that is, self-styled "strong," but whom Paul holds to be much in need of correction. So he does not include himself in ch. 14 in those who perceive themselves as "strong" but revises the designation to what we might term "the redefined strong" in such a way that he can include himself in the designation from 15:1.

It appears that this term was being used among the ethnē in Christ to denote a sense of superiority since the Roman public were inclined to view strength as an indication of honor and weakness as a term of contempt (Reasoner 1999: 54, Jewett 2007: 835); thus some despise (ἐξουθενεῖς deriving from οὐδέν nothing repeated from 14:3) the other (14:10). The verbal form, ἐξουθενέω "to despise," Esler regards as referring to the scornful rejection of another from a position of perceived superiority, often in an intergroup context (2003: 350). This may indicate the influence of Roman imperial attitudes toward weakness generally, an ethos favoring "strength" (Roman means strength). Harrison, commenting upon Seneca's condemnation of the Jewish people, notes how "victory" ideology totally shaped the Roman perception of the world (2020: 326). But, in Paul's perspective, "the weak" must be included among those welcomed whether or not their weakness involves dietary or festival laws.

Paul's paraenesis in ch. 14 aims to challenge the self-styled "strong" among the Christ-followers to accommodate the "weak." I have called them "self-styled strong" because Paul does not refer to anyone in ch. 14 with the label "strong." Pressure is put on these because they have the freedom to change their behavior pattern to accommodate "the weak" without necessarily damaging their own integrity. The "self-styled strong" are only negatively presented in ch. 14 in their destructive effect upon

---

[1] On this, we follow the findings of our discussion of "Synagogues and Craft Associations" in the "Introduction" chapter. We will return to this issue later in our reading of ch. 16.
[2] The heading "Paul's Measure of Strength" of this section is in analogy to "the measure of trust" (12:3).

"the weak." They are depicted in their failure to carry the "weak," in not abstaining from anything that acts as a hindrance, in not walking in love of the other. "The weak," on the other hand, have convictions that they feel demand abstinence from anything that may cause them to stumble and may result in their ruin if forced to yield to the power of "the strong" (14:15-20). Although not an exact parallel, there may be some resonance with a passage where Josephus describes the "most miserable end" of the Essene, who, having been rejected by his community, is still bound by his convictions as to what he may eat and with whom (*War* 2:143-44).[3]

Romans 14:5-12: "The Weak"—Not a Temporary Phenomenon

⁵The one person distinguishes one day from another, while the other judges all days [alike]. Let each be fully convinced in his own mind. ⁶The one observing the day, observes it in relation to the Lord. And the one eating, eats in relation to the Lord, since he gives thanks to God; while the one who does not eat, does not eat in relation to the Lord and gives thanks to God. ⁷For no one of us lives to himself, and no one dies to himself. ⁸If we live, we live in relation to the Lord, and if we die, we die in relation to the Lord; so then, whether we live or whether we die, we are the Lord's. ⁹For to this end Christ died and lived, so that he might be Lord over both the dead and the living. ¹⁰You, who are you to pass judgment on your brother? Or you, who are you to despise your brother? For we will all stand before the judgment seat of God. ¹¹For it is written, "As I live, says the Lord, to me shall every knee bow, and every tongue shall acknowledge God." ¹²So then, each of us shall give account of himself.

Even though we are advocating reading Paul's Romans as particular address, we must note some distinctive factors that require explanation before we proceed. We pause at this point to take note of the fact that "the Lord," that is, the God of Israel is an integral participant in the discussion. "The one who eats" or "the one who does not eat" must not be judged or despised "for God welcomed him." This verse (3.b) is similar in content to the imperatival construction of 14:1 "welcome the one who is weak," but not to antagonize him by quarrelling over different interpretations or distinctions, since God has welcomed him without discrimination (10:12) (Campbell 2018: 129–52). Here Paul continues in the interrogatory diatribal style, using the second-person singular σύ (14:4, 10, 22) to keep his rhetorical distance in giving guidance indirectly via the interlocutor, present at many points in the previous discussion. This guidance is sharply formulated in the interrogatory diatribal style, "Who are you to pass judgment on the οἰκέτης (household-slave) of another" (4)? Jewett stresses the οἰκέτης as a domestic slave, who could be an inalienable member of the household and who

---

[3] Cf. Baumgarten 2021.

functions almost as a family member (2007: 841–2). "He stands or falls before his own Lord. And he will be made to stand, for the Lord has the power to enable him to stand" (14:4). Via the analogy of an earthly lord or master, Paul reminds his audience that they too are household slaves, subject only to one Lord, and not to be determined by other human lords or masters, nor even by those who hold differing views of what is "good." Household slaves must not judge other household slaves, since they both have a master who will do this, and whose opinion is final. Similarly, in 14:10, the issue of judging and despising the other is repeated, again in diatribal style.

The hermeneutical significance of the diatribal style in texts such as 14:4 or 14:10 is that we cannot read these verses as identical with second-person plural address, since we must consider what Paul intends to signify by this style. The second-person singular, in particular, "serves as a distinct marker of the diatribe" and the diatribe form and its function presuppose a student–teacher relationship (Song 2004: 3, 108). Here in Romans 14, we read the recurrence of diatribal style as a sign of Paul's being careful in his limited leadership of the Romans. He did not found an ἐκκλησία in Rome, and so he carefully avoids any presumption of taking on the authority that such founding would give him, particularly in the use of imperatives. So he permits himself at certain points only to speak to the single imagined interlocutor, rather than addressing the Romans directly in the second-person plural. But this does not mean that the paraenesis is any less significant even if indirect. Paul thinks he cannot speak as if he had the same authority as a father-founder figure, and so carefully states what he wishes to say in terms in which the Romans would be able and willing to recognize his authority. In Romans, elements of the diatribal style (which included vivid interjections, sharp responses, and even exaggeration) serve an educational rather than a polemical function (Stowers 1981: 179). We would not wish to limit our understanding of the reason for Paul's use of diatribe only to his lack of familiarity with the actual situation (contra., e.g., Murphy O'Connor 1996: 334). Perhaps we need to reflect on whether Paul uses the diatribal style at points where he wishes himself to be identified as a philosophical teacher rather than as a pastor (Stowers 1981: 179).

Does the recurrence of diatribal elements in 14:4, 10, 14-22 perhaps indicate that here Paul, despite his interspersing these with normal first-person plural constructions, is still using the diatribal style to distance himself personally from some of the hortatory or imperatival constructions he directs at the Romans? Whatever the reason, Paul recognizes that the response must be voluntary, not forced, and that his authority does not permit any other pattern. We will return to this issue later in ch. 15.

Even though "the weak" may be weak, their trust is still valid, "they will be upheld because the Lord is able to make them stand." "The one thing Paul does demand from 'the weak' is the recognition that *other* believers can act otherwise" (Barclay 2015: 514). Paul's use of the term "weak" may in fact be an indicator of his critique of the Roman ethos of strength, which regarded non-Roman cultural patterns as "weak" (Rodriguez 2014: 267). Since the Lord is a participant in the personal as well as the corporate life of the Christ-followers, his power which Paul claims leads to rescue (1:16), is able (δυνατεῖ) to make the "weak one" stand (14:4). We note here the resonance with the δυνατοί of 15:1 (cf. also 1:16, 11:23). Thus, the standing of "the powerless one," that is, "the weak" is established firmly at the outset of the conversation because the Lord is with him to empower him. There is no suggestion here that "the weak" should be accepted temporarily on condition that they become more "enlightened" or more conforming. They are not viewed as being only a temporary phenomenon. Indeed, if their weakness were, partially at least, due to social status, it would not be something about which they would have a choice, and not something that would have potential easily to be removed. This is further developed in 14:5-12 where the emphasis is also on the presence of the Lord in the discussion, but with the focus on everyone being fully convinced in his or her own mind (5b). Those who observe certain days as special do so "in relation to the Lord," but so also those who do not, as well as those who eat or abstain from specific foods; in that sense all give thanks to God, whose presence must be taken into account in all decisions.

We do not consider that the giving of thanks clearly denotes meeting together for the Eucharist, though this possibly may be included. If there were communal meals, "the strong" would be obligated to accommodate their behavior to the scruples of "the weak" (Barclay 2015: 515). Giving thanks to a god was normal wherever meals were celebrated, and Christ-followers would give thanks to God, to the God of Israel through Christ. Paul is not concerned at difference in practices done in honor of the one and same God. His inclusive stance is "so then whether we live or die, we are the Lord's" (v. 8); this is the uniting formula that means that diversity in practice must not be a cause for strife. At several points in this chapter, the reference to "the Lord" could indicate the God of Israel, but at other points Christ as Lord is specifically mentioned. We take it as a rule that where it is not specifically noted, the reference is to God (through Jesus Christ). In v. 8, the reference to a "Lord" could mean either God or Christ in that the death of Christ is referenced in v. 9 as enabling him to rule over both the dead and the living. But it is the judgment seat of God that is mentioned in both v. 10 and v. 12, so the Lord who speaks in v. 11 must also refer to God. Fitzmyer reads 14:4-6 and 11 as meaning κύριος in the "Old Testament" sense of God, but in v. 9 Paul extends this lordship to Christ, and in v. 14 "it becomes clear that by Kyrios he means Christ Jesus" (1993: 691).[4]

Thus what the ethnē in Christ have in common is greater than any differing practices that might threaten to separate them. But it is significant that the focus is on "honoring the Lord," and the freedom that is commended is freedom in relation to him. "The weak" who eat in relation to the Lord, in their pattern of behavior must not be despised, because they belong to the Lord and his work in them must not be denied. Hence, the diatribal question "Why do you pass judgment on your brother?" The coherence and solidarity of the community depends on the recognition and remembrance that they are one family under God, and that even the "weakest" members of the community "have been welcomed by God" (14:3). The aorist tense here for God having welcomed him (προσελάβετο) may be referring to the occasion of baptism (cf. Esler 2003: 351). One might suggest that it is somewhat negative to regard "the weak" as likely to be a permanent feature among the ethnē in Christ. Since they are being judged on account of "weaknesses," not sins, "the weak" need not necessarily "grow" out of these, but harmonious love expressed in community should lessen the friction that may surround

---

[4] On this note, see also Keck's claim that "the Lordship of the resurrected and exalted Jesus as Lord does not compete with the Lordship of the one God, but expresses it" (2005: 255).

difference in practice. In fact, such support will enable the Lord to "strengthen" them through their shared fellowship.

Paul's strongest claims for his argument for mutual acceptance comes in v. 10b, "for we will all stand before the judgment seat of God." Paul supports this claim by citing Isa. 45:23, "As I live, says the Lord, every knee shall bow to me, and every tongue shall give praise to God." Paul uses this citation primarily as a reminder of another factor of commonality—"each will be accountable to God" (14:12). Since he could have found many other scriptural citations that make the same point, why did Paul cite this one? It resonates with giving God the honor due to him (13:7). The bending of the knee denotes worship of this God, and a refusal to worship any other. The crucial issue is to which god one gives honor, denoting a (Roman) context in which there is the option of loyalty to different gods.

Romans 14:1–15:13 Paul's Paraenesis Addresses Both "the Weak" and Those Who Despise and Judge Them

As we noted above, the Roman public in their imperial context were inclined to view "strength" as an indicator of honor and "weakness" as a term of contempt (Reasoner 1999: 58–62). Thus, there would be an incentive to seek to belong to a category indicating strength in the contemporary social standing that included the public acclaim for military and athletic prowess, the celebratory victory parades after successful military campaigns. This is the typically Roman ethos that is "strongly" influencing "self-styled strong" among Paul's addressees as demonstrated in their tendency to despise those whom they perceived and labeled as "weak." We might surmise that there was a minority of gentile Christ-followers of higher social standing who were exercising more influence upon the poorer members than was beneficial for the cohesion and positive development of the entire group of ethnē in Christ.

It is not possible to identify in each verse the precise group Paul addresses when telling them not to judge and to exert pressure or even despise. As Thorsteinsson notes, "The different attitudes towards eating, drinking, and judging days described in the text are no sure indicators of Jewish versus gentile dispositions" (2003: 97). The same claim is valid even when we are speaking only of differences among ethnē in Christ. Only by a certain stereotyping of "the weak" and "strong" can this be achieved, especially when these groups are identified as exemplifying modern theological stances such as "liberal 'gentiles'" or "conservative Jews." Although I have used these terms myself in the past, I now hold that these modern depictions seldom offer much worthwhile insight. It is also important that, in this discussion, social issues are emphasized, rather than designations of the proposed groups as entirely theological. Reasoner argues convincingly that some of the "strong" are of higher status (1999: 58–62, 202, 210–19). Jewett and Lampe have rightly stressed the low social level and immigrant status of the Roman Christ-followers,[5] but that there were a minority of people involved in the administrative machinery of Rome who were of higher social status cannot be ruled out. And, if that were so, then why

---

[5] Jewett (2007: 66–9), Lampe (2003: 143–8). Cf. also Longenecker (2010: 298–316) and Meggitt (1999).

did these not come to the aid of those Christ-followers who were forced to sell themselves into slavery as Lampe has questioned? (1991: 229). Could it have been because they did not fully accept "the weak"? Also, it must be recognized that this minority of higher social status would have had to make difficult choices because they were involved in the administration, and their stances on various issues would be very public. Paul's flexibility in his paraenesis may indicate his attempts to take such people into account. Hence, no one fixed pattern is recommended for everyone, but only the guiding principle—"let each be fully convinced in his own mind" (14:5b).

The verb προσλαμβάνω in 14:1 has a technical sense of "welcome someone" into one's home or circle of acquaintances, accept with an open heart (Fitzmyer 1993: 689). Donfried, notes that the verb "to welcome" is used to address someone who is not already in intimate communion with the one addressed (Donfried 1991: 110, cf. also Esler 2003: 347–8). We recognize the strength of the potential household connotations of this advice, though Jewett (1993: 23–43) and others strongly emphasize the context of accepting one another at the common meal in tenement buildings (*insulae*) or workshops (*tabernae*) as a likely setting beyond the household, and we recognize this as a real probability. But there are good reasons for acknowledging also the possibility that some of the Romans at least, lived as slaves or former slaves in the households of their masters (see section "The Beginnings of the Messianic Movement at Rome" in the "Introduction" chapter). Living in these large households or estates might help account for some of the differences noted between the "weak" and the "strong."

It is necessary that all the Roman gentile Christ-followers recognize that they are included within the sphere of Paul's address, in that it might only further divide the audience if it were clear that one group was seen to have an advantage over the others. Since the audience addressed here is non-Jewish, the older tendency to view those who judge as "conservative Jews" is not relevant. Non-Jews were equally capable of, and prone to, making biased judgments against the other. Non-acceptance of any brother or sister is ruled out by the example of Christ who has welcomed all who have responded to his call. Apart from the four instances of Paul's use of the term "welcome one another" in Romans, the only other occurrence of the verb "to welcome" προσλαμβάνεσθαι in Paul is Philemon 17, which certainly supports the nuance of household welcome and hospitality (cf. Acts 28:2.).

One of the most comprehensive discussions of 14:1–15:13 is provided by Hultgren in his Romans commentary (2011). He analyzes the issue of to whom does Paul speak, and of how does he do it, paying particular attention to the Greek verbs, whether past or present tense, singular or plural, indicative or imperative. He notes the use of the singular verbs as particularly effective if Paul is actually expressing diatribe within a framework of paraenesis (2011: 495–504, especially 501–4).

Hultgren helpfully subdivides the passage of 14:1–15:13 into five forms of address, noting the number of specific addresses to each, and the content of the verbal address to each. We will outline his analysis briefly.[6]

---

[6] I cite Hultgren as an example, although I differ from him in certain respects, for example, in the mixed composition of Paul's targeted audience, and the confidence with which at certain points one can identify these as Jewish or gentile; however, his careful investigation indicates the framework of Paul's argument on which differing readings can be based.

A. Paul addresses the Romans as a whole four times using *second-person plural verbs*:

   14:1, 15:7 προσλαμβάνεσθε—"welcome" is used twice, both in the imperative
   14:13 κρίνατε—"decide" is used once in the imperative
   15:6.1 δοξάζητε—"glorify" is used once in the subjunctive

B. Paul addresses the Romans as a whole *using first-person plural verbs* to include himself.
   Here, there are three examples:

   14:13 μηκέτι … κρίνωμεν, subjunctive—"no longer let us judge"
   14:19 διώκωμεν, subjunctive—"let us pursue"
   15:1 οφείλομεν, indicative—"we ought"

C. Paul addresses the Romans as a whole using a *third-person singular verb*.
   Here, there is just one example:

   14:5 πληροφορείσθω, imperative—"let [each person] be fully convinced"

D. Paul addresses "the strong" using *singular verbs*.
   Here, there are ten examples:

   14:3 μὴ ἐξουθενείτω, third-person singular, imperative—"let [him] not despise"
   14:4 εἶ, second-person singular, indicative—"you are"
   14:10b ἐξουθενεῖς, second-person singular, indicative—"you despise"
   14:15a περιπατεῖς, second-person singular, indicative—"you are walking"
   14:15b μὴ … ἀπόλλυε, second-person singular, imperative—"do not … cause ruin"
   14:16 μὴ βλασφημείσθω, third-person singular, imperative—"let [it] not be defamed"
   14.20 μὴ … κατάλυε, second-person singular, imperative—"do not … destroy"
   14:22 ἔχεις, second-person singular, indicative—"you have"
   14:22 ἔχε, second-person singular, imperative—"keep"
   15:1 ἀρεσκέτω, third-person singular, imperative—"let [each] please"

E. Paul addresses "the weak" using *singular* verbs[7]
   Here, there are two examples:

   14:3 μὴ κρινέτω, third-person singular, imperative—"let [him] not judge"
   14:10a κρίνεις, second-person singular, indicative—"you judge"

---

[7] I do not agree with this designation as to "the weak" but include it to indicate Hultgren's designation.

I repeat here the list of verbs Paul uses to demonstrate the greater number of occasions on which Paul possibly addresses "the strong," not because I am convinced that they are a clearly identified group but to show that it is the (self-perceived) powerful among the Christ-followers whom Paul most expects to change their ways. Even allowing for some uncertainty in the number of instances cited, much more attention is paid to the "failings" of these so-called strong persons than to those designated as "the weak." These seem to be specifically addressed only in two instances, 14:3 and 14:10a, but it is very difficult to distinguish the groups here in that those who abstain and those who do not appear in 14:3, and 14:10a opposes judgment of the other but is followed by opposition to despising. The Romans as a whole are addressed in seven instances as noted above, indicating Paul's policy of allowing those in each group conscientiously to "judge" for themselves, that is, where to situate themselves and what they ought to do. "The strong" are, according to Hultgren's analysis, addressed no less than ten times, but I would qualify this assessment in that, in ch. 14, I consider "the strong" are only indirectly "addressed" via Paul's descriptors of how they fail to support "the weak." Here they are "identified" by what they fail to do. The second reason for listing the number of Paul's specific addresses is to note that some of these are certainly in diatribal style. Some scholars (e.g., Stowers 1981: 115, Hultgren 2011: 502–4) see diatribal style in 14:4 and 10b to which I think 14:22 should be added. If these instances are allowed, we still need to consider the significance of the fact that the second-person singular extends almost throughout the chapter (i.e., to 14:22). This has significance in itself irrespective of the actual frequency of address to each group. We will return to this issue at the end of the chapter.

"The Good" Is Not Precisely Defined by Paul—What Is "Good" Varies According to Circumstances and Conscience

Also, since Paul has stated plainly that in Romans he addresses non-Jews, those traditional readings that are based on the supposition of a mixed audience require careful reformulation. Paul may imply, though cautiously, that he himself can be an exemplar in relation to the use of food and drink in that he declares, "It is good not to eat meat or drink wine or do anything that makes your brother stumble!" (14:21). He refrains from personal intrusion into the debate until 14:14. But he does not repeat 1 Cor. 8:13, "if food is a cause of their falling, I will never eat meat, so that I may not cause one of them to fall." I will not compare Romans 14–15 with 1 Corinthians 8–10 since I see the Roman context and Paul's purpose in addressing that, to be determinative, not a combined theological perspective, or a generalizing of the content of each particular letter (Jewett 1971). The Romans most likely would not have had access to 1 Corinthians and would know it most likely only from hearsay, if at all.

Not only so, but Paul advises, "Do not for the sake of food, destroy the work of God." This targeted arrogant behavior indicates most likely that of "self-styled strong" who fail to abstain despite damaging others. The weaker person must take priority over one's own (groups') preferences, implying that those whose conscience does not bind them to certain causes of action must be flexible in relation to the convictions of others. Here, the challenge is placed upon "the strong" who have the possibility of abstaining without hurting themselves, whereas "the weak" can only change their practice in conflict with their own conscience. But although it is convenient here to use again the designation "the strong," this label should not be used without qualification to refer to those who do not care for "the weak," who despise them, eat meat, and so on that may damage the "weak." This explains why Paul does not speak of "the strong" until 15:1. He could never associate himself with those who despised or were prepared to behave so arrogantly that "the weak" might possibly be destroyed, both in terms of allegiance to Christ and of their own personal existence, so they remain nameless in ch. 14. Paul reserves the label "the strong" for that group who share his sympathy and concern for "the weak." They are those strong enough not to squabble or regard with contempt those who abstain from meat, and so on. We conclude, therefore, that though this cannot be explicitly evidenced from ch. 14, there is, in ch. 15 a "group" titled as "the strong re-defined," but their strength does not lie in eating meat (which they can do) but in their care for the brother or sister. It is this category to which Paul can now attribute himself.

Paul's response implies an overall conception of "the good" (vv. 14, 16), even though Christ-followers differ in their conceptions since there is no agreement about what constitutes "the good." The acknowledged "good" is not some conception of ultimate ethical standards because the good action will always, according to Paul's perspective, be determined with respect to the needs of "those for whom Christ died." Thus, this is a flexible context where Paul hopes there may be some movement among the ethnē in Christ rather than a fixed confinement to stereotypical groupings. What behavior may be reckoned as "good" in a particular instance will have to be adjusted to take care of the needs of "the weak," and the relationship between "the good" and the Law is not unimportant, nor can it remain simply in the realm of private behavior (McMurray 2021: 175). This determines how they relate to one another over issues where they disagree on principle, perhaps over what is "good." In 14:1, Paul warned against διακρίσεις διαλογισμῶν, quarrelling about disputable matters (Fitzmyer 1993: 686). This follows immediately after the call for mutual acceptance, and thus denotes the boundary within which all discussion takes place, that is, between those who accept one another as equal brothers in Christ, however much they may differ, and who take care not to injure "the weak." All the ethnē in Christ are targeted by Paul, though some are more frequently addressed than others. But it is notable that the great extent of the use of second-person singular to address these Romans denotes that Paul, especially in the use of the imperatives, is careful at significant points to use diatribal features such as the second-person singular to signify the indirect address fitting for one who is not their father-in-Christ, and whose authority has been publicly questioned and misrepresented.

An earlier instance of Paul's usage of "welcoming one another" is Philemon 17, noted above, and this certainly would support a reference to "welcoming into one's household" or at least suggest that such a reading ought not to be ruled out. Welcoming others into one's social space, whatever that may be, is included, and the verb is also used for receiving cities in confederations and taking partners in marital relations (Jewett 2007: 835). Jewett is correct to connect the term to refer to welcome in the fullest sense, which in the earliest days of the Christ-movement certainly indicated a nuance of hospitality.

But "the weak" do not determine everything because what is done or not done is determined by each in association with their Lord, and therefore each "group" must stand up for their own particular conscientious application of their trust in the Lord. Paul probably does not know the extent of the precise groupings into which the various groups of ethnē in Christ had divided themselves, but he is certainly thinking in terms of groups rather than individuals. Nor is he saying simply that they ought to assert themselves, but rather to insist that since their Lord has been involved in their determining of what is ethical/permissible, any opposition to this pattern of action must take his will into account (and not merely that of another house slave). This means defending their pattern of behavior in Christ, that is, their "good" (they must not allow their "good" to be slandered, i.e., "be spoken of as evil," 14:16). Paul knows what this means in practice because he and his mission had been slandered (βλασφημούμεθα, 3:8). Since he addresses here the nations, we ought not to think that Paul's person and message were slandered by Jews—most likely this has happened among the ethnē in Christ. Thus, however little or much Paul is reputed or discussed in Rome, he certainly is known there. One's "good," whether Paul's or anyone else's must not be misrepresented as evil because it has been done out of allegiance to Christ, in honor of God. Since he, as Lord, has been included in the legitimation of this behavior, so he also must be involved in any revision or negation of this pattern. And this entire debate must be guided by a larger principle, "the kingdom of God which is righteousness, joy and peace," not merely food and drink (14:14-17). The significance of eating and drinking, or not eating and drinking, is determined by a governing principle that subordinates these practices to the values of the kingdom, significantly more extensive than the household or even the ἐκκλησία. And these may lead a group not to insist on their freedom to behave in this or that way, and not to please themselves in the pursuit of that which in itself is perfectly legitimate, all because of its negative effect upon others. But it may also indicate Paul's attempt to allow space for those whose work or status does not allow them to avoid making decisions about what is permissible, hence his inclusion of himself in the redefined "strong."

As noted above, there is a conception of "ultimate good," the good, which permeates this discussion, but the final arbiter in practical terms is "your good." This must be defended and practiced for "the good" of everyone in the group, including the weaker brother. This means mutual respect, especially where there exist strongly conflicting stances and resultant behaviors. Otherwise, if one is encouraged or forced to behave in ways incompatible with this, "whatever is not of trust" results in sin, and this forced conformity may lead to the "ruin of the one for whom Christ also died" (14:15). This is not to deny the value and legitimacy of a discussion of ultimate values, which are assumed here. There is light, but it is like the rainbow, the light is refracted into many strands all different in color within the same phenomenon. And all of this stands under the reminder that "each of us will be accountable to God" (14:12).

Romans 14:13-16: Guarding the Holiness of the Ethnē in Christ Community

¹³Let us therefore no longer judge one another, but judge instead never to put a stumbling block or hindrance in the way of the brother. ¹⁴I know and am persuaded in the Lord Jesus that nothing is profane in itself; but it is profane for anyone who reckons it profane. ¹⁵For if your brother is being pained by what you eat, you are no longer walking in love. Do not by means of your food destroy the one for whom Christ died. ¹⁶So do not let your good be slandered.

Commentators have noted Paul's mildness of tone and inclusive attitude in Romans 14–15, but this is partly because here he is dealing with vital issues that may hinder, or even destroy, not only a brother's trust but the persons themselves. Paul is discussing real life and death issues here, and his gentle approach does not obscure the seriousness of the conversation. That this is so is indicated by the effect of causing the other to "stumble." Hence, he calls upon them, rather than passing judgment to "judge instead never to put a stumbling block or hindrance in the way of the brother."[8] Paul sees that βρῶμα (food) may cause "the ruin" of the other. The term λυπεῖται, translated as being injured, here bears the connotation of causing grief or pain. In 14:15, this is followed by the second-person singular imperative μὴ ἀπόλλυε from the verb ἀπόλλυω denoting more devastating harm; it is the term used for Peter's fierce judgment of Simon, the magician in Acts 8:20, "May your silver perish with you." Paul is clear—do not let your food cause the destruction of a brother.

This could indicate kashrut-related issues, especially if pork were involved and if Jews were among the addressees. But, given Paul's clear address of this letter to non-Jews, the more likely issue is the perception of food involved in idolatry. Indeed, the term κοινός used by Paul in v. 14 sheds light on this. Rather than κοινός being the equivalent of "impure" (ἀκάθαρτος), it has been demonstrated that the term took on a specific meaning in Greek Jewish literature referring to all that did not conform to Jewish ways of life. It does not replicate a specific Hebrew term but developed in the Diaspora of the Second Temple period where Jews had to negotiate the boundaries to their host cultures (Eschner 2019: 91–2). Κοινός *refers to that which is common among non-Jewish peoples.* This can be food such as pork, or even generally relate to non-Jews and their way of life, which is decisively shaped by their worshipping of their gods (Eschner 2019: 95), characterized by Paul as confusion (1:18-32). If meat and wine were under discussion as an issue concerning kashrut rules, it would be relevant only for Jews and has been thought to be so in the majority of interpretations that assume that Paul also addressed Jews in Romans. But since he is here addressing non-Jews, kashrut cannot be directly relevant. This is not to ignore or fail to take into account that the issues and vocabulary of the debate concerning "the weak" and "the strong" do include terms such as stumbling, slandering, pure (κάθαρος) and common (κοινός),

---

[8] We translate κρίνατε here as "judge," and note the context of "judging" and judgment frequent since Rom. 2:1. Cf. Meeks (1987).

observance of certain days, and so on, which would feature in discussions relating to kashrut or other specifically Jewish issues. The Christ-following ethnē in Rome would not have been unaware of or been uninfluenced by these. What is relevant, however, is the risk of perceived idolatry, a real issue for ethnē in Christ, *living in a diverse society*. Since meat and wine production involved dedications to the gods, these could be considered as contaminated by these practices. To avoid any risk of being involved in idolatrous behavior, some ethnē in Christ may have avoided meat altogether, eating only vegetables as some Jews also did. There may be a deliberate exaggeration in Paul's diatribal style, in that it is unlikely that some were confident to eat anything and, similarly, in the reference to eating only λάχανα, vegetable leaves (14:2).

This may be significant since gentile Christ-followers most likely were former God-fearers. Not only this, but the Roman context was a context in which Jews were numerous, and in which there had been a long-term Jewish and non-Jewish interaction. Debates among Jews concerning what may be eaten would not be confined to inner-Jewish debates, and in any case, these probably included God-fearers and proselytes. But even apart from such shared history, non-Jewish Christ-followers needed to consider such issues as the consumption of food in such a way as to avoid contamination with idolatry. Since meals are at the center of piety in antiquity, gentile Christ-followers need to follow the same guidelines for the avoidance of idolatry as were common with Jews. In this, the commonality with Jews is greater by far than the ethnic commonality they share with their pagan neighbors.

If some Christ-followers were not sure, that is, if they were "weak in trust," and thought that meat and wine were not risk-free, then they would be harmed in being pressured to eat and drink against their conscience. It is their perception that is decisive for what is "good" for them, not some abstract principle that might theoretically be legitimate—what is κοινός is κοινός for the one who considers it κοινός, it is not based on some natural quality (14:20). For the one who perceives the food to be eaten as κοινός, it is for them the same as committing idolatry, and thus for Paul indicates sin. Idolatrous "gentiles," that is, those "apart from the law" are doomed to perish (Rom. 2:12). Conscientious gentile Christ-followers in response to Paul's teaching on idolatry and all that follows from it would consider themselves polluted. To push a brother or a sister in that direction causes serious harm not only to them but also to the community as a whole. As Ehrensperger states,

> The issue of food only comes into play in relation to the main concern of holiness. The food that the "weak gentiles" wish to abstain from eating could cause the stumbling of a brother. To act in a way that harms the brother or sister constitutes an immoral deed, and the impurity that is associated with such a deed, classified as sin, thus threatens to profane the holy community, that is, it threatens to "discredit your good." (cf. 14:16, 2010: 105)

In Paul's view, this stumbling not only exists as a limited perception of certain people but becomes a cause of sin for the entire community that would be broken by such behavior and weakened in its solidarity. Moreover, this is plainly in opposition to the welcoming of Christ, which embraced all in their diversity. The communal aspect of injuring a brother or sister further illustrates the seriousness with which Paul viewed such an action.

Thus, instead of indicating which things may be eaten or drunk, Paul states what behavior is permissible and what is prohibited. Paul is adamant, he knows and not only so, he is convinced in the Lord Jesus ὅτι οὐδὲν κοινὸν δι' ἑαυτοῦ, that nothing is κοινός in itself (14:14). The exception that renders some things κοινός is that for the one reckoning something to be κοινός, to that one it is κοινός. Since it is not the nature of the food in and by itself, but the perception of the one participating, the decision is guided not so much by innate food qualities or content but categories set out in the Law specifying Israel's identity as a holy people belonging to God. This also includes, especially in the Diaspora context, the avoidance of idolatry, hence the specialized vocabulary of holiness, idolatry, pollution, slandering, and stumbling that we find evidenced in Romans 14–15. This would not be unexpected if Jews are perceived as part of the addressees, but when Paul limits his audience to non-Jews, as he does in Romans, this might seem somewhat surprising. From this, we conclude that for non-Jews this focus is relevant particularly concerning the avoidance of idolatry, which has a significant effect on each one's behavior, on the rest of the community, and on their interaction with other groups in the neighborhood.

Paul regards the Romans as "beloved" even though they are not Jews (Rom. 1:7; 12:19). We noted already how in ch. 8, many of the descriptors of Israel as God's people, not only appeared in that chapter but were repeated in ch. 9. Paul is seeking to transform these non-Jews into a holy people, not as a replacement of Israel, but as an associate people representing the nations alongside God's people Israel. They do have a distinct identity, not as half-Jews or "culture-freed" ethnē, but as those from the nations who follow Christ, their elder brother, the Messiah of Israel. They neither take over Israel's identity and role, nor do they replace these. Nor is the Torah annulled or irrelevant. Although the Torah is Israel's peculiar possession, it is also not without relevance for non-Jews who are also called to serve Israel's God, and to identify in another pattern to his guidance for living. So even though non-Jewish Christ-followers are called "apart from the Law," the Law has abiding relevance in how it relates to non-Jews who also worship the God of Israel, hence the significance of the avoidance of idolatry, and the recurrence of the vocabulary of holiness and idolatry. When the issue of idolatry is in question, Christ-following Jews as well as non-Jews would find themselves in unison with other unpersuaded Jews in opposition to all forms of idolatry or appearances of such.

Romans 14:17-23: The Way of the Kingdom—Walking in Love

[17] For the kingdom of God is not food and drink but righteousness and peace and joy in the Holy Spirit. [18] The one who thus enslaves himself to the Christ is pleasing to God and has human approval. [19] Let us then pursue what makes for peace and for mutual upbuilding. [20] Do not, for the sake of food, destroy the work of God. Everything is indeed

pure, but it is wrong for a person who stumbles and eats; ²¹it is good not to eat meat or drink wine or anything else that makes your brother stumble. ²²You, the trust that you have, have it as your own before God. Blessed is the one who does not condemn himself by what he approves. ²³But the one who has doubts is judged if he eats, because he does not act out of trust; for whatever is not from trust is sin.

Paul's criterion is κατὰ ἀγάπην περιπατεῖς "walking in love," that is, a life guided by love of the brother, the individual as a member of a brotherhood or family, of a holy people. We must note and keep in our focus that in 13:8-10 Paul has interpreted love as the fulfilling of the Law, so this would not indicate, though he regards all things as κάθαρα pure (14:20), that Paul, from this stance, regards the Law as somehow annulled or rejected; rather love is the evidence of the Law being fulfilled (McMurray 2021: 171, 184).

According to Paul, the "polluting" factor for his holy communities of those in Christ is the effect of some of the group's behavior on the brother, which instead of building up (14:19)[9] pains the brother (14:15). For a non-Jew, to lose the support of other Christ-followers and to be damaged by their opposition or lack of support would leave such a person isolated and confused. If unable or unwilling to return to their former pagan way of life, and not finding acceptance and peace or joy with those in Christ, this is destruction of a very serious kind. Behavior is never purely one's own private business as an individual, but a community-oriented issue, and it is this extra-individual dimension that confirms its (the community's) holiness or lack of it. Transformation takes place in association with Christ, but it is actualized in the solidarity and koinonia of co-participants; thus, their presence facilitates growth in relation to Christ, and their absence would necessarily denote loss.

A lost person, having left one group behind and unable to find sustaining friendship and peace with the new group of ethnē in Christ, would be in a kind of limbo, and certainly on the way to ruin, not only in terms of belief but of life itself. It is out of a concern for such that Paul calls upon those in Christ not, for the sake of food, to destroy the work of God (14:20). The phrase that Paul repeats as if it were a slogan arising from the Romans' debates is not denied; for ethnē in Christ "all things are pure," but this is qualified with the addition of "it is good not to eat meat or drink wine or anything else that makes your brother stumble." Paul knows and is aware that such abstract principles are part of the general understanding of what is right and good, but in the particular application of these to "walking in love," good or bad is determined not only by the principle itself, but by its effect in one's actions on other people. Good and right principles are valued ultimately not by their expression in a theoretical vacuum but by the outcome and effect of their practice upon other people's lives. A person not ruled by compassion, but proud of their principles, is a clear example of trust without appropriate works (Rom. 2:13). Paul is more concerned about the effect of one's behavior upon others than upon it being demonstrated to be right in accordance with some theoretical argument.

---

[9] The language of building or construction can be taken as evidence for house building—it belongs to this linguistic context, but further see Adams (2013: 43–4).

Paul's solution is abstinence from such food or drink that causes others to stumble. It is "good" (καλόν) to live thus, but "it is wrong for a person who stumbles and eats" (14:21, cf. 1:32). This is not to demand that "the self-styled strong" who despise "the weak" or cause them to stumble (with whom Paul does not identify) should entirely give up their own conscientious principles of how to live according to Christ, but in those circumstances where there is a real risk of ruining or destroying the weaker ones, one ought in these circumstances to abstain from consuming what gives cause for offence. Each group can rightly hold on to their own convictions, but they retain these between themselves and God (14:22) and must not allow them to become a cause of stumbling for the other. God's blessing is on those who are not self-incriminated "by what they approve" (14:22). We take this to refer to the outcome of acting out their own convictions in a given situation. On the other hand, if some have conscientious concerns about the consumption of certain food or drink, but nevertheless proceed to consume this, they are self-judged, not because of the nature of what is consumed, but because they did not act in accordance with their trust. Paul's norm for behavior is "whatever is not of trust is sin" (14:23). Here one's trust can be a guide as to what is good, but if it is not allowed to be such, it becomes instead, via the conscience, an instrument of judgment, hence also an instantiation of sin.

Instead of risking or causing the destruction of the weaker brother or sister, the Christ-following community are called to mutual upbuilding following the criteria of the kingdom of God. Paul uses this theme sparingly, but whenever it occurs, it denotes something of significance. Here we have a broad definition of the kingdom in a neat summary of its nature and effects, which has *a wider horizon than the household*. The γάρ (for) connects Paul's statements to his preceding arguments as the rationale for a new kind of life. Rather than engaging in negative conflicts about what one should eat or drink, Christ-followers should pursue what makes for righteousness and peace, "for the kingdom of God is not food and drink, but righteousness and peace and joy in the Holy Spirit" (14:17). Nor should they be welcomed as a means of getting them to change their convictions (Jewett 2007: 836). Paul's summary just noted in v. 17 does not suggest "peace at any price," nor does it justify causing division among the people of God by an unyielding insistence on one group's pattern of conduct. Righteousness is noted first, but immediately followed by "peace and joy through the Holy Spirit." The unity of the Spirit is very high on Paul's list of priorities and indicates his continuing concern that these newly founded communities of Christ-followers do not live in conflict with one another but become communities of mutual support in which they can grow together and (together) realize the goals of the kingdom, righteousness, peace, and joy in the Holy Spirit. Starting from small beginnings, they cannot afford to lose any one of their members because of the destruction wrought by some who confuse and thus cause the ruin of one "on behalf of whom Christ died" (14:15). Those who live by this pattern of loving "the weak" will be acceptable to God, and should have human approval (v. 18). At this point, in contrast to Greco-Roman culture, Paul reverses the ordinary structure of obligation, though we do not hold that Paul is consistently counter-cultural. Rather than "the weak" being forced to submit to "the strong," the powerful are here under obligation to bear/carry the weaknesses of the powerless (Jewett 2007: 877). Not only this, Paul does not overrule but actually legitimates diversity of opinion and practice as in keeping with the pattern of Christ who has welcomed all of them.

Although much in agreement generally, here I differ from Barclay's claims concerning "strength" in relation to Rom. 12:1–15:13 (Barclay 2015: 508–19). As noted above, I contrast Paul's stance here with the dominant cultural pattern, what I have termed the "imperialistic ethos" that I detect in the dominating power exercised by "the strong" at Rome. So I agree on this emphasis, and similarly with Barclay's perception of "the deep commonality among the saints as evidence of a new *habitus* that disregards the taxonomies and 'schemas' of 'this age' (12:2) in a community 'formed by this recalibration of value'" (2015: 511). But where I cannot agree is on the claim, "The strength in their trust is the degree to which they have been able to dissociate their trust in Christ from every *norm* and value that is not derived from the good news itself" (Barclay 2015: 515). I cannot see that Paul's concern here is best encapsulated in this reading of "strength," which, in my view, moves the emphasis away from strength as conformity to Christ to strength as conformity to a trust independent of everything but gospel norms. Trust in Christ is relational, personal, and not didactic—nothing must be allowed to come between the bond of those in Christ with their Lord, not even the best and most carefully considered norms. The measure of strength must be relational and personal. What pollutes the community is not ill-considered norms, but injuring the weak person. This emphasis is particularly pertinent in the Roman context, especially with regard to the exercise of power by "the strong"; but it is crucial in the contemporary world where Christ-followers are being called on more and more to distance themselves from uncaring structures of power.

The Significance of Paul's Diatribal Style in the Argumentation in Romans 14:1–15:13

We noted the presence of diatribal elements earlier in 14:4 and 14:10b on stylistic grounds, and possibly also in 14:22. Following on from Excursus I and after having completed the exegesis of chs. 1–14 where diatribal style often was recognized, we thought it necessary at this point to come to some conclusion about the significance of diatribal style in these chapters. This is particularly important when the frequency of singular verbs in ch. 14 is noted. This diatribal feature is diminished and can lead to misleading interpretations in English translations where "you" singular and "you" plural cannot be distinguished, whereas, in German, grammar demands this distinction. The Luther, Zurich, and Einheits translations replicate the Greek grammatical distinctions precisely as singular or plural, whereas the inability in English speech to discern whether Paul addresses "you" plural, the normal pattern, or "you" singular, the diatribe pattern, obscures Paul's change of style and mode of address. While many commentators on Romans in the past two decades have noted to varying degrees the presence of diatribal style,[10] few have paid explicit attention to the significance of this specific style and

---

[10] For example, Stowers, Donfried, Thorsteinsson, Song, Tobin, Witherington, Keck, Jewett, Wengst, Matera, Rodriguez, and Hultgren. Jewett is comprehensive, devotes space to style, including a section on "Numerical Series" and "The Genre of Romans in Relation to Its Epistolary Type" (2007: 42–6).

its function in the letter. Hultgren considers the use of singular verbs as particularly effective in expressing diatribe within the framework of paraenesis, hence our use of his analysis above. Stowers is more aware of this issue than most—at least he perceives that "Paul presents himself to the Romans as a teacher" and that "the dialogical style of the diatribe is central to his self-presentation" (1981: 179). Paul's use of the diatribal style is not akin to such tendencies as a frequent use of present participles or the citation of the scriptures, though the latter may be more on a par with its significance. We keep in mind that in relation to Romans 11, we demonstrated that it seems via this diatribal style, Paul can be more critical in relation to specific behavior, without causing the offense that a more direct approach might possibly do, as, for example, in 11:17-19, the address to the wild olive shoot. This indirect approach is noticeable also in relation to style and content in ch. 14. Two references that can be agreed as diatribal are 14:4 and 14:10. It is evident that the content of these verses is very pointed, "Who are you to pass judgment on someone else's household-slave?" and "Who are you to pass judgment on your brother? Or you, why do you despise your brother?"

These verses imply a very critical stance in relation to those who do such things, but by stating these in diatribal style, Paul can, by this indirect means, offer critical evaluations of such behavior, which, as one who has never been in Rome, would have been difficult for him to give without offense. This is partly because Paul had to be more diplomatic since he also was not the first to bring the gospel to Rome. Although Rom. 11:17-24 is clearly diatribal, as we have already noted, this passage is set within Paul's normal epistolary form of address beginning in 11:13, "Now I am speaking to you 'gentiles.'" Thus, there may be a parallel between Romans 11 and 14, where the differing patterns of address, diatribal and epistolary, appear in conjunction with each other. Hultgren also considers the significance of Paul's rhetoric at this point in the letter. In addition to the useful analysis of Paul's verbal addresses we noted above, he is aware that Paul may be expressing diatribe within the framework of paraenesis as I have proposed. However, I cannot agree that Paul "addresses a concept, not a group of persons" (2011: 502–3). Hultgren's suggestion of "Paul resorting to the form of the diatribe, but one clothed in paraenesis" is a constructive proposal with which I am in agreement, but from which I draw a differing conclusion, that is, that the diatribal form serves the function/goal of the paraenesis, and that this is particular rather than general.

It is also possible that Paul's unique address only to the ethnē in Christ at Rome made the diatribal style more useful in relation to Rome, especially at those many points where he sought to draw a neat distinction between himself as a Jewish apostle and his audience as those from the nations. By a careful use of pronouns singular and plural, Paul can indicate clearly the points at which he is in complete solidarity with his addressees, and those where he clearly excludes himself from the "you" that includes them (cf. Rodriguez 2016, on Romans 5–8). The same applies to some extent to the use of "speech in character" in Rom. 7:7-25. The famous depiction of one with the Law but without Christ required this innovative presentation to enable Paul to portray what would otherwise have been an impossible situation, that is, where he anachronistically presents a picture of someone in bondage, not himself but a non-Jew with the Law yet without Christ.

It may be that Paul is stressing here his role as a teacher of those already in Christ (as the Romans were) rather than as an evangelist. If so, the presence of diatribal style may suggest something about Paul's teaching, his διδαχή, and thus his classroom style (cf. 6:17). His letters, and Romans in particular, are not documents dictated in brief pauses on his travels, but more likely reflect patterns not unique to the letters themselves but reflective of Paul's teaching in the wider context. Here we must stress again that Paul is not a lone apostle, but a team player, part of a traveling network of co-workers (Rom. 16:21-22) (Ehrensperger 2022b). The content of Romans and the style in which it is presented indicate patterns that most likely preceded and extended far beyond the content of the letters, but it was these teaching patterns that enabled the creation of such letters. This claim in no way suggests that Paul did not use secretarial help, or that he wrote independently of such, but it regards the letters as an expression of Paul's own teaching rather than of those who assisted in their creation. Paul's use of rhetorical questions as well of diatribal patterns such as μὴ γένοιτο are evidence of a good teacher drawing out the implications of stated positions to guide the student to further refinement and understanding of their views (and his), rather than to rudely interrupt their trend of thought. The teaching methods Paul used included drawing out the implications of students' stances, rather than merely rebutting false opinions of opponents (Stowers 1981: 174–9).

After these examples of diatribal style in Romans 14, and particularly the strange pattern of using the singular to address the Romans whether as a whole or as sub-groups in no less than thirteen instances (Hultgren 2011: 501–2), Paul will now continue to address directly the Christ-following ethnē in Rome in his normal pattern of address, which has not been dormant in this chapter but, as noted, has continued, being interspersed with diatribal elements throughout. This is very obvious when we note how Paul, in contrast to the "I" of ch. 7, draws himself (in his own voice and character) into the conversation, for example, "I know and am persuaded in the Lord Jesus that nothing is κοινός in itself" (14:14). We may, therefore, conclude from this mixing of diatribal and his normal epistolary style that Romans is a letter where Paul's epistolary and diatribal styles demonstrate complementary rhetoric, rather than adversative, in his attempt to persuade the Romans to live in harmony in honoring the God of Israel. But by incorporating both epistolary and diatribal styles together in a single address in the form of a paraenetic letter, Paul demonstrates his intent as one who was not their "father in Christ," but "apostle to the nations," to persuade the Romans to follow the pattern of trust in Christ in an appropriate manner. We note that the use of the singular to address the Romans as a whole (including sub-groups) is generally agreed as ending with ch. 14, suggesting that now Paul addresses the Romans directly as he nears the end of his letter, and no longer via an interlocutor, the change being indicated by the cessation of the dominant first-person singular to refer to the behavior of groups of people addressed in ch. 14, and the return to the plural address in 15:1 (cf. Song 2004: 107–8).

Romans 15:1-6: He Did Not Please Himself—Christ the Exemplar

¹Now we the strong are obligated to bear the weaknesses of the weak, and not to please ourselves. ²Each of us must please the neighbor for the good purpose of upbuilding. ³For even the Christ did not please himself; but, as it is written, "The insults of those who insult you have fallen on me." ⁴For whatever was previously written, was written for our instruction, so that by perseverance and by the encouragement of the scriptures we might have hope. ⁵May the God of perseverance and encouragement grant you to have the same mind among one another, in accordance with Christ Jesus, ⁶so that unanimously you may with one voice glorify the God and Father of our Lord Jesus Christ.

Continuity in subject matter is demonstrated by the term "weak" in 15:1. A major theme is presented as a focus for the paraenesis in 15:2, "pleasing God and others." By means of a flashback to ch. 12, Paul takes up again the topic of what is pleasing or acceptable to God (ἀρεσκέτω in 15:2 and εὐάρεστος in 12:1-2). Christ-followers must present their bodies as a pleasing sacrifice to God. Following the example of Christ, whom Paul proclaims as one who did not please himself, they must "please their neighbor" in self-denial of their own freedom, and in loving sacrificial giving thereby empower those who are "weak," enabling them to stand, rather than fall (McMurray 2021: 177). Each must please the neighbor "for the good" (τὸ ἀγαθόν) not only of the neighbor but of everyone, that is, the upbuilding of the "community." The great exemplar for this is Christ who did not please himself, and scripture is cited in evidence that he voluntarily denied himself for the sake of others (15:3). The importance Paul attaches to his call to mutual acceptance and welcoming one another is demonstrated by his use of the example of Christ himself as the basis for his paraenesis.

What follows in 15:4-5 appears to be, as previously instanced in 4:23-25, an argument that the scriptures were meant also for ethnē in Christ (and not only for Jews). Here Paul cites Ps. 69:9 and connects it with both perseverance ὑπομονή and encouragement παράκλησις qualities that he appears to link with the role of the scriptures. It seems strange that Paul should feel the need to stress this point if, as the tradition suggests, many of the Romans were former God-fearers who know the Law (7:1). There may be a resonance here with the rabbinic expression, "in order to teach you," εἰς τὴν ἡμετέραν διδασκαλίαν ἐγράφη (Jewett 2007: 880). It appears that Paul is pointing out to the ethnē in Christ that the scriptures are part of the Jewish symbolic universe into which they have been adopted through Christ, that these testify to Christ's death for all, and therefore enable hope (15:3-4). Not only this, Paul may also be making a specific link between the understanding of the meaning of Christ's life and death, and the content of the scriptures. Paul cites from Ps. 69:9 to indicate that "Christ did not please himself," but that "the insults of those who insult you have fallen on me." The psalmist confesses before God his unjustified suffering due to the hatred of the enemies of the God of Israel, and Paul applies this to Christ as the one who suffered on behalf of others. Keck somewhat surprisingly opposes the view that the citation here refers to the recurring pattern of suffering of God's faithful down the centuries (1990). But, despite Baur's earlier doubt about its authenticity, Jewett rightly indicates how Paul's inclusion of this text is most appropriate in its new context. He points out that Paul is conscious that his transfer of a reference to God to apply to his audience requires some explanation such as he offers here (2007: 881). It may even be possible that Paul reads the psalm as portraying Christ bearing the contempt intended for "the weak" (Rodriguez 2014: 280). But, in any case, to belong to Christ even as non-Jews, signifies a link with the scriptures and likewise a link with the people of Israel and their traditions. Learning and receiving encouragement from scripture, Christ's self-giving on behalf of all, and living a steadfast life of trust, are all in keeping with the purpose of God, which includes the welcome of the nations and faithfulness to Israel (15:4-5).

Marcion is reported to have omitted ch. 15 from his shortened version of Romans partly because of this obvious reference to the scriptures of Israel (Matera 2010: 328–30). It is difficult for us to envisage the cultural pattern of the nations in the early days of the Christ-movement, but the fact that Paul commends these to non-Jews, and that Marcion opposes the reading of the scriptures of Israel are, taken together, quite significant. It seems that already at the time of sending this letter, Paul was becoming aware of a lacuna in gentile catechetical instruction (15:4) that caused him to deny any suggestion that Israel may have been cast off from God's purpose, or that the Torah was entirely irrelevant for a gentile "community" of Christ-followers. As Das has correctly noted, Rom. 14:1–15:6 offers "some of the strongest evidence for a Jewish constituency among the Roman congregations" (2007: 109). I take account of this in that I also stress that what Paul addresses is not the issue of Jewish practices per se, but rather the observances of Jewish practices by "gentiles." This may be taken to mean that charismatic activity and experience of the Spirit may have seemed to be the central locus/focus of the gentile messianic experience, as Käsemann has strongly argued. Later at the time of Ignatius, the scriptures and who legitimately owned these would become a contested issue, when, as happened already at the time of Romans, a gentile community of Christ-followers is presumed and specifically addressed.[11] The continuity of gentile attitudes toward the scriptures is what is constant, and this may account for Paul's somewhat sweeping claims.

As noted above, the penultimate chapter of Paul's letter continues the theme of the previous chapter without interruption. This goes against any theories that would view ch. 14 as the end of a diatribe to which chs. 15–16 were later added. Chapter 15 begins almost as a repetition of 14:1, but with additional emphasis on not pleasing ourselves. It is noteworthy that here Paul includes himself in the "we who are strong" (v. 1).[12] Thus, "we, the strong," that is, οἱ δυνατοί "we who are able," ought to put up with or "bear" the weaknesses of "the weak," pointing to the reason for the label "weak." Not only are "the weak" more fully described, but the identity of "the strong" is now explicitly specified. They are those who are now called upon to carry or bear the weaknesses of "the weak." The call to bear or carry, βαστάζειν, the weaknesses of "the weak" links back directly to 11:18, which we noted was a high point of Paul's warning against the unwarranted proud self-understanding of the Romans, "If you do boast, remember it is not you who bears (βαστάζεις) *the root but the root that bears you.*" This call to carry "the weak" must necessarily apply to the entire community, that is, everyone who is not weak. This recognition again goes against a binary division between weak and strong in ch. 14, as if these labels encompassed all the ethnē in Christ. In 14:15 and 20, Paul has explicitly taken the side of "the weak" in ruling that it is wrong to cause someone to stumble by what one practices, so we must be careful not to misinterpret the significance of Paul's

---

[11] Runesson 2022: 259-91.
[12] Since this is the first occurrence of the term οἱ δυνατοί "the strong," this signifies that Paul *chose not to make this explicit connection earlier.*

inclusion among "the strong" in 15:1. This has led us to question the designation of οἱ δυνατοί as an opposing group to "the weak." The latter are clearly so designated more than once in ch. 14 as, for example, 14:1, whereas "strong" are only so designated as the subject of the first verse, that is, the δυνατοί in 15:1, and otherwise do not appear.

The Inversion of Roman Imperial Ethos

It appears that this label (i.e., "the strong") was being used by some among the ethnē in Christ to denote a sense of superiority. This is expressed in the attitude of those who eat anything and others who do not, which leads to the former despising the latter. The verbal form, ἐξουθενέω (to despise), is referring to the scornful rejection of another from a position of perceived superiority, often in an intergroup context, as noted (Esler 2003: 350). This may indicate the influence of Roman imperial attitudes toward weakness generally, an ethos favoring "strength." Thus Harrison, commenting upon Seneca's condemnation of the Jewish people, notes how "victory" ideology totally shaped the Roman perception of the world (2020: 326, 201–3). But, in Paul's perspective, "the weak" must be included among those welcomed whatever their weakness involves. As we argued earlier, even though "the weak" may be weak, their trust is still valid. Paul only demands from "the weak" that they recognize that others can legitimately act differently. (Barclay 2015: 514) Paul's use of the term "weak" may in fact be an indicator of his critique of the Roman ethos of strength, which regarded non-Roman cultural patterns as "weak" (Rodriguez 2014: 267). As noted above, the Roman public in their imperial context were accustomed to view "strength" as an indicator of honor and "weakness" as a term of contempt (Reasoner 1999: 58–62; Jewett 2007: 835). Thus, there would be an incentive to seek to belong to a category indicating "strength" in the contemporary social *value scale* that included the public acclaim for military and athletic prowess, and the celebratory victory parades after successful military campaigns. This is the Roman ethos that is potentially influencing the "so-called strong" among Paul's addressees as demonstrated in their tendency to despise those whom they perceived and labeled as "weak." The sharing of some common patterns of eating, drinking, and celebration of days with Jews may have assisted those fearing to eat meat possibly sacrificed to idols. It may also have alienated those ethnē in Christ, who, like Paul, would eat meat in the right context, and who may have reacted against what they perceived as unjustified limitations on their gentile "freedom" in Christ ("idols do not exist and have no power").

What extends the power and effect of this Roman self-perception of "strength" is that it may incite or encourage a devaluation of Jews and Judaism in light of their inclusion in the category of the subdued nations. For diverse reasons, particularly the (temporary) expulsion of some Jews, this perception could have found expression in Rome at this time. It could include, as we have noted above, the view that those who are not victorious have been deserted by their gods and that the gods of the victors were more powerful.[13] In any case, it encouraged a gentile ethos of superiority over Jews.

---

[13] After the fall of Jerusalem to Titus, outsiders inferred that the god of the Jews had been defeated by the gods of Rome, cf. Fredriksen (2021: 107–8).

Even though we have found no evidence for the presence of Jews or Jewish Christ-followers in Romans 14, the vocabulary associated with Jewish patterns in public life is present (e.g., idolatry, pollution, stumbling, and slandering). This indicates some discussion of, and possibly the existence of, both shared and disputed values by the ethnē in Christ with Jews concerning issues in the wider community. It could be that those who share patterns of behavior in relation to idolatry and things sacrificed to idols were despised by those who thought themselves superior, possibly under the influence of Roman imperial ideology. But Paul, in response to this perception, inverts the social operations of this system in challenging ways (Harrison 2020: 167). Elliott sees one of these as being to correct the Roman ethnē's misunderstanding of Christological benefits (Elliott 2010: 51).

In contrast, it is the Lord who empowers (δυνατεῖ) the weak to stand (14:4). We note here the resonance with the δυνατοί in 15:1 (cf. also 1:16, 11:23). Thus, the standing of "the weak" is established firmly at the outset of the conversation because the Lord is with them to empower them. "The weak" by themselves would remain "weak," but since the Lord has accepted them and is with them, they have access to divine power (cf. 1:16). However, there is no suggestion here that "the weak" should be accepted temporarily on condition that they become more "enlightened" or more conforming. They are not viewed as being only a temporary phenomenon. This is further elaborated in 14:5-12 where the emphasis is also on the presence of the Lord in the discussion, alongside the focus on all being fully convinced in their mind (14:5b). Those who observe certain days as special do so "in honor of the Lord," but so also do those who do not, as well as those who eat or abstain from specific foods; in that sense all give thanks to God, whose presence and whose Law must be taken into account as the norm through Christ in all decisions concerning idolatry, even for the ethnē.

The "strong" are called to "bear the weak," and to accept them, not merely as a temporary measure but as they are, since God has welcomed these without discrimination. In opposition to the Roman cultural pattern, Paul reverses the normal structure of obligation of "the weak" being obligated to submit to "the strong" (Jewett 2007: 877). In contrast, the "strong" are here obligated to bear with the weaknesses of "the weak," and not to please themselves. This is a redefinition of what constitutes strength: not to "lord it over" others, not to despise as would be the demonstration of strength according to Roman elite ideology, but rather the opposite. Strength means to provide support, empower, care for, and respect the other.

It seems best not to view the community as split into two distinct parties. What we have evidence for is a group who are weak in that they believe it is wrong to eat meat or drink wine and observe certain days, whether the Sabbath, or fast days or feast days, as more significant than others. The ethnicity of this group is not mentioned. Since Paul confines his audience in Rome to non-Jews, being Jewish or non-Jewish is not the issue, they are from the nations. Our presuppositions might lead us to read back Paul's self-identification as being among the οἱ δυνατοί in 15:1 into the previous chapter, something Paul did not do. Thus, if it might be assumed that some of the Christ-followers in ch. 14 were behaving selfishly and trying to force their strong opinions on those who are weak, even to the point of risking their destruction, then we cannot label these as οἱ δυνατοί, "the strong" with whom Paul explicitly identifies only at 15:1.

Paul would not associate himself without reservation with a group whose behavior he explicitly repudiates (Ehrensperger 2019: 88–90).

Thus, although it may be assumed that "the strong" can be read back into ch. 14, there are problems in doing so. In 15:1, "the strong" does not refer to an already existing "group," but to the category of those among the gentile Christ-followers who have the strength to consume certain foods without scruples or fear of contamination, as Paul and other like-minded Jews could do. The weaknesses of "the weak" consisted in their being unable to do so, even though they were non-Jews. This does not authorize such patterns to be regarded as "failings," as if these people were to be blamed for their conscientious stance with regard to viewing some days as more significant than others, possibly the Sabbath, or some foods as unacceptable. According to Paul's own reasoning, if they eat or do anything else with doubts about its legitimacy, for them this is sin (14:23), so they have no option but to abstain. If they were thus weak, they would be unable to find the strength to change their patterns of behavior, and to advise them to do so would injure rather than empower them. Hence, "'the strong' must help those who, through their own powerlessness [*sic*] have these 'weaknesses.'" They must support and encourage them, not browbeat them with demands for more "strength" than they can muster. The weaknesses here should not be regarded as failings worthy of blame (Wright 2002: 745). This is what love of the weaker ones demands. This also points to the reason for the (revised) appellation οἱ δυνατοί. These are those *who do have the strength* to follow certain patterns of behavior without unresolved conflicts because they have a trust that can cope successfully with these disputed issues. But they also are strong, that is, compassionate enough to abstain from certain practices voluntarily for the sake of the good of "the weak" even though they themselves are convinced that these are entirely permissible (Bartchy 2005: 49–60).

What is notable in ch. 15:1-6 is that Paul not only includes himself among "the strong," but also supplies now a positive description of their identity. We would not even have known the label "strong" if, like the Romans, we had still been waiting to hear the conclusion of Paul's references to "the weak" after ch. 14 in 15:1-6. "The strong" are not defined negatively in opposition to "the weak," as in binary groupings, but are here defined as those who care enough for the well being of "the weak" that they are willing and able to adjust their patterns of behavior for the benefit of these. They are sufficiently concerned about the upbuilding of the community that they refuse to endanger "the work of God" that these weak "gentiles" represent. Though previously not including himself within a particular group (i.e., "the strong"), Paul did give a hint as to his own stance in 14:14 where he agreed that nothing is "common" (κοινόν) in itself, and similarly in 14:20 where he acknowledged that all things are indeed pure (κάθαρα). Yet he did not, in ch. 14, explicitly identify a group as being strong, but it might have been gleaned that he held some views that we (later) discover coincided with the portrait of "the strong" in 15:1-13. It seems that here in 15:1, Paul slightly adjusts his description to indicate clearly in direct address his own view that the proper definition of strong people is *not* those who seek to exert force upon the ones who are weak in order to *overpower* them, but rather "the strong" are those who, like him, seek to *empower* weaker brothers and sisters by holding them up and by avoiding, or abstaining from, what causes them injury.

The goal of such a pattern of life is to enable all "to have the same mind among one another according to Christ Jesus" (14:5) "so that unanimously you may with one voice glorify the God and Father of our Lord Jesus Christ" (15:6). If Paul's advice is taken, as he hopes it will, it will bring harmony and unity in keeping with the acceptance of "the weak" and thus of ongoing diversity.

Romans 15:7-13

"Rejoice, Ethnē Together with His People"—the Dual Outcome of Christ's Servanthood

⁷Therefore welcome one another, just as Christ has welcomed you, into the glory of God. ⁸For I tell you that Christ has become a servant of the circumcision on behalf of the truth of God in order to confirm the promises given to the patriarchs, ⁹[and] to glorify God for his mercy towards the ethnē. As it is written, "Therefore I will acknowledge you among the ethnē, and sing praises to your name"; ¹⁰and again he says, "Rejoice, ethnē, with his people"; ¹¹and again, "Praise the Lord, all you ethnē, and let all the peoples praise him"; ¹²and again Isaiah says, "The root of Jesse shall come, the one who rises to rule the ethnē; in him the ethnē shall hope." ¹³May the God of hope fill you with all joy and peace in trusting, so that you may abound in this hope by the power of the Holy Spirit.

The understanding of scriptural citations has recently been comprehensively defined lest its contents should be too narrowly understood:

> It now appears that the epistles' indebtedness to the Old Testament goes far beyond the immediate scope of some explicit quotations, often marked with quotation formulas. The Old Testament is not merely confirming or corroborating what the epistle-writer wants to say. Rather it is constitutive; it is essential to the text: in some sense, it actually forms the text. The quotations of the Old Testament within the New thus emerge as the tip of a vast iceberg of literary connection and interconnection. (Brodie, Porter, and MacDonald 2006: 5)

We will consider this claim further in relation to the citations in 15:9-12.

Paul begins a summary Conclusion,[1] perhaps even the culmination[2] to his advice to the Romans by repeating the introductory exhortation of 14:1 to "welcome one another" (προσλαμβάνεσθε) with the additional weight of Christ's example in

---

[1] Note that though Jewett uses the same terminology of Conclusion here, he does not introduce the formal designation *peroration* until 15.14 (2007: 903); cf. also Witherington (2004: 16–22).
[2] Wagner states "climax" (2003: 307).

fully welcoming them into "the glory of God" (15:7). This pericope begins with the inferential conjunction διό (therefore), connecting back to the prayer for agreement in vv. 5-6. Significantly, in 15:9-12, this mutual welcoming is elaborated and strengthened by citations drawn from five different passages representing all three divisions of the Hebrew scriptures within the space of four verses. Before considering these further, we must clarify the identity of the groups addressed. If we consider 15:7, following the repeated imperative to welcome, as merely a repetition of the content of 14:1, we may conclude that Paul is simply here repeating the content of 14:1 for the sake of emphasis. But that view does not fully grasp the function of 15:7. As usual, Paul's pattern tends to be that though he may repeat himself, he simultaneously adds new content pointing both to the previous argument and to whence he is about to proceed.

The reference to "the glory of God" denotes a universalizing of the call to accept one another, also indicated by the phrase "as the Christ has welcomed you." As previously, Christ is included in the teaching, and likewise the "glory of God" is reflective of the ongoing purpose of God through the Christ. The ethnē in Christ are not alone in their disputes with each other, but God through the Christ is also involved, and all the characters in this narrative together combine as part(s) of the *messianic story*. The narrative into which the nations have now been called includes the people of Israel, and to become part of the narrative of God's saving purpose for the world means not only a (positive) relation to Jesus as the Christ of Israel and his welcome, now extended to the nations, but involves also a link with the people of Israel as a people. Since the Christ is the Messiah of Israel, he ought not and actually cannot scripturally be separated from the people of Israel; if the Christ does not originate in the promises and heritage of Israel, he cannot be the savior of the nations either. This means that the Messiah cannot be separated from the symbolic universe of Israel. A Messiah separated from historic Israel cannot evoke trust in the God of Israel. The identity of the Messiah from Israel for the ethnē will now be elaborated by Paul.

The progression and extension of Paul's argument in Romans is crowned by a fourfold series of citations that provide confirmation of the argument Paul has developed in ch. 14. Keck has drawn attention to the γάρ, which begins 15:8 as indicating that the function of vv. 8-12 is to provide the warrant for the mandate in v. 7 to accept one another; but he continues by claiming that "the content of vv. 8-12 discloses the horizon against which Paul's treatment of the conflict is to be seen—the role of Christ in overcoming the hiatus between Jews and Gentiles, yet without obscuring or erasing the differences between them" (2005: 353–4). Where we differ is on whether this paragraph summarizes the argument. I would extend Keck's statement concerning a summary to include also the content of the chapters that precede ch. 14, *viewing the citations as summing up Paul's teaching in the entire letter*. Yet the sequence of Paul's argument must still be taken into account. The fact that Paul did not explicitly affirm the identity of "the strong" until 15:1 means that what succeeds 15:1 cannot be read back into ch. 14. So too at 15:7-13, the extension of the horizon that Paul desires from the ethnē cannot be read back in such a way as to maintain that Paul was simply assuming this expanded horizon already prior to ch. 15. In fact, he does clearly build on the content of chs. 12–13, having furnished the ethnē with a λατρεία that replaces and corrects their misguided λατρεία of 1:25, and that operates in parallel with the λατρεία of their new brothers, the Israelites (McMurray 2021: 170-1). So we conclude that in 15:1 though there is continuity with what precedes, Paul not only continues but also *expands* his previous paraenesis in an expansion that includes explicitly for the first time "praising God with his people Israel." Lest there should be any doubt, he asks, as noted above, for full attention to what he is about to say (15:8) and follows with the solemn introduction of four powerful scriptural citations.

Paul begins in v. 8 with "For I tell you" (note the REB translates this as "remember") indicating he is making a solemn pronouncement to remind the Romans of the unfinished argument he has been putting forward up to this point in the letter. Paul is here telling his audience to pay careful attention to what he is now about to say concerning the role of Christ for Jews and non-Jews. Following Wagner's recognition of an ellipsis in v. 9 (1997: 481–2), Keck (2005: 354) notes how this results in a perfectly balanced statement, which he sets out as follows:

The Christ has become
a servant of the circumcision
on behalf of the truthfulness of God
in order to confirm the promises
And on behalf of the mercy shown to the ethnē
[in order] to glorify God. (Rom. 15:9)

This way of reading emphasizes the pivotal role of the Christ throughout, for in the last line it is he who glorifies God, not the "gentiles" (Keck 2005: 355). The perfect tense here implies that as a result of a past event (particularly the resurrection) Christ has become and now is a servant (διάκονος, not δοῦλος) of the circumcision. The Christ has become a διάκονος of the περιτομῆς, that is, of the Jewish people[3] on behalf of (ὑπέρ for the sake of) the truth of God, that is, the faithfulness of God. But there are two outcomes arising from Christ's work. If, in the words of Paul in v. 9 as cited above, there should be only one outcome, then the result of Christ's confirming the promises—would be that the nations glorify God, suggesting that it is this that is the τέλος of the divine purpose. But if we follow Wagner and Keck, and attend to the rhetorical construction then, in the second part of the sentence, beginning with "and," and with the repetition of "a servant," *two* outcomes are specified, Christ's servanthood now serves these *two* purposes, "to confirm the promises … *and* to glorify God for the mercy to the ethnē." This produces a perfectly balanced statement that makes the outcome of Christ's role clear in relation to both Jews and the nations rather than just for the latter. The infinitive verb βεβαιῶσαι "to confirm" (the promises to the patriarchs) resonates with the adjective βέβαιος in Rom. 4:16 where the promise to Abraham that he would become the father of many nations was confirmed or guaranteed. Not only this, βέβαιος carries the sense of "reaffirming" and also of "realizing the promises" (Michel 1978: 359). Because of what Christ has become, the promises to the patriarchs are ratified, not ignored or dissolved, God "has not abandoned his people" (Keck

---

[3] Contra Garroway's suggestion that Paul "calls Christ an agent of circumcision" (2012: 132). Cf. Tucker (2018: 224–8).

2005: 355). In the second half of his statement, Paul focuses on Christ's ministry to the "gentiles."

It is significant following this reading of Christ's servanthood as having two outcomes, not just one, that the incoming of the nations is indeed celebrated, but in a context where Christ's affirmation of the promises to Israel are equally and simultaneously emphasized. The high significance attaching to the content of 15:8 is indicated by the proclamation of Christ's agency as having dual roles in its effects, that is, for both Jews and those from the nations. In this depiction, Christ is the Messiah in whom the promises are confirmed, i.e., what he has achieved on behalf of Israel. Second, Christ glorifies God "on behalf of the mercy shown to the nations." It is the dual outcome of the work of Christ that provides for Paul the conclusion of Romans. He does not stress Jew and non-Jew separately but Jew and "gentile" together receiving the benefit of the Christ's activity.

Thus, the interpretation of the four citations Paul will introduce from 15:9 does not supply the theme of Christ's work on behalf of Jews and the nations. That is already introduced and presupposed from 15:8. The four citations illumine the sphere of Christ's work, but the proclamation of the dual agency of Christ for Jews and for the nations *precedes* the content of 15:9-12. The arena of his influence has already been determined and will now be more fully illustrated in four citations. *Thus, the challenge of the new element, that is, the challenge to expand reconciliation to the people of Israel is already decisively introduced beginning in 15:8, but not until then.*

Respecting the Sequence of Paul's Arguments in Romans 15

Just as we resisted the temptation to read back the content of 15:1 where "the strong" are explicitly identified, into ch. 14 where they are not, so too here we follow the order of Paul's writing in its sequence.

We do not read back this theme of worshipping God together into 14:1–15:6 where, according to our reading, Paul continues the address to non-Jews only. We reiterate, nowhere in Romans does Paul address actual Jews. When Paul calls the ethnē in Christ to praise God "with his people," he does not speak *to Jews* but only about *how ethnē in Christ should relate to them*. He may have sent greetings to all God's beloved in Rome and will request that further greetings be extended to a group of named people in ch. 16, but Paul has not changed his audience—it is still the same; only now, what he asks of them has been extended beyond the boundaries of the ethnē in Christ. Paul's argument here is clear: the nations must first accept one another and *then* praise God together with his people Israel.

One issue needs clarification—does the repetition of "welcome one another" demand that 15:7-13 be inextricably linked to 15:1-6, and thus to 14:1-4? Some commentators treat 15:1-13 as one unit rather than two (e.g., Rodriguez 2014: 277–8). However, the subject matter does not necessarily warrant such an approach. Jewett recognizes 15:1-6 as a separate unit and notes that most current commentators separate 15:1-6 and 15:7-13 (2007: 887, Matera 2010: 322). Thus, the theme of pleasing not one's self but one's neighbor as did the Christ is a dominant motif in 15:1-6. Here we acknowledge with Michel (1978: 444) that the reference in v. 3 has the titular form *ho christos* (the Christ) referring to Jesus's messianic role, perhaps his entire ministry (Thompson 1991: 221–3). But Paul does not continue to dwell even on such a significant topic as Christ's pleasing God in the acceptance of reproach but, after the citation of Psalm 68 (LXX 69) in 15:3b, moves to stress the role of the scriptures, only here related to "steadfastness," "encouragement," and "hope." Jewett reads the reference to τὴν ἐλπίδα not to hope in general but as meaning specifically "the hope in the conversion of the nations" (2007: 883), though this hope may not presently be common to all but the logic of the Christ-event and of Scripture will produce it. In 15:5, a homiletic benediction or prayer wish ties together major themes of the letter and serves as transition to the final paragraph of the paraenesis. Thus, the content of these six verses is not a close continuation of the previous pericope, nor is it any closer to what succeeds in 15:7-13, which might *seem* to simply repeat the introductory theme of 14:1. One obvious development is that the call to mutual acceptance is expanded beyond an appeal to mutual acceptance (i.e., not just of weak by strong).

We would stress instead that there is development in thought and content throughout 14:1–15:6, notable primarily in Paul's silence on identifying "the strong" in ch. 14, but also in that the reiterated words of 14:1 in 15:7 now are set in a more messianic universalizing context than the more "congregational setting" of the previous chapter. Rodriguez rightly notes the continuation in the new chapter of the exhortative section that began in Romans 14. But, more than that, "Romans 15 *expands* the exhortations by generalizing from the interaction between 'strong' and 'weak' Christians in Rome to the international scope of God's people" (2014: 278).

We hold that this development in thought, marked by the variation in content and the parallel benedictions in 15:5-6 and 15:13, gives additional reason why 15:1-6 be not linked too closely either to ch. 14 or to 15:7-13, the diverse content and vocabulary of which meriting, if not even requiring, distinctive treatment.

The fact that 15:3 refers to "the Christ" must not be underestimated in reading 15:1, especially when it is defined in terms of familial and ethnic instrumentality and in its aggregate rather than oppositional outcomes (McMurray 2021: 238, 243). The significance of "the Christ" for the future of Jews and ethnē is crucial. If, following Keck's stress, as already noted, that Jesus is the Jewish Messiah by virtue of the people from which he originates (and not merely the people he serves), then 15:1-6 introduces into the text another powerful new element that Paul stresses here, which has the effect of widening the sphere of his thinking beyond the inner gentile constituency addressed throughout the letter. This does not mean, as already stressed, a change to addressing Jews instead of, or as well as, "gentiles," but rather a reminder of the extent of the universal influence of Christ's Messiahship beyond the inclusion of "gentiles." By stressing their brotherhood with Christ (8:29) and thus with his people Israel, it sets their inclusion in its fuller dimension of the world of all peoples, and God's ethnically variegated purpose for these through the Christ. Thus, it serves as a bridge to the messianic perspective of ethnē worshipping God with his people, Israel.

It is both interesting and intriguing that Jewett repeats the concept of "recapitulating" in his headings for both 15:7 and 15:14. This indicates similarity between the two pericope and possibly some lack of clarity as to where the *peroratio* in Jewett's reading is actually to be located, not assisted by the (his) use of two terms, Conclusion and *peroratio*. I do not propose to repeat or even to debate the massive effort of Jewett to engage meaningfully with rhetorical categories and descriptions—there is no need for this to be repeated for this commentary, but merely to note that, at this point, I have found that a differing denotation of the Conclusion of Romans allows a differing perspective that changes the signification of 15:7-13. In Jewett's commentary his use of the term "Conclusion" at this point (2007: 900–3), is coherent with my perspective in that I emphasize 15:7-13 as the Conclusion not merely of 14:1–15:1-6 but of the entire letter though Jewett lists the formal *peroratio* as commencing only with 15:14 (2007: 903). My perspective accords to some extent with the view of Matera who lists no less than five scholars, including Dunn (1988b: 844–45), who have argued that this unit (15:7-13) has a triple function to conclude Paul's discussion of the weak and the strong (14:1–15:13), to conclude his paraenesis (12:1–15:13), *and to conclude the argument of the letter 1:18–15:13* (emphasis mine, Matera 2010: 322).

The Citations in Romans 15:8-12

Rom. 15:7-13 has been described as Paul's providing "a summary restatement of the principal themes of his letter" (Wagner 2003: 307. We include Rom. 15:8 under this heading because it is the beginning of the sentence in which the citations occur). This designation rightly recognizes the progress and development here from 15:1-6, rather than a continuation of themes of ch. 14 denoted by the repetition of 14:1. Until very recently, it was customary to read the citations in 15:9-12 from the perspective of Romans as a letter addressed to a mixed audience, including both Jews and non-Jews, and there is no doubt that the content of the citations here can easily be read in support of this position. Thus, the call for mutual acceptance could fruitfully be read as a call for acceptance between Jewish and non-Jewish Christ-followers, and the scriptural references viewed from this perspective, as depicting these differing groups of Christ-followers (cf. Wagner 2003: 35–59). Keck claims that the one complex Greek sentence in vv. 8-12 should be seen as a whole, and that implies taking seriously the disproportionate emphasis on Christ's significance for "gentiles"; "the word ethnē [gentiles] occurs in all four citations—the only word that does" (2005: 356). But when Romans is read, as has gradually been recognized, as a letter limited in address only to non-Jews, these citations can still be seen to cohere around the theme of the full acceptance of non-Jews as another "called" group, *but within a new perspective* (i.e., from 15:7-13). The united gentile entity (of 14:1–15:6) is called to praise God not only with one another as diverse groups but *now also alongside God's people Israel*. Mutual acceptance is applied first to non-Jews, that is, ethnē in Christ with differing life patterns who must accept one another. But with 15:7 this call to welcome is continued yet its scope is widened. With 15:9-12, those gentile Christ-followers, already called to "mutually accept one another as the Christ accepted you for the glory of God," are now exhorted in the second citation, to "rejoice ethnē with his people." Having exhorted those from the nations to unity through mutual acceptance, another dimension already featured at many points in Romans now comes clearly into focus, the relation of the ethnē in Christ to the people of Israel (Campbell 2021: 165–86).

The topic is still "accepting one another," but the constituency has been widened to include God's people Israel who likewise join in his praise. The psalmist in LXX Ps. 18:50 says, "Therefore I will confess you among the ethnē and sing praises to your name" (15:9). The praise of God extolled by the psalmist introduces a theme for this section; what follows can be perceived as an eschatological vision of a great choir of all nations praising God together with his people Israel whom God has already welcomed (Rom. 9:4-5, 24). This perspective is neatly summarized as noted in the second citation, "Rejoice, O ethnē, with his people" (Deut. 32:43). Paul is careful in his references to a "people" or a "nation," using λαός for Israel and ἔθνος for "gentiles," so we can be sure how Paul read Deut. 32:43c, εὐφράνθητε, ἔθνη, μετὰ τοῦ λαοῦ αὐτοῦ "it is clear that this is a summons for gentiles to worship *with* Israel" (Lincicum 2010: 165). Paul has had Deuteronomy in mind, as we have noted, especially in Romans 9–11. As Wagner notes, "God's plan for Israel has been hammered out in conversation with passages previously cited in Romans, particularly Deuteronomy 32 and Isaiah 65. These texts provide the conceptual and temporal framework for Paul's sweeping account of God's design to redeem Israel and, with them, the entire cosmos" (2003: 266).

The third citation, this time from LXX Ps. 116:1 repeats the same theme with the universalizing of the content, "Praise the Lord, all you ethnē, and let all the peoples praise him" (πάντες οἱ λαοί) *possibly meaning all the tribes of Israel*. In his final citation, this time from Isa. 11:10, Paul cites Isaiah as claiming "there will be a shoot of Jesse, and one who rises up to rule over the ethnē." These are still in focus but, depicted in this instance, as being ruled over by a "root of Jesse, the one who rises to rule the ethnē." Thus, the fourth and final citation focuses upon the nations via the Christ as "the root of Jesse" to indicate their dependence on him, and thus their connection with God's people Israel noted above. It is in this "root of Jesse," probably Jesse's son David (confirming Christ's Davidic Messiahship), that the "ethnē" shall hope (cf. Isa. 42:4, 52:5).

In Rom. 5:2, Paul has spoken of the gentile Christ followers who, having obtained access to grace and reconciliation through Christ (5:11), are boasting in "hope of the glory of God," and in 8:24, he stated "in hope we were saved." All this is implied when Paul claims "in him shall the ethnē hope"—the content of this hope has been gradually clarified and developed throughout the letter. Here, the gentile nations are *not* depicted as worshipping God in a multicultural, international choir, all perceived as one homogenous gentile entity, with perhaps individual Jews joining in, not as Jews, but *identical* with those from the nations. This is not the scenario of the praise of God that Paul envisages. Paul's vision is truly universal and also inclusive—it includes those from all the gentile nations, but it would not be complete without the people Israel *qua* Israel (or all the tribes of Israel) and not merely as individuals. The people Israel have not been removed from God's plan for the world, they retain their place but now an associate gentile people has emerged with whom they can glorify God together as the "totality" or "fullness" of God's people.

If disproportionate emphasis is placed upon Paul's supposed concern to unite differing factions among the gentile Christ-followers in Rome, it might seem as if Paul's fourfold citations in 15:8-12 are making such a concern more significant than it really is—does a local conflict really require such strong scriptural legitimation? We note here that Paul refers to the people of Israel without qualification (15:10). He is not speaking about a group of Christ-following Jews in Rome such as could be envisaged in an address to a mixed congregation of Christ-followers, that is, one that included both Jews and non-Jews. But if the expansion of Paul's theme of acceptance is noted as beginning from 15:7 to include the theme of the nations praising God *in concert with his people Israel* (Wagner 2003), then such a theme certainly is fully deserving of the combination of citations in its support that Paul offers here. The four citations do have the "gentiles" as their focus, but these citations are preceded by and form one complex sentence with v. 8, "for I tell you that Christ became a servant of the circumcision on behalf of the truth of God in order that he might confirm the promises given to the patriarchs." It is significant, that the term ethnē occurs uniquely in all of the four citations in 15:9-12. But this concentration on the term ethnē denotes only the addressees, not the guidance given in v. 8, which directs these ethnē to praise God "with his people Israel."

However, when the citations are misread as affirming only gentile inclusion (rather than giving due weight also to Christ's function in relation to Israel), then a disproportionate emphasis is placed upon Christ's significance for "gentiles," with a corresponding risk of gentile arrogance. In direct contrast to this, when the coming of Christ is read correctly as having more than one outcome, then the four citations are fully justified. With the repetition of "welcome one another" and the addition "just as Christ has welcomed you for the glory of God", Paul extends the call to mutual acceptance as reconciliation among the gentile Christ-followers to reconciliation with the Jewish people. This could refer primarily to Jewish people in Rome, but should not be limited to that, since Paul is about to reveal to the Romans his plans to visit Jerusalem with a collection from "the ἐκκλησίαι of the ethnē." The theme of the citations is no longer only the mutual acceptance of other Christ-followers who differ, now the theme is the representatives of gentile peoples, the ethnē in Christ, praising God with his people Israel. Paul concludes by citing the Greek text of Isa. 11:10 in which the term ethnē occurs, describing the root of Jesse as the "one who rises to rule the ethnē and the one in whom they shall hope."

Ethnē are now "co-participants in the praise of God ... this would not have happened had the Christ not belonged 'to the circumcised,' for only a member of this people can be the one through whom Gentiles join Israel in the praise of God. Only when he is the one in whom Gentiles hope do they 'rejoice *with* his people'" (Keck 2005: 359).

Paul's Stance and Strategy in 14:1–15:13

Romans 14:1–15:6

What Paul advocated in ch. 14 is encapsuled in the phrase "accept one another," a call to accept one another fully into their home and friendship, whatever the differences between them. It has emerged through our study of this chapter that instead of overcoming differences, what Paul intends is a positive recognition that differences may remain within a policy of mutual acceptance. This consists of a recognition of diversity not only in life and practice but also in valuing the other in their difference as exhibiting behavior in accordance with the will of God. The presupposition is that if each is fully convinced in their own mind as Paul has advocated (14:5), then each group can accept the stance of the other while maintaining their own practice. But what has happened thus far is that the groups define themselves antagonistically over against each other; those categorized as "other" are looked at with contempt or negatively judged by those seeking to maintain their identity in negatively differentiating between the groups. Paul, however, tries to show them that it is not difference that is the problem, but the fact that such difference leads to a negative assessment of the other, as was prevalent in Roman imperial ideology and its promotion of high-minded superiority claims. As noted, not all group formation is directed negatively against those who are not part of one's own group. Group formation can primarily consist of inward strengthening of identity (Bar-Tal 2000), which has not necessarily a negative impact on others, but the opposite, and could support positive relations out of security in one's own identity. Thus, Paul shows the groups that as long as they are firm in their own self-understanding, the other in their difference will not pose a threat as they are united in their giving honor to God.

Paul's self-understanding is indicated by the striking fact that he does not mention "the strong" except in 15:1. Paul's strategy here is that he delays naming and self-identifying with "the strong" until this verse. As noted this is because the conception of strength that "the strong" advocate implicitly mirrored Roman values determined by the dominant Roman ethos of victory. The Roman ethos of victory over the vanquished nations is leading to some being perceived as "weak," and to a neglect of their needs by "the self-styled strong" who regard themselves as the norm for all. Paul reveals something of his own views in 14:14 where he acknowledges that "nothing is κοινός in itself." In ch. 14, "the strong" are only described negatively in their destructive effect upon "the weak." This is because Paul cannot, without implied critique, associate with those who continue to injure "the weak." Only when he redefines the meaning of "strength" Christologically can he join in the label. He redefines the meaning of "the strong" as those who are strong enough to bear the burdens of "the weak" and so he is then able to attribute himself to the "strong" category. Paul's own understanding of "strength" has been reconceptualized with reference to Christ, so that from his perspective some who are labeled "weak" may in fact be potentially "strong." Paul's use of "the strong" designation is fluid to the extent that he envisages one group, "the self-styled strong" alongside another group with whom Paul identifies, that is, "the strong in Christ." The latter's "strength" encompasses and is reflected in their concern for those "weaker in conscience" than themselves. I find in this fluid labeling evidence of Paul's resistance to a Roman imperial ethos that has permeated the ethnē in Christ community.

Romans 15:7-13

This self-styled strong mentality was not visible only in this intercommunal conflict but emerges also in an exaggerated self-understanding of ethnē as the true people of God who through Christ are victorious—whereas Israel, perceived as having rejected

Christ as Messiah, is now considered has having been cast off from God's purpose in the Messiah just as other conquered nations are succeeded by the Roman victors. A Roman ethos of "strength" is central to the "high-mindedness" that is, inflated self-confidence of the gentile Christ-followers. This has been fueled in part by a negative attitude toward Israel (Elliott 2008: 25–40) combined with a misunderstanding of God's purpose in Christ (which must necessarily have a positive reference both for the Jewish people as well as for the nations), and a corresponding domineering militancy in relation to "the weak" and their conscience.

Paul's solution is a restatement of God's purpose in Christ for Israel and the nations. Whether or not it was being perceived in this way, Paul is resolute that the Messiah's coming must not be interpreted in an anti-Israelite perspective. Thus, the non-Jewish Christ-followers must be steered away from regarding their Jewish neighbors in the same arrogant and dismissive way that the Romans adopted toward those they had conquered (Harrison 2020: 13, following Elliott 2008: 25–47). Therefore, in contrast to Roman "victory" theology of the Roman gods over the defeated nations and their gods, Christ becomes the model of strength, but it (this model) encompasses the strength of one who suffered and died on the cross, the servant Christ (Elliott 2008: 52). This is stated in 15:7-13, which serves as a summary conclusion of the letter. As noted, Paul emphatically asserts that the Christ became a servant (διάκονος not δοῦλος) of the circumcision[4] for two reasons—to confirm the promises to the fathers and to glorify God for his grace to the nations. So, the call of the nations, demonstrated in four scriptural citations, is set out as including praising God together with his people Israel. This joint praise of God is a new element not as yet included in ch. 14 but first introduced into this summary conclusion in 15:7-13. When Paul, as in earlier reception and until recently, has been regarded as addressing a mixed congregation of Jews and ethnē in ch. 14, then it has been assumed that the scriptural citations refer to this same mixed group. But if, as we hold to be the case, Paul addresses only ethnē throughout, then the people Israel are only included in ch. 15 via the emphasis on the dual outcome of the work of the Christ and in the scriptural citations. So, Paul's advice to "welcome one another" serves two purposes. In ch. 14, it addresses all the ethnē in Christ to accept one another, and in 15:7-13 this is expanded to include the people of Israel. Ethnē in Christ are first exhorted to accept one another, and then to praise God with his people.

We can explain Paul's strategy fruitfully in the terminology of SIT. As we have noted in ch. 11:19, instead of stressing their common belonging to the one God of Israel, these non-Jewish Christ-followers emphasized their new-found status, as non-Jews in association with Christ, in contrast to Israel's majority who could not see or accept the significance of the Christ-event. They were hostile to Israel, believing that the Jews had been replaced by ethnē in Christ as God's new people. We turn here to the approach,

---

[4] Denoting the group to which Christ belongs, not the group he serves (Keck 2005: 355–6). This reading has important ramifications in reducing of the emphasis upon "gentiles" as central, indicating rather a parallel Jewish heritage and agency. But there is quite a difference. For the circumcised, it is significant—Christ having become a servant "of the circumcision" is because he belongs to them, and a servant "with respect to the gentiles" indicates those to whom he does not belong.

outlined in the "Introduction" chapter, that is, superordinate identity or common in-group identity approach that has been found valuable in the attempt to overcome hostility between groups. In this approach, groups are recategorized to see themselves as part of a larger superordinate group, which allows them to stress their commonality rather than their difference. By redefining the group boundaries, the bias against outgroup members, perceived by the Romans as the people of Israel, would hopefully be reduced or dissolved. By recategorizing the ethnē in Christ and the people of Israel as both being peoples of Israel's God, Israel could then be seen as also God's people, as one of "us" not of "them." Evidence demonstrates that such recategorizations actually do reduce intergroup tensions or problems in a number of culturally diverse settings (Dovidio et al. 2009). What Paul is seeking to do in his letter is to remind these non-Jews with their over-inflated estimate of themselves that they are only one element of the people of God. Even if Israel is now (temporarily) unpersuaded of the Christ-event, it does not mean that the Jews are outside of God's purpose. Exclusive worship of the God of Israel is a common identity marker despite present differentiation concerning the recognition of the Christ-event. Common in-group identity means that the ethnē in Christ must recognize Israel as also under the rule of the one God, and not presume wrongly that God's purpose is ethnically limited or subject to fluctuation. In the stress upon common in-group identity, attention is turned away from the ethnē in Christ themselves to the God of the Christ whom they worship and to the historic people of Israel associated with this God.

When the continuing emphasis upon Christ's messianic role in relation to two peoples—Jew and ethnē—is not adequately recognized, a lack of clarity results. Mutual acceptance of each other as differing both now and continuing into the future, each having a differing λατρεία (McMurray 2021: 170) and joining together with, rather than being merged or fused with the other in an ethnically indifferent company, would appear to be Paul's goal. But, as the concluding scriptural citations exhibit, difference and ethnically related patterns do not disappear, nor are overlooked. Neither do Israelite and (gentile) ethnic existence lose their place in the God of Israel's familial purposes for the world of humanity. Paul still plans to visit Jerusalem with the collection from the gentile ἐκκλησίαι in a vision of "the fullness of the ethnē" alongside "the restoration of Israel." Ongoing ethnic existence for both Jew and "ethnē" together within the purpose of God is affirmed, not abandoned or denied.

Romans 15:7-13: The Conclusion to the Argument of the Entire Letter

This choice concerning 15:7-13 as the conclusion leads to quite a differing interpretive outcome. It differentiates this pericope (15:7-13) from the specific argument concerning "the weak" and "the strong" as indicated by the shift in terminology from "weak and strong" in 14:1-15:6 to Jew-gentile from 15:7.

While not ignoring or diminishing the significance of 14:1-23, or of 15:1-6, it allows attention to be focused more on the added content of 15:7-13, specifically on the call to worship God with his people Israel. It recognizes the significance of the two parallel benedictions in 15:5-6 and 15:13 drawing attention, while differentiating, to the structural similarity between the two paragraphs—an admonition, followed by a scriptural proof and concluding with a homiletic benediction.

Differentiating 15:7-13 from the preceding pericope allows ongoing emphasis upon the recapitulation of some of the leading themes of the letter. But these are now set within the wider scope of the field encompassed particularly by the four scriptural citations, including the emphasis upon the Christ as proceeding from the people of Israel, and as the basis for welcoming one another as he has welcomed the ethnē. My reading of this pericope gives full recognition to the specific and peculiar content of the pericope itself rather than fusing it too closely with what precedes it (with the inevitable result that its specific unique content is thus diluted and diminished in significance). Hence, my refusal to allow the content of 15:7-13 to be read back into ch. 14.

As we have demonstrated with 15:7-13, the repeated "welcome one another" indicates not just *repetition* but *expansion* of the theme. This expanded theme in 15:7-13 is more significant than the conflict arising from non-acceptance of one another among the ethnē in Christ at Rome, even though that itself is crucial. With the repetition of "welcome one another" (15:7) and the addition "just as the Christ has welcomed you for the glory of God," Paul extends the call to mutual acceptance as reconciliation within the gentile Christ-followers to call them to reach out to extend to reconciliation with the Jewish people. This could refer to Jewish people in Rome but should not be limited to that, since Paul is about to reveal to the Romans his plans to visit Jerusalem with a collection from the gentile ἐκκλησίαι.

However we relate the issues in 14:1–15:13 to Paul's argument in Romans, it is clear that if the gentile Christ-followers mistakenly regard Israel as cast off from God's purpose, they would see no reason to associate with Jews or to respect their Law and the patterns of behavior resulting from its observance. They would also see no reason for reducing or discontinuing their unwarranted and mistaken boasting over (cast off) Israel in their own self-understanding. There could be no conciliatory relations with Jews of any kind in Rome so long as these ethnē in Christ continued to disparage Jews and to have a proud self-understanding of themselves as the focus of God's purpose through Christ. In light of Rome's previous disciplining punishment of Jews by exile from Rome, Paul knows that further conflicts of any kind within, or concerning, a messianic movement would result in catastrophe for all involved or related in any way. Paul no doubt was well aware that anti-imperial resistance was flourishing in Judaea since he was soon to be arriving there himself.

This reading offers an insight into Paul's global vision in which the Messiah underpins their new identity (cf. McMurray 2021: 210–11). Paul's ministry included the resolution of local gentile conflicts but extended far beyond these to Jerusalem and to Spain to include the messianic purpose of God for the reconciliation and peace of all the peoples of this world, hence the reference to "the glory of God." With the vision of the Christ as coming from "the root of Jesse" (v. 12) (cf. 11:16-18) to rule the nations, Paul, in a correlation with Rom. 1:3-4, links Christ as the Messiah of Israel (15:7) with the incoming of the nations as he does at points throughout Romans. Whereas in Rom. 11:17-24, Paul stressed the identity of the nations as a wild olive shoot grafted into the stem alongside Israel, here he, now in 15:7-13, presents them as the co-participant with Israel in the praise of God. But we do not see any convincing evidence here that Paul wished to have all the Roman Christ-followers, both Jewish and non-Jewish join together as one entity (contra Watson 1991: 203–15). Neither the identity of the nations nor the identity of Israel has been dissolved, but now both together as distinct but related corporate entities, can join in the praise of God through the Christ. Paul's global vision, emphasized in his linking in family brotherhood the Messiah from the Davidic seed of Jesse with the incoming of the nations, represents another stage in his hope for the world and merits the rejoicing that it introduces here.[5] As we noted in the "Introduction" chapter, Paul does not regard the promises as having already received fulfillment, but speaks of affirmation of the promises, looking forward to a consummation still to come. Jews and non-Jews join together under the umbrella of a superordinate collective identity under the one God in which each retain their particular social identity as part of their doxological identity. This identity, to include the people of Israel both prior to and after the Christ-event, must be a superordinate identity not under Christ but under the God of Israel. As each together, but differently, glorify the God of Israel, his glory will be enhanced and more fully expressed.

In 15:13, in a concluding doxology or prayer wish, Paul stresses "this hope of universal reconciliation ensuing from the reconciliation of the nations" via the description "the God of hope" meaning the source or ground of hope (Jewett 2007: 899). He prays that this hope, by the power of the Holy Spirit (cf. 1:16), will be realized in the outcome of the ethnē in Christ praising God together with his people Israel (*qua Israel*). We note Paul's use of περισσεύειν as the overflowing of charismatic blessing, here with Messianic overtones, strongly indicated in Paul's choice of citations in 15:8-12. This blessing can be read as referring back also as an outcome of the unity among the gentile addressees of ch. 14:1–15:6. But the primary referent here is the messianic outcome of the ethnē in Christ praising God in concert with his people Israel, the new theme, or rather the expanded theme that was introduced in 15:7. Paul seems to think of this in terms of fullness of God's blessing as his use of περισσεύειν indicates. Israel and the ethnē worshipping together will lead to a further realization and enhancement of the glory of the God of Israel.

Thus, we can distinguish our reading of 15:7–13 as a discussion within an inter-ethnic horizon in contrast to 14:1–15:6, which is an inner-gentile discussion. Paul has not changed his specified gentile audience and continues to address these, but he has widened the sphere of his exhortation to remind the Romans to include the Jewish people within their horizon. Through "the Christ," thus introduced in 15:7, it is now possible for the nations to join with Israel in praise of the Creator God. As Keck claims, "Christ's Messiahship is a necessary, but not sufficient, condition for this role. Only when he is the one in whom gentiles hope do they 'rejoice *with* his people'" (2005: 359). McMurray uses the distinction between aggregative and oppositional ethnic reasoning here: "the *ethnē* are now part of the Abrahamic lineage (aggregative), but as brothers are not identical to Israel(oppositional); the ethnē now appropriately worship the same

---

[5] It is noteworthy that Ekkehard Stegemann cites Rom. 15:10 as the Leitmotiv of his unpublished Habilitationsschrift "Der eine Gott und die eine Menschheit. Israels Erwählung und die Erlösung von Juden und Heiden nach dem Römerbrief" (1981).

God as the Jews (aggregative), but differently and so alongside their new brothers (oppositional)" (2021: 210–11). The rejoicing of Jews and ethnē together under the God of Israel is the expression and hope of their emerging doxological identity (see Introduction, pp. 31–2) at the dawn of the Messianic Time.

The outcome of our investigation of the role of Rom. 15:7-13 is a recognition both of its distinctiveness and its significance. It is more than a continuation of 14:1–15:6, and not just a conclusion to another section of the paraenesis of the letter, concerning "the weak" and "the strong." It does link not only with what immediately precedes but also with the leading themes and interests of the entirety of the body of Paul's letter. These include the promises, the patriarchs, the scriptures of Israel, the Messiah from Israel, the people of Israel, and the incoming of the ethnē, as well as the subsequent relation of Jew and gentile as distinct entities in the merciful purpose of God; not least, in their mutual relation in a new brotherhood of reconciliation. The messianic outcomes of trusting in peace and joy with the power of the Holy Spirit crown the content of this pericope and offer a fitting cumulative conclusion to the argument of the entire letter (once Paul's travel plans and greetings have been communicated after 15:14).

Reconciliation with God and reconciliation between Jew and non-Jew as a brotherhood of peoples are central to Paul's letter. When 15:7-13 is read merely as a scriptural substantiation of the call for mutual acceptance between a mixed group of Jews and non-Jews, the scriptural citations are undervalued as having their principal significance as a call to peaceful coexistence between people(s). If 15:7-13 is read as a final cumulative summary that rounds off the body of the letter, then it cannot just be merged with 14:1–15:6. In relation to all that precedes, 15:7-13 is the culmination and thus presents the actual implication of the conclusion to Romans 11 (all Israel will be restored). The argumentation up to this point was leading to the affirmation of the restoration of all Israel. But only after the end of Romans 11 can Paul first draw out the implications of the conclusion of this argumentation in a new consequence for the ethnē in Christ arising from it. Thus chs. 9–11 are the climax of the argumentation of Romans, whereas 15:7-13 represents the conclusion of the culmination of 12:1–15:6 and thus of the whole letter. Romans 9–11 as the climax of 1–11 implies that Romans 1–8 cannot be the center of Romans. These chapters need the added content of 9–11, to complete Paul's clarification for ethnē what it means to be in Christ. Only when they come to understand how to relate to God's people Israel will they be able to embody their own social identity in Christ. Thus, 12:1-15:6 are the culmination of the sustained argumentation of 1–8 and 9–11, and constitute the outworking of its implications in real life for ethnē in Christ. The conclusion of the argument of the entire letter includes everything that precedes this, both taking into account 1–8, 9–11, and 12:1–15:6, leading up to worshipping God with his people in 15:7-13.

When the focus on the ethnē is properly recognized, 15:7-13 emerges as a specific call for ethnē, now in fraternal union with the resurrected Christ as sons of God, to recognize, accept, and identify with, as brothers, the people of Israel as co-worshippers of the Creator God. The ethnē in Christ, do not merely consist in a company of individuals but are together perceived by Paul as the representatives of the nations in parallel to Israel. Christ's role as Messiah underpins the new status of the ethnē in association with Israel.

By drawing together the destinies of Israel and the nations under God in the overarching theme of the God of Israel's ethnically diverse family retaining the integrity of their particular identity rather than seeking to fuse these into one amorphous entity, Paul has stressed the inalienable call of the gospel of Christ to enable unity and full acceptance of all peoples in their difference and diversity of life.

Romans 15:14-33

As Ehrensperger has noted, "There can hardly be any doubt that Jerusalem is at the center of Paul's perception of the world rather than Rome. Those who are called from the nations cannot bypass Israel; their call is inherently linked to Israel through Christ, the διάκονος περιτομῆς" (2013: 221). This concluding section of Paul's letter repeats and elaborates on Paul's travel plans first expressed in 1:8-15. New elements are now added in the information given—the reason why he has been previously unable to visit them, and his plans to visit them en route for Spain and enjoy their company for a while. But only with v. 25 does he confess that, at present, he is not heading west for Spain, but going east to Jerusalem "in a ministry to the saints." Only after he has completed this sharing of resources, delivering what has been collected from gentile groups who have come to share in the Jewish people's spiritual blessings (Macedonia and Achaia are mentioned), will he set out by way of Rome for Spain. Obviously, Paul has been hesitant to disclose this information until this late point in his letter. But why? One reason seems clear—he did not want to admit until now that his plans to visit Rome would be further delayed by a visit to Jerusalem. Even if it was not Jerusalem, he would visit perhaps any place other than Rome would have caused offence, because of giving precedence to it rather than Rome. Interestingly, in the different context of 2 Corinthians, Paul similarly delays mention of the collection until more than half-way through the letter (Esler 2021a: 334).

Romans 15:14-21: Reiterating and Expanding on His Plans

¹⁴I myself feel confident about you, my brothers, that you yourselves are full of goodness, filled with all knowledge, and able to instruct one another. ¹⁵But I wrote to you even most boldly in part as one who reminds you because of the grace given to me by God ¹⁶so that I would be a minister of Christ Jesus to the ethnē in [priestly] service to the gospel of God, so that the offering of the ethnē might become acceptable, made holy by the Holy Spirit. ¹⁷I have therefore a boast in Christ Jesus, before God. ¹⁸For I will not be so bold as to speak of anything except what Christ has accomplished through me for the hearing in trust of the ethnē, by word and deed, ¹⁹in the power of signs and wonders, in the power of the Spirit of God, so that

> *from Jerusalem and circling around as far as Illyricum I have fulfilled the gospel of Christ. ²⁰Thus making it my ambition not to preach where Christ has already been named lest I build on another's foundation ²¹but as it is written, "They shall see who have never been informed about him, and those who have never heard of him shall understand."*

But if there was, as we have noted, a poor appreciation of Israel in Rome as one of the nations subjected and dominated by Rome, perhaps even the suggestion that Israel had been bypassed in God's future plans, then for Paul to travel to Jerusalem prior to his long-proposed visit to Rome might have alienated at least some of "the beloved" ethnē in Rome. Paul thought that the content of his letter required to be expressed and understood before he revealed his plans for Jerusalem in order to soften its impact and to avoid misunderstanding. It is obvious that Paul thinks he needs to approach the Romans with some caution. If it seems that he thought that some of the Roman gentile Christ-followers were over-influenced by Roman imperial attitudes and propaganda, it would not be fitting to elaborate on his visit to Jerusalem—going East to an under-appreciated minority people, rather than coming first to Rome. In 15:18-23, he acknowledges the delay in his long-planned visit based on the nature of his apostolic work to those who had never previously heard "the good news of Christ." But now, this work in these regions of the East has already been completed, so at last Paul is free to work elsewhere. He does not want the news of his future plans for the collection to Jerusalem to have a negative effect on his relationship with the Romans before he has had an opportunity to clarify delicate issues through his letter. So, the letter not only looks forward to Spain but also serves the function of clarifying misunderstandings and rebutting misinformation circulating in Rome about Paul's ministry.

Importantly, he now also needs the support of the ethnē, hospitality, financial, linguistic, and so on, in order for the visit to Spain to have any chance of success (since hospitality and any kind of support among Jews could be taken for granted, cf. Hezser 2011). One of the merits of Jewett's commentary on Romans is the detailed and ongoing attention he devotes to these various requirements. Thus, it is only after this long letter that Paul feels comfortable enough to disclose his plans and their implications. Now he returns to his previous links with them and acknowledges both his confidence in their good character and in the adequacy of their knowledge and ability to instruct one another. Paul is making it very clear that although they were not founded by him, they are nevertheless self-sufficient in that they do not require a second foundation (contra. Klein 1991) and are coping well despite his failure to visit. He has established already in 1:1-15 his apostolic credentials, and that they, as Christ-following ethnē, therefore, also come within his remit. Nevertheless, Paul admits that he has written in parts to them somewhat boldly (15:15), and he quickly justifies this bold speech as a partial *reminder* (ἐπαναμιμνῄσκων) of that which they already know. They are not Paul's own apostolic foundation, which, he acknowledges, he cannot possibly claim them to be, that is, "laying a foundation where Christ has not already been named" (15:20) but they do come within the sphere of his appointment to be a "minister of Christ Jesus" to the nations. And since he did not found them, his teaching is only a partial reminder of that which they already know, and in part, new teaching relating to where he, as apostle to the nations, sees them in need of correction. As Jewett notes, "Honest and effective rhetoric requires Paul to admit that part of his letter moves beyond reminder towards a timely and prophetic claim against their present and future behavior" (2007: 906).

Paul here presents himself in a very specific image of being appointed by God's grace to be a minister of Christ Jesus to the nations, note the term λειτουργός. This term may refer in the Septuagint to a royal attendant but more often to temple personnel. Jewett, in correlation with his perception of Paul's role as an ambassador of Christ, stresses Paul's ambassadorial rather than priestly role, following Spicq's emphasis on λειτουργοί who serve as ambassadors sent from particular Greek cities (2007: 906–15). However, despite the relevance and attraction of this perspective, perhaps Jewett should have given more weight to Paul's focus upon Paul's liturgical language, so emphatic at this point. Paul does compare (not contrast) his *diakonia* with that of Moses (Campbell 2016: 139–45) in 2 Cor. 3:12-15 and, as Munck (1959) has emphasized, viewed himself as having an important role in relation to all the nations, however we may describe this, as ambassadorial or not. The term ἱερουργοῦντα, to act in some cultic or sacred capacity, focuses also on the priestly offering of sacrifice. Thus, even though we give some significance to Paul's priestly imagery, we remember he was not from a priestly family, but of the tribe of Benjamin, and thus the ambassadorial aspect that Jewett stresses should not be dismissed entirely; perhaps it can be interpreted as "a verbalized form of priesthood" as Jewett suggests (2007: 107).

Rodriguez has sought to remedy Jewett's emphasis by underlining the cultic terminology that Paul uses here "so that I would be a priestly servant (λειτουργός) of Christ Jesus for the ethnē, offering priestly service (ἱερουργοῦντα) on behalf of the gospel of God, so that the offering (ἡ προσφορά) of the ethnē might be acceptable (εὐπρόσδεκτος), sanctified (ἡγιασμένη) by the Holy Spirit" (15:16) (2014: 285–7). This perspective fits better with the collection as being what is offered, rather than those who give this offering, though they themselves are also necessarily involved. Paul is "offering priestly service" in the gentile mission, which he is leading, as apostle, and also as ambassador for the incoming of the ethnē (Lim 2009: 124, 139).

The term εὐπρόσδεκτος (acceptable) is similar to its near synonym εὐάρεστος (pleasing, 12:1-2) to which we drew attention in relation to the sacrificial giving of one's body above. Ἡγιασμένη (sanctified) is likewise an *explicitly cultic term*, and it is striking how Paul uses it here to denote the full acceptance of the Romans into the family of God, as representatives of the nations. We have noted at several points a certain resonance that might imply Paul's implicit opposition to idolatry in Rome (alongside its explicit rejection), and this may be another point where Paul calls for complete self-giving and dedication to God alone in contrast to all the other gods.

But we would not limit Paul's offering only to the Roman ethnē. He views them as being within his sphere or field of mission—they are only a part of a larger entity "all the assemblies of the ethnē" (15:4). It this totality to which Paul is commissioned as apostle (Ehrensperger 2022b: 290, 297) as a linking person, perhaps as "travelling ambassador for the nations to Jerusalem." This self-designation of Paul as λειτουργός is not to be defined by any conceptuality that limits his representative and apostolic function *but should be enlarged so that the descriptor fits the content it conveys and the person it describes*. If Paul in 2 Cor. 3:12 feels able to compare his mediating task in relation to the nations with that of Moses, then this is no mean task, and his role in relation to all the ethnē must not be underestimated. Significantly, Paul does not depict himself specifically as apostle to all humans, but only to a specific section of humanity—to the gentile nations.

Thinking about his role in relation to the nations leads Paul to speak further about the gentile mission. Paul thinks he is justified in boasting in Christ about his gentile mission success, but then proceeds to claim he will speak only of what "Christ has accomplished through me for the hearing in trust of the ethnē by word and deed." He has "fully proclaimed the good news about Christ from Jerusalem circling around as far as Illyricum" (15:19). This statement and its context reveal Paul's explicit acknowledgment that he sees the work of Christ extending beyond his particular limited "field of service," implying that he could speak of work other than that which he had founded, but here limits himself to his own mission.

With this mention of Jerusalem, Paul comes closer to telling the Romans he is not now coming to visit them, but going to Jerusalem instead. By this means, he reminds them of his planned mission travels and that Jerusalem had always been included within his wide-ranging vision. Not only had Jerusalem been included, but it is depicted here as the center of Paul's Jewish world. The Temple acted as a bond or link between widely separated Jewish communities, the metropolis for all Jews, according to Philo (*Flacc.* 46, cf. Ehrensperger 2022b: 297). These former functions of the Temple probably became more significant after its destruction. If, due to the loss of the Temple, Jewish networks were intensified providing a route for rabbinic ideas to spread, this implies that such networks already existed, as the literary evidence suggests (Ehrensperger 2022b: 296–7, informed by Collar 2013). The introduction of his planned mission activity allows Paul to explain to the Roman gentile Christ-followers why, until now, he has been unable to find time to visit them. His mission policy is that he has not taken the gospel to where Christ has already been named "so that I do not build upon another man's foundation." He offers scriptural support from Isa. 52:15, "Those who have never been told of him shall see, and those who have never heard of him shall understand" (15:21).

By explaining his ongoing mission policy, Paul is able to tell the Romans why, hitherto, for many years (15:23) he has been unable to visit them (and also why he heads for Spain). It seems he is sensitive that he has not visited them earlier and feels the need to explain himself, particularly if 3:8 is read as indicative of misunderstandings. The term φιλοτιμούμενον (15:20) from the ancient honor/shame culture was used of persons who vied for the honor of doing the most for the city. Though Paul has not yet managed to visit Rome, this is because he is outstanding among the apostles in that he is excelling in the field of pioneer evangelism. This provides further explanation in that Paul claims he has concluded (fully proclaimed) the gospel in the mission areas where he has previously worked. We take this to mean that Paul had a policy in which he and his colleagues planted the gospel in a region and then moved on to a new area, leaving the new ethnē in Christ to evangelize further by themselves. The relevance of this policy of non-intervention (not building on another's foundation) for the Romans would be twofold—it signals Paul's recognition of their standing in Christ and also his reason for not hastening to visit them because of his, till now, unfinished work.

Romans 15:20-24: Not Where Christ Has Already Been Named—Paul's Prioritizing of Pioneer Areas

[20]Thus making it my ambition not to preach where Christ has already been named lest I build on another's foundation, [21]but as it is written, "Those who have never been told of him shall see, and those who have never heard of him shall understand." [22]This is the reason that I have so often been hindered from coming to you. [23]But now, with no further place for me in these regions, I desire, as I have for many years, to come to you [24]when I go to Spain. For I do hope to see you as I pass through and be sent there by you after I have fully enjoyed your company for a while.

Although Paul does not fully explain his mission strategy in Romans, this section is one of the more comprehensive coverages of his work. What is not explicit here is that Paul appears to consider that God allocates to each apostle a certain region or sphere of service, which is his particular responsibility. Aspects of this appear in the claim to avoid building on another's foundation (15:20). It seems that there must be some resonance here with the Galatians 2 narrative in which Paul claims there had been a public recognition of Cephas and himself as the respective leaders of two missions, Peter to the circumcision and he himself to the foreskin (Gal. 2:7-9). This claim correlates with the agreement apparently arrived at in the summit meeting reported in Acts15. But these two reports do not indicate whether there may have been other minor agreements within the sphere of the mission to the nations as to who should have authority to work in a specific region. Due to the significance of Paul's mission strategy, which I have interpreted as being an issue in 2 Corinthians (Campbell 2016). I will interpret Romans 15 in conjunction with this. In 2 Cor. 10:15 Paul claims, "We are not straining to exceed the limits of our jurisdiction/province" (κανώνα). I am convinced by the translation of κανώνα as jurisdiction since it carries both the idea of legitimate authority as well as the area over which it is exercised (Furnish 1984: 471–2). Paul asserted in 2 Cor. 10:13 that "we will keep within the limits God has prescribed to us," and that the Corinthians lie within that territory. It would seem that the area of a leader's work in proclaiming the gospel was regarded as somehow apportioned to them by God—God apportioned to Paul and his colleagues a certain sphere of mission (ὁ μέτρον τοῦ κανόνος οὗ ἐμέρισεν ἡμῖν ὁ θεὸς μέτρου). Paul also mentions that he was the first to proclaim the gospel in Corinth (2 Cor. 10:14). What motivated this statement? Is the issue here the question as to who has authority to preach the gospel and where, and how does this relate to ethnic groups as well as geographical regions?

The debate between Peter and Paul, as evidenced in Galatians 2, indicates only an agreement along ethnic lines with Paul regarding himself as of equivalent status to Peter in the latter's leadership in work among Jews. I agree in taking the reported division of work between Peter and Paul as an ethnic demarcation, though not that "another man's foundation" may refer to Moses (Rodriguez 2016: 289). Rodriguez's suggestion is interesting in light of Paul's comparison of his ministry διακονία with that of Moses, a view in my opinion emanating from the Corinthians themselves rather than Paul. It was they rather than Paul who wanted to compare or contrast old and new covenants (Campbell 2016: 149–50). Reading Rom. 15:20 from my perspective might suggest that the issue at Rome was not the possible building on another person's work in the mission to the nations, but that it was an even more serious issue of possible intrusion into the mission field of Peter. We have no texts that specifically indicate this, though inferences might be drawn from reports of the Christ-movement in Rome as having a Jewish foundation, and also from the Petrine traditions associated with Rome. This would help explain why Paul includes such a powerful rationale for his gentile mission, and similarly for his inclusion of the Roman ethnē within his apostolic sphere of labor. We have no hint from Paul in his references back to his previous links with the Romans of who may have first brought the gospel to Rome. Judge and Thomas in an earlier article stressed the emigration of Pauline converts from the East to Rome as the source of gentile Christianity (1966: 81–94). But if the Christ-movement possibly first came to Rome from Jerusalem, this would explain why Paul should avoid building on another's foundation since this division of labor was basic to the mutual recognition.[1]

But Paul is clear that he does not address Jews in his letter to Rome, so he is not interfering with the mission to the circumcision. He has explained carefully his own overarching (ethnic) sphere of authority (in all the assemblies of the ethnē ἐκκλησίαι τῶν ἐθνῶν, 16:4). Also, whoever may have been the first to establish an ἐκκλησία in Rome, Paul makes no claims for authority as a founder, and since he does not assert that the Christ-followers are deficient in a proper foundation, he must come to Rome as "a waterer" of a planting made by someone else (Ehrensperger 2021: 5). If that someone established a Jewish Christ-following group, Paul does not refer to it as a specific entity, and the only reason for this omission, if such an entity ever did exist, must be that Paul regards this as outside his sphere of legitimate influence. If Paul had some knowledge of how an ἐκκλησία in Rome first originated, and especially if it had a Jerusalem/Petrine mission association, this might partly explain his delay in visiting them.

Having outlined aspects of his mission policy, Paul provides the Romans with the reason why he has desired "for many years" to visit them. It is difficult to give an estimate of what Paul means by this, but anything less than ten years would not seem to be warranted, and it is probable that Christ followers existed prior to Paul's planning to come to visit. Taken together with Paul's explicit statements of their knowledge and competence to instruct one another, we must envisage a Christ-following group or groups as possibly having been in existence for up to fifteen years. This span would give substance to Paul's possibly generous description of their trust as "proclaimed throughout the world" (1:8). Initially in 1:12, Paul acknowledged their ὑπακοὴν πίστεως, but revised this first envisaged strengthening to become mutual encouragement. Here toward the end of his letter, Paul reiterates that despite his "bold reminder," the Romans are adequately equipped for mutual self-development—here he seems to be warding off any suggestion that without his presence they are somehow inadequate. Once again at this point, we find that Paul in his contact with the Romans treads most carefully,

---

[1] As noted above, we need to ask whether this text refers to the allocation of territories *within the gentile mission* or to the larger domain of the mission to the nations as a whole in distinction from that to the circumcision.

suggestive that there remained areas of possible misunderstanding of which both parties were aware.

Now Paul fills out the itinerary of his proposed mission travels. Having no further place in these regions, that is, in the East, he hopes to spend a little time with them on his way to Spain. It would be normal hospitality for him to anticipate being supported en route for a few days, but it is also likely that here Paul uses a technical word προπεμφθῆναι, common in Jewish and non-Jewish texts (15:24) that includes helping him and his team on the next stage of his journey and might involve financial support, translators, guides, and so on to facilitate the work. Such support would certainly imply interference in another's sphere of labor if there were such a tradition in Rome. As has recently been noted, Paul most likely operated via small group networks, probably following a pattern that existed among Diaspora Jews and other ethnic groups (Collar 2013: 229). These small global networks operated among local community groups and facilitated communication, business, and other connections between these, especially in the eastern Mediterranean. It would have been normal for Jewish groups to maintain links with one another over long distances, and particularly with their common connection with the Temple in Jerusalem as a common focus through pilgrimages and the half-shekel tax. As a result of both forced and voluntary migration, Jewish groups were widespread, and travelers via these would have contacts to assist and guide them on long dangerous journeys. It is highly probable that Paul would have traveled along networks of Jewish hubs that would have offered him a minimal framework for support, especially where there were local synagogues (Levine 2005: 81–134). These would have been Paul's first chosen resting place on his many journeys. To the extent that Spain may not offer such facilities, it differed from Paul's mission work in the past, and would intensify Paul's dependence for support from the Romans.

Paul as he writes Romans is at a major crossroads in his mission work. He has completed with some success his work in the East and after having delivered the collection, the fruit of that work, he will be free to visit Rome and to reformulate his plans.

Romans 15:25-29: "I Am Going to Jerusalem in Service of the Saints"

²⁵At present, however, I am going to Jerusalem in service of the saints; ²⁶for Macedonia and Achaia have been pleased to establish a particular fellowship with the poor among the saints at Jerusalem. ²⁷For they were pleased to do this, and indeed they owe it to them; for if the ethne shared in their spiritual matters, they ought also to be of service to them in material matters ²⁸So, when I have completed this, and sealed the fruit for them, I will set out by way of you to Spain; ²⁹and I know that when I come to you, I will come in the fullness of the blessing of Christ.

At last Paul is able to admit that he is not coming to Rome just now, but, instead, going to Jerusalem "in service of the saints." He has laid the foundation already in his explanations about his mission work being successfully completed in the East, and now he will explain the motivation and function of his forthcoming travel. The planned recipients of his ministering are described similarly to 1:7 as being to τοῖς ἁγίοις (the saints), with the limitation here to "the poor among the saints" (15:25). The limitation is not so much determined by Paul as by those, the gentile Christ-followers of Macedonia and Achaia who, Paul claims, voluntarily decided to share their resources with "the poor among the saints at Jerusalem." But having stressed the voluntary aspect of the gift, Paul also points out another feature that he seems not to view as being in contrast to the first. He repeats, "They were pleased" to do this, but adds that in view of the nations having come to share in their spiritual blessings (τοῖς πνευματιοῖς), "they ought also to be of service to them in material things (τοῖς σαρκικοῖς)." We take this designation here at its face value, as referring to the destitute in the Christ-following community (Keck 1965: 100–29; 2003: 365). Paul, as is common, does not speak explicitly about raising a fund or such like, but is rather more allusive and suggestive, emphasizing the corporate sharing, to make κοινωνία for the poor, that is, it is this that both originated and would sustain the sharing of resources. Paul is not so polite that he does not discuss financial matters, but he does so under the umbrella of the Christ-movement, which has as its template, "whether we live or die, we are the Lord's," 14:8). Paul is keen to stress the generosity of the ἐκκλησίαι who share their gifts with the Jerusalem poor, cf. 2 Cor. 8:1-4 where he uses χάρις relating to the Macedonian's generosity and the same terminology of κοινωνία as here.

The same point that Paul makes here with the Romans had been made earlier in relation to a desired equivalence ἰσότης between two groups—"your plenty will supply what they need, so that in turn their plenty will supply what you need" (2 Cor. 8:13-14, NIV). Here Paul stresses that the ethnē have come to share (ἐκοινώνησαν) the Jerusalemites' spiritual things, and so they are obligated ὀφείλουσιν to be of sacred service (λειτουργῆσαι) to them in material things (Keck 2005: 365). Paul is speaking in terms of an appropriate response from those from the nations. When a gift is exchanged there may be a gracious response, which of course is not legally binding, but morally to be anticipated. This is how Paul reasons in relation to the "assemblies of the ethnē." This way of presenting the issue is notably ethnic in orientation and demonstrates how at this advanced stage in his mission work Paul is still taking ethnic issues very much into account; indeed, this looks very much like what has been termed "ethnic reasoning." However, here the emphasis lies on the sharing of resources so that there is parity and equivalence among those who worship the same God whether Jews or non-Jews. Such a common fellowship of sharing reflects a commonality of mind and intention. This κοινωνία was fundamental to Paul's vision of Jews and non-Jews as distinct entities both sharing their life together, including their economic resources under the covenant (Longenecker 2010: 310).

When Paul addressed the Romans in 1:13, he had mentioned that he hoped to "get some fruit from among them" as with other non-Jews. Paul does not make any explicit request for the Romans to contribute to the collection, which we know he has been planning for some time (cf. Esler for a fine overview of its rationale and history from a social identity perspective, 2021a: 229–35; cf. similarly also Tucker 2014: 52–70). Paul's reasoning about the nations responding to the spiritual gifts they received from the Jews is as cogent for the Romans as for the other ἐκκλησίαι of the ethnē, so it may be that though he does not say so, Paul could be hoping that the Romans might volunteer. There can be no question of pressure or of compulsion as the possible parallel with various types of collection undertaken by differing voluntary associations clearly indicates (Kloppenborg 2019: 264–5). It is, however, probably already too late for the Romans to contribute to the collection (Wedderburn 1988: 72), other than through their prayerful support (if they were to contribute, there would be delay to allow time for collecting). Wedderburn considers but eventually drops the proposal that the Romans might contribute (2002: 109–10). Yet this acknowledgement of the Romans' non-participation must not be allowed to diminish the crucial significance of the collection in Paul's own thinking and activity. Paul feels responsible as "apostle to the ethnē" for their attitude as ethnē in Christ to the Jewish people in Jerusalem as well as in Rome. The important issue is how they view Paul's coming visit to Jerusalem and how that, in turn, may influence his reception with the collection.

The possibility of the Romans contributing to the collection puts more weight on the collection as the offering contributed rather than on the gentile contributors themselves (Ehrensperger 2019: 349–51). In Rom. 12:1-2, there is an accumulation of temple-related language, which calls Christ-followers to present their bodies as consecrated instruments for God's service in everyday life (Downs 2008, Ehrensperger 2019: 342–3). This is somewhat similar in emphasis to 15:27 but in neither place is there any suggestion that the presentation of one's body replaces any offerings. The collection is something that requires organization, contributing, and people to take it to the recipients. Even though there may be a symbolic aspect to this, the tangible expression still comprises the monetary offering, and this was sufficiently important to occupy a significant part of Paul's time and effort. With it he certainly wishes to create a concrete cultic link of his ἐκκλησίαι of the ethnē with Jerusalem, possibly even with the Temple (Ehrensperger 2019: 343–51; cf. also Acts 24:1-23).

Paul's role is that he plans to take the collection to Jerusalem with other representatives of the ἐκκλησίαι. How Paul describes his part in the διακονία εἰς Ἰερουσαλὴμ 15:31b seems to be as a courier, delegated by the ἅγιοι to deliver something. This makes Paul a delegate rather than one traveling in his own interests and highlights the voluntariness of the collection (Ehrensperger 2022b: 300). Ogereau has demonstrated that κοινωνίαν τινὰ ποιοῦμαι is a business or legal administrative term that does not refer to sharing resources or a generous giving of resources and so on, but it is a phrase used for contractual agreements between parties for a common project (2012: 360–78). Thus, the Macedonians and Achaians by sending these funds indicate a commitment to a partnership that would be beneficial for the poor of the saints in Jerusalem. Hence, Paul is part of a legal contract into which the Macedonian and Achaian assemblies had entered with the poor in Jerusalem. This distinguishes it from the promise to remember "the poor" (Gal. 2:10), which can be described as a concern for the poor generally in Jewish tradition. If this obligation had been agreed in Jerusalem with the pillars, why might there be some serious concern "that my ministry to Jerusalem might be acceptable" (15:31)? It is clear from his own statements that this collection symbolizes Paul's theological standpoint of the relation of his gentile communities to Jerusalem. He is the Jewish apostle to the nations, and his creation through the gospel of gentile ἐκκλησίαι was not an end in itself, nor had it the goal of creating an independent gentile entity totally emancipated from the Jewish Law and the Jewish cult. Paul may already have been sensitized to such a stance at Rome from earlier reports.

Romans 15:30-33: "Join Me in Earnest Prayer to God"

³⁰I appeal to you, brothers, by our Lord Jesus Christ and by the love of the Spirit, to agonize with me by praying on my behalf before God, ³¹in order that I may be delivered from the unconvinced in Judea, and that my service to Jerusalem might be acceptable to the saints, ³²so that in coming to you in joy through the will of God I may be refreshed together with you. ³³The God of peace be with all of you. Amen.

However, Paul's struggle for the full equality and rights of all those in Christ did not take place in a political vacuum, and so could not avoid challenges from voices for and against events in Jerusalem and Rome. Paul's concern for the non-acceptance of the collection may result from the fear that a gift specifically sent by gentile Christ-followers to poor Jews in Jerusalem might cause political unrest. It would not be identical with non-Jews giving gifts directly to the Temple, but it could arouse similar reactions if not well understood. So Paul intends to seal the delivery of the collection himself when he and those representatives of the ἐκκλησίαι eventually reach Jerusalem. But he has strong fears for his safety for which he asks that the Romans agonize (συναγωνίσασθαί) together in prayer with him for his safety, so that he might then come to visit in Rome. But we note that those whom Paul fears are not necessarily the Jewish leaders, since they are themselves subject to Roman control. So it is probable that the unconvinced οἱ ἀπειθούντοι from whom Paul prays to be delivered were the Romans or certain antagonistic Jewish leaders both of whom might intervene if there was any unrest or if there were serious doubts about the legitimacy of the collection. This was not the permitted half-shekel tax for the Temple and may not be regarded as a legitimate financial transaction. Jew–gentile relations were a dangerous subject since the time of Caligula at least, and Paul is very well aware that he is embarking on a potentially dangerous project. But it is typical of his entire activity as apostle to the nations, and fitting to the climax of a life of conflict in an inter-ethnic context.

Here, perhaps somewhat surprisingly, we find the repetition of the appeal, παρακαλῶ, which began the long paraenesis in ch. 12:1. We will return to this verse, but there can be no doubt that it intensifies Paul's requests to the Romans, and that his own well-being, even his life may be in the balance. The repeated appeal and the fact that παρακαλῶ did not appear in the normal form in ch. 1 indicates the distinctness of Romans as a Pauline letter.[2] A link has been made between the thanksgiving in Rom. 1:8ff and Paul's request for prayer support in 15:30-32. Normally in letters, these

---

[2] Note also the repetition in 16:17, which we will deal with separately because it is disputed.

two items should succeed each other immediately. And even though Romans differs with such vast separation between the two items, this should not prevent us from considering a link between them,[3] possibly making the παρακαλῶ (I appeal, urge) sentence in 15:30-32, the or a reason for Paul writing the letter (Bjerkelund 1967: 161). This possibility has been fully discussed by Wedderburn (1988: 67–75). We agree with Wedderburn's perspective on this connection in that he sees the repeated παρακαλῶ as somehow related to Paul's prayers in relation to the Jerusalem collection visit. A major feature in this discussion, which we also support, emerges in the emphasis upon the renewal of the minds of the Romans in light of the mercies of God outlined in chs. 9–11 (Bjerkelund 1967: 171, Wedderburn 1988: 86). This will involve a reorientation in their attitude to Israel and thus to Jerusalem (Tucker 2014).

Irrespective of the details, it is clear that Paul, with accompanying representatives of his gentile ἐκκλησίαι is still committed to links of some kind with Jerusalem. He reminds the Romans of the place of Jerusalem in his mission travels. This perspective goes in tandem with Paul's arguments that Israel has not been bypassed but still occupies a significant place in the divine purpose and the fact that there is demonstrated here an historic obligation from his gentile communities. They acknowledge in the giving of gifts their indebtedness to the people Israel, and this points to Paul's ongoing immersion in the symbolic universe of Israel, to which he sees his gentile ἐκκλησίαι connected. He remains the Jewish apostle to the nations.

By getting the Romans to share in his collection for the poor among the saints in Jerusalem, or at least to acknowledge it, Paul demonstrates to them his own interests and theological concerns. His early emphasis in Romans upon "the Jew first and also the Greek" (1:16, 2:9-10) revealed this. In a sense, by taking this collection to Jerusalem, it is as if Paul is hoping for a symbolically positive verdict on his apostolic ministry. But he is not sure how the collection will be received because of the conflicts that gentile gifts to Jerusalem might set alight. Ehrensperger has demonstrated that there may be much more significance than presently realized in Paul's cultic concerns with Jerusalem as indicated both by the collection and by his planned visit. "Nothing less than the actual worshipping of the God of Israel by 'Israel and the nations' at the center of the Jewish social and symbolic world is what Paul might hope for" (2019: 351).

---

[3] The subject matter of the thanksgiving is often directly connected to that of the request, in that the former somehow paves the way for the latter. Here the thanksgiving concerns Paul's desire to visit Rome, which is also mentioned in 15:22-24 alongside the request for the Romans to agonize with him in prayer.

Romans 16

Romans 16:1-2: "Now I Recommend to You Phoebe, Our Sister"

> ¹*Now, I recommend to you Phoebe our sister, who is a minister of the assembly at Cenchreae, ²that you may welcome her in the Lord in a manner worthy of the saints, and provide her in whatever she may require from you in the matter, for she has become a benefactor of many and of myself as well.*

This chapter begins like a letter of commendation for Phoebe in the normal pattern of contemporary Hellenistic letters. In her recent study on women in the greetings in ch. 16, Mathew concentrates on Paul's final greetings and categorizes these final greetings under three headings—first, second, and third, with reference to their apparent function (2014: 36–7). The first-person greeting is informative in that it has potential for spelling out the intended readership, and the second-person type of greeting informs of the relationships that exist beyond the scope of the letter (2014: 26). If Romans 16 ever existed separately from 1 to 15, this would offer a solid reason for this strange phenomenon of a letter, which mentions so many people in one chapter. This option is tied in with the issue of whether Romans 16 could have first existed as a letter to Ephesus (cf. Gamble 1977, Jewett 2007).

The verb συνίστημι here means to commend or introduce, and its placement at this point indicates Paul wants to give Phoebe the highest possible recommendation to those in Rome. Paul shows the importance he attaches to the content of 16:1-2 by setting it out as a separate pericope at the beginning of the last chapter of his letter. But it is attached to the contents of this long letter by the particle δέ ("now," indicating it is part of the foregoing, and not an entirely new document). Paul informs his hearers why he commends Phoebe. She serves as a διάκονος, not equivalent to the English word, deacon, but a leader, possibly the leader, in the ἐκκλησία at Cenchrea, the eastern port of Corinth. She is an established leader, and possibly more than just a local leader in view of her projected visit to Rome and even to Spain. She is probably someone already known to Prisca and Aquila (Mowczko 2021: 91–102) whose leadership and generosity Paul wishes to be recognized in Rome. Paul's recommending of Phoebe also informs the Romans that she has been a benefactor προστάτις of many, of whom he himself is one.

The activity in which she is credited of being a patron to many, including Paul, most likely refers to hospitality for differing people on different occasions, but probably includes substantial support other than only hospitality (Jewett 2007: 946). It may include coming to the aid of foreigners by providing housing and financial aid and by representing these before local authorities (Moo 1996: 916). Here it includes the function of courier of Paul's letter.[1] This indicates that Phoebe has sufficient resources to give assistance and hospitality to many followers of Christ. The term "benefactor" places Paul in debt to Phoebe, she is his benefactor, rather than presenting her as his helper, though Paul acts as Phoebe's patron in commending her to the Romans (MacDonald 2011: 274–5). The dynamics of patronage do not seem to completely explain the relationship between Paul, Phoebe, and assembly members. MacDonald notes a certain ambiguity in Paul's depiction of Phoebe as his patron, "certain elements are maintained, but others seem to be reversed or at least qualified" (2011: 274–5). Thus, MacDonald sees a near mutuality implied in Paul's descriptions; Paul tells the Romans to welcome her as appropriate in the Lord (possibly hinting at a reciprocal response to her reported generosity). They "should help her in whatever business she may require your help" (16:2). This is indicative of her high standing in Paul's eyes, but it also implies that she is coming with a purpose in view, and one that may require support from others. The recommendation of individuals to the attention of groups would suggest that Phoebe was introduced in this way to link her person and her subsequent activity to the content of the letter. The open request to help Phoebe indicates that the extent of what may be required remains as yet unclear, even to Paul, but it may be hinted at in the reference to Phoebe's previous activity as προστάτις. He is possibly presenting Phoebe as a generous patron who will ensure that the Romans by themselves will not be required to bear undue expense because of the mission to Spain. To refer to Phoebe as a sister, minister, and benefactor indicates her importance as a leader, representing in a prototypical way the ethos of the movement. So here there is a female leader embodying the characteristics of being in Christ. Jewett perhaps exaggerates somewhat when he extends her patronage role to underwriting the huge project of the forthcoming mission to Spain announced in 15:28 (2007: 947–8). Paul's hopes and expectations concerning Phoebe and her anticipated future role help explain his caution at many points in his relation with the Romans. He never risks offending them unduly or being too explicit in correcting them.

Not only Phoebe is the trusted bearer of an important letter, but there is also evidence that suggests that the carrier would be conversant with its contents. Cicero complains in a letter to one of his friends that a letter carrier did not provide some expected details for him (*Letters to Friends* 151 [IV.2.1]). It seems the sender here had written a shorter letter because he had expected the carrier to elaborate the details for the recipient. It was simply presumed that the carrier would provide additional information where something was ambiguous (Wilder 2016: 112). So, it is probable that Phoebe would be fully conversant with its contents so that she will also interpret

---

[1] It has been noted that Frederick W. Danker added "courier" to his list of activities possibly designated by the term διάκονος in Rom. 16:1 in the 2003 revision of (BDAG) Bauer's *Greek-English Lexicon of the New Testament and Early Christian Literature* (230). Cf. Terry L. Wilder (2016: 107–18, 112–13).

the letter as well. Whether it would be read on several occasions we cannot be sure, but it is rather likely since it would have been difficult to ensure the meeting of "all God's beloved in Rome" in one place at the same time, especially as there seems to have been so many differing groups of Christ-followers in Rome (Wolter 2019: 465).

Phoebe's Role as Indicative of Women's Leadership

It is highly significant that the bearer of Paul's letter is a woman, and that she will also present its contents to the Romans (Osiek and MacDonald 2006: 32, Jewett 1988). Lampe notes that of the twenty-six named individuals he can identify in Rom. 16:3-16, there are nine women, and that these are commended more than the men for being highly active in the ἐκκλησία (1991: 222–3). In addition to Phoebe, Prisca, Miriam, Junia, and Rufus's mother are specifically mentioned, while Lampe also adds Persis to this group. We note also Tryphaena and Tryphosa (v. 12) who possibly may be sisters. The verb ἐκοπίασεν denotes hard labor, wearying toil, but this activity can also include teaching and preaching (as in 1 Cor. 15:10) and in 1 Thess. 1:3, "the labour (κόπος) of love" (Keck 2005: 372). Here it refers to several others, all women (v. 12). After Prisca and Aquila, who had worked together with Paul in both manual activity and the ministry of the gospel in Corinth and Ephesus (Acts 18:2-3), one of the first (married?) couples to be mentioned is Andronicus and Junia (16:7). It might also be possible that these were a missionary couple, even celibate co-workers. Macdonald offers a finely nuanced discussion of the many varied options that might be relevant to the status of travelling co-workers, and notes the relevance of Paul's insistence in 1 Cor. 9:5 on his right not to be accompanied by ἀδελφὴν γυναῖκα, a sister as wife or female traveling companion on his journeys (2011: 275–8).

Most, though not all, medieval scribes of manuscripts made Junias a man. Modern grammars explained the fact that although "Junia" was a common name in the Roman empire, while "Junias" did not exist, the hypothesis that Junias was a short form of "Junianus" (without being able to give evidence)[2] justified assuming Junias was a man, one of a male missionary couple. The fathers and mothers of the early church knew better, always identifying Andronicus's companion as the woman Junia or even Julia in P46 (Lampe 1991: 223). As other apostles mentioned in 1 Cor. 9:5, Andronicus and Junia may have traveled together as a missionary couple (cf. Fitzmyer 1993: 737, Moo 1996: 921–2). Junia's elevated status in the earliest days of the Christ-movement is evidence that the New Testament places "no restrictions on the ministry of women" (Moo 1996: 923). The most natural understanding of this couple's description as ἐπίσημοι ἐν τοῖς ἀποστόλοις is that they were both outstanding apostles (here surprisingly Keck gives no reason for limiting the reference to "apostles" to its generic use, "emissaries," 2005: 372). At some point, they had been Paul's fellow prisoners. Like Andronicus and Herodion, they too were kin, that is, Jews (συγγενή not necessarily Paul's relatives), though they had been at some point his "fellow prisoners."

---

[2] Cf. Eldon Jay Epp's comprehensive rebuttal of the view that Junia was the shortened form of a male name and the significance of its denial, see *Junia: The First Woman Apostle* (2005).

A significant and crucially important fact is that historically Andronicus and Junia are reported as being in Christ before Paul. Since Paul's call, in my view, can be dated no later than 35 CE (cf. Jewett 1979: 99–100), this means this couple were part of the Christ-community virtually from the start (Keck 2005: 372). This almost incidental detail brings us very close via Paul to the earliest days of the Christ-movement in Antioch or Damascus in a witness that involves a woman leader (Wolter 2019: 476–7). The significance of Prisca (notably mentioned first) and Aquila as hosting the only ἐκκλησία reported in Rome (as they had done earlier in Ephesus?) should not be overlooked in the Roman context where Phoebe arrives as the bearer and expositor of Paul's letter. This is in keeping with Paul's other incidental references (e.g., vv. 6-7, 12-13), which indicate the apostle's consciousness of the indebtedness of the Christ-movement, and the gentile mission in particular, to the toil of many dedicated women (Schüssler Fiorenza 1986: 420–3). The mutuality between Paul and Phoebe that emerges in Paul's commendation does not reflect an aberration but a constant concern for genuine mutuality in Christ between fellow workers irrespective of their gender.

Romans 16:3-16: Paul Requests the Roman Ethnē to Transmit Greetings to Numerous People in Rome

³Greet Prisca and Aquila, my co-workers in Christ Jesus, ⁴who risked their necks for my life, to whom not only I give thanks, but also all the assemblies of the ethnē. ⁵Greet also the assembly in their home. Greet my beloved Epaenetus, who was the first fruit for Christ in Asia. ⁶Greet Miriam, who has labored much for you. ⁷Greet Andronicus and Junia, my compatriots and fellow prisoners who are outstanding among the apostles, and who were in Christ before I was. ⁸Greet Ampliatus, my beloved in the Lord. ⁹Greet Urbanus, our co-worker in Christ, and my beloved Stachys. ¹⁰Greet Apelles, the approved one in Christ. Greet those among you who belong to the household of Aristobulus. ¹¹Greet my compatriot Herodion. Greet those from the household of Narcissus who belong to the Lord. ¹²Greet Tryphaena and Tryphosa the laborers in the Lord. Greet the beloved Persis, who has labored much in the Lord. ¹³Greet Rufus, the chosen in the Lord and also his mother— and mine. ¹⁴Greet Asyncritus, Phlegon, Hermes, Patrobas, Hermas, and the brothers, who are with them. ¹⁵Greet Philologus, Julia, Nereus and his sister, and Olympas, and all the saints with them. ¹⁶Greet one another with a holy kiss. All the assemblies of Christ greet you.

We next encounter the beginning of a long list of people to whom Paul commissions greetings via the Roman ethnē in Christ. These we assume are not the same group addressed in Rom. 1:7, otherwise this would be needless duplication (to specifically greet some separately after all had been addressed, and subsequently greeted directly at the end of the letter, would be strange). Those greeted here, most likely, therefore, were not included among "those from the nations called by Jesus Christ," and Paul requests that the addressees pass on his greetings to them. This request indicates that "instead of being descriptive of the letter's audience, these greetings suggest that the persons meant to be greeted should *not* be counted among those to whom Paul wrote the letter" (Thorsteinsson 2003: 98–9). Thorsteinson's insights on the passing on of greetings have been ignored, sometimes undervalued, but not invalidated. In fact, with this second-person type of greeting Paul is actually instructing the addressees of the letter to greet other parties who are not part of the congregations addressed (Mathew 2014 32–3). We need to distinguish between those asked to transmit greetings and those who are in fact the precise recipients of (these) greetings (Wolter 2019: 483). The imperative form of greeting has the effect of Paul's own greetings being extended to a third party and thus establishing a mutual bond between all three parties (Mathew 2014: 39). If Paul addresses non-Jews in Romans, and these others here greeted separately are Jews, this would help explain that greetings are sent because these Jewish Christ-followers have not been included among the specific addressees of the letter. It is noteworthy that at least six of these greeted here can be explicitly identified as Jewish.[3] Our proposal is that these greeted are Christ-followers, mainly of Jewish origin, who share Paul's understanding of the gospel in the gentile mission. We have no clear proof that they are Jewish, but we need otherwise to explain why they are greeted separately. We consider that they are identified for several reasons: to show that Paul knows, has worked with, and is accepted by these Christ-followers, and that they will likely be willing to give further support in the planned mission to Spain, a not insignificant factor. Another reason is to suggest, even demonstrate, that Paul is already a part of the social network through which the Christ-followers in Rome are connected with each other (Wolter 2019: 483). Such leaders and former associates in mission, almost exclusively Jewish who shared Paul's convictions, and who had previously co-operated with him in differing situations, were proof that Paul would not be totally dependent on the addressees but had already a support base in Rome.

The Function of Paul's Greetings

In order to glean as much as is possible from this chapter, we will try to analyze it with a view to discover how what Paul says about those to whom he gets greetings sent can inform us about their relation to each other in terms of meeting, worship together, and so on. Though he uses these greetings to commend not only Phoebe but also himself, it is justified to claim that Paul wants to confer recognition, even honor on these people (Jewett 2007: 952). He possibly presents them in certain groupings because they are known to belong to particular areas of the city, have certain work skills, and so on (cf. Wolter 2019: 470–1).

1. The first people greeted appear to consist of close personal friends and other workers in the Christ-movement who now reside in Rome. There is a total of

---

[3] Jewett rightly decides that "since Paul refers to the persons in this chapter with Greek, Latin, and Jewish names, I have decided to break with the Latinized tradition of commentaries and translations in a manner that reflects their distinctive cultural identities" (2007: 953). He identifies nineteen Greek names and eight Latin names with some six or seven Jewish identities (Andronikos, Aquila, Junia, Herodian, Rufus, Rufus's mother, with Miriam having a Jewish name also strongly attested in the diaspora).

fifteen of these, who include women such as Prisca, Miriam, Junia, and Rufus's mother. The majority of the names are Greek or Latin, with Miriam being the only obviously Jewish name, though Mary was also a well-attested Roman name.
2. The second group listed are leaders of assemblies (Jewett 2007: 953), but who Paul does not seem to know at firsthand. There are eleven of these, again some of them being women as, for example, Julia and Nereus's sister (15:15). Ollrog thinks that many of these persons had not been in touch with Paul, he knows of them only through hearsay (1979: 236–41).
3. The third group are leaders of five house or tenement assemblies whose members Paul does not know, only their leaders:
   a. the ἐκκλησία in the οἰκία (home) of Prisca and Aquila (16:5a), the most prominent of those mentioned;
   b. those of the household (slaves) of Aristobulus (16:10.b);
   c. those of the household (slaves) of Narkissos (16:11b);
   d. the brothers who are with Asynkritos[4] et al. (16:14b); and
   e. the saints who are with Philologos et al. (16:15b).

It is noteworthy that the term συγγενεῖς, kin (v. 7) occurs also in vv. 11 and 21 (cf. also 9:3). There is some agreement concerning the recognition of these five groupings as Christ-groups (if not ἐκκλησίαι), for example, by Lampe, who considers that the rest of the names in ch. 16 imply at least two other groups (household slaves and dependents of Aristobulus or of Narcissus),[5] and that Paul may have founded another group when he arrived in Rome. I agree concerning the seven groups, but not to the latter proposal as this suggests (improbable) Pauline interference (1991: 229–30).

Meeting Places: Homes (Slaves in Households of the Rich), Rented Houses, Tabernae, and Tenements

On this reckoning, we have at least twenty-six people of the Christ-followers known by name in Rome with another seven groups of which we only know the leaders' names. These include Prisca and Aquila, Paul's "fellow-workers who risked their lives for [his] sake" (16:3). If they plied the same trade as Paul (Murphy O'Connor 1996: 49),[6] the "home in the house" here could indicate the workshop (*taberna*) or some part of a building necessary also for trade purposes, with living space included. This need not indicate the building was owned rather than merely rented—since this couple seemed to be very mobile. The οἶκοι in which their ἐκκλησίαι met in Rome as in Ephesus were most likely *tabernae* (i.e. workshops). The formula, "the at the home of X

---

[4] Since no patron is identified for these men and those with them, this omission indicates an egalitarian "tenement church" (Jewett 2007: 971), but Oakes considers that even a group meeting in rented accommodation, whether an upper apartment or a ground floor *taberna* would have required a host (2009: 92).

[5] These were probably not Christ-followers, otherwise Paul would have greeted them by name. If Aristobulus here refers to the grandson of Herod the Great, he would have been dead already (around 45 CE) by this time, but his household could have retained his identity.

[6] On *tabernae* as possible meeting places for Christ-following groups, see Adams (2013: 43–4).

church," certainly refers to someone's home, though οἶκος, οἰκία can refer to a variety of dwellings, not only to houses strictly understood, and it is likely that Philemon's house would not have been very large even though it contained an ξενία or guest room (Adams 2013: 17–39).

It is hard to evaluate the significance of the fact that only one ἐκκλησία is mentioned; τὴν κατ᾽ οἶκον αὐτῶν ἐκκλησίαν, "in the house of X assembly" occurs only four times in the entire Pauline corpus. Rom. 16:3-5 is connected with 1 Cor. 16:19 since the reference is also to the church in the house of Aquila and Prisca (this time in Ephesus). There is one other reference to the church in Philemon's house (v. 2), and one in Col. 4:15 where Nympha is greeted along with τὴν κατ᾽ οἶκον αὐτῆς ἐκκλησίαν. We take the other people mentioned in Romans 16 as representing groups equivalent to the group meeting in the οἰκία of Aquila and Prisca, but this does not indicate that these met in a home—it only tells us that they are somehow connected with one another by area of residence or place of meeting. How they are listed in groups seems to suggest Paul compiled his list with some rationale in mind. It seems that he has some information or knowledge that causes him to list them together. It could be that they live near each other, are related, or work in similar trades. We do not know the rationale for Paul's grouping, though contextual, geographical location and trade connections may be reflected. We will not at this point, reconsider the topic of associations already discussed in the "Introduction" chapter, though this topic has particular relevance at this stage in our commentary. This relevance is related to the possible umbrella organization under which the gentile Christ-followers may regularly have assembled, and to what extent it implied some connection/affiliation with the synagogue.

With a population in Rome of at least one million, it would have been practically impossible to operate one central organization across the city given the distance. Since Romans is a letter only to the non-Jews, then we are seeking to identify how these Christ-followers were connected with one another for worship or communal meals as we consider they possibly may have been.

One feature of note is that two of the five groupings consist of "those who belong to the household of Aristobulus (possibly the grandson of Herod the Great) or of Narcissus. This sequence may explain why Herodion is mentioned immediately after those who belong to the household of Aristobulus, who, perhaps was a freedman who, as was customary, took on the name of his former owner, somehow a member of the Herod family. After those who belong to the household of Aristobulus, Paul greets those who belong to the household of Narcissus. Together, the presence of Roman Christ-followers in these two households offers evidence that the Christ-movement had penetrated already two households of the upper social strata in Rome though not those strata themselves (Keck 2005: 373).

Another interesting feature of Paul's terminology in 16:16b is that Paul states "All the assemblies of Christ greet you." This designation is in accord with the ἐκκλησία in the house of Priscilla and Aquila, but none of the other groups are designated thus! Is this purely accidental, or are we missing something from Paul's categorization? It is somewhat strange to find a unique formulation without ethnic signification some twelve verses after the specific ethnic emphasis of 16:4, "all the assemblies of the ethnē."

Are "all the assemblies of Christ" different from these, and if so in what respects? Does this signify Paul being careless, or is he introducing a new designation stressing unity? But the important fact to note is that Paul here feels justified in passing on greetings from all the ἐκκλησίαι of the ethnē. At the end of his long letter, he emerges, as he introduced himself in ch. 1, thereby giving himself significant but warranted status, as one qualified to speak on behalf of all the ἐκκλησίαι, as the recipient of grace and apostleship to bring about the response of trust among all nations, apostle to the ethnē (1:5-6). As such his status and success among "all the ἐκκλησίαι of the ethnē" is publicly proclaimed, demanding an appropriate response in Rome.

Romans 16:17-20: Warning and Assurance

17I appeal to you, brothers, to look out for those who stir up dissentions and enticements, contrary to the teaching that you have learned; steer away from them. 18For such people do not serve our Lord Christ, but their own belly, and through their smooth talk and flattery they deceive the hearts of the simple-minded. 19For while your hearing in trust has extended to all, therefore I rejoice over you, I want you to be wise in what is good and innocent with regard to what is evil. 20And the God of peace will crush Satan under your feet, and soon. The grace of our Lord Jesus be with you.

The reason why we have chosen to deal separately with these verses is because there is some reason for considering they may be an interpolation, not a part of the original letter. The most important factor is because both the location of this paragraph and its content are unexpected, irrespective of whether it is accepted or not as genuine. Jewett gives the strongest case for recognizing this as an interpolation (2007: 986–8, cf. also Keck 2005: 375–9). Primary in his rationale is vv. 19-20a, which in contrast to other Pauline blessings "is a kind of curse related to the crushing of demonic heretics under the feet of true believers." There was some indication of harsh language already in 16:18, which offered a rather stereotypical description of the heretics criticized in terms more typical of later polemics—they "do not serve our Lord Christ, but their own appetites and by smooth talk and flattery they deceive the hearts of the simple-minded." These are not the typical theological criticisms of Paul anywhere else in Romans or his other letters. The sharp and authoritarian tone reflected in the admonitions against the schismatics in 16:17-20 contrasts vividly with the more irenic and solicitous tone of chs. 1–15 (Longenecker 2011: 23).

Also, in a letter where Paul has exercised much caution and reserve in expressing his opinions, it seems strange that he should be so extremely outspoken at this point. Already in 6:17 Paul acknowledged that the Romans "responded from the heart to the imprint of the teaching to which you were committed," which I take to mean that he himself agrees with this "imprint of teaching." And in 14:1–15:13 they were called upon to accept one another without disputing, but never were they told to avoid those with differing opinions, as in 16:17. In ch. 15:14, Paul has affirmed that the Romans are "full of goodness, filled with all knowledge, and able to instruct one another," whereas as Ziesler claims, "the most startling thing about 16:17-20 is … the fact that in them

Paul does not argue. He simply denounces." (1989: 353). Nor can any valid connections be established between "the weak" in chs 14–15 and those whose god or appetites is "their own belly" (v. 18). Decisively, there is a real contrast between all that precedes and the tone and content of this section.

The only possible, convincing explanation for the change of tone and content is that those referred to here are recent arrivals from elsewhere, and Paul has just been given this information near the conclusion of dictating his letter, responding in a postscript (cf. Weima 1994, Marshall 1999). We have not found specific opponents of any kind among the Romans. Only in readings where diatribal style is interpreted as polemical can opponents be envisaged (see Excursus I). I resist, therefore, speaking of interfering "teachers" or such lest I give credence to the proposal of entities that are in my view, lacking in solid foundation, but which can theoretically be posited to warrant certain discussions of the content of Romans.

However, is there any passage in Romans that actually gives evidence of teaching being offered contrary to Paul's teaching? The diatribal style that is typical of certain parts of the letter might offer a possible candidate for introducing contrary teachings to Paul, for example, "Let us remain in sin so that grace may proliferate?" (6:1). "Should we sin because we are not under law, but under grace?" (6:15). "What then should we say? The law is (the source) of sin, is it not?" (7:7). Such questions in diatribal exchange could indicate the presence of extreme opponents of Paul if taken literally. So, one possibility that may have encouraged the positing of radical opponents of Paul is a misunderstanding of the function of these questions aside from their rejection and or modification by Paul. But such a reading is to misunderstand Paul, and not to discern that it is Paul himself who introduces these stances only to deny them validity, even if they are not entirely without some possible basis in reality. But the basis in reality would be the opinions and practice of the ethnē themselves, not that of supposed opponents. Indeed, I think it possible that the sharp rejection of diatribal questions may offer a link between the body of Romans and the unexpectedly sharp tones of 16:17-20. But this would offer a reason for the interpolation rather than Pauline authorship?

Manuscript Evidence Relevant to Interpolation Theories

Other textual issues arise in relation to the placing of the doxology at 16:25-27 as in most manuscripts, or at the end of ch. 15 (i.e., at 15:33). Longenecker's summary clarifies the variation, "All of our present Greek MSS contain the long form of Romans, that is, 1.1-16.27, though they vary somewhat with regard to the various grace benedictions[7] at 16.20b, 16.24 and/or 16.28 (i.e. after the final doxology" (2011: 20 1).

However, there is good manuscript evidence that already in P46, the second of the Chester Beatty Papyri held in Trinity College Dublin, one of the earliest and most reliable of New Testament manuscripts,[8] chs. 1–14 are followed by 15:1-33

---

[7] In Paul's formulation of the first-century Hellenistic letter pattern, the grace benediction functions as the final wish (cf. Mathew 2014: 27).
[8] This dates from about 200 CE and contains extensive portions of the text of Romans covering 5:17–6:14, 8:15–15:9, and 15:11–16:27 (Longenecker 2011: 18).

but 16:25-27 surprisingly precedes 16:1-23, and is duplicated after 16:27. This may indicate that if the interpolation of 16:17-20 happened, it did so at an early date. As Keck states, "Since no manuscript lacks this paragraph, it must have been added before Paul's letters were compiled" (2005: 379). Wolter helpfully sets out the manuscript evidence that is supportive of the traditional text (2019: 17–23, cf. also his summary of the [limited] evidence for 16:17-20 as interpolation, 2019: 26–7). Wolter considers that too much has been read into Paul's warning here. He does not think that it (the warning) is based on solid information received from Rome, but rather that it reveals that Paul was not fully informed about the situation at Rome (2019: 494). It is clear that Paul warns generally against those who create unrest and produce divisions (17b), but he does not give further information about theological or other stances. (Wolter 2019: 487). The diatribal questions and reactions might point to Paul's suspicions of misunderstanding of his actions and theology, but may also indicate that he does not know with sufficient detail or accuracy to be able to say anything more in public.

It is sufficient for the interests and purposes of this commentary to note the evidence for and against an interpolation here (16:17-20) and at 16:25-27, and to show that the outcome of this investigation does not invalidate what we have written about Romans since no major premises or conclusions are based upon it, or invalidated by it. Also, our consideration of these verses demonstrates that they do not offer a substantial basis for regarding their sharp denunciation as in any way typical of Paul's otherwise irenic approach to the Romans, or a credible adequate basis for positing opponents of Paul.

They can be read in relation to the long list of commended people earlier in the chapter. Paul has stated clearly that these are trustworthy people with many of whom he has shared much successful cooperative activity, and hopefully will yet share, in the work of God. He is offering the ethnē in Christ at Rome excellent models to follow, and he does not want them to follow any guidance contrary to these, and the long letter that he has written. "He needed the Gentile believers in Rome to place themselves [on his terms] on the map of God's purposes for Israel and the world" (Barclay 2015: 158, n19).

Here I disagree with Douglas Campbell's substantial discussion of 16:17-20 in association with Phil. 3:2–4:3 and related texts in that I am not convinced that the evidence for his theorizing about opponents is easily discernible whether in Romans 2 or Rom. 16:17-20 (2014: 49–50, 141–44).[9] As Wolter notes, even the crushing of Satan "under your feet" is posited as God's activity, not that of the Romans (2019: 492–3).

The textual evidence for Romans 14–16 reveals numerous diversities and twists throughout its history in the period after Marcion, which explain part of its anomalies, but which must not be overlooked as if there were not still unanswered and abiding textual questions at certain points. But the manuscript evidence for Romans as a whole

---

[9] This is not to dismiss the merit of Campbell's project in *Framing Paul* (2014) as, for example, in his Chapter One, but I cannot possibly do justice to such comprehensive challenges in the minimum space available at this point.

is extremely strong in favor of the established text. On this, see the comprehensive overview, "Major Text-Critical Issues Today," by Longenecker (2011: 30–42).

Romans 16:21-23: Paul Conveys Greetings from Colleagues with Him

²¹Timothy, my co-worker, greets you as also do Lucius and Jason and Sosipater, my compatriots.
²²I Tertius, who wrote this letter, greet you in the Lord.
²³Gaius, my host along with the whole assembly, greets you. Erastus, the city treasurer, and our brother Quartus, greet you.

Alongside the list of people greeted in 16:1-16, Paul in 16:21-23, sends greetings from friends with him in Corinth from whence Paul sends this letter. Here, it is Paul himself who passes on the greetings rather than requesting the Romans to transmit them. Timothy, his co-worker is mentioned first, then three fellow countrymen; Tertius, the letter-writer, sends his own greeting as well as Gaius who is Paul's host as for many others. Erastus, the city treasurer, host to the entire ἐκκλησία, and brother Quartus also send greetings.

These varied greetings indicate that Paul operates in relation to "small group networks" common among Jews and other ethnic minorities, as we have already noted in relation to 15:14-33 (Collar 2013: 229). He is not a lone apostle but a collegial person who is closely attached to many co-workers. They greet each other as a group involved in the same enterprise, an activity that is not of their own creation, the "work of God," who through Christ is the Lord and Master of them all. They are his co-workers in the gentile branch of the family of God through Christ their elder brother (Rom. 8:29), though only Aquila, Prisca, and Urbanus are given prominence as co-workers of Paul by the use of the term συνέργος (Lampe 1991: 228). Whatever their previous history in the Christ-movement, this large group of over twenty people (and their associates) are referred to affectionately and encouragingly by Paul, bringing to memory again some of the previous activities and experiences they had shared over a number of years.

The number of named persons to whom greetings are sent in Romans is unique among Paul's letters. The second-person plural imperative ἀσπάσασθε ("you pl. greet") is repeated no less than fifteen times in 16:1-16. This seems surprising since Paul has not yet visited Rome, but perhaps it is this very fact that helps explain the extent of the greetings. As his letter demonstrates, Paul does not write as a complete stranger to Rome. He wants to show that he is not unacquainted with the Romans but has many fellow workers, friends, even relatives in Rome. The fact that in a number of instances Paul relates part of his past shared experiences denotes significant connections in the service of God. Even if it was not in Rome itself, Paul in the course of the gentile mission has worked closely with people now living in Rome. This demonstration of Paul's shared experiences in the gentile mission with named people, presumably in good standing with the Romans, acts as verification of Paul's previous activity and their approbation of it.

Romans 16:25-27: The Final Doxology

> ²⁵Now to the one who is able to strengthen you according to my gospel and the proclamation of Jesus Christ, according to the revelation of the mystery that was kept secret through the ages ²⁶but is now revealed, and through the prophetic writings is made known to all the ethnē, according to the command of the eternal God, to bring about the hearing in trust—²⁷to the only wise God, through Jesus Christ, to whom be the glory forever! Amen.

Despite the fact that there is some doubt as to the location of these verses or even if they are original to the letter as we have it (Jewett 2007: 997), this doxology is consistent with the content of the letter. The important theme of hearing and responding in trust to the divine revelation in Christ by the ethnē is like a bracket to the entire letter (Rom. 1:5) confirming that Paul addresses non-Jews in Christ only, and his clarifications and elaborations of the gospel are thus directed to, and significant for, those from the nations. Despite the significance of Christology throughout this letter, this final doxology is directed to the one and only God, who is able to strengthen them, and who is the one who through the prophetic writings revealed himself through Christ to the ethnē. So, the final emphasis repeats the theocentric focus of the entire letter. The Christ event is intrinsically linked to the entire history of Israel, at the heart of which is the God of Israel and Creation who works in all things for good. It is to him that this doxology is fittingly addressed indicating that what is final for Paul is the glory of God.

References

Abel, Frantisek, ed. (2021) *Israel and the Nations: Paul's Gospel in the Context of Jewish Expectation*, Lanham, MD: Lexington/Fortress Academic.
Abrams, Dominic, and Michael A. Hogg (1988). *Social Identifications: A Social Psychology of Intergroup Relations and Group Processes*. London: Taylor & Francis.
Achtemeier, Paul J. (1985). *Romans: Interpretation: A Bible Commentary for Teaching and Preaching*. Atlanta, GA: John Knox Press.
Achtemeier, Paul J. (1990). "Omne verbum sonat: The New Testament and the Oral Environment of Late Western Antiquity," *Journal of Biblical Literature* 109.1, 3–27.
Adams, Edward (1997). "Abraham's Faith and Gentile Disobedience: Textual Links between Romans 1 and 4," *Journal for the Study of the New Testament* 65: 47–66.
Adams, Edward (2000). *Constructing the World: A Study of Paul's Cosmological Language*. Edinburgh: T&T Clark.
Adams, Edward (2013). *The Earliest Christian Meeting Places: Almost Exclusively Houses?* London: Bloomsbury.
Aletti, Jean-Noël (1998). *Commentary to the Letter to the Romans*. Collegeville, MN: Liturgical Press.
Aletti, Jean-Noël (2011). "Interpreting Romans 11:14: What Is at Stake," in *Celebrating Paul: Festschrift in Honor of Jerome Murphy O'Connor and Joseph A. Fitzmyer*, ed. Peter Spitaler. Washington, DC: Catholic Biblical Association of America, 245–64.
Anderson, R. Dean (1999). *Ancient Rhetorical Theory*. Leuven: Peeters.
Ando, Clifford (2019). "Race and Citizenship in Roman Law and Administration," in *Xenofobia y Racismo en el Mundo Antiguo*. Barcelona: Edicions de la Universitat de Barcelona.
Arendt, Hannah (1958). *The Human Condition*. Chicago, IL: Chicago University Press.
Ascough, Richard (2015). "Paul, Synagogues, and Associations: Reframing the Question of Models for Pauline Christ Groups," *Journal of the Jesus Movement in its Jewish Setting* 2: 27–52.
Ascough, Richard S., Philip A. Harland, and John S. Kloppenborg (2012). *Associations in the Greco-Roman World: A Sourcebook*. Waco, TX: Baylor University Press.
Aune, David E. (1987). *The New Testament in its Literary Environment*. Philadelphia, PA: Westminster Press.
Aune, David E. (1991). "Romans as Logos Protreptikos," in *The Romans Debate*, ed. Karl P. Donfried. Peabody, MA: Hendrickson, 278–98.
Aus, Roger D. (1979). "Paul's Travel Plans to Spain and the 'Full Number of the Gentiles'", *Novum Testamentum* 21: 232–62.
Avemarie, Friedrich (2014). "The Notion of a 'New Covenant' in 2 Corinthians 3: Its Function in Paul's Argument and Its Jewish Background," in *Second Corinthians in the Perspective of Late Second Temple Judaism*, eds. Reimund Bieringer, Emmanuel Nathan, Didier Pollefey, and Peter J. Tomson. Leiden: Brill, 59–78.
Badenas, Robert (1985). *Christ, the End of the Law. Romans 10.4 in Pauline Perspective*. Sheffield: JSOT Press.

Bailey, Daniel P. (2000). "Jesus as the Mercy Seat: The Semantics and Theology of Paul's Use of Hilasterion in Romans 3:15," *Tyndale Bulletin* 51.1: 155–8.
Baker, Coleman, and J. Brian Tucker, eds. (2014). *The T&T Clark Handbook to Social Identity in the New Testament*. London: Bloomsbury.
Bakhos, Carol (2014). *The Family of Abraham: Jewish, Christian and Muslim Interpretations*. Cambridge, MA: Harvard University Press.
Barclay, John M. G. (2013). "Under Grace: The Christ-Gift and the Construction of a Christian *Habitus*," in *Apocalyptic Paul: Cosmos and Anthropos in Romans 5–8*, ed. Beverly Roberts Gaventa. Waco, TX: Baylor University Press, 59–76.
Barclay, John M. G. (2015). *Paul and the Gift*. Grand Rapids, MI: Eerdmans.
Barentsen, Jack (2011). *Emerging Leadership in the Pauline Mission: A Social Identiy Perspective on Local Leadership Development in Corinth and Ephesus*. Eugene, OR: Pickwick.
Barrett, Charles Kingsley (1957). *A Commentary on the Epistle to the Romans*. New York: Harper.
Barrett, Charles Kingsley (1962). *From First Adam to Last: A Study of Pauline Theology*. London: A&C Black.
Bar-Tal, Daniel (1990). *Group Beliefs. A Conception for Analysing Group Structure, Processes and Behavior*. Heidelberg: Springer.
Bar-Tal, Daniel (2000). *Shared Beliefs in a Society: Social Psychological Analysis*. Thousand Oaks, CA: Sage.
Bartchy, S. Scott (2005). "When I'm Weak, I'm Strong; A Pauline Paradox in Cultural Context," in *Kontexte der Schrift Band II: Kultur, Politik, Religion, Sprache—Text, Wolfgang Stegemann zum 60. Geburtstag*, ed. Christian Strecker. Stuttgart: Kohlhammer Verlag, 49–60.
Barth, Karl (1957). *Church Dogmatics* II.2. London: T&T Clark.
Barth, Markus (1969). "The Faith of the Messiah," *Heythrop Journal* 10: 363–70.
Barth, Markus (1974). *Ephesians 1–3. A New Translation with Introduction and Commentary*. New York: Doubleday.
Barth, Markus (1982). *St. Paul, the Good Jew*. Sheffield: Sheffield Academic Press.
Barth, Markus (1983). *The People of God*. Sheffield: Sheffield Academic Press.
Barth, Ulrich (2021). *Symbole des Christentums: Berliner Dogmatik Vorlesung*. Tübingen: Mohr Siebeck.
Barton, Carlin A. (2001). *Roman Honor: The Fire In the Bones*. Berkeley, CA: University of California Press.
Bartsch, Hans Werner (1967). "Die antisemitischen Gegner des Paulus im Römerbrief," in *Antijudaismus im Neuen Testament?* eds. Willehard Eckert, Nathan P. Levinson and Martin Stöhr, München: Kaiser, 27–43.
Bartsch, Hans Werner (1968). "Die historische Situation des Römerbriefes," *Studia Evangelica IV*: 281–91.
Bauer, Walter (1988). *Griechisch-Deutsches Wörterbuch zu den Schriften des Neuen Testaments und der Frühchristlichen Literatur*. Berlin: de Gruyter.
Baumgarten, Albert (2021). "Mary Douglas Memorial Lecture: Sectarian Factions in Ancient Judaism," Lecture held and recorded on May 26, 2021, https://www.academia.edu/49083392/Mary_Douglas_Memorial_Lecture_Sectarian_Factions_in_Ancient_Judaism, accessed May 18, 2022.
Baur, Ferdinand Christian (2003). *Paul the Apostle of Jesus Christ: His Life and Works, His Epistles and Teachings*. Originally published 1873. Peabody, MA: Hendrickson.

Beale, Gregory K. (1989). "The Old Testament Background of Reconciliation in 2 Corinthians 5–7 and Its Bearing on the Literary Problem of 2 Corinthians 6.14-7.1," *New Testament Studies* 35.4: 550–81.
Beker, J. Christiaan (1980). *Paul the Apostle: The Triumph of God in Life and Thought*. Philadelphia, PA: Fortress Press.
Beker, J. Christiaan (1986). "The Faithfulness of God and the Priority of Israel in Paul's Letter to the Romans," in *Christians among Jews and Gentiles. Essays in Honor of Krister Stendhal on his 65th Birthday*, eds. George W. E. Nickelsburg and George W. MacRae. Philadelphia, PA: Fortress Press, 10–16.
Bell, Richard H. (1994). *Provoked to Jealousy: The Origin and Purpose of the Jealousy Motif in Romans 9–11*. Tübingen: Mohr Siebeck.
Berthelot, Katell (2011). "Philo's Perception of the Roman Empire," *Journal for the Study of Judaism* 42.2: 166–87.
Berthelot, Katell (2016). "The Rabbis Write Back! L'Enjeu de la 'parente' entre Israel-Rome Edom," *Revue de L'histoire des religions* 2: 165–9.
Berthelot, Katell (2021). *Jews and Their Roman Rivals: Pagan Rome's Challenge to Israel*. Princeton, NJ: Princeton University Press.
Bjerkelund, Carl J. (1967). *Parakalo: Form und Funktion der Parakalo-Sätze in den paulinischen Briefen*. Oslo: Univeristätsverlag.
Black, Matthew (1974). *Romans*. New Century Bible. London: Oliphants.
Bodel, John (2017). "Death and Social Death in Ancient Rome," in *On Human Bondage: After Slavery and Social Death*, eds. John Bodel and Walter Scheidel. Hoboken, NJ: John Wiley, 81–108.
Bodel, John, and Walter Scheidel, eds. (2017). *On Human Bondage: After Slavery and Social Death*. Hoboken, NJ: John Wiley.
Bodenhausen, Galen V. (2010). "Diversity in the Person, Diversity in the Group: Challenges of Identity Complexity for Social Perception and Social Interaction," *European Journal of Social Psychology* 40: 1–16.
Bornkamm, Günther (1969). *Early Christian Experience*. London: SCM.
Bornkamm, Günther (1971). *Paul*. New York: Harper & Row.
Bornkamm, Günther (1991). "The Letter to the Romans as Paul's Last Will and Testament," in *The Romans Debate*, ed. Karl P. Donfried. Peabody, MA: Hendrickson, 16–28.
Brandenburger, Egon (1962). *Adam und Christus: Exegetisch-religionsgeschichtliche Untersuchung zu Röm. 5,12-21 (1. Kor. 15)*. Neukirchen-Vluyn: Neukirchener Verlag.
Brawley, Robert L. (2020). *Luke: A Social Identity Commentary*. London: T&T Clark.
Bremmer, Jan N. (2013). "Post Scriptum: Virgil and Jewish Literature," *Vergilius* 59: 157–64.
Brewer, Marilynn B. (2007). "The Importance of Being We: Human Nature and Intergroup Relations," *American Psychologist*, Nov.: 728–38.
Brewer, Marilynn B. (2010). "Social Identity Complexity and Acceptance of Diversity," in *The Psychology of Social and Cultural Diversity*, ed. Richard J. Crisp. Hoboken, NJ: Blackwell, 11–33.
Brewer, Marilynn, and Kathleen P. Pierce (2005). "Social Identity Complexity and Outgroup Tolerance," *Personality and Social Psychology Bulletin* 31.3: 428–37.
Breytenbach, Cilliers (1989). *Versöhnung. Eine Studie zur paulinischen Soteriologie*. Neukirchen-Vluyn: Neukirchener Verlag.
Brodie, Thomas L., Dennis R. MacDonald, and Stanley E. Porter, eds. (2006). *The Intertextuality of the Epistles: Explorations of Theory and Practice*. Sheffield: Phoenix Press.

Brooten, Bernadette. "Slavery," in *Encyclopedia of Jewish-Christian Relations*, eds. Walter Homolka, Amy-Jill Levine, Rainer Kampling, Amy-Jill Levine, Christoph Markschies, Peter Schäfer, and Martin Thurner. Berlin: de Gruyter, online resource.

Brown, Raymond E. (1983). "Not Jewish Christianity and Gentile Christianity, but Types of Jewish/Gentile Christianity," *Catholic Biblical Quarterly* 45: 74–9.

Brown, Raymond E., and J. P. Meier (1983). *Antioch and Rome: New Testament Cradles of Catholic Christianity*. New York: Paulist Press.

Bruce, Frederick F. (1981). "Anthony Tyrell Hanson: A Tribute", Essays in Honour of Anthony Tyrell Hanson, *Journal for the Study of the New Testament* 13: 3–8.

Brueggemann, Walter (1977a). *The Land: Place as Gift, Promise, and Challenge in Biblical Faith*. Philadelphia, PA: Fortress Press.

Brueggemann, Walter (1997b). *Theology of the Old Testament. Testimony, Dispute, Advocacy*. Minneapolis, MN: Fortress Press.

Buber, Martin (1937). *I and Thou*. Edinburgh: T&T Clark.

Bultmann, Rudolf (1910). *Der Stil der paulinischen Predigt und die kynisch-stoische Diatribe*. Göttingen: Vandenhoeck & Ruprecht.

Byron, John (2003). *Slavery Metaphors in Early Judaism and Pauline Christianity. A Tradition Historical and Exegetical Examination*. Tübingen: Mohr Siebeck.

Campbell, Douglas A. (2009). *The Deliverance of God: An Apocalyptic Reading of Justification in Paul*. Grand Rapids, MI: Eerdmans.

Campbell, Douglas A. (2014). *Framing Paul. An Epistolary Biography*. Grand Rapids, MI: Eerdmans.

Campbell, William S. (1979). "Paul's Use of the Old Testament in Romans 9–11," paper presented at the SNTS Annual Meeting, Durham, UK.

Campbell, William S. (1981). "Romans III as a Key to the Structure and Thought of the Letter," *Novum Testamentum* 23: 22–40.

Campbell, William S. (1982), 'The Place of Romans 9-11 within the Structure and Thought of the Letter', *Studia Evangelica*, Vol.VII, 90-99,Akademie Verlag: Berlin.

Campbell, William S. (1990). "Did Paul Advocate Separation from the Synagogue?" *Scottish Journal of Theology* 42: 457–67.

Campbell, William S. (1991a). *Paul's Gospel in an Intercultural Context: Jew and Gentile in the Letter to the Romans*. Bern, Paris: Peter Lang.

Campbell, William S. (1991b). "Romans III as a Key to the Structure and Thought of the Letter," in *The Romans Debate*, ed. Karl P. Donfried. Peabody, MA: Hendrickson, 251–65.

Campbell, William S. (1995). "The Rule of Faith in Romans 12:1–15:13," in *Pauline Theology*, vol. 3, eds. David M. Hay and E. Johnson. Minneapolis, MN: Augsburg Fortress Press, 259–86.

Campbell, William S. (2000). "Divergent Images of Paul and His Mission," in *Reading Israel in Romans: Legitimacy and Plausibility of Divergent Interpretations*. Romans Through History and Cultures Series, vol. I, eds. Cristina Grenholm and Daniel Patte. Harrisburg, PA: Trinity Press International, 187–211.

Campbell, William S. (2006). *Paul and the Creation of Christian Identity*. London: T&T Clark International.

Campbell, William S. (2007). "Reading Romans in Conversation with Medieval Interpreters: The Challenge of Cross-Fertilization," in *Medieval Readings of Romans*. Romans Through History and Cultures Series, eds. William S. Campbell, Peter S. Hawkins, and Brenda Deen Schildgen. London: T&T Clark, 202–12.

Campbell, William S. (2008). "Built on Tradition but Not Bound by Tradition," in *Reformation Readings of Romans*, Romans Through History and Cultures Series, eds. Kathy Ehrensperger and R. Ward Holder. London: T&T Clark, 166–70.
Campbell, William S. (2010). "The Addressees of Paul's Letter to the Romans: Assemblies of God in House Churches and Synagogues?" in *Between Gospel and Election*, eds. Florian Wilk and J. Ross Wagner. Tübingen: Mohr Siebeck, 171–95.
Campbell, William S. (2013). *Unity and Diversity in Christ: Interpreting Paul in Context. Collected Essays*. Eugene, OR: Wipf & Stock.
Campbell, William S. (2015). "'A Remnant of Them Will Be Saved' (Rom 9:27): Understanding Paul's Conception of the Faithfulness of God to Israel," *Journal of the Jesus Movement in Its Jewish Setting* 2: 79–101.
Campbell, William S. (2016). "Reading Paul in Relation to Judaism: Comparison or Contrast?" in *Early Christianity within the Boundaries of Judaism: Essays in Honor of Bruce Chilton*, eds. Leslie Avery-Peck, Craig Evans, and Jacob Neusner. Leiden: Brill, 120–50.
Campbell, William S. (2018). *The Nations in the Divine Economy: Paul's Covenantal Hermeneutics and Participation in Christ*. Lanham, MD: Lexington/Fortress Academic.
Campbell, William S. (2019). "Fulfilment Language in Paul," paper presented at the SBL Annual Meeting, Boston, MA.
Campbell, William S. (2021). "But It Is Not as Though the Word of God Had Failed: Israel as a Sub-Text in Romans," in *Israel and the Nations. Paul's Gospel in the Context of Jewish Expectation*, ed. František Abel. Lanham, MD: Lexington/Fortress Academic, 165–86.
Caragounis, Chrys C. (1985). "Romans 5.15-16 in the Context of 5.12-21: Contrast or Comparison?" *New Testament Studies* 31: 142–8.
Carter, Warren (2006). *The Roman Empire and the New Testament*. Nashville, TN: Abingdon Press.
Carter, Warren (2008). *John and Empire: Initial Explorations*. London: T&T Clark.
Casson, Sarah Helen (2019). *Textual Signposts in the Argument of Romans: A Relevance Theory Approach*. Atlanta, GA: SBL Press.
Ciampa, Roy (2008). "Scriptural Language and Ideas," in *As It Is Written: Studying Paul's Use of Scripture*, eds. Stanley Porter and Christopher D. Stanley. Atlanta, GA: Society of Biblical Literature, 41–57.
Clarke, Andrew, and J. Brian Tucker (2014). "Social History and Social Theory in the Study of Social Identity," in *T&T Clark Handbook to Social Identity in the New Testament*, eds. Coleman Baker and J. Brian Tucker, London: T&T Clark, 41–57.
Cohen, Naomi (1995). *Philo Judeaus: His Universe of Discourse*. New York: Peter Lang.
Cohen, Shaye J. D. (1989). "Crossing the Boundary and Becoming a Jew," *Harvard Theological Review*, 82.1: 13–33.
Cohen, Shaye J. D. (1994). "Judaism at the Time of Jesus," in *Jews and Christians Speak of Jesus*, ed. Arthur Zannoni. Minneapolis, MN: Fortress Press, 3–12.
Cohen, Shaye J. D. (1999). *The Beginnings of Jewishness*. Berkeley, CA: University of California Press.
Coleman, Thomas M. (1997). "Binding Obligations in Romans 13.7: A Semantic Field and Social Context," *Tyndale Bulletin* 48.2: 307–27.
Collar, Anna (2013). *Religious Networks in the Roman Empire: The Spread of New Ideas*. Cambridge: Cambridge University Press.
Collins, Adele Yarbro (2019). "The Metaphorical Use of ἱλαστήριον in Romans 3:25," in *Soteria: Salvations in Early Christianity and Antiquity. Festschrift in Honor of Cilliers*

Breytenbach on the Occasion of his 65th Birthday, eds. David Du Toit, Christine Gerber, and Christiane Zimmermann. Leiden: Brill, 273–86.
Cranfield, Charles E. B. (1975). *A Critical and Exegetical Commentary on the Epistle to the Romans*, vol. I. Edinburgh: T&T Clark.
Cranfield, Charles E. B. (1979). *A Critical and Exegetical Commentary on the Epistle to the Romans*, vol. II. Edinburgh: T&T Clark.
Cranfield, Charles E. B. (1980). "Romans 9:30–10:4," *Interpretation: A Journal of Bible and Theology* 34.1: 70–4.
Cranfield, Charles E. B. (1985). *Romans: A Shorter Commentary*. Edinburgh: T&T Clark.
Dabourne, Wendy (1999). *Purpose and Cause in Pauline Exegesis: Romans 1.16-4.25 and a New Approach to the Letters*. Cambridge: Cambridge University Press.
Dahl, Nils Alstrup (1976). *Jesus in the Memory of the Early Church: Essays*. Minneapolis, MN: Augsburg Publishing.
Dahl, Nils Alstrup (1977). *Studies in Paul: Theology for the Early Christian Mission*. Minneapolis, MN: Augsburg Publishing.
Das, Andrew (2007). *Paul and the Jews*. Peabody, MA: Hendrickson.
Das, Andrew (2012). "The Gentile-Encoded Audience of Romans: The Church Outside the Synagogue," in *Reading Paul's Letter to the Romans*, ed. Jerry L. Sumney. Atlanta, GA: SBL, 29–46.
Davis, Stephan (2002). *The Antithesis of the Ages: Paul's Reconfiguration of Torah*. Washington, DC: The Catholic Biblical Association of America.
Deissmann, Gustaf Adolf (1910). *Light from the Ancient Near East: The New Testament Illustrated by Recently Discovered Texts of the Greco-Roman World*. London: Hodder and Stoughton.
Dochhorn, Jan (2018). "Der Vorwurf des Tempelraubs in Röm 2,22b und seine politischen Hintergründe," *Zeitschrift für die neutestamentliche Wissenschaft* 109: 101–17.
Dodd, Charles H. (1932). *The Epistle of Paul to the Romans*. London: Hodder & Stoughton.
Doering, Lutz (2012). *Ancient Jewish Letters and the Beginnings of Christian Epistolography*. Tübingen: Mohr Siebeck.
Donfried, Karl P. (1977). *The Romans Debate*. Minneapolis, MN: Augsburg Fortress Press.
Donfried, Karl P. (1991). *The Romans Debate*, rev. and exp. Peabody, MA: Hendrickson.
Dovidio, John. F., Samuel. L. Gaertner, and Tamar Saguy (2009). "Commonality and the Complexity of 'We': Social Attitudes and Social Change," *Personality and Social Psychology Review* 13: 3–20.
Downs, David (2008). *The Offering of the Gentiles: Paul's Collection in Its Chronological, Cultural, and Cultic Contexts*. Tübingen: Mohr Siebeck.
Draper, Jonathan (1988). "Humble Submission to Almighty God and Its Biblical Foundation: Contextual Exegesis of Romans 13:1-7," *Journal of Theology for Southern Africa* 63, 30–55.
Dunn, James D. G. (1988a). *World Biblical Commentary, vol. I: Romans 1–8*. Dallas, TX: Word Books.
Dunn, James D. G. (1988b). *World Biblical Commentary, vol. II: Romans 9–16*. Dallas, TX: Word Books.
Dunn, James D. G. (2005). *The New Perspective on Paul*. Tübingen: Mohr Siebeck.
Eco, Umberto (2003). *Mouse or Rat? Translation as Negotiation*. London: Weidenfeld & Nicolson.
Ehrenkrook, Jason von (2011). *Sculpting Idolatry in Flavian Rome*. Atlanta, GA: SBL Press.
Ehrensperger, Kathy (2003). "'Be Imitators of Me as I Am of Christ': A Hidden Discourse of Power and Domination in Paul?," *Lexington Theological Quarterly* 38.4: 241–61.

Ehrensperger, Kathy (2005). "Scriptural Reasoning—the Dynamic That Informed Paul's Theologizing," *Journal of Scriptural Reasoning* 5.3.
Ehrensperger, Kathy (2007/2009). *Paul and the Dynamics of Power: Communication and Interaction in the Early Christ-Movement*. London: T&T Clark International.
Ehrensperger, Kathy (2010). "'Called to Be Saints'—the Identity-Shaping Dimension of Paul's Priestly Discourse in Romans," in *Reading Paul in Context: Explorations in Identity Formation: Essays in Honour of William S. Campbell*, eds. J. Brian Tucker and Kathy Ehrensperger. London: T&T Clark, 90–109.
Ehrensperger, Kathy (2013). *Paul at the Crossroads of Cultures: Theologizing in the Space Between*. London: T&T Clark.
Ehrensperger, Kathy (2016). "The Pauline Ἐκκλησίαι and Images of Community in Early Enoch Traditions in Bi-Cultural Perspective," in *Paul the Jew: Rereading the Apostle as a Figure of Second Temple Judaism*, ed. Gabriele Boccaccini. Minneapolis, MN: Fortress, 183–216.
Ehrensperger, Kathy (2019). *Searching Paul. Conversations with the Jewish Apostle to the Nations. Collected Essays*. Tübingen: Mohr Siebeck.
Ehrensperger, Kathy (2020). "Paul and Feminism," in *The Oxford Handbook of Pauline Studies*, ed. Matthew V. Novenson. Oxford: Oxford University Press,
Ehrensperger, Kathy (2021), 'Bending Knees and Acknowledging Tongues (Phil 2:9-11). The Nations' Loyalty to the God of Israel in the Shadow of the Empire", in *Israel and the Nations. Paul's Gospel in the Context of Jewish Expectation*, ed.by František Abel, 149–64, Lanham, MD: Lexington/Fortress Academic.
Ehrensperger, Kathy (2021). "Imagine—No Works of Law! Struggling with 'Erga Nomou' in Changing Times and Places," paper presented in the "Paul Within Judaism" section of SBL Annual Meeting 2019, San Diego.
Ehrensperger, Kathy (2022). "Romans," in *T&T Clark Handbook to the Historical Paul*, eds. Ryan S. Schellenberg and Heidi Wendt. London: T&T Clark, 289–305.
Ehrensperger, Kathy (2023). "Abraham Our Forefather and Herakles Our Cousin: Paul's Genealogical Reasoning and Jewish Narratives of Belonging," in *Paul within Judaism*, eds. Mike Bird and Jörg Frey, Tübingen: Mohr Siebeck.
Ehrensperger, Kathy, and J. Brian Tucker, eds. (2010). *Reading Paul in Context: Explorations in Identity Formation: Essays in Honour of William S. Campbell*. London: T&T Clark.
Ehrensperger, Kathy, and R. Ward Holder, eds. (2008). *Reformation Readings of Romans*. Edinburgh: T&T Clark.
Eisenbaum, Pamela (2004). "A Remedy for Having Been Born a Woman: Jesus, Gentiles and Genealogy in Romans," *Journal of Biblical Literature* 123.4: 671–702.
Elliott, Neil (1994). *Liberating Paul. The Justice of God and the Politics of the Apostle*. Maryknoll: Orbis.
Elliott, Neil (2004). "The Apostle's Self-Presentation as Anti-Imperial Performance," in *Paul and the Roman Imperial Order*, ed. Richard A. Horsley. Harrisburg: Trinity Press International, 67–88.
Elliott, Neil (2007). *The Rhetoric of Romans: Argumentative Constraint and Strategy and Paul's Dialogue with Judaism*. Minneapolis, MN: Fortress Press.
Elliott, Neil (2008). *The Arrogance of Nations: Reading Romans in the Shadow of Empire*. Minneapolis, MN: Fortress.
Elliott, Neil (2010). "Paul's Political Christology: Samples from Romans," in *Reading Paul in Context: Explorations in Identity Formation: Essays in Honour of William S. Campbell*, eds. Kathy Ehrensperger and J. Brian Tucker. London: T&T Clark, 39–51.

Epp, Eldon Jay (2005). *Junia. The First Woman Apostle*. Minneapolis, MN: Fortress Press.
Eschner, Christina (2019). *Essen im antiken Judentum und Urchristentum. Diskurse zur sozialen Bedeutung von Tischgemeinschaft, Speiseverboten und Reinheitsvorschriften*. Leiden: Brill.
Esler, Philip F. (2003). *Conflict and Identity in Romans*. Minneapolis, MN: Fortress.
Esler, Philip F. (2014). "Group Norms and Prototypes in Matt 5.3-12: A Social-Identity Interpretation of the Matthean Beatitudes," in *T&T Clark Handbook to Social Identity in the New Testament*, eds. A. Coleman Baker and J. Brian Tucker. London: Bloomsbury, 147–72.
Esler, Philip F. (2021a). *2 Corinthians. A Social Identity Commentary*. London: T&T Clark.
Esler, Philip F. (2021b). "The Adoption and Use of the Word ΕΚΚΛΗΣΙΑ in the Early Christ Movement," *Ecclesiology* 17: 109–30.
Eyl, Jennifer (2021). "Philo and Josephus on the Fidelity of Judeans," *Journal of Ancient Judaism* 12: 94–121.
Feldman, Louis H. (1993). *Jew and Gentile in the Ancient World: Attitudes and Interactions from Alexander to Justinian*. Princeton, NJ: Princeton University Press.
Fitzgerald, John T. (1989). "Paul and Paradigm Shifts: Reconciliation and Its Linkage Group," in *Paul Beyond the Judaism/Hellenism Divide*, ed. Troels Engberg-Pedersen. Louisville, KY: Westminster/John Knox, 241–62.
Fitzmyer, Joseph A. (1993). *Romans: A New Translation with Introduction and Commentary*. New York: Doubleday.
Flower, Harriet I. (2017). *The Dancing Lares and the Serpent in the Garden: Religion at the Roman Street Corner*. Princeton, NJ: Princeton University Press.
Forbes, Christopher (2016). "Paul and Rhetorical Comparison," in *Paul in the Greco-Roman World: A Handbook*, ed. J. Paul Sampley, 2nd ed. London: T&T Clark, 196–229.
Forman, Mark (2011). *The Politics of Inheritance in Romans*. Cambridge: Cambridge University Press.
Frankfurter, David T. M. (2001). "Jews or Not? Reconstructing the 'Other' in Rev 2:9 and 3:9," *The Harvard Theological Review* 94.4: 403–25.
Fredriksen, Paula (2010). "Judaizing the Nations: The Ritual Demands of Paul's Gospel," *New Testament Studies* 56: 232–52.
Fredriksen, Paula (2014). "Paul's Letter to the Romans, the Ten Commandments, and Pagan 'Justification by Faith,'" *Journal of Biblical Literature* 133.4: 803–10.
Fredriksen, Paula (2015). "If It Looks Like a Duck, and It Quacks Like a Duck … on Not Giving up on the Godfearers," in *A Most Reliable Witness: Essays in Honor of Ross Shepard Kraemer*, eds. Susan Ashbrook Harvey, Nathaniel DesRosiers, Shira L. Lander, Jacqueline Z. Pastis, and Daniel Ullucci, Providence, RI: Brown Judaic Studies, 25–34.
Fredriksen, Paula (2017). *Paul: The Pagan's Apostle*. New Haven, CT: Yale University Press.
Fredriksen, Paula (2019). "How Do the Nations Relate to Israel? Family, Ethnicity, and Eschatological Inclusion in the Apostle Paul," in *In the Crucible of Empire: The Impact of Roman Citizenship upon Greeks, Jews and Christians*, eds. Katell Berthelot and Jonathan Price, Leuven: Peeters, 131–40.
Fredriksen, Paula (2021). "Divinity, Ethnicity, Identity: 'Religion' as a Political Category in Christian Antiquity," in *Confronting Antisemitism through the Ages: A Historical Perspective*, eds. Armin Lange, Kerstin Mayerhofer, Dina Porat, and Lawrence H. Schiffman, Berlin: de Gruyter, 101–20.

Friedrich, Gerhard (1964). "εὐαγγέλιον," in *Theological Dictionary of the New Testament*, vol. 2, eds. Gerhard Kittel, Geoffrey William Bromiley, and Gerhard Friedrich. Grand Rapids, MI: Eerdmans, 724–5.

Fuller, Reginald H. (1963). *The New Testament in Current Study: Some Trends in the Years 1941–1962*. London: SCM Press.

Furnish, Victor P. (1968). *Theology and Ethics in Paul*. Louisville, KY: Westminster John Knox Press.

Furnish, Victor P. (1984). *II Corinthians*. Anchor Bible Series. New York: Doubleday.

Furnish, Victor P. (2012). "Living to God, Walking in Love: Theology and Ethics in Romans," in *Paul's Letter to the Romans*, ed. Jerry L. Sumney. Atlanta, GA: Society of Biblical Literature, 187–202.

Gaca, Kathy L. (1999). "Paul's Uncommon Declaration in Romans 1:18-32 and Its Problematic Legacy for Pagan and Christian Relations," *The Harvard Theological Review* 92.2: 165–98.

Gaertner, Samuel L., and Dovidio, John F. (2000). *Reducing Intergroup Bias: The Common Ingroup Identity Model*. Philadelphia, PA: Psychology Press.

Gagnon, Robert A. J. (1993). "Heart of Wax and a Teaching That Stamps: *Typos Didaches* (Rom.6.17b) Once More," *Journal of Biblical Literature* 112: 667–87.

Gamble, Harry (1977). *The Textual History of the Letter to the Romans: A Study in Textual and Literary Criticism*. Grand Rapids, MI: Eerdmans.

Garroway, Joshua D. (2012). *Paul's Gentile-Jews: Neither Jew nor Gentile but Both*. New York: Palgrave Macmillan.

Gaston, Lloyd (1982). "Israel's Enemies in Pauline Theology," *New Testament Studies* 28: 400–23.

Gaston, Lloyd (1987). *Paul and the Torah*. Vancouver: University of British Columbia Press.

Gathercole, Simon (2002). *Where Is Boasting? Early Jewish Soteriology and Paul's Response in Romans 1*. Grand Rapids, MI: Eerdmans.

Glaim, Aaron (2014). "Reciprocity, Sacrifice and Salvation in Judean Religion at the Turn of the Era," Brown University PhD Dissertation.

Godet, Frédéric Louis (1977). *Commentary on St. Paul's Epistle to the Romans*, rev. and ed. T. W. Chambers, 1883, repr. Grand Rapids, MI: Kregel.

Goodman, Martin (2007). *Rome and Jerusalem: The Clash of Ancient Civilizations*. London: Allen Lane.

Goodrich, John (2012). *Paul as an Administrator of God in 1 Corinthians*. Cambridge: Cambridge University Press.

Goodrich, John (2013). "From Slaves of Sin to Slaves of God: Reconsidering the Origin of Paul's Slavery Metaphors in Romans," *Bulletin for Biblical Research* 23.4: 509–30.

Goodwin, Mark (2001). *Apostle of the Living God: Kerygma and Conversion in 2 Corinthians*. Harrisburg, PA: Trinity Press International.

Gorman, Michael J. (2019). *Participating in Christ: Explorations in Paul's Theology and Spirituality*. Grand Rapids, MI: Baker Academic.

Gregerman, Adam (2018). "Is the Biblical Land Promise Irrevocable? *Post-Nostra-Aetate* Catholic Theologies of the Jewish Covenant and the Land of Israel," *Modern Theology* 34.2: 137–58.

Grenholm, Cristina, and Daniel Patte, eds. (2000). *Reading Israel in Romans: Legitimacy and Plausibility of Divergent Interpretations*. Romans Through History and Cultures Series. Harrisburg, PA: Trinity Press International.

Grieb, Katherine A. (2002). *The Story of Romans: A Narrative Defence of God's Righteousness.* Louisville, KY: Westminster John Knox Press.
Hanson, Anthony Tyrell (1974). *Studies in Paul's Technique and Theology,* London: Society for the Propagation of the Gospel.
Harding, Sarah (2016). *Paul's Eschatological Anthropology: The Dynamics of Human Transformation.* Minneapolis, MN: Fortress Press.
Harding, Sarah (2017). "Paul's Eschatological Anthropology: The *Esō Anthrōpos* and the Intermediate State," *Transformation: An International Journal of Holistic Mission Studies* 34.1: 50–65.
Harrill, Albert (2012). *Paul, the Apostle: His Life and Legacy in Their Roman Context.* Cambridge: Cambridge University Press.
Harrill, Albert (2016). "Paul and Slavery," in *Paul in the Greco-Roman World: A Handbook,* ed. Paul Sampley, vol. 2. 2nd edition, London, New York: Bloomsbury T&T Clark, 301–45.
Harrington, Daniel (1992). *Paul on the Mystery of Israel.* Collegeville, MN: Liturgical Press.
Harrison, James R. (2011). *Paul and the Imperial Authorities at Thessalonica and Rome.* Tübingen: Mohr Siebeck.
Harrison, James R. (2020). *Reading Romans with Roman Eyes: Studies on the Social Perspective of Paul.* Lanham, MD: Lexington Book/Fortress Academic Press.
Hays, Richard B. (1985). "'Have We Found Abraham to Be Our Forefather According to the Flesh?' A Reconsideration of Rom 4:1," *Novum Testamentum* 27.1: 76–98.
Hays, Richard B. (2005). *The Conversion of the Imagination. Paul as Interpreter of Israel's Scripture.* Grand Rapids, MI: Eerdmans.
Hester, James D. (1968). *Paul's Concept of Inheritance: A Contribution to the Understanding of Heilsgeschichte.* Edinburgh: Oliver & Boyd.
Hester, James (2004). "The Rhetoric of *Persona* in Romans: Re-Reading Romans 1.1-12," in *Celebrating Romans: Template for Christian Theology: Essays in Honor of Robert Jewett,* ed. Sheila E. McGinn. Grand Rapids, MI: Eerdmans, 83–105.
Hezser, Catherine (2005). *Jewish Slavery in Antiquity.* Oxford: Oxford University Press.
Hezser, Catherine (2011). *Jewish Travel in Antiquity.* Tübingen: Mohr Siebeck.
Hodson, Gordon, and Megan Earle (2017). "Social Identity Theory (SIT)," in *Encyclopedia of Personality and Individual Differences,* eds. Virgil Zeigler-Hilland and Todd K. Shackelford, New York: Springer.
Hogg, Michael A. (2006). "Social Identity Theory," in *Contemporary Social Psychology Theories,* ed. Peter J. Burke. Stanford: Stanford University, 113–36.
Hogg, Michael A. (2012). "The Social Identity Theory of Leadership: Theoretical Origins, Research Findings, and Conceptual Developments," *European Review of Social Psychology* 23.1: 258–304.
Hogg, Michael A. (2016). "Social Identity Theory," in *Understanding Peace and Conflict Through Social Identity Theory,* eds. Shelley McKeown, Reesham Haji, and Neil Ferguson. Heidelberg: Springer Verlag, 3–18.
Hogg, Michael A., and Joanne R. Smith (2007). "Attitudes in Social Context: A Social Identity Perspective," *European Review of Social Psychology* 18: 89–131.
Hogg, Michael A., Dominic Abrams, and Marilynn B. Brewer (2017). "Social Identity: The Role of Self in Group Processes and Intergroup Relations," *Group Processes & Intergroup Relations* 20.5: 570–81.
Hoklotubbe, Christopher (2017). *Civilized Piety: The Rhetoric of Pietas in the Pastoral Epistles and the Roman Empire.* Waco, TX: Baylor.

Hornsey, Matthew J., and Michael A. Hogg (2000). "Assimilation and Diversity: An Integrative Model of Subgroup Relations," *Personality and Social Psychology Review* 4.2: 143–56.
Horsley, Richard A. (1987). *Jesus and the Spiral of Violence: Popular Jewish Resistance in Roman Palestine*. San Francisco, CA: Harper & Row.
Horsley, Richard A. (1998). *1 Corinthians*. Abingdon New Testament Commentaries. Nashville, TN: Abingdon Press.
Horsley, Richard A., ed. (2000). *Paul and Politics. Ekklesia, Israel, Imperium, Interpretation*. Harrisburg, PA: Trinity Press International.
Horsley, Richard A., ed. (2004). *Paul and the Roman Imperial Order*. Harrisburg, PA: Trinity Press International.
Hübner, Hans (1984). *Gottes Ich and Israel. Zum Schriftgebrauch des Paulus in Römer 9–11*. Göttingen: Vandenhoeck & Ruprecht.
Hultgren, Arland J. (2011). *Paul's Letter to the Romans: A Commentary*. Grand Rapids, MI: Eerdmans.
Ilan, Tal (2009). "The Torah of the Jews in Ancient Rome," *Jewish Studies Quarterly* 16: 363–95.
Jackson, W. Daniel (2018). "The Logic of Divine Presence in Rom. 3.23," *Catholic Biblical Quarterly* 80.2: 293–305.
Jeffers, James S. (2002). "Slaves of God: The Impact of the Cult of the Roman Empire on Paul's Use of the Language of Power Relations," *Fides et Historia* 34: 123–39.
Jervell, Jacob (1991). "The Letter to Jerusalem," in *The Romans Debate*, ed. Karl Donfried. Peabody, MA: Hendrickson, 53–64.
Jervis, L. Ann (2012). "The Spirit Brings Christ's Life to Light," in *Reading Paul's Letter to the Romans*, ed. Jerry L. Sumney. Atlanta, GA: Society of Biblical Literature, 139–56.
Jetten, Jolanda, Russell Spears, and Tom Postmes (2004). "Intergroup Distinctiveness and Differentiation: A Meta-Analytic Integration," *Journal of Personality and Social Psychology*, 86.6: 862–79.
Jewett, Robert (1971). *Paul's Anthropological Terms: A Study of Their Use in Conflict Situations*. Leiden: Brill.
Jewett, Robert (1979). *A Chronology of Paul's Life*. Philadelphia, PA: Fortress Press.
Jewett, Robert (1982a). *Christian Tolerance: Paul's Message to the Modern Church*. Philadelphia, PA: Westminster.
Jewett, Robert (1982b). "Romans as an Ambassadorial Letter," *Interpretation: A Journal of Bible and Theology* 36.1: 5–20.
Jewett, Robert (1985). "The Redaction and Use of an Early Christian Confession in Romans 1.3-4," in *The Living Text: Essays in Honor of Ernest W. Saunders*, eds. Robert Jewett and Dennis E. Groh. Washington, DC: University Press of America, 99–122.
Jewett, Robert (1988). "Paul, Phoebe and the Spanish Mission," in *The Social World of Formative Christianity and Judaism: Essays in Tribute to Howard Clark Kee*, eds. Peter Borgen, Jacob Neusner, Ernest S. Frerichs, and Richard A. Horsley. Philadelphia: Fortress Press, 148–55.
Jewett, Robert (1993). "Tenement Churches and Communal Meals in the Early Church: The Implications of a Form-Critical Analysis of 2 Thessalonians 3.10," *Bible Review* 38: 23–42.
Jewett, Robert (2000). "The Social Context and Implications of Homoerotic References in Rom 1:24-27," in *Homosexuality, Science, and the "Plain Sense" of Scripture*, ed. David Balch. Grand Rapids, MI: Eerdmans, 223–41.

Jewett, Robert (2004). "The Corruption and Redemption of Creation: Reading Romans 8:18-23 within the Imperial Context," in *Paul and the Roman Imperial Order*, ed. Richard A. Horsley. Harrisburg: Trinity Press International, 25-46.

Jewett, Robert (2007). *Romans: A Commentary*. Minneapolis, MN: Fortress Press.

Jipp, Joshua W. (2016). "What Are the Implications of the Ethnic Identity of Paul's Interlocutor? Continuing the Conversation," in *The So-Called Jew in Paul's Letter to the Romans*, eds. Rafael Rodriguez and Matthew Thiessen. Minneapolis, MN: Fortress Press, 183-203.

Johnson Hodge, Caroline (2007). *If Sons, Then Heirs: A Study of Kinship and Ethnicity in the Letters of Paul*. Oxford: Oxford University Press.

Jonas, Kai J., and Amélie Mummendey (2008). "Positive Intergroup Relations: From Reduced Outgroup Rejection to Outgroup Support," in *Improving Intergroup Relations: Building on the Legacy of Thomas F. Pettigrew*, eds. Ulrich Wagner, Linda R. Tropp, Gillian Finchilescu, and Colin Tredoux. New York: Blackwell, 210-24.

Judge, Edwin A. (1966). "The Conflict of Educational Aims in New Testament Thought," *Journal of Christian Education* 9.1: 32-45.

Judge, Edwin A. (1972). "St. Paul and Classical Society," *Jahrbuch für Antike und Christentum*: 16-36.

Judge, Edwin A., and G. S. R. Thomas (1966). "The Origin of the Church at Rome: A New Solution?" *Reformed Theological Review* 25: 81-94.

Kameda, Tatsuya, and Daisuke Nakanishi (2003). "Does Social/Cultural Learning Increase Human Adaptability? Rogers's Question Revisited," *Evolution and Human Behavior* 24.4: 242-60.

Kaminsky, Joel, and Mark Reasoner (2019). "The Meaning and Telos of Israel's Election: An Interfaith Response to N. T. Wright's Reading of Paul," *The Harvard Theological Review* 112.4: 421-46.

Karris, Robert J. (1973). "Rom. 14:1-15:13 and the Occasion of Romans," *The Catholic Biblical Quarterly* 35.2: 155-78.

Karris, Robert J. (1991a). "Romans 14:1-15:13 and the Occasion of Romans," in *The Romans Debate*, ed. Karl P. Donfried. Peabody, MA: Hendrickson, 65-84.

Karris, Robert J. (1991b). "The Occasion of Romans: A Response to Professor Donfried," in *The Romans Debate*, ed. Karl P. Donfried. Peabody, MA: Hendrickson, 125-27.

Käsemann, Ernst (1969). "Worship in Everyday Life: A Note on Romans 12," in *New Testament Questions of Today*, ed. Ernst Käsemann. Philadelphia, PA: Fortress Press, 189-95.

Käsemann, Ernst (1971a). "The Faith of Abraham in Romans 4," in *Perspectives on Paul*, ed. Ernst Käsemann. London: SCM, 79-101.

Käsemann, Ernst (1971b). "Justification and Salvation History in the Epistle to the Romans," in *Perspectives on Paul*, ed. Ernst Käsemann. London: SCM, 60-78.

Käsemann, Ernst (1980). *Commentary on Romans*, trans.Geoffrey W. Bromiley. London: SCM.

Keck, Leander E. (1965). "The Poor among the Saints in the New Testament," *Zeitschrift für die neutestamentliche Wissenschaft* 56.1/2: 100-29.

Keck, Leander E. (1990). "Romans 15:4 an Interpolation?" in *Faith and History: Essays in Honor of Paul W. Meyer*, eds. John Carroll, Charles Cosgrove, and E. Elizabeth Johnson. Atlanta, GA: Scholars Press, 125-36.

Keck, Leander E. (2005). *Romans*. Abingdon New Testament Commentaries. Nashville, TN: Abingdon Press.

Keesmaat, Sylvia (1999). *Paul and his Story. (Re-)Interpreting the Exodus-Tradition*. Sheffield: Sheffield Academic Press.

Kim, Jin Young (2021). "The Function of Paul's Grief in Romans 9.1-2 in Light of Hellenistic Moral Philosophy: Transforming the Gentile Misunderstanding and Boasting," paper presented at the SBL San Antonio Pauline Epistles Section, 2021.

Kirk, J. R. Daniel (2007). "Reconsidering Dikaiōma in Romans 5:16," *Journal of Biblical Studies* 126.4: 787–92.

Klauck, Hans-Josef (1998). "Allegorie/Allegorese III.Bibel," in *Religion in Geschichte und Gegenwart*, 4th ed., vol. 1, Tübingen: Mohr Siebeck, 305–6.

Klawans, Jonathan (2006). *Purity, Sacrifice, and the Temple: Symbolism and Supersessionism in the Study of Ancient Judaism*. Oxford: Oxford University Press.

Klein, Günter (1963). "Römer 4 und die Idee der Heilsgeschichte," *Evangelische Theologie* 23: 424–47.

Klein, Günter (1991). "Paul's Purpose in Writing the Epistle to the Romans," in *The Romans Debate*, ed. Karl P. Donfried. Peadbody, MA: Hendrickson, 32–49.

Klepper Copeland, Deeana (2007). "First in Knowledge of Divine Law: The Jews and the Old Law in Nicholas of Lyra's Romans Commentary," in *Medieval Readings of Romans*. Romans Through History and Cultures Series, eds. William S. Campbell, Peter S. Hawkins, and Brenda Deen Schildgen, London: T&T Clark, 167–81.

Kloppenborg, John S. (2019). *Christ's Associations. Connecting and Belonging in the Ancient City*. New Haven, CT: Yale University Press.

Korner, Ralph (2015). "*Ekklesia* as a Jewish Synagogue Term: Some Implications for Paul's Socio-Religious Location," *The Journal of the Jesus Movement in its Jewish Setting* 2: 53–78.

Korner, Ralph (2017). *The Origin and Meaning of Ekklēsia in the Early Jesus Movement*. Brill: Leiden.

Krahn, Annika (2018). *Legitimation qua Adoption: Eine Inklusionsmaßnahme bei Paulus*. Weilerwist: Velbruck Wissenschaft.

Kümmel, Werner G. (1929). *Römer 7 und die Bekehrung des Paulus*. Leipzig: J. C. Hinrichs'sche Buchhandlung.

Kustas, George (1976). "Diatribe in Ancient Rhetorical Theory: Protocol of the Twenty Second Colloquy," *Center for Hermeneutical Studies in Hellenistic and Modern Culture*, 25 April.

Lampe, Peter (1991). "The Roman Christians of Romans 16," in *The Romans Debate*, ed. Karl P. Donfried. Peabody, MA: Hendrickson, 216–30.

Lampe, Peter (2003). *From Paul to Valentinus: Christians at Rome in the First Two Centuries*. Minneapolis, MN: Fortress Press.

Lampe, Peter (2015). "Roman Christians under Nero (54–68 CE)," in *The Last Years of Paul*, eds. Armand Puig I. Tarrech, John M. G. Barclay, and Jörg Frey. Tübingen Mohr Siebeck, 11–29.

Last, Richard (2016). "The Other Synagogues," *Journal for the Study of Judaism* 47: 330–63.

Leenhardt, Franz J. (1961). *The Epistle to the Romans*. Cambridge: Lutterworth.

Leonhard, Clemens (2019). "The Associations and the Others: Were the Rabbinic *Havurot* Greco-Roman Associations?" in *Private Associations and Jewish Communities in the Hellenistic and Roman Cities*, ed. Benedikt Eckhardt. Leiden: Brill, 179–205.

Levinas, Emmanuel (1969). *Totality and Infinity: An Essay on Exteriority*. Pittsburgh: Duquesne University Press.

Levine, Amy-Jill (2006). *The Misunderstood Jew: The Church and the Scandal of the Jewish Jesus*. San Francisco: Haper.

Levine, Amy-Jill (2021). "The Gospel and the Land Revisited: Exegesis, Hermeneutics, and Politics," in *Peace and Faith: Christian Churches and the Israeli–Palestinian Conflict*, eds. Cary Nelson and Michael C. Gizzi. Philadelphia: Academic Studies Press, 130–51.

Levine, Lee I. (2005). *The Ancient Synagogue. The First Thousand Years*. New Haven, CT: Yale University Press.

Levinson, Jon D. (2012). *Inheriting Abraham: The Legacy of the Patriarch in Judaism, Christianity, and Islam*. Princeton, NJ: Princeton University Press.

Lewis, Robert Brian (2016). *Paul's Spirit of Adoption in Its Imperial Context*. London: Bloomsbury T&T Clark.

Lietzmann, Hans (1971). *An die Römer. Handbuch zum Neuen Testament*. Tübingen: Mohr Siebeck.

Lim, Kar Yong (2009). *The Sufferings of Christ Are Abundant in Us: A Narrative Dynamics Investigation of Paul's Sufferings in 2 Corinthians*. London, New York: T&T Clark.

Lim, Kar Yong (2014). "Reading Romans 13.1-7 in a Multifaith Context: Some Reflections from Malaysia," in *What Young Asian Theologians Are Thinking*, ed. Leow Theng Huat, CSCA Christianity in Southeast Asia Series 7. Singapore: Trinity Theological College, 37–47.

Lincicum, David (2010). *Paul and the Early Jewish Encounter with Deuteronomy*. Tübingen: Mohr Siebeck.

Livesey, Nina (2010). *Circumcision as a Malleable Symbol*. Tübingen: Mohr Siebeck.

Livesey, Nina (2012). "Sounding Out the Heirs of Abraham (Rom. 4.9-12)," *Oral Tradition* 27.1: 273–90.

Longenecker, Bruce W. (2010). *Remember the Poor: Paul, Poverty, and the Greco-Roman World*. Grand Rapids, MI: Eerdmans.

Longenecker, Richard (1964). *Paul, Apostle of Liberty*. Grand Rapids, MI: Eerdmans.

Longenecker, Richard (2011). *Introducing Romans: Critical Issues in Paul's Most Famous Letter*. Grand Rapids, MI: Eerdmans.

Lopez, Davinia C. (2008). *Apostle to the Conquered: Reimagining Paul's Mission*. Minneapolis, MN: Fortress Press.

Lütgert, Wilhelm (1913). *Der Römerbrief als historisches Problem*. Gütersloh: Bertelsmann.

MacDonald, Margaret Y. (2011). "Women in the Pauline Churches," in *Blackwell Companion to Paul*, ed. Stephen Westerholm. Oxford: Blackwell, 268–84.

Maddux, William W., and Marilynn B. Brewer (2005). "Gender Differences in the Relational and Collective Bases for Trust," *Group Processes & Intergroup Relations* 8.2: 159–71.

Magnusson, Eva, and Jeanne Marecek (2017). "Feminisms, Psychologies, and the Study of Social Life," in *The Palgrave Handbook of Critical Social Psychology*, ed. Brendan Gough. London: Palgrave Macmillan, 17–35.

Malherbe, Abraham J. (1980). "Μὴ γένοιτο in the Diatribe and Paul," *The Harvard Theological Review* 73: 231–40.

Malherbe, Abraham J. (1986). *Moral Exhortation. A Greco-Roman Sourcebook*. Louisville, KY: Westminster John Knox Press.

Malherbe, Abraham J. (1987). *Paul and the Thessalonians. The Philosophic Tradition of Pastoral Care*. Philadelphia, PA: Fortress Press.

Malherbe, Abraham J. (1989). *Paul and the Popular Philosophers*. Minneapolis, MN: Fortress Press.

Manson, Thomas W. (1991). "St. Paul's Letter to the Romans-and Others," in *The Romans Debate*, ed. Karl Donfried. Peabody, MA: Hendrickson, 3–15.

Marcus, Joel (1989). "The Circumcision and the Uncircumcision in Rome," *New Testament Studies* 35.1: 67–81.

Marshall, I. Howard (1999). "Romans 16.25-27—an Apt Conclusion," in *Romans and the People of God. Essays in Honor of Gordon D. Fee on the Occasion of his 65th Birthday*, eds. S. K. Soderland and N. T. Wright. Grand Rapids, MI: Eerdmans, 170–84.

Martin, Dale B. (1990). *Slavery as Salvation. The Metaphor of Slavery in Pauline Christianity*. New Haven, CT: Yale University Press.

Martin, Dale B.(1993). "Slavery and the Ancient Jewish Family," in *The Jewish Family in Antiquity*, ed. Shaye J. D. Cohen. Atlanta, GA: Scholars Press, 113–29.

Martin, Ralph P. (1981). *Reconciliation. A Study of Paul's Theology*. Atlanta, GA: John Knox.

Matera, Frank J. (2010). *Romans*. Paideia Commentaries on the New Testament. Grand Rapids MI: Baker Academic.

Mathew, Susan. (2014). *Women in the Greetings of Romans 16.1-16: A Study of Mutuality and Women's Ministry in the Letter to the Romans*. London: Bloomsbury T&T Clark.

McCaulley, Esau (2019). *Sharing in the Inheritance: Davidic Messianism and Paul's Worldwide Interpretation of the Land Promise in Galatians*. London, New York: T&T Clark.

McMurray, Patrick (2021). *Sacrifice, Brotherhood, and the Body: Abraham and the Nations in Romans*. Lanham, MD: Lexington/Fortress Academic.

Meeks, Wayne (1983). *The First Urban Christians: The Social World of the Apostle Paul*. New Haven, CT: Yale University Press.

Meeks, Wayne A. (1986). *The Moral World of the First Christians*. Philadelphia, PA: Westminster.

Meeks, Wayne A. (1987). "Judgment and the Brother: Romans 14:1–15:13," in *Tradition and Interpretation in the New Testament. Essays in Honor of E. Earle Ellis*, ed. Gerald F. Hawthorne. Grand Rapids, MI: Eerdmans, 290–300.

Meeks, Wayne A. (1991). "On Trusting an Unpredictable God: A Hermeneutical Meditation on Romans 9-11," in *Faith and History: Essays in Honor of Paul W. Meyer*, eds. John T. Carroll, Charles Cosgrove, and E. Elisabeth Johnson. Atlanta, GA: Scholars Press, 105–24.

Meggitt, Justin (1999). *Paul, Poverty, and Survival*. Edinburgh: T&T Clark.

Mendes-Flohr, Paul (1999). *German Jews: Dual Identity*. New Haven, CT: Yale University Press.

Mermelstein, Ari (2021). *Power and Emotion in Ancient Judaism. Community and Identity in Formation*. Cambridge: Cambridge University Press.

Metzger, Bruce M. (1971). *A Textual Commentary on the Greek New Testament*, 3rd ed. London: United Bible Societies.

Metzger, Bruce M. (1994). *A Textual Commentary on the Greek New Testament*. Stuttgart: Deutsche Bibelgesellschaft.

Meyer, Paul (1980). "Romans 10.4 and the End of the Law," in *The Divine Helmsman: Studies on God's Control of Human Events, Presented to Lou H. Silberman*, eds. James Crenshaw and Samuel Sandmel. New York: KTAV, 59–78.

Michel, Otto (1978). *Der Brief an die Römer*. 14., neubearbeitete Auflage. Göttingen: Vandenhoeck & Ruprecht.

Miller, Patrick D. (1990). *Deuteronomy*. Interpretation. Louisville, KY: Westminster/John Knox.

Minear, Paul S. (1971). *The Obedience of Faith: The Purposes of Paul in the Epistle to the Romans*. London: SCM.

Moo, Douglas (1996). *The Epistle to the Romans*. The New International Commentary on the New Testament, Grand Rapids, MI: Eerdmans.
Morales, Rodrigo J. (2012). *Reading Paul's Letter to the Romans*. Atlanta, GA: SBL Press.
Morgan, Teresa (2017). *Roman Faith and Christian Faith. Pistis and Fides in the Early Roman Empire and Early Christianity*. Oxford: Oxford University Press.
Moule, Charles F. D. (1967). *The Phenomenon of the New Testament*. London: SCM Press.
Mowczko, Marg (2018). "What Did Phoebe's Position and Ministry as διάκονος of the Church at Cenchrea Involve?" in *Deacons and Diakonia in Early Christianity: The First Two Centuries*, eds. Bart J. Koet, Edwina Murphy, and Esko Ryökäs. Tübingen: Mohr Siebeck, 91–102.
Mühling, Anke (2011). *"Blickt auf Abraham, euren Vater." Abraham als Identifikationsfigur des Judentums in der Zeit des Exils und des Zweiten Tempels*. Göttingen: Vandenhoeck & Ruprecht.
Muilenberg, James (1961). *The Way of Israel. Biblical Faith and Ethics*. New York: Haper.
Muilenberg, James (1969). "Form Criticism and Beyond," *Journal of Biblical Literature* 88: 1–18.
Mullins, Terence Y. (1964). "Disclosure: A Literary Form in the New Testament," *Novum Testamentum* 7.1: 44–50.
Munck, Johannes (1954). *Paulus und die Heilsgeschichte*. Kobenhagen: Munksgaard.
Munck, Johannes (1959). *Paul and the Salvation of Mankind*. London: SCM.
Munck, Johannes (1967). *Christ and Israel: An Interpretation of Romans 9–11*. Minneapolis, MN: Fortress Press.
Murphy O'Connor, Jerome (1996). *Paul. A Critical Life*. Oxford: Clarendon Press.
Murphy O'Connor, Jerome (2010). *Keys to Second Corinthians: Revisiting the Major Issuess*. Oxford: Oxford University Press.
Nancy, Jean-Claude (2000). *Being Singular Plural*. Stanford, CA: Stanford University Press.
Nanos, Mark D. (1996). *The Mystery of Romans, The Jewish Context of Paul's Letter*. Minneapolis, MN: Fortress Press.
Nanos, Mark D. (1999). "The Jewish Context of the Gentile Audience Addressed in Paul's Letter to the Romans," *The Catholic Biblical Quarterly* 61: 283–330.
Nanos, Mark D. (2010a). "'Broken Branches': A Pauline Metaphor Gone Awry? (Romans 11:11-24)," in *Between Gospel and Election: Explorations in the Interpretation of Romans 9—11*, eds. Florian Wilk and J. Ross Wagner. Tübingen: Mohr Siebeck, 339–76, now also in Nanos (2018: 112–52).
Nanos, Mark D. (2010b). "'Callused, Not Hardened': Paul's Revelation of Temporary Protection Until All Israel Can Be Healed," in *Reading Paul in Context: Explorations in Identity Formation. Essays in Honour of William S. Campbell*, eds. Kathy Ehrensperger and J. Brian Tucker. London: T&T Clark International, 52–73.
Nanos, Mark D. (2012). "To the Churches Within the Synagogues of Rome," in *Reading Paul's Letter to the Romans*, ed. Jerry L. Sumney. Atlanta, GA: Society of Biblical Literature, 11–28.
Nanos, Mark D. (2017). "Romans," in *The Jewish Annotated New Testament*, rev. 2nd edition, eds. Amy Jill-Levine and Marc Zvi Brettler. New York: Oxford University Press, 285–320.
Nanos, Mark D. (2018). *Reading Romans within Judaism: Collected Essays of Mark D. Nanos*, vol. 2. Eugene, OR: Cascade Books.
Nanos, Mark D. (2021). "Re-Framing Paul's Opposition to Erga Nomou as 'Rites of a Custom' for Proselyte Conversion Completed by the Synecdoche 'Circumcision,'" *Journal of the Jesus Movement in its Jewish Setting* 8: 75–115.

Nanos, Mark, and Magnus Zetterholm, eds. (2015). *Paul Within Judaism. Restoring the First Century Context to the Apostle*. Minneapolis, MN: Fortress Press.

Neufeld, Scott D., and Michael T. Schmitt (2019). "Solidarity Not Homogeneity: Constructing a Superordinate Aboriginal Identity That Protects Subgroup Identities," *Political Psychology* 40.3: 599–616.

Neutel, Karin (2021). "Restoring Abraham's Foreskin: The Significance of *Akrobustia* for Paul's Argument about Circumcision in Romans 4:9-12," *Journal of the Jesus Movement in Its Jewish Setting* 8: 53–74.

Neville, David J. (2021). "Review of Sarah H. Casson, Textual Signposts in the Argument of Romans: A Relevance-Theory Approach," *Review of Biblical Literature* 3.

Nickelsburg, George W. E. (2001). *1 Enoch 1: A Commentary on the Book of Enoch 1 Chapters 1-36: 81-108*. Minneapolis, MN: Fortress Press.

Noack Bent, W. (1965). "Current and Backwater in the Epistle to the Romans," *Studia Theologica* 19: 155–66.

Nongbri, Brent (2013). *Before Religion. A History of a Modern Concept*. New Haven, CT: Yale University Press.

Novenson, Matthew V. (2012). *Christ among the Messiahs: Christ Language in Paul and Messiah Language in Ancient Judaism*. New York: Oxford University Press.

Novenson, Matthew V. (2016). "The Self-Styled Jew of Romans 2 and the Actual Jews of Romans 9–11," in *The So-Called Jew in Paul's Letter to the Romans*, eds. Rafael Rodriguez and Matthew Thiessen. Minneapolis, MN: Fortress Press, 133–62.

Oakes, Peter (2009). *Reading Romans in Pompeii: Paul's Letter at Ground Level*. Minneapolis, MN: Fortress Press.

Ogereau, Julien (2012). "The Jerusalem Collection as Κοινωνία: Paul's Global Politics of Socio-Economic Equality and Solidarity," *New Testament Studies* 58.3: 360–78.

Öhler, Markus (2016). "Das Bestehen das Kosmos vor dem Hintergrund frühjüdischer und frühchristlicher Apokalyptik," *Kerygma und Dogma*: 3–26.

Öhler, Markus (2021). "'If You Are Called a Judean …' (Rom 2:17): Paul and his Interlocutor," in *Israel and the Nations. Paul's Gospel in the Context of Jewish Expectation*, ed. František Abel. Lanham, MD: Lexington/Fortress Academic.

Ollrog, Wolf-Henning (1979). *Paulus und seine Mitarbeiter. Untersuchungen zu Theorie und Praxis the paulinischen Mission*. Neukirchen-Vluyn: Neukirchener Verlag.

Opitz, Peter (2008). "Bullinger on Romans," in *Reformation Readings of Romans*, eds. Kathy Ehrensperger and R. Ward Holder, London: T&T Clark International, 148–63.

Osiek, Carolyn, and Margaret Y. MacDonald (2006). *A Woman's Place: House Churches in Early Christianity*. Minneapolis, MN: Fortress Press.

Park, Young-Ho (2015). *Paul's Ekklesia as Civic Assembly*. Tübingen: Mohr Siebeck.

Patte, Daniel (1995). *Ethics of Biblical Interpretation: A Reevaluation*. Louisville, KY: Westminster/John Knox.

Patte, Daniel (2018). *Romans: Three Exegetical Interpretations and the History of Reception* (vol. 1 Romans 1:1-32). London: Bloomsbury T&T Clark.

Patte, Daniel, and Cristina Grenholm, eds. (2013). *Modern Interpretations of Romans: Tracing Their Hermeneutical/Theological Trajectory*. London: Bloomsbury T&T Clark.

Patterson, Orlando (2017). "Revisiting Slavery, Property, and Social Death," in *On Human Bondage: After Slavery and Social Death*, eds. John Bodel and Walter Scheidel. Hoboken, NJ: John Wiley, 265–95.

Pavlenko, Aneta (2005). *Emotions and Multilingualism*. Cambridge: Cambridge University Press.

Pavlenko, Aneta, ed. (2006). *Bilingual Minds: Emotional Experience, Expression and Representation*. Clevendon: Multilingual Matters.

Peppard, Michael (2019). "Son of God in Gentile Contexts (That Is, Almost Everywhere)," in *Son of God. Divine Sonship in Jewish and Christian Antiquity*, eds. Garrick V. Allen, Kai Akagi, Paul Sloan, and Madhavi Nevader. Winona Lake, IN: Eisenbrauns, 135–57.

Perdue, Leo G. (1981). "Paraenesis and the Epistle of James," *Zeitschrift fur die Neutestamentliche Wissenschaft* 72: 241–56.

Pickett, Cynthia. L., and Marilynn B. Brewer (2005). "The Role of Exclusion in Maintaining Ingroup Inclusion," in *The Social Psychology of Inclusion and Exclusion*, eds. David Abrams, Michael A. Hogg, and José M. Marques. London: Routledge, 89–111.

Porter, Stanley E. (1990). "Romans 13.1-7 as Pauline Political Rhetoric," *Filologica Neotestamentaria* 3: 113–37.

Porter, Stanley E. (1991). "The Argument of Romans 5: Can a Rhetorical Question Make a Difference?" *Journal of Biblical Literature* 110.4: 655–77.

Porter, Stanley E. (1995). "A Newer Perspective on Paul: Romans 1-8 through the Eyes of Literary Analysis," in *The Bible in Human Society: Essays in Honor of John Rogerson*, eds. M. Daniel Carroll R., David J. A. Clines, and Philip R. Davies. Sheffield: Sheffield Academic Press, 366–92.

Porter, Stanley E., ed. (2005). *Paul and His Opponents*. Leiden: Brill.

Portier-Young, Anthea E. (2013). *Apocalypse against Empire: Theologies of Resistance in Early Judaism*. Grand Rapids, MI: Eerdmans.

Portmann, Adolf W. (1971). *Wir sind unterwegs: Der Mensch in seiner Umwelt*. Olten: Walter Verlag.

Rainey, Brian (2018). *Religion, Ethnicity and Xenophobia in the Bible: A Theoretical, Exegetical and Theological Survey*. London: Routledge.

Rajak, Tessa (1991). "Friends, Romans, Subjects: Agrippa II's Speech in Josephus' Jewish War," in *Images of Empire*, ed. Loveday Alexander. Sheffield: Sheffield Academic Press, 122–34.

Rajak, Tessa (2009). *Translation and Survival: The Greek Bible of the Ancient Jewish Diaspora*. Oxford: Oxford University Press.

Reasoner, Mark (1999). *The Strong and the Weak. Romans 14.1-15.13 in Context*. Cambridge: Cambridge University Press.

Reasoner, Mark (2014). "The Redemptive Inversions of Jeremiah in Romans 9–11," *Biblica* 95.3: 388–404.

Reasoner, Mark (2019). "Paul's Letter against the Roman Gods," in *Romans and the Legacy of St. Paul. Historical, Theological and Social Perspectives*, eds. Peter G. Bolt and James R. Harrison. Sydney: Sydney College of Divinity Press, 71–90.

Reed, Annette Yoshiko (2014). "Messianism between Judaism and Christianity," in *Rethinking the Messianic Idea in Judaism*, eds. Michael L. Morgan and Steven Weitzman. Bloomington, IN: Indiana University Press, 23–62.

Reese, James M. (1970). *Hellenistic Influence on the Book of Wisdom and its Consequences*. Rome: Biblical Institute Press.

Reicher, Stephen D. (2004). "The Context of Social Identity: Domination, Resistance and Change," *Political Psychology* 25: 921–45.

Reinhartz, Adele (2014). "The Vanishing Jews of Antiquity," *The Marginalia Review*, June 24.

Remus, Harold (1986). "Justin Martyr's Argument with Judaism," in *Anti-Judaism in Early Christianity, vol. 2, Separation and Polemic*, ed. Stephen G. Wilson. Waterloo, ON: Canadian Corporation for Studies in Religion, 59–80.

Ricker, Aaron (2021). *Ancient Epistolary Association Culture and the Purpose of Romans*. London: T&T Clark.

Rillera, Andrew (2021). "Paul Does Not Have a Kipper Theology," paper presented at SBL San Antonio, Nov.

Rock, Ian E. (2010). "Another Reason for Romans—a Pastoral Response to Augustan Imperial Theology: Paul's Use of the Song of Moses in Romans 9–11 and 14–1," in *Reading Romans in Context: Explorations in Identity Formation. Essays in Honour of William S. Campbell*, eds. Kathy Ehrensperger and J. Brian Tucker, London: T&T Clark International, 74–89.

Rock, Ian E. (2012). *Paul's Letter to the Romans and Roman Imperialism*. Eugene, OR: Wipf & Stock.

Rodriguez, Rafael (2014). *If you Call Yourself a Jew: Reappraising Paul's Letter to the Romans*. Eugene, OR: Wipf & Stock.

Rodriguez, Rafael (2016). "Romans 5–8 in Light of Paul's Dialogue with a Gentile Who 'Calls Himself a Jew,'" in *The So-Called Jew in Paul's Letter to the Romans*, eds. Rafael Rodriguez and Matthew Thiessen. Minneapolis, MN: Fortress Press, 101–32.

Rodriguez, Rafael, and Matthew Thiessen, eds. (2016). *The So-Called Jew in Paul's Letter to the Romans*. Minneapolis, MN: Fortress Press.

Rosenfeld, Ben-Zion, and Joseph, Menira (1999). "The Ancient Synagogue as an Economic Center," *Journal of Near Eastern Studies* 58.4: 133–58.

Runesson, Anders (2016). *Divine Wrath and Salvation in Matthew: The Narrative World of the First Gospel*. Minneapolis, MN: Fortress Press.

Runesson, Anders (2022). *Judaism for Gentiles. Reading Paul Beyond the Parting of the Ways Paradigm*. Tübingen: Mohr Siebeck.

Sabou, Sorin (2005). *Between Horror and Hope: Paul's Metaphorical Language of Death in Romans 6.1-11*. Milton Keynes: Paternoster Press.

Saller, Richard P. (1994). *Patriarchy, Property and Death in the Roman Family*. Cambridge: Cambridge University Press.

Sanday, William, and Arthur C. Headlam (1895). *A Critical and Exegetical Commentary on the Epistle to the Romans*. Edinburgh: T&T Clark.

Sanders, Ed P. (1977). *Paul and Palestinian Judaism: A Comparison of Patterns of Religion*. London: SCM Press.

Sanders, Ed P. (1983). *Paul, the Law and the Jewish People*. Minneapolis, MN: Fortress.

Sanders, Ed P. (1994). *Judasim. Practice and Belief 63 BCE–66 CE*. London: SCM Press.

Sandnes, Karl Olav (2018). *Paul Perceived: An Interactionist Perspective on Paul and the Law*. Tübingen: Mohr Siebeck.

Scheid, John (2003). *An Introduction to Roman Religion*. Edinburgh: Edinburgh University Press.

Schmeller, Thomas (1987). *Paulus und die "Diatribe": Eine vergleichende Stilinterpretation*. Münster: Aschendorff.

Schmidt, Hans-Wilhelm (1963). *Der Brief des Paulus an die Römer*, ThHK 6. Berlin: Evangelische Verlagsanstalt.

Schnelle, Udo (2005). *Apostle Paul. His Life and Theology*. Grand Rapids, MI: Baker Academic.

Schottroff, Luise (1979). "Die Schreckensherrschaft der Sünde und die Befreiung durch Christus nach der Römerbrief," *Evangelische Theologie* 39: 497–510.

Schreiner, Thomas (1993). "Did Paul Believe in Justification by Works? Another Look at Romans," *Bulletin for Biblical Research* 3: 131–55.
Schüssler Fiorenza, Elisabeth (1986). "Missionaries, Apostles, Coworkers: Romans 16 and the Reconstruction of Women's Early Christian History," *Word and World* 6.4: 420–23.
Schwartz, Daniel R. (2016) "Rome and Alexandria: Why Was There No Jewish *Politeuma* in Rome?" in *Jewish and Christian Communal Identities in the Roman World*, ed. Yair Fürstenberg. Leiden: Brill, 153–66.
Scott, James C. (1985). *Weapons of the Weak: Everyday Forms of Peasant Resistance*. New Haven, CT: Yale University Press.
Scott, James C. (1990). *Domination and the Arts of Resistance: Hidden Transcripts*. New Haven, CT: Yale University Press.
Scroggs, Robin (1966). *The Last Adam: A Study in Pauline Anthropology*. Oxford: Basil Blackwell.
Segal, Alan (1990). *Paul the Convert: The Apostolate and Apostasy of Saul the Pharisee*. New Haven, CT: Yale University Press.
Setzer, Claudia (2001). "Resurrection of the Dead as Symbol and Strategy," *Journal of the American Academy of Religion* 69.1: 65–102.
Sharifian, Farzad (2011). *Cultural Conceptualizations and Language*. Amsterdam: John Benjamins.
Sievers, Joseph (1997). "Who Were the Pharisees?" in *Hillel and Jesus: Comparative Studies of Two Major Religious Leaders*, eds. James H. Charlesworth and Loren L. Johns. Minneapolis, MN: Fortress Press, 137–55.
Sievers, Joseph (2000). "God's Gifts and Call Are Irrevocable: The Reception of Romans 11.29 through the Centuries and Christian-Jewish Relations," in *Reading Israel in Romans: Legitimacy and Plausibility of Divergent Interpretations*, eds. Cristina Grenholm and Daniel Patte. Harrisburg, PA: Trinity Press International, 127–73.
Slingerland, H. Dixon (1997). *Claudian Policymaking and the Early Imperial Repression of Judaism at Rome*. Atlanta, GA: Scholars Press.
Song, Changwon (2004). *Reading Romans as a Diatribe*. New York: Lang.
Spicq, Ceslas (2007). *Agape in the New Testament*. Eugene, OR: Wipf & Stock.
Spilsbury, Paul (2002). "Josephus on the Burning of the Temple, the Flavian Triumph and the Providence of God," *SBL Seminar Papers* 41. Atlanta, GA: SBL, 306–27.
Spitaler, Peter, ed. (2011). *Celebrating Paul: Festschrift in Honor of Jerome Murphy O'Connor, O. P., and Joseph A. Fitzmyer S. J.* Washington, DC: The Catholic Biblical Association of America.
Stark, Rodney (1986). "Jewish Conversion and the Rise of Christianity: Rethinking the Received Wisdom," *SBL Seminar Papers*, 314–29.
Stark, Rodney (1996). *The Rise of Christianity: A Sociologist Reconsiders History*. Princeton: Princeton University Press.
Steffens, Niklas K. (2015). "'Of the Group' and 'For the Group.' How Followership Is shaped by Leaders. Prototypicality and Group Identifications,"*European Journal of Social Psychology* 45: 180–90.
Stegemann, Ekkehard W. (1981). *Der eine Gott und die eine Menschheit. Israels Erwählung und die Erlösung von Juden und Heiden nach dem Römerbrief*. Habilitationsschrift Heidelberg: University of Heidelberg.
Stegemann, Ekkehard W. (2005). "Der Jude Paulus und seine antijüdische Auslegung. Antijudaismus im Neuen Testament," in *Paulus und die Welt. Aufsätze*, eds. Christina Tuor-Kurth und Peter Wick. Zürich: Theologischer Verlag, 17–40.

Stegemann, Ekkehard W. (2010). "Coexistence and Transformation: Reading the Politics of Identity," in *Reading Romans in Context: Explorations in Identity Formation. Essays in Honour of William S. Campbell*, eds. Kathy Ehrensperger and J. Brian Tucker. London: T&T Clark, 3–23.
Stegemann, Ekkehard W. (2012). *Der Römerbrief. Brennpunkte der Rezeption. Aufsätze*. Zürich: Theologischer Verlag.
Stendahl, Krister (1976). *Paul among Jews and Gentiles and Other Essays*. Minneapolis, MN: Augsburg Fortress.
Sterling, Gregory E. (2019). "Monotheism as an Identity Norm: Philo of Alexandria on Community Identity," in *A Question of Identity. Social, Political, and Historical Aspects of Identity Dynamics in Jewish and Other Contexts*, eds. Dikla Rivlin Katz, Noah Hacham, Geoffrey Herman, and Lilach Sagiv. Berlin: de Gruyter, 245–64.
Stone, Michael J. (1988). "The Mission to the Jews in Acts: Unravelling Luke's Myth of the Myriads," in *Luke/Acts and the Jewish People: Eight Critical Perspectives*, ed. Joseph B. Tyson, Minneapolis, MN: Augsburg Fortress.
Stowers, Stanley K. (1981). *The Diatribe in Paul's Letter to the Romans*. Chico: Scholars Press.
Stowers, Stanley K. (1986). *Letter Writing in Greco-Roman Antiquity*. Atlanta, GA: Westminster John Knox.
Stowers, Stanley K. (1994). *A Rereading of Romans: Justice, Jews, and Gentiles*. New Haven, CT: Yale University Press.
Stowers, Stanley K. (1995). "Romans 7:7-25 as Construction of a Character (*Prosopopoiia*)," in *Paul in His Hellenistic Context*, ed. Troels Engberg-Pedersen. Philadelphia, PA: Fortress, 180–202.
Streett, R. Alan (2018). *Caesar and the Sacrament. Baptism: A Rite of Resistance*. Eugene, OR: Cascade Books.
Suggs, M. Jack (1967). "'The Word Is Near You': Romans 10.6-10 Within the Purpose of the Letter," in *Christian History and Interpretation: Studies Presented to John Knox*, eds. William R. Farmer, Charles F. D. Moule, and Reinhold Niebuhr. Cambridge: Cambridge University Press, 289–312.
Sumney, Jerry, ed. (2012). *Reading Paul's Letter to the Romans*. Atlanta, GA: SBL Press.
Tajfel, Henri (1978). "The Achievement of Inter-Group Differentiation," in *Differentiation Between Social Groups*, ed. Henri Tajfel. London: Academic Press, 77–100.
Tajfel, Henri, and John C. Turner (1979). "An Alternative Theory to Ingroup Conflict," in *The Social Psychology of Intergroup Relationships*, eds. William D. Austin and Stephen Worchel. Monterey, CA: Brooks-Cole, 33–47.
Talbert, Charles H. (2002). *Romans*. Smyth & Helwys Bible Commentary. Macon, GA: Smyth & Helwys.
Tamez, Elsa (1993). *The Amnesty of Grace: Justification by Faith from a Latin American Perspective*. Nashville, TN: Abingdon Press.
Taubes, Jacob (2004). *The Political Theology of Paul*, trans. Dana Hollander. Stanford, CA: Stanford University Press.
Thiessen, Matthew (2011). *Contesting Conversion: Genealogy, Circumcision, and Identity in Ancient Judaism and Christianity*. New York: Oxford University Press.
Thiessen, Matthew, and Rafael Rodriguez, eds. (2016). *The So-Called Jew in Paul's Letter to the Romans*. Minneapolis, MN: Fortress Press.
Thompson, Michael B. (1991). *Clothed with Christ: The Example and Teaching of Jesus in Romans 12.1-15.13*. Sheffield: JSOT Press.
Thorsteinsson, Runar M. (2003). *Paul's Interlocutor in Romans 2: Function and Identity in the Context of Ancient Epistolography*. Stockholm: Almqvist & Wiksell.

Thorsteinsson, Runar M. (2016). "Paul's Interlocutor in Romans: The Problem of Identification," in *The So-Called Jew in Paul's Letter to the Romans*, eds. Rafael Rodriguez and Matthew Thiessen. Minneapolis, MN: Fortress Press, 1–38.

Tobin, Thomas H. (2004). *Paul's Rhetoric in Its Context: The Argument of Romans*. Peabody, MA: Hendrickson.

Tomson, Peter J. (2019). "The Names Israel and Jew in Ancient Judaism and the New Testament—A Reconsideration", in Peter J. Tomson, *Studies on Christians and Jews in the First and Second Centuries*. Tübingen: Mohr Siebeck, 187–220.

Tucker, J. Brian (2010) *"You Belong to Christ": Paul and the Formation of Social Identity in 1 Corinthians 1–4*. Eugene, OR: Pickwick.

Tucker, J. Brian (2011). *"Remain in Your Calling": Paul and the Continuation of Social Identities in 1 Corinthians*. Eugene, OR: Wipf & Stock.

Tucker, J. Brian (2014) "The Jerusalem Collection, Economic Inequality, and Human Flourishing: Is Paul's Concern the *Redistribution* of Wealth, or a Relationship of Mutuality (or both)?" *Canadian Theological Review* 3.2: 52–70.

Tucker, J. Brian (2018). *Reading Romans after Supersessionism. The Continuation of Jewish Covenantal Identity*. Eugene, OR: Cascade.

Turner, John C. (1975). "Social Comparison and Social Identity: Some Prospects for Intergroup Behaviour," *Journal of Social Psychology* 5.1: 5–34.

Turner, John. C., and Katherine J. Reynolds (2001). "The Social Identity Perspective in Intergroup Relations: Theories, Themes, and Controversies," in *Blackwell Handbook of Social Psychology: Intergroup Processes*, eds. Rupert Brown and Sam L. Gaertner. Hoboken, NJ: Blackwell/Wiley, 133–52.

VanderKam, James (2012). *The Dead Sea Scrolls and the Bible*. Grand Rapids, MI: Eerdmans.

Wagner, J. Ross (1997). "The Christ, Servant of Jew and Gentile: A Fresh Approach to Romans 15.8-9," *Journal of Biblical Literature* 116: 473–85.

Wagner, J. Ross (2003). *Heralds of Good News: Isaiah and Paul "in Concert" in the Letter to the Romans*. Leiden: Brill.

Wagner, J. Ross, and Florian Wilk, eds. (2010). *Between Gospel and Election: Explorations in the Interpretation of Romans 9–11*. Tübingen: Mohr Siebeck.

Wasserman, Emma (2008). "Paul among the Philosophers: The Case of Sin in Romans 6–8," *Journal for the Study of the New Testament* 30.4: 387–415.

Wasserman, Emma (2018). *Apocalypse as Holy War: Divine Politics and Polemics in the Letters of Paul*. New Haven, CT: Yale University Press.

Watson, Francis (1991). "The Two Roman Congregations: Romans 14.1-15.13," in *The Romans Debate*, ed. Karl P. Donfried. Peabody, MA: Hendrickson, 202–15.

Watson, Francis (2007). *Paul, Judaism and the Gentiles: Beyond the New Perspective*. Grand Rapids, MI: Eerdmans.

Wedderburn, Alexander J. M. (1988). *The Reasons for Romans*. Edinburgh: T&T Clark.

Wedderburn, Alexander J. M. (2002). "Paul's Collection: Chronology and History," *New Testament Studies* 48: 95–110.

Weima, Jeffrey D. (1994). *Neglected Endings: The Significance of the Pauline Letter Closings*. Sheffield: JSOT Press.

Wendt, Heidi (2016). *At the Temple Gates: The Religion of Freelance Experts in the Roman Empire*. New York: Oxford University Press.

Wengst, Klaus (2008). *"Freut euch, ihr Völker, mit Gottes Volk!" Israel und die Völker als Thema das Paulus—ein Gang durch den Römerbrief*. Stuttgart: Kohlhammer.

Wengst, Klaus (2014). *Christsein mit Tora und Evangelium. Beiträge zum Umbau christlicher Theologie im Angesicht Israels*. Stuttgart: Kohlhammer.

Wenzel, Michael, Amélie Mummendey, and Sven Waldzus (2007). "Superordinate Identities and Intergroup Conflict: The Ingroup Projection Model," *European Review of Social Psychology* 18.1: 331–72.

Westcott, Brooke F., and Fenton J. A. Hort (1881). *The New Testament in the Original Greek*. New York: Harper and Brothers.

Westermann, William L. (1955). *The Slave Systems of Greek and Roman Antiquity*. Philadelphia, PA: American Philosophical Society.

Wiefel, Wolfgang (1991). "The Jewish Community in Ancient Rome and the Origins of Roman Christianity," in *The Romans Debate*, ed. Karl P Donfried. Peabody, MA: Hendrickson, 85–101.

Wilder, Terry L. (2016). "Phoebe, the Letter-Carrier of Romans, and the Impact of her Role in Biblical Theology," *Mid-Western Journal of Theology* 15.2: 107–18.

Williams, Sam K. (1980). "The Righteousness of God in Romans," *Journal of Biblical Literature* 99.2: 241–90.

Wilson, Mark (2017). "*Hilasterion* and Imperial Ideology: A New Reading of Romans 3:25," *HTS Teologiese Studies/Theological Studies* 73.3: 1–9. https://hts.org.za/index.php/hts/article/view/4067/9240, accessed May 18, 2022.

Witherington, Ben, III (2004). *Paul's Letter to the Romans: A Social-Rhetorical Commentary*. Grand Rapids, MI: Eerdmans.

Witherington, Ben, III (2012). "Wright and Wrong on the New Perspective on Paul," *The Bible & Culture: Patheos*. https://www.patheos.com/blogs/bibleandculture/2012/04/28/wright-and-wrong-on-the-new-perspective-on-paul/

Wolter, Michael (1978). *Rechtfertigung und zukünftiges Heil: Untersuchungen zu Römer 5.1-11*. Berlin: de Gruyter.

Wolter, Michael (2014). *Der Brief an die Römer*. Evangelisch-katholischer Kommentar zum Neuen Testament Band IV/1. Göttingen: Vandenhoeck & Ruprecht.

Wolter, Michael (2015). *Paul. An Outline of His Theology*, translated by Robert L. Brawley. Waco, TX: Baylor University Press.

Wolter, Michael (2018). "Ein exegetischer und theologischer Blick auf Röm 11.25-32," *New Testament Studies* 64: 123–42.

Wolter, Michael (2019). *Der Brief an die Römer*. Evangelisch-katholischer Kommentar zum Neuen Testament: Band IV/2: Röm 9-16. Göttingen: Vandenhoeck & Ruprecht.

Woodley, Randy S. (2022). *Indigenous Theology and the Western Worldview: A Decolonized Approach to Christian Doctrine*. Grand Rapids, MI: Baker Academic.

Wright, Benjamin G. (1998). "Ebed/doulos: Terms and Social Status in the Meeting of Hebrew Biblical and Hellenistic Roman Culture," *Semeia* 83/84: 83–111.

Wright, Nicolas T. (2002). "The Letter to the Romans," in *New Interpreter's Bible*, ed. Lee E. Keck, Nashville, TN: Abingdon, 10.393–770.

Wuellner, Wilhelm (1991). "Paul's Rhetoric of Argumentation in Romans," in *The Romans Debate*, ed. Karl P. Donfried. Peabody, MA: Hendrickson, 128–46.

Yeo, K. K., and Gene L. Green, eds. (2020). *The Land: Majority World and Minoritized Theologies of Land*. Eugene, OR: Cascade Books.

Young, Stephen L. (2015). "Paul's Ethnic Discourse on 'Faith': Christ's Faithfulness and Gentile Access to the Judean God in Romans 3.21-5.1," *The Harvard Theological Review* 108.1: 30–51.

Zacharias, H. Daniel (2020). "The Land Takes Care of Us: Recovering the Creator's Relational Design," in *The Land: Majority World and Minoritized Theologies of Land*, eds. K. K. Yeo and Gene L. Green. Eugene, OR: Cascade.

Zahn, Theodor (1910). *Der Brief des Paulus an die Römer*. Kommentar zum Neuen Testament 6. Leipzig: Deichert.

Zeller, Dieter (1976). *Juden und Heiden in der Mission des Paulus*. Studien zum Römerbrief. Stuttgart: Katholisches Bibelwerk.

Zetterholm, Karin (2019). "Jewish Teachings for Gentiles in the Pseudo-Clementine Homilies: A Reception of Ideas in Paul and Acts Shaped by a Jewish Milieu," *Journal of the Jesus Movement in Its Jewish Setting* 6: 68–87.

Zetterholm, Magnus (2009). *Approaches to Paul. A Student's Guide to Recent Scholarship*. Minneapolis, MN: Fortress Press.

Zetterholm, Magnus (2015). "Paul within Judaism: The State of the Question", in *Paul within Judaism. Restoring the First Century Context to the Apostle*, ed. Mark Nanos and Magnus Zetterholm, Minneapolis, MN: Fortress Press, 31–51.

Ziesler, John (1989). *Paul's Letter to the Romans*. London: SCM Press.

Zoccali, Christopher (2008). "And All Israel Will Be Saved: Competing Interpretations of Romans 11.26 in Pauline Scholarship," *Journal for the Study of the New Testament* 30: 289–318.

Index of Ancient Sources

Psalms of Solomon
17 152
17:29-30 152

Jubilees
11-12 153
14-15 252
15 79
38:2-3 253

Aristeas
45 346
151 282

Philo
Legum Allegroriae
3:81 331

De Ebrietate 251 331

De Congressu 16 276

De Specialibus Legibus
1:53 135, 209
Virt. 108 110
2:255-256 79

De Praemiis et Poenis 158 154

De Legatione ad Gaium
132 4
156-158 4
157 346
220 348
311 5

Josephus
Ant.
10:210 349
11:300 193
14:228-90, 240 6
14:258-60 3
16.43 3

16.163-171 4
18:81-84 100

War
2:143-44 359
2:197 346
2:390 350
6:312-314 351

Life 276-81, 294-5 4

Against Apion
2:76-77 346
2:247-249 135
2:10 4

4 Ezra
6:8-9 253

Cicero
Pro Flacco
46 402
66-69 4

De Officiis
1:15 352
1:58 353

Letters to Friends
151 412

Juvenal
14:96-106 102

Virgil
Aeneid 67
Aeneid 1:257-296 255
Aeneid 6:756-854 152

Quintilian
Institutio 4.1.63-70

Tacitus
Annales 13:50-51   346

Plutarch
Amatorius 75 E   275

Ehrensperger
Virt. 108   110

Suetonius
Claudius 25:4   2

Origen
Commentary on Romans 2.11.4   99

Index of Biblical Texts

HEBREW BIBLE/SEPTUAGINT

Genesis
8:20-22	313
9:1-17	313
12:1-3	153, 248
12:4	157
15:6	142
17	109, 159, 162
18:10	251
21:12	251, 252
22:16-18	248
28:13-16	254
32:28	261

Exodus
3	252
4:22	247
10:3	202
12:25-26	328
13:5	328
25:16-22	129
32:32	246
33:19	260
32-34	260, 263

Leviticus
11:44	326
16	129, 130
16:2-20	129
18:4-5	276
18:5	278
19:2	326
19:18	353, 354
20:26	326

Numbers
7:89	129
11:15	246
15:17-21	299

Deuteronomy
7:7	313
7:9-13	313
8:17	278
9:4	278
10:15	313
29:3	291
30	277
30:11-14	277, 278, 279
31:29	255
32	79, 254, 255, 256, 257, 389
32:1-43	255, 256
32:21	45, 213, 285, 306
32:28-33	341
32:35	340
32:36	50, 257
32:39	257
32:43	247, 389
33:12	313

Joshua
14:7	50
22:27	328

1 Samuel
19:20	8

2 Samuel
7:5	50

1 Kingdoms
19:18	290

1 Chronicles
28:11	129

Job
41:23-24	277

42:1-6	126	45:2	106
		45:9	50
Psalms		45:23	362
2:7	53	48:20	50
5:9	122, 125	49:3	249
5:10	121	52:5	104, 389
9:5-9	125	52:7	66
9:28	121	52:15	402
13:1-3	121	53:5	104
14	122	54	162
14:2	125	54:1-3	162
18:4	45	54:9-10	161
18:50	389	58:7-8	328
19:5	284	59:7-8	120, 121
35:2	121	59:20	127
35:7	122	59:20-21	311
43:23	238	65	389
43:43	242	65:1-2	45, 255
51:4	118	65:2	285
52:2-4	121		
68	387	**Jeremiah**	
69	292	1:10	50
69:9	376	7:25	50
71:20	277	9:25	109
105:37	255	10	79
115	79	12:15	150
116:1	389	26:27	50
127:2	313	31:33	171
		34:5-7	346
Proverbs			
3:7	307	**Ezekiel**	
3:12	313	20:11	276
8:15	346	20:13	276
25:21-22	340	20:21	276
		28:25	50
Isaiah		34:23	50
6:10	291	36:24-28	150
8:14	267, 268, 269	37:24	50
10:22	265	37:25	50
11:10	389	38:17	50
28:16	265, 268, 269, 275, 280	43:13-21	129
29:10	291	**Daniel**	
41:8	215, 313	2:21	346
41:14	127	2:36-38	346
42:4	389	2:44-45	349
43:14	127		
44:6-18	79	**Hosea**	
45:1-3	346	1-2	262

2:1	262	**Baruch**	
2:23	262	4:7	255
11:1	313		
14:4	313	**1 Maccabees**	
		2:19	328
Joel		2:22	328
3:5	281		
		2 Maccabees	
Amos		7:33	50, 309
3:7	50	8:29	50
9:1	129		
9:11-15	150	NEW TESTAMENT	
Micah		**Matthew**	
5:6-7	150	15:21-28	305
		15:24	305
Zephaniah			
1:18	77	**Mark**	
2:2	77	7:24-30	305
2:8	78		
2:10	78	**Luke**	
2:15	78	8:31	277
Zechariah		**John**	
1:7	50	6:2	278
Malachi		**Acts**	
1	263	7	309
1:2-3	252, 260	8:20	368
		11:26, 28	2
Judith		13:46	305
8:18	107	15	403
		18	5, 346
Wisdom of Solomon		18:2	2
1:1-6	80	18:2-3	413
1:11	80	24:1-23	407
2:24	177	28:2	363
6:16-20	80		
12-14	79	**Romans**	
13-14	79	1	13, **49**, 74
13:1-9	77	1:1	50, 298, 314
13:1-19	79	1:1-4	57
13-16	71	1:1-7	**49**
14:22-31	79	1:1-15	400
15	79	1:2-4	52
		1:2-6	61
Sirach		1:3	53, 145
10:4	346	1:3-6	50
		1:4	28, 68, 124

1:5	28, 49, 176, 186, 188, 314, 418, 422	1:24-28	215
		1:25	326, 384
1:5-7	18, 54, 206	1:26	192, 207, 222
1:6	17, 21, 418	1:27	207, 222
1:6-15	189	1:27-29	81
1:7	55, 314, 327, 370, 406, 414	1:28	192, 329
		1:29-30	305
1:8	41, 314, 404	1:32	104, 145, 372
1:8-9	58, 408		
1:8-12	41, **57**	2	**83**, 86, 105
1:8-15	49, 399	2:1	83, 84, 88, 89, 368
1:10-12	58	2:1-5	84, 85, 86, **88**, 89, 90, 93, 212
1:11	59, 185		
1:12	48, 185, 196, 323, 404	2:1-6	38, 91, 92, 107, 113
1:13	18, 167, 206, 207, 273, 306, 326	2:1-11	92, 105
		2:1-16	110
1:13-15	61, 206	2:1-24	103
1:13-18	**59**, 60	2:2	41, 77, 92, 121
1:14	49, 227	2:3	88, 93, 94
1:14-16	62	2:4	132
1:15	41, 62, 63, 72	2:4-5	90
1:16	38, 67, 68, 78, 103, 124, 144, 145, 284, 305, 314, 360, 379, 395, 409	2:5	77
		2:6-16	92, **93**
		2:9-10	68, 91, 97, 103, 145, 409
1:16-17	61, 62, 63, 64, 65, 70, 72, 74, 97, 115, 127, 165, 171, 278, 324	2:10	314
		2:11	91
		2:11-16	94
		2:12	124, 369
1:16-32	323, 360	2:12-16	95, 96, 97, 105
1:18	69, 74, 77, 131, 132, 167, 314, 368	2:13	371
		2:16	115
1:18-25	215	2:17	19, 20, 83, 84, 85, 86, 87, 88, 94, 98, 99, 104, 111, 212, 133, 139, 142
1:18-29	171, 174		
1:18-32	59, 71, 179		
1:19-32	49, **69**, 70, 71, 72, 73, 74, 75, 77, 79, 83, 84, 89, 90, 91, 92, 93, 95, 107, 113, 118, 123, 124, 126, 131, 132, 170, 174, 326, 327, 355, 368	2:17-24	
		2:17-29	75, 84, 89, 93, **97**, 101, 105, 110, 113, 219
		2:18	174, 196, 220
		2:19-20	98
		2:21	104
		2:21-22	100
1:20	71, 73, 74	2:25-27	145
1:21	327	2:25-29	87, 98, **108**, 109, 114
1:21-23	81		
1:22-28	90, 230	2:27	104, 106, 107, 214
1:24	104, 192	2:29	115

3	**113**	3:31	46, 115, 136, 137
3:1-2	**113**, 114, 116, 118, 119, 120, 143, 158, 210, 247	4	**139**
		4:1	47, 116, 140, 146, 213, 238
3:1-3	98	4:1-2	139
3:1-8	13, 39, 115, 126, 140, 257, 258	4:1-8	**139**
		4:1-16	158
3:1-9	108, 238	4:1-25	140
3:1-20	125	4:2	139, 140, 141
3:2	277	4:3	186
3:3	45, 46, 47, 119, 250	4:4	352
3:3-8	**115**, 117	4:5	71
3:4	46, 115	4:7	136
3:5	118, 119	4:7-8	143
3:6	46, 115, 119	4:9	121, 159
3:8	20, 42, 115, 136, 181, 188, 196, 197, 235, 367	4:9-12	139, **143**, 144, 147, 157, 159
		4:9-22	136
3:9	114, 116, 121, 140, 145, 214	4:10	107, 146
		4:11	186, 314
3:9-20	115, **119**, 120, 124, 128	4:11-12	145, 146, 147
		4:12	145
3:12	314	4:13	215
3:18	120	4:13-14	153
3:19	41	4:13-18	**149**, 150, 151
3:19-20	122, 314	4:13-21	162
3:20	120, 124, 135, 219	4:15	219
3:21	124, 160, 219, 234, 290	4:16	144, 145, 147, 148, 150, 153, 314
3:21-24	296	4:17-25	**160**, 161
3:21-26	**125**, 126, 127, 128, 133, 137, 149, 156, 162, 163, 165, 167, 168, 171, 175. 226, 278, 299	4:19	155
		4:20-21	153
		4:23	145, 166, 308
		4:23-24	145. 162, 376
3:21-31	152	4:24	164
3:22	96, 129, 160, 281, 314	4:25	165, 192, 376
3:23	167, 314	5	38, **165**
3:25	130, 131, 132	5:1	167
3:25-26	129	5:1-11	127, 129, **165**, 166, 172, 173, 174
3:26	118, 126, 128, 229, 290, 313	5:2	172, 186, 188, 389
3:27	272, 291, 352	5:3	145
3:27-31	**132**, 133, 135, 139, 140, 142	5:5	170
		5:6-7	170
3:28	186, 352	5:6-11	168
3:29	136, 144, 158, 159	5:8-10	171, 174
3:30	159	5:9	126, 173, 290

5:9-17	38	6:17-18	199
5:10	176	6:18	192
5:11	126, 145, 167, 168, 173, 174, 389	6:19	126, 136, 225
		6:20	218
5:12	314	6:22	126
5:12-21	38, **173**, 175, 178, 185	7	**205**
5:14	174	7:1	188, 220, 273, 306, 326, 376
5:15	46		
5:15-17	178	7:1-6	185, 187, **205**, 213, 231
5:17	172, 174		
5:18	314	7:2	205
5:19	176	7:4	206, 207, 273, 306, 326
5:20	118, 182, 219		
5:21	167, 178, 183	7:5	207, 213, 217
		7:6	201, 205, 209, 210, 213, 230
6	35, **181**		
6:1	47, 116, 119, 140, 178, 185, 190, 213, 214, 238, 419	7:7	46, 47, 115, 116, 175, 219, 238, 272, 419
6:1-10	184, 187	7:7-8	215
6:1-14	**181**, 184	7:7-12	**212**, 213
6:1-23	201	7:7-25	44, 133, 140, 177, 186, 209, 210, 211, 216, 218, 220, 221, 222, 223, 224, 230, 274, 276, 326
6:2	46, 115, 116, 188		
6:3	14, 187, 314		
6:3-8	212		
6:4	229		
6:4-6	206	7:9	207, 218, 219
6:6	187	7:10	199, 218, 219
6:7	185	7:12	218, 272, 273
6:8-9	187	7:12-14	127
6:9	199	7:13	46, 115, 117, 214, 219
6:10	184, 185, 189		
6:11	183, 187, 189, 194	7:13-25	**216**
6:11-13	182, 189, 222	7:14	14, 41
6:11-14	184	7:17	226
6:12	197, 199	7:18-19	218
6:12-23	197	7:22-23	218
6:13	328	7:24-25	209
6:13-19	327	7:25	225
6:14	186, 188		
6:14-15	185, 218	8	**221**
6:15	46, 115, 116, 117, 119, 140, 184, 185, 188, 191, 214, 419	8:1	126
		8:1-11	**221**
		8:1-13	328
6:15-23	**190**, 192, 326	8:1-17	186, 272
6:16	188, 191	8:2	211, 221, 222, 223, 224, 272
6:17	8, 195, 220, 230, 375, 418		
		8:3-11	223

8:4	191, 352	8:39	170, 242
8:5	226		
8:5-7	225	9	**245**
8:6	226	9:1	243
8:7-8	335	9:1-3	101
8:8	224	9:1-4	21, 304
8:9	224, 226	9:1-5	**245**, 246, 247, 250, 254, 276, 285, 326
8:11	226		
8:12	187, 206, 227, 230, 273, 306, 326	9:1-13	161, 253, 341
		9:2-3	271
8:12-17	**226**	9:3	61, 206, 306
8:13	227, 228, 230, 244	9:3-5	191
8:14	163, 228, 236, 244, 314, 326	9:4	153, 186, 220, 228, 247, 248, 249, 251, 311, 312, 324, 327, 328, 329, 389
8:15	192, 228, 230, 231, 243		
8:16	228, 229, 242	9:5	28, 145, 247, 248, 249, 251, 311, 312, 314, 327, 389
8:17	228, 229, 238		
8:18	229, 235, 290		
8:18-30	**233**	9:6	45, 46, 47, 246, 249, 250, 271, 275, 285, 299, 311, 314
8:19	229, 234, 235		
8:21	228		
8:22	41, 245	9:6-13	**248**, 250, 254, 259, 261
8:23	145, 234, 235		
8:23-29	67	9:7	314
8:24	389	9:8	229
8:25	234	9:8-13	251
8:26	239, 257	9:10	145
8:26-27	236	9:11	160, 254, 347
8:26-39	245	9:14	45, 46, 47, 115, 116, 119, 140, 254, 340
8:27	238, 257		
8:28	41, 235, 241, 243, 257, 263		
		9:14-29	**258**, 262
8:29	14, 112, 163, 190, 206, 228, 236, 237, 241, 257, 263, 279, 306, 326, 329, 387, 421	9:15	314
		9:17	314
		9:18	263
		9:19	116
		9:19-22	45
8:29-30	283	9:20	39
8:30	263, 290	9:20-21	263
8:30-35	45	9:21	340
8:31	46, 47, 116, 117, 140	9:21-24	260
		9:22-29	263
8:31-39	**238**, 239, 241, 243, 244	9:23	264
		9:24	145, 154, 215, 264, 389
8:32	167, 240, 344		
8:33	237	9:24-29	254
8:34	236, 237, 241, 257, 324	9:25	55
		9:25-26	265

9:27	265	11:1-7	292
9:30	45, 47, 116, 117, 140	11:1-10	**289**, 295
		11:2	45
9:30-33	292	11:4	290
9:30-10:3	**267**, 269	11:5	290
9:31	272	11:6	352
9:33	268, 269, 280	11:7	45, 116, 117, 291, 294
10	**267**	11:8-10	293, 294
10:1	273, 276, 306, 311, 326	11:9	292
		11:10	292, 390
10:1-8	275	11:11	45, 46, 47, 115, 116, 117, 119, 214, 241, 268, 271, 292, 319
10:2-3	270		
10:4	**271**, 272, 273, 274, 275, 276, 329, 352, 354		
		11:11-12	292, 294
10:4-5	277	11:11-16	**293**
10:4-13	278	11:11-24	295, 296, 300
10:5-10	**275**, 276	11:13	18, 43, 46, 222, 230, 298, 335, 374
10:6	39		
10:8	45, 279	11:13-24	39, 43, 68, 163, 297, 324
10:9	281		
10:9-11	279	11:13-32	42
10:10-13	314	11:14	299
10:11	275	11:15	168
10:11-13	**280**	11:16	299
10:12	96, 127, 275, 276, 281, 282, 314, 359	11:16-18	394
		11:17	18, 43, 89, 104, 206, 237, 260
10:13	275, 276		
10:14-15	45	11:17-19	31, 271, 374
10:14-21	**282**	11:17-24	20, 43, 55, 68, 135, 299, **301**, 304, 307, 319, 374, 394
10:15	66, 299		
10:16	299		
10:17	311	11:18	78, 303, 335, 377
10:18	306, 314	11:18-32	307
10:18-19	45, 47, 284, 286, 289	11:19	29, 144, 235, 236, 237, 241, 302, 307, 335, 392
10:19	213, 254, 285, 306, 340		
		11:20	303, 335, 335, 339
10:19-21	255	11:22	237
10:20	306	11:23	360, 379
10:21	285	11:25	43, 78, 297, 306, 315, 326, 339
10:26	314		
		11:25-27	255, 307
11	13, **289**	11:25-35	300, 304
11:1	45, 46, 47, 98, 115, 116, 117, 119, 214, 241, 247, 250, 257, 293, 319	11:25-36	**305**
		11:26	296
		11:26-27	309, 311
		11:28	55, 312, 313

Index of Biblical Texts

11:29	163, 310, 312, 313	14	32, 43, **357**
11:30	126	14:1	59, 363, 366, 377, 378, 383, 384, 387
11:30-31	290		
11:31	313	14:1-4	**357**, 386
11:32	314	14:1-23	321, 393
11:36	315	14:2	369
		14:3	358, 361, 365
12	**323**	14:4	43, 202, 359, 360, 365, 373, 374, 379
12:1	81, 184, 189, 206, 215, 223, 226, 253, 306, 329, 408	14:5	363, 381, 391
		14:5-12	**359**, 361, 379
12:1-2	197, 225, **323**, 324, 325, 326, 327, 329, 334, 376, 401, 407	14:10	43, 105, 358, 360, 365, 373, 374
		14:12	362, 367
12:1-6	195	14:13-16	**368**
12:2	58, 373	14:22	43, 359
12:3	173, 186, 246, 307, 319, 334, 335, 337, 339, 358	14:14	370, 375, 380, 391
		14:14-17	367
		14:14-22	360
12:3-8	**334**, 336	14:15	170, 371, 372, 377
12:3-21	344	14:15-20	359
12:4	336	14:16	330, 367, 369
12:6-8	210	14:17	226, 335, 372
12:9-21	326, **337**, 338	14:17-18	17
12:11	51	14:17-23	**370**
12:14	340, 343	14:18	51, 327, 372
12:14-21	340	14:19	169
12:16	307, 319, 339	14:20	369, 377, 380
12:18	226, 237	14:21	365, 372
12:18-21	339	14:22	365, 372, 373
12:19	55, 347, 349, 370	14:23	372, 380
12:21	343	15	13, **375**
		15:1	59, 303, 358, 366, 378, 379, 384, 385, 386, 387, 391
13	**343**		
13:1	350, 351		
13:1-7	**343**, 344, 345, 346, 347	15:1-3	380
		15:1-6	321, **375**, 376, 386, 388, 393
13:4	347		
13:5	145, 347	15:1-13	380
13:6	347	15:3	386
13:7	362	15:4	401
13:8	227	15:4-5	377
13:8-10	223, 352, 371	15:5	387
13:8-14	324, 344, **351**, 253	15:5-6	384, 394
13:9	136, 321, 353, 354	15:6	381
13:10	273, 353, 354	15:7	336, 384, 390
13:11	126, 182, 355	15:7-13	31, 231, 244, 328, 330, **383**, 386, 387,
13:12	355		

	388, 391, 392, 393, 394, 395, 396	16:16	417
		16:17	408
15:8	150, 153, 347, 384, 385, 386	16:17-20	**418**, 419
		16:18	51
15:8-12	389	16:21-22	375
15:9	385	16:21-23	**421**
15:9-12	32, 383, 384, 390	16:25	185
15:10	247, 322	16:25-27	419, 420, **422**
15:12	53		
15:13	41, 394	**1 Corinthians**	
15:14	308, 383, 387, 388, 396, 418	1:1	298
		4:9	298
15:14-15	196	6:19-20	202
15:14-21	**399**	7:7-16	194
15:14-33	421	7:17	334
15:15	172, 186, 333, 400, 416	7:20	194
		7:22	51, 191, 193
15:16	18, 56, 58, 183, 335, 401	8:6	315
		8:11	170
15:17	206	8:13	365
15:18-19	279	9:1-2	298
15:18-23	400	9:5	413
15:19	402	9:19-22	188
15:20	400, 402, 404	12:3	279
15:20-24	**403**	14:23	332
15:21	402	15:3	170
15:22	44, 60	15:9	298
15:22-24	58, 409	15:10	413
15:23	402	16:19	417
15:24	309, 405		
15:25	28, 406	**2 Corinthians**	
15:25-29	**405**	1:1	50, 298
15:27	352, 407	1:20	352
15:28	412	3:7-11	171
15:30-32	409	3:12-15	401
15:30-33	**408**	4:16	329
15:31	407	5:14	170
		5:17	329
16	5, 13, 41, 44, **411**	5:18-20	168
16:1-2	**411**	7:10	312
16:1-16	9, 421	8:1-4	406
16:1-23	420	8:13-14	406
16:3-5	7, 417	9:12-14	171
16:3-16	413, **414**, 416	10:13-14	403
16:4	404	11:5	298
16:7	17, 413	11:22	98
16:10-11	2	12:11-12	298
16:15	3	13:13	170

Galatians

Ref	Pages
1:1	298
1:17	298
1:22-23	110
2:7	107, 159
2:7-9	403
2:7-10	55
2:10	407
2:15	71, 98, 207, 215
2:16	123
3:12	278
4:1	73
5:1	195
5:11	107, 110

Ephesians

Ref	Pages
2:6	184
2:12-14	29
2:18	167
3:12	167
6:5-9	193

Philippians

Ref	Pages
1:1	51
2:6-11	278
3:2-4:3	420
3:6	211

Colossians

Ref	Pages
3:1	
4:15	417

1 Thessalonians

Ref	Pages
1:10	311
2:6	298
5:9-10	170

1 Timothy

2:9-10	193

Philemon

17	363, 366

1 Peter

Ref	Pages
2:18-25	193
4:16	2

Hebrews

9:5	129

Revelation

Ref	Pages
9:1-2	277
9:11	277

Index of Modern Authors

Abrams, Dominic 24
Achtemeier, Paul J. 38, 62, 63
Adams, Edward 145, 151, 153, 371, 416, 417
Aletti, Jean-Noël, 285, 287, 298, 299
Anderson, Hugh xiii
Anderson, R. Dean 300
Ando, Clifford 103
Arendt, Hannah 22, 27
Ascough, Richard E. 6
Aune, David E. 35, 36, 40, 41, 48, 80
Aus, Roger 283
Avemarie, Friedrich 205

Badenas, Robert 273, 275, 276
Bailey, Daniel 131
Baker, Coleman A. 23
Bakhos, Carol 159
Bar-Tal, Daniel 62, 166, 171, 181, 391
Barbour, Robin xiii
Barclay, John M.G. 96, 127, 145, 162, 195, 197, 207, 315, 334, 360, 361, 373, 378, 420
Barentsen, Jack 338
Barrett, Charles Kingsley 92, 101, 105, 263, 292
Bartchy, S. Scott 380
Barth, Karl xiii, 96, 274, 313
Barth, Markus xiv, 128, 148
Barth, Ulrich 329
Barton, Carlin A. 66, 172
Bartsch, Hans Werner 105, 297
Bassler, Jouette 97
Bauer, Walter 251, 412
Baumgarten, Albert I. 184, 359
Baur, Ferdinand Christian 11, 15, 28, 32, 312, 376
Beale, Gregory K. 168
Beker, J. Christiaan 96, 118, 186, 234, 352

Bell, Richard H. 254, 285
Bertholet, Katell 253, 348, 349
Bjerkelund, Carl J. 409
Black, Matthew 171
Bodel, John 193
Bodenhausen, Galen V. 26
Bornkamm, Günther 13, 34, 35, 93
Brandenburger, Egon 178
Brawley, Robert L. xiii, 23
Bremmer, Jan N. 67
Brewer, Marilynn B. 25, 26
Breytenbach, Cilliers 169
Brodie, Thomas L. 383
Brooten, Bernadette 200
Brown, Raymond E. 1, 28, 89
Brueggemann, Walter 150, 354
Buber, Martin 22
Bultmann, Rudolf 33, 195
Byron, John 200, 202

Campbell, Douglas A. 71, 420
Campbell, William S. 8, 10, 11, 12, 17, 20, 21, 34, 37, 39, 44, 48, 55, 56, 77, 96, 97, 103, 116, 155, 169, 171, 194, 195, 196, 209, 210, 214, 224, 241, 255, 260, 262, 264, 271, 272, 281, 283, 284, 296, 312, 322, 328, 330, 352, 354, 359, 374, 388, 401, 403, 404, 416
Caragounis, Chrys C. 46, 175, 251
Carter, Warren 74, 95
Casson, Sarah Helen 40, 56, 59, 62, 65, 85, 163, 221, 274, 275, 277, 324
Ciampa, Roy 201
Clarke, Andrew 22, 32
Cohen, Shaye J.D. 69, 98, 105, 108
Coleman, Thomas M. 346
Collar, Anna 4, 54, 402, 405, 421
Collins, Adele Yarbro 130

Index of Modern Authors

Cranfield, Charles E.B. xiv, 52, 83, 101, 114, 120, 147, 178, 272, 275, 276, 278, 284, 292, 299, 345

Dabourne, Wendy 84, 85, 88
Dahl, Nils Alstrup 62, 120, 156, 332
Danker, Frederick W. 412
Das, Andrew 218, 377
Davies, W.D., 272
Davis, Stephan 268, 270
Deissmann, Gustaf Adolf 53, 200
Dibelius, Martin 35, 325
Dochhorn, Jan 99
Dodd, Charles H. 99, 262
Doering, Lutz 281
Donfried, Karl P. 10, 32, 33, 34, 35, 38, 188, 363, 373
Dovidio, John F. 27, 393
Downs, David 407
Draper, Jonathan 344
Dunlop, John xiii
Dunn, James D.G. 80, 84, 117, 125, 126, 144, 148, 185, 263, 277, 279

Earle, Megan 24
Eckhardt, Benedikt 3, 5, 6, 7
Eco, Umberto 131
Ehrenkrook, Jason von 70
Ehrensperger, Kathy xii, xiv, 4, 16, 25, 26, 28, 50, 51, 54, 57, 64, 69, 72, 75, 86, 106, 110, 121, 122, 127, 130, 144, 174, 176, 196, 201, 202, 233, 261, 264, 265, 269, 272, 298, 307, 308, 318, 319, 347, 348, 349, 351, 369, 375, 379, 380, 399, 401, 402, 404, 407, 409
Elliott, Neil xiii, 11, 12, 14, 16, 34, 41, 44, 45, 46, 47, 58, 59, 60, 61, 66, 67, 69, 72, 83, 94, 95, 97, 114, 123, 125, 126, 136, 137, 190, 192, 206, 224, 243, 244, 258, 297, 298, 310, 312, 318, 323, 324, 325, 328, 329, 344, 379, 392
Epp, Eldon Jay 413
Eschner, Christina 368
Esler, Philip F. xii, 8, 12, 14, 23, 28, 32, 50, 51, 71, 84, 86, 89, 142, 155, 166, 189, 207, 247, 252, 265, 293, 300, 302, 303, 331, 332, 337, 358, 361, 363, 378, 399, 405, 406

Evans, Craig xiii
Eyl, Jennifer 349

Felderhof, Marius xiii
Feldman, Louis H. 253, 348, 349
Fitzgerald, John T. 169
Fitzmyer, Joseph A. 8, 114, 184, 186, 191, 196, 229, 237, 263, 275, 277, 361, 363, 366, 413
Flower, Harriet I. 91, 233, 239, 258, 339
Forman, Mark 150, 151, 152, 156, 162
Förster, Hans xiii
Frankfurter, David T.M. 98
Fredriksen, Paula xiii, 52, 53, 71, 90, 102, 141, 142, 208, 216, 225, 228, 229, 230, 232, 237, 240, 247, 257, 317, 353, 378
Friedrich, Gerhard 66
Fuller, Reginald H. 10
Furnish, Victor P. 35, 128, 188, 190, 323, 324, 328, 403

Gaca, Kathy L. 77
Gaertner, Samuel L. 26
Gagnon, Robert A. 196
Gamble, Harry 10, 54, 56, 411
Garroway, Joshua D. 116, 140, 141, 267, 385
Gaston, Lloyd 253, 270, 297
Gathercole, Simon 84
Georgi, Dieter 69
Glaim, Aaron 129
Godet, Frédéric 54, 315
Goodman, Martin 103
Goodrich, John 191, 193, 200, 201, 202
Goodwin, Mark 72
Gorman, Michael J. 182
Gregerman, Adam 150
Grenholm, Christina 13, 16, 17
Grieb, Katherine A. 139, 140, 181
Grove, John xiii

Hanson, Anthony Tyrell xiv, 17, 54
Harding, Sarah 178, 192
Harrill, Albert 191, 193, 199, 202
Harrington, Daniel 313
Harrison, James R. 15, 60, 67, 142, 255, 352, 353, 358, 378, 379, 392
Hays, Richard B. 139, 140, 275

Headlam, Arthur C. 147
Hester, James D. 57, 61, 152
Hezser, Catherine 191, 400
Hodson, Gordon 24
Hofius, Otfried 312
Hogg, Michael A. 18, 24, 30, 86, 87
Hoklotubbe, Christopher 67
Hoppe, Juni xiii
Hornsey, Matthew J. 30
Horsley, Richard A. 14, 69, 191, 199, 202
Hübner, Hans 249
Hultgren, Arland J. 34, 51, 63, 120, 173, 207, 213, 339, 344, 346, 347, 363, 364, 365, 373, 374, 375

Ilan, Tal 175

Jackson, W. Daniel 167, 173
Jeffers, James S. 200
Jervell, Jacob 13
Jervis, L. Ann 225
Jetten, Jolanda 25
Jewett, Robert xiii, 2, 10, 14, 15, 34, 42, 46, 51, 52, 54, 61, 62, 63, 73, 99, 145, 165, 166, 169, 170, 171, 173, 175, 178, 182, 184, 192, 193, 195, 196, 223, 227, 229, 234, 241, 242, 248, 250, 251, 261, 262, 265, 268, 277, 279, 284, 294, 296, 298, 300, 301, 302, 307, 312, 313, 314, 329, 336, 337, 338, 343, 345, 346, 358, 359, 360, 363, 365, 366, 367, 372, 373, 376, 378, 379, 383, 387, 388, 395, 401, 411, 412, 413, 414, 415, 416, 418, 422
Jipp, Joshua W. 155
Johnson Hodge, Caroline 187, 228
Jonas, Kai J. 25, 26
Judge, Edwin A. 35, 172, 404

Kameda, Tatsuya 23
Kaminsky, Joel 248
Karris, Robert J. 11, 13, 34, 188
Käsemann, Ernst xiii, xiv, 11, 34, 49, 66, 96, 104, 114, 155, 156, 178, 188, 214, 229, 235, 324, 326, 328, 329, 335, 336, 337, 344
Keck, Leander E. 34, 45, 46, 47, 71, 81, 97, 99, 103, 104, 123, 127, 128, 154, 168, 169, 170, 182, 183, 205, 214, 215, 217, 218, 225, 226, 241, 247, 248, 249, 252, 271, 274, 275, 276, 277, 279, 280, 283, 284, 290, 291, 292, 295, 302, 304, 311, 314, 352, 361, 373, 376, 384, 385, 386, 388, 390, 392, 395, 406, 413, 414, 417, 418, 420
Keesmaat, Sylvia 232
Kim, Jin Yong 246
Kirk, J.R. Daniel 224
Klauck, Hans-Josef 302
Klein, Günter 60, 155, 400
Klepper, Deeana Copeland 16
Kloppenborg, John S. 331, 407
Korner, Ralph 3, 4, 6, 7, 8, 331
Krahn, Annika 290
Kuecker, Aaron xii
Kümmel, Werner G. 213
Kustas, George 35, 39, 40

Lampe, Peter 1, 2, 250, 363, 413, 416, 421
Last, Richard 3, 5, 6
Leenhardt, Franz J., 253, 261, 274
Leonard, Clemens 7
Levinas, Emmanuel 22, 27
Levine, Lee I. 4, 405
Levine, Amy-Jill 32
Levinson, Jon D. 142, 254
Lewis, Robert Brian 183, 187, 231, 233, 237
Lietzmann, Hans 84
Lim, Kar Yong 344, 350, 401
Lincicum, David 255, 256, 258, 279, 389
Livesey, Nina 147, 148, 157, 159, 279
Longenecker, Bruce W. 362, 406
Longenecker, Richard 2, 8, 10, 49, 60, 128, 130, 272, 278, 418, 419, 421
Lopez, Davina C. 213
Luomanen, Petri xii
Lütgert, Wilhelm 60, 297

MacDonald, Margaret Y. 412, 413
Maddux, William W. 24
Magnusson, Eva 24
Malherbe, Abraham 33, 35, 37, 40, 116, 325
Manson, Thomas W. 13
Marcus, Joel 100, 107
Marecek, Jeanne 24
Marshall, I. Howard 419
Martin, Dale 168, 191

Matera, Frank J. 34, 42, 45, 46, 47, 116, 118, 219, 373, 377, 386, 388
Mathew, Susan 411, 415, 419
McCaulley, Esau 151, 152
McDonald, Dennis R. 383
McMurray, Patrick xiii, 9, 11, 16, 71, 73, 80, 90, 131, 132, 136, 160, 163, 167, 184, 186, 207, 223, 227, 228, 237, 298, 323, 325, 327, 330, 334, 339, 340, 344, 354, 366, 371, 376, 385, 387, 393, 394, 395, 396
Meeks, Wayne 270, 273, 280, 325, 330, 334, 368
Meggitt, Justin 362
Meier, John P. 28
Mendes-Flohr, Paul 25, 27
Menira, Joseph 4
Mermelstein, Ari 348
Metzger, Bruce M. 141, 222
Meyer, Paul 270
Michel, Otto xiii, 159, 249, 272, 284, 328, 329, 385, 386
Miller, Patrick D. 340
Minear, Paul S. 10, 11, 13, 28, 34, 55, 89
Moo, Douglas 412, 413
Moore, George Foot 85
Morales, Rodrigo J. 122, 265
Morgan, Teresa 126, 312
Moule, Charles F.D., 274
Mowczko, Marg 411
Mühling, Anke 153, 252
Muilenberg, James 326, 354
Mullins, Terence Y. 60
Mummendey, Amélie 25, 26, 27, 163
Munck, Johannes 11, 28, 52, 273, 299, 305, 306, 401
Murphy O'Connor, Jerome 42, 360, 416

Nakanishi, Daisuke 23
Nancy, Jean-Luc 17
Nanos, Mark D. xiii, 15, 21, 28, 60, 127, 136, 167, 271, 273, 275, 292, 293, 294, 300, 301, 302, 304, 307, 308, 309, 311, 313, 314, 322, 332
Neufeld, Scott D. 27, 31, 155, 164
Neutel, Karin 107, 108, 145, 146, 156, 157, 158
Neville, David J. xiii
Nickelsburg, George W.E. 123
Noack, Bent W. 11

Nongbri, Brent 208
Novenson, Matthew V. 98, 99, 100, 102, 105, 109
Nygren, Anders 83

Ogereau, Julien 407
Öhler, Markus 70, 99, 100
Ollrog, Wolf-Henning 416
Opitz, Peter 16
Osiek, Carolyn 413

Park, Young-Ho 331
Patte, Daniel xiii, 13, 16, 17, 18
Patterson, Orlando 193
Pavlenko, Aneta 25
Peppard, Michael 53, 69
Perdue, Leo G. 325, 331
Pickett, Cynthia 25
Pierce, Kathleen P. 26
Porter, Stanley E. 34, 36, 38, 46, 165, 174, 175, 251, 383
Portier-Young, Anthea E. 346
Portmann, Adolf W. 23
Postmes, Tom 25

Rainey, Brian 61, 64, 71, 79, 80, 107, 300
Rajak, Tessa 16, 67, 69, 201, 309, 349
Reasoner, Mark 237, 238, 240, 248, 265, 304, 358, 362, 378
Reed, Annette Yoshiko 287
Reese, James M. 80
Reicher, Stephen D. 22
Reinhartz, Adele 32
Remus, Harold 250
Reynolds, Katherine J. 24
Ricker, Aaron 331, 332, 333, 334
Rillera, Andrew 129
Rock, Ian E. 14, 15, 56, 67, 68, 74, 79, 80, 81, 152, 253, 255, 256, 257, 258, 340, 341, 344, 345, 347, 348, 349, 351
Rodriguez, Rafael 18, 34, 36, 41, 43, 45, 46, 47, 49, 57, 58, 71, 92, 98, 99, 101, 105, 107, 109, 110, 114, 116, 118, 121, 125, 126, 128, 129, 134, 136, 140, 165, 166, 175, 182, 184, 185, 186, 187, 188, 206, 209, 212, 218, 219, 220, 222, 223, 224, 225, 231, 245, 251, 252, 262, 264, 265, 267, 268, 274, 275, 277, 279, 298, 326,

328, 333, 338, 340, 344, 345, 350, 351, 352, 354, 358, 360, 373, 374, 376, 378, 386, 387, 401, 403
Rosenfeld, Ben-Zion 4
Runesson, Andrew 216, 317

Saller, Richard P. 290
Sanday, William 147
Sanders, Ed P. 11, 85, 86, 90, 101, 127, 272, 353
Sandnes, Karl Olav 43, 91
Scheidel, Walter 193, 315
Schmeller, Thomas 39
Schmidt, Hans Wilhelm 284, 314
Schmitt, Michael T. 27, 31, 155, 164
Schnelle, Udo 249
Schniewind, Julius 105
Schreiner, Thomas 85
Schrottroff, Luise 193
Schüssler Fiorenza, Elisabeth 414
Schwartz, Daniel R. 3, 4
Scott, James C. 347, 348
Scroggs, Robin 177
Segal, Alan 330
Setzer, Claudia 66, 68
Sharifian, Farzad 202
Sievers, Joseph 260, 313
Slingerland, H. Dixon 2
Song, Changwon 10, 33, 34, 35, 36, 38, 39, 41, 43, 44, 64, 71, 72, 83, 89, 101, 115, 119, 139, 165, 187, 189, 192, 193, 212, 284, 292, 293, 360, 373, 375
Spears, Russell 25
Spicq, Ceslas 401
Spilsbury, Paul 250
Stark, Rodney 268, 284, 299
Steffens, Niklas K. 166
Stegemann, Ekkehard W. xiii, 60, 249, 302, 318, 320, 349, 395
Stendahl, Krister 11, 28, 213, 245
Sterling, Gregory E. 31
Stone, Michael J. 335
Stowers, Stanley K. 18, 28, 33, 34, 35, 36, 37, 38, 39, 41, 42, 43, 60, 62, 67, 71, 77, 78, 80, 81, 84, 89, 93, 99, 101, 114, 126, 129, 130, 131, 133, 135, 139, 140, 141, 144, 161, 188, 211, 214, 219, 261, 273, 274, 276, 277, 278, 292, 323, 336, 360, 365, 373, 375

Streett, R. Alan 185
Suggs, M. Jack 13

Tajfel, Henri xi, 23, 107, 261
Talbert, Charles H. 172
Tamez, Elsa 131
Taubes, Jacob 67
Thiessen, Matthew 57, 71, 99, 108, 109, 114, 120, 136, 159, 333
Thompson, Michael B. 387
Thorsteinsson, Runar M. 20, 28, 35, 36, 41, 54, 57, 80, 83, 84, 88, 92, 93, 98, 99, 104, 114, 121, 122, 206, 325, 333, 362, 373, 415
Tobin, Thomas H. 13, 34, 37, 38, 39, 41, 42, 43, 45, 48, 88, 118, 178, 182, 188, 192, 212, 219, 250, 295, 298, 299, 300, 311, 344, 345, 346, 351, 373
Toland, John 312
Tomson, Peter 245
Tucker, J. Brian xii, xiii, 9, 16, 20, 22, 23, 26, 31, 32, 147, 150, 285, 296, 302, 310, 325, 385, 406. 409
Turner, John xi, 24, 107

VanderKam, James 306

Wagner, J. Ross 46, 47, 255, 256, 268, 278, 354, 383, 385, 388, 389, 390
Waldzus, Sven 27, 163
Wasserman, Emma 70, 71, 73, 75, 79, 183, 238, 239
Watson, Francis 395
Weber, Ferdinand 33, 85
Wedderburn, Alexander J.M. 407, 409
Weima, Jeffrey D. 419
Wendt, Heidi 100, 112
Wengst, Klaus 34, 46, 47, 145, 248, 250, 251, 262, 263, 268, 373
Wenzel, Michael 27, 163
Westermann, William L. 200
Wiefel, Wolfgang 2, 66
Wilder, Terry L. 412
Williams, Sam K. 248
Wilson, Mark 131
Witherington, Ben III 10, 11, 12, 31, 79, 93, 127, 139, 155, 171, 193, 248, 251, 285, 373, 383

Wolter, Michael 64, 169, 310, 311, 312, 315, 413, 414, 415, 420
Wright, Benjamin 202, 261
Wright, Nicholas T. 224, 246, 265, 380
Wuellner, Wilhelm 41

Young, Stephen 128, 141, 142, 155, 160, 259

Zacharias, H. Daniel 162
Zahn, Theodor 140, 284
Zeller, Dieter 313
Zetterholm, Karin 287
Zetterholm, Magnus 10, 17
Ziesler, John 418, 419
Zoccali, Christopher 310

www.ingramcontent.com/pod-product-compliance
Lightning Source LLC
Chambersburg PA
CBHW071233300426
44116CB00008B/1016